OUR DAILY BLOG

TO:

_____

FROM:

_____

DEVOTIONS BY PASTOR JIM LAFFOON

with Reflections by the

newsboys

OUR
DAILY
BLOG

MON   TUES   WED   THU

FRI   SAT   SUN

inspirio™

ACKNOWLEDGMENTS

I offer my deepest thanks and gratitude to: Katy Bennett, Anna Cosand, Bethany Cosand, Michaela Jackson, Rebekah Laffoon, Kristen Lutte, Lynn Nawata, and Julia Swain for their tireless work in typing and editing this manuscript. This devotional would not have been possible without their faithfulness.

To Wes Campbell of Inpop Music and the newsboys members: Peter Furler, Phil Joel, Jeff Frankenstein, and Duncan Phillips. Special thanks for all your work and collaboration on this project. I am continually inspired by your love for God and your heart to advance his kingdom.

To Tom Dean, Kim Zeilstra, Molly Detweiler Editorial Services, and everyone at Zondervan, my heartfelt thanks for making this devotional a reality. It has been a pleasure working with you.

To the leaders and members of the Every Nation family worldwide, your lives were my greatest inspiration for this devotional.

To my parents, Ray and Kathryn Laffoon, thank you for raising me in a home where the Bible was both honored and obeyed.

To my wife, Cathy, without your tireless editing and continual encouragement, this project would not have been possible. Aside from my relationship with Jesus Christ, being married to you is the greatest honor of my life.

INTRODUCTION

I had the privilege of growing up in an incredible Christian home. My dad pastored the same church all of his life and my mother taught Sunday school for over fifty years. The Bible was such a part of our lives that my younger siblings had some of their first reading lessons during our family devotions. In this atmosphere, I grew up with a deep love for the Word of God. By the time I was twelve, I was already teaching Sunday school. Through my mother's mentoring, I learned how to make the great characters of Scripture come alive to the children I was teaching. I have never forgotten these early moments in my life.

When I finished high school, I joined the army and served in the 82nd Airborne Division for three years. While I was stationed at Ft. Bragg, North Carolina, I became part of a church pastored by a man named Jerry Dailey. To this day, he is still one of the finest Bible teachers I have ever heard. One of his gifts is using the lives of Bible characters to illustrate biblical principles. Whether it was Ezra or David, I will never forget some of the messages I heard him preach.

In using this approach myself, I have discovered that audiences of every age around the world find it easier to grasp the great truths and principles of the Bible when they are applied to their lives through the characters of Scripture. With these things in mind, I decided to base this devotional on the lives of biblical characters. Like Jesus and the apostle Paul who also used the characters of Scripture to illustrate the reality of New Testament faith, I am convinced that there is much to be learned from the study of the lives of these men and women.

For each devotional, I have done three things. First, I have recorded the Scripture reference where each character's story is found.

Second, I have retold the story in my own words in order to help the reader capture the very real emotions of these characters and the situations they faced. We must never forget that they were ordinary humans just like you and me.

Third, I have asked the Holy Spirit to help us apply the principles that are found in these stories to our lives today. My prayer for you is that these devotionals will be used by God to strengthen your faith as you follow him with all your heart.

JIM LAFFOON

Lessons from the Lives of Adam and Eve:

DESIGNED FOR HIS PRESENCE

 So God created man in his own image, in the image of God he created him; male and female he created them.

GENESIS 1:27

JANUARY 1

Carefully digging his fingers into the soft clay, the Creator began to fashion what would become the crown jewel of all creation. Uniquely designed and intricately crafted, humans would be created in his very image. Although there would be many purposes for their lives, one purpose would stand out among them all: humans would be designed to know and to fellowship with God.

From our emotional makeup to the fact that each and every one of us has a spirit, it is clear that you and I have been created to walk with the invisible God. From Genesis to Revelation, God's heart is repeatedly unveiled, for he wants to bring us into his ultimate purpose for our lives.

Imagine what it must have been like for Adam and Eve to walk with God every evening in the garden. Not satisfied with being their Creator and Lord, God also chose to be their friend. I cannot comprehend what it must have been like to fellowship with God before the fall. What did his face look like? How did his voice sound?

Even after the fall, God continued to reach out in fellowship and friendship to his people. Abraham was called his friend. Moses walked in an amazing intimacy with him. Even more extraordinary is the fact that God's heart to fellowship with his people is not limited to the great leaders of Scripture; ordinary people like you and me can taste the joy and blessing of deep fellowship with God.

Jesus told his disciples if they would learn to obey him, they would not just be his servants, but they would be his friends (John 15:14–15). Jesus offers us the same friendship today. As we settle the issue of his lordship in our lives and learn to embrace the disciplines involved in seeking his face, he will bring us into a new place of intimacy and fellowship with him.

In ALL my tRAvels I hAve seen thousAn>s of people thAt >esiRe intimAcy with Go>. But BefoRe they cAn expeRience this type of intimAcy, he must Become theiR LoR>.

Peter Furler

Lessons from the Lives of Adam and Eve:

DESIGNED WITH A PURPOSE

The Lord God formed the man from the dust of the ground and breathed into his nostrils the breath of life.

GENESIS 2:7

As the Creator carefully cradled the still form, he pursed his lips and breathed his very life into the crown jewel of his creation. He would breathe more than life into us, though. I believe our Creator breathed his very purpose into the essence of Adam's being.

JANUARY 2   Throughout the pages of the Bible, it is clear that God desires to transform this planet through people like you and me. Whether it was David facing the giant Goliath, young Queen Esther presenting herself to King Xerxes, or Ananias confronting Saul, God has always used people to spread his influence throughout this planet.

How does this work? How does God express his authority and rule through people like us? The answer is simple: we must accept the biblical call to discipleship and destiny so our planet may be changed. Discipleship requires mentoring and training. Unless Christians like you and me embrace these disciplines, we will never have the character and maturity necessary for God to truly express his rule and authority through our lives. Until we begin to grasp the fact that each and every one of us has a unique destiny and purpose, we will lack the motivation we need to truly pay the cost that biblical discipleship entails.

Remember, God is yearning, through you, to change the history of this planet. From the moment you were born, God has been working in your life, both to draw you to him and to prepare you for your appointed task. In Ephesians 2:10, the apostle Paul says that God was already preparing a specific work for each and every one of us to do before the world was even created. As you and I embrace the process of discipleship, we will find our purpose, and God will find the kind of people he needs to express his loving rule in the midst of our hurting, dying world.

WheTheR it hAS Been in my own Life oR the Lives of other ChristiAns I hAve Known, until we figure out GoD's pLAn, ALL of ouRS wiLL Be seconD Best.

Peter Furler

WHO WILL WORK THE GROUND?

No shrub of the field had yet appeared on the earth and no plant of the field had yet sprung up, for the Lord God had not sent rain on the earth and there was no man to work the ground.

GENESIS 2:5

There was seed, and there was sun; yet the earth was still barren. In fact, everything was present to create and maintain the lush vegetation that would one day characterize the earth's surface, except for two things: there was neither water nor worker.

JANUARY 3

This principle is as true in the spiritual world as it is in the natural world. As we survey the earth today, it is not hard to find places on this planet that are *physically barren*; there are also many places that are *spiritually barren*. Whether these places are high schools, college campuses, neighborhoods, businesses, cities, or nations, all of our prayers for them seem to be in vain. Could it be when we think we are waiting on God, in reality God is waiting on us?

What is he waiting for? Could it be that God desires to send the worker before he sends the water? If Scripture, and the annals of history, are any indicator, many times this is the case. You and I must never forget that the spiritual rains of revival and outpouring can only bring to the surface what the church has faithfully sown. If God cannot find a worker, many times he will not send the rain. From the ivory towers of academia to the massive citadels of Islam, the need is always the same; God is looking for workers.

Could it be that you are one of these missing workers? Like John the Baptist, maybe you have been called by God to do the hard work it takes to prepare a dry and barren place for God's move (Luke 1:17). In fact, maybe you are already in that place. That's right—you may very well be the answer to the prayers you have been praying for your school, business, or neighborhood. If this is the case, you are not waiting on God, but God is waiting on you.

> GOD is the sAme yesterDAy, toDAy, AnD foREveR.
> AS AmAzinG AS it mAy seem, GoD hAs A plAn
> AnD we ARe it.
>
> Peter Furler

Lessons from the Lives of ADAM AND Eve:

PLACED FOR HIS PURPOSE

 The LORD God took the man and put him in the Garden of Eden to work it and take care of it.

GENESIS 2:15

JANUARY 4

As Adam stood in the middle of an earthly paradise, which would have been beyond our comprehension, he must have been stunned when his Creator and friend began to speak to him. "Adam, I have sovereignly placed you here. It is your job to tend this garden and to protect it. There will be no walls around this garden; your obedience will be its only protection."

Turning away for a moment from the virgin purity surrounding him, Adam may have gazed into the eyes of his Creator and whispered these words: "Yes, my Lord."

As incredible as this story may seem, we, too, have been divinely placed by God. Whether it is our families, marriages, churches, schools, or jobs, all of us have been sovereignly placed into situations and relationships which, if they are ever going to grow and flourish, will require all the care and protection we can give them. Like Adam, we are called to do what it takes in order to build, protect, and defend the "gardens" God has placed us in. Whether it is praying for our pastor daily, refusing to gossip, or always being quick to forgive, this is part of the price we must pay to develop and maintain a little bit of paradise in a fallen world.

Maybe you are in a situation or relationship that is not flourishing. As you survey the pain and decay around you, everything in you wants to run. Could it be that you have been divinely placed within this situation to ensure its growth and protection? What is missing? Could it be your faith, prayers, love, or obedience?

Let us never forget that today our hearts and lives are God's Garden of Eden. That's right—Isaiah says, "The men of Judah are the garden of his delight." Therefore, if you and I carefully guard our hearts and build our relationships, I am convinced we can all experience new levels of joy and fruitfulness as true gardens of God's delight.

FOR YOUR MARRIAGE, CHILDREN, CHURCH, CITY, AND the NATIONS—SURRENDER YOUR HAPPINESS, YOUR WILL, YOUR RIGHTS, AND YOUR LIFE. DO IT OUT OF REVERENCE FOR CHRIST; then you WILL FIND JOY UNSPEAKABLE AND pEACE THAT SURpASSES ALL UNDERSTANDING.

Peter Furler

HE BROUGHT THEM TO THE MAN

[God] brought [the animals] to the man to see what he would name them; and whatever the man called each living creature, that was its name. So the man gave names to all the livestock, the birds of the air and all the beasts of the field.

GENESIS 2:19–20

JANUARY 5

"Adam, what should we call these birds? What about this tawny, four-footed creature with spots? How about the big hairy one swinging from the branches?" **Although none of us will ever stand with God in the Garden of Eden and name the creatures of the earth, we too have been given an amazing privilege.** Even as God brought creatures into the life of Adam so that he could name them, so he brings humans, the crown jewel of his creation, into our lives—to name and even rename them.

As we give birth to natural children, we have been given the power to name them. With the message of the Gospel, however, we have been given the power to supernaturally rename those we lead to Christ: from lost to found, sinner to saint, and slave to child. Do you see the glorious power and privilege you and I have been given? Through the good news of the Gospel, people receive more than a new name. They are birthed into a new family and given a new future.

Whether you realize it or not, God is bringing people into your life on a regular basis to see if you will rename them. From the random encounter, to the friend who pours out his or her heart to you, these may well be divine appointments. Yet, this is more than a great privilege; it is also an awesome responsibility. Paul clearly delineates the awesomeness of our responsibility in Romans 10:14: "And how can they hear without someone preaching to them?"

If you do not speak to the people whom God is bringing to you, how will they ever hear the Gospel? As you take a moment to ponder this great opportunity, let the words of John 20:21–22 settle into your spirit: *"'As the Father has sent me, I am sending you.' And with that he breathed on them."* Can you feel your Master's gentle breath? Can you hear his loving voice? He is not only sending people to you; he is sending *you*.

As I pondered this devotional, this is the prayer that came to me: "Lord let me live to fearlessly make known the mystery of the Gospel."

Peter Furler

Lessons from the Lives of Adam and Eve:

AT REST FOR HIS BEST

> The LORD God caused the man to fall into a deep sleep; and while he was sleeping, he took one of the man's ribs and closed up the place with flesh. Then the LORD God made a woman from the rib.
>
> GENESIS 2:21–22

JANUARY 6

As he continued to survey the vast menagerie of creatures lined up before him, Adam began to notice a difference between him and all the other creatures. It may have been only coincidence, but they all seemed to be in pairs, while he was alone. He was definitely missing either something or someone.

As he heard the voice of his Creator, however, divine rest began to enter his soul. *If you want my best, you must enter into my rest.* As his Creator's hand brushed his brow, Adam fell into a deep sleep. When the Lord awakened him, the woman formed by God for him was standing by his side.

If you are a single man or woman, there is much you can learn from this passage. I cannot count the times I have watched men and women wear themselves out in a vain search to find the right person. They seem to spend all their time looking and wondering. Instead of wisely preparing themselves to meet the right person, they spend all their time pursuing the wrong person.

Is there any answer to our culture's vain and even deadly preoccupation with romantic fulfillment? Yes, if we will put this area of our life on the altar, God will bring us into an amazing place of peace and rest. This rest is critical because ultimately only God knows the type of man or woman you need to marry.

You may be thinking to yourself, *I have tried to rest in this area of my life before.* Never forget, resting in God is more than praying a prayer. God's rest also means learning the art of satisfying the deepest needs of your soul through God's presence and Word. As you do this, you will find yourself standing at the doorway of a divine rest that will never fail to bring you God's best.

With secret wisdom, GOD heals us when we are at rest in Him. This healing is important in preparing you for whatever relationship GOD has for you.

Peter Furler

Lessons from the Lives of Adam and Eve:
WHERE ARE YOU?

The man and his wife heard the sound of the LORD God as he was walking in the garden ... and they hid from the LORD God among the trees of the garden. But the LORD God called to the man, "Where are you?"

GENESIS 3:8–9

JANUARY 7

As she huddled in her husband's arms, trembling with fear, warm tears began to cascade down her cheeks. For the first time in her life, however, they were not tears of joy; they were tears of sorrow. The serpent's words had been so mesmerizing. For a moment, she had really doubted her Creator. Yet now, though it was too late, she knew the truth.

Adam, on the other hand, was numb with the shock of his rebellion. Unlike his precious wife, he could not claim deception as an excuse. For the first time in his life he knew what the word *death* meant. He could already sense its decay and feel its icy fingers clutching at his breast. As he buried his face in his wife's snarled tresses, the sobering words of his Creator's warning began to haunt the chambers of his heart: *"When you eat of it, you will surely die."*

Then they heard God's voice. He was looking for them. He hadn't given up. *"Adam, where are you?"* As his hand reached into their hiding place, they heard both the sternness of their awesome Creator and the love of a Father coming to bring them back home. Yes, there were consequences because sin always has consequences. His mercy, however, was far greater than the consequences.

Do you see it now? Can you hear your Creator's loving voice? *"Where are you? Why are you hiding from me?"* What has bound you, hurt you, and shamed you? No matter how much sin has stained your soul and marred your life, there is no reason for despair. There is no sin your Savior's blood cannot cleanse. There is no wound his sacrifice cannot heal. No matter what you are facing today, he is able to forgive you, change you, and strengthen you. Respond to him today. He is waiting to deliver and rescue your soul.

"Behold the LAMB of GOD who takes away the sins of the WORLD." This Scripture, which is one of my favorites, was freshly impressed on my heart as I considered GOD's love for ADAM and Eve.

Peter Furler

Lessons from the Life of Cain:
WHY ARE YOU ANGRY?

Cain brought some of the fruits of the soil as an offering to the LORD. But Abel brought fat portions from some of the firstborn of his flock. The LORD looked with favor on Abel and his offering, but on Cain and his offering he did not.... So Cain was very angry, and his face was downcast. Then the LORD said to Cain, "Why are you angry?... If you do what is right, will you not be accepted?"

GENESIS 4:3–7

JANUARY 8

In Cain's mind, he was a victim. Surely this was some cosmic prank. How could this fickle tyrant, who called himself a loving Creator, reject the very work of his hands? Somehow, that sniveling, spineless Abel had ingratiated himself with God and stolen his blessing.

Was this really the case? Had God's decision to reject Cain's offering really been the arbitrary whim of a mean-spirited despot? No! Cain had forfeited God's blessing through his own behavior. God had asked for the first fruits; Cain had offered just "some of the fruits." Worse yet, he now blamed God, and his brother Abel, for the consequences of his own actions.

How many times do we do the same? We blame God and man for the results of our own behavior. I have found that the people who groan and moan the loudest about the condition of their finances are the very people who refuse to give even 10% back to the Lord. Many of us whine about our lack of joy on the very days that we refuse to read the Bible, worship, or even pray. What makes any of us think that we can have the fullness of God's blessings without obeying him?

Where are you today? Are you angry with God? Could it be that you are blaming God or another human for the consequences of your own actions? If you are, it is time for you to rise above the self-pity and blame that have been paralyzing your soul. You must acknowledge your true condition before God and repent. This may mean returning to church or beginning to read the Bible consistently. It might involve reconciliation with another believer. Whatever the case may be, never forget that God is ready to restore your soul to a level of fellowship and blessing that is beyond your imagination.

Selfishness is ugly, and thinking that the world owes you something could be the first warning signs that the enemy is laying a trap for you. This trap I'm talking about is the selfishness of twisted thoughts that come to our mind when we blame God or people for the roots of our problems.

Peter Furler

Lessons from the Life of Cain:

GUARDING THE DOOR OF YOUR HEART

> [God said to Cain], "If you do not do what is right, sin is crouching at your door; it desires to have you, but you must master it."

GENESIS 4:7

As he walked away from the place of sacrifice, Cain was seething with anger. "How could any being want the bloody carcass of a pathetic lamb when he could have the finest fruit grown anywhere outside the Garden of Eden?" Well, he would show them both.

JANUARY 9   Why did it happen? How could the firstborn son of history's first family become a rebellious murderer? The answer is simple yet frightening. The sinful passions we fail to master will master us. The consequences of submitting our hearts to sin's raging power can be terrible beyond belief.

Therefore, God's powerful challenge to Cain is as relevant today as it was thousands of years ago. *"You must master sin."* Paul echoes these words again in Romans 6:14: "For sin shall not be your master." How can we master the sin that threatens to overwhelm us? Here are three critical principles:

First, we must never forget that, ultimately, it is our Master, not us, who will master the power of sin. As you follow and obey Jesus, you can tap into the power of the Holy Spirit living inside of you. Through his power, there is no sin that you cannot overcome (1 John 5:4–5). As you turn away from sin and look to God in faith, he will give you the power you need in order to change.

Second, you do not have to try to defeat the power of sin alone. Share your battles with others, especially with those who are mature in their own faith, and you can experience the reality of James 5:16: "Confess your sins to each other and pray for each other so that you may be healed."

Third, sin grows when you feed it by giving in to it. On the other hand, if you want your spirit to grow, you must feed it through fellowship with other Christians, reading God's word, and prayer.

No matter how powerful the grip of sin is on your life, it seems God is more than able to free you from its grasp.

What we let our eyes see, our ears hear, and our minds entertain, will determine who is our master. We are either slaves to sin or slaves to righteousness.

Peter Furler

Lessons from the Life of Cain:
OUR BROTHER'S KEEPER

The LORD said to Cain, "Where is your brother Abel?"
"I don't know," he replied. "Am I my brother's keeper?"

GENESIS 4:9

JANUARY 10

"Am I my brother's keeper?" With these words, Cain revealed the root of his problem. Indeed, at the very root of Cain's murderous anger was his refusal to live as his "brother's keeper."

What do I mean by this? Although Cain was a hard worker, the only type of relationships it seems he was committed to were those that would serve his personal purpose and agenda. Therefore, why work hard for a God who wasn't going to bless him? And why protect his brother who was threatening his position and status? Abel, it seems, had a radically different view of life. He was committed to nurturing and protecting the people that God had placed in his life.

As I survey our culture today, I find that there are two radically different approaches to relationships: networking and covenant keeping. Although networking works incredibly well in the business world, it is a horrible foundation on which to build a relationship. This is true because networking is based on mutual benefit. For example, if my spouse doesn't satisfy me, why should I stay with her? As for my friends, if they fail me, I can just make new ones.

On the other hand, covenant keeping is all about protecting and cherishing our relationships. God is calling us to build our relationships as covenant keepers, not as networkers. Will you stay with your spouse even when it gets tough? As for your friends, do they become disposable the minute they fail you? God longs for us to be men and women who will guard and cherish our relationships. May the words of Philippians 2:2–4 guide us as we seek to build our relationships God's way:

Then make my joy complete by being like-minded, having the same love, being one in spirit and purpose. Do nothing out of selfish ambition or vain conceit, but in humility consider others better than yourselves. Each of you should look not only to your own interests, but also to the interests of others.

One of the GReAtest fReeDoms in LiFe is to Be ABLe to Rejoice when GoD BLesses otheRs AnD in YouR heARt WANt His Best FoR Both YouR FRienDs AnD enemies.

Peter Furler

Lessons from the Life of Cain:

THE CURSE OF CAIN

Cain said to the LORD, "My punishment is more than I can bear. Today you are driving me from the land, and I will be hidden from your presence."

GENESIS 4:13–14

JANUARY 11

As Cain dropped to his knees, he cried out to his Creator in anguish and pain. "Oh my God, this is more than I can bear. It is one thing to be condemned to wander the earth as a vagabond, but to never have your presence again is a sentence of death." Even in his darkened state, Cain could not imagine life without the presence of God. This curse was the very reason Cain was doomed to live a life of emptiness and dissatisfaction. Without the presence of God in his life, there was no hope for him to ever be truly content or deeply satisfied.

It is no different today; the deep discontent gnawing at the heart of every unsaved man and woman is directly related to the fact that there is no true contentment outside of God's presence. I am convinced that the root of things such as divorce or constant job changes is that people are looking for a new spouse or new job to satisfy needs which only God himself can satisfy.

For a Christian to lose the familiarity of God's presence after once experiencing it, however, can even be worse. This was why the pain was so excruciating for Cain; he knew what he was losing. The same can be said for David after he sinned with Bathsheba. The very thought of losing God's presence caused him to cry out in anxiety and fear: "Do not cast me from your presence!" (Psalm 51:11).

Where are you today? How much of God's presence are you experiencing? If you have been neglecting spending time with God—through his Word and prayer—your ability to sense God's presence is greatly diminished. Perhaps busyness and stress have strangled some of the flow of his presence. Whatever the case may be, God is ready and waiting to meet you with a new measure of life-giving presence if you will seek his face again.

The eARth is full of the GLORY of the LORD. I think the "hell" of hell will be that GOD won't be there. He is present in His WORD—seek Him while He MAY Be found.

Peter Furler

Lessons from the Life of Cain:

LIVING IN THE LAND OF NOD

> Cain went out from the Lord's presence and lived in the Land of Nod.... Cain was then building a city.
>
> GENESIS 4:16–17

JANUARY 12

Cain stumbled blindly out of the presence of God. How would he ever survive in the harsh world to which he had been banished?

Maybe he could create a place for himself where he could find some life and joy he had lost when he was banished from God's presence. Instead of wandering through the land of Nod, he would stay right where he was and build a city. He would make it a place with so much activity and revelry that no one would even have time to contemplate what it must have been like to walk in the presence of God.

In the middle of a land meant to imprison him, he would build the world's first city. But Cain's city was fabricated around the lie that people can live happily without the presence of God. Yet, if history has proven anything in the thousands of years since this city's founding, it has proven that Cain's dream would never come true. As we survey the stories of the rise and fall of nations it is clear that there is no true peace and joy apart from God.

Tragically, thousands of Christians have seemingly bought into this lie. Although they claim to love God, they live as if position, power, possessions, or the right person are all they need for a fulfilling life. With their

Bibles unopened and prayer as an afterthought, they pursue their own dreams.

Have you bought into the lie that you can be satisfied apart from God's presence and purpose? Whether you believe it or not, your devotional life may well reflect the fact that you have bought into this lie. If you rarely read your Bible, pray, or seek God, this is a clear indicator that your passion for his presence has slipped. Even if this is the case, however, it is not too late. As you begin to seek his face, you can discover a new depth of God's presence, and you will find yourself in a new place where true joy and peace waits for you.

"Where else can we turn except to the LORD?
Who else is faithful except our God? LORD, lead
us to the ROCK that is higher than we are."
Peter Furler

Lessons from the Life of Cain:
CALLING ON THE LORD

Adam lay with his wife again, and she gave birth to a son and named him Seth.... At that time men began to call on the name of the LORD.

GENESIS 4:25–26

JANUARY 13

Seth had grown up hearing stories about his brothers. Cain had broken the heart of his parents. As for Abel, his parents still spoke in hushed tones about him. There had been so much pain in his family. In the midst of this sadness, Seth began to call out to God.

What will it take to bring us to our knees? Many times it comes because of a terrible disappointment or a major crisis. If the desperation of the moment does not become the discipline of a lifetime, however, these momentary bursts of passion will quickly fade away.

God wants to bring us into a lifestyle of calling on him. Like the early apostles, all of us need the revelation that "apart from me you can do nothing" (John 15:5). Once we really come to believe this, deep in our souls, the daily discipline of calling on the Lord will become second nature.

We are deeply in need of a fresh start if we are ever going to develop a lifestyle of seeking God. If this is your situation, I believe these four simple principles will help you.

First, start small. Fifteen minutes of Bible reading and prayer every day is better than one hour, once a week. As you are successful, you can add five minutes a week until you are spending more and more time with God.

Second, start simple. Read a chapter out of one of your favorite books of the Bible. Take the passage that touched you the most and think about it. Read it out loud. Finish by praying about whatever is on your heart.

Third, start strategically. The best time to develop your relationship with God is in the morning. I have found the longer I wait to seek God, the harder it is to find time to do it.

Fourth, start strong. Ask one of the leaders in your church or another mature Christian to hold you accountable on a weekly basis.

May God grant you the discipline to call out to him every day and you will meet him afresh this year.

"LORD give me the strength to break bad habits, the discipline to form good habits, and the love for your holy habitation."

Peter Furler

Lessons from the Life of Noah:
LAST MAN STANDING

After Noah was 500 years old, he became the father of Shem, Ham and Japheth.

GENESIS 5:32

JANUARY 14

Our planet was different then. The forces released by the sin of Adam and Eve had not yet totally marred its original beauty. Within this pristine beauty, however, there lurked an insidious and growing evil. As he stood on the crest of the lush, green hill he had been climbing, Noah felt starkly alone.

Noah probably lived as a single man for hundreds of years. Although we can only speculate, this seems to be the case because Scripture says that Noah had children when he was 500 years old, hundreds of years later in life than all of his forefathers. And since Scripture doesn't mention any barrenness on the part of Noah's wife, it seems to suggest that Noah married far later in life than was the norm. Even if this wasn't the case, we know that by the time he entered the ark at the age of 600, all but his immediate family had either died or been swept away by the sin and deception that had ravaged his culture.

How did he do it? How did Noah resist the diabolical seduction that deceived his whole generation? Although there are many reasons for Noah's faithfulness, one of the most important was the blessing of spiritual family in his life. Despite the fact that he may have remained single for centuries, with virtually no peers he could count on for spiritual encouragement, Noah still had spiritual family. Based on the genealogical table of Genesis 5, it is clear that there was still a remnant of older men and women on the earth who worshipped the Lord God. These people were probably mentors and models for Noah. By telling him the stories of God, passed down from generation to generation, they had prepared him, from the time of his infancy, to stand against evil.

Where are you today? Do you feel like you are the last man or woman standing in your school, campus, job, family, or neighborhood? Wherever you have been called to stand, God has definitely not called you to stand alone. God wants to bring you a spiritual family. With his help seek out mature Christians—leaders in your church, family members, and other faithful young people—to stand with you. As you learn to live transparently with them, God will use their prayers, counsel, and encouragement to give you the strength to make a strong stand for him.

He who separates himself seeks his own desire, he quarrels against all sound wisdom. PROVERBS 18:1 NASB

Peter Furler

Lessons from the Life of Noah:
HE WALKED WITH GOD

Noah was a righteous man, blameless among the people of his time, and he walked with God.

GENESIS 6:9

JANUARY 15

Noah was weary. Yet, as he sat down to rest, he was comforted by the presence that had been with him since his youth. It was the awesome Lord of the universe—his dearest friend. In spite of the deception that had engulfed his world, and the struggle to live a pure life in a lust-crazed culture, it was his special relationship with God that had kept Noah strong.

What was the secret of Noah's amazing relationship with God? Noah had learned to walk with God. What does this mean? Here are three different ways a Christian can walk with God.

First, all Christians are called to follow God. By this, I mean that you must settle the issue of who is in control of your life. Will you obey God? In John 15:14, Jesus said, "You are my friends if you do what I command."

Second, as you learn to follow the Lord, you will begin to have a true friendship with him. You will learn to hear his voice through the Bible and by the Holy Spirit and will experience the joys of hearing and understanding God's plan for you.

Third, as you mature in your walk with God, he will send you to prepare people to hear the Good News about him and to accept it (Luke 1:17). Your ability to walk with God will give you the strength you need in order to stand as a testimony for him anywhere—even in places that are dry and hard spiritually.

Although Noah seemed to be alone as he faced all the temptations of his culture, in reality he was never alone. He was walking in fellowship with the invisible God. Nothing could not drown out the whisper of his Creator's love.

Are you beginning to hear the whisper of your Savior's love? If you will only be willing to walk with him, you will be flooded with a sense of divine confidence and approval that will transcend your deepest insecurities and fears. Like Noah you, too, can experience the joy and power of walking with God.

> OUR FIRST STEP TO BECOMING FULLY ALIVE IS OUR FIRST STEP IN OUR WALK WITH GOD.
>
> Peter Furler

Lessons from the Life of Noah:
WILL YOU BUILD?

By faith Noah, when warned about things not yet seen,
in holy fear built an ark to save his family. By his faith he
condemned the world and became heir of the righteousness
that comes by faith.

HEBREWS 11:7

JANUARY 16

It was immense. As Noah stepped back from the finished
ark, he could hardly believe he had built it. Although the
completed ark was almost one hundred years old, he still
believed the word God had spoken to him—that the flood
would come.

What gave Noah the ability to believe words that a
normal human would find insane? The answer is simple; Noah simply
believed what God told him. This faith enabled him to preserve his family
from destruction and save the human race from extinction.

What about you and me? Do we really believe that the Bible is true?
After all, none of it can really be proven. In my experience, many Christians are not building their lives and ministries like people who *really*
believe the truths of the Bible. Noah, though he could not prove it, was so
gripped by the reality of the coming deluge that he built an ark that saved
his family. Could it be, if we truly grasped the reality of an eternity without
Jesus, we would share our faith more?

Noah based his whole life on the words of an invisible God who
rarely spoke audibly. Today we have the clear record of God's Word and
hundreds of years of Christian testimony, and that is still not enough.
What will it take for us to realize that the people of our culture are just as
doomed as the people of Noah's day? Although they probably will not per-

ish in a flood, sooner or later all of us will die. If our friends and loved ones have not accepted Christ as their Savior, they will face the judgment of an eternity without him.

Have you built your life in such a way that people can clearly see Christ in you? Like Noah, has your heart been gripped by the dire peril of those you love? May your heart be set ablaze with fresh passion for our lost and dying world as you ponder these words today.

"LORD Give US A heART FoR the LoST. HeLp US to Live up to ALL thAt You've ShowN US. TheN they wiLL Be AttRACTeD to YouR RestoRAtioN poweR withiN US."

Peter Furler

Lessons from the Life of Noah:

THEY CAME TO NOAH

 Pairs of clean and unclean animals, of birds and of all creatures that move along the ground, male and female, came to Noah and entered the ark.

GENESIS 7:8–9

JANUARY 17

In almost six hundred years of serving God, this was the most amazing miracle Noah had ever seen. In a mere seven days, thousands of creatures from all over the planet had entered the ark. Although he had never had trouble believing what he could not see, at this point Noah was struggling to comprehend what was happening in front of his very own eyes.

What does this amazing story have to do with us today? Although animals do not have free will as we do, it still makes me wonder if Christians have severely underestimated the power of the Holy Spirit to draw people into salvation. If God can draw wild beasts into his purpose for their lives, maybe we have given up too quickly on the people in our lives who seem the most unreachable. There are three lessons we can learn from Noah's story:

First of all, Noah built the ark according to God's exact specifications. Although he may have wondered why the beams had to be so large, he understood once he saw the elephants lumbering toward the ark. Today, Jesus knows best how his church should be built. When we listen to his voice and obey, we will be amazed to see what God can do.

Second, Noah brought all the provisions aboard the ark before the creatures arrived. Could it be that God will not bring needy people into your life until you have stored up God's Word in your heart? I am convinced, if you will do what it takes to become a true disciple, you will never lack divine appointments with people who need God.

Third, Noah spent one hundred years of his life building the ark. He believed God in the face of what seemed impossible. This same kind of faith is needed today. No matter how unreachable the people around you may seem, your faith in God's love for them is one of the keys to their salvation.

What about you? Could it be that you are God's "Noah" for your generation? If you will build, bring, and believe, I am convinced that God can bring you into a season of service and purpose beyond anything you have imagined.

The question to me is not, CAn GOD Be tRUSteD? He is wORtHy OF tRUSt; pROven to Be tRUStwORtHy. But CAn I Be tRUSteD to Be fULL OF His wORD, wALKing in COvenAnt witH Him AnD the peOpLe He's pLACeD in my LiFe, AnD ReADy fOR His Divine AppoihtmenIs.

Peter Furler

Lessons from the Life of Noah:
INSIDE YOUR TENT

 Noah, a man of the soil, proceeded to plant a vineyard. When he drank some of its wine, he became drunk and lay uncovered inside of his tent.

GENESIS 9:20–21

JANUARY 18

Noah hadn't meant to get drunk. He was simply trying to relax. After all, he was in the privacy of his own tent. What possible harm could come from another drink?

What had happened? How had the most righteous man in the world ended up drunk in bed? Maybe his spiritual disciplines really were slipping. After all, it's hard to believe Noah would not have been exhausted, and even burned out, after the stress and trauma he had experienced. Although we will never really know the exact condition of Noah's soul, one thing is certain: God's choice servant had been snared in a moment of weakness. What lessons can we learn from this tragic story?

First, no matter how spiritually mature we think we are, all of us have the potential to fall into sin. That's why it is essential for us to maintain spiritual disciplines. In my own life, I have found my time in the Word and prayer is the key to my ability to walk in God's strength and power. No matter how exhausted I am, when I come into the presence of God, my strength is renewed.

Second, what happens in the privacy of your personal "tent" is vital. What is the condition of your private life? Are you growing in faith, or are you giving in to the power of secret sin?

Third, until we get to Heaven, there is no final victory in the battle wage against sin and Satan. Noah had waged war against the darkness of the world for hundreds of years. Surely, this veteran spiritual warrior was beyond the point of ever being trapped by the enemy. Yet in just a moment, he let his guard down and was snared by sin.

Like Noah, you have been called to stand against the dark tide of deception and despair flooding into your culture. This task will not end until you are before the throne of God. As you stand on the foundation of a private life filled with God and his Word, I am convinced you can win the battles God has called you to face.

FOR me the eAsiest pLACe to Be stRoNG in the LORD is oh stAGe. But the GREAtest pLACe to Be stRoNG in the LORD is At home. In FACt, whAt hAppens in my home DeteRmines whAt hAppens oh stAGe.

Peter Furler

Lessons from the Life of ABRAM:

I WILL MAKE YOU A BLESSING

The LORD had said to Abram, "Leave your country, your people and your father's household and go to the land I will show you. I will make you into a great nation and I will bless you."

GENESIS 12:1 – 2

JANUARY 19

Abram's whole family had been destined to go to Canaan. Years before, his father had described this Promised Land to them in glowing terms. They left the beautiful city of Ur on the banks of the Euphrates and began their journey to Canaan. Sadly, they had never gotten any farther than the city of Haran.

Abram was not satisfied there, though. There was a deep restlessness in Abram's soul. A soft voice had begun to call his name, *"Abram ... Abram ..."*

Of late, the voice had grown more strident. Abram knew intrinsically it was the voice of God. Now, this voice was telling him to go to the Promised Land. The voice insisted that if Abram obeyed, he would somehow be made into a "great nation."

***A great nation**, he had thought. How will God make a great nation out of a man with a barren wife?*

Yet, despite his doubts, Abram left Haran, in obedience to God, and journeyed to the Land of Canaan. He would now live like a desert nomad, in a tent, for the rest of his life.

Through this journey Abram grew into the man the Bible calls "God's friend" (James 2:23). The faith of Abram, who God renamed Abraham, and his family would be used by God to bring the world salvation through Christ.

Are you willing to be made into the kind of person God has called you to be? Will you leave when he calls you to leave and go where he calls you to go? God might be guiding you into a different career or to attend a certain college. You might face something as dramatic as a call to live as a missionary in another country. No matter the call, God will give you the grace to follow it. As you ponder these thoughts today, let God's words resound in the chambers of your heart: *"I will make you into what I have called you to be."*

FAITH is the KEY to the DOOR of BLESSING. ABRAHAM'S FAITH not only BROUGHT the BLESSING of GOD; it MADE him A BLESSING to the WORLD.

Peter Furler

Lessons from the Life of ABRAM:

HE BUILT AN ALTAR

Abram was seventy-five years old when he set out from Haran.... They set out for the land of Canaan, and they arrived there.... He built an altar there to the LORD, who had appeared to him.

GENESIS 12:4-5, 7

JANUARY 20

The farther he journeyed into Canaan, the more often Abram heard the voice God. This awesome God reassured him that one day this land would belong to his descendents. As he camped one evening, Abram began building an altar. Even while he was gathering the stones, he could already feel the growing presence of God. Later, as the fragrance of sacrifice mingled with the smoke of the fire, Abram felt as if his whole being was being deeply cleansed. He lifted his hands in praise and thanksgiving. As he made his way back to his tent, Abram was filled with a fresh sense of confidence and joy. He hadn't made a mistake. Step by step, he was being led by the awesomeness of God of the whole universe.

Abram's ability to believe God year after year was directly related to the amount of time he spent with God at the altar. Whether it was confessing his sins, or pouring out his heart to God in prayer, these powerful times were the secret of his persevering faith. We need the same thing today—a powerful and sustaining faith is built as we spend time with God.

As an altar was built of many stones, so there are many parts to a healthy devotional life. Some of these include worship, reading the Bible, taking time to listen to God, and prayer. Never forget, though, that any time with God is better than no time with God. Jacob worshiped God by pouring oil on one stone (Genesis 28:18). This was his first attempt at altar building. In later years, Jacob's time with God would become deeper and longer. But even his first small act of worship pleased the heart of his loving God.

As you consider the story of Abram, never forget that when you're building your "altar," you're building your faith. Although your daily devotional time may seem like a small thing, it is at the very core of building the faith muscles you need to walk with God.

> One breath at a time, one sunrise at a time, one word, one mercy, one stone.
>
> **Peter Furler**

Lessons from the Life of Abram:
DOWN TO EGYPT

Now there was a famine in the land, and Abram went down to Egypt to live there for a while because the famine was severe.

GENESIS 12:10

JANUARY 21

Everywhere he looked, the landscape around the river was green and lush. Yes, the flood plane of the Nile, like that of the Euphrates, was a fertile paradise. After months of no-madic living, the sophistication and cosmopolitan lifestyle of Egypt were like a balm to Abram's soul.

Deep inside, however, Abram wondered about his decision to come to Egypt. Maybe it was only coincidence, but the farther he had journeyed, the fainter God's voice had become. Tragically, this trip was not God's will, and it would cost Abram for the rest of his life.

Sooner or later we all go through a period of famine, just like Abram. It will seem that neither God nor his people can satisfy the legitimate needs of your life. When this happens, everything within you will be tempted to return to "Egypt"—the places of bondage and oppression from which God delivered you when you were saved.

Whether it is returning to a lifestyle of substance abuse in order to handle the pressure and stress of your life, or finding comfort in the rush of unhealthy relationships, there are hundreds of ways to return to Egypt. Although, like Abram, you may only plan to stay there "for a while," the longer you stay, the harder it will become for you to ever return to the land of promise.

Where are you today? Are you selling your soul back into bondage in order to satisfy the burning needs of the moment? Where once you walked confidently in the light of God's Word, you now struggle along under the weight of shame.

If you find yourself bound up in Egypt today, take heart! If you will only return to God and his people, there is still hope for your soul. I include God's people for a reason; typically, it is not enough to simply go to God for help. He will normally use people to rescue you. Go, as quickly as you can, to your pastor or another leader. If you don't have a church, ask a Christian friend for help. Tell them where you are, and be open about your struggle. As you respond to their counsel, God himself will rescue your soul.

EGYpt [the WORLD] pROMiSES FREEDOM BUt eveRY CRY OF FREEDOM is jUSt the RAttLiNG OF its cLAiNS.

Peter Furler

Lessons in the Life of ABRAM:

WILL WE HIDE OUR RELATIONSHIP WITH GOD?

As [Abram] was about to enter Egypt, he said to his wife Sarai, "I know what a beautiful woman you are.... Say you are my sister, so that I will be treated well for your sake and my life will be spared because of you."

GENESIS 12:11, 13

JANUARY 22

Abram would never forget the indescribable pain in Sarai's eyes when he had asked her to lie about their relationship. Now it was too late. When the officials of Pharaoh had come to escort her to his harem, she had remained nobly silent. Yet, even in her silence there had been a plaintive cry for help. Every expression of her body language had been a plea for rescue and protection.

"What kind of man am I?" he cried. Abram continued to wail until there was no strength left in his body.

What kind of man would sacrifice his most cherished relationship in life to save himself? Probably someone just like you and me. I cannot count the times I have watched Christians hide the true nature of their relationship with Christ in order to escape the pain of rejection. Tragically, when Christians hide their faith, they are not only wounding the heart of their precious Savior, but they are also keeping the Good News from the people who need it the most. How many unbelievers never hear the Gospel because their Christian friends never share their faith?

Have you grieved your Savior's heart by hiding your relationship with him? If you have, it is time for you to be brutally honest with yourself. Your silence in the face of the stark human need around you has nothing to do with trying to be relevant. The fear of rejection, alienation, and being shunned has paralyzed your soul.

Is there any hope of deliverance for you? In Acts 4:31, when the disciples were facing rejection and even persecution, Luke says, "After they prayed ... they were all filled with the Holy Spirit and spoke the word of God boldly." God's answer for the fear plaguing your soul is a fresh baptism of his love and power. As you are freshly filled with God and his purposes, he will break the chains of fear that have bound you, and you will be given the courage to boldly share your faith.

Peter denied Jesus three times. Then, after the Resurrection, Jesus asked Peter three times: Do you love me more than these? How about you? Do we love Jesus more than life?

Peter Furler

Lessons in the Life of ABRAM:

LEAVING THE PROMISED LAND

Lot looked up and saw that the whole plain of the Jordan was well watered, like the garden of the Lord, like the land of Egypt, toward Zoar.... Abram lived in the land of Canaan, while Lot lived among the cities of the plain and pitched his tents near Sodom.

GENESIS 13:10, 12

JANUARY 23

As he paced restlessly, Abram's soul was in agony. "Not Sodom! How could Lot leave the land of Canaan and choose to live in a place of such darkness?" he cried. As Abram fell to the floor weeping, he begged God to spare Lot from the consequences of his folly.

Why did Lot choose to live outside of the Promised Land? The same thing still happens today. Sadly, I know many Christians who, like Lot, have walked away from God's purpose for their lives.

According to Genesis 13:10, the plains near Sodom and Gomorrah were like the land of Egypt. Lot's trip to Egypt had awakened desires in him that Canaan didn't satisfy. To Lot, the cities of Sodom and Gomorrah were now his true "Promised Land."

We never read about Lot having a wife and children until he moved to Sodom and Gomorrah. Could it be that Lot's ardent desire for companionship and sexual fulfillment were greater than his desire for God and his purposes?

In addition, unlike Abram, Lot did not seem to have a deep relationship with God. Whenever Abram got discouraged, he would meet with God until his faith was renewed. I have found in my own life that when things get hard, only God can sustain me. Each of us must come to our own place of faith and confidence through time in the Word and prayer.

Some of you have allowed the deep loneliness of your soul to dominate your life. As you have frantically searched for fulfillment you have wandered from God's purpose. Perhaps, though you were raised in a Christian home, your parents' faith no longer carries you. Unless you develop your own vital relationship with God, you will never have the faith you need to sustain you. No matter where you are today, it's not too late for you to return to your Promised Land. If you will cry out to God, he will bring you into his best for your life. May God give you grace to change today.

No one can walk with God for you. Even though Abraham was a mighty man of God, he couldn't walk with God for Lot.

Peter Furler

Lessons in the Life of ABRAM:

THEY CARRIED HIM OFF

The four kings seized all the goods of Sodom and Gomorrah and all their food; then they went away. They also carried off Abram's nephew Lot and his possessions, since he was living in Sodom.

GENESIS 14:11–12

JANUARY 24

As he shuffled along under the sun's scorching heat, with the whip of his new master cutting into his skin, Lot was in the grip of dark despair. When the armies of King Kedorlaomer had ransacked Sodom and Gomorrah, he had lost everything. With nothing but a life of bondage and servitude ahead of him, all hope seemed to be gone. Lot collapsed to the ground.

He was awakened by the clashing of swords. In the flickering firelight, he saw the leader of the small army: it was Abram! In a moment, his beloved uncle, with tears in his eyes, was pulling Lot to his feet and slashing his bonds. Lot had been rescued by the man whose purpose and lifestyle he had rejected.

Surely, he would learn his lesson. He would return with Abram to the land of Canaan. This, however, was not the case. Whether it was pride, deception, or relational ties, Lot returned to Sodom. Years later, when he had to be rescued again, the cost would be more painful than he could ever imagine.

How many times will we have to be rescued before we come to our senses and follow God's will? Many times the very people whose counsel

we resist are the same ones God has used to repeatedly rescue and help us. Sooner or later, however, God will allow us to learn the "hard way." When we continually resist his counsel, God will finally allow us to face the consequences of our actions. And then, the process will be more painful than it ever had to be.

But, through God's deep grace, there is still hope of deliverance. That's right; no matter where you are today, you can have hope. Your God is willing and able to rescue your soul. If you will begin to listen to God's voice and imitate the faith of mature Christians in your life, you can begin to grow. May God, in this critical hour, grant you the grace to follow him with all your heart.

MAN CAN send A ROCKet to the moon But he can't see the BACK of his head. We ARe Defined By the WORD of GOD And the mIRRORS [people] we ALLOW Him to pLACe in oUR Lives.

Peter Furler

Lessons in the Life of ABRAM:
TRAINED MEN

When Abram heard that his relative had been taken captive, he called out the 318 trained men born in his household and went in pursuit.

GENESIS 14:14

JANUARY 25

For over thirteen years, the armies of King Kedorlaomer had been invincible. But out of the darkness, Abram's small raiding party struck the sleeping army like a thunderbolt. As Kedorlaomer's causalities mounted, chaos and pandemonium began to break out in his camp—the panicked soldiers fled for their lives into the darkness.

How could a small war party led by 318 servants rout one of the finest professional armies in the Middle East? First, according to verse 14, all of Abram's men were trained. Far from being simple servants, every one of them had been trained in the art of war. Abram's men had become a highly effective fighting force.

Second, every one of Abram's servants had been born into his family—they were part of Abram's household. They cared about Abram's grief and their hearts were intent on rescuing the nephew of their beloved master.

What can this story teach us? Even as the servants of Abram were born into his family, God desires for us to realize that we are born into his spiritual family. In Ephesians 2:19, we find that every Christian is a member of God's household. You didn't just join a club when you were saved; you were supernaturally born again into the family of God.

Abram's servants were also placed into his army. It Is clear in Scripture that every Christian, too, is called to a life of spiritual battle, and is therefore a member of God's army. In Ephesians 6:10–18, Paul challenges us to put on the armor of a warrior and prepare for battle against Satan. You must learn how to hold up the shield of faith as you wield the Word of God like a mighty sword. If you haven't yet mastered these skills, it is not too late. Whether through instruction at your church or personal discipleship from a respected, mature Christian, you can find the training you need in order to be an effective soldier in God's armed forces. Ask God today to bring you into the family and to provide the training you need to successfully win the battles that he has called you to fight.

The enemy of our soul has a need — a need for us to be alone. God has a desire for us to have people in our lives with faith worth imitating.

Peter Furler

Lessons in the Life of ABRAM:

WHEN FAITH IS THE ONLY WAY

The word of the Lord came to Abram in a vision:
"Do not be afraid, Abram.
I am your shield,
your very great reward."

GENESIS 15:1

JANUARY 26

Abram finally faced the reality of his plight. Without a miracle, he would never experience the fullness of God's promise to make him into a "great nation" (Genesis 12:2). Lot had been more than a nephew to him, so Abram had secretly wondered if Lot was the "son" through whom all of his promises would be fulfilled. Even when Lot pitched his tent near Sodom, Abram had never given up hope that he would come to his senses and return home.

Now, however, he knew the truth; Lot was never coming home. All of Abram's pleadings with him to return had fallen on deaf ears. As Abram fell to his knees in prayer, he was overwhelmed by the stark sense of need that flooded his soul. "Oh my God, what can you give me since I remain childless?" he asked.

"A son coming from your own body will be your heir," was God's answer. The Holy Spirit drew Abram outside of his tent. He was amazed afresh by the beauty of the heavens. "Count the stars," he heard the Lord whisper. "So shall your offspring be."

Abram was stunned. How could an aging, barren couple have a family who would one day be as numerous as the stars? There was only one answer: God himself was going to give them a miracle.

Whether it's a physical condition with no medical answer, or a financial crisis far beyond your natural resources, there are times when all you have is your faith. Never forget, however, that many times God will allow you to lose your "Lot," so he can bring you your "Isaac." Remember, Isaac was the name of the miracle son through whom all of God's promises to Abram would be fulfilled (Genesis 21:1–7). In my own life, I have found that I don't trust God fully until all of my own resources are gone. Only then can I see clearly my true need for God's power.

So, stop mourning the loss of your "Lot" and begin to develop the faith you need to receive your "Isaac." As you begin to build your faith by trusting in the promises of God you can reach out, in his timing, and seize your miracle.

I believe this psalm captures the faith that sustained Abraham. "Find rest, O my soul, in God alone. My hope comes from Him. He alone is my rock and my salvation. He is my fortress, I will not be shaken. My salvation and my honor depend on God" (Psalm 62:5).

Peter Furler

Lessons from the Life of ABRAM:
HOW WILL I KNOW?

"I am the LORD, who brought you out of Ur of the Chaldeans to give you this land to take possession of it."

But Abram said, "O Sovereign LORD, how can I know that I will gain possession of it?"

GENESIS 15:7–8

JANUARY 27

Falling to his knees, Abram was awestruck by the implications of what he was hearing. "I will give you this land, and you will take possession of it."

"Oh God," he sighed, "how can I know that I will gain possession of it?"

At those moments when God is challenging us to believe, how can we have the faith that we so desperately need? I am convinced that God's instructions to Abram show us the path to full confidence in God's promises.

First, in verses 9 and 10, God requires Abram to offer creatures from each of the five species that were acceptable as sacrifices. This speaks of the fact that he desires that we give our lives fully to him.

Second, instead of placing the creatures on the altar, Abram cut the larger creatures in half and prepared the very pathway through which God would come to meet him (vv. 10, 17). When we order our lives according to God's will, we are preparing the way for him to come to our aid.

Third, in verse 11, we find that Abram had to battle predatory birds that were trying to eat the sacrifice he had prepared. Whenever we set our minds to do God's will, the enemy will send doubts and fears to keep us from believing in God's best. The battle we wage against these thoughts is part of the process of developing the faith we need to receive the very promises for which we are hoping.

Fourth, after the sun had fully set, a dreadful darkness encompassed Abram. However, as he trusted God, even in the midst of the darkness, he entered a new depth of relationship with God. (vv. 12–18). Times of darkness and confusion often come right before a breakthrough of faith. As we rest in the Lord, we will discover the fresh dimension of faith that we have desired.

No matter where you are in this process, God is able to give you the strength you need. Whether you are battling doubts and fears, or walking through a time of deep darkness and confusion, a new level of faith and victory lies just ahead of you.

> FAith Believes the Blessing. Obedience sees it. FAith in Action is obedience. ABRAhAM's fAith Resulted in the obedience thAt BROught God's Blessing.
>
> **Peter Furler**

Lessons from the Life of Abram:
"HARMLESS" DETOURS

Now Sarai, Abram's wife, had borne him no children. But she had an Egyptian maidservant named Hagar; so she said to Abram, "The Lord has kept me from having children. Go, Sleep with my maidservant; perhaps I can build a family through her."

GENESIS 16:1–2

JANUARY 28

Perhaps Sarai was right. After all, God hadn't been specific about whom the mother of the promised child would be. Yes, Abram would make Hagar his second wife. After ten years in Canaan, it was time to have a baby.

This decision was among the most costly mistakes that Abram ever made. Even though the idea had originated with Sarai, she became bitter and resentful, and eventually demanded that Hagar and Ishmael be sent away.

Sadly, I have watched many Christians bring unnecessary pain into their life by attempting to fulfill God's promises through their own strength and wisdom. Many Christians, after waiting on God for awhile, grow impatient and marry a person who is not God's best for them. Although any marriage can be blessed, by waiting on God's best, unnecessary pain could have been avoided.

Some Christians leave the place to which they were called because the right job wasn't materializing there. In some cases, within days of moving, the perfect job opens up for them in the place they just abandoned. Although every person must discern God's timing for their own life, it is critical that we do not compromise God's best because of our impatience.

There are certain promises in each of our lives that will only be fulfilled through the work of the Holy Spirit. In other words, if God does not help us, we will never get what we have been waiting for.

Maybe you have come to a moment like that in your life. Nothing you have done brought about the results you desired. Could it be that you are in a situation that will only be resolved through the supernatural work of the Holy Spirit? Be patient. God has not forgotten you. As you wait on him in active faith and expectation, he will fulfill every one of the promises he has given you.

To walk with no shepherd is to be lost. To walk ahead of the shepherd, we will become prey. To walk with the shepherd, we will know His will. When Abraham ran ahead of God, his whole family became prey to tension and turmoil.

Peter Furler

Lessons from the Life of ABRAHAM:

WAITING WITHOUT BELIEVING

The Lord said, "This is my covenant with you: You will be the father of many nations. No longer will you be called Abram; your name will be Abraham...."

God also said to Abraham, "As for Sarai your wife ... her name will be Sarah. I will bless her and will surely give you a son by her."

GENESIS 17:4–5, 15–16

JANUARY 29

The familiar presence of the Almighty God began to rush through Abraham's soul. Once again, the voice of his beloved Friend began to repeat the very promises that had become the foundation stones of his life.

"Abraham, I will give you a son."

"I thought I already had one."

"Your wife Sarah will bear you a son."

"What kind of joke is this?" Abraham wondered. "Who's ever heard of a ninety-year-old-barren woman getting pregnant with the help of her ninety-nine-year-old husband?"

"Yes Abraham, your wife will bear a son. I will establish my covenant with him as an everlasting covenant."

At that moment, in a flash of insight, Abraham saw the truth. He had harbored deep roots of unbelief. His love for Ishmael, combined with his desire to find an easier way to fulfill God's promises, had blinded him to the fact that he had forsaken the supernatural way of faith.

Are you, like Abraham, going through all the motions of faith, even though it has long since died in your heart? Maybe you're still praying for your miracle, even though you stopped really believing it would come months, or even years, ago. Could it be that the unbelief in your own heart has lengthened the process? Sadly, in some cases that may be what has happened.

Wherever you are it's time for you to be honest. If you will only face the reality of your heart's true condition, God will uproot the unbelief from your heart, so you can begin the process of planting fresh seeds of faith. It's time for you to begin to apply the Word of God to your own situation. As you plant these seeds of faith in your heart through studying God's Word and allowing it to take root, fresh dynamic faith will begin to grow in your spirit. This powerful infusion of faith will give you the power you need to fully believe in, and wait for, the promises of God to be fulfilled.

GOD is FAIthful AND tRUSTWORThy. A FAtheR that is hAppy to give His chilDReN ALL the things that we ASK FOR thAt He is pleASeD to give. I Believe the oNly ReASoN ALL my pRAyeRs hAve not BeeN ANsweReD is BeCAuSe GoD's timiNg is peRfect AND miNe isN't. SARAh's pROBLem WAS thAt She LOST fAith whiLe wAitiNg oN GoD's peRfect timiNg.

Peter Furler

Lessons from the Life of Abraham:

A PLACE BEYOND YOUR NEEDS

The LORD appeared to Abraham ... while he was sitting at the entrance to his tent.... Abraham looked up and saw three men standing nearby. When he saw them, he hurried from the entrance of his tent to meet them.

GENESIS 18:1–2

JANUARY 30

As the burning rays of the sun beat down on him, the old man felt them coming. Abraham had felt this presence before. "Could it be?" Abraham whispered to himself in astonishment. "Has my God somehow come to me in human form?"

Rising to his feet, Abraham ran out to meet them. Bowing low to the ground as he came into their presence, he begged his Friend to stay. He frantically made the preparations for the finest meal he could serve. Later, as they ate, Abraham simply stood by, basking in their presence.

As he rose to his feet, the Lord looked lovingly into the eyes of Abraham. "Where is Sarah?" he whispered. When Abraham heard this question, he knew that Sarah's barrenness had come to an end.

In this beautiful story, we find some of the principles on which Abraham's amazing friendship with God was built. First, Abraham had learned to recognize the presence of his friend. He knew what God's voice sounded like. If we are going to experience deep friendship with God, we too must learn to hear his voice.

Second, Abraham learned the principle of divine inconvenience. Although it can differ from person to person, you can be sure that your friendship with God will never be built at your convenience.

Third, Abraham took the initiative in his relationship with God. Instead of waiting on God to come into his tent, Abraham ran out into the heat of the desert to meet him. If we want friendship with God, we must seek him.

Fourth, true friendship with God is built beyond the point of our need. Abraham continues to walk down the road with God and the angels, even after Sarah's barrenness was healed. Many Christians seem to stop seeking God the moment their need is met. Therefore, when God finds a person who truly desires to fellowship with him, even after all of their needs have been provided for, he brings them into an amazing place of intimate friendship, just like he did with Abraham.

"Blessed are those whose strength is in you; who set their hearts on you. Those who pursue you; they go from strength to strength till each appears before you in your heavenly kingdom." This lifestyle was the secret to Abraham's strength.

Peter Furler

Lessons from the Life of Abraham:

WHERE IS SARAH?

"Is anything too hard for the Lord? I will return to you at the appointed time next year and Sarah will have a son."

GENESIS 18:14

JANUARY 31

"Abraham, where is your wife Sarah?" At the mention of her name, her ears perked up. "Easing her way to the entrance of the tent, she was astonished by what she heard.

"About this time next year, Sarah, your wife, will have a son." Although something in the depths of her spirit wanted to respond, her faith had become so small that she found herself laughing in disbelief.

"Why is Sarah laughing?"

"Oh no, he heard me," Sarah thought. The Lord quietly spoke again.

"Why did Sarah say, 'Will I really have a child now that I am old?'"

At that moment her laughter ceased, and her mouth gaped open in astonishment. "The Lord really does know me." Yet, even though her heart was softening, the old defense mechanisms were still in place.

"Lord, I didn't laugh." Hearing the pain in her voice, the Lord gently replied, "Yes, you did laugh."

Despite the pain and fear in her heart, the Lord would overcome her unbelief, and she would bear a son.

Have you ever wondered why the Lord did not address Sarah directly until the end of the conversation? Could it be that she had never taken the time to develop her relationship with him? Maybe all of her life she had been living off the faith and revelation that were present in Abraham's life. If this was the case, it is no wonder that she had so little faith.

How about you? Have you been living on someone else's faith, instead of cultivating your own? Whether it is the faith of your parents, spouse, best friend, or pastor, sooner or later any faith other than your own will not be enough. If you do not develop your own relationship with God, you will never have the faith to overcome the challenges and move the mountains that you will face in your journey with God.

Are you bound with unbelief, yet too afraid to admit it? No matter where you are today, God is coming in his love to confront you. Be honest! Face the true condition of your heart, for God himself has come to heal *your* barrenness and bring you into the reality of his promises.

> It breaks my heart to think of those who will come face-to-face with God and meet him for the first time. "Lord come let me walk with you now, so you will know then that it is me." Even though Abraham was God's friend, Sarah barely knew him.
>
> **Peter Furler**

Lessons from the Life of ABRAHAM:
THE ROAD LESS TRAVELED

When the men got up to leave, they looked down toward Sodom, and Abraham walked along with them to see them on their way. Then the Lord said, "Shall I hide from Abraham what I am about to do?"

GENESIS 18:16–17

FEBRUARY 1

Abraham was on a road few humans ever traveled. Even the angels were beginning to wonder why he was still walking with God. Every one of his needs had been dramatically met. What more could he want? Could it be that Abraham simply loved his Creator, instead of merely loving him for his blessings?

When the Almighty God stopped and turned toward Abraham, all of creation seemed to be watching in anticipation. "Should I hide from Abraham what I am about to do? Abraham, the outcry against Sodom and Gomorrah is so great and their sin is so grievous, that I will go down and see if what they have done is as bad as the outcry that has reached me."

Abraham spoke boldly to the Lord. There was no doubt in his heart that God would judge Sodom and Gomorrah. "What about Lot and his family?" Abraham worried.

"What will it take for you spare these cities, my Lord? If there are fifty righteous people will you spare these cities?"

"For fifty I will spare them," the Lord replied. Abraham continued to ask about smaller and smaller numbers—what about 45 ... 40 ... 30 ... 20 ... 10?

Yes, Abraham was on a road rarely traveled—the road to a deep relationship and true influence with God. For those who travel this road, their needs are secondary and the needs of the Kingdom of God are primary. They walk with God because they cherish *him*, not merely his promises. As their relationship with God grows, these Christians can experience levels of influence with God, and with other people, that are beyond comprehension.

Are you only spending enough time with God to get your needs met? If you are, it's time for you to grow beyond your needs-based relationship with God and into the place of intimacy and influence that awaits you. Won't you spend a little longer in his presence today? If you do, you, too, will begin to walk the road that Abraham walked—a road to intimacy and influence with God that is beyond your wildest dreams.

To know God and build a relationship with Him, we must spend both quality and quantity time with Him. Set a priority appointment to meet with God each day. Schedule a personal time to meet with Him every morning. For me, this is the number one priority of every day.

Phil Joel

Lessons in the Life of ABRAHAM:
LOT'S CAVE

The angels urged Lot, saying, "Hurry!... Or you will be swept away when the city is punished." When he hesitated, the men grasped his hand and the hands of his wife and of his two daughters and led them safely out of the city, for the LORD was merciful to them.

GENESIS 19:15-16

FEBRUARY 2

Lot had been overjoyed when the angels had first entered Sodom earlier that evening. It had been years since he had experienced the deep presence of God, or even that of an angel. As the night progressed, however, Lot had become increasingly frightened. He soon realized that the angels had not come to visit him; they had come to rescue him.

The angels took them by the hands and forcibly dragged them from the city. Then his wife cast one last glance at the city she loved and she too was killed. Now, a drafty cave on a mountain was his home. He had lost everything but his daughters. *Where did I go wrong? How did this happen?*

Where *did* Lot go wrong? The Bible says that Lot was a righteous man, who was tormented in his soul by the darkness and perversion around him (2 Peter 2:7–8). Yet neither his wife nor his daughters seem to have had any real spiritual life, and he had made no significant impact on the city in which he was a leader for years. Although there are many reasons for Lot's failure, three stand out.

First, Lot had no pastor. When Lot left Abraham, he left his spiritual mentor. Second, he had no people. Without spiritual family or godly friends, it was very difficult to penetrate the deep darkness around him. Third, Lot had no power. Unlike Abraham who had followed God's call, Lot had left God's will for his life behind years before.

Have you paid the cost to develop real spiritual strength? Or are you like Lot, tormented by what you see around you but powerless to do anything about it? Could it be that you need some spiritual mentoring? Maybe it's time for you to make a more serious commitment to the spiritual family God has called you to. Whatever the case is, it's not too late for you to return to God and the center of his will, where you will find true power in him.

"LORD, I THANK YOU FOR MY PASTOR AND ALSO FOR those GODLY MEN YOU'VE PLACED in MY LIFE. MAY those RELATIONSHIPS Continue to GROW STRONGER AND DEEPER."

Phil Joel

Lessons in the Life of ABRAHAM:
LAST LAUGH

Sarah said, "God has brought me laughter, and everyone who hears about this will laugh with me.... Who would have said to Abraham that Sarah would nurse children? Yet I have borne him a son in his old age."

GENESIS 21:6-7

FEBRUARY 3

She wept, she cried, she laughed. By this time, the midwives were also laughing hilariously. As Sarah looked into the eyes of her precious child, all her years of pain and frustration were washed away. Despite the intensity of her struggles with unbelief and resentment, God had given her a son.

Her laughter was contagious. It quickly spread from the birth tent throughout the whole camp. When Abraham held his son for the first time, even he could not contain the gales of laughter that rocked his soul. Later that night, as Sarah cradled the infant in her arms, her soul was flooded with joy and thankfulness. "God has brought me laughter," she said, "and everyone who hears about this will laugh with me."

Have you, like Sarah, been in an agonizing battle to believe? If you have, this is no time to give up. Whether you have been waiting for days, months, or even years, God wants to give you the last laugh. No matter how long the wait, when God brings your promise to pass, you will have the last laugh.

In John 16:21–22, Jesus likens this process to the birth of a baby. "A woman giving birth to a child has pain, because her time has come; but when her baby is born she forgets the anguish because of her joy that a child is born into the world. So it is with you: Now is your time of grief, but I will see you again and you will rejoice, and no one will take away your joy."

Although many of you are in your time of pain today, when your promise comes, the accompanying joy will wipe away all the pain of waiting. Therefore, no matter where you are, or what you are facing, be strong in faith. Your God intends to give you the last laugh.

Let faith arise as you spend time in stillness before the LORD praying, meditating, and remembering his faithfulness and goodness. We must remain in fellowship and in an attitude of worship. We must remain proactive in the faith-building process.

Phil Joel

Lessons from the Life of Abraham:

A WELL IN THE DESERT

> God heard the boy crying, and the angel of God called to Hagar from heaven and said to her, "What is the matter, Hagar? Do not be afraid; God has heard the boy crying as he lies there. Lift the boy up and take him by the hand, for I will make him into a great nation." Then God opened her eyes and she saw a well of water.
>
> GENESIS 21:17–19

FEBRUARY 4

The pain was more than she could bear. Her precious son was slowly dying before her eyes. Although she loved him more than life, she could bear his cries no longer and she left him under a sparse desert bush to die.

"Oh God, forgive me! I cannot take it anymore," she whispered. As she sat weeping, she heard a voice that she had never expected to hear again—the gentle voice of the Almighty God. Drawn to the death cries of young Ishmael, he had come to the rescue. "Go back to your child and take him by the hand," God said to Hagar. She opened her eyes and saw a well. With tears of thanksgiving streaming down her cheeks, she led her precious son to the well's cool water.

Perhaps in your life too, God has been drawing near to the very cries that have been driving you away. We often run from the people and places we love the most, because we can no longer bear the pain of facing a problem we cannot fix. Whether it is because of horrible pain in your family, a terrible gash in the depths of your soul, or a period of crushing pressure at school or work, running away will never bring healing.

In the middle of your worst struggles, God has hidden your "miracle well." Today, if you will turn around and face your responsibility for the very person or place you have been running from, you will discover the well of provision and strength that has always been there. Whether it is through a new measure of his presence, a fresh revelation from the Bible, or the encouragement of a Christian friend, God will give you the strength you need today.

DO YOU REALLY BELIEVE IN GOD'S PROVIDENCE? DO YOU REALLY BELIEVE THAT HE UNDERSTANDS THE DETAILS OF YOUR LIFE? IN THE END, YOUR RESPONSE TO THE PROBLEMS YOU ARE FACING ANSWERS THESE QUESTIONS MORE THAN ANYTHING ELSE.

Phil Joel

Lessons from the Life of Abraham:
TESTED

 God said, "Take your son, your only son, Isaac, whom you love, and go to the region of Moriah. Sacrifice him there as a burnt offering on one of the mountains I will tell you about."

GENESIS 22:2

FEBRUARY 5

It shouldn't have been a total shock. The gods of the peoples around him routinely asked their followers to sacrifice their own children. But Abraham knew his God was different. Maybe he hadn't really heard God's voice. With the mountain now looming in the distance, a battle began to rage in Abraham's heart.

Deep inside, though the command was unthinkable, he knew that it had been God's voice he had heard. He had no choice but to continue his journey into the uncertainty of this terrifying test. Would he really sacrifice his son? Yes, if God did not stop him, Abraham would kill the son of promise, knowing that God was able to raise the dead.

Now with his knife raised over his beloved son's bare chest, with no substitute in sight, resurrection was his last hope. "Abraham." The voice of his beloved friend immediately silenced the war that was raging through the corridors of his heart. "Do not lay a hand on the boy. Do not do anything to him. Now I know that you fear me."

Sooner or later every believer will face a test, just like Abraham. He may not ask you to physically sacrifice your children, but he may require you to put your home, career, or a relationship on the altar in order to follow him.

Today, some of you may be facing the loss of a promise that God supernaturally provided for you. Others of you may feel that God is calling you to give up something very precious in order to follow him. No matter what it is you are facing, take heart. Whether God spares you from this potential loss at the last moment, or resurrects it after it is seemingly gone, his promises to you will not fail. Remember the ending to the story of Abraham's test:

> Abraham looked up and there in a thicket he saw a ram caught by its horns. He went over and took the ram and sacrificed it as a burnt offering instead of his son. So Abraham called that place The LORD Will Provide."

GENESIS 22:13–14

In my own life, I have learned that where God's promises are concerned, even when I don't see his provision for their fulfillment, it will always come.

Phil Joel

Lessons from the Life of Isaac:
ISAAC AND REBEKAH

[Abraham said to his servant,] "The LORD, the God of heaven, who brought me out of my father's household and my native land and who spoke to me and promised me on oath, saying, 'To your offspring I will give this land'—he will send his angel before you so that you can get a wife for my son."

GENESIS 24:7

FEBRUARY 6

Faith began to stir in Abraham's heart as he looked into the eyes of his trusted servant and friend. "Eliezer, you must find Isaac a wife. She must not be a Canaanite, nor must Isaac ever leave the Promised Land to find her." As Abraham watched Eliezer leave a few days later, he knew that God would provide.

When Eliezer reached the town of Nahor, and the thirsty caravan waited their turn to drink, he began to pray. "Lord, as I ask these young women for a drink, may the one who also offers to water my camels be the one you have chosen for Isaac." As he opened his tired eyes, he beheld a beautiful young woman. When he asked for a drink, her face broke into a shy smile and she asked him if she could also water his camels. Surely this was the woman designed by God for his master's son.

If you are a single person waiting on God for your spouse, this story contains a great roadmap for your journey. First, even as Abraham did not want Isaac to marry a Canaanite, so a Christian to should not marry an unbeliever (2 Corinthians 6:14–16).

Second, if young Isaac could trust his father's servant to find him a wife, you can trust the Holy Spirit to bring the right person into your life.

Third, although Rebekah was beautiful, Eliezer was most concerned about the condition of her heart. Godly character is the foundation on which successful marriages are built.

Fourth, when Rebekah arrived, Isaac was in the field meditating on the Lord. This is a beautiful picture of waiting on the Lord for his best. If you will stay in your "field," the place God has called you to serve in right now, you will be ready to receive God's best. Furthermore, as you build your relationship with God you will have the power and fulfillment you need in order to wait patiently.

Never forget that if God could use Eliezer to bring Isaac the right bride, surely the Holy Spirit will not make a mistake in the lives of those he is drawing together today.

Do we realize that we are God's best for someone else? Are we letting Him shape and define our character?

Phil Joel

Lessons from the Life of Isaac:

BREAKING OUT OF BARRENNESS

 Isaac prayed to the LORD on behalf of his wife, because she was barren. The LORD answered his prayer, and his wife Rebekah became pregnant.

GENESIS 25:21

FEBRUARY 7

Lord, this isn't just about me and my dream," Isaac prayed. "You have seen the pain in my wife's heart. I'm willing to wait forever, but for her sake, please have mercy. Bring us a child." As the presence of God rushed through his soul, he knew his prayer had been heard.

Are you facing barrenness in some area of your life? (Remember that we are talking about times of barrenness as a metaphor. This doesn't apply to physical infertility.) If so, take heart. Even Abraham, Isaac, and Jacob had to face the issue of barrenness before they could experience the reality of God's promises in their lives.

You may be wondering to yourself how God could ever use a dry, unfruitful time of barrenness. First of all, it would have been a simple matter for God to give Sarah, Rebekah, and Rachel children right away. I am convinced that he did not heal their barrenness quickly because he wanted to mold their characters before he made them fruitful. Ironically, while these families thought they were waiting on God, in reality, he was waiting on them.

Second, God uses barrenness to bring character issues to the surface of our lives—things like unbelief, impatience, and misperceptions about

God. Every time we bring these dark attitudes into the light of God's Word, we are drawing closer to the fulfillment of God's promises in our lives.

Third, the frustration and pain associated with barrenness can also provide the spiritual motivation we need to draw close to God consistently. As we wait on him for the healing, we are also developing the spiritual skills and faith we will need for every other area of our lives.

No matter what kind of barrenness you are facing today, do not be afraid. Whether it is your business or investments that are barren of all profits, or the fact that your ministry seems to be barren of success, God is at work to prepare you for the fulfillment of the promises you have been waiting for.

Like God used barrenness in the lives of the patriarchs, He has used wilderness experiences to sanctify and equip me for my roles as a husband, a father, and a friend. In most cases, I never understood that I was being prepared for those things until I was out of the wilderness.

Phil Joel

Lessons From the Life of Jacob:

HAVE YOU SOLD YOUR BIRTHRIGHT?

Once when Jacob was cooking some stew, Esau came in from the open country, famished. He said to Jacob, "Quick, let me have some of that red stew! I'm famished!"

Jacob replied, "First sell me your birthright."

"Look, I am about to die,"Esau said. "What good is the birthright to me?"

GENESIS 25:29–32

FEBRUARY 8

Esau thought he was starving. Always a man of deep emotion and dark passion, he lived for the immediate gratification of his needs. Then he smelled it. "So the little momma's boy is cooking again," he snarled to himself. Striding up to Jacob, he immediately demanded a bowl of stew. Jacob replied in a whisper: "Sell me your birthright." This was a high price for a bowl of stew. The birthright would give the son who possessed it leadership over the whole family, as well as the right to possess all the promises given to them by Abraham.

"Take it! What good is a birthright to a man who is starving?" Esau said flippantly. Esau walked away, wolfing down his food. Little did he realize the consequences of his actions that day; for when a person loses their birthright, they will also lose their blessing.

Like Esau, we have been given a divine birthright. We are born again into the amazing promise of a life filled with righteousness, peace, and joy. Tragically, to many Christians, this birthright has no practical value. How quick we are to sell our righteousness for a quick fix of lust and our joy for a gulp of biting anger.

Sadly, like Esau in Genesis 27:36, once we have sold our birthright, we will also begin to lose God's blessing on our lives. The temporary thrill of sin can never replace the blessing of walking in God's peace, favor, and presence. Life without the joys of our birthright is no life at all.

What have you been selling your birthright for? Have you been playing with the dark side of the Internet and found yourself robbed of your peace? Have you lost a cherished friend because of pride or bitterness? Fortunately it is not too late for you to regain your birthright. If you will turn afresh to Christ in repentance and faith, you can experience again the joy and life that you thought was gone forever.

Don't eat the stew. It doesn't belong to you. What is yours is always best: purpose, calling, job, ministry, wife, and possessions. We lust for the present and tangible at the expense of the eternal and invisible.

Phil Joel

Lessons from the Life of ISAAC:

ARE YOU BLIND?

When Isaac was old and his eyes were so weak that he could no longer see, he called for Esau his older son and said to him, "My son."

"Here I am," he answered.

GENESIS 27:1

FEBRUARY 9

Ever since the Lord had told Rebekah that Esau would serve Jacob (Genesis 25:23), she had done everything in her power to make it happen. With a growing desperation to see Jacob properly acknowledged by her husband and with Esau on a hunting trip, Rebekah decided it was time to take matters into her own hands. "Jacob put on your brother's clothes, and wrap these goatskins around your neck and arms. When you feed him this stew I have prepared, ask him for Esau's birthright." Although Rebekah's deception would work, the consequences would be grim. Jacob would be forced to flee from Esau's murderous rage, while his parents would be left to deal with Esau's animosity and rebellion for the rest of their lives.

How could the very family through which God had chosen to redeem the world come to the brink of murder? Although Rebekah and Jacob's deceitfulness was obviously a factor, perhaps Isaac's blindness was also to blame. If he could have understood God's destiny for Jacob, this tragedy might have been averted.

Are you blinded to the true character and calling of someone in your life? Are you exalting your "favorites," while the people God has called you to mentor and prepare are left out? Or maybe you are the one being

left out. Just like Jacob, many young people put on a "skin" that does not belong to them in order to gain the opportunities and respect they crave.

If you are a leader in your church or in a ministry, remember that God wants to open your eyes to see the true potential of the people you lead. And if you are a young person longing to use your God-given talents and passions, don't give up on your leaders. Be faithful to your calling and keep following Jesus as you wait for your opportunity to shine for him. As you ask God to open the eyes of your leaders, you will be amazed to see how God uses the great calling he has given you.

Do we believe in a divine purpose for each person and not just ourself? It's different for every person. Some people find it easier to believe for themselves than they do for others. Other people find it easier to believe for other people. Whichever the case may be for you, never forget that God has enough faith to cover them both. As you are filled with God's faith, you'll be surprised to see His destiny and purpose both in your life and in those around you.

Phil Joel

Lessons from the Life of Jacob:
SPIRITUAL AWARENESS

"Surely the Lord is in this place, and I was not aware of it." … "How awesome is this place! This is none other than the house of God; this is the gate of heaven."

GENESIS 28:16–17

FEBRUARY 10

Forced to flee Esau's murderous wrath, Jacob felt as if the very fabric of his life had been torn to shreds. Now, as he finally lay down for the night, he was numb to everything but his own pain.

At that moment, a huge staircase came down out of the heavens to the earth. Angels began to ascend and descend on its steps, and then, a form of incredible glory stood at the top of the stairs and spoke to Jacob of his destiny. It was the God of his father and grandfather, the Almighty God of the universe.

As the heavens were closing, Jacob awakened. Still trembling from his close encounter with heaven, all he could do was mumble, "Surely the Lord is in this place, and I wasn't aware of it."

Why was Jacob so stunned by God's visit? After all, he had grown up hearing the stories of how God had supernaturally intervened in the life of his family. Although there are a number of possible reasons for Jacob's surprise, I only want to concentrate on three of them.

First, Jacob did not think he was in the right place to meet with God. He had no idea that God could meet with him at any place and any time, even as far away as from the Promised Land.

Second, Jacob didn't think that God would *want* to meet with him. Why would God want anything to do with him after the shameful way he had deceived his brother?

Third, I do not believe that Jacob possessed the skills and experience necessary to recognize and respond to the presence of God. Perhaps for this reason, God chose to reach out to Jacob in his dreams.

Have you lost your awareness of God's presence? God is closer to you than you can imagine. Even now, he desires to break into your life with fresh power and grace. God longs to meet you right where you are today if you will reach out to him in faith.

I CANNOT Count the times that I have Been so humBLED AFTER GOD has BROKen through my cynicism By meeting me in pLAces, WAYS, AND through peopLe that I never expected.

Phil Joel

Lessons From the Life of JACOB:
THE SECRET OF TRANSFORMATION

Jacob made a vow, saying, "If God will be with me and will watch over me on this journey I am taking and will give me food to eat and clothes to wear so that I return safely to my father's house, then the LORD will be my God and this stone that I have set up as a pillar will be God's house, and of all that you give me I will give you a tenth."

GENESIS 28:20–22

FEBRUARY II

Incredibly, even after his amazing experience with God, it seems that Jacob was trying to make deals—the time with the Lord of the universe. After grabbing a convenient stone he poured some oil on his makeshift altar and began to bargain with God. "Lord, if you will give me food, clothes, and keep me safe, I'll pay my tithes. In fact I'll even make this stone into a pillar in a permanent home for you."

What was it going to take to finally cut out the root of the deception and compromise in Jacob's heart? What is it going to take to really deal with the "Jacob" that lives in all of us?

If one of the greatest heavenly visitations in all of Scripture had little impact on Jacob's basic character, what hope do we have for lasting change? In my own experience, I have found that amazing church services and incredible Christian events are not enough to bring true transformation. If you do not diligently build upon what you have received in these incredible moments, you will never experience the fullness of what God intends for you.

When God has dramatically touched you in a church service or at a Christian event, he will normally continue to work on you for days, and even weeks. Whether you begin to study the Scriptures more deeply, or you simply begin to spend extra time in prayer, it is critical that you cooperate with the work of the Holy Spirit. As you pay the price to respond to the voice of God, you will begin to experience the lasting change you have been longing for.

There have been times when God has done a number on me but I have not paid the price in the days that followed to fully cooperate with God's work.

Phil Joel

Lessons from the Life of Jacob:
TRICKED

Laban replied, "It is not our custom here to give the younger daughter in marriage before the older one."

GENESIS 29:26

FEBRUARY 12

After seven years of working for Laban in exchange for the beautiful Rachel's hand, Jacob's wedding day finally came. But the next morning, his newfound bliss was quickly shattered. He who had lived by the wiles of deception had finally been tricked himself. Laban had given him his first daughter Leah, instead of the beautiful Rachel. Although he would marry Rachel a week later, it would cost him seven more years of servitude.

What could this sordid love triangle have to do with you and me? First, of all, I believe Leah was at the very center of God's plan for Jacob's life. Rachel was a nagging idol worshipper who suffered from barrenness for many years. Leah, on the other hand, was a woman of noble character who bore Jacob a number of children. Among them would be Levi, the founder of Israel's tribe of priests, and Judah, from whose family line Jesus Christ himself would come. Jacob was so caught up in Rachel's beauty that he ignored the godly character of her sister.

I believe that this story illustrates this truth: If you do not learn how to walk under the influence and power of the Holy Spirit, you will never experience the blessing of deep relationships that God intends for you. In my life, I have found that the more I seek to follow the guidance of the Holy Spirit, the more I want to walk in transparency and accountability with other people, which brings great depth and joy to these relationships.

Furthermore, the results of living under the Holy Spirit's leading are love, patience, gentleness, and self-control (Galatians 5:22–23). It is the power of the Holy Spirit that gives me the ability to humble myself, to admit my faults, and to remain teachable — all qualities that help relationships last and grow.

If you will learn to listen to the Holy Spirit, you will have the ability to both find and maintain the relationships that God brings into your life. With God's help and guidance you will find deep, lasting, and fulfilling relationships that bring glory to him.

The Holy Spirit is always about service. Like Jesus, He seeks not to be served but to serve. Through Laban, Jacob, who had been spoiled as a child, learned to serve the hard way. This doesn't have to be the case in your life. As we open ourselves to the Holy Spirit's leading, we will become greater servants, serving both God and His children.

Phil Joel

Lessons in the Life of JACOB:
TRANSFORMED

A man wrestled with [Jacob] till daybreak.... Jacob called the place Peniel, saying, "It is because I saw God face to face, and yet my life was spared."

GENESIS 32:24, 30

FEBRUARY 13

Suddenly, Jacob was face-to-face with *him*. As he bowed low to the ground, before a man he knew to be God in human form, the Lord picked him up, as if he was a child, and hurled him to the ground. They wrestled all through the night.

Finally the Lord grabbed Jacob's leg and ripped it from its socket. At the same time deep roots of deceit and unbelief were being pulled from his heart. Jacob cried out, *"I will not let you go unless you bless me."* He had finally realized that he could not live without God. He would forever be a transformed man, with a lifelong limp as a tangible reminder of his incredible encounter with God. What Jacob's vision at Bethel and twenty years of being cheated by Laban could not do, God did in one night when he stepped into Jacob's life in human form.

Although incredible church services and mission trips play a critical role in the transformation process, by themselves, they are not sufficient to bring change to our hearts. Even as God stepped into the life of Jacob in human form, so he wants to bring change in your life through other people. He took the form of a human, just as he did with Jacob, when Jesus came to earth. And today he will come to you through other believers to encourage you in your faith.

In my own life, I have found that I have never outgrown the need to have other believers intimately involved in my life. When I was young, I desperately needed older Christians who would train me in the ways of the faith. Today, although I no longer need training in the basics of the Christian faith, I still need the counsel and encouragement of trusted Christian friends.

As a young person, this is the perfect time for you to seek out people who will encourage your journey with God. Go to your pastor or another Christian leader and ask them to help you find the relationships you need. As you find these special people, you will experience a whole new level of growth and change. You will never be the same.

The older I get, the more I see my great need to have older men in my life. In Christian music, there are far too many "ALL I need is Jesus" songs. The Bible is clear — we also need His people.

Phil Joel

Lessons in the Life of Joseph:
LOVED BY HIS FATHER

Now Israel loved Joseph more than any of his other sons, because he had been born to him in his old age; and he made a richly ornamented robe for him.

GENESIS 37:3

FEBRUARY 14

He was the absolute joy of his father's heart. Now, as Jacob reached out to hand his son the richly ornamented robe, young Joseph began to realize for the first time just how much his father loved him. This was no ordinary coat. This was the coat of a prince. As he considered the coat's rich hues, with a fresh revelation of his father's love churning in his heart, Joseph began to dream. His incredible dreams would define the rest of his life because in them he would begin to see a glimpse of his future.

Joseph began to dream God's dream for his life after he received the "coat of many colors" from his father. Perhaps receiving this amazing token of his father's love gave him the security and confidence he needed to begin to receive the revelation of God's plan for his life. And perhaps, until you begin to realize the magnitude of your Heavenly Father's great love, you will never be able to accept his amazing purpose and plan for your life, either.

Just as Jacob clothed Joseph in an amazing garment, so your Heavenly Father has clothed you with every gift of grace you need to fulfill your destiny. Isaiah says that we have been clothed in the "garments of salvation" (Isaiah 61:10). Peter says God has "given us everything we need for life and godliness" (2 Peter 1:3).

Just as Jacob revealed his love to Joseph through an extravagant gift, so God has revealed his love by adopting you as his child. "How great is the love the Father has lavished on us, that we should be called children of God! And that is what we are!" (1 John 3:1) Let these words really sink in. This is what you are! You are a child of God! No matter how dark your past is, or how terrible your present may be, if you are born again, God calls you his beloved child. As the reality of how deeply God loves you begins to grow in your heart, you, too, will have the confidence you need to dream his dream for your life.

I think Jacob cast a vision for young Joseph. Even as a young boy he knew that God had something going on for him. This vision was imparted to young Joseph both verbally (he used his tongue) and practically (he gave him the coat of many colors). Most parents seem to gravitate to one or the other. We must tell our children we love them and demonstrate it as well.

Phil Joel

Lessons in the Life of Joseph:
HERE COMES THE DREAMER

"Here comes that dreamer!" [Joseph's brothers] said to each other. "Come now, let's kill him and throw him into one of these cisterns and say that a ferocious animal devoured him. Then we'll see what comes of his dreams."

GENESIS 37:19–20

FEBRUARY 15

Like many young people on fire with big dreams, Joseph was filled with both God and a lot of himself. Filled with the lethal combination of youthful exuberance and arrogance, Joseph was totally unaware of the hatred that had been growing in the hearts of his brothers. When they attacked him, he was stunned. Now as he lay bleeding in the depths of an abandoned cistern, he was not just broken in body—he was broken in spirit as well. When his brothers had finally pulled him out it was not to take him home, but to sell him into slavery. Joseph, the big dreamer, could only hang his head and weep.

Although there are a number of lessons we can learn from this story, let me share just two. First of all, even a God-given dream must be handled with wisdom and humility. Although Joseph's dreams were from God, he shared them in a way that was both unwise and arrogant. We must be very careful about how, and with whom, we share God's vision for our lives.

Second, although Joseph was unwise, he *had* received God's vision and dream for his life. In Psalms 105:17–19 it says that Joseph was sold as a slave and put in chains until what he foretold came to pass and the

Word of the Lord proved him true. The pain was part of the process. God will take the most painful circumstances of your life and use them as tools to mold you and shape you for the purpose for which you were born.

Are you in the middle of a painful situation that is being used by God to prepare you for your destiny? Maybe your own pride and arrogance about the vision God has given you has alienated you from some of the brothers and sisters you love the most. Take heart. Whether you need strength to walk through the circumstances you're facing, or grace to humble yourself before the brothers or sisters you have offended, God is able to give it to you.

We have to learn how to steward our dreams. Part of this stewardship includes the wisdom about how, when, and with whom to share them. This reiterates the importance of having people in our lives with whom we can entrust our dreams.

Phil Joel

Lessons from the Life of Joseph:
JOSEPH'S BROTHERS

When the Midianite merchants came by, his brothers pulled Joseph up out of the cistern and sold him for twenty shekels of silver to the Ishmaelites, who took him to Egypt.

GENESIS 37:28

FEBRUARY 16

As they watched Joseph being dragged away into slavery, his brothers' faces were as hard as their hearts. They were happy to dispose of the arrogant young braggart. Perhaps in time their father would see it was for the best too. Right now Jacob was too blinded by his love for Joseph's mother to see the wickedness of Joseph's heart. Yes, just as the manipulative Rachel had stolen their father's love from their mothers, so Joseph had also stolen his love for them.

Although Joseph's pride and lack of wisdom and Jacob's favoritism were factors in the brothers' actions, there were far darker issues at work here. First, eight of the twelve sons had been born to Leah or Zilpah. Both women had been denied Jacob's affection because he only had eyes for Rachel. Both of these women surely passed down their bitterness to their children. It was only natural for their sons to hate the son of the woman who had so deeply wronged their own mothers. When Joseph became the favorite son, the hatred already lurking in their hearts was only exasperated.

Tragically, this same terrible pattern is still affecting families today. Whether it is toward God, an ethnicity, a gender, the church, or a person, bitterness gets passed down through generations. In the words of Paul, it will "cause trouble and defile many" (Hebrews 12:15).

Another factor was that Joseph's obedience to his father and vision for his own life only exposed the spiritual poverty and lack of character in the lives of his brothers. If Joseph's brothers would have been secure in their own walk with God and in his purpose for them, they never would have been so deeply offended at the exuberance of their young brother.

Where are you today? Are you battling with bitterness and offense? Maybe someone else's blessing has exposed some bitterness that you've been holding on to. God wants to deliver you today. Don't let bitterness bring heartbreak to your life and to the lives of those you love. Ask God for forgiveness, and the power to give up your bitterness. As you pursue freedom, God will give you the strength you need to be delivered.

No matter how hard we try, there will always be a certain amount of misunderstanding or resistance surrounding the dreams God has given us. However, we don't need to perpetuate this or make it worse by our own lack of wisdom. I know for myself, I need to be careful about prematurely sharing the things God has revealed to me.

Phil Joel

Lessons from the Life of Joseph:
IN THE PIT

> When Joseph came to his brothers, they stripped him of his robe — the richly ornamented robe he was wearing.

GENESIS 37:23

FEBRUARY 17

As he attempted to move his bruised body, Joseph was still stunned by the vicious betrayal of his brothers. When he reached to cover himself with his robe he realized for the first time that they had taken it. "Lord" he whispered, "they have taken the mark of my father's favor."

We experience the same thing today. The devil cannot throw us into a pit of despair or depression until he has ripped away our sense of God's love and favor.

The primary way that the enemy attempts to destroy our sense of God's love and favor is through condemnation. Unlike the Holy Spirit's conviction, which condemns our *sin*, the enemy condemns our *person*. The result of surrendering your soul to an attack of condemnation is a lack of confidence in God's power (1 John 3:21) and a gradual sense of separation from God's presence and purpose (Psalm 13:1–2).

According to Romans 8:1, however, there is no condemnation to those who are in Christ Jesus. How can you experience the reality of this amazing statement? First of all, when the enemy is condemning you, you can stand on the fact that God's love for you is based on Jesus' death for you on the cross. You have received the gift of Jesus' righteousness (2 Corinthians 5:21).

Second, you are a child of God (1 John 3:1). Like any good parent, he loves you with an everlasting love. Even on your worst days, never forget that you are still his child.

Third, no matter how you have sinned, when you ask forgiveness, the blood of Jesus will cleanse you from all unrighteousness (1 John 1:9).

No matter where you are today, God is coming to set you free. Whether you are already in the pit or still fighting to keep the sense of God's love and favor, his grace is sufficient for you. It is time for you to rise up in the divine confidence that is yours as a child of the Almighty God. There is no pit that can hold you today and no lie from the enemy that can blind you to the reality of whom you are if you will only believe what the Word of God says about you.

When we are in the pit, it is critical that we find ways to hold on to the promises and truths God has given us. In my own life, I have done this through journaling. Time and time again, I have been sustained in the present by the things I wrote down from what God spoke to me in the past.

Phil Joel

Lessons from the Life of Joseph:
POTIPHAR'S HOUSE

The LORD was with Joseph and he prospered.... When his master saw that the LORD was with him and that the LORD gave him success in everything he did, Joseph found favor in his eyes and became his attendant.

GENESIS 39:2–4

FEBRUARY 18

At seventeen, it seemed to Joseph that his life was already over. After being brutally betrayed by his brothers and sold into slavery, he was now being taken into the heart of Egypt. Yet despite his overwhelming pain, he also had a growing sense of God's presence. By the time he had been sold to Potiphar, the captain of Pharaoh's guard, the injuries to his body and, even more importantly, his faith were healed.

Within months, he had become Potiphar's personal attendant—the steward of everything he owned. Everything Joseph touched prospered. Although his work ethic and leadership were excellent, it was also as if the young man was especially favored by the gods. *Yes*, Potiphar thought to himself, *slave or not, this young man has been born for great things.*

Are you in Potiphar's house today—the one place you never wanted to be? Whether you are in the school you hate, the last job you would have chosen, or the city you never desired to live in, maybe, like Joseph, you, too, are unknowingly in the very center of God's will for your life. God knew that the young man who would one day rule all of Egypt had to learn to serve before he could lead. God himself has placed you, too, in your "Potiphar's house" for a reason. He is working to prepare you for the next step in your destiny.

Until you acknowledge that God has placed you where you are today, you will have trouble experiencing his presence there. It is almost impossible to embrace God's person and presence when you are resisting his placement. Once you say yes to God's will, you begin to receive the power and the grace you need to be successful right where you are.

If you buy into the lie that it is always in some other place that God is going to bring you blessing, you will probably never experience any true prosperity at all. But as you accept his placement you will experience the divine success that only God's favor and blessing can bring.

We must learn to serve before we can lead. Even though Joseph never would have chosen Potiphar's house as the place to be taught, his submission to God's will made him the man he needed to be.

Phil Joel

Lessons from the Life of Joseph:
POTIPHAR'S WIFE

Though she spoke to Joseph day after day, he refused to go to bed with her or even be with her. One day he went into the house to attend to his duties, and none of the household servants was inside. She caught him by his cloak and said, "Come to bed with me!" But he left his cloak in her hand and ran out of the house.

GENESIS 39:10-12

FEBRUARY 19

Sultry, seductive, and gorgeous, Potiphar's wife was unlike any woman Joseph had ever seen. But there was death in her eyes and poison in her heart. Every time she cast her eyes his way, it was as if she was throwing out a net to capture Joseph. Thus far, he had avoided her entrapments by deliberately avoiding her. This time, however, all the other servants were gone and he had work to do inside the house. This time, when he turned away from her blatant seduction, she reached out and grabbed him. He tore himself away from her grip and ran for his life. Although his courageous stand against temptation would result in his imprisonment in Pharaoh's dungeons, to Joseph, no price was too great to pay to remain pure in the eyes of God.

Joseph's story holds some great lessons about how to resist temptation. First, Joseph had a clear definition of sin. It did not matter to him what Potiphar's wife wanted, or whether or not her husband would ever find out; Joseph refused to sin against God.

Second, he was able to resist seduction because he refused to linger near its source. He had the wisdom to never place himself in a situation where he could fall; he steered clear of Potiphar's wife deliberately.

Although he was a righteous young man, he did not overestimate his ability to resist her charms.

Third, when he found himself in the grasp of her temptations, Joseph literally tore himself away and ran for his life. He did not try to reason with her, or even to gently pull away from her grip. He exerted every bit of strength he had to escape.

Are you having trouble admitting that you are struggling with sin? As long as you rationalize that the things that tempt you are only little problems or slight weaknesses, you are in danger of letting these temptations trap you. Perhaps, unlike Joseph, you are spending time with the very thing or person that could destroy you. Do you continually hang out with the crowd that has led you down the wrong path repeatedly? Do you still allow yourself to surf the Internet late at night, knowing that it will be easy for you to look at things you shouldn't? First Corinthians 10:12 says, "If you think you're standing firm, be careful that you don't fall." Part of being careful that you don't fall is deliberately avoiding the places and activities that are bound to cause you to stumble.

Let me tell you now that your own willpower will not be enough to allow you to win the battle with temptation. Only the power of God can help you escape sin's insidious grasp. When you feel its tentacles clinging to you, invite the strongest Christians you know to help you battle for your soul. Through the power of God and the support of your brothers and sisters in Christ, you too can have the integrity of Joseph, and the joy of walking in the light of the Lord.

We must remain on the balls of our feet — always vigilant, always ready to run from the temptation that we are not yet strong enough to fight.

Phil Joel

Lessons in the Life of Joseph:
PHARAOH'S PRISON

When his master heard the story his wife told him, saying, "This is how your slave treated me," he burned with anger. Joseph's master took him and put him in prison, the place where the king's prisoners were confined. But while Joseph was there in the prison, the LORD was with him; he showed him kindness and granted him favor in the eyes of the prison warden. So the warden put Joseph in charge of all those held in the prison, and he was made responsible for all that was done there. The warden paid no attention to anything under Joseph's care, because the LORD was with Joseph and gave him success in whatever he did.

GENESIS 39:19–23

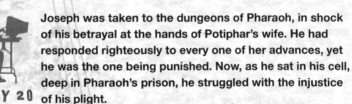

FEBRUARY 20

Joseph was taken to the dungeons of Pharaoh, in shock of his betrayal at the hands of Potiphar's wife. He had responded righteously to every one of her advances, yet he was the one being punished. Now, as he sat in his cell, deep in Pharaoh's prison, he struggled with the injustice of his plight.

Yet, there was a sense of peace beginning to permeate Joseph's soul. Even in this dark prison, God, his Friend, was with him. In the weeks to come, the blessing of God in Joseph's life would become apparent to the whole prison. The warden would entrust the whole prison to Joseph's oversight. What the enemy meant for evil, God meant for good. Pharaoh's prison would become the doorway to Pharaoh's palace.

We need to remember when the attacks and temptations of the enemy come, they often come in waves. Within moments of successfully rebuffing the advance of Potiphar's wife, Joseph was falsely accused and betrayed. When you find yourself under the relentless attacks of the enemy, it is critical that you don't lose your perspective. Be encouraged that strong attacks are normally a signal that you are approaching a spiritual breakthrough or transition.

Also, remember that God does his greatest work at the darkest moments in our lives. Joseph had to go to the prison before he was exalted to the palace. Despite the pain of his unjust imprisonment, God used the experience to prepare Joseph to fulfill his ultimate purpose (Psalms 105:18–21).

Are you in a dark period of your life today? God promises to be with you in a special way at this critical time in your life. And just like Joseph, he will bring you to a new and wonderful place of purpose and fulfillment as you trust him through the difficult times.

I Know FRom my own experience thAt the GReAtest heAt FRom the enemy ARRives when I'm on the threshold of A new BReAKthRough with the LORD.

Phil Joel

Lessons from the Life of Joseph:
FORGOTTEN

The chief cupbearer, however, did not remember Joseph; he forgot him.

GENESIS 40:23

FEBRUARY 21

In the darkness of Pharaoh's prison, Joseph shined like a burning beacon. Not only had he excelled as a leader, but he had also discovered the fullness of his spiritual gift. He was not only a dreamer of dreams; he was an interpreter of dreams. His interpretations had been exactly right. The cupbearer had been restored to his position in Pharaoh's court, just as Joseph predicted. Surely the cupbearer would speak to Pharaoh about Joseph's imprisonment now that he had been restored to his position of power. Yet as the days turned into months, Joseph knew the cupbearer had forgotten all about him.

Do you feel forgotten—by your coach, employer, friend, or significant other? Take heart, because your God has *not* forgotten you. According to Isaiah 49:15, God will never forget you: "Can a mother forget the baby at her breast and have no compassion on the child she has borne? Though she may forget, I will not forget you!"

You may be thinking to yourself, *If God has not forgotten me, what is happening?* Never forget that God's purpose for Joseph was far greater than merely freeing him from prison. He wanted to put him in the palace. Therefore, timing was everything. If Joseph would have been released from prison before Pharaoh dreamed a dream in need of Joseph's interpretation, everything might have been different. Joseph may never have reached the throne of Egypt.

Even in life's most painful moments, when we feel totally abandoned by God and others, our loving Father is at work to fulfill our ultimate destiny. He is both building the needed character into us, as well as working his perfect timing in the circumstances around us. As you face your own time of waiting, let the words of James 1:4 ignite a fresh flame of faith and hope in your heart:

> "Perseverance must finish its work so that you may be mature and complete, not lacking anything."

Sometimes in my own DARKest hours, I have fallen into despair because I have looked for God or expected him to come in the way that he had always done before. Although my faith has been tested during these times, no matter how badly I seem to fail, he is always willing to give me a retest.

Phil Joel

Lessons from the Life of Joseph:
PHARAOH'S PALACE

Joseph named his firstborn Manasseh and said, "It is because God has made me forget all my trouble and all my father's household." The second son he named Ephraim and said, "It is because God has made me fruitful in the land of my suffering."

GENESIS 41:51–52

FEBRUARY 22

Joseph's thirteen-year road to his destiny had taken him from the pit to Potiphar's house, to the prison, and finally, to the palace. As he held his new son in his arms, his heart was overflowing with thanksgiving. He would name the baby Ephraim, which means "twice fruitful." Joseph had named his first son Manasseh, or "forget," because God had healed him from the pain of his past. And now he had become fruitful in the very land where he had been enslaved and imprisoned.

After thirteen years of betrayal and suffering, how could Joseph be so free from the haunting memories of his painful past? First, there was no bitterness in his heart—toward his brothers, Potiphar's wife, or anyone else. Nowhere in his story is there even hint of Joseph using his power to take revenge on those who had hurt him. In fact, instead, an incredible reconciliation takes place between Joseph and his brothers.

Second, Joseph acknowledged that God had been working through everything he had suffered to position him for his destiny. As far he was concerned, God had sent him to Egypt. The betrayal of his brothers was merely the means to that end (Genesis 45:4–7).

With no bitterness in his heart, and the assurance that God had even been working through the most painful circumstances in his life, healing was the natural outcome for Joseph. Even more amazing is the fact that Joseph was healed long before he reached the palace and was able to see the good that came from the pain. The prosperity he experienced in the palace was simply a continuation of the blessing he had been experiencing for years.

Joseph's story can be yours too. If you will refuse to live in bitterness and embrace God's shaping hand in your circumstances, you, too, can begin to experience the prosperity and blessing that God has for your life. No matter who or what has wounded your soul, God is able to heal you. Let him take any bitterness out of your heart today and look forward to the blessings that are to come.

Although being in the palace was probably amazing and maybe even astonishing to Joseph, he was ready for it because he had experienced God's provision everywhere He had placed him.

Phil Joel

Lessons from the Life of Joseph:

FRUITFUL IN THE LAND OF HIS SUFFERING

 "God has made me fruitful in the land of my suffering."

GENESIS 41:52

FEBRUARY 23

He was the talk of the nation. His wisdom was already becoming a legend. At only thirty years old, Joseph was second only to Pharaoh in authority. He who had come to Egypt as a slave was now becoming the savior of the very nation that had imprisoned him. Yes, God truly had made him fruitful in the land of his suffering.

What was the secret of this young man's rise to power? In Potiphar's house, the prison, and ultimately the palace, Joseph had never failed to advance to leadership. Many factors brought about Joseph's success. The following are just a few of the lessons we can apply to our lives from the story of Joseph.

First, Joseph acknowledged the working of God's Spirit in the circumstances of his life. When Joseph was reunited with his brothers, he told them that their act of selling him into slavery had been used by God for great good. He saw that God had sent him into Egypt in order to save many lives during the famine. If we can have this perspective, we will strive for excellence no matter how menial the task or painful the circumstances. We, like Joseph, can then exemplify the words of Colossians 3:23: "Whatever you do, work at it with all your heart, as working for the Lord, not for men."

Second, Joseph was totally reliable. Neither Potiphar nor the prison warden ever worried about anything that had been entrusted to Joseph

(Genesis 39:6, 23). This level of integrity will always open incredible doors of opportunity.

Third, Joseph was remarkably humble. Even when he stood before the throne of Egypt, he refused to take any credit for interpreting the dreams that had been troubling Pharaoh (Genesis 41:15–16). Other men would have recommended themselves for the job of preparing for the famine, but Joseph asked Pharaoh to promote other people to the position (Genesis 41:32–37). His avoidance of self-promotion made way for God to promote him.

Could it be that these same principles will work in your life today? If you will allow God's Spirit to work in you, integrity to be your top priority, and humility to guide you, you will be amazed to see the doors of blessing and promotion that God will open just for you!

I have learned not to allow my circumstances to determine my joy. In other words, my joy must not pivot on my circumstances. Like Joseph, God is capable of giving us joy in the land of our suffering. In those tougher times, I need to press into God through worship more than ever if I am going to experience the joy I need.

Phil Joel

Lessons from the Life of Joseph:
I WILL MAKE YOU A BLESSING

"I will bless those who bless you, ... and all peoples on earth
will be blessed through you," [says the Lord].

G E N E S I S   1 2 : 3

All the countries came to Egypt to buy grain from Joseph,
because the famine was severe in all the world.

G E N E S I S   4 1 : 5 7

FEBRUARY 24

The whole court was stunned. Wasn't Pharaoh supposed
to be divine? Yet, this Hebrew nomad was bestowing a
blessing on him! First, Jacob's son Joseph had saved
Egypt from famine, and now Jacob was ministering the
most powerful leader in the ancient world!

The story of Jacob's family in Egypt clearly illustrates
that God's promise to make Abraham's descendants a blessing was already being fulfilled. Through the faithfulness and obedience of this single
family, much of the ancient world was saved from a catastrophic famine.
How could this small nomadic family walk out of the desert and change
the course of history?

First of all, this family had the paid the price for the favor and power
that the blessing of God brings. Joseph faithfully served God, even in
prison. Jacob literally wrestled with God all night for his blessing. God
made amazing promises but none of them were simply inherited. Each of
these chosen people paid the cost to develop the faith needed to receive
the blessings and promises that their family had been given. Whether it

was through blessing Pharaoh, saving an empire, or defeating the armies of five kings, the favor of God gave them the power to transcend their own culture and shape the world around them. As people living under the authority of the king of the universe, there was no earthly power to which they feared to speak.

In the process of developing faith, these people also developed deep intimacy with God. After years of walking with him, each of them could hear and follow the voice of God with deep confidence, giving them the ability to speak the word and wisdom of God into the troubled situations of their world.

As their faith was developed and they learned to walk with God, Abraham, Isaac, Jacob, and Joseph also developed tremendous character. They were separated from those around them by both the distinctions of their faith, and the excellence of their character. In the darkness of a pagan age, they shined.

If God can shape the course of human history and bless every nation in the world through one nomadic family, what can he do through you? If you will seek intimacy with God, he will make you a blessing to your school, neighborhood, coworkers, and family. He longs to see a generation of men and women who, in his power, will work to break the cycle of spiritual and moral famine that is devastating this world. Will you be a "Joseph" where you are today?

ASK the LORD to show you your condition and reveal those things that He desires you to move into at this time. Are there areas of faith and obedience that you have been avoiding that are actually keys to a greater level of influence? Joseph's faithfulness to obey God by storing up for a famine that in the natural there was no evidence of saved him, his whole family, and the nation of Egypt.

Phil Joel

Lessons from the Life of Joseph:

THE VISION STILL LIVED

Joseph said to his brothers, "I am about to die. But God will
surely come to your aid and take you up out of this land
to the land he promised on oath to Abraham, Isaac and
Jacob.... Then you must carry my bones up from this place."

GENESIS 50:24–25

Joseph had become a legend in his own time—the savior
of an empire. Yet, as he neared death, it was not monu-
ments or state funerals that were on his mind—it was
the Promised Land. A vision of his family's future came to
him and he spoke these amazing words: "God will surely

FEBRUARY 25 come to your aid, and then you must carry my bones up
from this place."

Joseph's prophecy that his family would one day return to the Promised Land is also a moving testament to the fact that he longed to return
there himself. The fabulous success and stunning wealth that he had
received in Egypt had never quenched Joseph's passion for the promises
of God.

We can find a great lesson in Joseph's faithfulness God's plan.
Sometimes the greatest threat to the divine vision you possess is the very
success that it brings. Many Christians see their burning vision and faith
quenched when they focus on the rewards that godly character brings
them. How can you and I maintain our vision for the king and his kingdom
in the face of the temptations that success brings?

Like Joseph, all of us need a Jacob in our lives. Jacob was a continual
reminder to Joseph of the promises that God had made to his family. The

humility and wisdom that characterized his father's life are a potent anti-
dote to the traps that come with success.

Joseph's relationship with God was not desperation-based. No matter the situation, he had always maintained a deep, life-giving relationship with God. Although he no longer lived in the Promised Land, he still
walked intimately with the God of the promise. He never lost sight of the
invisible. He saw beyond the seductive beauty of Egypt to a better world
and to the promises of his God.

If we, too, will look to our spiritual mentors for wisdom, walk in intimacy with God, and cultivate a faith in what we cannot yet see, we, too,
can pass the tests of success and keep our eyes on the Promised Land.

Joseph's success never stifled or quenched his passion for the generations that were to come. He never lost sight of their future purpose.

Phil Joel

Lessons in the Life of Moses:
PHARAOH'S STRATEGY

The Israelites were fruitful and multiplied greatly and became exceedingly numerous, so that the land was filled with them. Then a new king, who did not know about Joseph, came to power in Egypt. "Look," he said to his people, "the Israelites have become much too numerous for us. Come, we must deal shrewdly with them."

EXODUS 1:7-10

FEBRUARY 26

In the nearly three hundred years since the death of Joseph, the family of Jacob had grown from a small band of seventy to a population of two million. The Israelites' rapidly growing numbers were seen as a looming threat to Pharaoh. So, with Joseph long forgotten, Israel became a persecuted minority.

Pharaoh's solution to the Israelite "problem" was to forcibly draft the Jewish people into large-scale construction projects. Under Egypt's burning sun and the crack of the taskmaster's whip, the sons of Jacob plunged into the destitution of slavery. According to the book of Exodus, though, the more the Israelites were oppressed, the more they multiplied and spread. Even when their labor quotas were increased, and their schedules made more rigorous, the people of Israel continued to grow at an alarming rate, bringing even greater oppression upon them.

We face oppression from evil forces today as well. Just as Pharaoh feared the continued multiplication of Israel, so our enemy, the devil, fears true church growth—growth that comes from evangelism and discipleship. Whenever the devil is faced with the threat of a growing church or ministry, he will release his most insidious strategies in order to stop it.

One of Satan's primary strategies is to torment the people who are accomplishing the most for God's kingdom. He will do whatever it takes to keep the people of God from bearing fruit. I have seen the enemy use anything from unexpected sickness to discouragements at school or work to distract God's people from their primary purpose.

Whenever you are faced with the retaliation of the devil, you must remember to stay on the offensive. When you face an enemy attack that is the very time when you should work even harder at God's purpose for you. An attack means that you're doing exactly what God wants you to do and it is a threat to the enemy. Never forget, as you are faithful to meet God's foes, he will be faithful to defeat your woes!

When I am tempted to compromise what God has called me to do, I refuse to even indulge in these thoughts. The words of Nehemiah 6:3 have been very important to me in these times of temptation, "I am carrying on a great project and cannot go down. Why should the work stop while I leave it and go down to you?"

Phil Joel

Lessons from the Life of Moses:

PHARAOH'S ATTACK

The king of Egypt said to the Hebrew midwives, ... "When you help the Hebrew women in childbirth and observe them on the delivery stool, if it is a boy, kill him; but if it is a girl, let her live." The midwives, however, feared God and did not do what the king of Egypt had told them to do; they let the boys live.

So God was kind to the midwives and the people increased and became even more numerous. And because the midwives feared God, he gave them families of their own.

Then Pharaoh gave this order to all his people: "Every boy that is born you must throw into the Nile, but let every girl live."

EXODUS 1:15–17, 20–22

FEBRUARY 27

When the children of Israel continued to multiply, Pharaoh's anger turned into a burning rage. His plan to destroy them was diabolical; he would ask the Hebrew midwives to kill every baby boy they delivered. But his plans were thwarted. Although they feared the wrath of Pharaoh, the midwives feared the almighty God more. No matter how hard Pharaoh pressed them, they refused to kill the infant boys. When this attack failed, Pharaoh released his full wrath against the people of God. He gave every Egyptian citizen the order to drown any Hebrew male baby they found in the Nile River.

Sadly, even as Pharaoh tried to intimidate the Hebrew midwives into murdering the baby boys they were delivering, so today the devil tries to get Christians to spiritually kill "baby" Christians by keeping us from dis-

cipling them. Just like newborn babies, new Christians are vulnerable and need the care of older Christians if they are to grow.

When Satan fails at using ignorance and selfishness to kill brand-new faith, he will come to destroy it himself—just like Pharaoh had to resort to using his own citizens against the Hebrews. The first year in a new Christian's life is one of the most critical periods of his or her spiritual development. If these new Christians are not properly cared for, they can easily fall away.

There is a real devil who has declared a real war on the human race. Both new and older Christians need to be on guard and ready for battle. If you are a new Christian, make sure you find seasoned veterans to help you grow strong and ready for the fight. If you have been a Christian for a long time, keep your eyes open for young believers that need you to stand beside them in the battle.

If Christians like you and me will rise up and wage war on the enemy, we can be mighty in destroying his strongholds on this planet! May God fill your heart with a fresh passion as you stand strong in the battle for new souls and for your world!

HAve we plAced ourselves in A position where we hAve Been Discipled And Are continuing thAt process As we Disciple the next generAtion? These Are our sons And DAughters. Jesus spent three yeArs teAching And trAining His Disciples. I know for myself, the LORD hAd to tAke me through A seAson of intense Discipleship to prepAre me to Disciple others.

Phil Joel

Lessons in the Life of Moses:
NO ORDINARY CHILD

[A Levite woman] became pregnant and gave birth to a son. When she saw that he was a fine child, she hid him for three months. But when she could hide him no longer, she got a papyrus basket for him and coated it with tar and pitch. Then she placed the child in it and put it among the reeds along the bank of the Nile.

EXODUS 2:2–4

FEBRUARY 28

Murder and mayhem were the order of the day. Most of the women were afraid to become pregnant. Those who did would try to have their child in some hidden place and hide it once it was born. Faced with the birth of her third child, Jochebed did the same. From the moment of his birth, she saw an almost divine presence around this little one. As she clutched her infant son to her breast, tears streaming down her cheeks, Jochebed knew deep within her heart that this child would have a unique destiny. She would do whatever it took to keep this child alive.

After three months in hiding, Jochebed and her husband knew they couldn't conceal their precious son any longer. Pharaoh's spies or the never-ending patrols of Egyptian soldiers would soon discover him. As she prayed, a plan began to form in Jochebed's heart. After carefully constructing a small floating basket, she set her infant son inside and placed the craft on the gently undulating waters of the Nile—the very place which had been used to destroy her son's generation. God assured her that it would instead become a place of salvation for her little son. In spite of her fear, Jochebed felt an incredible sense of peace as well. Her son was not floating into the jaws of death but into the arms of destiny.

We are facing a world full of danger today as well. As a young person, you are under the assault by the enemy every day. I believe this is because you are part of no ordinary generation. The magnitude of the attacks you are facing is a sign of your divine calling to bring life and transformation to our hurting planet.

At times you may feel you are struggling to survive in a raging sea of darkness. But there is reason for great hope! As a born-again member of God's family, you are definitely "no ordinary child." Your heavenly Father is the king of the universe and he has given you an extraordinary destiny. You have been sent to this planet for a purpose. Even in the midst of your own "crocodile-infested Nile" you are safe because you are in God's hands. Continue to follow your calling, knowing that God will give you the grace to find your place and to seize your destiny!

Do we at times miss out on the realization that God has a great call on our children's lives? We have not sought to understand God's call on our own lives and have not experienced victory in living counterculturally in our own generation. When this is the case, we may well miss the calling in the lives of the very people who are closest to us. In other words, we don't see the potential in our children's lives because much of the time we don't see the potential in our own lives.

Phil Joel

RIVER RIDE

When she could hide him no longer, she got a papyrus basket for him and coated it with tar and pitch. Then she placed the child in it and put it among the reeds along the bank of the Nile. His sister stood at a distance to see what would happen to him. Then Pharaoh's daughter went down to the Nile to bathe, and her attendants were walking along the river bank. She saw the basket among the reeds and sent her slave girl to get it. She opened it and saw the baby. He was crying, and she felt sorry for him.

"This is one of the Hebrew babies," she said.

Then his sister asked Pharaoh's daughter, "Shall I go and get one of the Hebrew women to nurse the baby for you?"

"Yes, go," she answered. And the girl went and got the baby's mother.

Pharaoh's daughter said to her, "Take this baby and nurse him for me, and I will pay you." So the woman took the baby and nursed him.

EXODUS 2:3–9

FEBRUARY 29

To save her little son's life, Jochebed would put Moses in a papyrus basket coated with tar and pitch and float him down the Nile. With a whispered prayer, she pushed him out onto the river with the hope that she was sending him to his destiny and not his doom.

After instructing Miriam to follow the basket from a distance, she waited on the banks of the Nile until her baby was out of sight. When a breathless Miriam returned hours later with her report, Jochebed could hardly believe what she was hearing.

"The baby has been rescued by the daughter of Pharaoh, and she wants to hire you to be his nurse!" With tears of thanksgiving streaming down her cheeks, Jochebed, who had thought that she would never see her son again, would now care for him again, without fear for his life.

Sooner or later, like Moses parents, your parents will have to trust the life and future of their children to God and let them go. As a young person, it is probably hard for you to understand the struggle that your parents face between fear and faith as they send you on your way "down the Nile." You are full of big dreams—perhaps you are headed off to college, entering the military, or falling in love. No matter what the next chapter of your life holds, never forget that the same God who cared for little Moses as he floated on the dangerous waters of the Nile is there to guide you as well.

And when you face hard times, the God who used the daughter of Pharaoh to raise little Moses, can also provide you with the mentors and friends you need to stay strong in your faith. Maybe you are worrying about how you will overcome the pressures and temptations that you know are waiting for you in the "real world." Remember—the same God that has been taking care of you and guiding you since you were a baby is going with you wherever life takes you. He won't let you face your struggles alone. You belong to the God of the universe. Your earthly parents will have to let you go, but your heavenly Father never will. As you step out into the big, wide world, remember that you are still in his hands. Just like little Moses, you can have peace and security as you embark on your journey "down the Nile," knowing that God is guiding you on your way.

"LORD, THANK YOU FOR A FRESH REVELATION THAT YOU LOVE MY CHILDREN EVEN MORE THAN I DO. I TRUST YOU AND LOVE YOU."

Phil Joel

Lessons in the Life of Moses:

BURDENED BUT NOT BLESSED

[Moses] went out to where his own people were and watched them at their hard labor. He saw an Egyptian beating a Hebrew.... He killed the Egyptian and hid him in the sand. The next day, he went out and saw two Hebrews fighting. He asked the one in the wrong, "Why are you hitting your fellow Hebrew?"

The man said, "Who made you ruler and judge over us? Are you thinking of killing me as you killed the Egyptian?" Then Moses was afraid and thought, "What I did must have become known."

When Pharaoh heard of this, he tried to kill Moses, but Moses fled.

EXODUS 2:11–15

MARCH 1

At the age of forty, the secret of Moses' true identity was becoming more than he could bear. Born to Hebrew slaves, he had been raised as the son of Pharaoh's daughter. And yet, he had never forgotten the words of his real mother who had been hired to nurse him. She had told him that the Almighty God had rescued him from death for a special purpose. No matter how hard he tried to forget, her words had continued to haunt his soul with troubling conviction.

Everywhere he went, Moses saw Hebrews being brutally mistreated. As he watched, one of the taskmasters began to viciously beat a Hebrew man. Moses snapped. With no training in discerning the ways of God, he gave into his rage, and easily killed the overseer. Soon he found himself fleeing from the wrath of Pharaoh into the desert—an outcast to both the Egyptians and the Hebrews.

Moses had a legitimate burden and calling from God, but his spiritual immaturity caused him to respond improperly to the need he had been called to meet. I have seen many young Christians do the same thing. They respond to a divine opportunity in an inappropriate way because they lack training. They spiritually "murder" their own testimonies and make a mess of the very opportunities God has given them because they haven't taken the time to gain some maturity first.

Moses' violent act cost him the credibility he needed to lead the people he wanted to help. This principle also applies when we lack Christ-like character in our attempts to follow God—it can cost us the very reputation we need to fulfill our mission. Because of this immaturity, the same question asked of Moses is still being asked of Christians today: "Who made you ruler and judge over us?"

The children of God spent an additional forty years in bondage because their deliverer ran away in the face of his failure. We are all going to fail sometimes when we try to follow God. Maybe harshness or impatience caused you to hurt someone you were trying to help. In spite of the hurt and embarrassment you may feel, you must never let failures keep you from God's call.

If you are struggling with failure today, take heart: "God's gifts and his call are irrevocable" (Romans 11:29). God hasn't disqualified you for his service because of your mistakes. No matter how you have failed, if you will seek to be restored and to learn from your mistakes, God will be faithful to fulfill his purpose for you.

Jesus came to serve. If we keep humility at our call, we should escape most potential shortcomings. Integrity, honor, grace, and mercy are almost scorned upon in our culture but are crucial and integral parts of being a Christian. There is a consequence for our every action for which we will one day be judged. Very sobering!

Duncan Phillips

Lessons in the Life of Moses:
THE BUSH STILL BURNS

Moses was tending the flock of Jethro, his father-in-law, the priest of Midian, and he led the flock to the far side of the desert and came to Horeb, the mountain of God. There the angel of the Lord appeared to him in flames of fire from within a bush. Moses saw that though the bush was on fire, it did not burn up. So Moses thought, "I will go over and see this strange sight — why the bush does not burn up."

When the Lord saw that he had gone over to look, God called to him from within the bush. "Moses! Moses!"

And Moses said, "Here I am."

EXODUS 3:1–4

MARCH 2

The bush was burning with an intense fire, but it was not being consumed. Its glowing radiance did more than warm Moses' body; it ignited a strange sense of destiny within his spirit, as if he stood between two worlds. Was this something divine, or was it a mirage — the fevered fantasy of a man who had lost hope? When he stepped out in faith, Moses heard God's voice. It was the very same voice that had spoken to his ancestors long ago; it was the God of Abraham, Isaac, and Jacob.

How long have you been searching for God's destiny and purpose for your life? No matter how long you've been looking, God's purpose still burns for you. No matter how long you have been imprisoned in the desert of failure and mediocrity, if you will take a step toward his purposes for your life, you too will hear his voice of calling and deliverance.

You may be asking yourself, "Where will I find my burning bush?" In my own experience, I have found God's burning bush of deliverance and destiny in every spiritual desert. Some of you may discover your burning bush in your church; others of you may find it at a conference or retreat. Still others may find a fresh revelation of destiny as you seek God's face through prayer and his Word. Wherever you find it, however, like Moses you must turn aside and approach it. Turning aside may mean some priority changes, new time commitments, deep repentance, or renewed commitment to Jesus. Whatever it involves, it is worth it. As you open your heart to God's calling on your life, you will be filled with the guidance, confidence, and strength that only God's powerful voice can bring.

GOD HAS A PERFECT DESTINY FOR US ALL. MOST OF US FROM TIME TO TIME WALK OUTSIDE OF IT. THE BEGINNING OF TRUE HAPPINESS IS WHEN WE TURN TO GAZE UPON OUR "BURNING BUSH."

Duncan Phillips

Lessons in the Life of Moses:
"DON'T COME ANY CLOSER"

"Do not come any closer," God said. "Take off your sandals, for the place where you are standing is holy ground." Then he said, "I am the God of your father, the God of Abraham, the God of Isaac and the God of Jacob." At this, Moses hid his face because he was afraid to look at God.

EXODUS 3:5–6

MARCH 3

The moment Moses heard the Lord call him by name it was if years of shame began to be stripped away from his soul. Even after what he had done, God had not forgotten him. Yet, when he stepped toward the reassuring voice of his God, it was as if Moses hit an invisible barrier. As he tried to push through it, he was startled by the words he heard: *"Don't come any closer."*

Have you experienced this invisible barrier? As much as God desires to bring you into deep intimacy and fellowship with him, if you have unconfessed sin and rebellion in your life, it will keep you from him. To some of you, this thought may be revolutionary. After all, you have been born into a generation who considers itself highly spiritual. But just "being spiritual" is not what God requires. True holiness is required if you are to experience real and lasting intimacy with God.

Doesn't it seem unfair of God to allow Moses to taste his presence, then deny him further access only moments later? This seeming unfairness, however, is a display of God's wisdom. He knew that until Moses had tasted the freshness of his presence, he would never have the motivation to discover true holiness for himself. God does the same for us today. Whether it is the early days of our salvation or some other period of spiritual vulnerability in our life, God will allow us to experience just enough of his presence so that we are longing for more. When you truly begin to thirst for more of God, you will be willing to follow him with all of your heart.

If you have hit the "don't come any closer" barrier in your spiritual life, let me give you some suggestions: First, although Christ's blood has given you the access you need to enter into the Father's presence, you must also continually "take off" the sin keeping you from experiencing the fullness of that promised access (Hebrews 10:19–22). Moses was required to take off his shoes because they represented the earthly part of his life that he needed to give up. In the same way, we must be willing to turn from anything that would separate us from God's full presence. Sin keeps us from the freedoms that are ours in Christ. Thankfully, through the blood of Christ we have the righteousness we need to boldly come into his presence, even while we are struggling to be delivered from the very sin we are confessing.

Another key to truly experiencing God's incredible presence is remembering his true nature. Moses hid his face at the overwhelming revelation of God's holiness. Far from being some "cosmic buddy" or mere angelic "spirit guide," God is the awesome Creator of the universe, who has chosen to be our Savior, Lord, Father, and Friend.

When we come to realize the deep love of a holy God for us, we will find ourselves longing to know him more and more. When we are inspired by this longing to throw off our sin and seek God's presence we will find the "invisible barriers" falling down and the open arms of God waiting to embrace us.

The Father is calling us to intimacy with Himself. Read Matthew 7:21-23. These men looked like model Christians but didn't have intimacy with Him. I think we'll be surprised when we see who will truly be rewarded in heaven. This also is very sobering. Never judge a book by its cover ... God doesn't.

Duncan Phillips

Lessons from the Life of Moses:
I AM SENDING YOU

The LORD said, "I have indeed seen the misery of my people in Egypt. I have heard them crying out because of their slave drivers, and I am concerned about their suffering. So I have come down to rescue them from the hand of the Egyptians and to bring them up out of that land into a good and spacious land, a land flowing with milk and honey.... And now the cry of the Israelites has reached me, and I have seen the way the Egyptians are oppressing them. So now, go. I am sending you to Pharaoh to bring my people the Israelites out of Egypt."

But Moses said to God, "Who am I, that I should go to Pharaoh and bring the Israelites out of Egypt?"

And God said, "I will be with you."

EXODUS 3:7–12

MARCH 4

As Moses continued to hide his face, he was overwhelmed with the quiet whisper of a powerful voice. "Moses, I have indeed seen the misery of my people ..." While the Lord expressed his heart for the Israelites' deliverance and his willingness to come down and rescue them, Moses was filled with fresh faith. God was going to come to the aid of the Hebrews. Surely their time of oppression was at an end. Yet, as he continued to wait in trembling and silence before the Lord, he was jarred by what the Lord said next: "So now, go. I am sending you to Pharaoh ..."

Moses didn't know whether to laugh or cry. "Me? How could God send a broken failure like me on a mission like this?" Yet, the voice Moses heard was firm and sure and it left no room for doubt—he had been called to be God's instrument of deliverance.

Just as in the case of Moses, God has a two-part message for us today. God has seen the suffering and pain of your nation, city, company, or campus. He has been so moved by your plight that he has decided to exercise his mighty arm on behalf of your deliverance. But, guess what? He has decided to exercise his mighty arm of deliverance through *you!* You may well be God's sovereign answer to the very needs you have been lifting up to him.

You may be thinking, *I thought my pastor or some other great Christian leader was called to be the answer to these needs.* According to Ephesians 4:12 your pastor's job is actually to prepare other Christians, like you and me, to go. Go where? To the people you have been praying for and the places you have been longing to see transformed!

When the revelation that God desires to send *you* has gripped your heart, you may quickly begin to ask the very question that Moses asked: "Who am I, that I should go?" If that is where you are today, let the Lord's answer to Moses bring strength and grace to your heart: "I will be with you." The same God who enabled Moses to deliver Israel from the power and oppression of the Egyptian empire is with you today to give you the strength you need to go where he has called *you* to go.

> We are all ministers of the Gospel. Our every action is a testament to our Father. He promises that He will never leave us nor forsake us. He gives us a job and is with us all the way.
>
> Duncan Phillips

Lessons in the Life of Moses:

WHAT IF THEY DON'T BELIEVE ME?

The LORD said [to Moses], "Throw [the staff] on the ground." Moses threw it on the ground and it became a snake, and he ran from it. Then the LORD said to him, "Reach out your hand, and take it by the tail." So Moses reached out and took hold of the snake, and it turned back into a staff in his hand. "This," said the LORD, "is so that they may believe that the LORD, the God of their fathers—the God of Abraham, the God of Isaac and the God of Jacob—has appeared to you."

Then the LORD said, "Put your hand inside your cloak." So Moses put his hand into his cloak, and when he took it out of his cloak it was leprous, like snow.

"Now put it back into your cloak," he said. So Moses put his hand back into his cloak, and when he took it out, it was restored, like the rest of his flesh.

EXODUS 4:3–7

MARCH 5

Moses held his shepherd's rod in his hand; it was the symbol of all his earthly authority and power. When he dropped the rod on the ground, as God told him to, he jumped back in astonishment and ran for his life. The rod had become a huge, writhing, hissing serpent! When he finally stopped running and breathlessly turned around, he heard God's voice again: "Reach out your hand, and take it by the tail." When he obeyed, the serpent once again became a solid staff in his hand.

As Moses looked with amazement at his simple staff, he was instructed by the Lord to place his hand inside his robe. The moment he obeyed, he was seized with terrible pain; it was as if his hand was being eaten alive. When he pulled it out of his robe, he was stunned—his whole hand was covered with leprosy. Unlike the serpent, he could not outrun this. Yet, when he obeyed the Lord and put his hand back inside his robe, his hand was healed.

What does this miraculous story have to do with you? First, in the ancient world the serpent was a symbol of wisdom. In Exodus 7:8–13, Moses's staff once again became a serpent and ate snakes that Pharaoh's magicians had produced. God was demonstrating that his wisdom and power were far greater than the Egyptians'. Today, God wants to give us the wisdom of his Holy Spirit and his Word. When the people around you see this otherworldly wisdom in your life they will want to know why you are so different and you'll be able to shine God's love to them.

Also, as God was able to heal leprosy in Moses' hand, so he is able to bring radical change to your life. When people see this in you, it will give you the credibility you need to boldly speak to them. No matter how hard they try to deny the reality and existence of God, they won't be able to deny the evidence they see so clearly displayed through the changes in you. You will become proof of the greatness of your God to the world around you!

THIS STORY MAKES ME WONDER ... WHAT IF MOSES DIDN'T PICK UP THE SERPENT? WHAT IF HE DIDN'T PUT HIS HAND BACK INSIDE HIS ROBE THE SECOND TIME? HE WAS OBEDIENT AND GOD USED HIM MIGHTILY. HIS UNBELIEF WAS QUASHED BY HIS OBEDIENCE.

Duncan Phillips

Lessons in the Life of Moses:
RUNNING FROM THE ROD

The LORD said, "Throw [your staff] on the ground." Moses threw it on the ground and it became a snake and he ran from it. Then the LORD said to him, "Reach out your hand and take it by the tail." So Moses reached out and took hold of the snake, and it turned back into a staff in his hand.... "Take this staff in your hand so you can perform miraculous signs with it."

EXODUS 4:3-4, 17

MARCH 6

Moses was stunned. What had once been a rod in his hand was now a writhing serpent. The snake was so real and threatening that Moses ran for his life. Yet when the Lord told him to come back and take the serpent by its tail, Moses obeyed and received an instrument of miracles. With this staff and God's power, Moses would free his people. But if he had been arrogant during that first demonstration, and not humbled by God's power, that power could have come back to bite him.

From this story it is clear that the power of God should never be handled lightly. In fact, until you understand risks involved, you may well be in danger yourself. Among the clearest of these dangers is the insidious sin of pride. I have seen too many people bitten by the serpent of pride after being dramatically used in God's service. Tragically, a person who was once humble and teachable becomes arrogant, haughty, and hard.

Another danger is wielding the power of God without the maturity necessary to handle it correctly. Perhaps this was why the second miraculous sign God showed Moses was to give him leprosy. Moses needed to truly understand his own weakness and sin, and his need for God, so he would humbly use the power given him. The same holds true for you and me. One of the greatest deterrents to misusing God's authority is the clear revelation of our own weakness.

Once a person has been "burned," through the misuse of God's delegated authority or the consequences of spiritual pride, he or she may be reluctant to ever use God-given authority again. The challenge is to "learn from the burn" and to use caution and humility the next time. Always be willing to seek a new measure of God's power, but at the same time, seek the wisdom you need to use it honorably.

The STORY OF the ROD OF MOSES REMINDS me of the "AUTHORITY" OR RESPONSIBILITY we in the BAND hAve. THeRe is A temptAtion to Be pRideFUL OR hAUGHTY. ONe of MY GREAtest BAttLes is At A "meet AND GReet." I feeL I Give it ALL in A show But peopLe wANt moRe. But, sAyiNG thAt, I woULD hAte to think I DisseD A YouNG fAN BeCAUse of MY seLfishNess.

Duncan Phillips

Lessons in the Life of Moses:

AARON IS ON THE WAY

Moses said to the LORD, "O Lord, I have never been eloquent, neither in the past, nor since you have spoken to your servant. I am slow of speech and tongue."

The LORD said to him, "Who gave man his mouth?... Is it not I, the LORD? Now go; I will help you speak and will teach you what to say."

But Moses said, "O LORD, please send someone else to do it."

Then the LORD's anger burned against Moses and he said, "What about your brother, Aaron the Levite? I know he can speak well. He is already on his way to meet you."

EXODUS 4:10-14

MARCH 7

Despite the incredible sense of God's presence and the many miraculous signs he had experienced, Moses still struggled to believe that God could use him. He still felt that his poor speaking ability disqualified him.

"Lord, please send someone else," he moaned. For a moment he could even feel the singe of God's anger burning in the silence. Then God answered: "Your brother Aaron is a great speaker, and he is already on the way."

What lessons can we learn from the Moses' struggle to overcome his unbelief? First of all, many times the answer we are struggling to believe in is already on the way! Jesus taught that the Father knows what we need before we can even ask (Matthew 6:8). In my own experience, I have discovered that the battle of faith intensifies right before I receive

God's answer. Whether you are waiting and trying to believe for financial provisions, a health need, or a relational issue, take heart! Your answer is already on the way.

Another lesson we learn from this story is that there are times in our lives when God's answer takes the form of another person. God, in his wisdom, is doesn't give any one man or woman all the gifts and talents necessary to fulfill his plan. He wants us to need each other. You have been designed for team ministry. God delights in bringing teams of his people together who have just the right mix of gifts, talents, and abilities needed for his purposes. Even as Aaron was the great speaker that Moses wasn't, so God will never fail to bring the right people into your life as you walk humbly before him.

This shows the importance of the church. If you don't go, how can the Father use the brethren to help you? His timing is always perfect.
Duncan Phillips

Lessons in the Life of Moses:
GIVE AARON YOUR STAFF

The LORD said to Moses and Aaron, "When Pharaoh says to you, 'Perform a miracle,' then say to Aaron, 'Take your staff and throw it down before Pharaoh,' and it will become a snake." So Moses and Aaron went to Pharaoh and did just as the LORD commanded. Aaron threw his staff down … and it became a snake. Pharaoh then summoned wise men and sorcerers, … Each one threw down his staff and it became a snake. But Aaron's staff swallowed up their staffs.

EXODUS 7:8–12

MARCH 8

As he stood in the center of Pharaoh's court, Moses was flooded with memories. He had spent countless hours in the courts of Pharaoh as a young boy. He even knew some of the older servants, and the court officials still recognized him. Yet this was no time for nostalgia—now he was seen as an enemy. As he gripped his staff and prepared to do the first of the amazing signs God had given him, he was stunned by what he heard. It was the voice of God commanding him to give the miracle staff into the hands of his brother, Aaron.

When he obeyed and placed the staff in Aaron's hands, it was as if Aaron became another man. His whole being was filled with power as he threw down the staff at Pharaoh's feet. Although the Egyptians were able to reproduce this miracle, every one of their serpents was totally consumed by the serpent that had once been the rod of Moses.

Why did God have Moses give the staff to Aaron? God was using this situation to reveal his nature to humanity. First, as Moses was to work this first miracle through Aaron, God chooses to work his miracles through people, just like you and me.

Second, God was also reminding Moses and those who read his story about the importance of humility and the danger of spiritual pride. He had Moses hand the rod to Aaron in order to show Moses it was not his own power, but the power of God that would set the Hebrew children free. Although God's command may have frustrated Moses, it was a critical lesson for him, and for us. We must never forget that all true power comes from God.

"Give your staff to Aaron." God's test seemed to be a small one, but when Moses obeyed, he was laying a foundation upon which he would build the rest of his ministry. Through this act of obedience, Moses demonstrated both his humility and his realization that God was the true source of real power—a lesson that continues to teach us even today.

Awesome! It's been my experience that when I let go and give it to the Lord, He comes in like a loving Father and floods me with the answer. Before I joined the Newsboys, things weren't going all that great. I was in Nashville "treading water." I was confused. I was where I believed the Lord had led me. But nothing ... for months I cleaned windows in apartments where I lived. At a point of desperation I told the Lord that if He wanted me to go back to Australia and be the best builder I could be, that's what I would do. The very next day I got a call from the Newsboys. I believe the Father was seeing if I would let it go and give it back to Him. His timing was perfect.

Duncan Phillips

Lessons in the Life of Moses:
THE LONG WAY

When Pharaoh let the people go, God did not lead them on the road through the Philistine country, though that was shorter. For God said, "If they face war, they might change their minds and return to Egypt." So God led the people around by the desert road toward the Red Sea. The Israelites went up out of Egypt armed for battle.

EXODUS 13:17-18

MARCH 9

In a series of events that was beyond human comprehension God had shattered the power of the greatest empire in the world. Using frogs, gnats, and flies, and finally the power of death itself, Moses had watched the God of his fathers humiliate a proud nation and its "gods." Now, after hundreds of years of slavery and oppression, the people of God were free—free to return to the very land which had been promised to Abraham, Isaac, and Jacob.

As usual, however, God had given Moses a series of orders he could not understand. God was making the Israelites take the long route through the desert—even though they could simply march through the land of the Philistines and right into the Promised Land. *Why*, Moses thought, *does the Lord always choose the hard way?* Once again, his frustration was interrupted by the voice of God: "Moses, my children are not ready for the battles they will face in the land of the Philistines. If they go that way, they may quit and return to Egypt." Although Moses doubted that any Israelite would ever return to Egypt, he chose to trust God and go the long way.

Like Moses, have you ever wondered why God always seems to choose paths for your life which seem harder or longer than necessary? In my own experience, I have found that there are some really good reasons why God chooses to work this way. First, God uses both the length of the road as well as the hard times we may face to prepare us for the challenges which await us when we reach our "promised land." The very faith the Israelites learned in the desert—when they had to believe God for the daily necessities of life—was the faith they would later need to face giants and besiege walled cities. God in his wisdom is using the path you are on to enable you to succeed in the future. If you run from your path, you will be missing out on the very lessons you will need in order to receive the promises you long for.

Second, God was not only using the longer path to prepare his people—he was using it to protect them. Many times, though we do not see it, the shorter way is also the dangerous way. Only God knows the perils and pitfalls that may await us on the paths of life. Sometimes he will call us to walk in a way which may seem much harder in the short term in order to protect us from conflicts and trials we have neither the strength nor the character to endure. Be careful not to leave the path of safety because you think that the path you choose will be easier and better than the one God has chosen for you. No matter how long or how hard the path you are walking on may seem, never forget your loving heavenly Father is using it to both protect you from evil and prepare you for your "promised land." Keep traveling that long road—it will give you the faith you need to fulfill your God-given destiny.

This speaks to me personally. While in Australia in my younger years, I knew the Lord had told me of what He had in store which, by the way, is exactly what happened. But at the time, I was working on a construction site. It seemed I was going in exactly the opposite direction I believed God has promised. Now with 20/20 hindsight, I see that he was not only building my faith but preparing my heart.

Duncan Phillips

Lessons in the Life of Moses:
TURN BACK

The LORD said to Moses, "Tell the Israelites to turn back and encamp near Pi Hagiroth, between Migdol and the sea. They are to encamp by the sea, directly opposite Baal Zephon. Pharaoh will think, 'The Israelites are wandering around the land in confusion, hemmed in by the desert.' And I will harden Pharaoh's heart, and he will pursue them. But I will gain glory for myself through Pharaoh and all his army, and the Egyptians will know that I am the LORD." So the Israelites did this.

EXODUS 14:1–4

MARCH 10

The euphoria was spreading through the whole nation. Every mile they walked was another mile farther from the horrors of slavery and mass infanticide. Yes, Moses was the man of the hour, and their God was the awesome God. Nothing could stop them now—they were on their way to the Promised Land. Nothing, that is, but the voice of God. Even Moses couldn't believe it: "Moses, tell my people to march back toward Egypt and camp near Pi Hagiroth."

"March back toward Egypt? I thought you told me to lead your people out of Egypt, not back into Egypt." Yet, if Moses had learned anything, he had learned to obey the voice of God, even when it didn't make much sense.

Why would God tell his people to turn around and wait for their enemies to catch up with them? And why, sooner or later, will you, too, be told to turn around and face your enemies? First, like the Hebrews, God has not called you to spend the rest of your life running from your past. As

wonderful as the Promised Land would be, the Hebrews would have lived the rest of their lives in terror, always wondering if Pharaoh would eventually find them, if they had not seen God's deliverance for themselves. Whether you have been running from a deeply troubled family situation, guilt and shame from your past, or depression that haunts you, sooner and later God will call you to turn around and face that which has been pursuing you. When he does, no matter how frightening it may be, take heart. God will never call you to face anything without giving you the grace needed to defeat it.

Perhaps for you, this moment of facing your fear has already come. Even as you are reading these words, you hear the Holy Spirit telling you to turn around and face your past. Whether it is more time in the Word and prayer, or the strength of a trusted Christian brother or sister, God will help you to find what you need to face whatever has been chasing you.

God may also call you to walk into a circumstance where you are obviously weak and vulnerable. When God wins a victory over the enemy through you, even when you are at your weakest, God will get all the glory. Let me encourage you not to panic when this moment comes—you are about to show the world what your God can do! For even as God destroyed the chariot forces of Egypt when they were thundering down on his seemingly helpless and confused people, so he will rout every one of your enemies as they rush down on you. Trust, obey, and see God's deliverance in your life too!

The FATHER MADE me turn towARDS my "enemy." The FEAR OF hAViNG to WORK iN CONStRUCTioN FOR the REST OF my LiFe. iN DiRECT CONTRASt to whAt the LORD hAD toLD me. But, He is ALWAYS FAithFUL ANd neveR DisAppoiNtS. GLORY to GOD!
Duncan Phillips

CROSSING THE RED SEA

Moses [said], "Do not be afraid. Stand firm and you will see the deliverance the Lord will bring you today. The Egyptians you see today you will never see again. The Lord will fight for you; you need only to be still."

Then the Lord said to Moses, "Why are you crying out to me? Tell the Israelites to move on. Raise your staff and stretch out your hand over the sea to divide the water so that the Israelites can go through the sea on dry ground."

EXODUS 14:13–16

MARCH 11

Everywhere Moses turned was unbelievable danger. On the one side stood the Red Sea. On the other side came Pharaoh's army. And now, his own people were turning against him. "Don't be afraid," he shouted to the Hebrews. "All you have to do is stand here and the Lord himself will fight for you."

Looking up to heaven, Moses waited for a word of comfort and confirmation from the Lord. The reply he heard, however, was anything but comforting. "Why are you crying out to me? Tell the people to move on toward the sea." As Moses stood, shocked by what he had heard, the Lord's voice thundered again: "Raise your staff and stretch out your hand over the sea." Moses turned and obeyed. With a mighty wind, the Lord cut a path of dry ground through the heart of the raging sea. By the time the morning came, all the Hebrews had safely crossed through the sea, and the Egyptian army was drowned beneath it.

What does God want to teach us through this incredible story? First, when God asked Moses why he was crying out to him, God was not being hard or uncaring. He asked this as a way to show Moses that he had already been given everything he needed. Moses was ready. He was equipped. He just needed to act. No matter what type of challenge or seemingly impassable obstacle you are facing, God will give you everything you need to experience victory—maybe it is simply time for you to take a step of faith and act.

Second, like Moses' staff, you and I have been given a powerful instrument of God—his Word. No matter what raging sea you are facing, you can overcome through the promises and power of the Bible. I have found in my own life—whether it was my wife's cancer or any of the other major challenges I have faced—when I fully trust the Word of God for my needs, two things happen: fresh faith is ignited in my heart, and the power of God is released to meet my need.

Third, like Moses and the Hebrew children, many times when faced with a time of crisis we are tempted to freeze up and "stand still." Although there are times when waiting in faith is exactly the right thing to do, there are other moments when acting in faith is what God is calling you to do. Until the Israelites took that first step of faith toward the sea, it did not part. Perhaps you have been asked to obey by giving money to someone else, even though you have a financial need too. Or maybe the Holy Spirit is guiding you to share your faith with someone even though you see no sign of openness in that person. When you obey, and take that step of faith, you will begin to see incredible results. May God give you fresh faith to cross the seas you are facing today!

"You can only turn a moving ship." This little saying has helped me through the years. The temptation is to be "still." There are certainly times for that. But my experience has been: if I go, He will steer.

Duncan Phillips

Lessons in the Life of Moses:

MANNA IN THE DESERT

The LORD said to Moses, "I will rain down bread from heaven for you. The people are to go out each day and gather enough for that day."

EXODUS 16:4

MARCH 12

Although the Lord had supernaturally met their need for water only days before, now the Israelites were grumbling and complaining about their lack of food. *Will they ever learn?* **Moses wondered to himself. As Moses considered the Israelites' ingratitude, he heard the whisper of the Almighty God, promising to rain down bread from heaven.**

There were, however, some instructions to follow. The bread, called *manna*, had to be gathered early every morning, because it would melt under the sun's heat. It had to be collected on a daily basis and not kept overnight, or it would rot. As long as they followed these conditions, the Israelites would be well fed from God's miraculous hand.

God has given us an even more miraculous gift than manna—his precious Son, who is called "the Bread of Life" (John 6:35). In my own experience, I have discovered the primary way I can feed on this Bread of Life is through the time in the Bible. When I take time to soak in God's word, my spiritual life is strengthened, and my faith grows.

Another lesson we can learn from the story of manna is how God's rules for collecting it correspond to the best way to "collect" his words. I have found that the longer I wait to read my Bible during the day, the less I receive from it. Like manna, it seems to melt away in the heat of the day's busyness. You will find that starting your day in the Word will mean a richer and more fulfilling "feast."

I have also found that like manna, yesterday's time in the Word isn't going to sustain me today as well as a new portion today. God meets our needs one day at a time because he wants us to lean on him every single day. Psalm 68:19 says that God *daily* bears our burdens. Lamentations 3:22–23 say that his compassions are *new every morning*. The Scriptures testify to the fact that God delights in meeting with his children every day. So no matter what your day holds, remember to seek the Bread of Life for breakfast.

Like our bodies need daily sustenance, so do our spirits. Whatever you feed will grow. Unfortunately, this also works in the negative. Feed fear, disbelief and disobedience and that will grow. Feed faith, love, and hope and they will also grow. It's been my observation that you can actually see fear and desperation on people's faces. I believe you can also see peace and joy on their faces. What you feed on spiritually also affects you physically.

Duncan Phillips

Lessons in the Life of Joshua:
THE POWER OF PRAYER

The Amalekites came and attacked the Israelites at Rephidim. Moses said to Joshua, "Choose some of our men and go out to fight the Amalekites. Tomorrow I will stand on top of the hill with the staff of God in my hands."

So Joshua fought the Amalekites as Moses had ordered, and Moses, Aaron, and Hur went to the top of the hill. As long as Moses held up his hands, the Israelites were winning, but whenever he lowered his hands, the Amalekites were winning.

EXODUS 17:8–11

MARCH 13

The army of the Amalekites had come out of nowhere and brutally attacked the Israelites who had been straggling along at the rear of the huge group of travelers. Now, young Joshua had been appointed by Moses to lead the armies of Israel as they retaliated against the Amalekites for their cowardly attacks. Moses would climb to the top of a hill, overlooking the battle, and pray for them, leaving Joshua and his men to do the man-to-man fighting.

The fighting had been going for hours; the conflict had gone back and forth all day. Time and time again the Israelites had been at the point of seeming victory, only to see the Amalekites attack with new vigor. As the weariness of the long battle began to take its toll, Joshua turned his eyes to Moses on the top of the hill. What he saw stunned him. Whenever Moses would hold up the staff of God, the armies of Israel would begin to win, but the moment his strength would wane, and the rod would begin to drop, the tide of battle would begin to turn in the favor of the Amalekites.

The connection was plain to see; what Moses was doing on the hill was determining the fate of the thousands who battled in the valley below.

The same principle is true in our churches today. No matter how well planned and staffed our outreaches, programs, church services, and ministries are, none of them will be effective without people who will faithfully lift it all up to the Lord in prayer. As Christians we are often drawn to the more "high profile" work in ministry because it is easier to see the results of our labors. Although these activities are of critical importance, one of the church's most desperate needs is for faithful prayer warriors, who, like Moses, have learned the true secrets of releasing the power of God. These are the people that know that what happens on the mountain of prayer will always determine the outcome of the church's battles.

As we do battle for souls as part of God's army, we must remember that true spiritual power flows through the Word of God and prayer. As we learn to use the awesome power of prayer, we will find ourselves winning the battle for the kingdom of our God.

JAMes 5:16 SAYS, "The effectuAL, fervent prayer of a righteous man avaiLs much to the pulling Down of Strongholds." Read Job 22:27, Isaiah 65:24, and Matthew 18:19.

Duncan Phillips

Lessons in the Life of Moses:
DARKNESS SURROUNDS HIM

> When the people saw the thunder and lightning and heard the trumpet and saw the mountain in smoke, they trembled with fear.... The people remained at a distance while Moses approached the thick darkness where God was.
>
> EXODUS 20:18, 21

MARCH 14

The whole mountain was shaking as the presence of God was manifested on the summit and inky black smoke billowed into the sky as if from a fiery volcano. A shroud of huge, dark clouds emitting bolts of lightning and growls of thunder enveloped the massive rock.

As the Hebrew children trembled in terror at the foot of the mountain, God spoke to Moses. He alone would be allowed to approach the fiery inferno—and the Almighty God. As he climbed, Moses could sense he was drawing closer and closer to the awesome presence of his God. And then, as he reached the very center of this awesome display of God's power, he found ... utter darkness. It was not the darkness of evil, though, but the darkness of deep mystery.

Darkness is not something we are used to associating with God, even though Scripture, such as Psalms 18:11, says that God makes darkness his covering. This darkness, however, has nothing to do with sin. This darkness is the unfathomable mystery surrounding a completely holy God.

In my own life, I have found the most difficult periods are not the times when my faith is being tested by hard times or attacks of the enemy. The hardest times for me have been the times of deep darkness. I feel disoriented, confused, and paralyzed by the lack of direction. Amazingly, though, I have discovered in these moments that God is closer to me than ever. And when I simply trusted in him and walked through the darkness in faith, I found a new and deeper intimacy with the Lord.

If you are walking through a dark and mysterious place right now, take the strength and encouragement of Isaiah 50:10 to heart:

> Who among you fears the Lord
>   and obeys the word of his servant?
> Let him who walks in the dark,
>   who has no light,
> trust in the name of the Lord
>   and rely on his God.

Isaiah addresses this passage to people who are obeying and serving the Lord. This is important to remember, because many times when we are walking through a dark period in our lives, we feel we are being punished. Many times the opposite is true. All of God's children will go through periods of darkness and confusion as they learn to serve him. In fact, these periods have been so common to serious Christians throughout the ages that the term "dark night of the soul" has been coined to describe them.

During these dark nights of the soul, Isaiah encourages us to put our trust in the Lord instead of relying on our own strength. For no matter how dark it is around you, or how confused you may be, your God has not abandoned you. In fact, you are probably far closer to him than you can even imagine. If you will simply trust in his Word and the guidance of the Holy Spirit, God will bring you out of the darkness and into the light of his presence.

His ways are not our ways. It never ceases to amaze me looking back on situations how differently God orchestrated sequences of events in my life. Typically quite different to what I would have thought but far exceeding my expectations. This is faith in full effect.

Duncan Phillips

Lessons in the Life of Moses:
THE SPIRIT OF EXCELLENCE

The LORD said to Moses, "See, I have chosen Bezalel ... and I have filled him with the spirit of God, with skill ability and knowledge in all kinds of crafts—to make artistic designs for work in gold, silver, and bronze, to cut and set stones, to work in wood, and to engage in all kinds of craftsmanship. Moreover, I have appointed Oholiab ... to help him. Also I have given skill to all the craftsmen to make everything I have commanded you."

EXODUS 31:1–6

The LORD showed me four craftsmen. I asked, "What are these coming to do?"

He answered, "These are the horns that scattered Judah so that no one could raise his head, but the craftsmen have come to terrify them and throw down these horns of the nations who lifted up their horns against the land of Judah to scatter its people."

ZECHARIAH 1:20–21

MARCH 15

By now, all of Israel realized that Moses, Aaron, Miriam, and even Joshua had been anointed with the spirit of God. But Bezalel and Oholiab were not even from the priestly tribe of Levi. Yet, God had declared that his spirit would enable these two simple craftsmen to build things that had never been built by mere mortals. Not only would they construct the furnishings of God's house, but they would also build the Ark of the Covenant—the tangible sign of God's presence on the earth.

The story of Bezalel and Oholiab isn't one most of us learn in Sunday school, but it has some important lessons for us, even today. First of all, it shows us God doesn't only anoint people who have received a calling into what we would call full-time ministry. Even as God gave these ordinary men the anointing to perfect their skills and practice their craft at unprecedented levels, so he wants to anoint you, no matter what profession you choose. God is calling you and your generation to become leaders in every area of society. He wants to anoint you to work at it with excellence and skill that will bring him glory.

In Zechariah 1:20–21, we see another powerful use of God-given skills. God's answer to the demonic empires destroying the people of God was four craftsmen. Although these craftsmen were probably angels, I believe this passage can also be applied to the skills God gives us. God is raising up people like you to break his power of evil in our world. He wants to make you so skilled in what he has called you to do, and so excellent in your character, that even the world's leaders will have no choice but to listen to you. As you faithfully follow God's ways in your profession, God may anoint you to rise to amazing positions of power and influence. From these positions, you can bring dramatic change for the kingdom of God to your world. Seek God's calling today. Accept by faith the reality of what he wants to do through you, because the same God who anointed Bezalel and Oholiab is waiting to anoint you for excellence.

We are all ministers of the Gospel. Whether we realize it or not, the world is watching us, noting our attitudes and conversations. Most times, it's our actions that speak more than what comes out of our mouths. Excellence in any field will be noticed. You won't have to look for promotions. They will find you.

Duncan Phillips

Lessons in the Life of Moses:
THE GOLDEN CALF

When the people saw that Moses was so long in coming down from the mountain, they gathered around Aaron and said, "Come, make us gods who will go before us...."

Aaron answered them, "Take off the gold earrings that your wives, your sons, and your daughters are wearing, and bring them to me." So all the people took off their earrings and brought them to Aaron. He took what they handed him and made it into an idol cast in the shape of a calf."

EXODUS 32:1–4

MARCH 16

During these incredible days, Moses had received the Ten Commandments, instructions on how to build the tabernacle, and the social laws that would govern the nation of Israel. To the Israelites waiting below, these forty days seemed like an eternity. The longer Moses was gone, the more abandoned they felt. Where was this man who led them out of Egypt? Maybe Moses had left them to die in the desert. To the Hebrews it seemed that he had just disappeared—and taken his God with him.

Perhaps the reaction of the Israelites is understandable, but you would think that Aaron would have known better. But Aaron was insecure about his leadership and fearful of the growing discontent of the people. He quickly caved in to their demands and built them another "god."

How could these people who had seen God's destruction of the Egyptian empire, who had crossed miraculously through the Red Sea, and who had been sustained in the desert by the provision of heaven so quickly turn away from God who had loved them and rescued them? The truth is, these people did not have a relationship with the Lord. Their only relationship with God had been through Moses. So when he disappeared, the Israelites felt God had also disappeared.

I have seen this tragic story repeated today. Many Christians—just like Aaron and the Hebrews—never really develop a relationship with God on their own. So, when they are no longer near the person or people through whom they related to God, these Christians easily fall prey to unbelief and discouragement. Young people are especially vulnerable to this trap. It's a lot easier to coast along on your parents' faith than to work at a real relationship with God. But soon, you'll be on your own and you will need a true faith of your own to sustain you.

Are you relating directly to God, or are you still relating to God through the words and experiences of someone else? Although God wants us to be fed and inspired by the words of leaders and fellow Christians, this was never meant to replace the joys of hearing God's voice and receiving from his Word for ourselves. Learn from the mistakes of the Israelites. Seek out God for yourself. Ask him to make himself very real to you today and don't settle for any man-made substitutes!

We see this a lot in Christendom today. Mom and Dad are Christians and go to church. But their children don't have a personal relationship with God. Many times, these same children are the ones that fall away from church. I saw this personally when I was growing up. One of the biggest reasons, I believe, was that we were never discipled. Because I lacked the example of godly men to follow, I ended up with a distorted image of the Lord for that season in my life. I just didn't see much I wanted to be like.

Duncan Phillips

Lessons in the Life of Moses:
DEFINING MOMENT

Moses saw that the people were running wild.... So he stood at the entrance to the camp and said, "Whoever is for the LORD, come to me." And all the Levites rallied to him. Then he said to them, "This is what the LORD, the God of Israel, says: ... 'Go back and forth through the camp from one end to the other, each killing his brother and friend and neighbor.'" The Levites did as Moses commanded, and that day about three thousand of the people died. Then Moses said, "You have been set apart to the LORD today, for you were against your own sons and brothers and he has blessed you this day."

EXODUS 32:25–29

MARCH 17

Moses was burning with anger over the people's rebellion—and at the same time his heart was breaking. He had only been on the mountain forty days, and yet the Israelites had given up on him, on God, and were wallowing in sin. Every one of them had been chosen by God to be his special people. But because of the rebellion in their hearts, they had forfeited their incredible calling.

As Moses stepped down into the encampment his voice cut through the madness like a thunder bold. "Whoever is for the Lord, come to me!" Out of the hundreds of thousands of Hebrews, only the men of the tribe of Levi responded. Their response would define their destiny for generations to come.

And then came a terrible order. God commanded them to kill the Levites who had not responded to his call for repentance—their brothers, friends, and neighbors. When God saw the willingness of these men to

purge the sins of their own families, at the cost of the lives of those they loved, their tribe alone was chosen to represent Israel as priests before God.

The Levites paid a terrible price for the awesome privilege of serving a holy God. Today, we often take for granted the privilege we have to come before God in worship. Until Jesus paid the terrible price for us, the privilege of approaching the presence of God was granted to only one man, once a year—the high priest of the tribe of Levi. When you struggle with having passion for worshiping God, ask him to remind you of this awesome privilege.

If the Levites were willing to draw their swords and kill that which was most precious to them in order to obey God, how much more should we be willing to apply the sword of the Spirit, God's Word, to our lives? If you are not experiencing the presence of God in your life it may be because you have refused to cut out the sins that have been separating you from him. Today, it is time for you to respond to God's call on your life. Can you hear his voice?

I'm truly sobered by this topic. Sometimes I wish I could physically see into the spiritual realm to see what is really going on. We get so cheated by our senses. We think, "this is it." But the Lord says it's all going to burn and rust. That's why He says to lay up treasures in heaven where rust cannot destroy. "Lord lift the scales from my eyes."

Duncan Phillips

Lessons in the Life of Moses:
SPIRITUAL INFLUENCE

[God said,] "I will send an angel before you and drive out the Canaanites, Amorites, Hittites, Perizzites, Hivites, and Jebusites. Go up to the land flowing with milk and honey. But I will not go with you, because you are a stiff-necked people, and I might destroy you on the way."

Moses said to him, "If your Presence does not go with us, do not send us up from here. How will anyone know that you are pleased with me and with your people unless you go with us? What else will distinguish me and your people from all the other people on the face of the earth?"

And the LORD said to Moses, "I will do the very thing you have asked, because I am pleased with you and I know you by name."

EXODUS 33:2-4, 15-17

MARCH 18

As the Lord finished speaking, Moses thought his heart would break. Despite their rebellion, the children of Israel would still be allowed to go to the Promised Land—but God would not go with them. Instead, God would send an angel ahead of them because if he went with them, he would end up having to kill them all because of their sin. Moses now faced a horrible choice. God offered to give him a new nation to lead. Yet, despite the ungratefulness of the Hebrews, Moses could not bear the thought of leaving these people to be destroyed (Exodus 32:9, 10) or trying to lead them without the presence and strength of his Lord.

As Moses raised his hands in prayer, he began a dialogue with the Almighty that is probably the most amazing conversation a mortal man has ever had with God. Moses reminded the Lord of the promises he had made to never leave him or forsake him. Moses went on to tell the Lord that if he was going to leave the Israelites, then he was also leaving Moses, since Moses had been commanded to lead that nation. The next words out of his mouth were unlike any ever heard on the earth before. "If your presence does not go with us, do not send us up from here."

In essence Moses was saying "I would rather live in the desert with you than go into the Promised Land without you." After a poignant moment of silence, God responded. "I will do the very thing you have asked, because I am pleased with you, and I know you by name."

God loved Moses so much that he was willing to give the rebellious and ungrateful Hebrews another chance—for Moses' sake. This is the reality of spiritual influence. When we love and obey God and walk in friendship and intimacy with him, we come to a new place of influence with him. Imagine how different your campus, neighborhood, or workplace might be if your life, like the life of Moses, was marked by the radiant presence of God. May God ignite in you a fresh desire for true influence with him on behalf of your world today.

TODAY IS ALSO EXTREMELY SOBERING AND REMINDS ME OF A SHORT PASSAGE OF SCRIPTURE FROM MATTHEW 7:21-23. READ THIS PASSAGE. THE FATHER IS QUITE UNENAMORED BY WHAT WE DO FOR HIM BUT INCREDIBLY MOTIVATED BY US SEEKING A RELATIONSHIP WITH HIM.

Duncan Phillips

Lessons in the Life of Moses:
THE TENT OF MEETING

Moses used to take a tent and pitch it outside the camp some distance away, calling it the "tent of meeting." Anyone inquiring of the Lord would go to the tent of meeting outside the camp…. As Moses went into the tent, the pillar of cloud would come down and stay at the entrance while the Lord spoke with Moses…. The Lord would speak to Moses face to face, as a man speaks with his friend.

EXODUS 33:7, 9, 11

MARCH 19

God had spared the Hebrew nation from destruction and had promised to lead them into the land of Canaan after all. This amazing turn of events was due to the faith of one man: Moses. His ardent prayers had influenced the Lord to spare a whole nation from annihilation. How could one human achieve a place of such powerful influence with the God of all creation?

In Exodus 33 we see that *proximity* is important if we are going to develop a deep relationship with God. Moses erected a tent outside the boundaries of the Hebrew camp for the purpose of meeting with God. Moses realized that he was only going to develop deep intimacy with God if he spent time alone with him. In the same way, unless we are willing to spend quality time alone with God, we will never develop a deep relationship with him.

Moses called the place where he met with God the "Tent of Meeting." This name is more than a simple designation, for it also captures the purpose of the place. Moses wanted a place where he could fellowship with his Friend and Creator. To Moses, God was more than a source of strength or resources. He was a friend. God is not some distant cosmic force. He is a personal being who craves time with the humans he has created. When you begin to understand God's deep longing to have a personal relationship with you, it will change how you look at your time with God.

Of all the places that God could have fellowshipped with Moses, God met him in a tent. A tent isn't meant to be permanent—it's a place you can take with you. God's desire for a relationship with us goes far beyond a Sunday morning service in a church. He desires to remain in contact with us wherever we go, every day. Moses' tent shows us that we should never limit our contact with God to weekly church services and a few moments of quiet time. Instead, we should seek to include God in every moment of our lives.

And like a tent, our relationship with God has to be "pitched." Relating closely to God is not something that just happens. We must work on our relationship with God, day by day through things such as worship, prayer, and studying his Word. As you seek to walk more closely with your best friend, day after day, may you begin to hear his voice, just like Moses did—*"face to face, as a man speaks to his friend."*

Our culture has trivialized relationships. Divorce is al an all-time high. Hollywood promotes promiscuity and selfishness to heights never before seen. Relationships take time and are not always easy. But if we push through, they can be the most rewarding experiences of our lives. We are all eternal beings. It is our relationships, especially our relationship with God that we will take with us to eternity.

Duncan Phillips

Lessons in the Life of Moses:
MORE THAN A SPECTATOR

Whenever Moses went out to the tent, all the people rose and stood at the entrance to their tents, watching Moses until he entered the tent. As Moses went into the tent, the pillar of cloud would come down and stay at the entrance while the LORD spoke with Moses. Whenever the people saw the pillar of cloud standing at the entrance to the tent, they all stood and worshipped, each at the entrance to his tent. The LORD would speak to Moses face to face, as a man speaks with his friend. Then Moses would return to the camp, but his young aid Joshua, the son of Nun, did not leave the tent.

EXODUS 33: 8–11

MARCH 20

Whenever Moses would begin the long walk to the Tent of Meeting, every Hebrew would run to the door of their tent to watch the massive pillar of cloud begin to move. As Moses entered the tent, he would be enveloped in this manifestation of God's presence and power. The Israelites would worship God at a distance, from the doorways of their own tents. But one young man was not content to be merely a spectator of someone else's relationship with God. Whether Moses asked him, or he just decided to follow Moses into the tent, Joshua, the son of Nun, entered the presence of the Lord.

God wants to bring all of us from a long-distance relationship with him into one of closeness. Every Sunday, whether standing at their pew or watching on television, millions of Christians worship at a distance. They watch one great man or woman of God intimately commune with him, not realizing that this intimacy could be theirs too. If only they would step away from their seats or get off their couches and seek to experience intimacy with God for themselves.

Has your relationship with God turned into a spectator sport? Are you sitting by and watching the vital faith of someone else, wishing you could have the same but not doing anything to seek it? It's not too late for you to be like Joshua. Ask that growing, more experienced Christian to pray and study the Bible with you. Join in on opportunities in your church for intimate times of prayer and worship. Do not miss these opportunities to experience a deeper level of God's presence.

When you are willing to spend time in prayer or worship with people who have a more intimate relationship with God than you do, you will be ushered into a level of God's presence you could never experience on your own. And as you continue to pray with them you will learn how to obtain and maintain a level of intimacy with God on your own. May God help you to experience new levels of intimacy day after day as you are inspired by the faith of Joshua.

"LORD, it says in YOUR WORD that you give us the desires of our hearts. Give me a desire for YOUR WORD, prayer, and fellowship. TAKE the scales from my eyes. Reveal yourself. Remove deception from my life. I'm only going to see my destiny fulfilled as I deepen my intimacy with you."

Duncan Phillips

Lessons in the Life of Moses:

THE RADIANCE OF HIS PRESENCE

When Moses came down from Mount Sinai with the two tablets of the Testimony in his hands, he was not aware that his face was radiant because he had spoken with the LORD. When Aaron and all the Israelites saw Moses, his face was radiant, and they were afraid to come near him.

EXODUS 34:29–30

Now if the ministry that brought death, which was engraved in letters on stone, came with glory, so that the Israelites could not look steadily at the face of Moses because of its glory, fading though it was, will not the ministry of the Spirit be even more glorious? If the ministry that condemns men is glorious, how much more glorious is the ministry that brings righteousness!

2 CORINTHIANS 3:7–9

MARCH 21

Moses had spent forty glorious days and nights in the presence of God. He had spent his time writing down the Ten Commandments and fellowshipping with his God. When he finally left the presence of God and began his descent down the mountain, he was unaware of the heavenly glory that radiated from his face. As he reached the camp, Moses was confused by the reaction of his friends and family. Some covered their mouths, gasping for breath; others simply pointed at him and then ran away. The white brilliance of the glow radiating from his face was more than any human could bear to look at.

According to 2 Corinthians 3:7–8, the power and glory released to believers through Jesus Christ is even *more* powerful than the glory Moses received on the mountain. If the face of Moses became radiant with holy glory while fellowshipping with God on Mt. Sinai, how much more will our lives be transformed by the power and presence of the Holy Spirit as we fellowship with Christ? Although our faces will probably not glow like Moses', there will be a real sense of supernatural joy, life, and power that will radiate from our lives.

Furthermore, the effects of being in God's presence are not just spiritual. When we spend time in the presence of God, our outward appearance will begin to change too. People will notice a new glow in our smile that only the joy of the Lord can bring. We may even stand a bit straighter because the burdens of sin and guilt have been taken away! The prophet Isaiah says God will bestow on his people *"a crown of beauty instead of ashes."* Spending time with God is the least known, but most effective, beauty secret! May God continue to bring transformation in your life as you spend time in his presence today—a transformation that will shine the light of Jesus into the lives of others, as well.

I have seen bitterness and unforgiveness. I have seen what bitterness and unforgiveness can do to a human body. It twists and distorts, makes hard and calloused. I believe that a lot of physical sickness comes from these negative attitudes. We weren't made to accommodate this negativity. It makes perfect sense that if you fill your life with love, joy, and peace that you cannot help but "shine." If you will fill yourself with God's presence, there will not be room for the other things we are tempted to fill our lives with.

Duncan Phillips

Lessons in the Life of Moses:

THE POWER OF BUILDING RIGHT

 "Make this tabernacle and all its furnishings exactly like the pattern I will show you," [said the Lord]....

The Israelites had done all the work just as the Lord had commanded Moses. Moses inspected the work and saw that they had done it just as the Lord had commanded. So Moses blessed them....

Then the cloud covered the Tent of Meeting, and the glory of the Lord filled the tabernacle. Moses could not enter the Tent of Meeting because the cloud had settled upon it, and the glory of the Lord filled the tabernacle.

EXODUS 25:9; 39:42–43; 40:34–35

MARCH 22

As soon as they had finished the final details of the tabernacle, the cloud of God's glory began to descend upon it. The cloud was so thick and immense it changed the very atmosphere of the camp. As the cloud settled over the tabernacle, the whole nation of Israel began to radiate with the presence of God. Although the children of Israel had seen the cloud of God's presence many times, this was different. God wasn't just coming to visit them; he was coming to live with them in the holy house they had built.

Why did the completion of this simple structure bring such an incredible manifestation of God's presence? God's presence came in a powerful way because the people built him a home according to the exact specifications he had given them. Unlike many of God's people today, who think

they can build their lives, families, and businesses any way they choose and still have his blessing; Moses realized God would only inhabit that which was built according to his own plan.

Throughout Scripture, God has given us specific instructions about how we should live our lives. When God doesn't seem to be blessing our relationships, jobs, or even the work done for him, it may be because we aren't following God's instructions in these areas. Although I do not expect a gigantic cloud to hover over my home if I treat my wife and children the way God has told me to, I do believe obeying God in these areas will bring a tremendous release of his blessing and power upon my home and family. We have to remember that we will never get God's blessings until we are willing to live life God's way.

While it may seem obvious that we should live the way God tells us to, it is one thing to know this principle to be true, and a whole other thing to follow it. May God give you the grace to make the simple connection between your obedience to his instructions and his blessings in your life.

OBeDieNCe = BLessiNG

Duncan Phillips

Lessons in the Life of Moses:
THE WORK AND THE WEIGHT

[Moses] asked the LORD, "Why have you brought this trouble on your servant? What have I done to displease you that you put the burden of all these people on me?… I cannot carry all these people by myself; the burden is too heavy for me. If this is how you are going to treat me, put me to death right now—if I have found favor in your eyes—and do not let me face my own ruin."

The LORD said to Moses: "Bring me seventy of Israel's elders…. Have them come to the Tent of Meeting…. I will come down and speak with you there, and I will take of the Spirit that is on you and put the Spirit on them. They will help you carry the burden of the people so that you will not have to carry it alone."

NUMBERS 11:11, 14–17

MARCH 23

No matter how much God blessed the Israelites and provided for them, it was never enough—they were constantly whining, wailing, and groaning. Finally, something snapped inside of Moses, and he vented all his pent-up frustration to God. "I cannot bear the heavy weight of leading them any longer. Either send me some help or kill me now." God didn't get angry with Moses for his rant, but answered him with love: "Get seventy of your best elders and bring them into the Tent of Meeting with you. I will give these leaders the same burden you have, so you will not have to carry the leadership by yourself."

We can learn a lot about leadership through this story of Moses' frustration and struggle. Moses had thousands of "small group leaders" helping him (Exodus 18), but there is a big difference between having people help you do the *work* of the ministry and having them help you to carry the *weight*.

The vision, provision, and decisions involved in leadership are the heaviest burdens for a leader to carry. Although Moses had plenty of people to help him perform tasks, he was trying to inspire the Hebrews with a vision of their future, provide for their basic necessities, and make major decisions for them, all on his own. God told Moses to find responsible leaders who would help him to carry the great weight of leadership. God told him to find a team.

When you are called to lead, you must realize it is not enough to merely delegate tasks. You must find a team to help you make big decisions, provide for the needs of those you lead, and who will carry the group's vision into the future. Even as Moses brought the seventy elders into the Tent of Meeting, so you must be willing to bring others into your life and ask for their help.

If you are not a leader right now, but are being lead, your leaders need your support. The best way to help is to ask that God will give them the wisdom and the strength they need to carry the burden of leadership. And be prepared to be part of the answer to your own prayer—you might be one of the people that your leaders need to join them in their mission.

No one is an island. We're not wired that way. Not only do we need help to carry our burdens but also we need accountability partners. Even the president surrounds himself with people who have his best interest at heart — people he knows and trusts to give good counsel.

Duncan Phillips

Lessons in the Life of Moses:
ELDAD AND MEDAD

The LORD came down in the cloud and spoke with him, and he took of the Spirit that was on him and put the Spirit on the seventy elders. When the Spirit rested on them, they prophesized, but they did not do so again.

However, two men, whose names were Eldad and Medad, had remained in the camp. They were listed among the elders, but did not go out to the Tent. Yet the Spirit also rested on them, and they prophesied in the camp. A young man ran and told Moses, "Eldad and Medad are prophesying in the camp."

Joshua son of Nun, who had been Moses' aid since youth, spoke up and said, "Moses, my lord, stop them!"

But Moses replied, "Are you jealous for my sake? I wish that all the LORD's people were prophets and that the LORD would put His Spirit on them!"

NUMBERS 11:25–29

MARCH 24

The people were incredulous. Never before had Moses brought so many people to the Tent of Meeting. As the people gasped with astonishment, the cloud of God's presence began to descend on the small company of leaders surrounding Moses, and each of the men began to prophesy under the anointing of God.

Two of the men, however, Eldad and Medad, were late for the meeting. As they were running through the camp, they too were struck by the power of God's Spirit. Much to the astonishment of the people, they also

began to prophesy. When a young man brought a report of this strange occurrence to Joshua he spoke out of his insecurity. "Moses, we need to put a stop to the prophesying of Eldad and Medad. They are doing it in the wrong place, away from our authority." The response of Moses to Joshua's insecurity is prophetic for our day: "Are you jealous for my sake? I wish all the Lord's people were prophets and that the Lord would put His Spirit on them."

Far from being insecure and jealous about his position and anointing, Moses desired for every one of God's people to experience the power of the Holy Spirit. Perhaps without knowing it, Moses was foretelling of the day when the anointing of God would not be reserved for leaders, but would be given to every one who believes in Jesus.

In Joel 2:28–29, the prophet tells of a time on earth when every one of God's servants, men and women, young and old, will be anointed with his power and Spirit. Several hundred years later, while trying to explain what happened on the day of Pentecost, the apostle Peter preached about the outpouring of the Spirit. This outpouring in "the upper room," which took place with a small group of ordinary people, was the beginning of the fulfillment of Joel's prophecy. And today, no matter your age or gender or race, one thing is for certain: God wants to give you more of his power and might. If you will ask, he will give you a new measure of the incredible power of the Holy Spirit.

"LORD, MAY YOUR SPIRIT LAY ON MY LIFE. AS I SEEK YOU MORE FERVENTLY, WOULD YOU ILLUMINATE MY MIND. REMOVE THE BLINDERS FROM MY EYES. HELP ME TO SUBMIT TO YOUR WAYS SO THAT YOU WILL HAVE YOUR WAY IN MY LIFE."

Duncan Phillips

Lessons in the Life of Moses:
ARE YOU JEALOUS (OR INSECURE)?

Two men, whose names were Eldad and Medad, had remained in the camp. They were listed among the elders, but did not go out to the Tent. Yet the Spirit also rested on them, and they prophesied in the camp. A young man ran and told Moses, "Eldad and Medad are prophesying in the camp."

Joshua son of Nun, who had been Moses' aid since youth, spoke up and said, "Moses, my lord, stop them!"

But Moses replied, "Are you jealous for my sake? I wish that all the LORD's people were prophets and the LORD would put his Spirit on them!"

NUMBERS 11:26 – 29

MARCH 25

The people were used to seeing the anointing of God on Moses, but when the cloud had enveloped sixty-eight other leaders, the Hebrews were astonished. Each of the men began to prophesy the word of the Lord as they remained under the cloud of his glory. Even, Eldad, and Medad had begun to prophesy under the anointing of God's Spirit and they weren't even inside the Tent of Meeting.

Sadly, not all of the Israelites were excited by this amazing move of God's Spirit. Joshua, for one, was troubled. When he heard the report of Eldad and Medad prophesying, Joshua immediately asked Moses to stop them. Surely the Lord would not want just anyone to prophecy. They should be under the direct covering of a great leader such as Moses or himself. What good could come of it? If God were to anoint everyone, what would be so special about it? Yes, it would be far better if God left the whole business of leadership and power to the select few who could handle it. Moses, however, saw through Joshua's words and into his heart: "Are you jealous for my sake? I wish that all the Lord's people were prophets and the Lord would put his Spirit on them."

Just like Joshua, it is easy to allow our own insecurities to influence our judgment when it comes to spiritual leadership. Sometimes these insecurities keep us from training and empowering other gifted people who are also desperately needed in the body of Christ. Tragically, to the insecure leader, any person with a calling or gift from God will be seen as a potential threat to his or her own position, instead of a vital part of God's purpose. When we find ourselves feeling insecure, we must let the Lord help us change.

On the other hand, a mature, secure leader like Moses desires to see every person realize his or her calling and gifts. Although mature leaders definitely believe in the importance of mentoring and training, this is not based on their insecurities, but on their passion to see new people develop into strong leaders. In Ephesians 4:11–12, we see that the primary purpose of Christian leadership is *"to prepare God's people for works of service, so that the body of Christ may be built up."*

So whether you are a leader who needs to help mentor new leaders, or you are the one being mentored, remember that we are all on the same team and that we all have the same purpose.

I have seen this insecurity with an acquaintance. I think it was pride at its core but he would never fully delegate and wanted "hands on" everything. Partly fearing the success of others, he realized he could claim the victory if he was hands on at every step of the process. People under him and over him found it very difficult to work with him.

Duncan Phillips

Lessons in the Life of Moses:
MIRACULOUS PROVISION

[The LORD said,] "Tell the people: ..." The LORD heard you when you wailed, "If only we had meat to eat! We were better off in Egypt!" Now the LORD will give you meat, and you will eat it. You will not eat it for just one day, or two days, or five, ten or twenty days, but for a whole month—until it comes out of your nostrils and you loathe it—because you have rejected the LORD, who is among you, and have wailed before him, saying, 'Why did we ever leave Egypt?'"

But Moses said, "Here I am among six hundred thousand men on foot, and you say, 'I will give them meat to eat for a whole month!' Would they have enough if flocks and herds were slaughtered for them? Would they have enough if all the fish in the sea were caught for them?"

The LORD answered Moses, "Is the LORD's arm too short? You will now see whether or not what I say will come true for you."

Now a wind went out from the LORD and drove quail in from the sea. It brought them down all around the camp to about three feet above the ground, as far as a day's walk in any direction.

NUMBERS 11:18–22, 31

MARCH 26

The Hebrews looked around in amazement—everywhere they looked quail were piled three feet high. The supply was so abundant it took the Israelites thirty-six hours to collect it all. Even Moses was amazed. He had seen God part the Red Sea and provide food for a whole nation in the heat of the desert, but this new miracle was beyond his comprehension. If God had done this in response to the wailing and

whining of his unbelieving people, what would God do if Israel would learn to cry out in faith?

The most amazing thing about this story is not the millions of quail. Rather, it is the fact that God gave this abundant provision in spite of the unbelief and ingratitude of his people. Even Moses, who had faithfully trusted God through so much, had struggled to believe that God could really provide like he said he would.

No matter what type of need you are facing today, God can provide abundantly. Philippians 4:19 declares, "God will meet all your needs according to his glorious riches in Christ Jesus." If you will trust him, the unlimited resources of God are yours through Christ.

From this miraculous story we also learn that no matter how much faith we have, there are always deeper levels that God desires us to experience. Even Moses, who had incredible faith on a daily basis for the needs of two and a half million people, had not yet achieved the full depths of faith that God had for him. In spite of everything he had seen God do, Moses still couldn't imagine the true extent of God's power and provision.

Ephesians 3:20 praises God with this wonderful declaration: "To him who is able to do immeasurably more than all we ask or imagine, according to his power that is at work within us, to him be glory in the church and in Christ Jesus throughout all generations, for ever and ever!" What a great promise! No matter how much faith you have, God's abundant provision is still beyond anything you could ever imagine. Today, whatever your need, do not be afraid. God is able to meet your needs in miraculous ways as you trust him in faith.

WHAT A GREAT STORY. JUST READING THIS TODAY SHOULD STIR YOUR HEARTS TO ACTION. IF WE WOULD ONLY CONSISTENTLY AND SYSTEMATICALLY EXERCISE OUR FAITH, WE WOULDN'T CONSTANTLY BE SHORT-CIRCUITING WHAT THE FATHER HAS FOR US.

Duncan Phillips

Lessons in the Life of Moses:

THE MOST HUMBLE MAN ON THE FACE OF THE EARTH

 "Has the LORD spoken only through Moses?" [Miriam and Aaron] asked. "Hasn't he also spoken through us?" And the LORD heard this.

(Now Moses was a very humble man, more humble than anyone else on the face of the earth.)

At once the LORD said to Moses, Aaron and Miriam, "Come out to the Tent of Meeting, all three of you." So the three of them came out. Then the LORD came down in a pillar of cloud; he stood at the entrance to the Tent and summoned Aaron and Miriam. When both of them stepped forward, he said, "Listen to my words:

' … [Moses] is faithful in all my house. With him I speak face to face, clearly and not in riddles; he sees the form of the Lord. Why then were you not afraid to speak against my servant Moses?"

The anger of the LORD burned against them, and he left them. When the cloud lifted from above the Tent there stood Miriam — leprous, like snow.

NUMBERS 12:2–10

MARCH 27

With a growing sense of their own giftedness and anointing, Aaron and Miriam's hidden resentment toward their brother's leadership was finally coming to the surface. "What makes him think he's so special?" they grumbled. Unfortunately for Aaron and Miriam, the Lord heard them,

and his judgment came like a thunderclap out of heaven. Miriam was struck with a horrible case of leprosy. She would not be healed until Moses prayed for her.

Why was God so quick to come to Moses' defense? Was Moses perfect? No, Scripture records Moses' failings as well as his triumphs. If he wasn't perfect, was God just playing favorites? No. God repeatedly rushed to his defense because Moses was humble. In fact, the Bible says Moses was the *most humble* man on the face of the earth. Whenever Moses was attacked or criticized, instead of defending himself, he would simply wait for God to come to his defense.

How about you? Do you wait for God to defend you when you're attacked unfairly? I have found when I am patient, God himself *will* come to my defense. Over and over again, people who have wronged me have been convicted and have come to apologize to me when I have simply waited on the Lord and allowed him to work on my behalf in their hearts.

If you are struggling with someone's unfair criticism or mistreatment right now, it might be that God is allowing it for a very good reason. Sometimes, whether we like it or not, criticism and being misunderstood are the very ways God works his divine characteristic of humility into our lives. Only when we learn to be truly humble can we peacefully wait on God and allow him to defend us. May God give you the grace to walk in humility no matter what harsh words you face. God will use it to make you stronger if you'll let him work in you.

I WRESTLE WITH this. I tend to be REACTIONARY. But the times when I've WAITED have ALWAYS WORKED out FOR the Best. "VENGEANCE is mine," SAYS the LORD. He CAN have it!

Duncan Phillips

Lessons in the Life of Joshua and Caleb:

NEW EYES

Caleb silenced the people before Moses and said, "We should go up and take possession of the land, for we can certainly do it."

But the men who had gone up with him said, "We can't attack those people; they are stronger than we are." And they spread among the Israelites a bad report about the land they had explored. They said, "The land we explored devours those living in it. All the people we saw there are of great size. We saw the Nephilim there (the descendants of Anak come from the Nephilim). We seemed like grasshoppers in our own eyes, and we looked the same to them."

NUMBERS 13:30–33

MARCH 28

Every claim Moses had made about the Promised Land has proven true. This was a place of incredible abundance and fertility. God had brought them to the land of milk and honey. But abundant provision was not the only thing they noticed about this beautiful land. It may have been the land of promise, but it was also a land of danger.

Already living in the Promised Land was a race of vicious warrior giants. These monstrous men were unlike any foe the Hebrew children had faced. The cities seemed impregnable. Most of the scouts who had surveyed the land had come back with their hearts full of fear. But Joshua and Caleb came back full of faith and optimism. Although they tried to encourage the people to rise up in faith, the nation was so frightened by the bad report of the other ten spies, they gave up all hope of ever possessing the land.

How could the report of Joshua and Caleb be so radically different than the report given their fellow scouts? Ten of the spies had an "eye"

problem. They said, "We seemed like grasshoppers in our own eyes." Because their hearts were not filled with faith, they saw things through their own natural eyes. When faced with giants all they could see was themselves as bugs ready for the squashing.

Joshua and Caleb, on the other hand, had eyes full of faith. Their reality was not determined by their own natural sight—they saw everything through the lens of God's promise and power. It was as if they had put on a special pair of glasses that enabled them to see the world as God sees it. So what if these people were giants? All that mattered was God had promised this land to them. In Joshua and Caleb's minds these giants would either leave the land or they would have to be destroyed—and that was that.

Are you looking at your world through the eyes of faith? If you need God's special glasses to view your situation today, here is a prescription:

First, take time to read and study God's Word. As you do, it will change the way you see *everything* around you. As you learn and are filled with God's truth, you can begin to target the "giants" in your life with specific verses that apply to them and that will help you defeat them. As you are faithful in filling God's prescription for your eyes of faith, you will begin to see even the most difficult things in your life in a drastically different light. Your "giants" may just start looking like "grasshoppers" instead!

PERSONALLY, I HAVE FOUND the MORE time I spend MEDITATING on the WORD AND pRAYING, the MORE I'm AWARE of His pResence. MY DAYS HAVE A DIFFERENT emphASIS. TYpICALLY, I find the pASSAGE of SCRiptuRE I've BEEN FOCUSING on will APPLY to A SituATION thAt DAY. The WORD is LIVING AND ACtive. Living thROUGH FAith is incREDIBLY exCiting—you just Don't Know when the LORD will TuRN up AND Do A miRACLE.

Duncan Phillips

WHO'S EATING WHOM?

They spread among the Israelites a bad report about the land they had explored. They said, "The land we explored devours those living in it. All the people we saw there are of great size."

NUMBERS 13:32

[Joshua and Caleb said,] "Do not rebel against the LORD. And do not be afraid of the people of the land, because we will swallow them up. Their protection is gone, but the LORD is with us. Do not be afraid of them."

NUMBERS 14:9

MARCH 29

The whole nation had been terrorized by the reports of the ten spies. The Promised Land was a beautiful paradise—but it was filled with deadly perils. For centuries Canaan had been the place of dreams and now it was seen as a sinister land full of giants that would eat the people of God alive. Although Caleb and Joshua did everything in their power to stand against the unbelief sweeping through the hearts and minds of the people, they were fighting a losing battle. "The Cannanites' protection has left them," Caleb and Joshua had announced. "They won't eat us because we're going to eat them!"

This story captures the essence of the challenges all of us will face as we attempt to enter our own Promised Land. Like the Israelites, you too will discover that the size of your promises will determine the size of your problems. In other words, the gigantic problems you may be facing today should be a clear sign to you of the even bigger promises awaiting you. Why does our loving heavenly Father allow us to face such terrifying challenges before we can receive our greatest happiness and joy? It is because he knows that by overcoming the challenges we will grow the faith and strength we need to fulfill the promised purpose awaiting us.

In reality, the calamities, assaults, and obstacles that mark the road to our destiny are the food that feeds our faith. Caleb and Joshua had to face giants and, spiritually speaking, "swallow them" before they could walk into God's promised blessing. We too must rise up and "feed" on the very situations threatening to eat us alive.

So ... who's going to eat whom? The gigantic problems you are facing are either going to eat you alive through worry, fear, or anxiety, or you are going to "eat them up" through the power of God's Word and Spirit. In Isaiah 41:15, God promises to make you into a *"threshing sledge, new and sharp, with many teeth"* — which is Old Testament talk for something really sharp and really powerful — a tool that can cut down mountains of opposition and crush them. As you fill your heart and mind with the Word of God, it will become the teeth you need to chew up any challenge that comes your way.

The battle we face is in the mind. That is why the Lord says to "Renew our minds." If our minds are renewed daily, the battle will be more easily won. We just have to walk it out. The Father is interested in building character and spiritual stamina in his people.

Duncan Phillips

Lessons in the Life of Moses:
FACING THE CONSEQUENCES

The LORD replied, "I have forgiven them, as you asked. Nevertheless, as surely as I live and as surely as the glory of the LORD fills the whole earth, not one of the men who saw my glory and the miraculous signs I performed in Egypt and in the desert but who disobeyed me and tested me ten times — not one of them will ever see the land I promised on oath to their forefathers. No one who has treated me with contempt will ever see it. But because my servant Caleb has a different spirit and follows me wholeheartedly, I will bring him into the land he went to and his descendants will inherit it."

NUMBERS 14:20–24

MARCH 30

Moses almost felt consumed by the hot breath of God's anger. God was determined to punish the Hebrews for their persistent unbelief, and sadly, Moses knew he was justified in doing so. After all, what other people on the face of the planet would still refuse to enter their Promised Land after all the miraculous signs and wonders God had performed on their behalf? Didn't they realize that the same God who had destroyed the Egyptian empire could easily dispatch a few giants?

Yet, in spite of his own frustration with the people's attitudes, Moses cried out in prayer for God to have mercy on them. And in response to those prayers, God decided to forgive the people and to let them live. But God's amazing act of forgiveness did not wipe away the painful consequences of Israel's unbelief. Although God desired for all of his children to enter the Promised Land, he knew the unbelief in their hearts would never allow them to go forward. Therefore, no Israelite over twenty years old,

except for the faithful Caleb and Joshua, would ever be allowed to enter the Promised Land. The whole nation would be forced to wander in the desert until every one of them had died.

Unfortunately, like the Hebrews, many modern-day Christians believe it does not matter how they live, because God will always forgive them when they ask. What they are forgetting is the fact that God forgives, but he does not always take away the consequences of our actions.

Does God forgive things like drunk driving, drug abuse, sexual promiscuity, or cheating? Absolutely. This doesn't mean, however, that your behavior will not scar you, and others, physically, mentally, and spiritually. As a pastor, I have spent countless hours helping people deal with the horrible consequences of sin. Sadly, these people have learned the hard way that while there is forgiveness, there are also consequences.

My hope for you today is that you will not have to learn the hard way. Although God can heal the scars that sin can bring, why face unnecessary pain when you can obey God and avoid it in the first place? Take the example of Joshua and Caleb—stay faithful and know that you will be rewarded.

The relationship Moses had with the Father never ceases to amaze me. Time after time, we see the prayers of Moses influencing the heart of God. Because of his obedience, the Father would hear the prayers of Moses and his judgment would be withheld from Israel. If we would only bend our knees, pray, and be obedient, how much more could we bring about his will on the earth?

Duncan Phillips

Lessons in the Life of Moses:
DESTRUCTION

Moses said, "Why are you disobeying the LORD's command? This will not succeed! Do not go up, because the LORD is not with you. You will be defeated by your enemies, for the Amalekites and Canaanites will face you there. Because you have turned away from the LORD, he will not be with you and you will fall by the sword."

Nevertheless, in their presumption they went up toward the high hill country, though neither Moses nor the ark of the LORD's covenant moved from the camp. Then the Amalekites and Canaanites who lived in that hill country came down and attacked them and beat them down all the way to Hormah.

NUMBERS 14:41–45

MARCH 31

The Hebrew children were inconsolable. Not only had they been forbidden to enter the Promised Land, but their children would also be made to wander in the scorching desert until every one of their parents had died. Far from bringing deep repentance to the Hebrews, however, their punishment only exposed the deeper levels of rebellion hidden in their hearts. No matter how Moses had pleaded with them, they decided to march into the Promised Land with or without the presence of God. After a massacre on the border of the Promised Land, the Amalekites and the Canaanites drove the Israelites all the way to a place called *Hormah*—a name that means "destruction."

What lessons can we take from this story so that we can avoid being driven to our own "Hormah"? First, the Hebrews followed their own plan, instead of God's. The Israelites presumed they could do whatever they

wanted and still have the blessings and protection of God. They had some how convinced themselves they could still receive their Promised Land. Sadly, their thinking would prove to be fatal.

Second, they were so blinded by their pride that they believed they could possess God's promises without his help or the help of their leader, Moses. They left Moses, and the ark of the covenant, the symbol of God's presence, behind and went their own way as if these obviously vital things did not matter.

How many times are we blinded by our own presumption and pride as well? Like the Hebrews, we think that we can live outside of God's authority and yet still receive the blessings he promises to the faithful. Sadly, just as in the time of Moses, people who walk in this type of presumption normally end up at Hormah—destruction. Whether it is Christian couples who live like unbelievers and still expect a healthy marriage, or business people who lie and cheat while still anticipating God's blessings, many times presumption can lead to the destruction of the people and things we love most. Don't let the enemy trick you into making the same mistake that Israel made. Seek God's plan and purpose and you will see your Promised Land.

The children of Israel were deceived. Deceived into thinking they could take on their enemies without the covering of Moses and the tabernacle. Let us not be deceived into thinking we can take on the wiles of the enemy without the Armor of God. Read Ephesians 6:10 – 20.

Duncan Phillips

Lessons in the Life of Moses:
BEING EQUAL AND TEACHABLE

Korah ... Dathan and Abiram,... and On ... became insolent and rose up against Moses. With them were 250 Israelite men, well-known community leaders who had been appointed members of the council. They came as a group to oppose Moses and Aaron and said to them, "You have gone too far! The whole community is holy, every one of them, and the Lord is with them. Why then do you set yourselves above the Lord's assembly?"

Then Moses summoned Dathan and Abiram, the sons of Eliab. But they said, "We will not come! Isn't it enough that you have brought us up out of a land flowing with milk and honey to kill us in the desert? And now you also want to lord it over us?"

NUMBERS 16:1–3, 12–13

APRIL 1

After all he had done for the people and the sacrifices he had made to lead them, a small group of Moses' finest leaders had chosen to challenge his God-given authority. Angry over what they perceived as his failure to lead them into the Promised Land, they had decided he was now unworthy to lead them. They felt they had outgrown any need for human leadership in their lives. After all, hadn't the Lord said the Hebrews were all called to be a holy nation of priests? Therefore, from now on these leaders would simply approach God themselves.

As Moses fell on his face in response to their accusations, God quickly rushed to his defense. When the rebellious leaders crowded around the Tent of Meeting and attempted to offer incense, every one of them was destroyed in an awesome display of God's judgment. The earth convulsed and Dathan and Abiram were swallowed alive. The rest of the rebels were burned to death with fire from heaven.

Although God's children are all equal in his sight, he has chosen certain people to be leaders. The fact that God uses humans to mentor and lead his people is clearly supported by Scripture. In 1 Peter 5:2 leaders are called to "be shepherds of God's flock that is under your care, serving as overseers."

I have seen many Christians today blame their leader for their own failures, just as this group of Hebrews. When life gets difficult and things go wrong because they aren't living the way God wants them to, they search for someone else to blame for their own failures. Many times pastors and other ministry leaders are the prime targets for this blame.

No matter how spiritual you think you may be, or how close you have really become to God, you will never outgrow your need for the wise counsel and help of mature Christian leaders. Thankfully, God does not punish like he did in the Old Testament, even when we reject the advice of the people he has placed in our lives. But the consequences of ignoring sound advice and biblical wisdom can be costly. On the other hand, learning and growing under the guidance of strong leaders will help you develop the relationship with God that will bring you power when you need it the most.

Even though God has used the Newsboys in a mighty way many times, this devotional helped me to realize that no matter how spiritually mature we are, we never outgrow our need for help. No matter how many albums we sell, I realize we'll never outgrow our need for the men God places in our lives.

Jeff Frankenstein

Lessons in the Life of Moses:
THE FEAR OF THE LORD

The LORD said to Moses, "Tell Eleazar son of Aaron, the priest, to take the censers out of the smoldering remains and scatter the coals some distance away, for the censers are holy — the censors of the men who sinned at the cost of their lives.... So Eleazar the priest collected the bronze censers brought by those who had been burned up."

NUMBERS 16:36–38, 39

APRIL 2

Young Eleazar was sick with the pungent smell of burning flesh in his nostrils. So many men, his friends, and neighbors had been consumed with fire from heaven when they had attempted to come before the Lord in their rebellious pride. As Eleazar tried to comprehend their deaths and the great judgment he had just witnessed, he was roused by the voice of his uncle, Moses. "Eleazar, you have been commanded by the Lord to collect the censers of those who wrongly attempted to offer incense before the Lord."

It was like a nightmare. As he bent down and began to rake through the charred human remains scattered on the ground, Eleazar could see through the tears. As he pulled the censers out from the piles of ashes that had once been living, breathing men, Eleazar's heart was filled with a new resolve to walk in obedience and holiness all the days of his life.

It was not out of cruelty that God required young Eleazar to sift through the charred human remains looking for the holy censers. No, it

was out of love, for God did not want to lose Eleazar to rebellion and sin. Therefore, he gave the young man a terrible task in order to instill both a healthy fear of the Lord and a deep hatred of sin within his heart.

There are times God will give you a close look at the horrible consequences of sin through the life of another person. God's intention is not for you to become judgmental or to feel superior to that person. He is showing you, rather, the grim consequences of sin, in order to keep you from that same end.

In my own life, God has allowed me to see the destructive power of sin more times than I care to count. Every time I have to face the horrible consequences of rebellion and sin in the life of a person I love, it makes me fear God and hate sin all the more. These close encounters with God's judgments have helped to make me a wiser man today. When you are faced with sin's consequences in the life of another, watch and learn. May your heart be filled with the fear of the Lord and a hunger for holiness as you do.

As the son of a pastor and a Christian who has been involved in many ministries, I've seen situation after situation that's broken my heart. Even to think of them makes me sad. Yet, I realize that, like young Eleazar, God has used these situations to make me hate sin and love him all the more.

Jeff Frankenstein

BETWEEN THE LIVING AND THE DEAD

The plague had already started among the people, but Aaron offered the incense and made atonement for them. He stood between the living and the dead, and the plague stopped. But 14,700 people died from the plague, in addition to those who had died because of Korah. Then Aaron returned to Moses at the entrance to the Tent of Meeting, for the plague had stopped.

NUMBERS 16:47–50

APRIL 3

Surely the children of Israel would have learned their lesson after seeing God's judgment on Korah and the leaders who had rebelled with him. Sadly, this was not the case. The morning after Korah's rebellion, a large mob of Israelites formed around the Tent of Meeting. The mob called for retribution against Moses and Aaron because of their role in God's judgment. As the cloud of God's presence enveloped the Tent of Meeting, Moses could already feel God's growing wrath. The moment he and Aaron fell on their faces, a terrible plague began. Within seconds, hundred of Israelites had already died. Although these people had been ready to kill him only moments before, Moses still ordered Aaron to make atonement for the Israelites' rebellion and sin by using his censer to make an incense offering to the Lord. With people dropping all around him, Aaron courageously stood in the path of the horrible plague and faithfully called on God's mercy and grace until his judgment ceased.

This is an amazing story of courage and self-sacrifice. Even though the Israelites had come with threats of murder, Moses and Aaron were still willing to risk their lives to save them. God calls us today to the same selflessness. No matter how obnoxiously people treat us, or how threatened we are by their actions, we too must be willing to pray for their salvation and deliverance. This is also true when it comes to the sins and wickedness of our nation today. At times, like Aaron, you and I may even be called to stand between the "living and the dead." God may call you to personally reach out to the very people you have been praying for from a distance. Whether it is someone bound in a homosexual lifestyle, drug addict, or a homeless person, God may call you to act as an answer to your prayers.

Where are you today? Are you worried or angry over the condition of your school, neighborhood, business, or city, but aren't really doing anything to make it better? Will you, like Aaron, be willing to stand for God between the "living and the dead"? Today, the Holy Spirit is calling you out of your comfort zone into his service. When you obey his voice it will change both your heart and the hearts of those around you.

AFTER READING this DevotionAL, I hAD to ASK myself this question: WouLD I Be willing to RISK my Life to sAve the veRy peopLe who weRe tRying to kill me? WhetheR it is AARoh in this stoRy oR Jesus oh the cRoss, I Am contihuALLy chALLehGeD to Be moRe seLf-sAcRificihG wheh I consiDeR theiR Lives.

Jeff Frankenstein

Lessons in the Life of Moses:
THE BUDDING ROD

The LORD said to Moses, "Speak to the Israelites and get twelve staffs from them, one from the leader of each of their ancestral tribes. Write the name of each man on his staff. On the staff of Levi write Aaron's name, for there must be one staff for the head of each ancestral tribe. Place them in the Tent of Meeting in front of the Testimony, where I meet with you. The staff belonging to the man I choose will sprout, and I will rid myself of this constant grumbling against you by the Israelites."

NUMBERS 17:1 – 5

APRIL 4

Both God and his faithful servant Moses were grieved. There seemed to be no end to the Israelites' constant grumbling and complaining. Over fourteen thousand people had been killed by a horrible plague when they had rebelled against the leadership of Moses and Aaron. With families mourning the loss of their loved ones throughout the camp, Moses' heart was breaking. He longed to find a way to end the constant rebellion of God's people. The response of God to Moses' longing is an amazing demonstration of his compassion and his wisdom.

God told Moses to take a staff from the leader of each of the twelve tribes; these rods were to be placed in the tabernacle overnight. The man whose staff budded and bore fruit was the man God had chosen. The next morning, the fragrance of fresh life filled the whole tabernacle—from one end to the other, Aaron's staff was filled with blossoms and fruit. When the Israelites saw this amazing confirmation of God's hand on the life of Aaron, they never questioned his leadership again.

In this story, God demonstrates what it will take to restrain the rebellion which lives in the human heart. The manifestation of God's judgment could not restrain the evil and wickedness running rampant in the nation. It was only the beauty of the fruit of God's kingdom that finally stopped the endless cycle of rebellion paralyzing the progress of the Israelites.

The same principle applies to our world today. The greatest deterrent to a nation's wickedness is not the consequences of their actions, but the beauty of the fruit of a life filled with God's joy and peace. When Christians like you and I are truly bearing the fruit of the Holy Spirit—love, joy, patience, and humility—those around us will begin to be transformed.

This story also shows us the secret to divine fruitfulness. If an inanimate object like Aaron's rod can bear fruit after one night in God's presence, how much will you and I live a life of abundant fruitfulness if we are willing to spend time with God on a regular basis? The fruitfulness of Aaron's rod was maintained because it was kept in the tabernacle, in the constant presence of God. If we will purposefully walk in God's presence every day, we will continually bear the fruit necessary to change the world around us.

When I consider my own generation, it's clear they're sick of words. If words alone could change the world, it would already be changed. My generation really wants to see something. Like the Israelites, they are looking for the fruit of a changed life.

Jeff Frankenstein

Lessons in the Life of Moses:

DON'T STRIKE THE ROCK

[The LORD said to Moses,] "Take the staff, and you and your brother Aaron gather the assembly together. Speak to that rock before their eyes and it will pour out its water.... He and Aaron gathered the assembly together in front of the rock and Moses said to them, "Listen, you rebels, must we bring you water out of this rock?"

Moses raised his arm and struck the rock twice with his staff. Water gushed out....

But the LORD said to Moses and Aaron, "Because you did not trust in me enough to honor me as holy in the sight of the Israelites, you will not bring this community into the land I give them."

NUMBERS 20:8, 10–12

APRIL 5

The Israelites were complaining once again—this time it was about the lack of water. Even after God had provided them with food and water everyday for months, they still refused to trust him.

God told Moses to go into the tabernacle and get Aaron's rod, which had budded with life and fruit, and to simply *speak* to the rock to bring forth water, not to hit it with the staff. But in his anger, Moses smashed Aaron's rod against the rock twice. Although water gushed out of the rock as promised, Moses was immediately sickened by his own disobedience. And then he heard these terrible words from the Lord he loved: "You will not bring this community into the land I will give them."

Even after God clearly told Moses to speak to the rock, he chose to strike it. You must never forget that it is not enough to simply do what God

says; it is just as important that you do it in the *way* he says to do it. With the Lord, the means are just as important as the end.

Another mistake Moses made was his misrepresentation of God's emotions. God was not judging the people at this point. The only reason God had Moses carry the budding rod was to remind the people that he had chosen Moses and Aaron to lead them. Moses, however, was filled with judgment and frustration, so he struck the rock in anger. This rash act violated the way God had chosen to deal with his people. We must remember that it is not enough for us to simply hear and obey God's Word, we must also show people his love.

Moses also made the mistake of having pride in his position of authority. When Moses asked the question, "Must we bring you water out of this rock?" he was taking credit for something only God could do. Tragically, Moses' attempt to establish his own authority was totally unnecessary; God had already given him the credibility he needed. Many times we make this same mistake today. Whether it is using our anger to motivate people, or continually bragging about our ministry accomplishments, we are attempting to establish our authority in the wrong way. If we will spend more time in the presence of God and less time trying to prove ourselves, we will have the fruit we need to win the hearts of the people we have been called to serve. Trust God to prove your worth to others and he will do it in wonderful ways that will bring life to others.

When I read this devotional, I was struck by the fact of how easy it is to misrepresent God. Even when we're saying the right words, if we are coming across as angry, mean-spirited, or critical, we too are running the danger of misrepresenting our loving God.

Jeff Frankenstein

Lessons in the Life of Moses:
THE BRONZE SNAKE

The LORD sent venomous snakes among them; they bit the people and many Israelites died. The people came to Moses and said, "We sinned when we spoke against the LORD and against you. Pray that the LORD will take the snakes away from us." So Moses prayed for the people.

The LORD said to Moses, "Make a snake and put it up on a pole; anyone who is bitten can look at it and live." So Moses made a bronze snake and put it up on a pole. Then when anyone was bitten by a snake and looked at the bronze snake, he lived.

NUMBERS 21:6–9

Just as Moses lifted up the snake in the dessert, so the Son of Man must be lifted up, that everyone who believes in him may have eternal life.

JOHN 3:14–15

APRIL 6

The hissing, biting serpents were everywhere! The camp of the Israelites was filled with terror. People ran screaming for their lives; others lay dying from the serpents' venomous bites. Finally, in desperation, the Hebrews came to Moses and repented of their complaining and ingratitude. God's response to the people's repentance would point prophetically to the ultimate sacrifice of his Son, centuries later. God had Moses cast a bronze serpent and mount it on a tall pole. God promised that those who looked at the serpent on the pole with repentance in their hearts would be immediately healed from the deadly bites.

No matter what has "bitten" you today, God is able and willing to heal you. Whether you have been poisoned with the venom of immorality, substance abuse, bitterness, anger, or jealousy, it does not matter. God has the power to totally heal you. If you will look to Jesus and his sacrifice for you on the cross, just as the Israelites looked to the serpent mounted on the pole, healing and deliverance can begin in your life right now. Turn away from your sins and realize that its power over you has been broken by Jesus and your healing is certain.

Let me give you three steps that will help you through this process of healing. First, if you are struggling to quit a specific sin, find and study Scriptures that talk about that sin. God's word will make your conscience so sensitive to that sin that you will be uncomfortable until you stop and ask for forgiveness.

Second, in order for you to build your faith in the power of God to deliver, you should read about God's deliverance. Romans chapters 6–8 is a good place to start.

Last, it is important for you to remember to spend more time looking at your Savior than looking at your sin. Focusing on the snakes was not going to bring the Israelites healing—only looking to the symbol of God's deliverance would do that. As you seek to more deeply understand Jesus' sacrifice for you, you will discover the power you need to be delivered from the sins you are wrestling with today.

AFTER I'D READ this DEVOTIONAL, I WAS STRUCK AFRESH BY the POWER OF GOD'S WORD. In my own Life, I hAVE DISCOVERED thAT even when I DON'T wANT to READ the WORD OR I feel Like I'm not Getting Anything out of it; it is powerfully Affecting my Life. No mAtter whAT I feel when I'm REAding it, I'm DIFFERENT when I'm DONE.

Jeff Frankenstein

Lessons in the Life of Moses:

BATTLES AT THE BORDER OF THE PROMISED LAND

The Israelites ... turned and went up along the road toward Bashan, and Og king of Bashan, and his whole army marched out to meet them.... The LORD said to Moses, "Do not be afraid of him, for I have handed him over to you with his whole army and his land." So they struck him down, together with his sons and his whole army, leaving them no survivors. And they took possession of his land.

NUMBERS 21:32–35

APRIL 7

The closer the children of Israel came to the borders of the Promised Land, the more powerful their enemies had been. Now, as they went up the road to Bashan, they were confronted by the fiercest foe so far. His name was Og, King of Bashan, one of the last members of a race of giants. The Israelites had heard that his bed was thirteen feet long. *What kind of monster would need a bed this large?* the Hebrew soldiers wondered. To top it off, all sixty cities within Og's kingdom were impregnable fortresses with high walls and reinforced gates.

How would they survive with this huge threat now rushing to meet them? As Moses prepared them to meet this powerful foe, he was reassured by the quiet voice of the Almighty God: "Do not be afraid of him, for I have handed him over to you with his whole army and his land."

In the ensuing battle, the armies of Israel were wildly successful. The power of God made them invincible. All sixty cities were sacked, and all of the Amorite armies were destroyed as the victorious Hebrews systematically conquered Og's entire kingdom.

Just like the Israelites, the closer you get to your Promised Land, the more powerful and sophisticated your enemy will become. In fact, one of the sure signs that you are on your way to a big victory for God is a change in the intensity of the battles you are facing. If your "giants" are becoming larger, and your battles harder than ever, keep fighting! You are about to enter into the greatest days of your life.

As you face battles in your journey with the Lord, remember that just like Og, King of Bashan, the enemy's reputation is far greater than the reality of his ability to harm you. Whether it was the tales of Og's fortified cities or his giant bed, his fearsome legend had caused other foes to lose heart before the battle even began. But the Israelites' perspective on Og came from Word of the Lord and his promises. No matter what you are facing, if you will allow the Word of God and the Holy Spirit to define your perception of the foes you are facing, you will be better equipped to defeat them.

Remember during your fight, just as Moses *totally* annihilated the armies of Og, so you, too, must work to completely destroy the enemy's influence in your life. Stomp out even little sins. Run fast away from temptation. With the power of God, relentlessly attack these forces until you have utterly destroyed them. May you see victory today as you continue to march to your own Promised Land!

Whether it is in my own personal life or the life of my family, I have discovered that there is always a battle before the breakthrough. In fact, the bigger the battle is, the bigger the breakthrough will be. Once the breakthrough has come, however, I always realize afresh that the enemy that I have been facing is far smaller than the God I serve.

Jeff Frankenstein

Lessons in the Life of BALAAM:
BALAAM AND THE ANGEL

Moab was filled with dread because of the Israelites....

So Balak, son of Zippor, who was king of Moab at the time, sent messengers to summon Balaam....

Balak said:

"A people has come out of Egypt; they cover the face of the land and have settled next to me. Now come and put a curse on these people because they are too powerful for me. Perhaps then I will be able to defeat them and drive them out of the country. For I know that those you bless are blessed and those you curse are cursed."

But ... the angel of the Lord stood in the road to oppose [Balaam.]

NUMBERS 22:3–6, 22

APRIL 8

Balak, king of Moab, was trembling in terror on his throne. When he had heard the reports of Og's destruction, he knew Moab would have no chance of defeating Israel. Then Balak remembered the stories he had heard of Balaam—a powerful warlock who lived in a neighboring nation. Allegedly he commanded such dark, demonic power that he could curse people and they would die. If he could entice Balaam to curse the Hebrew nation, Balak knew they would be destroyed.

But although he was a powerful warlock, Balaam still feared the God of Israel. He was not a follower of Jehovah, but believed in his existence and had heard of his might. In the end, however, Balaam's greed overcame his fear. Despite the warnings of Israel's God, Balaam accepted Balak's offer.

But God sent a powerful angel to confront Balaam on the road (Numbers 22:21–35). This angelic encounter so frightened him that he promised to speak only the words God put into his mouth, no matter how much Balak offered to pay him to do otherwise. This divine protection saved Israel from the demonic storm that Balaam intended to release.

This story is a powerful example of God's protection. It is an incredible picture of what is described in Psalms 34:7: "The angel of the Lord encamps around those who fear him, and he delivers them." No matter how hard Balaam tried to avoid the angel, there was no escape. He was cornered and faced with death if he did not yield to the Lord. Balaam's power was no match for Israel's God.

Even as God's angel protected Israel, so his angels are protecting you now. Although their battles for your life take place in an invisible realm, you can be sure they are guarding you even at this very moment. While it is easy to focus only on the enemies that you can see all around you, there is a wonderful reality beyond what your eyes can perceive. May God open your spiritual eyes to see his armies standing in protection all around you today.

When I think over my last twelve years with the newsboys, there is no doubt in my mind that we've been saved by angels over and over again. Whether it is being shot at in Brazil or being kidnapped in Panama, I have experienced the supernatural protection of God countless times. That is why the newsboys and I are not afraid to go anywhere that God sends us.

Jeff Frankenstein

Lessons in the Life of BALAAM:
BALAAM AND THE DONKEY

Then the LORD opened Balaam's eyes and he saw the angel of the LORD standing in the road with his sword drawn. So he bowed low and fell facedown.

The angel of the LORD asked him, "Why have you beaten your donkey?... I have come here to oppose you because your path is a reckless one before me. The donkey saw me and turned away from me.... If she had not turned away, I would certainly have killed you by now, but I would have spared her."

NUMBERS 22:31–33

APRIL 9

Balaam was incensed. With all his power over the forces of darkness, he couldn't even control a stupid donkey. No matter how he had beaten and cursed the idiotic creature, the donkey had continued to resist. Then suddenly, the donkey talked back to him!

Well he was a wizard, wasn't he? Although most of us would have been speechless when faced with a talking donkey, it didn't seem to faze Balaam all that much. As the donkey chastened him for his cruel treatment, God finally opened the greedy wizard's eyes to the danger that was right in front of him. When Balaam saw what the donkey had been seeing, he fell on his face, trembling in fear. A fearsome angel with a drawn sword who had been sent by the Lord to kill him stood in the path ahead. Despite his unjust and cruel treatment of his faithful beast, the donkey had still saved his life.

Do you sometimes treat the people in your life the same way that Balaam treated his donkey? Do you hurt them with angry words even as

they try to steer you from the danger they see you heading toward? Much of the time, especially when we are young, we are blind to the things that are threatening to destroy us. Don't ignore the warnings of those that love you the most, like your parents, or your youth group leaders. While to you it may look like they are trying to keep you from having fun and experiencing freedom, they are really trying to keep you from ruining your future.

Many times, your safety and success in life will come down to your response to this simple truth: If the only people you listen to are those who tell you what you want to hear, sooner or later you will be ambushed by an attack of the enemy. May God give you the grace to love and cherish the counsel of the people he has put in your life, even when their words are painful to hear.

AS A memBER OF the newsBoys, it's never hARD to finD peopLe who WAnt to hEAR whAt we hAve to SAy AnD those who ARe ALSo GLAD to teLL us whAt we wANt to hEAR. In my own Life I hAve DiscovereD thAt the KinD of peopLe I ReALLy neeD to Be ARounD ARe the peopLe who wiLL teLL me the tRuth whetheR I wAnt to hEAR it oR not.
Jeff Frankenstein

Lessons in the Life of BALAAM:
BALAAM'S BLESSINGS

[Balaam said,]
"How can I curse
   those whom God has not cursed?
How can I denounce
   those whom the LORD has not denounced?"...

Balak said to Balaam, "What have you done to me? I brought you to curse my enemies, but you have done nothing but bless them!"

He answered, "Must I not speak what the LORD puts in my mouth?"

NUMBERS 23:8, 11-12

APRIL 10

Balaam was filled with fury. It was bad enough that he could not curse the Hebrew nation, but now their crafty God was even making him bless them. Balak suggested Balaam view the people of Israel from another vantage point, in hopes Balaam might be able to curse them if he had a new perspective. Balaam was more than willing to comply. Yet no matter which group of Hebrews Balaam viewed, or from what perspective he looked, all he could do was blessings of the Lord upon them. Finally, in exasperation, Balak fired him. "I summoned you here to curse the Hebrews, but all you have done is bless them," Balak roared. As Balaam left to go home, he was so gripped by the influence of God's Spirit that he involuntarily spoke even more incredible words about Israel's destiny.

What a wonderful picture of God's protective love. Even though the children of Israel had been rebellious and unbelieving, God intervened on their behalf. No matter how Balaam tried to curse them, God's Spirit would force him instead to bless the people of God. If blessings rained down even on rebellious Israel, how much more will they flood us when we are faithfully following the Lord? If you will call out to God in repentance and faith, you will experience the reality of his shielding love over you too.

No matter who or what is trying to accuse you today, according to Numbers 23:8, the blessing of the Lord far outweighs any curse directed toward your life. Whether it is someone who is spreading lies about you, a struggle with sin, or a secret that has been tearing your family apart for years, your God can deliver you today.

Remember that no matter how strong the enemy may seem, the only power he has over you is the power you give him. Jesus said in John 14:30, "The prince of this world is coming. He has no hold on me." When we trust Jesus with our lives, the prince of this world has no hold on us either!

The enemy's accusations or attempts to make you feel that you are under his control cannot penetrate your life unless you willingly open your heart to sin and rebellion. And even when we do sin, the forgiveness we can receive in Christ when we repent builds invincible wall of protection around us where the enemy cannot reach.

AS A minister AND A CHRISTIAN musician, being laughed at, mocked, and slammed comes with the territory. Many times, when people hear that I'm a Christian musician, they go out of their way to mock what I'm doing. I have learned through experience that God's blessing is far more powerful than anything people may say about me.

Jeff Frankenstein

Lessons in the Life of BALAAM:
BALAAM'S REVENGE

While Israel was staying in Shittim, the men began to indulge in sexual immorality with Moabite women, who invited them to the sacrifices to their gods. The people ate and bowed down before these gods. So Israel joined in worshiping the Baal of Peor. And the LORD's anger burned against them.

The Lord said to Moses, "Take all the leaders of these people, kill them, and expose them in broad daylight before the LORD, so that the LORD's fierce anger may turn away from Israel.

But those who died in the plague numbered 24,000.

NUMBERS 25:1-4, 9

APRIL II

Despite Balaam's failure to curse the people of God, King Balak still listened intently to the wizard's diabolical advice. Balaam encouraged the king to find some means through which the men of Israel could be enticed into sin and rebellion. Once they had broken the divine commands of their God, Balaam assured the king, their own God would judge them. And tragically, the plan worked to perfection. The men of Israel were seduced into sex and idol worship by the beautiful Moabite women and God's anger had burned. The resulting plague killed twenty-four thousand Israelites.

This was a brand-new generation of Israelites—the up and coming young leaders of their nation. And just like their parents before them, they were facing choices of life and death—to follow God or their own destructive path. Every generation of Christians will go through its own time of testing and attack in preparation for entering the Promised Land. The young men of Israel were attacked with the seductive beauty of the god-less Moabites. And you, as part of a new generation, are being attacked too. If you simply look around at TV, magazines, and movies, you will see today's equivalent of the seducing Moabite women. The enemy is using the same old tactics, just in a new wrapper.

Just as Balaam's attempt to curse the Israelites failed, so that he was forced to try a new plan of destruction, when the enemy cannot breach your defenses, he will do everything in his power to entice you into sin. Your God-given destiny—and that of your generation—is so powerful that the enemy will do anything he can to derail you through rebellion and sin.

Sex is probably one of the most potent weapons in the enemy's arsenal. He is taking something wonderfully powerful when experienced in the protection of marriage, and twisting it for his own purposes. A great weapon in your own arsenal against this tactic is to be accountable to a more mature Christian of your own gender. The sinful sexual thoughts that seem to appear in your mind so easily will not remain when you bring them into the light by confessing them to a loving Christian friend. In addition, use the powerful Word of God to break down the enemy's strongholds. Take time to read and really soak in Scriptures such as Job 31:1 and Matthew 5:27–28 and God will reduce these strongholds to harmless rubble. Remember—you will never be able to live in your own Promised Land until God conquers the sin that is living in you.

AS I've TRAVELED the ROADS OF AMERICA, there's no DOUBT in my mind that SEXUAL LUST is the GREATEST enemy that CHRISTIAN YOUNG peopLe FACE. WITH A CULTURE that seems MORE AND MORE OUT OF CONTROL in this AREA, everywhere you LOOK YOU ARE INUNDATED WITH UNGODLY iMAGES. It's ONLY BY the GRACE OF GOD. AND BY putting on his ARMOR OF pROTECTION. that ANY OF US CAN BE FREE.

Jeff Frankenstein

Lessons in the Life of Phinehas:
ZEALOUS FOR THE LORD

An Israelite man brought to his family a Midianite woman right before the eyes of Moses and the whole assembly of Israel while they were weeping at the entrance to the Tent of Meeting. When Phinehas, son of Eleazar, son of Aaron, the priest, saw this, he left the assembly, took a spear in his hand, and followed the Israelite into the tent. He drove the spear through both of them—through the Israelite and into the woman's body. Then the plague against the Israelites was stopped; but those who died in the plague numbered 24,000.

The LORD said to Moses, "Phinehas, son of Eleazar, the son of Aaron, the priest, has turned my anger away from the Israelites; for he was as zealous as I am for my honor among them, so that in my zeal, I did not put an end to them."

NUMBERS 25:6–11

APRIL 12

Moses was heartbroken. Hadn't this new generation learned anything from the failure of their parents to enter the Promised Land? As he continued to lead the people in weeping and repentance in front of the Tent of Meeting, what he saw stunned him. In broad daylight, in front of the whole nation, a Hebrew leader brazenly took a Moabite woman into his tent and began to have sex with her. Immediately, the plague God had sent as judgment began to grow in intensity. Before Moses could think to respond, a young man named Phinehas was on his feet, sprinting toward the man's tent. Burning with the fear of the Lord and a passion for the purity of his generation, he killed the couple with a spear

while they were in the very act of immorality. His bold response stopped the plague and spared the whole nation from destruction.

This is a pretty gruesome story, but it captures one of the most critical needs of our own world today. We desperately need young men and women like you who will walk in the spirit of Phinehas. The world needs young people with a passionate love for God and burning hatred of sin that will cause them to stand strong in the midst of the darkness that is threatening to destroy so many people today. While God doesn't call us to fight these battles with swords, spears, and guns, he will arm you with even more powerful spiritual weapons. Armed with the "sword of the Spirit" which is the Word of God and the shield of faith, you will be ready to meet the battle of your own generation.

Young people like you may well be the last hope for your own friends. The world needs young Christian leaders to rise up and hold both themselves and their peers spiritually accountable. When I talk about accountability, I am not talking about being judgmental with one another. I am talking about the loving confrontation and voluntary transparency necessary for true Christian growth at every age. Will you be a "Phinehas" in your generation and stand strong for God today? The world needs you!

AS I meditated on the story of young Phinehas, I began to ask myself a question: Do I have enough passion to take a stand against sin like Phinehas did? Will you ask yourself that question today too?

Jeff Frankenstein

Lessons in the Life of Moses:
THE DESERTERS

Moses said to the Gadites and Reubenites, "Shall your countrymen go to war while you sit here? Why do you discourage the Israelites from going over into the land the LORD has given them? This is what your fathers did when I sent them from Kadesh Barnea to look over the land. After they went up to the valley of Eshcol and viewed the land, they discouraged the Israelites from entering the land the LORD had given them....

And here you are, a brood of sinners, standing in the place of your fathers and making the LORD even more angry with Israel. If you turn away from following him, he will again leave all this people in the desert, and you will be the cause of their destruction."

NUMBERS 32:6–9, 14–15

APRIL 13

Moses couldn't believe the request. The tribes of Reuben and Gad were refusing to cross the Jordan into the Promised Land. Instead they begged to stay just outside because the land was more suitable for their large herds and flocks. As Moses listened to their reasoning, his grief quickly turned to anger. Finally his words lashed back at them like a whip.

"Don't you realize what you're doing? You are deserting your brothers as they battle for the Promised Land. Your parents were kept from entering the land through this same kind of selfishness and disbelief! Your desertion will break the hearts of your brethren and discourage them from fully conquering the land. If you leave your brothers, God may well leave both you and the whole nation."

Fortunately, that day Reuben and Gad rose out of their self-absorption and promised to cross over and fight with the rest of the nation until the whole Promised Land had been conquered.

Like the Reubenites and the Gadites, many Christians have made their own needs the highest priority of their lives. Once their needs are met, their commitment to the church that met those needs grows cold. Many young people who were very involved in youth group activities in high school drift away once they graduate as they find friends and activities in college or in the workplace. But now that they are growing and maturing, the church needs those young people more than ever to help continue its ministry!

Do you realize how much your church needs you and the special gifts God has given you? You may not realize how discouraging it will be to others when you stop being involved like you once were. Others count on you—for your help, your creativity, and your example.

So don't check out of church once your needs are met. There are many people who need you and your encouragement. Remember all those who helped you through hard times and ask God to allow you to be that person for someone else. Giving and receiving like this is what makes the family of God so great!

So many American Christians I have met remind me of the Reubenites and the Gadites. As long as they have what they need, nothing else seems to matter. We need God to pop our "Bubbles" of self-absorption so we can be loving brothers and sisters to each other in the family of God.

Jeff Frankenstein

Lessons in the Life of Joshua:
THE DEATH OF MOSES

The LORD said to Joshua, son of Nun, Moses' aid, "Moses my servant is dead. Now then, you and all these people, get ready to cross the Jordan River into the land I am about to give them — to the Israelites. I will give you every place where you set your foot, as I promised Moses.... No one will be able to stand up against you all the days of your life.... I will never leave you nor forsake you.

Be strong and courageous, because you will lead these people to inherit the land I swore to their forefathers to give them.... Be careful to obey all the law my servant Moses gave you; do not turn from it to the right or to the left, that you may be successful wherever you go. Do not let the Book of the Law depart from your mouth; meditate on it day and night, so that you may be careful to do everything written in it. Then you will be prosperous and successful."

JOSHUA 1:1-3, 5-8

APRIL 14

The Israelites had grieved for Moses for thirty days. Among those who had wept the most had been Joshua. Moses had been more than just Joshua's leader — he had been like a father to him. Now with the crushing burden of leading over two million people into their destiny, Joshua sorely missed the presence of his mentor and friend. How could he ever take the place of the man God had called the most humble on the face of the earth? And yet, the same God that had been with Moses had just promised to be with him as well.

First, God gave Joshua the straight truth: *"Moses, my servant, is dead."* Joshua had to be assured that the past was truly over and that he would now lead the people into the future. Chapters in our lives will come and go as well. We have to allow the Lord to put the past behind us, both the good and the bad, when it is time to focus on his mission for our future.

After helping Joshua come to terms with the loss of Moses and his new role, God assured Joshua although people and seasons may change, *he* is unchanging. God promised to be with Joshua, just as he was with Moses. Jesus made this same promise to us in Matthew 28:20: "I am with you always, to the very end of the age." Even though your "Moses" may be gone, your God has not gone anywhere. In fact, a loss like this may be just the motivation you need to seek God for yourself in a new way.

When you are faced with a big change and a huge mission like Joshua was, carefully and courageously continue to obey God's commands. You might be facing some big, scary challenges, but the even bigger God you serve is with you. In him you will find the strength to head into the Promised Land of your future. May God encourage you like he encouraged Joshua as you continue toward your destiny.

WHEN I CONSIDERED the LOSS that JOSHUA must have felt at the DEAth of MOSES, I WAS REMINDED of the pAIN I experienceD when my GRANDFATHER DIED OF CANCER. He WAS the MAN who tAUght me to plAY the KeyBOARD AND inspireD me to DO the very things I'm DOING toDAY. Even though his LOSS Left A hOLE in my LIfe, I DISCOVERED thAt the unchANGING GOD of the BIBLE WAS WELL ABLE to FILL it.

Jeff Frankenstein

Lessons in the Life of Joshua:
LIONS AND THICKETS

Early in the morning, Joshua and all the Israelites set out from Shittim and went to the Jordan, where they camped before crossing over.

JOSHUA 3:1

If you stumble in safe country,
how will you manage in the thickets by the Jordan?

JEREMIAH 12:5

APRIL 15

Joshua had heard that the banks of the Jordan were not a safe place, but this was even more deadly than he had expected. The Jordan was at flood tide. The current was flowing rapidly and the water was at least ten feet deep. If this impassable obstacle wasn't enough, there were also ferocious lions roaming through the thick underbrush which covered the river's banks.

Even as the nation of Israel faced lions when they crossed the Jordan, so you will face your own set of spiritual lions on the banks of your destiny. Just before you come into God's best for your life, you will always face the savage roar of the enemy. Peter says that "your enemy the devil prowls around like a roaring lion looking for someone to devour" (1 Peter 5:8). Although he will threaten to destroy your life in every possible way, he has no true power over you when you are safe under Jesus' protection.

Although Satan cannot devour any Christian eternally, he can devour the courage and strength you need to enter the Promised Land. Your response to the roar of the devil must be the roar of the lion of Judah who lives inside you. His roar of faith will release the strength you need to face the enemy.

Like the Hebrews, you will also face a tangled maze of thickets, like the ones that were growing along the Jordan's banks. These thickets represent the confusion that every believer faces when they attempt to cross into their Promised Land. This disorientation should be no cause for alarm. Instead, it should drive you to trust God to guide you—he knows the way. As you trust God and reach out for help from those he has placed in your life, you will not fail to find your way into the land God has promised to you. So, take heart, for even as God was with Joshua, he is with you too and he will guide you into his best when the time is right.

One of the most confusing times in my own life surrounded my decision to join the news-Boys. As a young person only months out of high school. I can still remember the confusion that surrounded what has proven to be one of the most important decisions of my life. Although there wasn't much money and I had more lucrative offers, even in the midst of my confusion. there was the sense that Being with the newsBoys was my destiny. In the twelve years that have gone By since I made that decision, I've never regretted obeying God. No matter how confused you are today, the same God that guided me will also guide you.

Jeff Frankenstein

Lessons in the Life of Joshua:
THE CLOUD WAS GONE

The officers went throughout the camp, giving orders to the people: "When you see the ark of the covenant of the L ORD your God, and the priests, who are Levites, carrying it, you are to move out from your positions and follow it. Then you will know which way to go, since you have never been this way before."

JOSHUA 3:2–4

APRIL 16

They were finally there. After wandering in the desert for forty years the nation of Israel stood on the banks of the Jordan River and prepared to cross over into the Promised Land. The people were filled with an overwhelming sense of both excitement and fear. So many things were changing and the unknown loomed large ahead of them. Moses, their faithful and patient leader, was gone. They were now to follow Joshua. And on this final leg of their journey, they were told to depend on the guidance of the priests by following them as they carried the ark of the covenant. They had followed the fiery cloud, the symbol of God's presence, for so many years. And yet, in spite of the uncertainty they must have felt, the Israelites obeyed and saw miracles again as they entered the land of milk and honey.

Just like Israel, we too may need to receive guidance and direction from the Lord in a whole new way in order to finally receive God's best for our lives. If you have become too dependent on others, you might begin to notice that the people that you normally count on won't have the answers or direction you need. This is a signal that God is calling you to lean more fully on him before you can see the fulfillment of his promise to you. As

you respond by seeking his face alone, you will receive both the direction you need and a more intimate, confident relationship with him.

On the other hand, if you have been trying to go it alone, without the support of other Christians, God will put you in situations that require you to receive the direction and encouragement of your brothers and sisters in the Lord. This may mean that God will have to do some healing work in your heart of the betrayals and the rejections that have kept you from trusting people in the first place. This is never easy, but if you will allow God's healing touch and the encouragement of the people into your life, you will discover a whole new relationship with both God and with others. May God give you the guidance and direction you need today as you prepare to cross your "Jordan."

I think, like the Israelites, all of us have "clouds." Although the clouds are different for every Christian, they are basically the significant ways that God has guided us and provided for us. This devotional made me realize that we need to make sure our lives are balanced between following our "clouds" and following the people God has prepared to lead us. We need both to find God's best for us.

Jeff Frankenstein

Lessons in the Life of Joshua:
CROSSING THE JORDAN

So when the people broke camp to cross the Jordan, the priests carrying the ark of the covenant went ahead of them. Now the Jordan is at flood stage all during harvest. Yet as soon as the priests who carried the ark reached the Jordan and their feet touched the water's edge, the water from upstream stopped flowing ... while the water flowing down to the Sea of the Arabah (the Salt Sea) was completely cut off. So the people crossed over opposite Jericho. The priests who carried the ark of the covenant of the LORD stood firm on dry ground in the middle of the Jordan while all the nation passed by until the whole nation had completed the crossing on dry ground.

JOSHUA 3:14–17

APRIL 17

As they approached the churning flood tide of the Jordan, the hearts of the priests who were carrying the ark pounded with fear. As much as they trusted Joshua, it was hard to control the natural instinct of fright in the face of deep, rushing water. But in spite of the battle raging in their hearts, they continued to walk confidently toward the swollen Jordan. The moment their toes touched the water, the river began to part. The waters of the Jordan stopped flowing miles downstream. As the priests bravely stood in the middle of the riverbed, the whole nation crossed over on dry ground.

There are times in your life where simply *standing* in faith is not enough. God just might be waiting for you to take a step of faith into the middle of the challenge you are facing. Like the priests of Israel, you have to put your "toes in the water" before the waters will part.

How do we find the courage to make that first step? The priests had faith to step into the teeming waters of the Jordan because they were carrying the ark of the Lord. We can have much more faith because God is actually living in us! God's power and strength is all you need to get past the barriers you are facing.

As we face obstacles that we must cross in faith, we have to realize that we can't do it alone. Even as Israel was required to follow the priests, so you, too, need other Christians to be a part of your journey into God's best for your life. When God does this, he is not merely trying to teach *you*. He is using another human because that will be the most effective way to meet your need while at the same time helping the other person grow too. The comfort of the Holy Spirit and the presence of God will often come most powerfully to us through the counsel and encouragement of our brothers and sisters in Jesus.

As you face your own raging rivers, may the Lord give you the courage to step out in faith, with his power and love in your heart and your fellow Christians by your side. This is God's formula for bringing you great things and it won't fail when you follow it!

In my own life, I have found that many times faith requires taking a step. When I joined the band, I didn't have the luxury of waiting and finding everything out. I had never been on the road or made my livelihood as a musician before. Once I stepped out, however, the floods of my own fears and worries parted and I entered my "promised land."

Jeff Frankenstein

Lessons in the Life of Joshua:

WHERE HAD THE MANNA GONE?

The day after the Passover, that very day, they ate some of the produce of the land: unleavened bread and roasted grain. The manna stopped the day after they ate this food from the land; there was no longer any manna for the Israelites, but that year they ate of the produce of Canaan.

JOSHUA 5:11-12

APRIL 18

It was another big change. The manna was gone. If they had been honest, the Israelites would have to admit that they were pretty sick of manna, anyway. After all, how many ways could you cook the stuff? Still, the fact that they had to work for their food instead of just collecting it on a daily basis was a big change after all those years. Even as Israel experienced a change in the way God had provided for them after they had entered the Promised Land, so you, too, may also experience a change in provision. Many times when people are in a period of spiritual transition, their finances are also affected. You may be quitting your job to go into a new career or into ministry. Maybe you've had to use some of your savings as a part of your new mission for the Lord. In spite of these changes, this is no need to panic. In many cases, God is not just changing the *way* he provides for you, he is also changing the level at which he provides for you. Just as the diet of the Israelites in the Promised Land had far more variety and richness, so your loving heavenly Father desires to bring you more of his abundant provision.

Are you in the middle of a tight financial time right now? If you will continue to obey God with what money you do have, by giving to the church, and using it wisely, God will be faithful to open the "floodgates of heaven" and meet your needs (Malachi 3:10). So if God has stopped raining down "manna" in your life, hang on and stay faithful. He is about to provide for you in a new and even more abundant way. While this could mean that you'll be blessed with more money, it also might mean that you'll be blessed more abundantly in some other way—with new help from friends and family, with a new job that you are passionate about, or even with a sense of contentment, even when you're pretty broke. Trust the Lord and no matter what, he will provide you with the spiritual prosperity that only he can give.

My wife and I were just talking the other day about all the times our "manna" was seemingly gone. This conversation arose out of a discussion about whether or not we could afford to go on vacation. Within twenty minutes of our discussion, the phone rang and God had provided all the money we needed. In all my years of following God he has never failed to provide.

Jeff Frankenstein

CIRCUMCISED AT GILGAL

At that time the Lord said to Joshua, "Make flint knives and circumcise the Israelites again." So Joshua made flint knives and circumcised the Israelites at Gibeah Haaraloth.

Now this is why he did so: All those who came out of Egypt—all the men of military age—died in the desert on the way after leaving Egypt. All the people that came out had been circumcised, but all the people born in the desert during the journey from Egypt had not.... After the whole nation had been circumcised, they remained where they were encamped until they were healed.

JOSHUA 5:2–5, 8

APRIL 19

Although the children of Israel had miraculously crossed through the flooded Jordan River, they still had one last major act of obedience to do before they began their conquest of the Promised Land. All those that had been born during their desert wanderings had not circumcised. Circumcision was important because it was the visible sign of being part of God's family.

What does a story about mass circumcision have to do with us? First of all, our entrance into our Promised Land is normally followed by an intense period of God working in our hearts and lives. We need to respond to God in obedience during this time so that we will be prepared for the fulfillment of God's plan for our lives.

Second, like the children of Israel who were born in the wilderness, many people are born into unbelieving families and become Christians without the guidance of their earthly families. Unlike children born into

Christian homes, they haven't been taught about God all their lives and have a lot they need to learn about their new Father. If they are to grow into strong members of God's Kingdom, it is vital that they receive discipleship and mentoring from older Christians. If you are one of these young Christians, make it a priority to find spiritual "moms and dads" who can help you learn and grow in your walk with God.

The uncircumcised men of Israel had to allow other men to work in the most private areas of their lives. We need to allow the same kind of work in hidden parts of our spiritual lives. We need loving Christian mentors to apply the Word of God to our most sensitive and private areas of life. While it is difficult and sometimes painful, an important part of discipleship and growth is the willingness to be open and honest with our brothers and sisters in Jesus.

The process of "spiritual circumcision" can be painful. Even as the children of Israel stayed in the camp until they were healed, so it may take some time for you to recover from an intense period of God working in your heart. Never forget, however, God is just preparing you to receive your full inheritance in your Promised Land. There will be great joy on the other side of the pain.

Like the Israelites, all of us will go through painful times of spiritual growth, especially when God is cutting away sensitive areas of our lives. At times it may take days or even weeks to fully recover from the process of God dealing in our lives. In my own life, I have discovered that no matter how bad it hurts or how long it takes, transformation and discipleship are always worth it.

Jeff Frankenstein

Lessons in the Life of Joshua:
COMMANDER OF THE LORD'S ARMY

[Joshua] looked up and saw a man standing in front of him with a drawn sword in his hand. Joshua went up to him and asked, "Are you for us or for our enemies?"

"Neither," he replied, "but as commander of the army of the LORD I have now come." Then Joshua fell facedown to the ground in reverence, and asked him, "What message does my Lord have for his servant?"

The commander of the LORD's army replied, "Take off your sandals, for the place where you are standing is holy." And Joshua did so.

JOSHUA 5:13–15

APRIL 20

With the crossing of the Jordan now accomplished, the weight of his new mission now settled on Joshua's shoulders. Although Jericho's citizens were terrified of Israel's armies, Joshua could not discover any weakness in the impregnable walls surrounding the city. As he turned over the problem in his mind, Joshua looked up, and saw a large man in full battle armor standing before him.

"Are you for us or against us?" Joshua asked.

"Neither, I am the commander of the army of the Lord."

At these words, Joshua crumpled to his knees and fell on his face. As Joshua lay with his face buried in the ground, he responded to the great warrior's pronouncement. "Lord, what are my orders?"

"Take off your sandals, Joshua, for the place where you are standing is holy."

What lessons can you and I learn from Joshua's miraculous encounter with the angelic commander of the Lord's armies? First, the heavenly warrior had his sword drawn. In the same way, God has declared war on every enemy you may be facing. As a great warrior, he is able to destroy all of the seemingly impenetrable barriers in your path and defeat the foes that are tormenting you.

As commander, (many scholars think that this warrior was God himself and not just an angel that appeared to Joshua) God had not come to solicit Joshua's advice, but to take charge of the battle. When the Lord steps onto the battlefields of your life, he does not come as your "cosmic buddy." He comes as the awesome Lord of the universe whose commands you must obey in order to be victorious in your battle.

Strangely, when Joshua asks what God's order is for him, it isn't to march into to Jericho or draw his sword and run to the fight. He was simply ordered to remove his shoes. Joshua's shoes symbolized the plans and strategies *he* had been devising to conquer Jericho. He had to be willing to lay down his own tactics in order to receive God's plan of victory.

Even as God came to the aid of Joshua and the Hebrew nation so he has come to your rescue. He has all the resources of heaven at his disposal to destroy the barriers between you and your Promised Land. When you let God become the commander of your life, you too can experience a great victory over the struggles the enemy puts in your way.

To me, Joshua's sandals represented the way he was going about his job as commander. By telling him to take off his sandals, God was saying, "If you're going to come into my best, you must be willing to stop doing it the old way and embrace my way." Is God calling me to take off my sandals today? Although it's a scary thought, I've decided to tell God that I'm willing to take my sandals off!

Jeff Frankenstein

Lessons in the Life of Joshua:
THE WALLS OF JERICHO

The Lord said to Joshua, "See, I have delivered Jericho into your hands, along with its king and its fighting men. March around the city once with all the armed men. Do this for six days.... On the seventh day, march around the city seven times, with the priests blowing the trumpets. When you hear them sound a long trumpet blast on the trumpets, have all the people give a loud shout; then the wall of the city will collapse and the people will go up, every man straight in."

JOSHUA 6:2–5

APRIL 21

The walls of Jericho were massive, thick, and high. And the plan they had been given to defeat this impenetrable city was so crazy only God could have come up with it. Joshua had been told to march around the walls of Jericho every day for six days. On the seventh day they were to march around the walls seven times and then the priests were to blow the trumpets. God himself would then destroy the city walls.

And so the Israelites began to march. By the fifth and sixth days, there still were no cracks in the giant walls. Yet, the army continued its parade around the city. As the Hebrews finished their seventh march on the seventh day, they blew the trumpets—and the walls of Jericho imploded. God had kept his promise!

Just as God reduced Jericho to rubble, he will also destroy every obstacle keeping you out of your "promised land." And as Joshua obeyed the strange plan that God gave him, so we need to do the same. God's plan to destroy Jericho involved seven days of seemingly pointless marching. It takes patience—for what can seem like a long time—for God to completely remove the obstacles we are facing. But if we allow ourselves to give in to frustration and quit, we will miss God's awesome answer—an answer that will solve our problem and bring us closer to him.

We can imagine that the longer that they marched, the harder it was for the Israelite army to continue marching. With physical, and probably mental, exhaustion setting in, these men were probably at a breaking point by that seventh day. Are you at a breaking point, too? Don't give up! Right before the walls of your obstacles come tumbling down, you will often feel like quitting. But remember—that isn't God talking—that's the enemy! He would like nothing more than for you to give up right before he is defeated—so stand strong!

Major spiritual battles are not won easily or quickly. The walls of the enemy will be shattered, slowly but surely, through the power of the Word of God and prayer. May God give you the faith you need to see every barrier shattered and every stronghold reduced as you follow him in your march around the walls of your Jericho.

DID you notice that GOD used music to BREAK DOWN the WALLS of JERICHO? Recently, the BAND played in a spiritually unreached part of the WORLD. EVERY MEMBER OF the BAND WAS STRUCK By the FACT that music still has the power to BREAK DOWN WALLS. Even though our audience that day did not speak ENGLISH and were part of a different religion, their souls were deeply touched as we worshiped.

Jeff Frankenstein

Lessons in the Life of Joshua:
ACHAN'S SIN

📖 And Joshua said, "Ah, Sovereign LORD, why did you ever bring this people across the Jordan to deliver us into the hands of the Amorites to destroy us?... The Canaanites and the other people of the country will hear about this and will surround us and wipe out our name from the earth."...

The LORD said to Joshua, "Stand up! What are you doing down on your face? Israel has sinned.... They have taken some of the devoted things; ... they have put them with their own possessions."

JOSHUA 7:7, 9–11

APRIL 22

Joshua's army had been triumphant over mighty Jericho but beat soundly by the smaller forces of Ai. How could the same God, who had crushed Jericho under the feet of Israel, now allow them to be humiliated by the far smaller city of Ai?

As he waited face down before the ark of the Lord, God spoke. The more Joshua heard, the sicker his heart became. One of the soldiers had stolen some of the spoils of Jericho that were supposed to be devoted to the Lord.

The next morning, Joshua and the elders searched until they found the guilty man. Achan confessed to stealing a beautiful robe and 250 shekels of silver and gold. Joshua and the elders then stoned him and his entire family.

The story of Achan is hard to understand from a twenty-first-century worldview, but it shows us some important things about God and our relationship with him. First, sin really does matter. Your sin will bring defeat and judgment to your life, and can affect the lives of your loved ones as well. The sin of one Christian also affects the health of the Church. If I come to church on Sunday morning with a rebellious attitude and a heart full of unconfessed sin, it is going to have an affect on God's presence in that service. The more people who come to a worship service holding onto sin, the harder it will be for the whole congregation to worship because sin separates us from God's presence.

Like Israel, many churches and ministries have stopped growing because they aren't lovingly dealing with the sin of their members. There are a lot of "Achans" in churches today who are being allowed to live any way they choose. No one is willing to do the hard thing and confront a brother or sister who is struggling with sin. But minding your own business is not what God calls us to do when it comes to fellow members of the body of Christ!

Maybe you, like Achan, have hidden some sin in the depths of your heart. Whatever your secret, you need to face the fact that it is endangering both your life, the lives of those you love, and your church. Hiding sin will only kill your joy and fulfillment that is yours in Christ. But when you bring it into the light before God, and to loving Christian friends, you will find abundant grace that will set you free.

Like ACHAN, there is no DOUBT in my mind that our sin Doesn't just MAR our lives. When I sin, I AM not the only one to pAy the price. Every one of my ACtions AFFects my wife, my fellow BAnD memBers, AnD my cHurcH. This reALizAtion hAs cAuseD me to Be more thAnkful thAn ever FOR the powerFuL BLOOD of cHrist. Through his WORK on the cross, there is no sin thAt we cAnnot overcome.

Jeff Frankenstein

THE SUN STANDS STILL

The LORD hurled large hailstones down on [the Amorite armies] from the sky, and more of them died from the hailstones than were killed by the swords of the Israelites....

Joshua said to the LORD in the presence of Israel:

"O sun, stand still over Gibeon,
O moon, over the Valley of Aijalon."
So the sun stood still,
and the moon stopped,
till the nation avenged itself....

There has never been a day like it before or since, a day when the LORD listened to a man. Surely the LORD was fighting for Israel!

JOSHUA 10:11–14

APRIL 23

Joshua and the armies of Israel had been commanded to destroy every inhabitant of the Promised Land. Among the tribes to be destroyed were the Gibeonites, but they fooled the leaders of Israel into thinking that they were from a distant country in an attempt to avoid destruction. Instead of asking the Lord for his discernment, the men of Israel made a treaty with the Gibeonites. Three days later, the Hebrews discovered the Gibeonites' deception, but it was too late. They had made a covenant with them before the Lord. The Gibeonites were punished—made to be servants to Israel for the rest of their lives—but Israel was now responsible for their provision and welfare. When the five kings of the Amorites heard about the treaty, they gathered all their armies together and attacked Gibeon.

As Joshua and his men fought for the Gibeonites, God provided the victory by actually stopping the sun for what the Bible says was almost a full day and by throwing down huge hailstones to wipe out the rest of the Amorite army as they ran away. Joshua summarized God's amazing intervention with these words: "There has never been a day like it before or since, a day when the Lord listened to a man. Surely the Lord was fighting for Israel!"

Just as the Gibeonites hid their true identities in order to be accepted by the people of God, I have seen people spend years in church never revealing the true nature of the sins that are destroying them. Their fear of being misunderstood, rejected, or even gossiped about keeps them in a silent prison of shame and pain. What these people desperately need is the compassion and love of Christ and the church needs to be the place where they can receive it.

When we as Christians learn to step out of our comfort zones and into the pain and difficulties of others, God will perform miracles. Israel went to rescue a part of their culture that was despised and rejected because of their sin and lies, and when they did God poured out amazing power to help them. May God give us the grace to reach out and rescue the Gibeonites of our day, for God loves them too.

The thing that hit me the hardest from this devotional was the fact that God displayed tremendous power in order to save the Gibeonites even though they had lied and deceived their way into his protection. If he was willing to do this for the Gibeonites how much more will he do for me today if I'm to believe his promises?

Jeff Frankenstein

Lessons in the Life of Joshua:

THE SPIRIT OF CALEB

"Now then, just as the LORD promised, he has kept me alive for forty-five years since the time he said this to Moses, while Israel moved about in the desert. So here I am today, eighty-five years old! I am still as strong today as the day Moses sent me out; I'm just as vigorous to go out to battle now as I was then. Now give me this hill country that the LORD promised me that day. You yourself heard then that the Anakites were there and their cities were large and fortified, but, the LORD helping me, I will drive them out just as he said."

JOSHUA 14:10–12

APRIL 24

Although he was eighty-five years old, Caleb's step was still strong and his eyes burned with fire. He had been Israel's hero when the spies brought back their bad report, and now the day he had been waiting for had come. *"Give me the hill country,"* he said confidently. *"Giants or not, I will kill them, for it is the inheritance that Moses promised me."* Joshua's eyes must have welled up with tears as he heard the faith-filled words of his friend. For a moment his mind was flooded with the wars they had waged and daring escapes they had experienced. They had a rare friendship, for they had been the only two men of their generation to enter the Promised Land.

Yet now, as Caleb stood before him, Joshua was also concerned. Did his oldest and dearest friend really still have the strength to face the Anakites? But, Caleb, bold as always, looked Joshua straight in the eye and put his concerns to rest. "I am still as strong today as the day Moses sent me out; I'm just as vigorous to go out to battle now as I was then."

What gave Caleb the vision and strength he needed to conquer the most powerful tribe of giants in the Promised Land? Moses had described it as a "different spirit" (Numbers 14:24). When everyone else was quaking in fear and unbelief forty years earlier, Caleb and Joshua had boldly stood in faith and proclaimed the promises of God. This same spirit had kept Caleb strong in body and steadfast in heart. Moses had also pronounced that Caleb followed the Lord "wholeheartedly." In every area of his life, Caleb was determined to obey the Lord. This faith and obedience gave him the strength and vision he needed to walk with confidence all his life.

How about you? You may not be old in body—but what about your spirit? The Bible says, in Proverbs 18:14, that it is a person's spirit that sustains them. The secret to living strong your whole life, just like Caleb, has far more to do with your spiritual health than your physical health. Strength of spirit will give you the anointing, determination, and power to live your whole life strong and confident in God's grace. May God bless you with a "different spirit" and "wholeheartedness" today!

The greatest examples of faith I have ever seen have not been at our concerts but in the eyes of Christians who are filled with joy and faith even though they are facing huge struggles. Like Caleb, they have learned the secret of being sustained through God's Spirit. I want God to make me a man like Caleb—strong and confident in the Lord, no matter the odds.

Jeff Frankenstein

Lessons in the Life of Joshua:
HIS LEGACY

Joshua son of Nun, the servant of the LORD died at the age of a hundred and ten. They buried him in the land of his inheritance....

Israel served the LORD throughout the lifetime of Joshua and of the elders who outlived him and who had experienced everything the LORD had done for Israel.

JOSHUA 24:29–31

APRIL 25

Joshua was one hundred and ten years old. He had conquered the Promised Land and divided it up among the tribes. He had appointed a group of trustworthy men who would continue to lead Israel successfully long after he was gone. These men had experienced everything the Lord had done for his people, and all of them were proven and tested. They were mighty in battle and wise in counsel. Even more important than the victories of Joshua's lifetime was this legacy he was leaving behind.

Despite all of Joshua's accomplishments, his greatest achievement was to nurture a group of men who would continue to lead Israel long after he was gone. The lack of this type of legacy-building discipleship might just be the greatest shortcoming of our churches today. When ministries are personality-driven, depending solely on one superstar leader, they can come to a screeching halt the moment that leader dies, moves on to another ministry, or falls into sin. If Jesus placed a high priority on the intense training of twelve men, though he could have spent all of his time basking in fame and the love of the crowd, shouldn't we do the same?

As a young adult, you are in the prime time of your life to begin a lifetime relationship with your own "Joshua." You are going to be the legacy of the generation before you—the future's leaders. Now is the time to seek out opportunities to learn from older Christians and to test your gifts in different ministries. Make time spent with your mentor a high priority. Let him or her be involved in every aspect of your life—spend time studying the Word and praying together, but also make time to have fun together and to share the things that bring you joy. Spending meaningful time with an older Christian will give you a visible example to follow in all aspects of your life.

Once you have spent some meaningful time with your mentor, it is critical that you take the opportunities they give you to minister to others yourself. Don't be afraid to fall a few times. You'll never learn the skills necessary to have a successful ministry if you don't practice them. May God grant you the courage to be the legacy of today's leaders as you learn from their example.

WHAT LEGACY WILL I LEAVE WHEN I'm GONE? Not my PERSONAL LEGACY BUT the WORK GOD'S Given me to DO. LiKe ALL of the BAND memBERS, I Am more CONCERNED ABOUT CHANGED LiVes thAN I Am with PERSONAL SUCCESS OR ALBUM SALES.

Jeff Frankenstein

DEBORAH — A MOTHER IN ISRAEL

Deborah ... was leading Israel at that time. She held court under the Palm of Deborah ... and the Israelites came to her to have their disputes decided. She sent for Barak ... and said to him, "The LORD, the God of Israel, commands you: 'Go, take with you ten thousand men of Naphtali and Zebulun and lead the way to Mount Tabor. I will lure Sisera, the commander of Jabin's army, with his chariot and his troops to the Kishon River and give him into your hands.'"

JUDGES 4:4–7

"Village life in Israel ceased,
    ceased until I, Deborah, arose,
    arose a mother in Israel."

JUDGES 5:7

APRIL 26

All of Israel had been cruelly oppressed for more than twenty years. Crushed repeatedly by Sisera, they had been reduced to an impoverished and broken nation. God, however, had not forgotten his people. In answer to their prayers, he raised up a leader—Deborah. Through her gift of prophecy and wise counsel, she challenged Israel to rise up against their oppressors. Finally, because of her faith, an obscure warrior named Barak answered her call to lead the armies of Israel. Under their leadership, Sisera and his diabolical legions were destroyed.

What can we learn from this one woman who changed a nation? First, wherever you look in the body of Christ today, it is clear that God is calling women into special work for his kingdom. God is calling them to take their place at the forefront of the spiritual battles that we face today.

Second, just as Deborah was a prophetess, all of God's daughters have been given unique gifts. If you are going to fully realize God's unique purpose for your life, it is critical that you understand the gifts that he has given you. Taking time to discover and practice your spiritual gifts is important to fulfilling your destiny.

While Deborah was a judge and prophetess, she was also a mother—both literally to her own children, and spiritually to the nation of Israel. While society today may not give mothers the respect they deserve, it is important for Christians to see their vital importance. Motherhood is at the very essence of God's plan to change history. He has given mothers the power and privilege of shaping the lives of their children in their most formative years. But when natural mothers fail, God often uses spiritual mothers to do the same for young people just like you. If you are missing your own mother's spiritual guidance, make it a priority to seek out a Christian woman who can fill that role for you.

No matter who you are, or how old you are, remember to honor the mother you've been given, and to pay special attention to the words God gives you through her, or through a spiritual mother. God has given these women a special calling—listen to them, and love them as gifts from him!

It is so important to know what gifts God has given us. As a prophetess, Deborah changed Israel. We have all received a gift from God that is vital to the kingdom of God and that can change the world.

Jeff Frankenstein

Lessons from the Life of the Judges:

JAEL— THE STAY-AT-HOME MOM

Jael went out to meet Sisera and said to him, "Come, my lord, come right in. Don't be afraid." So he entered her tent and she put a covering over him.

"Stand in the doorway of the tent," he told her. "If someone comes by and asks you, 'Is anyone here?' say 'No,'"

But Jael, Heber's wife, picked up a tent peg and a hammer and went quietly to him while he lay fast asleep, exhausted. She drove the peg through his temple into the ground, and he died.

JUDGES 4:18–21

"Most blessed of women be Jael,
    the wife of Heber the Kenite,
    most blessed of tent dwelling women [stay-at-home moms].

JUDGES 5:24

APRIL 27

A faithful wife and tremendous mother, Jael had no aspirations beyond the life she had grown accustomed to. Yet, God had a surprise for his faithful servant—his name was Sisera; the ruthless commander of Israel's most hated enemies. He claimed to be her husband's friend, but she knew that he was a ruthless butcher. Now, with Sisera in her door, her heart was pounding with fear as she invited him in. He had been to her home on other occasions, but this was one of the first times she had ever been alone with him. As she considered her vulnerability, she realized that God had given this mass murderer into her hands. As Sisera fell asleep, Jael searched frantically for a weapon. When he was sleeping soundly, she took a sharpened tent peg and drove it into his head with the blows of a hammer. With those strokes, she ensured the freedom of her friends and family for a whole generation.

If you are a stay-at-home mom, or simply considering that as an option for your future, the message of this story is critical for you. One of the great lies of the enemy is that your role as a mother is simply a menial task that anyone can do. This, however, is far from the truth. Even as God brought Sisera to Jael's door, so there are a number of enemies standing at the door of your home which he has called you to kill. Whether it is the immorality flooding the airwaves, the deceptive lies that are shaping our society's perspective of motherhood, or the loneliness and depression that seems to be the constant companion of many young mothers, your ability to defeat these enemies will have an incredible impact on many people. That's right, whether you realize it or not, you have an audience. Other mothers are watching the way you raise your children. The very fact that you live your life joyfully has caused them to question the enemy's lies—lies that tell them that their only hope for lasting fulfillment lies outside the confines of home and family. May God give you the grace to defeat the enemies that are knocking at your door as you ponder these words today.

We live in a culture that continually denigrates the role of mothers. Being a full-time mom is made to seem as if it is not even a "real job." I am so thankful that my own mother saw the importance of staying home to raise her children. The wisdom and mentoring I received from her form part of the very foundation of who I am as a man today.

Jeff Frankenstein

Lessons from the Life of the Judges:
STOLEN HARVEST

Again the Israelites did evil in the eyes of the LORD, and for seven years he gave them into the hands of the Midianites. Because the power of Midian was so oppressive, the Israelites prepared shelters for themselves in mountain clefts, caves and strongholds. Whenever the Israelites planted the crops, the Midianites, Amalekites and other eastern peoples invaded the country. They camped on the land and ruined the crops ... and did not spare a living thing for Israel, neither sheep nor cattle nor donkeys. ... Midian so impoverished the Israelites that they cried out to the LORD for help.

JUDGES 6:1–4, 6

APRIL 28

For seven years, the ruthless Midianites had stolen Israel's harvests. Like a swarm of ravenous locusts, they were systematically destroying the wealth and prosperity of God's people. Instead of fighting for their harvest, the Israelites fled to the mountains, where they were hiding in caves and holes in the ground. Finally, in desperation, they cried out to the Lord. His answer to them was anything but reassuring. He told them that they were being judged because they had left him behind and turned to idols. Yet, in spite of their cowardice and sin, God was already preparing a young man named Gideon to deliver them.

Just as the Midianites were stealing Israel's harvest, so the enemy wants to rob us of our spiritual harvest. The enemy will do everything in his power to discourage the people we have been sharing our faith with and blind them to the true answer to their spiritual needs.

And yet, though he has great power, the enemy can only steal our harvest if we let him have it. We need to fight for the souls of our loved ones and friends and never run away from that fight, even when it seems like they aren't listening to us anymore. When a person you've been sharing Jesus with seems to be rejecting the message, don't give up—that's just what the enemy wants. It may be that your friend is actually on the verge of trusting Christ and you are in the final battle for their soul!

Have you been driven out of your harvest field by the ruthless attack of the enemy? Maybe you've been ostracized and rejected because of your faith and you're finding it hard to talk about God with your unbelieving friends anymore. Remember, in these hard times, that you are in a battle with a strong enemy—and battles are never easy. The victory that God desires to give you, though, will make everything you have been suffering more than worth it. Step out in faith again today and ask God for help. The Lord will give you the strength to fight for your harvest—the hearts of those you love.

If you're like me, many of you have been tempted to hide in your own special cave when you feel rejected for your faith. Hiding away by yourself seems like the safest thing to do. In reality this is one of the most dangerous places to be, because there you can easily fall prey to the devil's lies. Get BACK out into the harvest field with GOD and let him fight for you again.

Jeff Frankenstein

GIDEON'S NEW NAME

The angel of the LORD came and sat ... where ... Gideon was threshing wheat in a winepress to keep it from the Midianites. When the angel of the LORD appeared to Gideon, he said, "The LORD is with you, mighty warrior."

JUDGES 6:11–12

APRIL 29

As Gideon hid down inside the winepress trough and threshed wheat he had no idea that he had come to the greatest moment of his life. "The Lord is with you, mighty warrior." Gideon almost didn't turn around. Whoever it was must be talking to someone else. After all, who would call a coward like him a "mighty warrior"? But when the angel of the Lord sat down in front of him, Gideon realized the message was for him after all.

As the Lord met Gideon's gaze, the unbelief and pain in his soul began to bubble up. "You've got to be kidding me!" Gideon replied. God's reply stunned him and began to revive the spark of faith that nearly died inside him. "Gideon, go in the strength you have, and save Israel."

God's words were like water to a man dying of thirst—and yet he was still afraid to hope. He began to list the reasons why he was not qualified. "I come from the weakest clan in Israel, and I'm considered the dumbest of my brothers." But the Lord was not moved. "I will be with you," he replied. "Lord," Gideon whispered, "if this is really you, don't disappear, but wait and let me prepare you a meal." When the Lord consumed the meal with fire and he disappeared, Gideon fell trembling to the ground—he had seen God!

No matter what you think of yourself, God wants to come meet you right where you are, like he did with Gideon. This young man was truly a coward, but God called him a mighty warrior. God clearly saw who Gideon could become and ignored what he was at the moment. If you listen carefully, you will hear God call you by a new name—one not based on what you are now, but on what you can become.

No matter how unqualified you may feel for this new role, never forget that God's "power is made perfect in weakness" (2 Corinthians 12:9). The more conscious you are of your weaknesses, the more you rely on God for strength. The more you trust him, the more strength you receive.

Just as we need to understand our weakness and God's strength, we also need to grasp the depth of God's love for us. Gideon begged the Lord not to leave until he could bring a meal for him. He feared that God would not stay and actually eat with someone like him. But when he returned God was waiting.

No matter where you have been hiding or what you've been hiding from, God is calling you by a new name. Your weakness doesn't matter because he promises to make you strong. No matter how rejected you feel, God loves you and wants to be with you. When you hear God call your new name, step out into his strength and love—it will change your life forever.

As both a Christian and a newsboy, I have discovered over and over again that God is strongest when I feel the weakest. Although it's hard to figure out, God seems to touch the most people through the concerts and shows in which we have felt the worst! Every time this happens, we are all struck again by the fact that God's strength is made perfect in our weakness.

Jeff Frankenstein

Lessons in the Life of the Judges:
GIDEON'S ALTAR

 Gideon built an altar to the LORD ... and called it The LORD is Peace....

That same night the LORD said to him, "Take the second bull from your father's herd, the one seven years old. Tear down your father's altar to Baal and cut down the Asherah pole beside it. Then build a proper kind of altar to the LORD your God on the top of this height. Using the wood of the Asherah pole that you cut down, offer the second bull as a burnt offering."

So Gideon took ten of his servants and did as the LORD told him. But because he was afraid of his family and the men of the town, he did it at night rather than in the daytime.

In the morning when the men of the town got up, there was Baal's altar, demolished, with the Asherah pole beside it cut down and the second bull sacrificed on the newly built altar!

They asked each other, "Who did this?"

When they carefully investigated, they were told, "Gideon son of Joash did it."

JUDGES 6:24–29

APRIL 30

Gideon and his ten servants crept toward his family's shrine through the dark. He was scared to death. God had asked him to tear down his family's altar and shrine to Baal. All the men in his family were utterly committed to this foreign god. But the Lord's message was clear and firm. Gideon couldn't build a new altar to the true God until he tore the old one down. As he and his men began the

demolition, they were all afraid. It was even worse when Gideon finally laid the trunk of the axe to the Asherah pole. By the time the altar had been destroyed, they were in a cold sweat.

As they began to build the new altar to the Lord, however, it seemed as if light was shining in the darkness. Their fear was replaced with a sense of confidence and peace. Although the men of the village wanted to kill Gideon the next morning, his father mocked the villagers and told them if Baal was a real god, he would kill Gideon himself. Gideon's courage in the face of the wrath of his neighbors and family was the beginning of his rise to a place of power and leadership.

Like Gideon, you too have been called to build an altar—a place to offer your life to God through prayer, worship, and time spent in his Word. Time spent in worship and study, time at your altar, is key to receiving the faith and strength we need to live for God.

Many Christians attempt to build a new altar without first tearing down the old altars of the idols in their lives. You can't build a life of true worship and faithfulness to God on top of a hidden life of sinful things. This is probably one of the main reasons Christians struggle to spend time with God every day. Hidden sin keeps us from having the faith and confidence to approach God on a regular basis. We need to learn from Gideon and tear down our idols through the power of God.

Whether you are tearing down an old altar, or building a new one, God has promised to give you the strength you need. When you are obediently offering yourself to him, he will be there beside you, helping you have an even deeper relationship with him.

When I thought about Gideon tearing down the altars of Baal, I was struck by the importance of demolishing idols in our lives today. Through discipleship and the blood of Jesus we can get rid of the idols that we've built and begin to offer ourselves as living sacrifices to the one true God.

Jeff Frankenstein

Lessons in the Life of the Judges:
GIDEON'S ARMY

The Lord said to Gideon, "You have too many men.... In order that Israel may not boast against me that her own strength has saved her, announce now to the people, 'Anyone who trembles with fear may turn back....'" So twenty-two thousand men left, while ten thousand remained. But the Lord said to Gideon, "There are still too many men. Take them down to the water, and I will sift them for you there...." Three hundred men lapped with their hands to their mouths. All the rest got down on their knees to drink. The Lord said to Gideon, "With the three hundred men that lapped I will save you."

JUDGES 7:2–4, 6–7

MAY 1

As he surveyed the 32,000 ragged soldiers who had responded to his call, Gideon's heart sank in fear. What hope did this broken band of cowards have against the 135,000 seasoned warriors of Midian? With the army already badly outnumbered, the Lord began to test Gideon. He was to let anyone who was frightened go back home. His knees buckled as 22,000 men turned tail and headed back. He was so frightened, he felt like joining them.

God spoke again: "Bring them down to the water and I'll sort them for you. Watch closely as they drink. Those that lie down and drink like dogs are to be sent home. Those who simply kneel and drink from their hands should stay." After all the sorting, Gideon's army of 32,000 was down to 300.

Why did God take an already outnumbered army and reduce it to a handful of men? First of all, God was leaving no room for doubt that *he* was the one who would win the battle for Israel. It would be impossible for Gideon's army to think that they had won using their own strength when they were so badly out manned.

In addition, God is more concerned about the *quality* of his servants than their quantity. If he allowed men full of fear to remain, their terror would affect the faith and morale of the whole army. The remaining three hundred continued to carefully scan the horizons for enemies, even while they were drinking, proving that they had not let their personal needs make them lose sight of the pressing battle.

As Christians, we need to be careful not to be like the fearful and self-absorbed Israelite soldiers. We need to seek God's power over our fears and insecurities so that we can be focused on the battles we are called to fight. Keep your head up and your eyes focused on God so that you will be qualified to be a part of his army today.

"MANY CLAIM to hAVE unFAILING LoVE BUt A FAIthFUL peRSon who CAn FIND?" EVen AS GoD tesTeD GIDEon's men to see IF they weRE FAIthFUL, So he wILL test you. Be commItteD to BeinG FounD FAIthFUL!

Peter Furler

GIDEON'S ENEMY

Now the camp of Midian lay below him in the valley. During that night, the LORD said to Gideon, "Get up, go down against the camp, because I am going to give it into your hands. If you are afraid to attack, go down to the camp with your servant Purah and listen to what they are saying. Afterward, you will be encouraged to attack the camp." So he and Purah his servant went down to the outpost of the camp.... Gideon arrived just as a man was telling a friend his dream.

"I had a dream," he was saying. "A round loaf of barley bread came tumbling into the Midianite camp. It struck the tent with such force that the tent overturned and collapsed."

His friend responded, "This can be nothing other than the sword of Gideon son of Joash, the Israelite. God has given the Midianites and the whole camp into his hands."

When Gideon heard the dream and its interpretation, he worshiped God. He returned to the camp of Israel and called out, "Get up! The LORD has given the Midianite camp into your hands."

JUDGES 7:8–11, 13–15

On the eve of battle, Gideon was awakened from a restless and fear-filled sleep by the voice of God. Once again God assured him that he would win the battle. He was even given another sign.

As Gideon and Purah crept into the enemy's camp, they heard two Midianites talking in frightened voices.

MAY 2

"I had a terrible dream," one said. "A giant loaf of barley bread rolled over our whole tent and crushed us."

"I know what that means," the other Midianite said anxiously. "Gideon and his gigantic army, coming to destroy us!" Gideon was thrilled. Far from being an invincible force, the armies of Midian were terrified of the Lord ... and of Gideon!

Although our enemy, the devil, and his army may seem like fearless and invincible foes, this is not the truth. When we fight Satan with faith and the Word of God he runs fast the other way. James 4:7 says, "Resist the devil, and he will flee from you."

Gideon's story also shows us the extent of God's patience. God had given Gideon sign after sign, and yet he was still willing to give him one more opportunity to build his faith before the battle. If you are struggling with fear, God in his love and patience will do whatever it takes to give you the faith you need.

This story also has an interesting twist. Doesn't it seem weird that the Midianites dreamed about a loaf of bread destroying their camp? Earlier in the story God tells Gideon that he is going to *sift* his army. Sifting is something you do when you're making bread. All of the strange tests God gave to Gideon's army were part of the process of making them into a force for victory—a giant loaf of bread which would smash their enemies. When God allows us to go through hard times that we don't understand, we need to remember that this is part of his process of making us into a weapon he can use for victory. May God give you the grace to become mighty in his army today.

GOD is BUILDING his CHURCH AND no enemy, GATE, OR BORDER WILL pREVAIL AGAINST it. This is his pURpOSE FOR ALL who LOVE GOD. When we ARE SERVING his pURpOSES WE WILL FIND THAT ALL OUR STRUGGLES WILL ONE DAY WORK TOGETHER FOR GREAT GOOD.

Peter Furler

Lessons in the Life of the Judges:
GIDEON'S VICTORY

Dividing the three hundred men into three companies, he placed trumpets and empty jars in the hands of all of them, with torches inside. "Watch me," he told them. "Follow my lead. When I get to the edge of the camp, do exactly as I do. When I and all who are with me blow our trumpets, then from all around the camp blow yours and shout, 'For the LORD and for Gideon.'" Gideon and the hundred men with him reached the edge of the camp at the beginning of the middle watch.... They blew their trumpets and broke the jars.... They shouted, "A sword for the LORD and for Gideon!" ... When the three hundred trumpets sounded, the LORD caused the men throughout the camp to turn on each other with their swords.

JUDGES 7:16–20, 22

MAY 3

The battle plan God had given the Israelites was strange to say the least. Gideon, however, had no trouble believing it would work. All doubt had finally been uprooted from his heart. Quickly gathering his forces together, he gave each of them a trumpet, an empty jar, and a torch. When they got to the edge of the enemy camp, he told them the plan. They were to watch him and do exactly what he did.

When the Israelites blew their trumpets and shattered the jars they were carrying with torches inside, madness struck the Midianite camp. As they stumbled out of their tents, they were blinded by the fire of hundreds of torches. The cry of, "For the Lord and for Gideon!" roared all around them. In confusion and panic, the Midianites began to fight and kill one another. Within a few hours, almost 100,000 Midianites had been slaugh-

tered, and the rest were fleeing for their lives. Indeed, God had fought for his servant Gideon that night.

The battle of Gideon is an incredible story of God's power and love for his people. It shows us that God does not need a gigantic army to win the fight. He used a mere three hundred men to defeat an army of over 100,000! All God needs is a few committed men and women who are willing to be instruments in his hands. When you offer yourself to him fully, he will give you all that you need to stand for him and win.

Another lesson we can learn from this story is that because Gideon's three hundred men were probably not trained soldiers they were more willing to follow Gideon's commands. It is important for us to follow the godly leaders God has placed in our lives and imitate their faith, especially when we are young and still "in training."

Another amazing part of this story is how God used trumpets, empty jars, and torches to defeat a whole army! This shows us just how much God can accomplish with ordinary people like you and me. When we will allow God to clean our hearts and then fill them with the fire of the Holy Spirit, he will be able to do amazing things through our lives.

One of the most awesome aspects of Gideon's story is that the Israelites did very little fighting in the initial battle. They were called to simply be obedient to God's strange plan. When the words of faith thundered from their lips God's power destroyed their enemies. Today, if you will simply do what God is telling you to do and say what he is telling you to say, you will experience a whole new level of victory in your life too. May God give you the grace to follow his "battle plan," even when it seems strange. God knows just what it takes to send your enemies running and give you the victory!

> Obedience to God is our greatest offense and our greatest defense.
> **Peter Furler**

Lessons in the Life of the Judges:
GIDEON'S FAILURE

[Gideon said]: "I do have one request, that each of you give me an earring from your share of the plunder." ... [The Israelites] answered, "We'll be glad to give them." ... The weight of the gold rings he asked for came to seventeen hundred shekels.... Gideon made the gold into an ephod, which he placed in Ophrah, his town. All Israel prostituted themselves by worshipping it there, and it became a snare to Gideon and his family.

JUDGES 8:24–27

No sooner had Gideon died than the Israelites again prostituted themselves to the Baals. They set up Baal-Berith as their god and did not remember the Lord their God, who had rescued them from the hands of all their enemies on every side. They also failed to show kindness to the family of ... Gideon for all the good things he had done for them.

JUDGES 8:33–35

MAY 4

It was better that Gideon was dead, for almost the moment he had died, the whole nation had resumed its worship of Baal. It was as if the Israelites had mass amnesia. They had seen God's miracles and experienced his deliverance, but once Gideon was gone, their desire to serve God died as well. As shrines to Baal and Asherah were rebuilt across the countryside, a deep spiritual darkness settled over the land. Sadly, Gideon was partially responsible for this resurgence of idol worship. After their miraculous victory over Midian he had crafted the golden ephod that opened the door for Israel's spiritual demise.

The ephod was a garment worn by a priest of Israel, but somehow Gideon allowed it to become an idol. Gideon, like many Christian leaders today, mistakenly believed that the right system or ceremony was what God wanted. But great religious programs and systems can never take the place of a close relationship with the true God. If we aren't careful, we can turn good things, like great worship music or powerful messages into idols—we end up worshiping these things instead of God.

Awesome music, cool presentations, and strong speakers are all great parts of worshiping God. We need to be careful, however, not to let these things become our primary focus. When we do, we lose sight of the one thing we were born to do, and that is to give God the glory in everything. Ask the Lord today to keep your eyes focused on him as your main goal, remembering that everything else pales in comparison to his greatness!

AS CHRISTIAN MUSICIANS WE PRAY THAT OUR MUSIC WILL ALWAYS POINT PEOPLE TO GOD AND NEVER POINT TO US. WE DON'T WANT TO BE IDOLS BUT SIMPLY MESSENGERS OF THE GLORY OF GOD!

Peter Furler

Lessons in the Life of the Judges:
SAMSON'S BIRTH

Again the Israelites did evil in the eyes of the LORD, so the LORD delivered them into the hands of the Philistines for forty years. A certain man of Zorah, named Manoah, from the clan of the Danites, had a wife that was sterile and remained childless. The angel of the LORD appeared to her and said, "You are sterile and childless, but you are going to conceive and have a son. Now see to it that you drink no wine or other fermented drink and that you do not eat anything unclean, because you will conceive and give birth to a son. No razor may be used on his head, because the boy is to be a Nazarite, set apart to God from birth, and he will begin the deliverance of Israel from the hands of the Philistines."

JUDGES 13:1–5

MAY 5

Supernaturally born to a childless couple, Samson was the new hope of Israel. After forty years of Philistine oppression, he was the answer to their prayers. He would be the strongest man in the history of our planet. He would tear apart a lion with his bare hands and kill a thousand men with only a donkey's jawbone. Yet, despite his incredible life of purpose and his amazing strength, Samson's anointing was a fragile thing. Unlike other Israelites, who would make a Nazarite vow to be set apart for short periods of their lives, Samson was called to live as a Nazarite until the day he died. This unique commitment to the Lord was the secret of Samson's power. Tragically, the young man who would not listen to his parents became the old man who would not listen to God. By

the end of his life, Samson was a blind prisoner hoping for one last chance to fulfill his destiny.

Although there are many lessons that can be drawn from Samson's life, the central message is this: Purpose and destiny alone are not enough. It takes commitment and the willingness to be different to live in the power of God. Although the sacrifice of Christ has given us all access to God's promises, our faithfulness and holiness are also part of the plan. Some ancient Israelites set themselves apart for God for limited periods of time. Christians today do the same thing. Whether it is the emotional promise made at a teary altar call, or the a promise of renewed dedication following a unique encounter with God, a commitment that fades once the feelings are gone is not going to bring us the relationship with God we need. Truly following the Lord, every day, has very little to do with external things or emotions. It has everything to do with our hearts.

In Acts 2:42 it says that the first Christians "devoted themselves to the apostles' teaching and to the fellowship, to the breaking of bread and to prayer." This list gives us a good place to start from as we work to set ourselves completely apart for God. Sincerely taking time to learn and grow through the study of God's Word, spending time sharing with other Christians, and building your relationship with God through prayer are all great ways to strengthen your commitment to the Lord. Take a lesson from Samson and don't abandon your relationship with God. Walking with him will never fail to bring you blessing.

"LORD keep my heart set on keeping your decrees until the very end." I need GOD's GRACE to give me the kind of faith that perseveres to the end.

Peter Furler

Lessons in the Life of the Judges:
SAMSON'S PARENTS

Then the woman went to her husband and told him, "A man of God came to me. He looked like an angel of God, very awesome. I didn't ask him where he came from, and he didn't tell me his name. But he said to me, 'You will conceive and give birth to a son. Now then, drink no wine or other fermented drink and do not eat anything unclean, because the boy will be a Nazarite of God from birth until the day of his death.'"

Then Manoah prayed to the LORD: "O Lord, I beg you, let the man of God you sent to us come again to teach us how to bring up the boy who is to be born." God heard Manoah, and the angel of God came again.... So Manoah asked him, "When your words are fulfilled, what is to be the rule for the boy's life and work?"

The angel of the LORD answered, "Your wife must do all that I have told her."

JUDGES 13:6–9, 12–13

MAY 6

After years of barrenness and sterility, Manoah's wife would see the answer to her prayers. As she ran to tell her husband the incredible news, her face was flooded with joy. She hadn't been sure if the messenger was human or angelic—but she knew that God had spoken to her. Her husband was astonished at her story. Falling to his knees, he cried out to God for the messenger to return and teach them how to raise this amazing child of promise. When the angel reappeared, both Manoah and his wife were amazed at the divine messenger's reply.

Instead of giving instructions for the child's rearing, he talked to them only about how *they* should live. The essence of the angel's message was simple, yet profound: Live in the way you want your child to live.

The story of Samson's parents can teach us many things. First, barrenness isn't a barrier to God's power. We may all experience times when we feel barren of relationships, money, or even of spiritual growth. But when we wait and trust God he will cause you to be fruitful when the time is right.

Like Manoah, who missed his wife's first encounter with the angelic messenger, maybe you are wondering if you have missed out on a divine moment in your own life. Maybe you thought you heard God's call, but were unsure and didn't respond. Now you are full of regrets, worrying that you may never experience another opportunity like the one you lost. And yet we see that Manoah simply prayed for another opportunity—and he received it. Ask, and you may just find another moment of divine opportunity right in front of you.

The angel's instructions to Manoah and his wife also give us the key to being good parents. Instead of emphasizing how the child should be raised, the angel told Samson's mother how she should live. Successful parenting consists of far more than bringing your children to church and telling them to read their Bibles. Good parenting involves living the kind of life that you would want your kids to imitate. In the end, *you* will influence your children far more than any church service they will ever attend.

Whether you are facing a barren time in your life, the need for a new divine opportunity, or simply a desire to raise godly children, simply ask God to provide. He loves to bring fruitfulness to the barren, purpose to the searching, and knowledge to those who need it most.

Seek the guidance of the LORD today. You will only affect the world for the kingdom of God as much as the kingdom of God has affected you.

Peter Furler

SAMSON'S WEDDING

Samson went down to Timnah and saw there a young Philistine woman. When he returned, he said to his father and mother, "I have seen a Philistine woman in Timnah; now get her for me as my wife."

His father and mother replied, "Isn't there an acceptable woman among your relatives or among all our people? Must you go to the uncircumcised Philistines to get a wife?"

But Samson said to his father, "Get her for me. She's the right one for me." (His parents did not know that this was from the LORD, who was seeking an occasion to confront the Philistines; for at that time they were ruling over Israel.)...

Samson's wife was given to the friend who had attended him at his wedding.... So [Sampson] went out and caught three hundred foxes and tied them tail to tail in pairs. He then fastened a torch to every pair of tails, lit the torches and let the foxes loose in the standing grain of the Philistines. He burned up the shocks and standing grain, together with the vineyards and olive groves. When the Philistines asked, "Who did this?" they were told, "Samson, the Timnite's son-in-law, because his wife was given to his friend." So the Philistines went up and burned her and her father to death.

JUDGES 14:1–4, 20; 15:4–6

The moment Samson saw her he had to have her. The fact that she was a Philistine didn't matter. His parents begged him to consider a Hebrew woman, but he would not be deterred. Samson's relationship with the Philistine woman would bring him nothing but grief. And then his new father-

in-law gave his new bride away to another man. Samson took revenge on the Philistines, burning their fields and vineyards and bringing about the brutal deaths of his new wife and her father.

Samson's story is a living example of Proverbs 14:12: "There is a way that seems right to a man, but in the end it leads to death." Samson's rebellious desire to marry a forbidden woman ended in nothing but heartbreak. And no matter how right our actions may "feel," if they violate the Word of God or go against the wise counsel of other mature Christians, they will lead only to pain.

The story of Samson's marriage has a strange twist to it as well, though. Judges 14:4 says that God was working through Samson's rebellious act. Scripture commanded the Hebrews to only marry other Hebrews, and yet God had a plan that worked even through Samson's disobedience. Later he would wreak more havoc on the Philistines by tearing off their city gates—after his visit to a prostitute. Then he would attack them as a result of his illicit relationship with Delilah. God used Samson many times, but always in spite of his sin.

God's work through Samson is difficult to understand. But if Samson was given power and used in mighty ways, even when he was rebellious, we can be sure that we will receive a power even greater when we are faithfully following God's plan. May God give us a new passion for obedience to his mighty will so that we might be found faithful and useful for his purposes.

OuR Decisions should ALWAYS Be confiRmeD By the WoRD of GoD, the Spirit of GoD, And the peopLe of GoD. SAmsoh's fAiLuRe to consider these three checkpoints cost him terribly. Don't mAke his mistAke.

Peter Furler

Lessons from the Life of the Judges:
SAMSON'S VICTORY

 [The men from Judah] said to [Samson], "We've come to tie you up and hand you over to the Philistines."

Samson said, "Swear to me that you won't kill me yourselves."

"Agreed," they answered. "We will only tie you up and hand you over to them. We will not kill you." So they bound him with two new ropes.... As he approached Lehi, the Philistines came toward him shouting. The Spirit of the LORD came upon him in power. The ropes on his arms became like charred flax, and the bindings dropped from his hands. Finding a fresh jawbone of a donkey, he grabbed it and struck down a thousand men.

Then Samson said,

"With a donkey's jawbone
I have made donkeys of them.
With a donkey's jawbone
I have killed a thousand men."

When he finished speaking, he threw away the jawbone.

JUDGES 15:12–17

MAY 8

As they pulled the bonds tighter and tighter, Samson's heart was full of hurt and anger. These weren't Philistines binding him, but his own countrymen. After the slaughter he had unleashed on the Philistines, Samson had thought the whole nation of Israel would rise up and join him in rebellion against them. But instead of following him into

battle they were turning him over to their oppressors in order to appease them.

The Israelites led Samson to a hill and left him alone there. Soon he could see the Philistine henchmen running up the hill to get him—thousands of them, screaming their battle cries, all set on killing him. But before the Philistines could reach him the power of God hit Samson like a lightning bolt. The ropes that bound him were burned to ashes and the power of the Holy Spirit turned him into an invincible warrior. Looking for any weapon he could find, Samson grabbed the jawbone of a donkey he found lying on the hill. With this makeshift weapon, Samson slaughtered one thousand Philistines single-handedly. The rest fled for their lives.

Even as the people of Israel bound Samson because they were afraid to fight, so I have seen churches bind their young Samsons out of fear. Many times they use the flaws of these young champions as the excuse for binding them, but in reality the church simply fears the passion and new ideas that these warriors bring. Young leaders certainly need to be trained and even, sometimes, tamed a bit. But if their youthful passion and enthusiasm is destroyed because it threatens our comfort zones, the church may well lose her greatest resources. If you are a leader in ministry, be careful not to stifle the young people that you lead in their fire for the Lord. And if you are a passionate young person, don't let your enthusiasm be squashed. Keep looking until you find a mentor who will help you develop and grow while encouraging your passion and gifts.

The church today is in desperate need of young warriors full of God's fire and passion for our lost world. May today's leaders recognize and have the courage to train and encourage the young people in their lives today. And may the future soldiers hold on to their passion and continue to grow. God is calling you both to bring hope to a hopeless world!

The passion of God, burning in the hearts of young and old, is the powerful force that the world is longing for today!

Peter Furler

Lessons from the Life of the Judges:
SAMSON'S REFRESHING

Because he was very thirsty, he cried out to the LORD, "You have given your servant this great victory. Must I now die of thirst and fall into the hands of the uncircumcised?" Then God opened up the hollow place in Lehi, and water came out of it. When Samson drank, his strength returned and he revived. So the spring was called En Hakkore, and it is still there in Lehi.

JUDGES 15:18–19

MAY 9

Samson fell to his knees in exhaustion after his great victory over the Philistines. With his thirst and fatigue growing, he cried out to the Lord with the last bit of his strength. "Lord, don't let me die of thirst after the great victory you have given me!" God's response was miraculous—the moment he had finished praying, water began to bubble out of the ground. Samson's strength was revived by this supernatural spring, and it remained there for many years as source of refreshment for the nation of Israel.

Like Samson, we can become just as exhausted by our victories as we can by our defeats. Whether it was Elijah running from Jezebel after his great victory over the prophets of Baal, or Moses coming down from the glory of Mt. Sinai and discovering the horrible sin of Israel, oftentimes the enemy mounts his greatest assaults against us when we are already tired from achieving a great victory. But if you will just call out to the Lord in prayer when you are weary from battle, he will bring a fresh spring of the Holy Spirit's power to refresh you. This may come from a new insight into a Bible verse or even the kindness of a trusted friend. In whatever

form your "spring" comes, it will bubble up when you choose to trust and act on the promises of God's Word.

It is also important for you to remember that the spring God opened for Samson wasn't only for him. According to Scripture, it continued to be a place of refreshing for Israelites for years to come. And the springs of refreshing resulting from our prayers are never just for us alone, either. God wants us to use the lessons we have learned and the power we have received to strengthen the people around us. May God both refresh you and make your life a source of refreshment for others today.

LORD LET US BE LIKE A WELL-WATERED GARDEN, LIKE A SPRING WHOSE WATERS NEVER FAIL (ISAIAH 58:11). WHETHER IT'S THROUGH THE WORD OF GOD OR OUR SPIRITUAL FAMILIES, GOD IS ALWAYS FAITHFUL TO WATER OUR SOULS.

Peter Furler

Lessons from the Life of the Judges:
SAMSON AND DELILAH

Having put [Samson] to sleep on her lap, [Delilah] called a man to shave off the seven braids of his hair, and so began to subdue him. And his strength left him. Then she called, "Samson, the Philistines are upon you!"

He awoke from his sleep and thought, "I'll go out as before and shake myself free." But he did not know that the LORD had left him. Then the Philistines seized him, gouged out his eyes.... Binding him with bronze shackles, they set him to grinding in the prison. But the hair on his head began to grow again after it had been shaved.

JUDGES 16:19–22

MAY 10

Her name was Delilah, and she was the love of Samson's life. Finally here was a woman would meet all his needs. She would do for him what the prostitutes he'd frequented could never do. Little did he realize that the woman he loved was being paid to destroy him.

Patiently, Delilah let Samson romance her, all the while enticing him to reveal the secret of his great strength. Although he was reluctant to tell her, his lust for her finally overcame his hesitation. When at last she knew the truth, Delilah sprung her trap. With Samson asleep on her lap she had his long braids shaved off—the symbol of his commitment to God. When Delilah woke him with a warning that the Philistines were coming Samson's strength was gone—God had left him. The Philistines bound him, gouged out his eyes, and set him to grinding flour in the dungeon like an animal. But in the darkness there two things began to grow: a repentant heart within Samson, and his hair.

Though many Christians speak of "falling" into sin, in reality we usually "walk" into it. Delilah slowly enticed Samson into breaking his vow to the Lord, but in the end he knew what he was doing was wrong, and chose to sin anyway. We too allow sin to slowly take over as we willingly yield to little temptations. And just like Samson, we are given plenty of warnings that we are putting ourselves in danger, and yet the deception that sin always brings often causes us to be blind to the threat.

Once Samson found himself in crisis his sin had already caused him to lose the presence and power of God in his life that was necessary to deliver him. When sin is allowed to grow in our lives we become desensitized to the voice of the Holy Spirit and we may not even notice the silence until you need him the most, but can no longer hear him. We must not be fooled into thinking that no matter how we live God will always come to our rescue when we call. Sooner or later, because of his great love for you, he will allow you to experience the consequences of your sin to teach you to fear and obey him.

Though we may face the painful consequences of our sin, God does not abandon us forever. Samson found himself blind and imprisoned, but it was in that prison that both his relationship with God and his hair grew. And with the return of both of these things, so returned his power. Though he had destroyed his testimony, God would still use him in a mighty way one last time before he died. May your eyes be opened to any sin that is trying to entangle you today so that you can avoid the pain of learning obedience the way Samson did—the hard way.

This is one of the most important prayers of my life: "MAY those who hope in you not be disgraced because of me, O LORD, the Almighty; may those who seek you not be put to shame because of me, O God of Israel" (PSALM 69:6).

Peter Furler

Lessons from the Life of the Judges:
SAMSON'S DEATH

The rulers of the Philistines assembled to offer a great sacrifice to Dagon their god and to celebrate, saying, "Our god has delivered Samson, our enemy, into our hands....Bring out Samson to entertain us." ...

When they stood him among the pillars, Samson said to the servant who held his hand, "Put me where I can feel the pillars that support the temple, so that I may lean against them." Now the temple was crowded with men and women; all the rulers of the Philistines were there, and on the roof were about three thousand men and women.... Then Samson prayed to the Lord, "O Sovereign Lord, remember me. O God, please strengthen me just once more, and let me with one blow get revenge on the Philistines for my two eyes." Then Samson reached toward the two central pillars on which the temple stood. Bracing himself against them ...he pushed with all his might, and down came the temple on the rulers and all the people in it. Thus he killed many more when he died than while he lived.

JUDGES 16:23, 25–30

MAY 11

The greatest leaders of the Philistine empire were assembled that day. They had come to celebrate the victory of their god Dagon and to taunt their enemy. With three thousand people gathered to watch, Samson was brought out to be mocked and tormented for their entertainment. Little did they realize, however, that more than his hair had been growing in the depths of the prison. The rebellious will of Israel's great champion

had finally been broken, and Samson had returned to the God of his youth in repentance. Now with the taunts and jeers of the Philistines filling his ears, Samson felt the power of God that he thought he had lost forever. He cried out, "God, strengthen me just once more!" Placing his hands on the temple's central pillars, he pushed with all his might. The great temple crashed down upon them all. Although Samson died that day, he took three thousand Philistines with him. The planet's strongest man killed more of his enemies in his death than he had ever killed during his life.

God is the God of the second chance. Samson's story is clear proof of that fact. No matter how far you have fallen or how many times you have sinned, God is ready and willing to restore you today. If you will truly seek God's forgiveness, your strength and spiritual health will return to you, even through the darkness of your pain—just as Samson's faith, and his hair, were restored in the dungeon.

And, just as Samson accomplished more for God in his death than he did in his life, so spiritually speaking, the same is true for you and me. When we die to our will and follow God into a new level of obedience, we will be amazed to see what God can do through us. As you consider Samson's end today, may God make Galatians 2:20 true in your life: *"I have been crucified with Christ and I no longer live, but Christ lives in me. The life I live in the body, I live by faith in the Son of God, who loved me and gave himself for me."*

> I pray that I will always be willing to die to my own desires so that God's infinitely better plan can live in me.
> **Peter Furler**

Lessons from the Book of Ruth:
ELIMELECH'S MISTAKE

In the days when the judges ruled, there was a famine in the land, and a man from Bethlehem in Judah, together with his wife and two sons, went to live for a while in the country of Moab. The man's name was Elimelech, his wife's name Naomi, and the names of his two sons were Mahlon and Kilion. They were Ephrathites from Bethlehem, Judah.... Now Elimelech, Naomi's husband, died, and she was left with her two sons. They married Moabite women, one named Orpah and the other Ruth. After they had lived there about ten years, both Mahlon and Kilion also died,... When she heard in Moab that the LORD had come to the aid of his people by providing food for them, Naomi and her daughters-in-law prepared to return home from there. With her two daughters-in-law she left the place where she had been living and set out on the road that would take them back to the land of Judah.

RUTH 1:1-7

MAY 12

In desperation, Elimelech had left the promised land of his people and moved to Moab. At the time, it seemed like the right thing to do. After all, he had heard that conditions were far better there. Yet despite the apparent wisdom of this move, both he and his two precious sons were to die, leaving their wives widows, and destitute. But God did not abandon them. At the end of ten years, Naomi and one of her daughters-in-law (the other turned back) would return to Bethlehem and find the blessing of God.

Whether it is financial, relational, spiritual, or emotional, you have, or will one day, come into a time of famine. And when famine hits, you wonder if a radical change is the only answer—perhaps you should leave the church, job, or city God called you to and retreat to a place where provision seems more certain. However, we need to avoid the urge to panic and retreat. You felt God call you to this place at one time, so be careful to run away from it without the assurance that God is releasing you to go. God may want you to stay in your "Bethlehem" and trust him through the famine.

Maybe, like Elimelech, you have allowed a crisis to make you run away from God's will. Maybe your new job is stressful and unfulfilling, unlike the one you had before you ran. Maybe you're struggling to find new relationships that were as deep and encouraging as the ones you left. No matter how long you've been gone or how far you've run from the center of God's will, it is never too late for you to return. Naomi returned broken and bitter to Bethlehem, but she still found renewal in the Lord.

Although there may be many steps in your journey home, the first is simple repentance. In fact, repentance literally means to "turn around," to get back on the right road. When you turn around and start walking back to God, he will give you all the grace you need to find your way home to his will and all the blessings it will bring.

"The sacrifices of God are a broken spirit. A broken and contrite heart, God, you will not despise." Even if you feel like you've taken a thousand steps away from God, repentance and brokenness will produce the one step that will take you back.

Peter Furler

Lessons from the Book of Ruth:
NAOMI'S BITTERNESS

So the two women went on until they came to Bethlehem. When they arrived in Bethlehem, the whole town was stirred because of them, and the women exclaimed, "Can this be Naomi?"

"Don't call me Naomi," she told them. "Call me Mara, because the Almighty has made my life very bitter. I went away full, but the LORD has brought me back empty. Why call me Naomi? The LORD has afflicted me; the Almighty has brought misfortune upon me." So Naomi returned from Moab accompanied by Ruth the Moabitess, her daughter-in-law, arriving in Bethlehem as the barley harvest was beginning.

RUTH 1:19–22

MAY 13

Naomi was returning to Bethlehem a radically different woman. The tragedies she had experienced in Moab had broken her and she was full of bitterness. When her friends saw her, they hardly recognized her. "Can this be Naomi?" they had cried. Her response to their question only served to reveal the depths of her bitterness. "Don't even call me Naomi anymore," she had snapped at them. "My new name is Mara, for God has made my life bitter." But even in the darkness of her despair God had not forgotten Naomi. She would soon experience the greatest fulfillment of her life.

What can we learn from Naomi and her struggle with bitterness? First, her real problem was not the pain she had experienced in Moab; it was the fact that she had allowed bitterness to be her reaction. Instead of looking to God for healing, she had blamed God for everything. We often make the same mistake. We are all going to face difficult and painful things in life. But we can avoid bitterness by choosing to look past the pain and into the loving eyes of our Heavenly Father. He can bring joy even out of the hardest circumstances.

When Naomi called herself "Mara" which means "bitter," she was only cursing herself. When we believe the enemies' lies and begin to call ourselves bitter, ugly, stupid, or hopeless, we are letting him have power over us. It does not matter what you think about yourself or your situation; all that matters is what God has to say about it. Listen to what he has to say about you through his Word and choose to believe the Author of Truth and not the father of lies. Bitterness isn't a way to get revenge on people or even on God for your pain. Bitterness, most of all, just hurts you and keeps you from God's healing power. Don't let your circumstances rename you "Mara." Instead, look to the Lord and let him give you a new name of hope.

When BAD things happen, there is a greater question to answer than "Why?" And that is, "What am I going to do about it?" Bitterness is poison to your soul. Until Naomi was able to stop BLAMING GOD for her circumstances, she would never be able to walk into God's promises for her life.

Peter Furler

RUTH'S JOURNEY

Naomi said to her two daughters-in-law, "Go back, each of you, to your mother's home." ... Then she kissed them and they wept aloud and said to her, "We will go back with you to your people."

But Naomi said,..."No, my daughters. It is more bitter for me than for you, because the LORD's hand has gone out against me!"

At this they wept again. Then Orpah kissed her mother-in-law good-by, but Ruth clung to her.... "Don't urge me to leave you or to turn back from you. Where you go I will go, and where you stay I will stay. Your people will be my people and your God my God. Where you die I will die, and there I will be buried. May the LORD deal with me, be it ever so severely, if anything but death separates you and me."

RUTH 1:8–11, 13–14, 16–17

MAY 14

Both Ruth and Orpah had promised to return with Naomi to Bethlehem — but only Ruth fulfilled her promise. As she approached Bethlehem that day, Ruth surely wondered what awaited her in this foreign land. She remembered how Naomi had described the God of her people. The only religion Ruth had ever known had been the violent, immoral rites of Moab; the thought that there was a God who loved her and cared for her was almost more than she dared hope for. Therefore, it was not just her love for Naomi that had brought her to Bethlehem; it was her deep longing for Naomi's God. Although Naomi had nothing to offer her, deep in her heart Ruth believed Naomi's God did. Ruth had no idea of the transformation and blessings that awaited her because of her faith.

The story of Ruth is one of the most amazing tales of commitment in all of Scripture. In fact, Ruth exemplifies the level of commitment God desires for us today. This young woman was from a country that had been an enemy of Israel for decades—she knew that not everyone in Bethlehem would accept her like Naomi had. Her hunger for God, however, overcame barriers of ethnic tension and historic hatred and brought her into the fullness of her destiny.

Ruth's story also shows us the importance of trusting God's guidance over our own sense. Ruth had no logical reason to follow God. Naomi was destitute, bitter, and impoverished. All she could offer Ruth was a life of poverty and pain. Yet Ruth, in spite of the fact that she didn't yet know God, still took a step of faith to seek him. Even more amazing is the fact that she continued to seek the one true God before she could see the promise of any earthly blessings.

Maybe you, like Ruth, are facing the barriers in your search for the Almighty God today. Or, perhaps you're a Christian who is facing God's call to take a step of faith, even though it seems like a crazy thing to do. No matter where you are or what you are facing, remember the story of Ruth and her illogical pursuit of a God she didn't yet know. When you run after the Lord, he will run to you and bring you blessings you've never imagined.

God blesses us when we commit ourselves to others out of reverence for him. Ruth's pure commitment to Naomi brought abundance to both of their lives.

Peter Furler

Lessons from the Book of Ruth:
THE KINSMAN REDEEMER

[Naomi] asked [Ruth], "Where did you glean today? Where did you work? Blessed be the man who took notice of you!" Then Ruth told her mother-in-law about the one at whose place she had been working.

"The name of the man I worked with today is Boaz," she said.

"The LORD bless him!" Naomi said to her daughter-in-law. "He has not stopped showing his kindness to the living and the dead." She added, "That man is our close relative; he is one of our kinsman-redeemers."

RUTH 2:19–20

MAY 15

Naomi had told Ruth that under Israelite law, widows were allowed to pick up the grain that the workers had left behind in the fields. But that day, as she had gathered, she had received more than she expected. This owner of the field, Boaz, had allowed her to gather the finest grain in the fields and had even fed her a meal. *Why had he shown such kindness? What did he want?* she wondered to herself.

When Ruth returned home to Naomi that evening, her heart was full of joy. "What was his name?" Naomi asked when she recounted the day's events. "Boaz," Ruth whispered. The moment Naomi heard his name her eyes filled with tears. Her face was transformed as she was too flooded with joy. "God has not forgotten us!" Naomi sobbed. "Boaz is one of our kinsman-redeemers."

The story of Ruth and Boaz is a beautiful tale of redemption. Under Israelite law, one of the responsibilities of a close relative or kinsman-redeemer was to marry and care for the widow of his relative. So, although

Boaz was later to fall in love with Ruth, his initial kindness to her in his fields was based on his faithfulness to God's laws.

The love story of the book of Ruth also points to another story of redemption. You and I also have a Kinsman-Redeemer—Jesus Christ! He has redeemed us from spiritual poverty and shame and has promised to care for us with all the resources and power of heaven. If life has left you feeling widowed, impoverished, afflicted, or abandoned, your heavenly Kinsman-Redeemer is waiting with open arms for you. As you accept his offer of love in faith, he will fulfill every promise he has made to you through his living Word.

"PRAISE BE to the LORD, to GOD OUR SAVIOR, WHO DAILY BEARS OUR BURDENS" (PSALM 68:19). GOD is FAITHFUL to BEAR YOUR BURDENS AND meet YOUR needs DAILY.

Peter Furler

Lessons from the Book of Ruth:
RUTH'S CONSOLATION

One day Naomi her mother-in-law said to her, "My daughter, should I not try to find a home for you, where you will be well provided for? Is not Boaz, with whose servant girls you have been, a kinsman of ours? Tonight he will be winnowing barley on the threshing floor. Wash and perfume yourself, and put on your best clothes. Then go down to the threshing floor, but don't let him know you are there until he has finished eating and drinking. When he lies down, note the place where he is lying. Then go and uncover his feet and lie down. He will tell you what to do."

RUTH 3:1–4

MAY 16

Naomi knew what needed to be done. Ruth did not need to settle for the leftovers of Boaz's field any longer; it was time for her to go and ask him to fulfill his responsibilities as her kinsman-redeemer. So Naomi told Ruth to put on her most beautiful clothes and some perfume. When darkness fell, she was to go down to the threshing floor where Boaz would be working and lay down at the feet of Boaz as he slept near the harvest.

That night, when she revealed her identity to Boaz, his reply had thrilled her heart. After complimenting her character, he told her not to be afraid, for he would make sure that the duties of her kinsman-redeemer were fulfilled. The next morning, when the closest kinsman declined to redeem her, Boaz took Ruth as his wife.

Like Ruth, we don't have to settle for anything other than God's best for us. Ruth could have resigned herself to living off Boaz's charity for the rest of her life. Instead she took a risk and asked for her rights to be his wife. As a member of God's family, you have the right to all the privileges of a child—you don't have to settle for living like an orphan.

Another lesson we learn from Ruth is in her careful preparation. Before she went down to Boaz that night, she put on her finest clothes and perfume—making herself beautiful out of respect and honor for Boaz. We show our respect and honor for our heavenly Father by putting on the righteousness of Jesus and entering his presence through Christ's cleansing blood.

After Ruth had come to the threshing floor, and placed herself at the feet of Boaz, she asked him to cover her with a blanket. Ruth was asking to come under Boaz's covering, protection, and authority as his wife. When we come to Jesus and kneel at his feet, we need to ask him for his covering, protection, and authority over our lives. We can only receive the full blessings of God when we are willing to make him King of our lives. May God use the principles found in Ruth's story to guide your life today as you seek a deeper relationship with your heavenly Kinsman-Redeemer.

Like Ruth's perfume, may we have righteous lives that spread a sweet fragrance that honors God and brings others to him.

Peter Furler

Lessons from the Book of Ruth:
RUTH'S BLESSING

The elders and all those at the gate said, "We are witnesses. May the LORD make the woman who is coming into your home like Rachel and Leah, who together built up the house of Israel. May you have standing in Ephrathah and be famous in Bethlehem. Through the offspring the LORD gives you by this young woman, may your family be like that of Perez, whom Tamar bore to Judah."

RUTH 4:11–12

MAY 17

It was probably the wedding of the year. Boaz, one of Bethlehem's most eligible bachelors, was taking Ruth, the beautiful young widow from Moab, to be his wife. The whole city was ecstatic; Boaz had always been one of the city's favorite sons, and no one could remember a widow as virtuous as Ruth. The elders of the city blessed their coming union by asking God to give Ruth the blessing of Rachel and Leah their future children the blessing of "Perez, whom Tamar bore to Judah."

In this blessing, we find some incredible history and words of prophecy. Perez, and his mother Tamar, were Boaz's ancestors, and frankly, this part of his family tree had some bad branches. According to Genesis 38, Tamar's first two husbands were so wicked that God killed them. Although her father-in-law, Judah, promised his third son to her as well, according to the kinsman-redeemer law, he never fulfilled his promise. So Tamar took matters into her own hands, dressed up as a temple prostitute and seduced her own father-in-law. When she became pregnant, Judah sentenced her to death for adultery. Once she proved to him, however, that he was the father of her child, Judah cancelled the death sentence.

As Tamar was giving birth to her twin sons, one baby's hand appeared out of the birth canal first. The midwife thought this baby would be the firstborn. But then, the other baby was born first, pushing his way past his brother. He was named Perez which means "breaking out."

So when the elders asked for the blessing of Perez to be on Ruth's children, they were asking God to give them a "spirit of breakthrough." Despite deception and sin surrounding Perez's birth, he would become the head of the leading clan of the tribe of Judah, the ancestor of King David and ultimately, of Jesus the Messiah. Like their forefather Perez, Boaz and Ruth, their grandson, King David, and their divine descendant Jesus all show us that through faith and obedience to the Lord, there is no barrier we cannot break.

God wants to give you the spirit of Perez. You may be suffering the pain of the past or the struggle of your present circumstances. But remember—God can help you break through every obstacle. Don't be discouraged, though, if your breakthrough doesn't come all at once. Although we would love for our struggles to simply disappear, God often allows us to go through the slow process of growing out of our problems instead. This process requires a consistent time spent in God's Word and daily conversations with the Lord through prayer. So while you're waiting, keep seeking God, and asking him for the spirit of Perez so you too can break through into the blessings in store for you.

The LORD will be the sure foundation for your times" (ISAIAH 33:6). While you're waiting and growing toward your breakthrough, God will give you the stability you need to stand firm and not give up.

Peter Furler

Lessons from the Book of Ruth:
NAUMI'S REDEMPTION

So Boaz took Ruth and she became his wife. Then he went to her, and the LORD enabled her to conceive, and she gave birth to a son. The women said to Naomi: "Praise be to the LORD, who this day has not left you without a kinsman-redeemer. May he become famous throughout Israel! He will renew your life and sustain you in your old age. For your daughter-in-law, who loves you and who is better to you than seven sons, has given him birth." Then Naomi took the child, laid him in her lap and cared for him.

RUTH 4:13–16

MAY 18

Naomi, who had been so filled with bitterness, had now been transformed by the blessing of the Lord. Naomi wept for joy as she cradled her first grandchild. She had felt so destitute and forsaken by God. In her bitterness, all she could see was a life of pain. But now, everything had changed! She had a new son in Boaz, Ruth, the daughter-in-law who loved her so much, and this new little grandson as her legacy.

Through Naomi's redemption we see the power of God to rescue the human soul from the darkness of bitterness and despair. No matter how bitter and destitute you may feel, seeking the presence of God is something you should never abandon. You may find it hard to pray or even step inside a church, but if you are going to see your soul restored, you need the encouragement of Christian fellowship and God's Word.

Your feelings are not going to change overnight, so don't rely on them to tell you whether or not you should go to church or spend time with Christian friends. Like Naomi, you may need to find some trustworthy people with whom you can be brutally honest about your struggle. You can even "vent" to God and tell him exactly how you feel. Naomi didn't stay silent about her pain, but she did return to God's presence and to his people, and that is where her restoration and healing took place.

Being surrounded by other people who have faith, even when you have little, will help you begin to see God working again. Once Naomi was back in Bethlehem, even though the situation hadn't changed, her ability to see God working in her life began to be restored. When Ruth told her about Boaz's kindness, she realized that God had "not stopped showing his kindness to the living and the dead" (Ruth 2:20). Authentic faith is contagious. When you're around people who have it, eventually you are bound to catch it too.

Once Naomi saw that God did still love her she had to be willing to place her full trust in him again. When Naomi sent Ruth to ask Boaz to redeem them, her willingness to take a risk demonstrated that she had found renewed faith in God and in his ability to bring her healing and redemption.

Wherever you are in this process, whether you are still in the depths of bitterness, or you are coming out the other side with a newfound faith, remember the example of Naomi and God's faithfulness to her. His love and healing power are still the same and available to you today.

The only hope of full restoration is through the LORD, his WORD, his people, and his purpose. Once all of these things are working in your life, like Naomi, you will be fully restored to the blessings God has for your life.

Peter Furler

LeSSoNS FROM the BOoK oF FiRST SAMueL:
HANNAH'S BARRENNESS

There was a certain man ... whose name was Elkanah.... He had two wives; one was called Hannah and the other Peninnah. Peninnah had children, but Hannah had none. Year after year this man went up from his town to worship and sacrifice to the LORD Almighty at Shiloh....Because the LORD had closed [Hannah's] womb, her rival kept provoking her in order to irritate her....Whenever Hannah went up to the house of the LORD, her rival provoked her till she wept and would not eat.

1 SAMUEL 1:1–3, 6–7

MAY 19

Despite the incredible love Elkanah and Hannah had for one another, their union had produced no children—Hannah was barren. It broke Elkanah's heart to see Hannah's pain, a pain that was only compounded by Peninnah, Elkanah's second wife who produced child after child, deepening Hannah's shame and sadness.

Adding insult to injury, every year Hannah had to journey with Elkanah, Peninnah and her ever-growing brood to worship at Shiloh. With Peninnah seeking every opportunity to mock her, Hannah would end up heartbroken and weeping by the end of each trip. But even in the middle of her deep anguish, God was already working to bring Hannah a great blessing. He would answer her prayers and give her a son.

Hannah's story helps us understand the pain and frustration of infertility, but also gives us lessons on God's process of healing spiritual barrenness. First of all, even though Hannah was deeply in love with her husband, nothing could replace the joy and honor that motherhood would bring. For Christians, no matter how deep our relationship is with Christ, if we are not being fruitful as a result of that relationship, we will never be satisfied. No matter how many Bible studies or church services we attend, songs we sing, or books we read we won't find our heart's deepest longing until we begin to pour ourselves out in service to the Lord.

Sometimes, God will use other people to motivate us toward his purposes. God used Peninnah to provoke Hannah, to make her so uncomfortable that she was driven to seek God with her whole heart. I see God using the passion of younger Christians today to provoke older Christians into a deeper pursuit of God's purposes. Their passion for evangelism and heart for making new disciples for Jesus drives veteran Christians, like me, into action. Their vibrant faith and desire to change the world has been one of the greatest motivations to continued fruitfulness in my own life.

Have you faced the fact that nothing but a renewed commitment to God's purposes will satisfy the emptiness in your soul? Perhaps you are surrounded by people that make you uncomfortable—and that is just what God has put them there to do! Or maybe you are a young person full of passion. If so, you might just be God's agent for change and new fruitfulness in your church. Chase hard after God's purposes and prepare to be blessed as you serve him.

I do not believe that Jesus saved us to have us pack our bags and wait on our rooftops for his return. His will is for us to make disciples, training them to go out and do the same. This is the purpose for everyone who follows Jesus. This is the secrets to abundant life in Christ.

Peter Furler

Lessons from the Book of First Samuel:
HANNAH'S SON

In bitterness of soul Hannah wept much and prayed to the LORD. And she made a vow, saying, "O LORD Almighty, if you will only ... remember me, and not forget your servant but give her a son, then I will give him to the LORD for all the days of his life" ... Hannah was praying in her heart, and her lips were moving but her voice was not heard.

Eli thought she was drunk.

"Not so, my lord," Hannah replied, "I am a woman who is deeply troubled. I have not been drinking wine or beer; I was pouring out my soul to the LORD." ...

Eli answered, "Go in peace, and may the God of Israel grant you what you have asked of him....

So in the course of time Hannah conceived and gave birth to a son. She named him Samuel, saying, "Because I asked the LORD for him."

1 SAMUEL 1:10–11, 13, 15, 17, 20

MAY 20

Hannah couldn't stand it any longer. In her desperation, she went to the tabernacle and began to cry out to God. As the pain and sorrow poured out of her heart, she made a vow to the Lord. "If you will give me a son, I will dedicate him to you all the days of his life." Hannah's story can teach us many things about our own relationship with God. First, God used the pain and emptiness in Hannah's life to drive her to her knees. God will often allow us to go through difficult times so that we will be driven to our knees to seek an answer from him. When we are at our weakest God's power can be at its strongest in our lives. When you face emptiness, don't let it drive you away from God. Instead run to him with open arms and ask to be filled.

Another lesson from Hannah is seen in her vow. Her promise to give her son back to the Lord, to set him apart for the Lord's service, may have been the commitment that God had been waiting to hear. God sometimes uses the desperation of his people to bring them to the place they need to be and into the commitment that he longs for them to make. The *process* of God's deliverance in your life is just as important as the *product* it will create.

As a part of God's process of healing, you may, like Hannah, find yourself misunderstood. Hannah was obviously wounded when Eli thought she was drunk. And your Christian friends may not always understand your desperation when you're in the midst of an empty time. But don't allow misunderstandings to stop you from finding the fulfillment Christ has promised for your life. Like Hannah, keep trusting and believing, and like Eli, your friends will see the truth in time.

Remember—emptiness isn't a sign that God has abandoned you. In fact, it is probably a sign that God is waiting with open arms for you to come running to him. He wants a deep commitment from you so that he can fill your life with blessings. Allow yourself to be driven to your knees today and believe that God will renew your hope and joy. He will do it!

We either FALL At the feet of Jesus OR we just FALL. Which will you DO when emptiness pLAGues you?

Peter Furler

LESSONS FROM THE BOOK OF FIRST SAMUEL:
SAMUEL'S CHILDHOOD

After he was weaned, she took the boy with her, young as he was ... and brought him to the house of the LORD at Shiloh.... They brought the boy to Eli, and she said to him, "As surely as you live, my lord, I am the woman who stood here beside you praying to the LORD. I prayed for this child, and the LORD has granted me what I asked of him. So now I give him to the LORD. For his whole life he will be given over to the LORD."

1 SAMUEL 1:24–28

Eli's sons were wicked men; they had no regard for the Lord... But Samuel was ministering before the Lord—a boy wearing a linen ephod.

1 SAMUEL 2:12, 18

MAY 21

Hannah had never once doubted God's call to dedicate her son to the Lord. Therefore, the moment he was weaned, she made preparations to take him to Shiloh and put him in the care of Eli the high priest. As she approached Shiloh, however, her heart must have been heavy. Things were not going well with Eli's own sons. She had heard terrible stories of how sinful and rebellious they were. How could her son walk purely before the Lord in an atmosphere like this? In spite of her concerns, she didn't waver in the commitment she had made to the Lord. When she arrived at Shiloh, she committed her precious Samuel into Eli's care.

When she arrived back home, Hannah began to pray for her son with a greater passion than ever before. And every year when she would journey to Shiloh to worship, she would give Samuel a new robe and encourage him to stand strong. This mother's prayers and encouragement would not be in vain—Samuel would grow up to become one of Israel's greatest prophets.

We can relate to the circumstances that Hannah and Samuel faced. Our world is full of compromise and immorality too. Parents are concerned for their children. Young people who are striving to follow God face a lot of obstacles. So what can we learn from the story of Samuel about how to life pure lives in an impure world? First Samuel 2:18 says that Samuel ministered before the Lord. This means he spent time both *serving* God and *worshiping* God. Both of these things are vital to maintaining a walk with God in a dark place. Service and worship will provide the passion needed to walk in purity, no matter what is going on around us.

We are also told that Samuel served the Lord while wearing a linen ephod or robe. This robe symbolized purity and transparency. As you seek to live a life of holiness, transparency with God and with other Christians will help you stay pure.

Finally, Samuel's story shows us the power of prayer—especially the prayers of a godly parent. Hannah's prayers, encouragement, and yearly visits played a vital role in Samuel's spiritual growth. No matter our age, we will have a hard time making it without the love and prayers of our spiritual families. Make it a priority to spend time with other Christians and to ask for their prayers. And if you are a parent, don't underestimate the power you have to lift your children up to the Lord. A praying parent is a powerful force in any child's life, whether they are 2, 22, or 62!

In a world every bit as dark and full of sin as it was during Hannah's time, we don't have to be discouraged. The God of Hannah is our God too. When we seek his holiness for ourselves and our children he will be faithful to provide and protect.

"Even in DARKness Light DAWns FOR the upRight" (PSALM 112:4). Even though young SAMuel WAS Living with ELi AnD his ReBeLLious sons, the Light in him still GREW BeCAuse oF his FAithFulness.

Peter Furler

Lessons from the Book of First Samuel:
SAMUEL'S CALLING

The boy Samuel ministered before the LORD under Eli. In those days the word of the LORD was rare; there were not many visions. One night ... Samuel was lying down in the temple of the LORD, where the ark of God was. Then the LORD called Samuel.... And he ran to Eli and said, "Here I am; you called me." ...

Eli realized that the LORD was calling the boy. So Eli told Samuel, "Go and lie down, and if he calls you, say, 'Speak, LORD, for your servant is listening.'" So Samuel went and lay down in his place.

The LORD came and stood there, calling as at the other times, "Samuel! Samuel!"

Then Samuel said, "Speak, for your servant is listening."

1 SAMUEL 3:1–5, 8–10

MAY 22

As Samuel lay down to sleep one night, the voice of the Lord began to call: "Samuel!" Samuel not yet able to recognize the voice of God, ran to Eli, thinking it was the priest who had called. "I didn't call you," Eli mumbled sleepily. But after Samuel came and woke him two more times, Eli figured it out. "Samuel," Eli said, "It is not me speaking to you; it is the Lord."

As Samuel lay back down in his bed, his whole body was trembling with anticipation. At that moment, he felt the presence of the Lord coming through his door like a wave of the sea. "Samuel!" the voice called again. "Speak, for your servant is listening," the young boy whispered. So began a friendship with the Lord that would change the course of Samuel's life, as well as that of his nation.

Many Christians today are just like young Samuel. They have grown up in the church and are living according to God's Word, but they have yet to experience the deep intimacy with God that comes from learning to hear his voice. Although the Bible is the primary and most authoritative way God communicates with his people, he also speaks to us through the whispered voice of the Holy Spirit. If you, like young Samuel, are longing to hear God's voice, there are a few things you can do to tune your heart to God's frequency.

First, it took young Samuel four times to discern the Lord's voice—it takes practice to hear God speak. A good way to practice is to spend time every day waiting in quiet on the Lord. When I first started learning how to hear God's voice, I would typically read my Bible and then sit quietly for a while, asking the Holy Spirit to speak to me. This is a great way to develop your relationship with the Lord so that you can hear him when he speaks.

Second, even as Samuel had Eli as a mentor, it is important for you to find a more experienced Christian to guide you as you listen for the Lord. When you do hear something, he or she will help you to know if you are really hearing from God or not. With a mentor's help, you will soon be able to recognize the Holy Spirit's leading in your life and you will know how to seek and receive the guidance you need.

God most often chooses to speak to us in our conscious minds through the Holy Spirit and through the Bible. As you grow in your ability to discern and respond to his whispered voice, you will not just receive the wisdom you need, you will also gain a deeper intimacy with the God who loves you so much. May God increase your hunger to know him and hear him today.

One of the first steps to knowing God's voice in my life has been reading his Word. As I began to read the Bible daily, it became clearer to me what God's voice sounded like because I had heard it through his Word.

Peter Furler

Lesson from the Book of First Samuel:
SAMUEL'S INFLUENCE

The Lord was with Samuel as he grew up, and he let none of his words fall to the ground. And all Israel from Dan to Beersheba recognized that Samuel was attested as a prophet of the Lord. The Lord continued to appear at Shiloh, and there he revealed himself to Samuel through his word.

1 SAMUEL 3:19–21

MAY 23

Things were changing at Shiloh. A growing sense of God's presence filled the tabernacle. And old Eli knew what was happening. His wicked sons had so grieved the heart of God that he had begun to withdraw his presence from the tabernacle. But now, for the first time in years, Eli's heart began to hope again as he saw things change. He knew as Samuel continued to grow in his relationship with the Lord, God's presence would grow with him. Whenever God finds a faithful man or woman with an open heart, the intimate companionship it produces is marked by God's presence and power.

After years of progressively withdrawing his presence from the tabernacle at Shiloh, the Lord returned in power and might because he had finally found a person with whom he could fellowship. One young person's relationship with God was affecting a whole nation. Samuel's faithfulness was counteracting the effects of the sin of Eli's wicked sons and the apathy and unbelief of Israel. God was visiting his people again.

If young Samuel's new and growing relationship with God could affect the spiritual life of a whole nation, what might he do through you? When you simply open your heart to God like Samuel did, your school, campus, neighborhood, or workplace could be radically impacted by God's pres-

ence. When you are willing to seek God with all your heart, nothing in this world can stop him from coming to be with you—and his presence comes with great blessing that will spill out to all around you. May God stir your heart to seek him passionately today!

GOD DOESN'T NEED CHRISTIAN ROCK STARS, TREND-SETTERS, OR FISHES ON CARS. ALL he NEEDS is the FAITHFUL AND the OBEDIENT to TURN the WORLD UPSIDE DOWN.

Peter Furler

Lessons from the Book of First Samuel:
ICHABOD'S BIRTH

[Eli's] daughter-in-law, the wife of Phinehas, was pregnant and near the time of delivery. When she heard the news that the ark of God had been captured and that her father-in-law and her husband were dead, she went into labor and gave birth, but was overcome by her labor pains. As she was dying, the women attending her said, "Don't despair; you have given birth to a son." But she did not respond or pay any attention.

She named the boy Ichabod, saying, "The glory has departed from Israel"—because of the capture of the ark of God and the deaths of her father-in-law and her husband.

1 SAMUEL 4:19–21

MAY 24

It was one of the darkest days in Israel's history. Eli, the high priest, and his two sons, Hophni and Phinehas, were dead and the Philistines army had captured the Ark of the Covenant. When Phinehas' pregnant wife heard the news, the shock sent her into labor. Tragically, the grim news she had received, combined with a difficult delivery, were more than her weary spirit could bear. She was dying. The midwives attempted to rouse her out of her deathly despair with the news that the baby was a son, but even that was not enough to save her. With her last breath, she cursed her own child by calling him Ichabod, which means "the glory has departed from Israel."

Even as the news of her husband's death began this young woman's labor pains, many times God "births" new life in us through pain. Sometimes it takes coming to the edge of divorce to help a couple give birth

to a deeper and more solid marriage. A new passion for God is often born out of the pain of a time of running from God. Time after time, I have watched God bring life out of death in wonderful ways.

This process, though, is not without danger. Phinehas' wife was so overwhelmed by her pain, that she lost sight of the hope she could have in the life of her new son. When God is bringing you through the "delivery" of new life out of some crisis or tragedy, you will have to choose whether this time will be defined by your *pain* or by God's *promises*. Holding on to God's promises in these painful moments will keep you from being overwhelmed.

Because Phinehas's wife lost sight of the promise of new life and instead focused on the pain, she cursed the blessing she was receiving. Ichabod means "no glory." As far as she was concerned, the death of Eli and his sons, as well as the capture of the Ark, was the end of the nation she loved and any hope for the future of her child. In reality however, their deaths would usher in the age of Samuel and David, who would lead Israel into her greatest years of glory. When we face terrible heartaches we feel as if all our hopes and dreams are dead. Like the wife of Phinehas, you simply want to quit. You have even been tempted to curse the precious new life God is creating for you. If this is where you are today, don't give in to the despair. The great pain you are experiencing is a sign of the even greater promise that will follow it.

The closer pain brings us to God, the more God will use it for his glory.

Peter Furler

Lessons from the Book of First Samuel:

THE POWER OF HIS PRESENCE

After the Philistines had captured the ark of God, they took it from Ebenezer to Ashdod.... The Lord's hand was heavy upon the people of Ashdod and its vicinity; he brought devastation upon them and afflicted them with tumors....

The Philistines called for the priests and the diviners and said, "What shall we do with the ark of the Lord? Tell us how we should send it back to its place."...

"Get a new cart ready, with two cows that have calved and have never been yoked. Hitch the cows to the cart, but take their calves away and pen them up. Take the ark of the Lord and put it on the cart.... If it goes up to its own territory, toward Beth Shemesh, then the Lord has brought this great disaster on us."

So they did this.... Then the cows went straight up toward Beth Shemesh, keeping on the road and lowing all the way; they did not turn to the right or to the left.

1 SAMUEL 5:1, 6; 6:2, 7–10, 12

MAY 25

The Philistines had celebrated prematurely. When they had defeated Israel's armies, they also thought they had defeated Israel's God. Now, because of the horrible plagues and infestation of rats, they knew they had made a big mistake. In order to discern the source of the calamities they were experiencing, the priests and diviners of the Philistines devised a strange test. Philistine soldiers were ordered to find two wild cows. These cows, totally unbroken, were to be hitched to a cart. Then their calves were to be taken away from them and pinned up in a place where they could still be seen and heard. Finally the Ark of the Covenant was to be placed in the cart. If the two cows would leave their calves and pull the cart all the way back to Israel, the Philistines would know they had been judged by Israel's God.

With the rulers of the Philistines following them, the cows pulled the Ark all the way to Israel without straying from the road even once. As the Philistine rulers watched they began to tremble with fear. They knew beyond the shadow of a doubt Israel's God had indeed been judging them.

What lessons can we learn from this strange story? First of all, the judgments of God alone are not enough to transform a culture. Like the leaders of the Philistines, the people of our world will not believe until they see the power of God to transform. People need to see that we are different because of the Lord.

Second, if the Ark of the Covenant had the power to transform two dumb cows, how much more power does Jesus Christ have to transform you? When we struggle in our Christian lives, we need to remember that the power of heaven is alive in our hearts and can do amazing things through us.

Third, when the Philistine rulers saw God's transforming power, they followed the cart all the way to Israel's borders. God's light shining in our lives will draw people to follow us too—and that is when we have the opportunity to lead them to the foot of the cross.

The same God who changed wild cows into evidence of his power wants to transform you into a light for him. Just as he caused cows to rise above their natural instincts for his purposes, he will free you from your sinful nature and give you access to the fullness of Christ.

Jesus transformed fishermen into church leaders; thieves into the trustworthy; adulterers into the faithful; liars into voices of truth. Transformation is attractive and contagious!

Peter Furler

Lessons from the Book of First Samuel:
SAUL'S DONKEYS

[Saul was] an impressive young man without equal among the Israelites—a head taller than any of the others. Now the donkeys belonging to Saul's father Kish were lost, and Kish said to his son Saul, "Take one of the servants with you and go and look for the donkeys."...

When they reached the district of Zuph, Saul said to the servant ..., "Come, let's go back, or my father will ... start worrying about us."

But the servant replied, "Look, in this town there is a man of God; he is highly respected, and everything he says comes true.... Perhaps he will tell us what way to take...."

When Samuel caught sight of Saul, the Lord said to him, "This is the man I spoke to you about; he will govern my people." Saul approached Samuel ... and asked, "Would you please tell me where the seer's house is?"

"I am the seer," Samuel replied. "Go up ahead of me to the high place, for today you are to eat with me, and in the morning I will let you go and will tell you all that is in your heart.... And to whom is all the desire of Israel turned, if not to you and all your father's family?"

1 SAMUEL 9:2–3; 5–6; 17–20

MAY 26

On the outside, young Saul was a giant of a man, a head taller than any other person in Israel. On the inside, though, he was deeply insecure himself. He came from a small tribe with little status. But in spite of his low self-esteem, he was soon to become Israel's first king. Kingship was the last thing on his mind as our story begins; in fact, Saul was far more concerned about finding his father's lost donkeys than he was with finding his destiny. After searching for three days with no luck, Saul's servant finally suggested that they talk to Samuel, the great seer. When Saul and his servant arrived at Samuel's house, the great prophet was waiting for them. God had told Samuel that the man he was going to anoint as king would come to see him. Although young Saul didn't believe it when Samuel first told him about his calling to become king, the miraculous signs he received in confirmation gave Saul the faith he needed to accept God's will for his life.

Even as God used the loss of his family's donkeys to bring Saul into his destiny, so God will use the natural circumstances in your life to show you your purpose. Saul would never have come to Samuel unless he had lost something of value that he could not find on his own. And sometimes we will be motivated to seek the Lord through loss of something we value or because of the desire for something we cannot get on our own. When we lose our health or our job, we are driven to seek God for healing and provision. Or maybe we are longing to find that person who will become our spouse and we know that only God can bring us a true love. Whatever your loss or your longing, God in his wisdom will use these needs to bring us into his purposes.

AND we know that in ALL things GOD WORKS FOR the GOOD of those who Love Him, who hAve Been CALLED ACCORDing to His pURpOSE" (ROMANS 8:28). Even in SAUL'S SEARCh FOR his fATheRS' DONKEYS, GOD WAS WORKING to BRing him into his pURpose.

Peter Furler

Lessons from the Book of First Samuel:
SAUL'S PROVISION

Samuel took a flask of oil and poured it on Saul's head and kissed him, saying, "Has not the LORD anointed you leader over his inheritance? When you leave me today, you will meet two men near Rachel's tomb.... They will say to you, 'The donkeys you set out to look for have been found. And now your father has stopped thinking about them and is worried about you. He is asking, 'What shall I do about my son?'

"Then you will go on from there until you reach the great tree of Tabor. Three men going up to God at Bethel will meet you there. One will be carrying three young goats, another three loaves of bread, and another a skin of wine. They will greet you and offer you two loaves of bread, which you will accept from them. After that you will go to Gibeah of God, where there is a Philistine outpost. As you approach the town, you will meet a procession of prophets coming down from the high place with lyres, tambourines, flutes and harps being played before them, and they will be prophesying. The Spirit of the LORD will come upon you in power, and you will prophesy with them; and you will be changed into a different person. Once these signs are fulfilled, do whatever your hand finds to do, for God is with you."

1 SAMUEL 10:1–7

MAY 27

Samuel slowly raised the flask of anointing oil and poured it on Saul's head. With the holy oil of God running down his face and Samuel continuing to call out the words of his destiny, Saul felt for a moment that he had been trans-

ported into another world. After helping Saul to his feet, Samuel described three other supernatural signs Saul would receive, confirming God's calling on his life: the knowledge of the lost donkeys, material provision, and an incredible encounter with a group of prophets—which would change Saul into a different man.

In these three miraculous signs that brought undeniable confirmation to Saul, we also find three lessons for our lives today. First, even as Saul heard that his father's donkeys had been found, so God will meet your particular need as you submit to his overall purpose for your life. Furthermore, the very fact that the first sign took place at Rachel's tomb was also significant. Rachel, one of the most illustrious women in Israel's history, was the mother of Benjamin, who was the patriarch of Saul's tribe. In this encounter, God was touching Saul's insecurities about his family by reminding him of the honorable origins of his tribe.

Second, when Saul reached the great tree of Tabor, he met three men who were going to seek God at Bethel. Between them, these men were carrying three young goats, three loaves of bread, and a skin of wine. As they gave some of these provisions to Saul, God was showing him that he would provide. You, too, will never lack provision as you follow God with all your heart.

Third, when Saul encountered the prophets at Gibeah, he was so impacted by the power of God that he also began to prophesy. As he was prophesying, Scripture records that he was changed into a different person. As you are willing to follow God, he will change you into the person you need to be to fulfill your destiny—the person you were born to be. May you find joy and strength in that fact that the God who provided so miraculously for Saul is your God as well.

"I WAS YOUNG AND now I'm OLD, yet I hAVe never seen the RiGHTeous FORSAKen OR their CHiLDRen BeGGiNG BREAD" (PSALM 37:25). When we Give ouRSeLVes to GOD he GiVes us ALL we neeD in RetuRn.
Peter Furler

Lessons from the Book of First Samuel:
SAUL'S BAGGAGE

 [Samuel said], "And to whom is all the desire of Israel turned, if not to you and all your father's family?"

Saul answered, "But am I not a Benjamite, from the smallest tribe of Israel, and is not my clan the least of all the clans of the tribe of Benjamin? Why do you say such a thing to me?"

1 SAMUEL 9:20–21

Samuel summoned the people of Israel to the Lord at Mizpah.... "Present yourselves before the Lord by your tribes and clans." ... Then he brought forward the tribe of Benjamin, clan by clan, and Matri's clan was chosen. Finally Saul son of Kish was chosen. But when they looked for him, he was not to be found.

So they inquired further of the Lord, "Has the man come here yet?"

And the Lord said, "Yes, he has hidden himself among the baggage." They ran and brought him out, and as he stood among the people he was a head taller than any of the others.

Samuel said to all the people, "Do you see the man the Lord has chosen? There is no one like him among all the people." Then the people shouted, "Long live the king!"

1 SAMUEL 10:17, 19, 21–24

MAY 28

All day the nation had been waiting to meet the man who would be their king. When Samuel brought all the tribes of Israel together, the tribe of Benjamin had been selected. From Benjamin, Samuel had gone clan by clan until the

family of Matri had been chosen. Finally he called out the name, "Saul, son of Kish!" But Saul was nowhere to be found. As the people grumbled, Samuel began to seek the Lord about Saul's whereabouts. God answered him saying, "Saul has hidden himself among the baggage." After they had pulled Saul out of his hiding place, Samuel introduced him to his new subjects. When the people saw this tall, handsome young man they shouted, "Long live the king!"

Why was Saul hiding from his destiny among the baggage? His reasons were the same as ours when we hide from God's purpose for us. While Saul was hiding in actual baggage—piles of clothing and supplies—he, like many of us, was also hiding behind his spiritual baggage. These are the emotional wounds, wrecked dreams, and shattered hopes that make us feel that we aren't fit for our destiny. Spiritual baggage does not come from God—it is piled on us by the enemy. So, just as Samuel sent men to pull Saul from the baggage, so God will send his Holy Spirit and other Christians to pull you out of your baggage.

Another important part of this story is that Saul hid himself among the baggage—it didn't just fall on top of him. He had to purposely climb into it. You may feel as if the baggage of your past is holding on to you. In reality, however, you are holding on to it. And the good news is that when you are holding on to something you have the power to let go of it as well. It may not be easy. You may need God's help to pry your hands open and release it. But know that, once you let go, the freedom you'll find in Jesus will be well worth the struggle.

LOOK to the WORD, Listen to the HOLY SpiRit. REACH OUT YOUR hANDS to YOUR SpiRitUAL FAMily AND come OUT FROM UNDER the BAGGAGE. FREEDOM is ONLY A Step OF FAith AWAY.

Peter Furler

Lessons from the Book of First Samuel:
SAUL'S FAILURE

Saul remained at Gilgal, and all the troops with him were quaking with fear. He waited seven days, the time set by Samuel; but Samuel did not come to Gilgal, and Saul's men began to scatter.

So he said, "Bring me the burnt offering and the fellowship offerings." And Saul offered up the burnt offering. Just as he finished making the offering, Samuel arrived, and Saul went out to greet him.

"What have you done?" asked Samuel.

Saul replied, "When I saw that the men were scattering, and that you did not come at the set time … I felt compelled to offer the burnt offering."

"You acted foolishly," Samuel said. "You have not kept the command the Lord your God gave you; if you had, he would have established your kingdom over Israel for all time. But now your kingdom will not endure."

1 SAMUEL 13:7–14

MAY 29

Saul was in the worst crisis of his young kingship. With thousands of Philistine soldiers surrounding his small army, his men were deserting him—hiding and running for their lives. Now, with the remainder of his army sticking with him, but quaking in fear, Saul decided to take matters into his own hands. He had waited the full seven days that Samuel had instructed him to wait and yet the prophet still hadn't shown up. Maybe he had been captured or even killed by the Philistines! Surely Samuel would expect him to use his own initiative. So going against Samuel's express orders, Saul sacrificed to the Lord on his own.

Just as he was completing the sacrifices, Samuel arrived. When he saw that Saul had not waited for him, he was heartbroken. "Saul, you have been foolish," Samuel said. "Because you have not learned to wait upon the Lord, your kingdom will not last."

Like Saul, when we are hard pressed by the crises in our lives, we have a natural tendency to panic and take matters into our own hands. We decide not to tithe because we are in a financial crisis. We quit a ministry because the going gets rough instead of seeking God's strength and guidance. Saul's story has become the story of many Christians over the years.

In this story we also find the frustration and mystery associated with trying to understand God's timing. When Samuel did not show up in seven 24-hour days, Saul gave up on him. Maybe Samuel had meant the number seven to be symbolic since, in Scripture, it is used as an expression of completion of perfection. The reason for his delay isn't really important, though. Saul was told what to do and he disobeyed—that's the bottom line.

To avoid the same mistake, we need to understand that God's timing is not our timing. What we think should happen tomorrow sometimes takes years. On the other hand, what we would like to put off for years may be what God is calling us to do today. Our job is not to understand the when of God's will—it is to obey it. His promises to you *will* be fulfilled, but in his time, not yours.

Saul's story also shows us that God takes our impatience personally. Because Saul didn't wait on the Lord it cost him the kingdom. When you run ahead of God you are actually trying to *be* God yourself—you are attempting to do what only he can do.

Learn from Saul's mistake. Don't second guess God's timing. Follow him and don't run ahead. The waiting will be worth it in the end.

Not waiting on God is distrust. Not walking with God results in restlessness. Not following God is foolish. Saul made all three of these mistakes and it cost him everything.

Peter Furler

Lessons from the Book of First Samuel:
JONATHAN'S ATTACK

Jonathan said to his young armor-bearer, "Come, let's go over to the outpost of those uncircumcised fellows. Perhaps the LORD will act in our behalf. Nothing can hinder the LORD from saving, whether by many or by few."

"Do all that you have in mind," his armor-bearer said. "Go ahead; I am with you heart and soul."

Jonathan said, "Come, then; we will cross over toward the men and let them see us. If they say to us, 'Wait there until we come to you,' we will stay where we are and not go up to them. But if they say, 'Come up to us,' we will climb up, because that will be our sign that the LORD has given them into our hands." So both of them showed themselves to the Philistine outpost.

"Look!" said the Philistines. "The Hebrews are crawling out of the holes they were hiding in." The men of the outpost shouted to Jonathan and his armor-bearer, "Come up to us and we'll teach you a lesson."

So Jonathan said to his armor-bearer, "Climb up after me; the LORD has given them into the hand of Israel." Jonathan climbed up, using his hands and feet, with his armor-bearer right behind him. The Philistines fell before Jonathan, and his armor-bearer followed and killed behind him.

1 SAMUEL 14:6-13

MAY 30

While Israel's army was paralyzed with fear, one young man and his courageous armor-bearer decided to rise up and win the day. The name of the young man was Jonathan; he was the son of Saul and the prince of Israel. Their

battle was not just dangerous—it was absurd. So absurd, in fact, that it would only work because God had devised it.

The Philistine outpost was perched high on the cliffs making it impossible to approach without being spotted and killed. And even if Jonathan and his armor-bearer could reach the top, they would be horribly outnumbered. Yet, out of a courage forged by faith in their God, the two young men set out on this impossible task. They had only asked for one sign: "Lord, if the Philistines taunt us by saying, 'Climb up to us,' let that be a sign that you have given them over to Israel." Not a very convincing sign when you really think about it! Through the eyes of faith, however, what seemed to be a logical response from the Philistines became a sign from God to attack. Once they miraculously reached the top of the cliff, Jonathan and the armor-bearer began to slaughter the Philistine garrison. Then the Lord struck the Philistine armies with a violent earthquake, and they ran for their lives.

Jonathan faced impossible odds. And we will many times face spiritual enemies that seem too strong to overcome. But if we will trust God and obey him, we have every reason to believe that he can change our world through us. When we take a leap of faith, and assault the enemy's fortresses, we will find they are not as invincible as we thought.

And with that leap of faith will come a release of God's power that will shake the enemy's foundations. God sent an earthquake when Jonathan and his armor-bearer trusted and went into battle! What might he do for you when you do the same? God will give us the power we need to change our world—all we need is faith and the willingness to obey him.

"There is no wisdom, no insight, no plan that can succeed against the Lord" (Proverbs 21:30). Jonathan's faith in God's plan brought him a great victory.

Peter Furler

Lessons from the Book of First Samuel:
SAUL'S REJECTION

Then Saul attacked the Amalekites.... Saul and the army spared Agag and the best of the sheep and cattle, the fat calves and lambs — everything that was good ... but everything that was despised and weak they totally destroyed. Then the word of the Lord came to Samuel: "I am grieved that I have made Saul king, because he has turned away from me and has not carried out my instructions...."

[Samuel said to Saul]: "Why did you not obey the Lord?... You have rejected the word of the Lord, and the Lord has rejected you as king over Israel!"

1 SAMUEL 15:7, 9–11, 19, 26

MAY 31

The Lord's instructions to Saul had been very specific. He was to totally destroy the Amalekites. Nothing, including their livestock, was to be spared. Saul slaughtered their army, but he spared the life of Agag, their king. He also kept the finest livestock, rationalizing his disobedience by devoting them to be sacrifices to the Lord.

When Samuel heard from God what Saul had done, he was both heartbroken and angry. "Why didn't you obey the Lord?" he asked Saul.

"I thought God would be pleased with my sacrifices," Saul whimpered.

"God wants your obedience more than your sacrifices," Samuel answered angrily. Saul pleaded with Samuel to forgive him. With a piercing gaze, Samuel told Saul that God had rejected him as king over Israel. Then he turned his back on Saul and began to walk away. Saul grabbed him so forcibly that the hem of his robe was torn. Turning once again toward the

fallen king, Samuel released God's prophetic judgment like an arrow into Saul's rebellious heart: "The Lord has torn the kingdom of Israel from you today and has given it to one of your neighbors" (verse 28).

Saul's story is a dramatic and tragic account of the results of disobeying God. The beginning of Saul's downfall came when he spared the best of the livestock because he was only willing to kill that which was "despised and weak." When we are only willing to give up the things in our lives that we see as worthless anyway, we are being just as disobedient as Saul. We find it pretty easy to give up sins that are making us feel depressed and weak. But what about those sinful things that we honestly find fun, entertaining, or pleasurable? We know that we shouldn't be dating that unbelieving guy or girl, but he or she is just so good-looking. We know we shouldn't sit and gossip with our friends, but it's so fun when you have juicy news to spread. God never said we could keep the "fun sins" and just give him the ones that make us feel bad. He requires us to rid ourselves of every sin if we are to have a relationship with him.

Saul deceived himself, through his rebellion, into believing that he was pleasing God, even while he was being disobedient. It's easy for us to do the same. God, through his Word and the conviction of the Holy Spirit, must be the final authority over what is right and wrong in our lives. And sometimes God will also use another Christian to challenge us about the stuff we're holding on to. It's never fun or easy to be made aware of your sin, but it is necessary if you are to avoid sin's consequences—which are even more painful. Remember that "fun sin" will eventually hurt you just as much as any other. Search your heart carefully today and ask God to help you kill *all* the roots of sin in your life.

"THERE IS A WAY THAT SEEMS RIGHT TO A MAN BUT IN THE END IT LEADS TO DEATH" (PROVERBS 14:12). LIKE MANY CHRISTIANS, SAUL FELT HIS PARTIAL OBEDIENCE WOULD SATISFY GOD'S COMMANDS—BUT FULL OBEDIENCE IS THE ONLY WAY TO PLEASE THE LORD.

Peter Furler

Lessons from the Book of First Samuel:
SAMUEL'S RENEWAL

The LORD said to Samuel, "How long will you mourn for Saul, since I have rejected him as king over Israel? Fill your horn with oil and be on your way; I am sending you to Jesse of Bethlehem. I have chosen one of his sons to be king."

1 SAMUEL 16:1

JUNE 1

Saul's downfall had broken Samuel's heart. In spite of the young man's rebellion and insecurities, the prophet had loved him like a son. When Samuel felt the presence of God begin to stir in his heart, he rose to his feet, but his spirits did not rise with him. "Samuel," the Lord called out, "how long will you grieve over what is gone forever?" With tears streaming down his face, Samuel fell on his knees before the Lord. And then he heard the words that would revive his broken heart and prove that his life had not been in vain. Samuel was to go to Bethlehem for there he would anoint the new king.

Like Samuel, are you still mourning over some loss in your life? It may be time for you to let go of the past and face the promise of your future. While grieving over a loss is natural, and something we must do before we can move on, there comes a time when God will call us to get back on the path and head into the new life he has for us.

In preparation for his trip to Bethlehem, God told Samuel to fill his anointing horn with oil. Before we set out on the road toward our new life, we too should be freshly filled with the power and might of the Holy Spirit. His strength will enable you to walk away from the grief and sorrows of your past. Take time to worship, study God's Word, and spend time talking to the Lord. Through these things, God will fill you with Spirit and with strength for your journey.

As a replacement for the loss he had experienced, Samuel received a new mission. When you lose something precious, God will give you a fresh vision for your future and a new mission to bring you hope. As you let go of your sorrow and receive a fresh filling of the Holy Spirit's power and joy, God will set you on his path of purpose and help you walk confidently toward your new life.

Just as Samuel filled his anointing horn with oil, we too must open ourselves to God's refreshing through setting aside a specific time, preferably morning, to meet with Him one on one.

Phil Joel

Lessons from the Book of First Samuel:
DAVID'S ANOINTING

Jesse had seven of his sons pass before Samuel, but Samuel said to him, "The Lord has not chosen these." So he asked Jesse, "Are these all the sons you have?"

"There is still the youngest," Jesse answered, "but he is tending the sheep."

Samuel said, "Send for him; we will not sit down until he arrives." So he sent and had him brought in....

Then the Lord said, "Rise and anoint him; he is the one."

1 SAMUEL 16:10 – 12

JUNE 2

Young David's thoughts were back home, where the great prophet, Samuel, was visiting. As the baby of the family, he was stuck with sheep duty so the rest of his brothers could meet the man of God. "It's not fair," he sighed to himself. To console himself, he picked up his harp and began to worship God.

His song was interrupted by one of the household servants. "David!" the servant yelled, "Come quickly! The prophet is waiting for you! He has told your father he will not even sit down until he meets you."

Samuel waited anxiously for David's arrival. He'd met all the rest of Jesse's tall, powerfully built sons, and God had rejected each one in turn. When the breathless teenager finally appeared before him, Samuel knew that he was looking at the hope of his nation. Samuel asked David to kneel before him. When the anointing oil began to cover David, the Spirit of the Lord came on him.

Do you feel like David sometimes—left out and treated unfairly because you are young? It's hard to be the one who is always missing out and being left behind. Remember, though, that this won't last forever. One day, God is going to come to you with your "big break" so use this time of waiting to prepare yourself. Then you'll be ready, like David was, to run when God calls your name.

And just like Samuel, who would not even sit down until he had met with David, God is standing and waiting for you. You are precious and important to the Lord—he's given you special gifts that only you can use. When you hear him call, know that he will be waiting for you with open arms when you come running.

And while Jesse's other sons certainly looked to be much more qualified for ruling Israel than a shepherd boy like David, they were not God's chosen ones. People may judge your ability to be effective for God by your age or even your looks, but God sees far beyond all of that. He looks into the depths of the heart and calls people who love him deeply. Those are the people he can use in powerful ways!

So remember—God is not concerned with your family background, appearance, education or finances. He cares most about the state of your soul. If you are open to his will and purpose then you are more than qualified for his call. In the end, you see, it is these things that are your destiny.

PATIENCE IS OFTEN THE KEY TO ALLOWING GOD'S WAY TO RULE IN OUR LIVES. HIS TIMING IS ALWAYS BEST. BE DILIGENT IN YOUR PURSUIT OF GOD THROUGH HIS WORD, WORSHIP AND FELLOWSHIP. BUT DON'T BE LURED INTO FAST-TRACKING GOD'S PLAN FOR YOUR LIFE. PATIENTLY SEEK HIM, BEING CONFIDENT THAT HIS WAYS AND TIMING ARE BEST.

Phil Joel

Lessons from the Book of First Samuel:
DAVID'S MUSIC

The Spirit of the LORD had departed from Saul, and an evil spirit from the LORD tormented him. Saul's attendants said to him, "See, an evil spirit from God is tormenting you. Let our lord command his servants here to search for someone who can play the harp. He will play when the evil spirit from God comes upon you, and you will feel better."

So Saul said to his attendants, "Find someone who plays well and bring him to me." ... Whenever the spirit from God came upon Saul, David would take his harp and play. Then relief would come to Saul; he would feel better, and the evil spirit would leave him.

1 SAMUEL 16:14–17, 23

JUNE 3

Saul had been tormented by the devil since the day he had rebelled against God's command to totally destroy the Amalekites. At times the depression, despair, and anger he felt threatened to crush him to death. Saul's servants and friends had done everything they could think of to help him, but at times, his rage grew so great that they feared for their lives. Finally, someone suggested that music might help. "Find me someone who is skilled on the harp," Saul agreed. One of the servants had heard of David's skill on the harp, and so the newly anointed king came to minister to the rejected one.

When David walked into Saul's court for the first time, he was immediately confronted with the darkness and despair filling the broken king. David had faced and defeated both a lion and a bear, but this was much worse. After bowing before the king, David began to strum his harp. As

the songs of God's protection, power, and might began to flow out of his lips, the atmosphere of the room was changed. Saul's court was amazed at the difference. Saul, too, visibly relaxed—a peace came over him that he hadn't had in a long time. He was actually smiling again.

This story demonstrates the great spiritual power of music. If one young man on a harp could lift the demonic depression of a rebellious king, how much more can singing in worship and praise do for you? You have a wonderful, show-stopping voice, or a voice that stops the show for an entirely different reason—it doesn't matter. If you worship from your heart, God's joy, power, and delight will come to you. In my own life, I have found worshipful music plays a critical role in my spiritual development. When I am under the attack of the enemy, praising God with song sends him running. I learned long ago, too, that the music I listen to can have a huge affect on my attitude and outlook. You've probably noticed the same thing. So fill your house or car with songs of praise today and you'll find yourself filled with God's joy and peace.

We are a spiritual people. We must feed on things that will nurture us and edify us. Music is a tool and a resource that can lead us into greater depths of intimacy with God and build our faith. It's power goes far beyond what we can see and hear because it has a tremendous affect in the invisible realm as well.

Phil Joel

Lessons from the Book of First Samuel:
THE GIANT

A champion named Goliath, who was from Gath, came out of the Philistine camp. He was over nine feet tall. He had a bronze helmet on his head and wore a coat of scale armor of bronze weighing five thousand shekels, on his legs he wore bronze greaves, and a bronze javelin was slung on his back. His spear shaft was like a weaver's rod, and its iron point weighed six hundred shekels. His shield bearer went ahead of him. Goliath stood and shouted to the ranks of Israel, "Why do you come out and line up for battle? Am I not a Philistine, and are you not the servants of Saul? Choose a man and have him come down to me. If he is able to fight and kill me, we will become your subjects; but if I overcome him and kill him, you will become our subjects and serve us." Then the Philistine said, "This day I defy the ranks of Israel! Give me a man and let us fight each other." On hearing the Philistine's words, Saul and all the Israelites were dismayed and terrified…. For forty days the Philistine came forward every morning and evening and took his stand.

1 SAMUEL 17: 4–11, 16

JUNE 4

He was more monster than man. At over nine feet tall, the armor-clad champion of the Philistines had never been defeated in combat. He was a being of mythological proportions; there was not a man alive who would dare face him. For forty days, he had been taunting the armies of Israel. "Give me a man to fight with," he would bellow, as he cursed the God of Israel. Every time the priests would make their sacrifices, Israel's worship would be interrupted by the defiant challenges of this invincible giant.

As for Saul and the armies of Israel, they were terrified. Goliath was calling for a trial by combat, a fight between two men that would decide the fate of both armies. While the armies of Israel sat paralyzed in fear, a young teenager entered the valley. His name was David, and he would hear the voice of destiny in the giant's taunts when everyone else heard the voice of doom.

Just as Israel faced a giant, so the body of Christ today faces giant spiritual enemies. Giants like substance abuse, false spirituality, and the anti-God philosophy that seems so "cool" right now all threaten to destroy people's souls. Like Goliath these giants seem invincible.

Goliath taunted Israel for forty days. In Scripture, the number forty often symbolizes a time of testing and trial (the rains of the flood lasted forty days and nights and Jesus was tempted by Satan for forty days in the desert). Like Israel, when I am faced with a time of testing, it seems like no matter what I do, the enemy's challenge is constantly in my face. Even when I try to read my Bible or pray, I can still hear the devil's whispered lies. God allows this challenge though, to make me strong. The Lord is forcing me into a fight, because he knows that when I fight at his side, I will win.

While all of Saul's army heard the voice of doom in Goliath's challenge, David heard the sound of God's call. Many times, God will allow the sin and pain around us to become so oppressive that we have no choice but to rise up and make a difference—to fight. May God bring you to that place as you face the giants of our world today.

AS I READ this I find myself saying, "It's on!" There's A BATTLE RAGING AND I REFUSE to BE intimidateD. "LORD, use me!"
Phil Joel

Lessons from the Book of First Samuel:
DAVID'S PREPARATION

 David said to Saul, "Let no one lose heart on account of this Philistine; your servant will go and fight him."

Saul replied, "You are not able to go out against this Philistine and fight him; you are only a boy."...

But David said to Saul,... "When a lion or a bear came and carried off a sheep from the flock, I went after it,... and killed it. Your servant has killed both the lion and the bear; this uncircumcised Philistine will be like one of them, because he has defied the armies of the living God. The LORD who delivered me from the paw of the lion and the paw of the bear will deliver me from the hand of this Philistine."

Saul said to David, "Go, and the LORD be with you." Then Saul ... put a coat of armor on him and a bronze helmet on his head. David ... tried walking around, because he was not used to them. "I cannot go in these," he said to Saul, "because I am not used to them." So he took them off.

1 SAMUEL 17:32 – 39

JUNE 5

David burned to go to war against the Philistines. But once again, he was left at home with the sheep. Now as he approached the battle lines to bring food to his brothers, he heard Goliath's mocking challenge for the first time. How dare this foul creature defy the armies of the living God? If no one else would fight him, David would!

When he was taken before Saul to make his declaration, the king gave him the brush-off. "You're only a boy. What hope do you have against this invincible giant?"

"I have already killed a lion and a bear," David replied. "This giant will be no different because he has defied the armies of the almighty God." Saul shrugged his shoulders and decided to let the kid try. He offered David his own armor for the battle, but after trying it on, David took it off and left it. He wasn't used to it and it would only hold him back. With the fate of his nation now resting on his shoulders, the young man left Saul's tent and approached the Philistine ranks.

We can learn a lot from David and his bold faith. First of all, David was not intimidated by Goliath's size. David knew that God was his only hope for victory, so size just didn't matter. Once you realize the enormity and power of the God you serve, you won't be threatened by the size of your enemies either.

Second, although the giant was a far greater challenge than either the bear or lion he had once killed, David knew the same God who had given him strength in the past would be more than sufficient to destroy the monster that he now faced. The giants we face may grow larger over the years, but the principles and promises we used to defeat to them in the past will still bring us victory in the future because they are based on our unchangeable God.

Finally, David's refusal to wear Saul's armor was an important part of his victory. As tempting as the offer may have been, David realized that he couldn't go to war wearing armor he didn't know how to use. And you will only be able to defeat your enemy with the weapons that you have practice using. In other words, if you have not been praying, worshiping, and reading the Bible on a regular basis, you won't be able to use them as weapons in a time of crisis. So take time to do some battle training before the battle comes. Then you'll fight your giant with confidence from the Lord, just like David.

THERE IS SO MUCH in this STORY AND once AGAIN I feel my FAITH Rise up AS I ReReAD this AMAZiNG ACCOUNT. "LORD, LEAD me in GREATER pRepARATion to Be A GiANT SLAYer."

Phil Joel

Lessons from the Book of First Samuel:

DAVID'S VICTORY OVER GOLIATH

[Goliath] said to David, "Am I a dog, that you come at me with sticks?" And the Philistine cursed David by his gods. "Come here," he said, "and I'll give your flesh to the birds of the air and the beasts of the field!"

David said to the Philistine,… "This day the LORD will hand you over to me, and I'll strike you down and cut off your head … and the whole world will know that there is a God in Israel."…

David ran quickly toward the battle line to meet [Goliath.] Reaching into his bag and taking out a stone, he slung it and struck the Philistine on the forehead. The stone sank into his forehead, and he fell facedown on the ground. So David triumphed over the Philistine with a sling and a stone; without a sword in his hand he struck down the Philistine and killed him.… [David] took hold of the Philistine's sword and … cut off his head.… When the Philistines saw that their hero was dead, they turned and ran.

1 SAMUEL 17:43–46, 48–51

JUNE 6

Both armies were shaking their heads in disbelief. Who was this young teenager challenging the greatest warrior any of them had ever seen? When Goliath saw David, he actually felt insulted: "Am I a dog, that you would threaten me with a small stick?" As he lumbered toward David he cursed him in the names of his gods.

Although he could see his huge foe coming, David was far more conscious of the power of the Lord filling his body. With words that came straight from the Holy Spirit, David answered the giant's threats with a

challenge of his own: "This day, by the power of God, I will strike you down and behead you."

Goliath was a powerful giant, but for David his size only meant a bigger target. With a stone between his eyes, Goliath toppled to the ground. Then David took Goliath's own sword and chopped off his giant head. The Philistines fled for their lives with the armies of Israel in full pursuit.

The story of David and Goliath is one of those stories we all know. But even if you've heard it a hundred times, there are new insights to be found. First, instead of waiting to be attacked, David initiated the conflict. In our lives there are times when we too must charge the enemy before he has a chance to charge us.

Second, it's interesting to note that David told Goliath that he was going to cut off his head and he didn't even have a sword. He was inspired by the prophetic words of the Lord and he had the faith that God would make them come true. When we speak the words of God in faith, he can make even the impossible come true for us as well

Lastly, isn't it incredible that David seemed to have no fear of defeat? He had been born for this moment and because he trusted God, he was given the assurance that he would not fail at his appointed task. Ephesians 2:10 describes these tasks as *"works which God prepared in advance for us to do."* Like David, you also have divine purpose—the reason you were put on this earth. When you discover your purpose, you will also discover the power of God to fulfill that purpose, no matter how impossible it may seem. May God give you the grace to destroy the Goliaths you have been born to face, and may you meet the battle with the fearlessness and confidence of David.

READ this AGAIN. (I SAM 17:46) "This DAY, the LORD will hAND you over to me. AND I'LL strike you DOWN AND Cut off YOUR heAD." He Knew GOD'S power. GOD'S plAN. GOD'S equipping, AND GOD'S presence. He Knew whAt must Be Done AND By whose power it WOULD Be ACCOMPLISheD.

Phil Joel

Lessons from the Book of First Samuel:
DAVID AND JONATHAN

After David had finished talking with Saul, Jonathan became one in spirit with David, and he loved him as himself. From that day Saul kept David with him and did not let him return to his father's house. And Jonathan made a covenant with David because he loved him as himself. Jonathan took off the robe he was wearing and gave it to David, along with his tunic, and even his sword, his bow and his belt.

1 SAMUEL 18:1–4

JUNE 7

When David was brought before Saul, he was still carrying the gory head of Goliath in his hands. David was so transformed by the anointing power of the Lord that the glory of God was still radiating from his whole being. Every eye in Saul's court was on this young hero who had saved the nation of Israel. However, Jonathan, Saul's son and the crown prince of Israel, was feeling something far different. From the moment David walked into his father's tent, Jonathan sensed that he shared a joint destiny with this young warrior. Far from being insecure or jealous over David's miraculous victory, Jonathan felt as if his own heart was being knit together with that of Israel's new champion.

When Saul had finished speaking with David, Jonathan jumped to his feet and took the young hero by the hand. As he looked into David's eyes, Jonathan made a covenant of friendship with David that would result in one of Scripture's most amazing relationships. Their friendship would weather the storms of kingdom politics, and eventually King Saul's insane hatred for David. After Jonathan died in battle years later, David would take in his crippled son and treat him like one of his own.

What secrets of lasting friendship can we learn from David and Jonathan? First, when Jonathan saw him, David was carrying the head of Goliath. Jonathan took one look at this battle trophy and was filled with respect for David—a respect that would become one of the foundation stones of their relationship. Mutual respect between friends is the cornerstone on which deep trust and love can be built. In the end, no one will stay friends with someone they do not respect.

Second, the Bible says that David and Jonathan "became one in spirit." God did something supernatural in their lives—he gave them a deep bond of unity from the very start. Many of my greatest friendships have started like this as well. Although I may hardly know the person, there is such a sense of joint destiny and common calling that we are inexplicitly drawn together.

Third, Jonathan made a covenant with David. Although we may not call it a "covenant" today, true, deep friendships *are* built on a covenant—the promise to trust, to care for and always watch out for each other. These are the ingredients of friendship straight from God's Word. May God give you a friendship like David and Jonathan's that will last your whole lifetime. A friend like that is one of God's greatest gifts.

"MAY those special FRIENDSHIPS I hAve with the men who ARE my tRue COMRADeS GROW even stRONGeR. LORD I pRAY FOR YOUR pROteCtion oveR the Lives OF these vALueD BROthers."

Phil Joel

Lessons from the Book of First Samuel:
SAUL'S JEALOUSY

When the men were returning home after David had killed the Philistine, the women came out from all the towns of Israel to meet King Saul with singing and dancing, with joyful songs and with tambourines and lutes.

As they danced, they sang:

"Saul has slain his thousands,
and David his tens of thousands."

Saul was very angry; this refrain galled him. "They have credited David with tens of thousands," he thought, "but me with only thousands. What more can he get but the kingdom?" And from that time on Saul kept a jealous eye on David. The next day an evil spirit from God came forcefully upon Saul. He was prophesying in his house, while David was playing the harp, as he usually did. Saul had a spear in his hand and he hurled it, saying to himself, "I'll pin David to the wall." But David eluded him twice. Saul was afraid of David, because the LORD was with David but had left Saul.

1 SAMUEL 18:6–12

JUNE 8

The songs of the women of Israel had haunted King Saul for days. Every time he saw young David, it only became worse. "How dare they sing that David has slain tens of thousands, while the great Saul has only slain thousands?" Finally, one day when David was playing the harp for him, Saul exploded into a murderous rage and hurled a spear at David. Al-

though David got out of the way in time, this was the beginning of the end of their relationship. Soon David would be forced to live in the mountains like a common criminal, while Saul pursued him with an army.

Why did King Saul attempt to murder the young man who had always served him faithfully? What drove Saul to reject the young man who had soothed his soul with music, and saved his skin in battle? First of all, Saul was jealous of David's success; jealousy is a sure way to destroy any relationship. God's Word tells us to "rejoice with those who rejoice" (Romans 12:15). True friends are delighted to see the victories in each others' lives and are quick to celebrate them. When you let jealousy keep you from sharing your friend's joy, you're not only missing out on a blessing, you're putting your friendship in danger.

Second, the fact that Saul had lost God's presence in his life was a major factor in the deterioration of his relationship with David. Without the confidence and security that God's love and presence bring, Saul could only feel threatened by David's success. We, too, need to be careful to hold on to a deep sense of God's presence and purpose in our lives so that we will have the security we need to truly enjoy the accomplishments of our friends. May God give you the grace to resist jealousy and insecurity and to sincerely "rejoice with those who rejoice."

"LORD I pRAY FOR the ALARMS to Go oFF in my mind if I step neAR jeALousy. I wAnt to Rejoice AS others ARe BlesseD By youR hAnd."

Phil Joel

Lessons in the Book of First Samuel:
BOARD AND SWORD

[Ahimelech] the priest [said to] David, "I don't have any ordinary bread on hand; however, there is some consecrated bread here — provided the men have kept themselves from women." … So the priest gave him the consecrated bread, since there was no bread there except the bread of the Presence that had been removed from before the Lord and replaced by hot bread…. David asked Ahimelech, "Don't you have a spear or a sword here?" … The priest replied, "The sword of Goliath … is here; it is wrapped in a cloth behind the ephod. If you want it, take it; there is no sword here but that one."

David said, "There is none like it; give it to me."

1 SAMUEL 21:4, 6, 8–9

JUNE 9

One moment David had been the nation's hero; now he was a fugitive. Despite Saul's attempts to murder him, David still deeply loved him — he was heartbroken at all that had happened. Now, David was on the run and desperate for supplies. When he came to the tabernacle at Nob, he breathlessly asked Ahimelech the priest for bread. "The only loaves I have are the consecrated loaves removed from the Holy Place just this morning," the priest told him. "You and your men can have them if you are pure." David accepted the extraordinary offer and made one last request: "Do you have a sword or spear?"

"The only weapon in the house of God is the sword you took in battle from the giant, Goliath."

These words momentarily transported David back in time. After defeating the giant he had entrusted the huge sword to the care of the

priests. Could it be that the Lord wanted him to have this great weapon again as he faced the crisis of his life? With new hope blazing in his heart, David unwrapped the legendary sword from the cloth that had covered it in the temple and carried it with him as he faced the journey ahead.

David was facing a terrible time and overwhelming odds—and yet he knew where to go to seek God's help. He ran to the house of God. Many times when Christians are hurting they run away from the church instead. When we do this we are running away from the one place that can truly provide the strength and healing we need.

When we run to the Lord and ask for help, just like David, we will find that God gives us special provision. The bread that the priest gave David had never been eaten by anyone but other priests for hundreds of years—according to God's law. But when David, with a pure heart, came with a need, he was taken care of without hesitation. No matter what type of crisis you are facing, God will provide for you, too, without hesitation.

In addition to providing for our needs, God will also arm us for our battles when we come to him. Just as Ahimelech gave David the sword of Goliath, so the Lord has the spiritual weapon you need to face your enemies. This weapon may be a new understanding from Scripture, a new power in your prayer life, or the strengthening encouragement of a close Christian friend. When you receive it, like David receiving Goliath's sword, you will say, "There is nothing like it." So run to God today, no matter what enemy is on your tail. When you do you'll receive all you need to stand, fight, and win your battle.

> The STORY OF AHIMELECH AND GOLIATH'S SWORD is like something out of An epic movie. I love it And it inspires me to think of my life As just that — An epic tale full of GREAT surprises, strange provision And Amazing escapes.
>
> **Phil Joel**

LESSONS FROM THE BOOK OF FIRST SAMUEL:
DAVID'S CONSCIENCE

The men said, "This is the day the LORD spoke of when he said to you, 'I will give your enemy into your hands for you to deal with as you wish.'" Then David crept up unnoticed and cut off a corner of Saul's robe. Afterward, David was conscience-stricken for having cut off a corner of his robe. He said to his men, "The LORD forbid that I should do such a thing to my master, the LORD's anointed, or lift my hand against him; for he is the anointed of the LORD."

1 SAMUEL 24:4–6

JUNE 10

For months, David and his men had lived in mountain caves like animals while Saul and his armies pursued them. Now, however, David had his chance. Saul was inside a cave, totally unguarded. All David had to do was slip into the cave and kill him, and all his problems would be over. "Surely the Lord has given Saul into your hands," his men told him. Yet when David had crept into the cave, he could not bring himself to kill the Lord's anointed. Instead, he cut off a small corner of Saul's robe, so king would realize that David had had the power to kill him, but had chosen to spare his life.

David returned to his men brokenhearted by his act. They simply couldn't understand his reasoning when he said that he had sinned against the Lord through what he had done. But David's conscience had kept him from committing an act that would destroy the foundations of the very kingdom he had been called to establish, even though it had seemed to everyone around him that it was the right thing to do.

David's life is an extraordinary example of sensitivity to the leading of God. He didn't live according to the dictates of his passions and personal needs. He lived by the Word of God and the divine conviction of the Holy Spirit. David's men would have murdered Saul without a second thought. After all, Saul had become an insane tyrant who was threatening the lives of the very subjects he had sworn to protect. But David valued the anointing and calling of God so much that his conscience would not allow him to harm Saul, who in spite of everything, had been chosen by the Lord. In the months to come, David would spare Saul again and again, trusting the leading of the Spirit. It was that leading that would provide him with the clarity and direction he needed throughout his life.

What about you? Are you ruled by your emotions or by the convictions of the Holy Spirit? God has given you a conscience that was created to be used by the Holy Spirit to show you right from wrong. But it can be rendered ineffective if you allow sin to crowd out its voice. Your conscience can also be used by the enemy if you aren't in tune with the Lord. Then it will lie to you and fill you with guilt for things that you need not feel guilty about. Therefore, it is important to develop your conscience, like David did, through spending time in God's Word. As you listen to God's voice through the Bible, your conscience will begin to be the instrument of the Holy Spirit that it was meant to be. This inner voice is a great gift from God. It will never lead you astray if you will keep it in tune with heaven's frequency.

The WORLD's idea of conscience is relative. A mind renewed by God is clear and absolute. We must measure our conscience by the WORD of God and not by our feelings, personal preference or experience. Read Romans 12:2.

Phil Joel

Lessons from the Book of First Samuel:
SAUL'S PERIL

The Philistines assembled and came and set up camp at Shunem, while Saul gathered all the Israelites and set up camp at Gilboa. When Saul saw the Philistine army, he was afraid; terror filled his heart. He inquired of the LORD, but the LORD did not answer him by dreams or Urim or prophets. Saul then said to his attendants, "Find me a woman who is a medium, so I may go and inquire of her."

"There is one in Endor," they said....

The [medium] asked, "Whom shall I bring up for you?"

"Bring up Samuel," he said.

1 SAMUEL 28:4–7, 11

JUNE 11

Saul was desperate. No matter how hard he had tried to seek the Lord, there was no response. The prophets were silent, and even the mysterious Urim, a sort of prophesying set of dice, had failed in the hands of the high priest to provide Saul with an answer. And Samuel was dead. Although they had been estranged because of Saul's rebellion, Samuel had been the only man that the king had ever really trusted. No matter how angry he had gotten at Samuel, when he was completely honest with himself, he realized how much he had cherished his wisdom.

Finally, with the host of the Philistines pressing his army from all sides, Saul disguised himself and went to visit a witch in the village of Endor. Despite the fact that Saul hated witchcraft, he hoped this renowned medium could call Samuel down from heaven to speak with him. Although God in his mercy allowed Saul's old mentor to appear to him, the mes-

sage Samuel delivered left Saul a broken and shattered man. The next day, Samuel prophesied from beyond the grave, Saul and his sons would die on the battlefield.

The story of Saul and the witch may be one of the saddest tales in all of Scripture. Saul had been called to a great destiny but threw it all away through sin and rebellion. Many Christians today have been given incredible missions from the Lord, and yet they are throwing away their destinies by living for themselves instead. And just like Saul, a life lived outside of God's purpose leads only to emptiness and heartbreak in the end.

By the end of his life, when it was too late, Saul was desperate for the counsel of Samuel. If only he hadn't ignored the prophet's wisdom when Samuel was alive! In spite of Samuel's miraculous appearance from beyond death, he could no longer help Saul—he could only prophesy the inevitable.

Is there someone in your life today who is trying to give you godly wisdom and advice? Are you listening or are you stubbornly going your own way? Ignoring the advice of strong Christians in your life, whether it be a pastor, youth leader or a parent, can be more dangerous than you realize. Without the loving counsel of other Christians you can easily become blind to the very things that are threatening to destroy you. But unlike Saul in this story, it isn't too late for you. Ask for a humble and teachable heart. Seek out the help and advice of the mature Christians in your life. Take their words seriously and test them by comparing them to the word of God. Let Saul's story remind you of the incredible value of godly advice today.

You need to ASK the LORD whose counsel you have spurned. Once you have discovered this, do whatever it takes to be reconciled to these precious people.

Phil Joel

Lessons from the Book of First Samuel:
DAVID AT ZIKLAG

When David and his men came to Ziklag, they found it destroyed by fire and their wives and sons and daughters taken captive. So David and his men wept aloud until they had no strength left to weep.... David was greatly distressed because the men were talking of stoning him; each one was bitter in spirit because of his sons and daughters. But David found strength in the Lord his God.... David inquired of the LORD, "Shall I pursue this raiding party? Will I overtake them?"

"Pursue them," he answered. "You will certainly overtake them and succeed in the rescue."

1 SAMUEL 30:3–4, 6, 8

JUNE 12

As David and his men slowly marched into Ziklag, they looked around in anguish. All their homes had been burned, their wives and children had been taken captive. The shock was so great that even David's mightiest warriors began to weep uncontrollably. The men were so angry and heartbroken, they began grumble to each other about stoning David for his failure to prevent the tragedy.

With all his men looking on, David asked the Lord for direction. "Pursue them," the Lord replied, "You will certainly overtake them and succeed in the rescue." David's forces quickly overtook the raiding party and utterly destroyed them. They recovered all of their wives and children and every one of their possessions.

David had been only days away from beginning his triumphant march to the throne of Israel when this story takes place. We may find the same events happening in our lives. When we are about to do something great for God, the enemy will launch a surprise attack to break our spirits. Often, like the Amalekites attacking David's home and family, the enemy will attack those closest to us in order to distract us from God's great purpose. When these attacks come don't give in and let the enemy have his way. Fight on!

Like David and his men, when we are surprised by the vicious attack of the enemy on our lives and the lives of those we love, it is easy to fall into despair and bitterness. But allowing these emotions to take over will only blind us to wisdom and direction we need. When we start to be over-whelmed, we should follow the example of David, who realized that he had to experience the Lord's encouragement and strength before he could receive the Lord's direction. Your first reaction to despair and bitterness should be worship and prayer. These are their only antidotes.

Once David had sought God's direction and received new strength, he went into battle, and he and his men recovered everything they had lost. Likewise, as you and I are faithful to obey God, we will regain what the enemy has stolen from us. So when the attacks come, don't give up and don't give in, but give yourself to the Lord and you will be restored.

To experience the Lord's encouragement and strength we must consistently put ourselves in a place where we are hearing, learning and being reminded of His goodness and faithfulness. Again, this comes from time alone with Him, worship and fellowship. David's response in this story is a beautiful example of Psalm 143:8 ASV, "Cause me to hear thy lovingkindness in the morning, for in thee do I trust. Cause me to know the way wherein I should walk, for I lift up my soul unto thee."

Phil Joel

Lessons from the Book of
Second Samuel:

ASAHEL'S DEATH

The three sons of Zeruiah were ... Joab, Abishai and Asahel.
Now Asahel was as fleet-footed as a wild gazelle. He chased
Abner, turning neither to the right nor to the left as he pursued him....

Abner warned Asahel, "Stop chasing me! Why should I strike you
down? How could I look your brother Joab in the face?" But Asahel
refused to give up the pursuit; so Abner thrust the butt of his spear into
Asahel's stomach, and the spear came out through his back. He fell
there and died on the spot.

2 SAMUEL 2:18–19, 22–23

JUNE 13

**Asahel was the youngest son of the Zeruiah family. His
older brothers were Joab and Abishai, two of the most famous warriors in all the land. Although young Asahel was
not yet as great a warrior as his brothers, he was considered by many to be the fastest runner in all of Israel. Now,
in the heat of battle, he saw Abner, the general of Saul's
armies and David's mortal enemy, running away from
the fray. Whether it was youthful adrenaline or a battle-induced delirium,
Asahel decided to chase down Saul's great champion that day. Even when
Abner, out of his fear of Joab, asked the young man to turn around and
stop chasing him, Asahel, because of his pride, would not stop. Finally,
Abner accidentally killed Asahel when he tried to stop the young man's
charge by using the blunt end of his spear. Tragically, this young man's
impulsive attack on Abner led to his own needless death and the beginning of a horrible blood feud.**

In Abner's response to Asahel's attack, we find a number of important lessons. First, Abner told Asahel to fight with one of the young warriors instead of fighting him. With these words, he was warning Asahel that he was not ready for battle with a warrior of his experience. We too may be full of passion to fight a battle that we just aren't prepared to win. For example, maybe you've just been delivered from a problem with drinking and now you want to hang out with your old friends again so you can help them overcome the same problem. Or perhaps you believe you are ready for a serious relationship with a member of the opposite sex, even though you are still working through the pain of a previous unhealthy relationship. While your intentions and motives may be pure, you need to be careful not to step into a battle that you're not yet strong enough to fight. You could end up falling again.

Even as young Asahel was killed by the blunt end of a spear, so you too need to watch out for things that seem harmless, but are really dangerous to your young faith. It might be a TV show—just a little brainless entertainment—but it is filling your mind with evil images and emotions that are crowding out God's Word. Maybe you have a friend who isn't doing anything really bad, but the person's attitude about God is starting to make you lazy in your Christian walk. Pay attention to these "harmless" things—don't let them end up killing your faith in the end.

Take a hard look at yourself and your faith today. Seek God's guidance and that of some seasoned soldiers of the Lord and avoid Asahel's mistake.

We must remain vigilant. Always on the balls of our feet. Ready for those seemingly good opportunities that may be merciless attacks from the enemy. We must also surround ourselves with more seasoned men and women in the faith who, as we submit to their authority will be able to help us see through the lies.

Phil Joel

LESSONS FROM THE BOOK OF SECOND SAMUEL:

DAVID'S CONQUEST OF JERUSALEM

The Jebusites said to David, "You will not get in here; even the blind and the lame can ward you off." They thought, "David cannot get in here."

... David said, "Anyone who conquers the Jebusites will have to use the water shaft to reach those 'lame and blind' who are David's enemies." That is why they say, "The 'blind and lame' will not enter the palace."

David then took up residence in the fortress and called it the City of David.... And he became more and more powerful, because the LORD God Almighty was with him.

2 SAMUEL 5:6, 8-10

JUNE 14

For hundreds of years, the impregnable fortress of Mount Zion had remained under Jebusite control. Even the armies had not been able to enter this citadel while they were conquering the Promised Land. Now as David surveyed his newly won kingdom, he realized this fortress had to be taken. By this time, however, the fortress's defenses had reached almost mythological proportions. But David had discovered a weakness in the defenses of the fortress.

The king had asked for one volunteer to enter the darkness of the fortress's water system. Once inside, he was to climb up through the shaft, into the fortress, and then stealthily open the gates so Israel's army could walk right in. Although the bravery of David's men was legendary, they were wondering if anyone would have the audacity to attempt David's seemingly reckless plan. Joab, without hesitation, took the challenge. Just hours later, the gates opened and the fortress was conquered. Through the bravery of one man, David's control over his kingdom was secured.

What does Joab's courage teach us? First, even as the fortress of Zion had remained under Jebusite control for hundreds of years, so there are things in our world on which the church has yet to make a real impact. Whether it is the media and entertainment world, the educational system, or the political field, the church will never be able to truly influence our world until strategic areas like these are penetrated with the Gospel.

In spite of the reputation that these areas of our world have for being impossible to penetrate, nothing is beyond the power of God. Sooner or later, someone must be willing to penetrate these places personally with the Gospel of Christ.

The fortress of Zion could only be taken from the inside out. Today a new generation of Christians must find their way into the inner circles of their professions so they can transform them from the inside out. Like Joab, through courage and the power of God we too can liberate the influential areas of our culture from the darkness that has controlled them. May God give you a fresh passion to change your world from the inside out today.

can cities, nations, and cultures be changed by the power of the Gospel through the lives of God's servants here on earth? Let this question set your mind to thinking about your faith in the power of God to use one man who is carrying out a mission uniquely designed by God. That person is you: What is your unique mission?

Phil Joel

Lessons from the Book of Second Samuel:

DAVID AT BAAL PERAZIM

 David inquired of the LORD, "Shall I go and attack the Philistines? Will you hand them over to me?"

The LORD answered him, "Go, for I will surely hand the Philistines over to you." So David went to Baal Perazim, and there he defeated them.

Once more the Philistines came up and spread out in the Valley of Rephaim; so David inquired of the LORD, and he answered, "Do not go straight up, but circle around behind them and attack them in front of the balsam trees. As soon as you hear the sound of marching in the tops of the balsam trees, move quickly, because that will mean the LORD has gone out in front of you to strike the Philistine army." So David did as the LORD commanded him, and he struck down the Philistines.

2 SAMUEL 5:19–20, 22–25

JUNE 15

The Philistines had not been this frightened since David had slain Goliath. Now that their mortal enemy had been made king, the Philistines decided to immediately attack Israel. David, however, wisely retreated to his stronghold and waited on the Lord for instructions. When the Lord told him to attack, he and his army struck the host of the Philistines and destroyed them.

When the Philistine armies attacked Israel for the second time, however, the Lord's instructions were different. He told David to circle his army behind the host of the Philistines and hide next to a grove of balsam trees. David's signal to attack would be the sound of an invisible army marching through the tops of the trees. Most of us would have thought these instructions were pretty strange, but David's faith made him confident in the Lord's commands.

When Israel's army positioned themselves near the balsam trees they could all feel the presence of the Lord and the angelic armies that were rustling the branches. The armies of the Philistines were shattered before Israel could even begin their attack. God's army may not have been visible, but it was powerful.

What lessons can we learn from David's victories? First of all, the moment David became king, the Philistines made an all-out assault on him. And the moment God gives you a position in his service, you can expect the full onslaught of the enemy. As you take refuge in the stronghold of God's presence and promises, however, he will show you how to shatter the dark army coming against you.

Second, many times we will not fully understand the plans of God for our lives, just as David probably didn't fully understand why he was supposed to hide behind trees. But God is working for us in the invisible realm, behind the scenes. Even as God's angelic armies were invisible and yet overwhelmingly powerful, so God's angels are fighting for us today, even though we cannot see them. Be patient as you wait for God's deliverance—he is working, even when there is no evidence. Soon, you'll see your enemies flee before his mighty hand.

On this side of heaven we won't know the extent of GOD's WORK for us Behind the scenes. He is A FATHER who WORKS tirelessly on Behalf of his children to provide for them. He provides counsel, instruction And victory if we are faithful to listen And Be obedient to His ways which Are so much higher than our own.

Phil Joel

LESSONS FROM THE BOOK OF SECOND SAMUEL:

DAVID AND THE ARK

📖 [David and his men] set the ark of God on a new cart.... Uzzah and Ahio ... were guiding the new cart with the ark of God on it.... David and the whole house of Israel were celebrating with all their might before the Lord.... When they came to the threshing floor of Nacon, Uzzah reached out and took hold of the ark of God, because the oxen stumbled. The Lord's anger burned against Uzzah because of his irreverent act; therefore God struck him down and he died there beside the ark of God. Then David was angry because the LORD's wrath had broken out against Uzzah.

2 SAMUEL 6:3–8

JUNE 16

The great symbol of God's presence, the Ark of the Covenant, was finally coming home. As the procession continued on its way to Jerusalem, the cart carrying the ark came to the rough surface of a threshing floor, and the oxen stumbled. Uzzah reached out to steady it, but when he touched it he dropped dead. Everyone around the ark could feel the burning of God's anger.

For three long months, David brooded over God's judgment of Uzzah. Meanwhile, the ark was kept in the house of a man named Obed-Edom and God blessed everything he did because he was housing the ark. Finally, David realized that the ark must be carried on the shoulders of the Levites and not by an ox cart—according to the law God gave Moses. David was ashamed. He should have known better and treated the ark with the respect it deserved.

So David gathered the tribes of Israel, had the Levites lift the ark and take their place at the front of the procession. With David and a grateful nation following, the Levites brought the ark to the tabernacle in Jerusalem. That day the joyous celebration was renewed for God blessed the obedience of his people with an outpouring of his presence.

So why did God judge Uzzah and Israel so harshly? This extreme judgment shows us the incredible holiness of God. In spite of his good intentions, David failed to follow the clear instructions for handling the symbol of God's presence. In our lives we must be careful, too, of doing the wrong thing with the right intentions. Meaning well isn't always enough. If you don't live your life God's way, you will not receive his blessing.

An amazing part of this story is the fact that the ark stayed in the house of Obed-Edom for three months. God allowed his ark to live with a simple family while David worked through his fear and came to understand what God required. Even when we make big mistakes, God will be patient with us when we are trying to learn and grow from them.

In this story we see that God would only allow the special people that he had set apart for that purpose to carry his holy presence. And elaborate rituals or strategic evangelism plans mean nothing unless real people, who love Jesus, are willing to carry God's presence and power into the world we have been called to change. May we learn to take our mission seriously and take God's presence into the places that need him most.

GOD'S WAYS ARE ALWAYS BEST. They ARE not SUGGESTIONS OR OPTIONS. they ARE his DIREC-tions FOR LIFE AND in them Lies the ABUNDANT LIFE. One OF the REASONS there's Been so much DISAppointment Among Christians in my GENERATION is BECAUSE they hAve tAken the BIBLE AS A BOOK OF SUGGESTIONS AND not A BOOK OF COMMANDS.

Phil Joel

Lesson's from the Book of Second Samuel:

MICHAL'S BITTERNESS

As the ark of the Lord was entering the City of David, Michal daughter of Saul, watched from a window. And when she saw King David leaping and dancing before the Lord, she despised him in her heart … When David returned home to bless his household, Michal daughter of Saul came out to meet him and said, "How the king of Israel has distinguished himself today, disrobing in the sight of the slave girls of his servants as any vulgar fellow would!"

David said to Michal, "It was before the Lord, who chose me rather than your father or anyone from his house when he appointed me ruler over the Lord's people Israel—I will celebrate before the Lord. I will become even more undignified than this, and I will be humiliated in my own eyes. But by these slave girls you spoke of, I will be held in honor." And Michal daughter of Saul had no children to the day of her death.

2 SAMUEL 6:16, 20–23

JUNE 17

As all of Israel celebrated the ark's return to Jerusalem, David's heart was bursting with the joy and presence of the Lord. He couldn't contain himself. David began to dance and leap before the Lord because the God whom he loved so much would finally have a home again. The whole nation was amazed when they saw their king dancing with the unbridled joy of a little child. His passion for the Lord made his people trust and love him all the more.

There was one person in Israel that day who was not rejoicing, though. In fact, she despised the fact that her king was dancing like some drunken commoner. Her name was Michal—the daughter of Saul and David's wife. Embittered by the loss of her father and the kingdom he had ruled, she hated David's passionate expression of love for God. "I was ashamed of you today," Michal told David when he arrived home. "Your foolish dancing was disgraceful. Kings should never behave like that." David, knowing the bitterness in Michal's heart turned to her and gently said, "I will never allow my own sense of dignity to get in the way of my worship of the Lord." Sadly, Michal's bitterness resulted in barrenness. She would be childless all the days of her life.

Bitterness will radically affect your fruitfulness for the Lord, just as it did Michal's. No matter how deeply you have been wounded bitterness won't do anything but hurt you even more. Don't miss out on God's healing by letting bitterness separate you from his love.

Michal's disdain for David's passionate worship caused her to reject the very thing that could have delivered her soul from the bitterness that was eating her alive. If she would have humbled herself and joined her husband in worship and praise, her story would have had a radically different end. Don't make Michal's mistake. Differences in age, religious traditions, or musical taste, should never make us reject the sincere worship of our fellow Christians. We can learn so much from each other's worship styles if we will be open to them. Sometimes, finding a whole new way to worship God will even bring you a whole new understanding of his love for you. So when you watch someone give all they've got to praising God, don't despise them—join them!

Let us never ALLOW OUR own sense of Dignity to keep us FROM WORShiping the LORD with uNBRiDLeD pAssioN AND joy.

Phil Joel

Lesson's from the Book of Second Samuel:

DAVID'S TABERNACLE

 They brought the ark of the LORD and set it in its place inside the tent that David had pitched for it, and David sacrificed burnt offerings and fellowship offerings before the LORD.

2 SAMUEL 6:17

[David] appointed some of the Levites to minister before the ark of the Lord, to make petition, to give thanks, and to praise the Lord the God of Israel.

1 CHRONICLES 16:4

After this I will return
and rebuild David's fallen tent.
Its ruins I will rebuild,
and I will restore it,
that the remnant of men may seek the Lord,
and all the Gentiles who bear my name,
says the Lord, who does these things.

ACTS 15:16 – 17

 Why wasn't David placing the ark in the tabernacle of Moses at Gibeon? Instead, David had simply pitched a tent on Mount Zion. There were no elaborate veils—all of the other tabernacle furnishings were still at Gibeon. In David's tabernacle, the unveiled ark was surrounded by Levites who worshiped and prayed in shifts, twenty-four hours a

JUNE 18

day. And yet God was obviously not displeased for his mighty presence poured out of the simple tent like a rushing river.

Due to the time he had spent shepherding sheep as a boy, and the years he had spent hiding from Saul in the wilderness, David had spent most of his life alone with God. Unlike most of the Israelites, who only experienced God's presence at the sacrifices and feasts associated with the tabernacle of Moses, David had developed his own vital intimate relationship with the Lord. Therefore, when the Lord allowed him to erect a new tabernacle, David's deep desire was for the Levites, and the nation as a whole, to experience the same presence of God that he had been enjoying all of his life.

Through his lifelong relationship with the Lord, David understood God's desire to be worshiped and adored by his people. David filled his simple tabernacle with music and songs of praise because he knew those were special gifts he could give that God would cherish. God's desires haven't changed in all these thousands of years. He longs for people who will come into his presence and worship him deeply, with all of their hearts.

In the New Testament, Peter says that worship like David's, is one of the keys to drawing unbelievers to the Lord. In other words, as God's presence is released in response to our passionate worship, even people who know nothing of God will find themselves inexplicably drawn to him. So whether it is at church, in your small group, or even when you are taking a stroll through the mall, sing a song to the Lord. You'll bring joy to his heart and maybe even an unbeliever to him.

DAVID'S WORSHIP CORpORATELY WAS AN extension AND FURther expRESSION OF his intimAte peR-sonAL RELATIONShip with the LORD. WhAt mADe DAVID'S WORShip pOWERFUL WAS not just the stYLE OF WORShip; it WAS the FACt thAt it FLOWeD out OF A heARt FiLLeD with the pASSION to WORShip.

Phil Joel

DAVID AND MEPHIBOSHETH

When Mephibosheth, son of Jonathan, the son of Saul, came to David, he bowed down to pay him honor…. David said, "Mephibosheth!" "Your servant," he replied.

"Don't be afraid," David said to him, "for I will surely show you kindness for the sake of your father Jonathan. I will restore to you all the land that belonged to your grandfather Saul, and you will always eat at my table."

2 SAMUEL 9:6–7

JUNE 19

David had enjoyed many victories and was now king of an incredible kingdom that God had blessed. He longed to share his blessings, and since his dear friend Jonathan, was gone, he would make a point of finding Jonathan's family so he could bless them. David's servant told him that one of Jonathan's sons, Mephibosheth, who was crippled in both feet, was still alive. Perhaps God would allow him to honor his best friend by helping this disabled son. David immediately told soldiers to bring Mephibosheth to the palace.

When Jonathan's son arrived in Jerusalem, he was filled with uncertainty. David's men had been gracious, but through Saul, Mephibosheth had a legitimate claim to the throne. Perhaps he had been brought to the palace to be imprisoned or killed. As he faced David, he was full of terror.

David, however, was overwhelmed with joy when he saw the son of his beloved Jonathan. He rose up from his throne and urged the boy not to be afraid. Mephibosheth bowed before the king, and blurted out, "Why should you care about a dead dog like me?" David replied, "For the sake of your father, Jonathan, who was my best friend, I will restore every one of your lands to you, and you will live under my royal protection forever," he assured him.

If King David restored Mephibosheth to a place of honor and protection because of his relationship with Jonathan, how much more will the king of heaven do for you because of Jesus Christ? Maybe, like Mephibosheth, you feel like a "dead dog" in God's sight. Sin, both your own and that of others, has so marred your life that you have been left with little hope for the future. Perhaps the pain has left you emotionally crippled and deeply scarred in your soul.

If you're feeling crushed and disabled today, God has good news for you. Through the sacrifice of Christ, you have full access to all the riches of God's kingdom. Just like Mephibosheth, you are invited to sit at God's table and be a part of his family forever! If you come to God's throne and ask him to be your king he will adopt you as his child and become your Father as well.

As David had Mephibosheth brought into his presence, so God is drawing you into his presence. He is not a tyrant who is simply looking for a chance to punish you. Your Heavenly Father wants you to come to him so he can bless you!

Like Mephibosheth's response, it can all seem too good to be true. But we must embrace the fact that God also has a wonderful inheritance of health and freedom for us that can at times seem too good to be true.

Phil Joel

Lessons from the Book of Second Samuel:

DAVID AND BATHSHEBA

David sent Joab out with the king's men and the whole Isra-
elite army.... But David remained in Jerusalem. One evening
David got up from his bed and walked around on the roof of the palace.
From the roof he saw a woman bathing. The woman was very beautiful,
and David sent someone to find out about her. The man said, "Isn't this
Bathsheba,... the wife of Uriah the Hittite?"
Then David sent messengers to get her. She came to him, and he slept
with her.

2 SAMUEL 11:1–4

JUNE 20

For the first time in his life, David was not going to war.
After all, he was the king now. He would stay home and
enjoy the comforts of his palace and let his army do the
fighting. But as he watched Joab and the troops leaving
for the campaign, his heart was torn. Many of them were
his boyhood friends, the very men that had secured his
kingdom for him. When he saw the Levites and the ark of the covenant
going out at the head of the army, he wondered if he had made a mistake
by remaining at home.

As he walked on the roof of his palace to cool off, he saw her—a
beautiful young woman bathing on the roof of her nearby home. In spite
of discovering that she was the wife of Uriah, one of his finest soldiers, he
sent for her anyway. He would commit adultery with the young Bathsheba,
try to cover up his sin by murdering her husband, and in the process,

break the heart of his God. Although God would forgive him, David's life, and that of his family and kingdom, would never be the same.

How could David, who was called "a man after God's own heart," sin in such a horrible way? First of all, when David stayed home from battle, he stepped out of God's purpose for his life. If David would have been with his army, he would have avoided the temptation of Bathsheba.

When Joab and the army went off to battle, David was left without the people God had placed in his life to protect him. Joab and his brother had spent their whole lives serving David; therefore they had the relationship necessary to speak candidly with him. Perhaps if they had been there, they could have kept David from falling into sin. We, too, need to surround ourselves with people who will speak the truth to us in love and help us stand up to temptation.

In addition, when the ark left Jerusalem the symbol of God's presence was no longer there to remind David every day of his commitment to the Lord. When we stop attending church, reading the Bible, or praying, the reminders that we need to remain pure are missing.

So as you follow God's purpose for your life today, be sure to include Christian friends in your journey, and keep the reminders of God's presence always with you. These are the keys to avoiding David's tragic mistake.

ARE YOU BACKING OFF AND GIVING YOURSELF A "BREAK" FROM PURSUING THE LORD WHOLE-HEARTEDLY? ARE YOU BACKING AWAY FROM THE PEOPLE GOD HAS PLACED IN YOUR LIFE TO WALK WITH AND HOLD YOU ACCOUNTABLE? ARE YOU BACKING OFF FROM WORSHIP, PRAYER AND CHURCH? DON'T BE LURED INTO THINKING THAT THE ANSWERS TO THESE QUESTIONS ARE NOT CRITICAL TO YOUR SPIRITUAL WELL-BEING.

Phil Joel

LESSONS FROM THE BOOK OF SECOND SAMUEL:

DAVID'S RESPONSE TO CRISIS

The whole countryside wept aloud as all the people [who were fleeing with David] passed by. The king also crossed the Kidron Valley, and all the people moved on toward the desert. Zadok was there, too, and all the Levites who were with him were carrying the ark of the covenant of God. They set down the ark of God, and Abiathar offered sacrifices until all the people had finished leaving the city. Then the king said to Zadok, "Take the ark of God back into the city. If I find favor in the LORD's eyes, he will bring me back and let me see it and his dwelling place again."

2 SAMUEL 15:23–25

JUNE 21

People throughout the nation wept. David had been betrayed by his own son, Absalom, and was now being forced to flee for his life into the mountains. As David and his men began to climb the Mount of Olives, however, they were met by Zadok, the high priest. The priests had removed the ark from the tabernacle and brought it to be a protection for David. Although David realized the ark would probably guarantee him the loyalty of the whole nation, he instructed Zadok to take it back to its rightful place. When Zadok hesitated, David said, "If God wants me to see his holy ark again, he will bring me back home."

What lessons can we learn from David's attitude during one of the worst crises of his life? First of all, even though both Absalom and Ahithophel had betrayed him, David never lost sight of his own sin. He realized that his immorality with Bathsheba (Ahithophel's granddaughter) and his failure to punish his other son for the rape of Absalom's sister had led to the betrayal. Therefore, although he would deal with their rebellion, his own heart remained broken and pliable before the Lord. Many times when we are rejected or betrayed, we easily lose sight of our own responsibility in the situation. We must allow the Holy Spirit and trusted fellow believers to help us see and face the truth.

And even though the presence of the Ark of the Covenant would probably have guaranteed the security of the kingdom, David refused to take it with him. His trust in God was so strong that he realized no power on the earth could keep him off the throne except that of God himself. In those moments when our place or position has come under attack, instead of responding with panic and insecurity, we can trust in the God who gave us the position in the first place. He will bring us back into our purpose when the time is right.

Although the bitterness and rebellion of Absalom was due in part to David, David didn't wallow in self pity. He faced the consequences and did what needed to be done. He was humble and repentant and trusted God for restoration no matter how difficult the process may have been. If this is where you find yourself today, no matter how hard the process may be, like David, you too can be restored.

Phil Joel

LESSONS FROM THE BOOK OF
SECOND SAMUEL:

AHITHOPHEL'S DEATH

Now in those days the advice Ahithophel gave was like that of one who inquires of God. That was how both David and Absalom regarded all of Ahithophel's advice.

2 SAMUEL 16:23

When Ahithophel saw that his advice had not been followed, he saddled his donkey and set out for his house in his hometown. He put his house in order and then hanged himself. So he died and was buried in his father's tomb.

2 SAMUEL 17:23

JUNE 22

When David heard Ahithophel had joined Absalom's rebellion, he was afraid. Ahithophel was widely regarded as the wisest man in the whole kingdom. His advice was treated like the very word of the Lord. To David, this man was more dangerous than a whole army. Yet, as his onetime best friend, David knew Ahithophel's weakness—if his advice was ever rejected, his own insecurities would destroy him. With this in mind, David sent his dear friend Hushai into the camp of Absalom. Hushai would do his best to frustrate the counsel of Ahithophel.

Eventually Hushai's advice was accepted and Ahithophel's was rejected. Ahithophel stormed away, mounted his donkey and headed home. By the time he arrived there, his burning anger had been replaced by a dark despair. Since Absalom had not listened, his rebellion against David was now doomed to failure. Ahithophel had set his affairs in order and hung himself.

When a person is full of pride they cannot stand to be rejected. Since their self-worth is based on their own success and the approval of other people, when they lose these things, the foundation of who they are is destroyed. In my own life, I have found that unless the righteousness of Christ and the approval of God are the basis for my self-worth, sooner or later I will be left feeling worthless.

When Ahithophel's counsel was disregarded, he quit and went home. And if we end up feeling worthless because we aren't basing our lives on God's love for us, we, too, will end up giving up and giving in when we face rejection from people.

Quitting church, a ministry, a job, or even your marriage when things don't go your way is never going to make you feel better. It will only make you more vulnerable to the enemy's attacks.

Ahithophel became so despondent that the enemy convinced him to end his life. In the same way the enemy would like nothing more than to persuade you to commit spiritual suicide when the going gets tough. He might convince you to leave your church or the ministry God called you to when you don't receive the position or recognition you feel you deserve. Satan's main goal, though, would be to get you to walk away from your relationship with God rather than swallow your pride or deal with your insecurities. Don't let the enemy win! Ask God to dig up any roots of pride in your heart and kill the vines of insecurity that are threatening to choke your soul. Don't let your story end like Ahithophel's did.

ALL OF US, LIKE Ahithophel, ARE insecure in one AREA OR Another. ASK GOD to ReveAL the ROOTS OF YOUR insecurities toDAY. Insecurity is FAR more thAn wishing you weRe BetteR LookiNG OR weReh't so shy — insecurity is A vAin Attempt to finD YOUR iDentify outsiDe of chRist.

Phil Joel

Lessons from the Book of
Second Samuel:

ABSALOM'S DEATH

In all Israel there was not a man so highly praised for his handsome appearance as Absalom. From the top of his head to the sole of his foot there was no blemish in him. Whenever he cut the hair of his head — he used to cut his hair from time to time when it became too heavy for him — he would weigh it, and its weight was 200 shekels by the royal standard.

2 SAMUEL 14:25–26

Absalom happened to meet David's men. He was riding his mule, and as the mule went under the thick branches of a large oak, Absalom's head got caught in the tree. He was left hanging in midair, while the mule he was riding kept on going.... So [Joab] took three javelins in his hand and plunged them into Absalom's heart while Absalom was still alive in the oak tree.

2 SAMUEL 18:9, 14

JUNE 23

Absalom was the most handsome man in the whole nation. He was especially proud of his gorgeous hair. In fact, Absalom would grow his hair so long that when he cut it, its weight would be in pounds. This day, however, the beautiful hair he was so proud of would be his downfall. While Absalom was riding toward the battle where his men were fighting his father's army, he inadvertently met up with some of David's soldiers. When he attempted to flee, however, his hair was tangled in the tree branches over his head. He was jerked off the saddle of the donkey

and suspended in midair. Helpless and exposed, he was discovered and Joab and his armor bearers brutally murdered him.

We are all like Absalom in some ways. We all take pride in things that aren't truly valuable, whether it be our looks, the cool car we drive, or our good grades. And many times these things that we are most proud of are the very things the devil uses to try and destroy us. We become so proud of all our knowledge that we refuse any correction and advice—and then find out the hard way that we really don't know it all. Or we think that we are so "spiritual" that we begin to take dangerous spiritual risks—like ignoring time reading the Bible or toying around with temptation—only to find ourselves in deep trouble when sin catches up with us after all.

We also have to ask ourselves why Absalom did not cut himself free from the tree branches. Surely a warrior of his magnitude was wearing a sword, or at least a dagger. He could have simply cut through his hair and escaped. Could it be that Absalom, in his vanity, refused to cut his lovely hair, even though it was about to cost him his life? Although it is hard to believe that anyone could be that vain, people put themselves in danger like this every day. We refuse to take off the happy mask we wear in front of others and admit that we need help with depression because we don't want to seem weak. Or we refuse to get rid of that flashy car or newest gadget, even though it has us deep in debt.

When you find yourself facing decisions like this, take a good look at your situation. You might just find that you, too, are hanging from a tree by your hair. May God give you the grace to cut through your pride with the sharp, two-edged sword of his Word.

ABSALOM'S point of pride was worn on his head and easily seen by others. But some of the most DANGEROUS and potentially DEADLY forms of pride are subtle and cleverly disguised. Ask the LORD to alert you to these areas of DANGER in your own life. MAY GOD give you the GRACE to KILL YOUR pride before it KILLS YOU.

Phil Joel

LessoNs fRoM the BooK of SecoND SAMueL:
DAVID'S RESCUE

Once again there was a battle between the Philistines and Israel. David went down with his men to fight against the Philistines, and he became exhausted. And Ishbi-Benob, one of the descendants of Rapha, whose bronze spearhead weighed three hundred shekels and who was armed with a new sword, said he would kill David. But Abishai son of Zeruiah came to David's rescue; he struck the Philistine down and killed him. Then David's men swore to him, saying, "Never again will you go out with us to battle, so that the lamp of Israel will not be extinguished."

2 SAMUEL 21:15–17

JUNE 24

David was weakening by the moment. He who had once slain "tens of thousands" of Philistines was now in danger of being slain by them. Ishbi-Benob, another Philistine giant, had been boasting for weeks that he would kill David in battle. As he ran to attack against Israel's king, Ishbi-Benob felt certain of victory. At the last minute, though, Abishai, one of David's best friends, came to the rescue. Before the giant could slay David, Abishai had attacked and put an end to Ishbi-Benob.

As his armies marched home, David was ashamed. His men had been so frightened by his near death on the battlefield that they had made him promise never to go to war again. After slaying Goliath as a teenager he had been nearly killed in the prime of his life by a boasting Philistine nowhere near Goliath's size. Where had David's legendary strength gone?

We face the same question in our lives sometimes. We get frustrated when the spiritual enemies that we seemed to easily defeat when we were younger become almost too much for us when we should be at our most spiritually mature. Maybe you are facing a major struggle with doubt and you can't understand what has happened to your once strong, yet child-like faith. Maybe you won the battle with drugs or alcohol as a teenager, but now you're feeling tempted by the same old habits all over again.

There are many things that can cause Christians to lose their spiritual strength and vigor. First, although God had forgiven David for his immorality with Bathsheba, the consequences of his sin were still affecting him. He had lost his son and had struggled to crush a rebellion that had almost destroyed his kingdom. David's soul was deeply scarred and battered. Second, while David loved God, I believe his faith had been shaken by the repeated assaults on his kingdom. His confidence in God's protection had been shaken, leaving him vulnerable to Ishbi-Benob's ferocious attack.

When we find ourselves struggling and vulnerable, we need an Abishai of our own. We too must allow trusted friends into the vulnerable areas of our lives. Unless our Christian friends know our weaknesses, they will not be able to come to our aid in the heat of conflict. So if you are feeling weak and defeated today, don't go it alone. Seek the companionship of other Christians, and of God himself to help you in your fight.

We can't let our sharing of our vulnerabilities with friends be a one time thing. We must remain humble and transparent before one another. Helping each other keep our way clear and our hearts yielded to the Holy Spirit is vital at every age. Much of our spiritual life boils down to a choice between humility and pride.

Phil Joel

Lessons from the Book of First Chronicles:

THE WEAVER'S SON

> In another battle with the Philistines, Elhanan son of Jair killed Lahmi the brother of Goliath the Gittite, who had a spear with a shaft like a weaver's rod.

1 CHRONICLES 20:5

JUNE 25

To the armies of Israel, Lahmi was an invincible giant. Like his brother Goliath, the shaft of Lahmi's spear was as large as a weaver's beam. Still bitter over the death of his brother at the hands of David, Lahmi was filled with fury when he attacked the armies of Israel that day. As this giant bellowed his war cries, once again, one man had the courage to step out of the ranks of Israel's army to face him: Elhanan, the son of Jair the weaver. While everyone else had been intimidated by the giant's stature and the size of his spear, Elhanan had been unshaken. His boldness stunned the giant. Although he defended himself furiously, the great champion of the Philistines was quickly dispatched by Elhanan's flashing blade.

One has to wonder if Elhanan's fearlessness when faced with the giant's massive spear came partially from being raised by a weaver. Yes, the spear was big—but only as big as the weaver's rods that his father used to make rugs every day. Perhaps if we take the time to learn about and become familiar with the nature of the enemy's weapons, we won't be surprised or intimidated when we are faced with them. Second Corinthians 2:11 says that we should be aware of schemes. We will find it far easier to withstand an assault when we are expecting it.

Elhanan also had the will and skill necessary to attack the giant. We can have lots of knowledge about God, and even about our enemy, but we also must have the passion to truly apply that knowledge in our every day lives. Passion comes as we seek and discover God's purpose for us. When we catch a glimpse of the great mission we've been given we will have the motivation to be disciplined in our training for that mission. May God give us the will and the skill as we prepare to serve him today.

We must not let pride and fear of losing our reputation keep us from sharing our own personal experiences of how the enemy has attempted to destroy us. Many times this could save the life of another person. I wish there would have been more men who would have shared their testimonies and insights into their lives with me when I was younger.

Phil Joel

Lessons from the Book of First Kings:
SOLOMON'S PRAYER

The LORD appeared to Solomon during the night in a dream, and God said, "Ask for whatever you want me to give you."…

"O LORD my God, you have made your servant king in place of my father David. But I am only a little child and do not know how to carry out my duties.… So give your servant a discerning heart to govern your people and to distinguish between right and wrong."…

So God said to him, "Since you have asked for this and not for long life or wealth for yourself, nor have asked for the death of your enemies but for discernment in administering justice, I will do what you have asked.… Moreover, I will give you what you have not asked for—both riches and honor—so that in your lifetime you will have no equal among kings."

1 KINGS 3:5, 7, 9, 11–13

JUNE 26

As young Solomon looked out on the kingdom he had received from his father, his heart was heavy. Where would he ever get the wisdom he needed to rule all these people? To seek some answers, Solomon went to the tabernacle. After offering a thousand sacrifices to the Lord, Solomon quieted his soul and waited.

When he finally fell into a restless sleep, the Lord appeared to him in his dreams—promising to give the young king whatever he wanted. Without hesitation Solomon answered: "Without your help, I will never be able to rule this great people. Please give me the discernment and wisdom I need to govern them, for without your wisdom, I am doomed to failure."

"Solomon," the Lord whispered, "because you have not asked for the death of your enemies or for wealth, I will the wisdom and discernment you require. In your lifetime, there will be no king greater than you." In the years to come, the gift of God's wisdom he received that night would make Solomon the world's most famous man.

What lessons can we learn from Solomon's encounter with God? First, at the foundation of Solomon's prayer was the revelation of his own need for God. Solomon wasn't blinded by pride and youthful zeal—instead he realized his desperate need for God. When we face a God-sized task, our first step should be to acknowledge our need for God-sized help.

Second, by asking God for wisdom, Solomon was acknowledging that his own wisdom wasn't enough. Furthermore, Solomon asked for more from God than just an answer to his immediate needs; he wanted the wisdom and knowledge that would give him the answers he would need for problems he would face in the future as well.

Like Solomon, God wants to give you wisdom that will take you far beyond the solution to today's problems. As you humble yourself before him, he will give you the knowledge and direction you need to walk with him all the days of your life.

Notice that in Solomon's prayer, even though he was the King, he still referred to himself as God's servant. No matter what our positions may be, it is important that we never forget that we are all God's servants, not the other way around. Never forget that God is not your "genie in a bottle."

Phil Joel

Lessons from the Book of First Kings:
SOLOMON'S FALL

King Solomon … loved many foreign women besides Pharaoh's daughter — Moabites, Ammonites, Edomites, Sidonians and Hittites. They were from nations about which the Lord had told the Israelites, "You must not intermarry with them, because they will surely turn your hearts after their gods." Nevertheless, Solomon held fast to them in love. He had seven hundred wives of royal birth and three hundred concubines, and his wives led him astray. As Solomon grew old, his wives turned his heart after other gods, and his heart was not fully devoted to the Lord his God, as the heart of David his father had been. He followed Ashtoreth the goddess of the Sidonians, and Molech the detestable god of the Ammonites. So Solomon did evil in the eyes of the Lord; he did not follow the Lord completely, as David his father had done.

1 KINGS 11:1 – 6

JUNE 27

Moses had clearly instructed the kings of Israel not to take too many wives, lest their hearts be led astray from the Lord. As Solomon's power and splendor grew, however, he felt that he had the right to live like any other king. Therefore, he chose to seal his alliances with other nations by marrying into their families. By the end of his life, he had taken seven hundred wives and three hundred concubines. And as Solomon grew older, his wives led him into the worship of their gods. From the immorality of Ashtoreth worship to the human sacrifices associated with Molech, Solomon defiled the nation of Israel with idolatry.

How could the wisest man in the history of our planet fall into such horrible sin and deception? First of all, as Solomon's power and wealth grew, he felt that he was exempt from the words of wisdom that he preached to others. Perhaps he thought that a man of his wisdom and nobility could never be enticed by the false gods of the women he had married. Tragically, this self-deception opened his life to sins that would eventually destroy his kingdom. Like Solomon, no matter how successful you have become, if you choose to go against God's Word the consequences of your disobedience will eventually catch up with you.

Even when we go off the path and disobey, God is always willing to forgive and guide us back to the right road. But we have to be willing to give up our sin and go back to God. Solomon refused to repent of his sins. Even when God confronted him, he continued in his idol worship. Although God would grant Solomon mercy because of his love for David, Solomon's son would see the kingdom fall apart as a result of his father's sin. Remember, the consequences of your sin will only grow larger the longer you harbor them. Don't be like Solomon. When God points out a sin, get rid of it quickly and get back on the right track toward God's blessings.

Like Solomon, eventually all of us have the tendency to become the company we keep. Before Solomon died, he was worshipping the gods of all the many women he had married.

Phil Joel

SOLOMON'S ADVERSARIES

Although [the Lord] had forbidden Solomon to follow other gods, Solomon did not keep the Lord's command. So the Lord said to Solomon, "Since this is your attitude and you have not kept my covenant and my decrees, which I commanded you, I will most certainly tear the kingdom away from you and give it to one of your subordinates. Nevertheless, for the sake of David your father, I will not do it during your lifetime. I will tear it out of the hand of your son. Yet I will not tear the whole kingdom from him, but will give him one tribe for the sake of David my servant and for the sake of Jerusalem, which I have chosen."

Then the Lord raised up against Solomon an adversary, Hadad the Edomite, from the royal line of Edom. And God raised up against Solomon another adversary, Rezon son of Eliada … He gathered men around him and became the leader of a band of rebels when David destroyed the forces of Zobah; the rebels went to Damascus, where they settled and took control. Rezon was Israel's adversary as long as Solomon lived … So Rezon ruled in Aram and was hostile toward Israel.

1 KINGS 11:10-14, 23-24

JUNE 28

God was heartbroken over Solomon. As much as God loved David's son he could not let his sin go unpunished. So God slowly began to remove his divine protection from his chosen nation. After years of peace, Israel now found itself in a series of minor skirmishes and small wars. And yet Solomon continued in the sin that was causing the

peace of his kingdom to be removed. While he would be spared the full consequences of his sin because of God's love for his father, Solomon's son Rehoboam would not be so fortunate. During his rule he would lose all but one of Israel's tribes.

Like Solomon, the consequences of your sin may well affect the lives of the people you love the most. Even as Solomon's sin affected the kingdom of his son, so the sinful patterns in your life can mar the marriages, friendships, and careers of your family. These destructive effects may be passed on to your children because they follow your example. And sometimes, sinful patterns can actually bring hurt and pain that can affect our families for decades. So be careful to never ignore the Holy Spirit's voice of conviction. Root sin out of your life as soon as you're aware of it so it doesn't cause pain for the people you love the most. And remember, God is full of mercy. As our loving Father, he will always forgive us if we simply repent.

In Jesus' teaching on prayer, part of that teaching involves what needs to be a daily dealing with our sin. Daily asking the Lord to reveal to us those areas which need attention and that He wants to change is very important. Matthew 6:12-13 should be part of how we deal with sin: "Forgive us our debts as we also have forgiven our debtors. And lead us not into temptation but deliver us from the evil one."

Phil Joel

Lessons from the Life of Elijah:
ELIJAH'S PROVISION

Now Elijah ... said to Ahab, "As the Lord, the God of Israel, lives, whom I serve, there will be neither dew nor rain in the next few years except at my word."

Then the word of the Lord came to Elijah: "Leave here, turn eastward and hide in the Kerith Ravine, east of the Jordan. You will drink from the brook, and I have ordered the ravens to feed you there." So he did what the Lord had told him. He went to the Kerith Ravine, east of the Jordan, and stayed there. The ravens brought him bread and meat in the morning and bread and meat in the evening, and he drank from the brook. Some time later the brook dried up because there had been no rain in the land. Then the word of the Lord came to him: "Go at once to Zarephath of Sidon and stay there. I have commanded a widow in that place to supply you with food."

                                        1 KINGS 17:1-9

JUNE 29

In spite of the horrible drought facing the nation of Israel, God's miraculous provision for Elijah had never ceased. When God had told him to hide in the Kerith Ravine, Elijah had wondered how he would survive. Now, however, he had no doubts about God's ability to provide for him; he had been receiving his water from a small brook that never seemed to run dry. His food had been supernaturally delivered to him by ravens—they had brought him bread and meat twice a day. Who but God could command ravens to do his bidding?

But now the brook had dried up so God told him to go to the city of Zarephath and live with a widow there and she would supply him with food. Even though Zarephath was located in the wicked nation of Sidon, Elijah knew better than to disobey the God who had never failed him. Through his obedience, he would receive the provision he needed to be sustained until the famine was over.

No matter what type of "famine" you are facing, God will provide for you too. Maybe you have lost your job through no fault of your own and you're not sure how your bills are going to get paid. Maybe that scholarship you were counting on to pay for college has fallen through and now you're wondering if you'll be able to get an education after all. No matter what you are facing, you don't need to despair. The same God who sent food to Elijah—on the wings of ravens—can meet your needs in miraculous ways as well.

When we are in need, simple faith is our first step to receiving the miraculous provision of God, but we also need humility. Elijah, the greatest prophet in all of Israel, had to ask a destitute widow who lived in a pagan country to support him. It was probably one of the most humbling moments in his life. I cannot count the times I have been humbled, too, by the people God has used to bring his provision into my life. Sometimes everything in me wanted to give the money back just to avoid the embarrassment. But pride, like unbelief, has the ability to quickly disrupt the flow of God's provision. May God give you the grace to trust him for all your needs and the faith and humility to accept his miracles when they come.

GOD'S PROVISION ALMOST NEVER COMES IN WAYS WE EXPECT IT TO. HE LOVES TO SURPRISE US WITH CREATIVE WAYS OF PROVIDING FOR US. TRUSTING GOD IS A SERIOUS BUSINESS YET IT CAN BE HIGHLY AMUSING.
Phil Joel

Lessons from the Life of Elijah:

THE WIDOW OF ZAREPHATH

[Elijah] went to Zarephath. When he came to the town gate, a widow was there gathering sticks. He called to her and asked, "Would you bring me a little water in a jar so I may have a drink?" As she was going to get it, he called, "And bring me, please, a piece of bread."

"As surely as the LORD your God lives," she replied, "I don't have any bread—only a handful of flour in a jar and a little oil in a jug. I am gathering a few sticks to take home and make a meal for myself and my son, that we may eat it—and die." Elijah said to her, "Don't be afraid. Go home and do as you have said. But first make a small cake of bread for me from what you have and bring it to me, and then make something for yourself and your son. For this is what the LORD, the God of Israel, says: 'The jar of flour will not be used up and the jug of oil will not run dry until the day the LORD gives rain on the land.'" She went away and did as Elijah had told her. So there was food every day for Elijah and for the woman and her family.

1 KINGS 17:10–15

JUNE 30

When Elijah entered Zarephath he began to search for the widow God had said would feed him. What he found was a destitute woman who was at the point of death. How could God expect him to ask this poor, dying woman to give him what she obviously didn't even have?

But, in obedience, Elijah asked the woman to bring him a drink of water—and a piece of bread. "Bread!" she

snarled, "As your God lives, I am down to my last handful of flour and my oil is almost gone. Once I make this last meal, my son and I will eat it and die." Far from being angered by the woman's reply, Elijah was touched by her pain and brokenness. With tears in his eyes, he told her not to be afraid. Then he gave her the prophecy that would change her life: "If you will use your last bit of flour to make me a small cake, the God of Israel says that your jar of flour will not be used up, and your oil will not run dry, until the drought has ended." Elijah's faith was contagious—without another word she did what the prophet asked, and his words were fulfilled. Through her obedience, God provided for both Elijah and her whole family until the drought was over.

In spite of the stark reality of her own poverty, this widow obeyed God with the little she had to give. This act of obedience opened the channels of God's supernatural provision into her life. Many times, when we are at our greatest point of need, God will ask us to give. Whether it is the tithe that we do not have or the special offering we cannot afford, when we give out of our poverty, God's supernatural flow of blessings will be released. In Malachi 3:10, God tells us to test him in this area. He says that if we will be faithful in giving to him, he will open the floodgates of heaven and pour out so much blessing that we will not have enough room to receive it! May you, in your need, find the faith to give. Like the widow of Zarephath, you'll see the miracles as a result.

GOD'S PROVISION FOR US IS ALWAYS ABOUT MORE THAN JUST OUR OWN NEEDS. IT'S ALSO ABOUT the NEEDS OF OTHERS. HIS PROVIDENCE FOR US WILL ALWAYS OVERFLOW FOR OTHERS. AND THAT to me is the BEST PART.

Phil Joel

Lessons from the Life of Elijah:
ELIJAH AND THE DROUGHT

And Elijah said to Ahab, "Go, eat and drink, for there is the sound of a heavy rain." So Ahab went off to eat and drink, but Elijah climbed to the top of Carmel, bent down to the ground and put his face between his knees.

"Go and look toward the sea," he told his servant. And he went up and looked.

"There is nothing there," he said.

Seven times Elijah said, "Go back."

The seventh time the servant reported, "A cloud as small as a man's hand is rising from the sea."

So Elijah said, "Go and tell Ahab, 'Hitch up your chariot and go down before the rain stops you.'" Meanwhile, the sky grew black with clouds, the wind rose, a heavy rain came on and Ahab rode off to Jezreel.

1 KINGS 18:41–45

JULY 1

It had been the most amazing day of Elijah's life. Fire had fallen from heaven, and 450 prophets of Baal had been killed by God. Shortly afterward, he heard a sound deep within his spirit, almost like rain falling on the ground. In a flash, he knew it was time for the drought to end.

Elijah climbed to the top of Mount Carmel. Although he was exhausted, he knew he could not avoid the task that God had given him. As he bent down with his face to the ground, he began to fervently pray for rain. He sent his servant to look for rain clouds while he continued to pray. Finally, the seventh time, his servant spotted a small rain cloud. This sign was enough to stoke the fires of Elijah's burning faith. "Tell Ahab to get into his chariot and return to his palace before the rain stops him," he cried out. As he spoke, the sky grew black, the winds began to howl, and a heavy rain began to fall. After three-and-a-half years, the horrible drought had ended because of Elijah's prayers .

What can we learn from this amazing story? First, when Elijah heard the sound of rain in his spirit, he immediately began to pray. How many times have you and I sensed that God wants to do something for us, yet it never seems to happen? Whether we are audibly hearing the message or sensing it in our spirit, it makes no difference. Unless we are willing to pay the price in prayer, whatever we sense will never take place. Sadly, most of us, simply go about our business and leave the real work of prayer to the few who are willing to do it.

Second, Elijah was persistent. Simply stated, he did not quit until he received his answer! This is also an important principle for your life today. If you do not persevere in prayer, you will never receive many of the answers you desperately need. I cannot count the times I have watched Christians quit praying at the moment God was ready to answer them.

Third, when rain was heard, Elijah went to pray, and Ahab went to party. Things are no different today. While there are a few Christians who, like Elijah, really pray, the majority of Christians, like Ahab, live a self-absorbed life because they believe their prayers don't really matter. May God give you the spirit of Elijah as you ponder these words today.

It AMAzes me the Authority he hAS given to us. Even though God could have made it rain whenever he wished, he didn't until a man started to pray. I'm convinced if Elijah hadn't been so faithful in his prayers, the drought wouldn't have been broken until God found someone else who was willing to pray. Spiritual Authority has been given to us. Believe it today.

Duncan Phillips

Lessons from the Life of Elijah:
ELIJAH'S JOURNEY

Elijah was afraid and ran for his life. When he came to Beer-sheba in Judah, he left his servant there, while he himself went a day's journey into the desert…. "I have had enough, Lord," he said. "Take my life; I am no better than my ancestors." Then he lay down under [a] tree and fell asleep.

All at once an angel touched him and said, "Get up and eat." He looked around, and there by his head was a cake of bread baked over hot coals, and a jar of water. He ate and drank and then lay down again.

The angel of the Lord came back a second time and touched him and said, "Get up and eat, for the journey is too much for you." So he got up and ate and drank. Strengthened by that food, he traveled forty days and forty nights until he reached Horeb, the mountain of God. There he went into a cave and spent the night.

1 KINGS 19:3–9

JULY 2

Elijah's faith was so shattered by Jezebel's threats that he ran for his life. Now, hidden from Jezebel in the vastness of the desert, he sat in the depths of despair. Just as the depression was threatening to overwhelm the last remnants of his faith, Elijah fell into a troubled sleep.

God knew that the prophet was utterly committed to serving him. Considering his servant's plight, he sent an angel to strengthen Elijah. When Elijah was awakened by the angel, the place he had been sleeping had been permeated with the presence of God and filled with the fragrance of fresh-baked bread. The angel had cooked a

meal to give Elijah the strength to complete his journey. Once he finished his meal, Elijah fell into a deep sleep.

When the angel awakened Elijah the second time, he told the prophet to get up and eat for the journey was too much for him. When Elijah had completed his second meal, he was strengthened by the power of God and he traveled for forty days and forty nights without ceasing.

There are three main lessons that can be drawn from Elijah's miraculous meals. First, as God provided the food that Elijah needed for his journey, so he provides spiritual food for us today through his Word and the Holy Spirit.

Second, the angel touched Elijah and told him to get up and eat. Unlike Elijah, many Christians whom God has touched refuse to get up and "eat." Your life will never be transformed until you embrace the daily disciplines of seeking God through the Bible. Third, Elijah did not receive the strength he needed until he ate the bread a second time. There will be times of stress and crisis in your life when the normal amount of time you spend with God will not be sufficient to give you the strength you need. In seasons like these, it is critical that you find the additional time it takes to receive the new levels of strength. May God give you a new hunger for heaven's bread as you contemplate the lessons of this incredible story.

1 Thessalonians 5:12-28. This passage is really a picture of Christian conduct. I've always been amused by verse 17. How can I possibly pray without ceasing? It's impossible, right? You've heard people say, "I've worried all day" or "I was continually afraid." We have the ability to be consumed by an emotion. It can invade every second of every day. So then, if we can be consumed by negative emotions, surely we can be consumed every day with prayer and faith.

Duncan Phillips

Lessons from the Life of Elijah:
ELIJAH AND THE STILL, SMALL VOICE

The LORD said, "Go out and stand on the mountain in the presence of the LORD, for the LORD is about to pass by."

Then a great and powerful wind tore the mountains apart and shattered the rocks before the LORD, but the LORD was not in the wind. After the wind there was an earthquake, but the LORD was not in the earthquake. After the earthquake came a fire, but the LORD was not in the fire. And after the fire came a gentle whisper. When Elijah heard it, he pulled his cloak over his face and went out and stood at the mouth of the cave.

1 KINGS 19:11–14

JULY 3

Elijah had finally reached the mountain of God. That night, he heard the voice of God. "Elijah," God whispered, "what are you doing here?" Elijah could not contain the emotions tearing at his heart. Tears streaming down his cheeks, he poured out his complaints to God. "Lord, your people have rejected your covenant, destroyed your holy altars, and killed your prophets. I am so afraid, and now they're trying to kill me," he cried.

"Elijah," God replied, "come out of your cave, for I am going to visit you through the manifestation of My powerful presence." Suddenly, a howling wind struck the mountain with such force that whole rock formations were shattered. Then the mountain began to convulse as it was shaken by an earthquake. When the fire came, it was as if the mountain began to glow with radiant heat. However, God was not in these acts of nature.

Then, Elijah heard the gentle whisper. What the wind, quake, and fire had not been able to do, God's voice did do, for Elijah came out of his cave.

What lessons can be learned from Elijah's miraculous encounter with God? First of all, God was unwilling to answer Elijah's questions (verse 10) until he came out of his cave. Until you let God lead you out of the spiritual cave of unbelief and discouragement in which you have been hiding, God will not give you the direction you need to follow him.

Second, God did not speak through a storm, but in a gentle whisper. Sometimes, Christians expect God to come to them through some miraculous sign or event. This expectation can blind them to the fact that God is already speaking to them through the words of Scripture and the gentle voice of the Holy Spirit. I have found that when God speaks to me, it almost always comes in the form of words that are quietly spoken within my conscious mind. Although the words of Scripture are the final authority in my life, I have also learned to trust my perception of God's voice. May God give you the grace to discern his voice in the midst of the storms you encounter.

WHAT A GREAT STORY OF HOW OUR GOD OPERATES. NORMALLY, WHEN THE SPIRITUAL REALM IS DEPICTED IN MOVIES, IT'S ALL FIRE, BRIMSTONE AND SPECIAL EFFECTS. WE HAVE BEEN CONDITIONED TO THINK THAT GOD ALWAYS REVEALS HIMSELF IN THIS MANNER. I DON'T KNOW IF THIS WILL HELP BUT I OFTEN, AFTER PRAYING, JUST SIT IN HIS PRESENCE TO ALLOW THE FATHER TO TALK WITH ME. AT TIMES IT SEEMS ALMOST AUDIBLE. BUT MOST TIMES IT IS WORDS THAT ARE DROPPED INTO MY SPIRIT OR A RECOLLECTION OF SCRIPTURES THAT I'VE RECENTLY READ. CERTAINLY, IF HE WANTED TO SEND AN ANGEL, THAT WOULD BE GREAT TOO!

Duncan Phillips

Lessons from the Life of Elijah:
ELIJAH'S MANDATE

The Lord said to him, "Go back the way you came, and go to the Desert of Damascus. When you get there, anoint Hazael king over Aram. Also, anoint Jehu son of Nimshi king over Israel, and anoint Elisha son of Shaphat from Abel Meholah to succeed you as prophet. Jehu will put to death any who escape the sword of Hazael, and Elisha will put to death any who escape the sword of Jehu. Yet I reserve seven thousand in Israel—all whose knees have not bowed down to Baal and all whose mouths have not kissed him."

1 KINGS 19:15–18

JULY 4

As Elijah stepped out of his cave into the night air, the whole mountain was still trembling from the presence of the Lord. When Elijah repeated his complaints to the Lord, the Lord answered him with a new mandate. Although the prophet was to go back to Israel, this time he was to minister differently. He was commanded to anoint three men: Hazael, the politician; Jehu, the soldier; and Elisha, the businessman. Through these three men, the enemies who were pursuing Elijah would be destroyed. The Lord also told Elijah that, unlike what his emotions were telling him, he was not the last righteous man left in Israel. In fact, there were seven thousand other Israelites who had refused to bow their knees to Baal. Armed with both a new mandate and a new mindset, Elijah returned to Israel in the power of God's Spirit.

There are several lessons that can be learned from this story. After his triumph over the prophets of Baal, Elijah became discouraged because he had been unable to turn Israel back to the Almighty God. He knew that if fire falling from heaven and the end of a three-and-a-half year drought had not transformed his nation, there was nothing else he could personally do. But isn't it true that when we come to the end of our own strength, we often find that God is simply working to bring us into a new measure of his strength?

God not only had new strength for Elijah, but he had a new plan for the prophet, as well. Although Elijah would still operate in God's miraculous power, he was now commanded to impart this supernatural power to other men. As these new disciples received both the anointing of God and the necessary training, they would bring about the changes in Israel that Elijah would never have been able to accomplish alone. This principle is also critical for our time: If we do not impart to others, through discipleship, the passion and power God has given to us, we will never see the cultures of our world transformed. This type of impartation is not limited to only men and women who have been called into a full-time ministry. God desires to bring a new level of his anointing into the lives of every Christian, no matter what profession they have chosen.

Awesome! This is the spirit behind discipleship — that it's not really about me. When a ministry revolves around one man, sadly the effectiveness of that ministry is limited to what one man can accomplish. But if its mindset is discipleship and nurturing the next generation, we will do exceedingly more for the kingdom than we can accomplish alone.
Duncan Phillips

Lessons from the Life of Elisha:
THE CALL OF ELISHA

So Elijah went from there and found Elisha son of Shaphat. He was plowing with twelve yoke of oxen, and he himself was driving the twelfth pair. Elijah went up to him and threw his cloak around him. Elisha then left his oxen and ran after Elijah. "Let me kiss my father and mother good-by," he said, "and then I will come with you."

"Go back," Elijah replied. "What have I done to you?"

So Elisha left him and went back. He took his yoke of oxen and slaughtered them. He burned the plowing equipment to cook the meat and gave it to the people, and they ate. Then he set out to follow Elijah and became his attendant.

1 KINGS 19:19–21

JULY 5

Elisha was a wealthy farmer, and when the old prophet came and stood in his field, he was so busy plowing that he didn't even notice. But when Elisha saw Elijah, his whole being began to shake. With fire burning in his eyes, Elijah simply took the mantle of the Lord off his own shoulders and threw it on top of Elisha. When Elisha looked up into the eyes of the stern, austere prophet, he meekly asked him if he could tell his parents goodbye before he began his training to become a prophet. "What have I done to you?" Elijah growled. As Elisha turned around and looked at the fields and family he loved so much, he knew his old life was gone forever.

Even though there were at least fifty men training in the prophetic schools of Israel (2 Kings 2), God chose a young businessman to bring his message to the people. This does not mean that leadership training or

theological education is not important, but God has priorities that are even higher than these. Unlike the rest of Israel's young, well-trained prophets, Elisha would be personally mentored by an eccentric, crotchety old prophet—Elijah. While Christian education is important, personal discipleship and mentoring have always been at the heart of God's plan to raise up leaders.

Then, when Elisha was called into the ministry, Elijah cast his cloak over him. There is often a supernatural element that is present when God calls a person into the ministry: Some people are called by God in a dream or through hearing his voice. Others face the reality of their call while reading the Bible or hearing a message preached. No matter how it happens, there is always a very real sense of God's call.

Finally, when Elisha asked to tell his parents goodbye, Elijah answered him: "What have I done to you?" Elijah wanted this young businessman to know that it was God himself, not merely his servant, who was calling Elisha into the ministry. No person can call you into God's ministry—it must be God who does so, but when he does, you are certain to succeed.

PEOPLE often SAY to me, "I DON'T KNOW how you DO it. The tRAVELING, BEING AWAY FROM YOUR FAMILY." AND yes, it is hARD; especiAlly AS my chILDREN GROW theRe will Be times thAt I'll miss importAht events in theiR Lives. But, I Know without A DOUBt thAt I've Been CALLED to DO this At this time. The ALL-Knowing GOD in his infinite wisDOM CREATED me with the peRsonALity AND tALehts I woulD heeD to fulfill this CALLING.

Duncan Phillips

Lessons from the Life of Elisha:
AHAB'S FOOLISHNESS

[King Ben Hadad's] officials said to him, "Look, we have heard that the kings of the house of Israel are merciful. Let us go to the king of Israel with sackcloth around our waists and ropes around our heads. Perhaps he will spare your life."

Wearing sackcloth around their waists and ropes around their heads, they went to the king of Israel and said, "Your servant Ben-Hadad says: 'Please let me live.'"

The king answered, "Is he still alive? He is my brother."

The men took this as a good sign and were quick to pick up his word. "Yes, your brother Ben-Hadad!" they said.

"Go and get him," the king said. When Ben-Hadad came out, Ahab had him come up into his chariot.

"I will return the cities my father took from your father," Ben-Hadad offered. "You may set up your own market areas in Damascus, as my father did in Samaria." Ahab said, "On the basis of a treaty I will set you free." So he made a treaty with him, and let him go.

1 KINGS 20:31–34

JULY 6

The battle had been miraculous. Ahab's small army had crushed the hosts of Aram. After losing one hundred thousand men in the battle, the armies of Aram took refuge in the city of Aphek. As they prepared to be besieged by Israel's armies, another twenty seven thousand of the Aramean soldiers were killed when the walls of the city collapsed on them. With all hope gone, Ben-Hadad, the king of Aram, decided to surrender, but he devised a plan to insure that the king of Israel would be merciful to him.

Much to Israel's amazement, the leaders of Aram came out of the rubble wearing sackcloth and asking for mercy. Ahab was astonished. Perhaps his mortal enemies had repented. "Go and get Ben-Hadad," Ahab said. When he had gently lifted the wicked king of Aram into his chariot, Ben-Hadad quietly articulated his surrender proposal: "I will return the cities my father stole from you, and you may also set up small markets in Damascus." Ahab was so overjoyed at his enemy's contrition that he accepted the treaty and let his enemy go free. God, however, was not pleased. While Ahab was returning to his palace, he was confronted by a prophet of the Lord and told that he would die because he had failed to execute the wicked king.

Ahab was duped by his enemies into settling for less than total victory. The leaders of Aram pretended to mourn, and they convinced Ahab that they had repented. We make this same mistake today. Time after time, we settle for what I call "cosmetic conversions"—people who walk down the aisle, cry, and say all the right things, but whose lives never change. We can't forget to look for the fruit of true change in the lives of people who claim to be converted.

Like Ben-Hadad, who offered to give back the cities that had been stolen, the devil may offer to return what he has stolen from you, but if you settle for that, you've missed the point of the battle you've been fighting. God wants to give us far more than what we've lost—he wants us to take ground for him! Lord, help us not to act foolishly like Ahab did, but instead, believe God for total victory.

Awesome! What a message for our times. I believe the Father is constantly challenging us to expand our territories and boundaries. Read 1 Chronicles 4:9-10. It is within the nature of the enemy to offer us what we already have.

Duncan Phillips

Lessons from the Life of Elisha:
ELISHA AND THE DOUBLE PORTION

Elijah said to Elisha, "Tell me, what can I do for you before I am taken from you?"

"Let me inherit a double portion of your spirit," Elisha replied.

"You have asked a difficult thing," Elijah said, "yet if you see me when I am taken from you, it will be yours—otherwise not."

As they were walking along and talking together, suddenly a chariot of fire and horses of fire appeared and separated the two of them, and Elijah went up to heaven in a whirlwind. Elisha saw this and cried out, "My father! My father! The chariots and horsemen of Israel!" And Elisha saw him no more.

2 KINGS 2:9–12

JULY 7

Elisha knew that it was time for Elijah to leave the earth. He had heard prophets say: "The Lord is going to take your master today." Finally, Elijah turned and asked Elisha the question that would change his life forever: "What can I do for you before I am taken from you?" "Let me inherit a double portion of your spirit," Elisha replied. "You ask a difficult thing," Elijah whispered. "But if you see me when I am taken, what you ask for will be yours."

Out of nowhere, two fiery horses appeared, pulling a chariot behind them. One moment Elijah was there, and then he was gone, taken to heaven in the chariot. As Elisha looked into the heavens, he saw his master's mantle fluttering to the ground. Elisha reached down and took the mantle as he was filled with the rushing torrent of God's power and anointing. When he approached the Jordan River, he struck it with the mantle. "Where is the God of Elijah?" Elisha thundered. After the waters had parted, he walked across the river bed and approached the prophets who were waiting for him. Both Elisha and all the prophets knew he was a new man—God's chosen prophet, the man who had been given the double portion.

In Israel the firstborn son always received a double portion of his father's inheritance. As the firstborn "spiritual son" of Elijah, Elisha was simply asking for what was rightfully his. Although we as Christians are not God's firstborn, we are still his precious children, and we can ask him for the fullness of his Spirit and power.

Elijah told Elisha that he could only have the double portion if he saw him when he was taken. This was not a game; Elijah realized that if Elisha had applied himself in developing his prophetic gifts, he would have what he needed to see Elijah's supernatural transition to the next world. This was Elisha's "final exam." It is the same for you today. Although Jesus Christ has given you access to the Holy Spirit's power and gifts, you will never be able to experience their full reality until you are willing to master the disciplines involved in their operation. May God give you a new hunger for his power as you meditate on these words today.

Some things he desires to give us swiftly and surely. We'll never reach our full potential until we recognize and start to operate within our giftings. The Father even encourages us to desire these gifts. Read 1 Corinthians 12:30-31.

Duncan Phillips

Lessons from the Life of Elisha:
ELISHA'S DITCHES

📖 The hand of the Lord came upon Elisha, and he said, "This is
what the Lord says: Make this valley full of ditches. For this
is what the Lord says: You will see neither wind nor rain, yet this valley
will be filled with water, and you, your cattle and your other animals will
drink…. the Lord … will also hand Moab over to you. You will overthrow
every fortified city and every major town. You will cut down every good
tree, stop up all the springs, and ruin every good field with stones."

The next morning, about the time for offering the sacrifice, there it
was—water flowing from the direction of Edom! And the land was filled
with water.

2 KINGS 3:15-20

JULY 8

The armies of Israel were dying. After seven days of
marching, they were totally out of water. As the kings
met together in the desert's burning heat, Jehoshaphat
asked Ahab if he had a prophet who could inquire of the
Lord for them. Ahab answered, "The only prophet we
have is Elisha, who served that crazy old Elijah for years."
Finally, Jehoshaphat insisted that Ahab call him, and although Elisha
had no respect for Ahab, he knew Jehoshaphat was a godly man, so he
responded to his request.

Elisha began to wait on God. When the presence and power of God
came over him, the plan God gave him was almost beyond his comprehension. The kings were to have their dying armies fill the whole valley
with a series of ditches; while they would see neither wind nor rain, the
whole valley would be filled to overflowing with enough water for every

soldier and all of their animals. The kings realized they had no choice but to obey the prophet's word. The next day, while the armies of Israel and Judah were worshiping God at the morning sacrifice, they heard the sound of a rushing torrent of water. Before their eyes, the valley filled with water, and after they had refreshed themselves, they attacked their enemies and destroyed them.

Just as the armies were to dig ditches even though there was no sign of water, God may also require something of you that can only be done by faith. But when you obey him as Elisha and the armies of Israel and Judah did, you, too, will experience God's miraculous provision.

God wants to meet the needs of his people for spiritual water, as well. In 1 Kings 18, Elijah broke a drought by climbing on top of a hill and praying until the rain came. When we follow his example, we go up to the mountain and intercede for revival until our culture is transformed. On the other hand, Elisha, was called to go down into the valley of human need and dig the very ditches that God had promised to fill with water.

Although both examples are important, could it be that God wants his Church to come down from its lofty, religious mountain and face the needs of a culture that is dying around it? May God give us the grace to dig the ditches of love, mercy, service, and relationships in the heart of a culture that is desperate for hope.

Being a musician, I'm continually amazed at the role music plays in the ways of the Spirit. The wonderful psalmist, David, danced before the Lord, wrote incredible psalms of praise, and was a chief musician. The musicians would march before the armies of the Lord. I believe music can bypass our head and connect instantly with our spirits, opening our hearts to hear from God.

Duncan Phillips

THE SHUNAMMITE'S BUILDING

Elisha went to Shunem. And a well-to-do woman was there, who urged him to stay for a meal. So whenever he came by, he stopped there to eat. She said to her husband, "I know that this man who often comes our way is a holy man of God. Let's make a small room on the roof and put in it a bed and a table, a chair and a lamp for him. Then he can stay there whenever he comes to us."

2 KINGS 4:8-10

JULY 9

The Shunammite woman and her husband were very wealthy. She had no physical needs, yet deep within her heart, there was secret pain. From time to time, the prophet Elisha would take a meal with them. But after he left, there was a sense of God's presence. Finally, she decided to ask her husband to build a small bedroom on the very top of their home where the prophet could stay. "Perhaps if we build Elisha a room," she told her husband, "he won't simply visit us—he will stay with us."

After the room was completed, Elisha came to visit. The prophet was amazed by the couple's generosity and decided to spend the night. As he lay in bed pondering their amazing attitude of service, he told his servant, Gehazi, to call the Shunammite woman to him. "You have been so generous to me," Elisha said. "I would like to do something for you." But the woman said, "I have no needs."

After the woman had left, Elisha asked Gehazi if the woman was being honest. "She only has one need, my lord," Gehazi replied. "She has never had a son, and her husband is aging." "Call her back into my room," Elisha said. As the woman stood in the doorway, she Elisha saw the pain of her barrenness. With faith in his heart, Elisha spoke. "About this time next year, you will hold a son in your arms."

"No, my lord," she objected. "Don't get my hopes up. I can't take the pain of hoping anymore." But twelve months later, the prophet's word came true, and the Shunammite gave birth to a son.

The Shunammite was blessed because of her generosity—and because she wanted the presence of God in her home. God wants to have the same attitude. He delights in people who are not satisfied with merely worshiping him on Sunday mornings, but who want to make room for him in their lives on a daily basis.

The woman took action by building a room for the prophet. Just as she built a special room for God's prophet to inhabit, so we must create space in our busy lives for God through worship, the Word, and waiting on him. The Bible tells us that the Almighty God searches the earth for a place to rest (Isaiah 66:1). I have found that God has many houses, but very few homes—people who have made him the priority of their lives. May God grant you the desire to make more room in your life for him today!

FATHER, YOU ARE WELCOME IN MY HOUSE. THIS LESSON REMINDS ME OF A SMALL PICTURE THAT HUNG ABOVE THE KITCHEN TABLE WHEN I WAS A KID.

CHRIST IS THE HEAD OF THIS HOUSE
THE UNSEEN GUEST AT EVERY MEAL
THE SILENT LISTENER TO EVERY CONVERSATION.

THIS SPEAKS TO ME OF MY PARENTS' DESIRE TO HAVE HIS PRESENCE IN OUR HOME. THE HOLY GHOST IS A GENTLEMAN AND WILL NEVER GO WHERE HE'S NOT INVITED.

Duncan Phillips

Lessons from the Life of Elisha:
THE SHUNAMMITE'S BATTLE

 But the woman became pregnant, and ... she gave birth to a son, just as Elisha had told her.

The child grew, and one day he went out to his father, who was with the reapers. "My head! My head!" he said to his father.

His father told a servant, "Carry him to his mother." After the servant had lifted him up and carried him to his mother, the boy sat on her lap until noon, and then he died. She went up and laid him on the bed of the man of God....

She called her husband and said, "Please send me one of the servants and a donkey so I can go to the man of God quickly and return." ...

When she reached the man of God at the mountain, she took hold of his feet....

"Did I ask you for a son, my lord?" she said. "Didn't I tell you, 'Don't raise my hopes'?"

2 KINGS 4:17–22, 27–28

JULY 10

The Shunammite and her husband were ecstatic; their son was finally old enough to go out into the harvest fields with his father. When the boy reached the field, though, his head began to hurt. When the pain worsened, the father had a servant carry him to his mother. As she lifted her child out of the servant's arms, she cried out to God, but despite her prayers, her son of promise was dead by noon.

Something in the Shunammite refused to accept that her child was gone forever. With faith burning in her heart, she saddled a donkey and began her search for the prophet.

When Elisha saw her approaching, he knew she was deeply troubled. The woman threw herself at Elisha's feet and began to weep. "Didn't I beg you not to raise my hopes?" she cried. With tears streaming down his cheeks, Elisha handed his staff to Gehazi. "Run, my son," he said. "Do not stop for anyone or anything. When you come to the child, lay my anointed staff on his face." The Shunammite, however, refused to go with Gehazi, for she realized it was Elisha who had the power she needed. When Elisha saw that she would not go without him, he followed the woman to the body of her precious son.

When the child died, the Shunammite carried him upstairs and placed him on the prophet's bed. Her response to this terrible crisis provides a tremendous example for us today. You must claim the promises of God's Word (over the death you are experiencing) until his promised resurrection comes. Whether that death is spiritual, relational, financial, or professional, God is able to resurrect his promises in your life.

Even though the Shunammite knew that Gehazi was a respected servant of the prophet, she also realized where the true power lay. It is no different for us today. As much as we should respect the people whom God has placed in our lives, when the crises come, we must tap into the deep reservoirs of power that only our awesome God can provide. May God give you the Shunammite's perseverance as you believe God to resurrect your dream today.

MAy he Give us ALL the peRSeVeRANce to RecLAim the LoST pRomise.

Duncan Phillips

THE SHUNAMMITE'S BLESSING

When Elisha reached the house, there was the boy lying dead on his couch. He went in, shut the door on the two of them, and prayed to the Lᴏʀᴅ. Then he got on the bed and lay upon the boy, mouth to mouth, eyes to eyes, hands to hands. As he stretched himself out upon him, the boy's body grew warm. Elisha turned away and walked back and forth in the room and then got on the bed and stretched out upon him once more. The boy sneezed seven times and opened his eyes.

Elisha summoned Gehazi and said, "Call the Shunammite." And he did. When she came, he said, "Take your son." She came in, fell at his feet and bowed to the ground. Then she took her son and went out.

2 KINGS 4:32–37

JULY 11

When Gehazi reached the boy's still form, he laid the rod of his mentor on the child's face. When nothing happened, he simply gave up and left the room. Elisha, however, was not to be deterred. By the time he entered the woman's home, he was also experiencing the Lord's anger. How dare the evil one touch the child whom God had promised to this woman! In a moment, Elisha had climbed the stairs and was standing over the child's small body.

After shutting the door, he began to cry out in prayer. When that didn't work, he crawled up on the bed and stretched his body out across the child's still form. After spending another season in prayer, the prophet

climbed back into the bed and stretched out on the child for the second time. The boy was revived! When the Shunammite entered the room and saw that her son was alive, she was overwhelmed with thanksgiving and fell at the prophet's feet as she thanked him and the God he served.

Unlike Gehazi, who quit too quickly, Elisha persevered until the child had actually been raised from the dead. It is no different for you and me today: There are certain things in the Kingdom of God that take both faith and patience before they become reality.

When Elisha entered the room where the child was lying, he shut the door, which was not just a natural act. When Elisha shut the door, he was shutting out all the despair and unbelief radiating from both the Shunammite's husband and their extended family. This is a critical principle for your life. There are times when your need for faith will require you to shut yourself away with God until you have received the faith you need. May God give you the faith to experience the fullness of his resurrection power as you contemplate Elisha's example today.

I love ELISHA'S tENACITY. He WAS A "never quit" KIND OF GUY. AS A READ this STUDY. I felt ELISHA'S SpiRituAL ANGeR AS he BURST into the RooM. HOW DARE SATAN TAKE WHAT the LORD HAD GiveN! I Believe he WAS filleD With A RighteouS ANGeR WhICh GAVe him the perSeVeRANCe to see the BoY RAiSeD. LORD, BuilD in me A BACKBone LiKe ELISHA.

Duncan Phillips

Lessons from the Life of Elisha:
DEATH IN THE POT

Elisha returned to Gilgal and there was a famine in that region. While the company of the prophets was meeting with him, he said to his servant, "Put on the large pot and cook some stew for these men."

One of them went out into the fields to gather herbs and found a wild vine. He gathered some of its gourds and filled the fold of his cloak. When he returned, he cut them up into the pot of stew, though no one knew what they were. The stew was poured out for the men, but as they began to eat it, they cried out, "O man of God, there is death in the pot!" And they could not eat it.

Elisha said, "Get some flour." He put it into the pot and said, "Serve it to the people to eat." And there was nothing harmful in the pot.

2 KINGS 4:38–41

JULY 12

When Elisha arrived at the school of the prophets for one of his regular visits, he asked his servant to cook a large pot of stew. One of the men who was sent to collect some herbs for the stew also gathered some gourds from a wild vine. Although he had no idea what type of plant the vine was, he still put the gourds into the pot of stew. As the men were eating the stew, they began to scream out in agonizing pain, "Man of God, help us! There is death in the pot!" Elisha responded by asking one of the men to pour some flour into the stew. From that moment, the stew was perfect, and everyone present could eat in safety.

This strange story has unique ramifications for the day in which we live. I say this because even as there was death in the pot of stew, so there are subtle forms of death being served to those of us in the body of Christ. This death has to do with a "wild vine" which is the way I see Christians relating to Jesus.

First of all, songs like "You're All I Need" capture one of my greatest concerns. Although Jesus is truly all we need for salvation, many Christians seem to forget that he has also called them to walk with other people on this earth. In my own life, I have found that he has used other Christians to encourage me and to help me change. Unlike those Christians who arrogantly claim only God himself can speak to them, I have chosen to live with an utterly different spirit. While Jesus, through the written Word of God, is my primary authority, I readily acknowledge his right to use other people in my life.

The second problem I have seen involves the responsibility of every Christian to be a witness for Christ. I cannot count the number of Christians I have seen who have become so self-absorbed in their relationship with Christ that they are totally oblivious to the needs of the hurting people around them. As much as the Lord desires to be intimate with each and every one of us, he also yearns to see us bring hurting people into the love and joy that only he can provide for them. May God help you not to forget his people or the dying world around you as you passionately pursue him with all of your heart.

The first point of today's lesson got my attention. Indeed, if he was all we needed, why do we go to church? Why do we have pastors, teachers, and prophets to exhort us? Even Christ had twelve close companions. I also think it's dangerous to say that only God speaks to you. Where is your accountability? Thank God for the relationships he puts us in.

Duncan Phillips

NAAMAN'S SERVANT

Now Naaman was commander of the army of the king of Aram. He was a great man in the sight of his master and highly regarded, because through him the LORD had given victory to Aram. He was a valiant soldier, but he had leprosy.

Now bands from Aram had gone out and had taken captive a young girl from Israel, and she served Naaman's wife. She said to her mistress, "If only my master would see the prophet who is in Samaria! He would cure him of his leprosy."

Naaman went to his master and told him what the girl from Israel had said. "By all means, go," the king of Aram replied.... So Naaman left, taking with him ten talents of silver, six thousand shekels of gold and ten sets of clothing.

2 KINGS 5:1–5

JULY 13

Naaman's battle prowess was legendary; under his leadership, the armies of Aram had been invincible. Yet, underneath his armor, unknown to everyone but those closest to him, he was dying from leprosy. Although he didn't realize it, his one hope for deliverance was living in his home. Scripture doesn't tell us her name—we only know she was a young Israelite girl who had been captured and was used as a slave. Yet, despite her personal grief, when she heard about Naaman's condition, her heart melted. She approached Naaman's wife that day, "Mistress, there is a prophet in my country who can cure leprosy," she said. Naaman's wife was overwhelmed by the girl's kindness. When her husband heard the

young girl's report, he immediately went to the king of Aram and asked permission to seek a cure from the prophet.

Like Naaman, there are people around us whose lives are being eaten up by the spiritual leprosy of sin. Underneath their hardened souls they are in desperate need for God. Unless we allow the Holy Spirit to bring us into relationships with the hurting unbelievers around us, we may not see their needs in time to help them.

Also, despite all she had suffered at the hands of her captors, the servant was able to rise above her own pain and show love to her masters. In my own experience, I have found that many Christians have become so offended and sickened by the darkness of their cultures that they have lost sight of the fact that people around them are dying. Although God wants us to hate sin, he also wants us to love sinners with all of our hearts.

Lastly, the slave did not allow the bitterness of her captivity and the loss of her family to rob her of her faith in God. Her attitude is far different from the countless Christians I have seen who hate where God has placed them and they end up missing the purpose for which he brought them there. Could it be that in the midst of the job or school you hate so much, there is a Naaman waiting for you? May God give you the same heart that burned in the little servant girl.

What a great lesson in mercy and compassion. The Israelite girl would have been quite within her "rights" to be resentful and bitter toward her captors. The word says to love the unlovely and to love your enemies. Just think, we were once enemies of God, unlovely in his sight. But someone took the chance and shared Christ with us. Where might we be now if they hadn't?

Duncan Phillips

Lessons from the Life of Elisha:
NAAMAN'S MIRACLE

Elisha sent a messenger to say to [Naaman], "Go, wash yourself seven times in the Jordan, and your flesh will be restored and you will be cleansed."

But Naaman went away angry and said, "I thought that he would surely come out to me and stand and call on the name of the Lord his God, wave his hand over the spot and cure me of my leprosy. Are not ... the rivers of Damascus, better than any of the waters of Israel? Couldn't I wash in them and be cleansed?"...

Naaman's servants went to him and said, "My father, if the prophet had told you to do some great thing, would you not have done it? How much more, then, when he tells you, 'wash and be cleansed'!" So he went down and dipped himself in the Jordan seven times, as the man of God had told him, and his flesh was restored and became clean like that of a young boy.

2 KINGS 5:10-14

JULY 14

Elisha sent one of his servants to tell Naaman. "The prophet of the Lord says you are to go and wash yourself seven times in the Jordan River. When you do this, you will be completely healed," the servant said. *How dare he relay his message through some worthless servant?* As Naaman turned to leave, he angrily spoke to his servants. "Our own rivers are far better than this filthy Jordan."

When his servants finally caught up with his chariot, they entreated him, "I beg you not to let your expectations keep you from submitting to the prophet's instructions." Hearing this plea, Naaman stopped at the bank of the Jordan—deep inside he knew that he had no other choice. As he waded into the Jordan, he was assailed by doubt and fear. He undoubtedly thought: *What if it doesn't work? Everyone will think I'm a fool!* Yet, on the inside, his obedience was already beginning to make him into a different man. After the seventh time, his leprosy was gone, and his skin had been completely restored. Naaman would go home a radically different man, for the leprosy of his body and his heart was gone.

Like many people I have met, Naaman had a distinct set of expectations about how he thought he would be healed. The expectation for God to heal him through some elaborate ritual or religious ceremony almost cost him the miracle he needed. I have watched well-meaning Christians reject the very healing God desired to give them because it did not come the way they expected. Whether it is an unexpected negative prognosis from a doctor or an uneffective marriage counselor, many people lose their faith when their expectations are not met.

Naaman was also not healed the first time he dipped himself in the Jordan—he had to dip *seven times* before he was healed. It almost always takes longer than I expect for me to be healed, as well. As much as this frustrates me, it is simply part of the way God works. May God give you the grace to submit to his treatment plan for your own life!

FOR his WAYS ARE not OUR WAYS. IF we GOT whAT we WANTED when we WANTED it, we WOULDn't need FAith. His timing is perfect even though it mAy not seem so At the time. Let's keep in mind thAt this extended time of FAith-BuILDing is nothing compARED to eteRnity.

Duncan Phillips

Lessons from the Life of Elisha:
GEHAZI'S SIN

After Naaman had traveled some distance, Gehazi, the servant of Elisha the man of God, said to himself, "My master was too easy on Naaman,... by not accepting from him what he brought.... I will run after him and get something from him.".... When Naaman saw him, he got down from the chariot ...

Gehazi [said]. "My master sent me to say, 'Two young men from the company of the prophets have just come to me ... Please give them a talent of silver and two sets of clothing.'"

"By all means," said Naaman... and then tied up the two talents of silver in two bags, with two sets of clothing ... When Gehazi came to the hill, he took the things ... and put them away in the house....

"Where have you been, Gehazi?" Elisha asked. "Your servant didn't go anywhere," Gehazi answered.

But Elisha said, "Was not my spirit with you when the man got down from his chariot to meet you? ... Naaman's leprosy will cling to you and to your descendants forever." Then Gehazi went from Elisha's presence and he was leprous.

2 KINGS 5:19–27

JULY 15

Gehazi couldn't believe his ears. Why did Elisha treat Naaman as a friend—he was an enemy. Surely God wanted them to take the treasure Naaman was offering as payment for his healing. *Well, if Elisha doesn't have the sense to receive God's provision, I'll just help myself,* Gehazi thought.

Gehazi whispered to Naaman, "My master was wondering if you could give us a talent of silver and two sets of clothes because two needy young prophets arrived right after you left." When Naaman responded to his request, Gehazi hid the gifts in his home and reported back to Elisha.

Elisha thundered, "Was this the time for you to enrich yourself? Naaman's leprosy will cling to you for the rest of your life." When Gehazi heard these words of doom from Elisha, his very skin began to be eaten away immediately, for he had become a leper.

The lesson of this story is a frightening one. No matter how well you think you have hidden your sin, God sees and knows all. If you are in secret sin today, do not deceive yourself into thinking that it will stay a secret forever. Jesus himself, in the Sermon on the Mount, said that our Father in heaven sees what is done in secret (Matthew 6:4).

The choice you have today is whether or not you will confess your sin. In my own experience, I have discovered that once sin is brought into the light, it begins to lose its power. When this happens, you will have the power and the help you need to be set free. May God give you the grace to walk in humility as you follow him with all your heart.

WHAT'S funny is that somehow we think our sin is a secret. Are we that deceived to think that the Creator of Space and time doesn't know our every thought? LORD, Rend the tentacles of deception from our minds and expose us to your Light. Help me with humility and obedience. Amen.

Duncan Phillips

ELISHA AND THE ARAMEANS

[The king of Aram] summoned his officers and demanded of them, "Will you not tell me which of us is on the side of the king of Israel?"

"None of us, my lord the king," said one of his officers, "but Elisha, the prophet who is in Israel, tells the king of Israel the very words you speak in your bedroom."

"Go, find out where he is," the king ordered, "so I can send men and capture him." The report came back: "He is in Dothan." Then he sent horses and chariots and a strong force there. They went by night and surrounded the city. When the servant of the man of God got up and went out early the next morning, an army with horses and chariots had surrounded the city. "Oh, my lord, what shall we do?" the servant asked.

"Don't be afraid," the prophet answered. "Those who are with us are more than those who are with them." And Elisha prayed, "O LORD, open his eyes so he may see." Then the LORD opened the servant's eyes, and he looked and saw the hills full of horses and chariots of fire all around Elisha.

2 KINGS 6:11–17

JULY 16

The king of Aram was enraged. There must be a spy among his most trusted counselors! Every one of his plans had been discovered by the king of Israel. After much investigation, the king discovered the source of his betrayal: To his amazement, the spy was Elisha, the prophet of Israel. The king of Aram was determined to kill or capture God's prophet.

When Elisha's servant awakened that morning, he was paralyzed with fear. The city of Dothan had been surrounded. Screaming their war cries, they were preparing to assault the city. Far from being alarmed, or even concerned, Elisha acted as if the armies of Aram did not even exist. *Has the old prophet gone crazy?* the servant wondered. *Maybe he is blind, or simply denying reality.* When Elisha saw his servant's fear, he smiled and said, "Don't be afraid. The armies of Aram are outnumbered." *Outnumbered?!* the servant thought. *He's definitely gone crazy!* At that moment, Elisha began to pray, "Lord, open his eyes." With a blinding flash, everything changed for Elisha's servant. He saw a large heavenly army of fiery chariots surrounding their besiegers.

No matter how many enemies you face, you will never be outnumbered. The psalmist tells us, "The angel of the LORD encamps around those who fear him, and he delivers them" (Psalm 34:7). Jesus himself told Peter to put away his sword because his Father had plenty of angels to deliver him (Matthew 26:53).

God wants to open your eyes to the reality of his power to protect you. Whether he does it through the written Word of God, or through the gifts of the Holy Spirit, it is critical that you begin to see the world around you through the eyes of faith. May God open your eyes today just as he opened the eyes of Elisha's servant so long ago.

WHAT A GREAT STORY! ELISHA'S CONFIDENCE WAS not in WHAT HIS NATURAL SENSES TOLD HIM BUT WHAT HE KNEW OF GOD. WOULDN'T IT BE GREAT TO see WHAT WAS REALLY HAPPENING? WHAT I'M REALIZING AS I GROW IN MY WALK IS THAT THE SPIRITUAL REALM IS MORE "REAL" THAN THIS ONE. IT'S LIKE WE'RE BLINDED BY THIS WORLD BUT REALLY LIVE IN ANOTHER ONE.

Duncan Phillips

Lessons from the Life of Elisha:
ELISHA AND THE SIEGE

There was a great famine in the city;... [King Ahab] said, "May God deal with me, be it ever so severely, if the head of Elisha son of Shaphat remains on his shoulders today!"

Now Elisha was sitting in his house, and the elders were sitting with him. The king sent a messenger ahead, but before he arrived, Elisha said to the elders, "Don't you see how this murderer is sending someone to cut off my head? Look, when the messenger comes, shut the door and hold it shut against him. Is not the sound of his master's footsteps behind him?"

2 KINGS 6:25, 31–32

JULY 17

This time, the king of Aram mobilized his entire army, determined to besiege Samaria until he had destroyed it. As the siege continued, life for the city's inhabitants became almost unbearable. With the strength of his army melting away and the morale of his people plummeting, the king of Israel became desperate for someone to blame. "Surely this must be Elisha's fault. He's done nothing but judge me and my family since the moment he began to prophesy. Maybe if I kill him, the judgment he pronounced on our nation will end."

Meanwhile, Elisha was also suffering from the effects of the siege. Although he knew the Lord would deliver the city, he had no idea how long it would take. While Elisha was seeking God for wisdom, he was warned by the Lord that the king wanted to kill him. Elisha immediately spoke to the elders: "No matter what, keep the door shut when the king's messen-

ger comes. If you open it, the king and his men will come in and kill me."
At that moment, someone began to pound on the door.

The messenger said, "His Majesty says, 'If this siege is sent by the
Lord, why should I serve him anymore?'" Elisha responded to the king's
unbelief with a powerful prophetic word, but he refused to open the door.
Even when the king's men tried to break through the door, the elders
who were with Elisha barred their way. Their stubborn resistance saved
Elisha's life, as well as the lives of the city's inhabitants. The next day, in
accordance with Elisha's word, the armies of Aram were routed by the
Lord, and the siege ended.

Even as King Ahab sent his courier to get inside Elisha's house, so
the enemy of our souls will also send his messengers to us today. In our
case, however, the enemy wants to do more than merely get into our
homes—he wants to get into our hearts. Whether his messenger is a lust-
ful fantasy, a terrifying thought, or a shooting pain in our body, if we open
our hearts to him, the enemy will come in and try to steal our righteousness, peace, and joy.

Elisha asked his friends to help him hold the door shut against the
king's messenger. There are times when I also need the strength of the
friends whom God has placed in my life to hold the doors of my heart and
mind firmly shut against the enemy. May God give you the strength to
close every doorway in your life against the subtle couriers of the enemy
and the death they try to bring.

This is another testimony to the power of
having men in your life. For years I struggled
because I was very independent. It's only been
the last few years that I've experienced this
amazing freedom of having godly men in my
life.

Duncan Phillips

Lessons from the Life of Jehu:
JEHU'S ANOINTING

Jehu got up and went into the house. Then the prophet poured the oil on Jehu's head and declared, "This is what the LORD, the God of Israel, says: 'I anoint you king over the LORD's people Israel. You are to destroy the house of Ahab your master, and I will avenge the blood of my servants the prophets and the blood of all the Lord's servants shed by Jezebel. The whole house of Ahab will perish. I will cut off from Ahab every last male in Israel—slave or free.'"

When Jehu went out to his fellow officers, one of them asked him, "Is everything all right? Why did this madman come to you?"...

Jehu said, "Here is what he told me: 'This is what the LORD says: I anoint you king over Israel.' They hurried and took their cloaks and spread them under him on the bare steps. Then they blew the trumpet and shouted, "Jehu is king!"

2 KINGS 9:6–8, 11–13

JULY 18

In obedience to the prophecy God had given him, Elisha sent a prophet to anoint Jehu as king. Although Jehu was one of the outstanding officers in the army of Israel, being king was the last thing on his mind. When the young prophet arrived at the camp, he immediately approached a group of officers. "I have a message for you, Commander," he said. "Which one of us?" Jehu asked.

"You, sir," the prophet replied. Then the prophet turned toward Jehu, took a horn of anointing oil, and poured it over Jehu's head. The next moment brought prophetic words that shook Jehu to the very depths of his being: "The Lord said, 'I have anointed you king over Israel. You are to destroy the house of Ahab, for I will take my vengeance on him and his family'"

His friends, already wondering about this extraordinary event, were so startled by Jehu's appearance that they exclaimed, "What did this madman want with you? Tell us what he said to you." Jehu replied, "The Lord has anointed me king over Israel!" Then, his friends took off their cloaks and placed them under his feet in acknowledgement of what the Lord had said. After they had blown the trumpets, they hailed him as king.

We serve a God who has a plan for our lives that is far beyond anything we can imagine! Our future in God is full of divine surprises. *You must never forget that you have been born into this world for a purpose—a purpose that may be far different than you have ever expected.* Although Jehu was astonished at the Lord's message, deep in his heart he also knew Elisha and the men serving with him were credible messengers of the God whom they served.

Jehu had to overcome his own doubts and the initial unbelief of his friends. It will be no different for you. In many ways, the unbelief of our own hearts (and of those who love us) is a great threat to our destiny. In other words, without God's help, we all are our own worst enemies! May God give us the grace to overcome the limitations of our own unbelief so that we might embrace the incredible calling he has for our lives.

I've experienced this personally. The knowing in my heart that God had something for me but it not having materialized yet in the natural. We will always face this battle at the door of our destiny.

Duncan Phillips

Lessons from the Life of Jehu:

JEHU'S BATTLE WITH THE KINGS

Joram king of Israel and Ahaziah king of Judah rode out, ... to meet Jehu.... When Joram saw Jehu he asked, "Have you come in peace, Jehu?" "How can there be peace," Jehu replied, "as long as all the idolatry and witchcraft of your mother Jezebel abound?" Joram turned about and fled, calling out to Ahaziah, "Treachery, Ahaziah!" Then Jehu drew his bow and shot Joram between the shoulders. The arrow pierced his heart and he slumped down.

Jehu said to Bidkar, his chariot officer, " ... Remember ... when the LORD made this prophecy about him: 'Yesterday I saw the blood of Naboth and the blood of his sons, ... and I will surely make you pay for it on this plot of ground, ...' Now then, pick him up and throw him on that plot, in accordance with the word of the LORD." When Ahaziah king of Judah saw what had happened, he fled.... Jehu chased him, shouting, "Kill him too!" They wounded him ... but he escaped to Megiddo and died there.

2 KINGS 9 : 21 – 27

JULY 19

Despite the confidence that the prophet's word had given him, Jehu knew it wouldn't be to destroy King Joram. Like his father, King Ahab, Joram and his henchmen held a death grip over the kingdom of Israel. While Jehu was still some distance from Jezreel, King Joram sent horsemen to meet him. "Have you come in peace, Jehu?" asked the king.

"How can there be peace when Jezebel, your mother, has filled God's chosen nation with idolatry and witchcraft?" replied Jehu.

"This is treason!" Joram shouted, and raced away.

As he fled toward Ahaziah, Joram looked down and realized where he was: the very plot of ground that had once been owned by Naboth, the man whom his father, Ahab, had ordered to be murdered in order to steal his property. When the prophet Elijah had heard of this atrocity, he had predicted Ahab would die for what he had done. Jehu also remembered this prophecy, and as his faith was bolstered by its power, he drew his bow and killed the wicked king.

As Jehu began to consolidate his kingdom, he had to conquer his old master in order to fulfill his destiny. Sooner or later you, too, will have to face the things that have threatened to master you. Whether it is a sinful habit, a weakness in your soul, or an ungodly relationship, any master other than God will keep you from your destiny until you have conquered it with the Word of God and the power of the Holy Spirit.

Jehu had the confidence to kill King Joram because he faced him on the very plot of ground where God had promised to destroy Joram and his whole family. This is an important principle for you to learn, because there is no enemy you cannot defeat through the promises of God's Word. May God give us the grace to defeat every enemy we meet on the pathway to our destiny!

Sooner or later, you're going to have to face that which was king over your life before Jesus became king. When this clash comes, you must stand on the promises of God's Word.

Duncan Phillips

Lessons from the Life of Jehu:
JEHU AND JEZEBEL

Then Jehu went to Jezreel. When Jezebel heard about it, she painted her eyes, arranged her hair and looked out of a window. As Jehu entered the gate, she asked, "Have you come in peace, Zimri, you murderer of your master?"

He looked up at the window and called out, "Who is on my side? Who?" Two or three eunuchs looked down at him. "Throw her down!" Jehu said. So they threw her down, and some of her blood spattered the wall and the horses as they trampled her underfoot.

2 KINGS 9:30-33

JULY 20

Although both King Joram and King Ahaziah were dead, Jehu still felt a great deal of fear because the real power behind Israel's throne—Jezebel—was still alive. Jezebel had filled the nation of Israel with the worship of Asheroth and Baal, and she was not alarmed when she heard of Jehu's rebellion. She had no doubt that he, like any other man, would succumb to her charms. Never bothering to call for her guards, she arranged her hair and gazed seductively out the window as she awaited the king's arrival.

When Jehu and his troops arrived, Jezebel spoke to him from her window: "Have you come in peace, Zimri?" When Jehu heard her voice, rather than being drawn in by her seductions, he was repulsed by the degradation emanating from the darkness of her soul. Unwilling to even touch her, he frantically looked for someone to help him. Finally in desperation he called out, "Who is on my side?" Much to his amazement, the eunuchs gathering around her replied, "We are!"

"Throw her out the window!" Jehu said. Before Jezebel knew what was happening, the very men assigned to protect her had thrown her to her death. When Jehu and his troops returned to her palace later that day, the city's dogs had devoured her corpse—just as the prophet Elijah had declared.

Sooner or later, every Christian must overcome the temptation of sexual lust. This is one of those areas where any amount of compromise will open the door of your heart to destruction. There can be no neutrality where sexual lust is concerned. If you do not defeat it, it will eventually destroy you. Whether it destroys your morality, your marriage, or your conscience, it will definitely bring death to your soul.

But Jezebel wasn't just a beautiful woman; she also embodied the very spirit that was destroying the nation of Israel. Today we live in a culture permeated by spirits of immorality and lust. Like every Christian on the planet, you are not just facing human beings, but the all-out attack of the forces of darkness. Human willpower alone is not enough to achieve victory: You must use all the weapons God has given you in order to win this crucial fight.

Unlike many Christians today, Jehu realized he alone could not defeat Jezebel and the spirits she represented, and he cried out for help. Fortunately, there were eunuchs present—men who weren't seduced by Jezebel's charms. If you are not willing to live in accountability to others, you may never conquer the sin in your life. May God give you the grace to defeat sexual lust and live in his victory.

This is probably for men the biggest battle they'll ever face, but such an important one to conquer. Like Jehu, we must find godly men to stand with us. Almost no one can conquer this alone.

Duncan Phillips

Lessons from the Life of Jehu:
JEHU AND JEHONADAB

After he left there, he came upon Jehonadab son of Recab, who was on his way to meet him. Jehu greeted him and said, "Are you in accord with me, as I am with you?"

"I am," Jehonadab answered.

"If so," said Jehu, "give me your hand." So he did, and Jehu helped him up into the chariot. Jehu said, "Come with me and see my zeal for the Lord." Then he had him ride along in his chariot.

2 KINGS 10:15–16

JULY 21

Jehu's power was growing by the moment. With King Joram and his mother, Jezebel, dead, it seemed to the Israelite nation that Jehu had a clear path to the throne. Jehu himself, however, was not so confident. Although he had been a tremendous military leader, he had no experience in politics, nor had he developed all the skills necessary to rule a kingdom. Now, as he was on the way to confront the priests of Baal in their high temple, he keenly felt his need for wise counsel and advice. As he thundered on toward the temple of Baal, he saw a man walking beside the road. This man also was neither a great soldier nor a powerful politician. He was, however, widely considered to be one of the most righteous and wisest men in all Israel. In fact, his sage counsel had kept every member of his own family free from the sins that were polluting Israel.

His name was Jehonadab, the son of Recab. And amazingly, he was searching for Jehu. When Jehu had reined in his horses, he looked

down at this humble man. "Do you approve of what I'm doing?" he asked Jehonadab.

"I do," he replied.

"Give me your hand," Jehu said, "so I can help you up into my chariot." Much to the amazement of Jehu's entire entourage, this humble man remained by the king's side. With his help and wise counsel, the priests of Baal were executed, and their temple was demolished. Jehu's relationship with Jehonadab may be one of the most compelling examples of a godly friendship in the whole Bible. Although there are many lessons for our day in this story, we will examine only two of them.

First, despite his extraordinary rise to power, Jehu acknowledged his need for the counsel and advice of other men. Tragically, this is not the attitude most successful people maintain. I cannot count the times I have seen godly people deceived—and even destroyed—by the very success they have achieved in their pursuit of God. This happens to them because their successes cause them to become so arrogant and filled with pride that they lose their need for human help.

Second, Jehu not only asked Jehonadab into his chariot—he also asked him into his life. This humble spirit and open heart gave him the help he needed to destroy the false religion that had been seducing his kingdom. It is no different for your life today; if you will humbly open your heart to the counsel of other godly men and women, you will never lack the advice and wisdom you need. May your desire for accountability grow along with your success as you ponder Jehu's humility today.

No matter how successful we get, may we all have that desire for godly counsel in our lives because in it is such freedom. It's a comfort to have that confirmation from godly men around you.

Duncan Phillips

Lessons from the Life of Hezekiah:
HEZEKIAH'S PAIN

Ahaz was twenty years old when he became king, and he reigned in Jerusalem sixteen years. Unlike David his father, he did not do what was right in the eyes of the LORD his God. He walked in the ways of the kings of Israel and even sacrificed his son in the fire, following the detestable ways of the nations the LORD had driven out before the Israelites.... In the third year of Hoshea son of Elah king of Israel, Hezekiah son of Ahaz king of Judah began to reign. He was twenty-five years old when he became king, and he reigned in Jerusalem twenty-nine years. His mother's name was Abijah daughter of Zechariah. He did what was right in the eyes of the LORD, just as his father David had done. He removed the high places, smashed the sacred stones and cut down the Asherah poles. He broke into pieces the bronze snake Moses had made, for up to that time the Israelites had been burning incense to it.

2 KINGS 16:1–3; 18:1–4

JULY 22

When Hezekiah ascended the throne, no one would have believed that he would go down in history as one of Judah's greatest kings. His father, Ahaz, had been a wicked king who had led Judah into the worship of false gods. Hezekiah grew up under one of Judah's most wicked kings.

Young Hezekiah should have been no more than a spiritual and moral misfit, yet Scripture records that he rose above his past to lead Judah into some of her greatest days of revival and renewal.

Even when he was confronted by the might of the Assyrian empire, Hezekiah trusted in the Lord and watched as his enemies were miraculously slaughtered. His bold stand was amazing, because he had watched this very same empire destroy the other eleven tribes of Israel. King Hezekiah is one of the greatest examples of faith in the Bible.

What lessons can we learn from this king's amazing reign? Scripture says that he walked in the ways of his father, David. Even though Hezekiah had no real role models in his own life, he was still able to develop a dynamic relationship with God because he emulated the ways of David, his ancestor and Israel's most successful king. So many people of our generation have been wounded and traumatized by the pain of divorce and family dysfunction. If Hezekiah was able to learn from a man who had his own share of family troubles, certainly you can receive from the precious Christians whom God has placed in your life!

Unlike almost every other king in Israel or Judah's history, Hezekiah destroyed the "high places," locations throughout the nation where people would worship God without the teaching of the priests, Levites, or prophets of the Lord. In many cases, this type of independence opened the door to the worship of false gods. Sadly, we find this same dead spirituality in our culture today. In the United States, more than 90 percent of the people claim to believe in God, but in reality, the majority of them don't serve the God of the Bible at all. They have simply designed their own ideas of how he should be worshiped. May God give you the grace to rise above the pain of your past and worship him in spirit and in truth.

ALL OF US WHEN WE LOOK BACK AT OUR CHILDHOOD CAN PROBABLY FIND CERTAIN ELEMENTS OF DYSFUNCTION IN OUR FAMILIES. THE TEMPTATION IS TO SAY, "THAT'S HOW MY FAMILY WAS SO THAT'S HOW I'LL BE." BUT IT DOESN'T HAVE TO BE LIKE THAT. YOU CAN MAKE DECISIONS BY THE POWER OF GOD THAT IT'S NOT GOING TO BE THAT WAY IN YOUR LIFE OR THE LIFE OF YOUR FAMILY.

Duncan Phillips

Lessons from the Life of Hezekiah:
HEZEKIAH'S POWER

Hezekiah trusted in the LORD, the God of Israel. There was no one like him among all the kings of Judah, either before him or after him. He held fast to the LORD and did not cease to follow him; he kept the commands the LORD had given Moses. And the LORD was with him; he was successful in whatever he undertook. He rebelled against the king of Assyria and did not serve him. From watchtower to fortified city, he defeated the Philistines, as far as Gaza and its territory.

2 KINGS 18:5–8

JULY 23

Hezekiah lived in a world dominated by the power of Egypt and the might of the bloodthirsty Assyrian empire. Despite the influence of these tremendous empires, Judah experienced one of the greatest periods in all of Israel's history under Hezekiah's reign. Biblical worship was reinstated, the Philistines were crushed, and the Assyrian empire's finest legions were shattered.

What were the secrets of Hezekiah's amazing reign? First, the Bible says very clearly that Hezekiah trusted in the Lord, the God of Israel. Although both he and his kingdom were threatened with countless crises, he never once failed to put his faith in the Lord. His dynamic faith was the true source of his success. Whether it was restoring Solomon's temple after it had suffered years of neglect, or defying Sennacherib with a holy boldness, in the end Hezekiah refused to live his life based on the dictates of his circumstances. It should be the same for you today. No matter what you are facing, if you will simply choose to put your trust in God and the promises of his Word, he will give you all the power you need.

Second, Hezekiah not only trusted in the Lord, but he also walked in full obedience to him. The Bible says, "He held fast to the Lord and did not cease to follow him." Although faith is critical, without obedience you will never come into the fullness of what God has promised you. *You must never forget that it is one thing to believe God for his promises; it is an entirely different matter, however, to pay the price that is required to possess these promises.* For example, many Christians believe God wants them to have a tremendous marriage. Yet if they don't follow God's plan for marriage, all the belief in the world will never help them have the marriage they desire. Even worse is the fact that many of these same Christians will end up being frustrated with God and even disillusioned because they have never received the kind of marriage they felt the Word had promised them. Tragically, like many of their contemporaries, they have conveniently forgotten the sobering words of James: "Faith without works is dead" (James 2:17, NKJV) May you walk in the faith and obedience you need to fully possess God's promises for your life.

AS GREAT AS FAITH IS, WE WILL NEVER BE ABLE TO WALK INTO OUR DESTINY UNTIL WE ARE WILLING TO WALK IN OBEDIENCE.

Duncan Phillips

Lessons from the Life of Hezekiah:
HEZEKIAH'S PERIL

"This is what the king of Assyria says: Make peace with me and come out to me. Then every one of you will eat from his own vine and fig tree and drink water from his own cistern, until I come and take you to a land like your own, a land of grain and new wine, a land of bread and vineyards, a land of olive trees and honey. Choose life and not death! Do not listen to Hezekiah, for he is misleading you when he says, 'The LORD will deliver us.' Has the god of any nation ever delivered his land from the hand of the king of Assyria?... Who of all the gods of these countries has been able to save his land from me? How then can the LORD deliver Jerusalem from my hand?"

2 KINGS 18:31–33, 35

JULY 24

It had been one of the most amazing times in Judah's history. After the temple had been cleansed and restored, the people of God had celebrated the Passover in its fullness for the first time in years. But just as the people of Judah began to enjoy the fruits of their labor, the armies of Assyria began their invasion of the nation. Their military forces had never been defeated.

Now with their armies surrounding Jerusalem, even some of Judah's stoutest soldiers were beginning to despair. What hope did Judah have against the might of an empire that had destroyed nations far greater than theirs? The Assyrians were filled with arrogant confidence. Day after day, they mocked the faith of Jerusalem's inhabitants by telling them their God would not save them.

Finally, with the Assyrian propaganda grinding down the morale of his people, Hezekiah tore his clothes, put on sackcloth, and went into the temple of the Lord. While they were presenting their nation's needs to the prophet, he cried out to the Lord in prayer. When God heard the prayers of Hezekiah, he gave a prophetic word of hope through Isaiah, and eventually the angel of the Lord destroyed the Assyrian army, killing 85,000 of their soldiers.

Judah experienced one of the greatest threats in her history just when she was in the middle of spiritual renewal. Many times when we are in a period of spiritual growth, the enemy will launch an assault because he is threatened by the change we are experiencing. Although these attacks can be unsettling, I have learned to see the good in them because if I were not making spiritual progress, the enemy would not be threatened!

The enemy's favorite lies and deceptions show up in the propaganda of the Assyrians. When the enemy is trying to break down your defenses, he will remind you of everyone you know who has fallen into sin, given up, or been deceived. In moments of attack like these, it is critical that you stand on the promises of God's written Word.

Hezekiah responded to the Assyrian crisis by seeking the counsel and help of both God and his prophet. If you are to receive the strength and direction you need, it is important that you learn to go to both God and godly people in your time of need. May God give you the strength to defeat your enemies as you contemplate this story of divine deliverance!

The effectual, fervent prayer of a righteous man avails much. No matter what surrounds you today, God is able to deliver you.

Duncan Phillips

LESSONS FROM THE LIFE OF HEZEKIAH:
HEZEKIAH'S PROGNOSIS

In those days Hezekiah became ill and was at the point of death. The prophet Isaiah, son of Amoz, went to him and said, "This is what the LORD says: Put your house in order, because you are going to die; you will not recover."

Hezekiah turned his face to the wall and prayed to the LORD, "Remember, O LORD, how I have walked before you faithfully and with wholehearted devotion and have done what is good in your eyes." And Hezekiah wept bitterly.

Before Isaiah had left the middle court, the word of the LORD came to him: "Go back and tell Hezekiah, the leader of my people, 'This is what the LORD, the God of your father David, says: I have heard your prayer and seen your tears; I will heal you. On the third day from now you will go up to the temple of the LORD. I will add fifteen years to your life. And I will deliver you and this city from the hand of the king of Assyria. I will defend this city for my sake and for the sake of my servant David.'"

2 KINGS 20:1–6

JULY 25

Hezekiah couldn't believe it. After being used by God to restore the temple and see his people delivered from the hand of Assyria, he was dying. *Surely God will deliver me!* he thought. At that moment, Isaiah entered the royal apartments. "Yes, God has answered my prayers," Hezekiah whispered. "The great prophet has come to announce my healing!" But the words from the prophet's mouth left him anything but encouraged: "Put your house in order because you are going to die; you will not recover."

"God," Hezekiah wept, "if your prophet has pronounced my doom, what hope is there for me? How can I have any grounds for faith without a word of encouragement from you?" Yet even in the depths of despair, the spirit of faith in Hezekiah refused to be denied. Isaiah, who hadn't left the palace yet, felt the presence of God. The Lord said, "Isaiah, go back and tell Hezekiah that I will heal him because I have heard his prayers." After Isaiah returned to Hezekiah, the king asked for a sign. When the Lord gave him the sign he had asked for, Hezekiah knew he was healed.

Even though Hezekiah had received a bad prognosis, he did not give up. Rather, the king continued to battle in faith for his healing. In my own life, I have seen God's miraculous hand countless times. Whether it was the time I was dying from hepatitis after returning from the mission field or facing my wife's battle with cancer, God has never failed to heal me or my family.

More amazing was the fact that Hezekiah continued to believe in his healing even when it seemed that God himself was unwilling to help. Imagine what it must have been like for Hezekiah when Isaiah told him that he was going to die. When you are battling an illness in your life or someone else's, you must stand on the promises of God's Word.

There are times when God does not heal in this lifetime. Even in those times, however, I know that he is sovereign, and I have determined to submit to his will with faith and joy in my heart.

Even though the WORD came down from the LORD's prophet that he WAS going to die, Hezekiah's faith rose within him. He cried out to the LORD with such faith that God responded to him and he WAS healed.

Duncan Phillips

Lessons from the Life of Josiah:

THE SECRETS OF JOSIAH'S SUCCESS

[Josiah] did what was right in the eyes of the Lord and walked in the ways of his father David, not turning aside to the right or to the left.... In his twelfth year he began to purge Judah and Jerusalem of high places, Asherah poles, carved idols and cast images.... In the eighteenth year of Josiah's reign, to purify the land and the temple, he sent Shaphan son of Azaliah and Maaseiah the ruler of the city, with Joah son of Joahaz, the recorder, to repair the temple of the Lord his God.... While they were bringing out the money that had been taken into the temple of the Lord, Hilkiah the priest found the Book of the Law of the Lord that had been given through Moses.... When the king heard the words of the Law, he tore his robes. He gave these orders to Hilkiah, Ahikam son of Shaphan, Abdon son of Micah, Shaphan the secretary and Asaiah the king's attendant: "Go and inquire of the Lord for me and for the remnant in Israel and Judah about what is written in this book that has been found. Great is the Lord's anger that is poured out on us because our fathers have not kept the word of the Lord."

2 CHRONICLES 34:2–3,8,14,19–21

How could an eight-year-old king with such a dark spiritual heritage develop into one of the greatest kings in all of Judah's history? There are three principles that explain Josiah's rise to greatness. First, after reigning for eight

JULY 26 **years, the Bible says that Josiah began to seek the Lord:**

when he was sixteen, something changed inside the heart of this young king. Instead of leaving the faith, Josiah began to develop his own faith by seeking the Lord. No matter how godly your family is, if you don't learn to seek the Lord on your own, sooner or later, you will no longer follow the faith of your parents. Proverbs 8:17 clearly states that those who *seek* him will find him. Are you looking for the Lord?

Second, when he was twenty, Josiah began a campaign to restore the nation's faith. In my own experience, I have found that until we can see the destiny God has for us, we are usually unwilling to fully embrace the spiritual disciplines required to follow God, but once we grasp our destiny, we have the vision and direction we need to live our lives for him.

Third, when he was twenty-six, he began to repair and restore the temple that Solomon had built. While the workmen were repairing the temple, Hilkiah the priest found the book of the law. When the priest read the words of Moses to the king, he tore his clothes because his heart was broken. For the first, he fully realized how badly the nation he loved had sinned against God. Throughout his youth, Josiah never had a copy of God's Word, but today we are surrounded by Bibles. We often take them for granted because we have never learned how to practically apply the Bible's promises to our lives and we remain unchanged. May God give you the grace to seek him with all your heart and personally discover the reality of his promises for your life.

GOD HAS A DESTINY FOR ALL OF US. NO MATTER WHAT AGE WE ARE. WE CAN'T RIDE INTO HEAVEN ON THE SHIRT TAILS OF OUR PARENTS. WE HAVE TO HAVE OUR OWN RELATIONSHIP WITH GOD AND SEEK HIM WITH ALL OUR MIGHT.

Duncan Phillips

Lessons from the Life of Josiah:
THE DEATH OF JOSIAH

 Neco king of Egypt went up to fight at Carchemish on the Euphrates, and Josiah marched out to meet him in battle. But Neco sent messengers to him, saying, "What quarrel is there between you and me, O king of Judah? It is not you I am attacking at this time but the house with which I am at war. God has told me to hurry; so stop opposing God, who is with me, or he will destroy you." Josiah, however, would not turn away from him, but disguised himself to engage him in battle. He would not listen to what Neco had said at God's command but went to fight him on the plain of Megiddo.

Archers shot King Josiah, and he told his officers, "Take me away; I am badly wounded." So they took him out of his chariot, put him in the other chariot he had, and brought him to Jerusalem, where he died.

2 CHRONICLES 35:20–24

JULY 27

Josiah was at the peak of his power. With his kingdom in revival, he felt there was nothing that could stop him. Therefore, when Neco, king of Egypt, allied himself with the king of Assyria, Josiah declared war. Although the king of Egypt warned Josiah that he would be opposing God by attacking him, Josiah would not listen. Instead, Josiah disguised himself in the armor of another person. Tragically, Neco had been truthfully prophesying, for Josiah was killed in the ensuing battle. When Jeremiah heard of the king's demise, he was so heartbroken that he composed a lament to mourn his death.

Like many men in their late thirties, Josiah might have become very insecure. Although he had experienced remarkable success, he may have

felt the need to prove himself. He decided to become a warrior king, and this rash act cost him his life. Sadly, Josiah's foolishness is being repeated by many men in our culture today. For some of them, their insecurities will only cost them time and money. Other men, however, will lose their marriages or businesses. Their attempts to satisfy the needs of their soul through their accomplishments are doomed to failure, for only God himself can satisfy the ultimate longings of the human heart.

Josiah made the foolish decision to disguise himself in the armor of another man. Many men do the same thing today. Whether it is the pastor who tries to become a businessman or the couch-potato who tries to once again prove his manhood by running a marathon in his forties, even when they accomplish these feats, their souls remain unsatisfied.

Unfortunately, Josiah was in such a hurry to go to war that he missed the divine warning from Neco. It is clear in Scripture that God himself was speaking to Josiah. The state of Josiah's soul caused him to miss the warnings he normally would have discerned. I have found that when a person is being driven by their own pride and insecurities, they can easily miss the warnings that God sends, instead of being led by the Spirit. May God give you the grace to negotiate the traps that come in each stage of your life.

Because of his insecurities, Josiah got out from under God's covering and was foolishly killed. Who knows what might have happened to his nation if he had lived a full life as king?

Duncan Phillips

Lessons from the Life of Jeremiah:
THE CALLING OF JEREMIAH

 The word of the Lord came to me, saying,

"Before I formed you in the womb I knew you,
before you were born I set you apart;
I appointed you as a prophet to the nations."

"Ah, Sovereign Lord ," I said, "I do not know how to speak; I am only a child."

But the Lord said to me, "Do not say, 'I am only a child.' You must go to everyone I send you to and say whatever I command you. Do not be afraid of them, for I am with you and will rescue you," declares the Lord. Then the Lord reached out his hand and touched my mouth and said to me, "Now, I have put my words in your mouth. See, today I appoint you over nations and kingdoms to uproot and tear down, to destroy and overthrow, to build and to plant.... Get yourself ready! Stand up and say to them whatever I command you. Do not be terrified by them, or I will terrify you before them."

JEREMIAH 1:4–10, 17

The young man was astonished. Although he had been born into the family of a priest, he had never before experienced the presence of God like this. As he tried to process what he was experiencing, he could hear the voice of God resounding in his heart: "Before I formed you, I knew you.

JULY 28 **You were set apart before you were born to be a prophet to the nations." As the weight of these words began to settle on him, he** fell to his knees. "Lord," he cried. "How can I speak for you? I am only a young boy."

"Do not say you are only a child," the Lord thundered. "You must go everywhere I send you and say whatever I command you." Before Jeremiah could draw back, the fingers of God brushed his lips and the very words of God were imparted deep within his soul: "You have authority over nations now," the Lord said. Finally, with the words "get ready" echoing in his spirit, Jeremiah's first encounter with the Lord was over.

Like Jeremiah, you have been born into this world for a purpose. You may have been called to advance God's kingdom as a professional, or you may have been called to serve God in full-time ministry. No matter what your calling, do not be afraid. The same God that promised to give Jeremiah the strength and power he needed is more than able to do the same for you.

God refused to allow Jeremiah's concerns about his age to keep him from fulfilling his calling. Whether you are thirteen or thirty-three, God has a plan and a destiny for your life!

Jeremiah was told to "get ready" for amazing things to come. You must never forget that it is God's job to give you a purpose, and it is your job to prepare yourself for that purpose. Stay committed to your church and to other believers. Stay in God's Word, and seek him in prayer. May God give you a heart for these things today as you ponder the story of Jeremiah's calling.

Like Jeremiah, all of us are tempted to run from God's calling on our lives and the responsibility it brings. No matter how weak or young we are, God has the strength we need to fulfill our calling.

Duncan Phillips

Lessons from the Life of Jeremiah:
JEREMIAH'S COMPLAINT

O LORD, you deceived me, and I was deceived;
　　you overpowered me and prevailed.
I am ridiculed all day long;
　　everyone mocks me....
But if I say, "I will not mention him
　　or speak any more in his name,"
his word is in my heart like a fire,
　　a fire shut up in my bones....
I hear many whispering,
　　"Terror on every side!
　　Report him! Let's report him!"
All my friends
　　are waiting for me to slip, saying,
"Perhaps he will be deceived;
　　then we will prevail over him
　　and take our revenge on him."

JEREMIAH 20:7, 9–10

Jeremiah was heartbroken because it seemed to him that the whole nation despised him. When he prophesied that God was going to judge the nation of Judah for their sins, he was branded as a traitor. One day a chief priest even had him brutally beaten and put in stocks. After being mocked all day by the jeering crowds, they finally released

JULY 29

him, but no one really knew how long he would remain free, for Zedekiah, Judah's current king, was already his mortal enemy.

After the horrible beating, something in Jeremiah finally broke. "O God," Jeremiah wept, "I am ridiculed all day long. Even my own friends want to kill me! The words you give me become more judgmental and harsh. Your word is like a burning fire deep within my heart—the more I try to contain it, the more it burns. O God! Is there any hope for my soul?"

No matter how called and anointed you are, sooner or later, you will face dark times. When you face these times, remember that the mission God has given you may well bring you into a season of persecution, rejection, and spiritual conflict.

Where are you today? Maybe like Jeremiah, you feel deeply rejected and even misunderstood by the very people who should understand you the most. God promises to give you everything you need. If you will simply take your stand on his promises, the light of his Word can break through the darkness and change your life.

Like Jeremiah, we all have moments when we want to quit. In moments like this, it's no time to make major decisions about anything.

Duncan Phillips

Lessons from the Life of Jeremiah:
JEREMIAH'S BATTLE

But the LORD is with me like a mighty warrior;
so my persecutors will stumble and not prevail....
O LORD...
let me see your vengeance upon them,
for to you I have committed my cause.
Sing to the LORD!
Give praise to the LORD!
He rescues the life of the needy
from the hands of the wicked.
Cursed be the day I was born!...
Cursed be the man who brought my father the news, ...
May that man be like the towns
the LORD overthrew without pity.
May he hear wailing in the morning,
a battle cry at noon.
For he did not kill me in the womb,
with my mother as my grave,
her womb enlarged forever.
Why did I ever come out of the womb
to see trouble and sorrow
and to end my days in shame?

JEREMIAH 20:11-18

JULY 30

Even worse than the pain of Jeremiah's battered body was the brokenness of his heart. He felt very alone, but despite all of his pain, he was beginning to feel the stirrings of

fresh faith. After a verbal confession of God's faithfulness and power, the tide of faith began to rapidly rise in Jeremiah's heart. The next thing he knew, he was singing and worshiping the Lord.

But suddenly it seemed as if the bottom fell out of his faith. Where once his soul had soared on the wings of praise and prayer, it now plummeted in despair, and Jeremiah chose to go down the pathway of spiritual passivity and paralysis. As the atmosphere created through his worship slowly dissipated, the praises that had come from his lips were replaced by curses of bitterness and hopelessness.

Notice that Jeremiah did not experience any form of victory until he began to confess the promises of God. It is clear in Scripture that both hearing and speaking the Word of God play a critical role in building our faith.

Once Jeremiah had confessed the Word of God, he began to worship the Lord. When you are willing to offer a sacrifice of praise, God will respond to you with a fresh manifestation of his presence and power.

Unfortunately, right at the moment of victory, Jeremiah fell back into the depths of bitterness and despair. Christians throughout the ages have faced this struggle. They want to worship God with all their hearts, but there are places of pain within their souls that make it almost impossible. You must rise up and take dominion over your soul by the power of God, so that you will be able to defeat the darkness that is threatening to overwhelm you. May God give you the grace to walk in his divine power as you worship and praise him today!

We ALL have times in our lives when the only encouragement we may get is self-encouragement. At these moments, you'll probably find that no one is answering their phone. If you don't encourage yourself in the LORD, you won't be encouraged.

Duncan Phillips

Lessons from the Life of Jonah:
JONAH'S REBELLION

The word of the LORD came to Jonah son of Amittai: "Go to the great city of Nineveh and preach against it, because its wickedness has come up before me." But Jonah ran away from the LORD and headed for Tarshish. He went down to Joppa, where he found a ship bound for that port. After paying the fare, he went aboard and sailed for Tarshish to flee from the LORD. Then the LORD sent a great wind on the sea, and such a violent storm arose that the ship threatened to break up. All the sailors were afraid and each cried out to his own god. And they threw the cargo into the sea to lighten the ship. But Jonah had gone below deck, where he lay down and fell into a deep sleep.

The captain went to him and said, "How can you sleep? Get up and call on your god! Maybe he will take notice of us, and we will not perish."

Then the sailors said to each other, "Come, let us cast lots to find out who is responsible for this calamity." They cast lots and the lot fell on Jonah.

JONAH 1:1–7

JULY 31

This can't be from God!" the Johah shouted, "After all, I'm the Lord's great prophet to Israel! Surely the God I serve would never waste his powerful prophet on the likes of a brutal, idol-worshiping, barbaric nation like Assyria. As for Nineveh," the angry prophet wailed, "that foul city is no more than a human pigpen of degradation and filth."

Despite Jonah's stubbornness, God was persistent. "Jonah," God whispered, "go to the great city of Nineveh and preach, because I have seen its wickedness." "If you've seen its wickedness," Jonah replied, "why don't you just destroy it and save me the trouble of going?" "Jonah, you must go!" God entreated him. Finally, Jonah decided to run away.

When Jonah finally arrived in Joppa, he found a ship bound for the Port of Tarshish. After Jonah had boarded the ship, he went down into the hold and fell into a deep, restful sleep. his newfound tranquility, however, was to be short-lived.

Once the ship was on its way, the winds of a violent storm began to blow. With the ship threatening to break, all of the sailors began to call out to their own gods. In desperation, they woke Jonah. "How can you sleep? Get up and pray. Maybe your God will save us," they cried. But all Jonah could do was hang his head in shame. When the sailors decided to cast lots to determine who was responsible for the horrible storm, the lot fell to Jonah. The prophet knew in his heart that there would only be one way to calm the storm.

Although God delights in the happiness of his people, this is not his highest priority. Whether we like it or not, all of us have been given a divine mandate, which, will decide God's placement in our lives. When Jonah arrived in Joppa, a boat was waiting for him—rebellion is frequently more convenient and easier than obedience. Although Jonah thought that Tarshish would be a more peaceful place than Nineveh, he actually ran right into a storm. Don't run away from God's will for your life! Instead, may God give you the grace to run after him will all your heart today.

Jonah's problem wasn't just rebellion, it was discrimination. His hatred of the Ninevites caused him to take a course of action that he typically would not have taken. What will you do when God calls you to a person or people that you don't like or are not accustomed to being around?

Duncan Phillips

Lessons from the Life of Jonah:
JONAH AND THE GREAT FISH

 The L ORD provided a great fish to swallow Jonah, and Jonah was inside the fish three days and three nights. From inside the fish Jonah prayed to the L ORD his God. He said:

"In my distress I called to the L ORD,
    and he answered me....
You hurled me into the deep,
    into the very heart of the seas,
    and the currents swirled about me ...
But you brought my life up from the pit,
    O L ORD my God.
When my life was ebbing away,
I remembered you, L ORD,
    and my prayer rose to you,
    to your holy temple."...

And the L ORD commanded the fish, and it vomited Jonah onto dry land.

JONAH 1:17 — 2:3, 6 – 7, 10

AUGUST 1

As the storm continued to grow in intensity, Jonah told the crew to throw him overboard. Although they knew Jonah was running from the Lord, they had no desire to drown him, but they cried out to the Lord to forgive them and threw Jonah into the churning depths of the sea.

Slowly but surely, Jonah was drowning. After fighting for one last breath, his body began to descend into the depths of the sea. Suddenly he was swallowed alive by a gigantic fish. He found himself lying in a foot of water, the air reeking with the smell of rotten fish. From time to time, fresh air would be released into the chamber, as well as faint rays of light.

As horrible as his situation was, Jonah knew that he had been shown tremendous mercy by the God against whom he had rebelled. "Lord, forgive me," Jonah wept. "If you release me from this whale, I *will* go to Nineveh, but even if you don't free me, I will die worshiping you." When the Lord saw Jonah's repentance, he commanded the fish to vomit Jonah out of its mouth. This time, when God spoke to Jonah, Jonah obeyed.

Where are you today? Maybe you have been swallowed up by the consequences of your sin and rebellion. Take heart, the same God who delivered Jonah is also able to deliver you. The timing of your deliverance, however, will be determined by you, for you will not be set free until you have learned the lessons God is teaching you and you repent. Instead of blaming God for his horrible circumstances, Jonah faced the fact that his own rebellion had been the cause of his terrible plight.

Jonah had true sorrow for what he'd done—he was not repenting in order to escape from the stomach of the whale, but because he had grieved the heart of God. When he promised to fulfill his vows, he was committing to obey God for the rest of his life, no matter how long it lasted, and at that moment, God released him from his imprisonment. Once you have fully responded to God, like Jonah, you, too, will be projected into your destiny!

UNLIKE MANY CHRISTIANS I HAVE MET, JONAH DID NOT BLAME GOD FOR THE HORRIBLE ORDEAL HE EXPERIENCED IN THE WHALE'S BELLY. HE REALIZED THAT HIS OWN SIN AND REBELLION HAD BROUGHT HIM INTO THE WHALE. THIS IS IMPORTANT BECAUSE UNTIL YOU STOP BLAMING GOD FOR YOUR PROBLEMS, YOU'LL NEVER BE ABLE TO COME TO HIM.

Jeff Frankenstein

JONAH'S MINISTRY

Then the word of the LORD came to Jonah a second time: "Go to the great city of Nineveh and proclaim to it the message I give you."

Jonah obeyed the word of the LORD and went to Nineveh. Now Nineveh was a very important city—a visit required three days. On the first day, Jonah started into the city. He proclaimed: "Forty more days and Nineveh will be overturned." The Ninevites believed God. They declared a fast, and all of them, from the greatest to the least, put on sackcloth....

When God saw what they did and how they turned from their evil ways, he had compassion and did not bring upon them the destruction he had threatened.

JONAH 3:1-5, 10

AUGUST 2

When Jonah reached Nineveh, he was almost overwhelmed by the size and grandeur of the capitol of the Assyrian empire. Yet, there was no doubt in his heart that God had sent him to this city. With their legendary reputation for brutality, he fully expected to be persecuted and even martyred. He knew the message that God had given him would not be easily received. God had commanded Jonah to tell the Assyrians that they would be destroyed in forty days unless they repented from their wicked ways.

As he walked through the city preaching these grim tidings, he was stunned by the response of the Assyrians. Far from persecuting him, they received his message with brokenness and weeping. Even the king of Assyria took off his royal robes and covered himself with ashes and sack-

cloth. Jonah was even more amazed when the king commanded every person within his empire to repent of their wicked ways and to fast and pray until God's judgment was averted. When God saw the city's response, he decided to spare them from the destruction they deserved.

How encouraging this story should be to us! If God can transform the capitol city of one of history's most brutal empires, what can he do in your city, school, neighborhood, or workplace? If God can use a stubborn prophet who didn't even love the people to whom he was preaching, surely God can use you to radically change your world! Like Jonah, God has given you the command to go and tell people to repent and be saved. If you would just obey him and begin to proclaim the simple message of the Gospel, perhaps you would begin to see the same kind of results that Jonah experienced.

Tragically, many Christians have become so "seeker-sensitive" that we now run the risk of blunting the sharp edge of the Gospel. The lordship of Christ is rarely mentioned. *Discipleship* has become a dirty word in many circles, and the subject of hell is a great taboo. Far from being tepid and politically correct, Jonah told the Ninevites that they would be destroyed in forty days if they did not repent. Although I do not despise cultural sensitivity and creative methods of spreading the Gospel, these things alone cannot transform the human heart. Unless we boldly, yet lovingly, proclaim the message of the Gospel—that Jesus Christ alone is Savior and Lord—we will never experience the fullness of the Holy Spirit's convicting power in the lives of those Christ came to save.

When I saw how Jonah's simple message of repentance changed a whole city, I was reminded again of the power of the Gospel. Every time we are tempted as Christian artists to rely on our talents or the incredible technology we have been given, the Holy Spirit reminds us that it is only the power of the Gospel that changes people.

Jeff Frankenstein

Lessons from the Life of Jonah:
JONAH'S ATTITUDE

But Jonah was greatly displeased and became angry. He prayed to the LORD, "O LORD, is this not what I said when I was still at home? That is why I was so quick to flee to Tarshish. I knew that you are a gracious and compassionate God, slow to anger and abounding in love, a God who relents from sending calamity. Now, O LORD, take away my life, for it is better for me to die than to live."

But the LORD replied, "Have you any right to be angry?"

JONAH 4:1–4

AUGUST 3

Surely God's mighty prophet would be overjoyed! After all, Nineveh had been spared from the wrath and judgment of God because the people had turned from their wickedness and repented. But instead, Jonah was far from overjoyed. "I knew it!" he pouted to himself. "God judged his special prophet by sending a whale to eat him, and yet he spares these brutal, pig-headed Assyrian dogs and gives them no punishment at all! Why did God have to choose me? He knew how much I hated these unclean barbarians! I figured this would happen all along. In fact, this is one of the main reasons I ran away. If there was even a chance that God would spare these infidels, I wanted nothing to do with it," Jonah fumed. "God, it's unfair!" he screamed. "The Ninevites are a people I wanted to see destroyed, yet you used me to save them!" As Jonah grew silent, the heart of God was grieved. It was clear that his servant had not learned all the lessons he had needed to learn in the belly of the whale. Jonah's heart was still filled with anger and bitterness.

What does this story have to do with you? Sadly, like Jonah, you may despise—or even hate—the very people who need you the most. Although you claim to simply hate their sin, in reality, you find *them* to be despicable, as well. The truth is, typically you spend far more time talking *about* them than you do talking *to* them.

Unlike Jesus, who is the friend of sinners, the only people you befriend are those who share your vision, values, and standards. In the name of holiness and spiritual compatibility, you may have turned your back on the very people whom God has called you to reach. You may think you have to stay away from sinners in order to maintain your lofty standards of holiness. This may be the case for new believers, but if *your* own holiness is that fragile, perhaps you should examine your heart. I am convinced that God may well be more grieved by the hardness of his own people's hearts than by the rebellion of those who don't even know him.

Until you, and other Christians, as well, allow God to fill your heart with his love and compassion, those segments of our culture that need God the most will remained unchanged. But if you open up to him and allow him to work through you, there is no limit to what he can do through your life!

My wife and I were recently commenting on how sensitive non-Christians are to the attitudes of Christians. No matter how articulate we are, if they do not feel that we're truly interested in them as people, they will never listen to our message. I have made it one of my life goals not to be like Jonah. I'm asking God to fill me with his love and compassion for people more and more every day.

Jeff Frankenstein

Lessons from the Life of Jonah:
JONAH'S VINE

[Jonah] made himself a shelter, sat in its shade and waited to see what would happen to the city. Then the LORD God provided a vine and made it grow up over Jonah to give shade for his head to ease his discomfort, and Jonah was very happy about the vine. But at dawn the next day God provided a worm, which chewed the vine so that it withered. When the sun rose, God provided a scorching east wind, and the sun blazed on Jonah's head so that he grew faint. He wanted to die, and said, "It would be better for me to die than to live."

But God said to Jonah, "Do you have a right to be angry about the vine?"

"I do," he said. "I am angry enough to die."

But the LORD said, "You have been concerned about this vine, though you did not tend it or make it grow. It sprang up overnight and died overnight. But Nineveh has more than a hundred and twenty thousand people who cannot tell their right hand from their left, and many cattle as well. Should I not be concerned about that great city?"

JONAH 4 : 5 – 11

AUGUST 4

Jonah had gone on strike. After building a small shelter east of the city, he refused to budge from its shade until God destroyed Nineveh. Even when God confronted him, Jonah's response was to pout silently. However, while Jonah was pouting, God miraculously caused a beautiful plant to grow up over the prophet's shelter. Jonah was comforted by the shade this miracle plant provided and smiled for the first time in days. But his smile would be short-lived.

The next day, God sent a voracious worm to visit Jonah's plant. Before Jonah even had a chance to squash the worm, the plant withered and died. If this wasn't enough, when the sun was at its brightest, God sent a burning wind to scorch the skin of his hardened prophet. Jonah became so miserable that he wanted to die. "Jonah!" the Lord thundered. "Do you have the right to be angry?"

"I'm angry enough to die!" Jonah retorted. The Lord responded, "You have been grieved over the death of a plant that you neither planted nor tended. How dare you question my love for the inhabitants of Nineveh who were so blinded by their own sin that they could not even tell the difference between right and wrong?"

Are you more concerned about your own comfort than about the salvation of a dying world? This desire for comfort and lack of concern for the lost may well be the greatest sin of the Church today. While millions are searching to find the God they so desperately need, the majority of Christians are basking in the comfort of their salvation. While millions are dying, the Church waits for God to judge the culture they have come to hate. The truth is, "it is time for judgment to begin with the family of God" (1 Peter 4:17), and God typically deals with the comfortable before he judges those in need of comfort.

When I thought about Jonah's vine, I couldn't help but think of all the ways that God has blessed me. Whether it is my finances, my wonderful wife, good health or the joy of the Lord, I realize that these things are not simply for me. Everything God has given my wife and me is not just for our enjoyment and pleasure. He has given us these things so we can reach the hurting people around us.

Jeff Frankenstein

Lessons from the Life of the Shulammite:
IT'S NOT MY FAULT

Let him kiss me with the kisses of his mouth—
     for your love is more delightful than wine.
Pleasing is the fragrance of your perfumes;
     your name is like perfume poured out.
No wonder the maidens love you!
Take me away with you—let us hurry!
     Let the king bring me into his chambers.
We rejoice and delight in you;
     we will praise your love more than wine.
How right they are to adore you!
Dark am I, yet lovely,
O daughters of Jerusalem,
     dark like the tents of Kedar,
     like the tent curtains of Solomon.
Do not stare at me because I am dark,
     because I am darkened by the sun.

SONG OF SONGS 1:1–6

AUGUST 5

She was young, she was beautiful, and the king loved her with all of his heart. However, it was a struggle for the Shulammite to believe in his love. She was not of royal birth like the rest of his wives. She was just a simple farm girl who had caught the king's eye while he was traveling throughout his kingdom. But unlike his other wives whom he had married for the sake of political alliances, she was his one true love.

The Shulammite couldn't understand this. After all, his other wives were beautiful. Raised from birth to be queens, they had advantages she never experienced. Her own hands were rough, and her skin had been permanently tanned by the rays of the sun as she had labored in her family's vineyards. Though she loved the king with all her heart, she found herself unable to respond to his affection. Like a beautiful garden surrounded by high walls, with a locked gate, something within her resisted the fact that anyone could really love her.

What is locking up your heart today? Are you like the Shulammite, unable to receive the love of the great King who adores you—the Lord Jesus Christ? If so, there is no reason for despair. Even as the heroine of this love story received the healing she longed for, so Christ fully intends to heal you.

To receive this healing you must first acknowledge your need to be healed. On one hand, the Shulammite said that "she was Dark, yet lovely." On the other hand, she acknowledged that she was insecure because of the color and condition of her skin. Until you acknowledge the reality of your pain, you will never experience the fullness of God's promises for your life.

Far from being a hopeless victim, you are a child of God (1 John 3:1) and the bride of His beloved Son (Revelation 19:7). As the revelation of who you really are in Christ begins to penetrate into the depths of your soul, you will have the security and confidence you need to receive the healing that is yours for the asking.

BLAme shifting is probably one of the main reasons that many Christians aren't healed from their wounds. No matter how you've been hurt, sooner or later you must take responsibility for your own life. In my own life I have learned that no matter how people hurt me or let me down, if I blame them I will never be healed.

Jeff Frankenstein

FOLLOW THE TRACKS OF THE SHEEP

Tell me, you whom I love, where you graze your flock
    and where you rest your sheep at midday.
Why should I be like a veiled woman
    beside the flocks of your friends?
If you do not know, most beautiful of women,
    follow the tracks of the sheep
and graze your young goats
    by the tents of the shepherds.
I liken you, my darling, to a mare
    harnessed to one of the chariots of Pharaoh.

SONG OF SONGS 1:7–9

AUGUST 6

It was the Shulammite's strong will that had kept her functioning, even when the pain was more than she could bear. Now, however, her stubborn will was about to become her greatest enemy. "Why do I have to be like the rest of your wives," she asked the king. "I refuse to wear that stupid veil. After all, if you consider me to be so beautiful, why not let everyone gaze upon me?" The king was amazed how this beautiful young woman could be so wounded and broken one moment, yet become a stubborn, raging fury the next moment.

    When he patiently explained the laws and traditions of his kingdom to her, she refused to listen. "Darling," he explained, "if you ever want to experience the fullness of my love and favor, there are certain ways you

must walk." Finally, when she remained obstinate, he likened her to one of the mares pulling Pharaoh's chariot. Although she responded with a small smile, she had no idea how much truth the king's simple analogy contained for her life.

Maybe this story reminds you of someone you know; maybe even yourself. If it does, take heart, for your loving God has an answer for your willfulness—as well as for the pain of your heart. In my experience, I have discovered that people who have been deeply wounded are also, in many cases, deeply willful. This happens because it takes tremendous willpower to cope with the pain of a horrible childhood or an abusive relationship. Sadly, the independence and stubbornness these people develop can eventually become a barrier to healing.

The words "... follow the tracks of the sheep and graze your young goats by the tents of the shepherd" (verse 8) are very important. Although God delights in an intimate relationship with you, you will never experience the fullness of healing outside of the Church. In the right church, you will find the fellowship and counsel that healing requires. Even as the Shulammite was encouraged to follow the tracks of the sheep, so it is vital for you to follow the commands of Scripture. Unlike the "designer religions" being adopted within our culture today, the God of the Bible has a plan of healing for your life which must be followed exactly if you desire his promised results. God is not something you try; he is Someone you follow.

Although all of us would protest that we're willing to be healed, if you're anything like me, there's probably a bit of stubbornness hiding inside of you. Whether we're stubborn about admitting we're wrong or about asking for help, this attitude can become one of the major barriers to the healing you need so badly.

Jeff Frankenstein

Lessons from the Life of Shulammite:
I CAN'T FOLLOW YOU NOW

My lover spoke and said to me,
"Arise, my darling,
   my beautiful one, and come with me.
See! The winter is past;
   the rains are over and gone.
Flowers appear on the earth;
   the season of singing has come,
   the cooing of doves
   is heard in our land "...
My lover is mine and I am his;
   he browses among the lilies.
Until the day breaks
   and the shadows flee,
turn, my lover,
   and be like a gazelle ...
   on the rugged hills.

SONG OF SONGS 2:10–12, 16–17

AUGUST 7

"Darling, please come out," the king begged her. "The seasons have changed; it's not winter anymore. I know how much you hate winter weather, but it's gone." Solomon entreated her, "There are flowers everywhere, and the doves are cooing. The fragrance of spring is filling the air."

"I won't come out," the Shulammite pouted. "It is still dark and there are frightening shadows everywhere I look."

"How would you know?" the king asked. "You haven't been out of your chambers for weeks. It's only dark because you have refused to come out into the light of day." The king sighed.

"I'm sorry," she wept. "Go without me; I will not come out until this stifling darkness is gone."

What a sad tale this is. The Shulammite woman had not even realized that the seasons had changed, because she had locked herself in her room and refused to come out. Whether it was because of her wounding or her willfulness, she was missing the very spring season her soul so desperately needed.

Do you see it? Like the springtime that came to the Shulammite woman's life, a new season is dawning for you. The horrible winter of your wounding is coming to an end, and a springtime of new growth and hope is on the way. If you listen carefully, you will even hear the sound of the dove of the Holy Spirit at work in your life. He is comforting you, he is calling you, and he is convicting you. Even if you cannot see the fruit of change in your life yet, the buds preceding this fruit are steadily growing and soon will be ready to blossom. Jesus Christ himself promises to take you by the hand, through the Bible and the power of the Holy Spirit, and lead you out of the pain that has entrapped your soul. Take a deep breath now, and let the Holy Spirit fill your whole being with the fragrance of the healing that has been promised to you.

When I read this, it makes me never want to miss my time — my time to be healed; my time to be changed; my time to be blessed. I have discovered that if we allow our circumstances to dictate whether or not we follow God, we may never experience the blessings He has for us.

Jeff Frankenstein

Lessons from the Life of the Shulammite:

COME OUT OF YOUR CAVE

My dove in the clefts of the rock,
    in the hiding places on the mountainside,
show me your face,
    let me hear your voice;
for your voice is sweet,
    and your face is lovely.

SONG OF SONGS 2:14

Until the day breaks
    and the shadows flee,
I will go to the mountain of myrrh
    and to the hill of incense.
All beautiful you are, my darling;
    there is no flaw in you.
Come with me from Lebanon, my bride,…
Descend from the crest of Amana,
    from the top of Senir, the summit of Hermon,
    from the lions' dens
and the mountain haunts of the leopards.

SONG OF SONGS 4:6–8

AUGUST 8

Even though her husband and king pleaded with her, the woman refused to come out of her chambers. Although she had almost opened the door when Solomon had told her that her face was lovely, in her heart she had not believed him. After all, her skin was so coarse and dark

compared to the other women in the palace. Far from being truthful, she believed he was simply taking pity on her wretched condition.

Yet for the Shulammite, far more was at stake than missing the changing seasons. In fact, the longer she stayed in her chambers, the more endangered she would become. Whether her refusal to come out of her room was based on the pain of her poor self-esteem or the stubbornness of her own heart is not the issue. Either way, she was resisting the love that only King Solomon could give her.

Where are you today? Are you still trapped in the cave of self-pity, rejection, and depression? If so, you may be in more danger than you even realize. In Song of Songs 2:11–17, we find that the Shulammite was in danger of missing her new season. By the time you come to Song of Songs 4:8, her peril, however, had grown exponentially, for the room where she had been hiding had now become the den of lions and the haunt of leopards. If you remain isolated and depressed because of the pain of your own heart, sooner or later, there is an enemy who will come to rend your soul.

Even if this is the predicament in which you find yourself, don't despair. No matter how battered your self-esteem is, or how many lies you have believed, Jesus Christ says that your voice is sweet to him, and your face is lovely. Deep in your heart, you have been wondering if he was calling you out so he could rebuke you or correct you for your wickedness. Fortunately, your perceptions could not be farther from the truth. Jesus, the lover of your soul, is not calling you into punishment and pain. He is calling you into a loving embrace that will begin the healing in your troubled soul.

Isn't it amazing that the very things that we think will bring us happiness and security can be the very things the devil uses to destroy us? Whether it is an ungodly relationship or a deep pattern of self-pity, we must let Jesus bring us out of these things.

Jeff Frankenstein

Lessons from the Life of the Shulammite:

FOXES IN THE VINEYARD

Catch for us the foxes,
   the little foxes
that ruin the vineyards,
   our vineyards that are in bloom.

SONG OF SONGS 2:15

AUGUST 9

"My darling," the king whispered through the door, "if you do not deal with these attitudes, you will destroy our relationship."

"What relationship?" she whimpered. "No matter how hard I try, I'm never good enough. I know you must secretly despise how I look. I want your love, not your pity."

"You have both," the king replied. "Yet if you do not deal with your unforgiveness, stubbornness, and self-pity, these attitudes, like little foxes, will destroy the blossom of our love."

How about you? Are any attitudes running loose in your heart threatening to destroy your relationship with Christ? If so, according to Song of Songs 2:15, you are the only one who can stop them. That's right—as much as God loves you, he is not going to deal with these attitudes for you. You may be wondering to yourself, *How do I stop these deadly attitudes? I don't even know what they are.* You're right. Before you can deal with them, you must first identify them. Perhaps you are threatened by the sins of unforgiveness, bitterness, anger, and stubbornness. Or you may need to deal with the rejection, depression, fear, and loneliness that have been stalking the chambers of your heart.

No matter what attitudes you are facing, they can all be stopped in basically the same way. After you have identified them as either a sin of which you need to repent, or a wound from which you need healing, you must bring them to Christ through the promises of His Word. Once you have applied the specific promise to your area of need, your faith for deliverance will begin to grow. As your faith grows, you will begin to experience the strength you need to completely uproot the mindsets and sins that have been damaging your soul.

Even with the promises of God's Word, however, you may still have trouble capturing your thoughts and bringing them under the obedience of Christ. Second Corinthians 10:4–5 makes it clear that there are certain mental, emotional, and spiritual strongholds that must be demolished before you can begin the process of placing your thoughts and attitudes under the captivity of Christ and his Word. These strongholds could include deeply ingrained patterns of bitterness or longstanding struggles with depression, but God is well able to shatter *all* entrenched bondages through the power of the Holy Spirit. Never forget: God wants to do more in your life than simply set you free. He wants to bring you to a place where you have captured the very things that had once captured you.

ALL of us in the BAND hAve hAD to LeARn how to CAtch the Little "foxes" thAt this DevotionAL DescRiBes. Whether it is selfishness, gRumpiness fRom Being on the ROAD, or Losing ouR tempeR, we have LeARneD thAt if we Do not "CAtch" these things, they will fRACtuRe ouR unity AnD keep us fRom ACComplishing GoD's Best foR ouR Lives.

Jeff Frankenstein

Lessons from the Life of the Shulammite:

HIDE AND SEEK

All night long on my bed,
I looked for the one my heart loves;
    I looked for him but did not find him.
I will get up now and go about the city,
    through its streets and squares;
I will search for the one my heart loves.
So I looked for him but did not find him.
The watchmen found me
    as they made their rounds in the city.
"Have you seen the one my heart loves?"
Scarcely had I passed them
    when I found the one my heart loves.
I held him and would not let him go.

SONG OF SONGS 3:1–4

AUGUST 10

How could he leave me alone in this frightening room? He knows how scared I get," the Shulammite groaned to herself. "I knew he didn't really love me," she pouted. "I didn't really mean it when I locked the door and told him to go away. If he was any kind of man at all, he would have broken the door down and rescued me from myself. After all, it's not really my fault. I had a bad childhood."

Finally, in her desperation to find the king, the woman unlocked the door. At this point, all she wanted was the love that only her husband, King Solomon, could give. As she searched the darkened streets of the city, her desire for him grew by the moment. When she saw one of the city's powerful watchmen, she was not deterred. "Have you seen the one my heart loves?" she cried. At that very moment, however, she found the one she was seeking. With tears streaming down her cheeks, she began to whisper these words: "Now that I have found you, I will never let you go."

How could King Solomon have been so unkind to his fearful young bride? Surely he would have waited by her door no matter how long it took for her to finally open it. Unfortunately, that was not the case, for when she opened the door he was gone. I am afraid this is an area where God is much like Solomon; if you choose to play "hide and seek" with him, he is more than willing to play along. Although God doesn't play games, he may hide himself from you for a season.

The prophet Isaiah wrote, "You are a God who hides himself" (Isaiah 45:15). When you refuse to seek him, God, because of his great love, may hide from you. Then you will have no choice but to seek him. Don't let this thought frighten you, however, because the same God makes this promise: "Those who seek me find me" (Proverbs 8:17). He will allow himself to be found—when you seek him with your whole heart.

Fortunately for us, God's hiding places are very predictable. God is not hiding in horoscopes, bars, or New Age religion. The search for God is actually far simpler than that. I have found that God typically hides in church services, the Bible, prayer, and Christian fellowship. If you can't find him in any of these places, it's probably because he wants to spend more time alone with you. When that is the case, simply do the same things, but go deeper and longer. Then, you will find him, just as you always have before.

I don't know about you, but I have played hide and go seek with God more times than I can count. Even when he hides, however, I have found that he's easy to find. He's easy to find because he's always hiding in the same places — places like prayer, worship, Bible study, and church.

Jeff Frankenstein

Lessons from the Life of the Shulammite:
LOCKED UP

You are a garden locked up, my sister, my bride;
   you are a spring enclosed, a sealed fountain....
You are a garden fountain,
   a well of flowing water
   streaming down from Lebanon.
Awake, north wind,
   and come, south wind!
Blow on my garden,
   that its fragrance may spread abroad.
Let my lover come into his garden
   and taste its choice fruits.

SONG OF SONGS 4:12, 15-16

AUGUST 11

By this time, she could hardly stand to be away from him. Far from being an unhealthy case of codependence, the Shulammite woman had finally realized the reality of the love they shared. But despite this revelation, her soul was still locked up. No matter how hard she tried, something deep within her refused to trust her husband; it seemed almost as if she was helpless to combat the forces raging in her heart. Finally, in desperation, she began to share some of her most painful secrets with him. "No matter what it takes, don't let me shut you out," she pled. "I know that at one point I was both wounded and willful, but I'm not that way anymore. No matter how wounded I am, I have set my will to do what is right. Please, I beg you, don't let me destroy the love you have so freely given me."

Upon hearing these words, the heart of the king was broken. Although he realized she had been severely crippled by her pain, he also realized she would do whatever it took to find the healing she so badly needed. Despite the agony of her soul, the Shulammite woman had accepted the very revelations that would ensure her healing. Where once she had been in denial, she was now willing to face reality. In addition, she had settled the question of authority in her life. Relinquishing her stubbornness, she had finally come to the place where she would do whatever it took to be delivered.

Have you come to this place in your life yet? If you have, then there is hope for you today, no matter how badly you have been hurt. The Shulammite was so desperate for freedom that she even asked for the north wind, the coldness of winter, to blow into the garden of her soul. Where once she refused to follow the king because she thought it was wintertime, she was now willing to face anything, even the frigid temperatures, in order to be healed. It should be no different for you today. If you are unwilling to trust God with your whole life, you don't trust him enough to be healed. *Wait a minute*, you may think, *I don't want to trust God until he heals me*. Let me stop you right there, because that kind of thinking could be the very reason you're not healed. People who are waiting to trust God until he heals them will wait forever. No matter how locked up your soul is today, if you simply trust him enough to invite him in, he will scale the walls you have erected and bring healing and light to your soul.

I've learned in my own life that no matter how "locked up" I am, Jesus has the key that is needed to open me up. I have found that if I am simply willing to let Him touch me, there is nothing that He cannot accomplish in my life.

Jeff Frankenstein

Lessons from the Life of the Shulammite:

SEALED WITH HIS LOVE

Place me like a seal over your heart,
    like a seal on your arm;
for love is as strong as death,
    its jealousy unyielding as the grave.
It burns like blazing fire,
    like a mighty flame.
Many waters cannot quench love;
    rivers cannot wash it away.
If one were to give
    all the wealth of his house for love,
    it would be utterly scorned.

SONG OF SONGS 8:6–7

AUGUST 12

My darling," she whispered, "I want to be like the signet ring that you wear on the chain around your neck. I want to stay that close to your heart, that secure in your arms. I want our love to grow stronger than we ever imagined. Let it burn with righteous jealousy. Not the self-absorbed feelings of insecurity, but a holy jealousy for God's best for our lives." With tears streaming down her cheeks, she sighed one last time and said, "When we have this kind of love, nothing will quench it. Nothing will destroy it, for all the money in the world cannot buy it."

Where once she had been afraid to both give love and receive love, now her whole soul was bubbling with a love she had never imagined possible. This love was finishing the work of healing in her heart. With her will submitted to her king, and her wounds being healed, she had no greater passion than to please the one who loved her so deeply.

It should be no different for you. In the end, the revelation of how much God loves you will free your soul to finally love him in return. Once you have this revelation, you will become so jealous for his best in your life that resisting him will rarely even be an option. As your passion for him grows like a fire, it will begin to consume the sinful attitudes that have plagued your soul. This raging fire of love will be nearly impossible to quench.

Do you understand? Just as the king was waiting for the Shulammite to finally realize the great love he had for her, so your loving Savior is waiting on you today. Don't break his heart by resisting him, but allow his love to fill your heart and your life. Many waters cannot quench his love; not even a mighty river can wash it away. Like the signet ring around the neck of the king, you are close to his heart; he has even engraved your name on the palms of his hands. Run to him and experience his love today.

The kind of love this devotional describes is the kind of love I want to have for God. A love that no circumstance can quench and no trial can squelch. When I consider the passion that this story displays, it makes me want to love God with all my heart.

Jeff Frankenstein

Lessons from the Life of the Shulammite:

HIS EYES

Thus I have become in his eyes
like one bringing contentment.

SONG OF SONGS 8:10

AUGUST 13

The Shulammite had always despised her body. When she had come to the palace and seen the voluptuous figures of the other queens, her self-esteem had become even worse. Now, finally, it wasn't an issue. In the king's eyes, she was beautiful, and that was all that mattered.

How about you? Have you, like the Shulammite woman, learned the secret of seeing yourself through his eyes? Not through the eyes of King Solomon, but instead through the eyes of Jesus Christ, your beloved Savior. Sooner or later, you must choose whose opinion will define your reality: the opinion of your Lord or the opinions of the people and the culture around you.

You may have allowed your self-worth to be defined by the faces, fashions, and forms that shape our culture today. If these are the forces shaping the basis of your self-worth, you must be miserable, because only a person with the form and figure of a Greek god or goddess could survive in this cultural fantasy world.

Or perhaps you have allowed the essence of who you are to be twisted by the pain and brokenness of a hurting past. No matter how much you have accomplished, or how beautiful you have become, deep inside you have never been able to escape the pain that has been etched so deeply into your soul.

No matter what has defined your self-esteem, God has an answer for you today. His answer, however, is not a philosophy or an esoteric principle: It is the person of his precious son. Jesus says if you know the truth about yourself, you will be set free (John 8:32). God's son calls you his brother or sister. He also calls you his friend. Through the voice of King Solomon, he says you are without a flaw. Although these truths have the power to set you free, only you can determine their outcome in your life. If you will accept them as the ultimate truth in your life, they will change you forever. If you don't, you will continue to be defined by the whims and wants of a culture much more confused than you are. God wants to give you new eyes today: eyes of faith, that see you just the way that your God, who loves you so much, sees you. May the Lord give you new eyes as you ponder the Shulammite and her understanding of her king's unconditional love.

As much as I appreciate and value the opinions of other people, I have learned that the opinion that counts the most is God's. Even on my worst day, his love for me never changes. This revelation has given me the confidence I have needed to perform with the newsboys in countless concerts and festivals.

Jeff Frankenstein

Lessons from the Life of the Shulammite:

FRIENDS

Where has your lover gone,
   most beautiful of women?
Which way did your lover turn,
   that we may look for him with you?…
Come back, come back, O Shulammite;
   come back, come back, that we may gaze on you!

SONG OF SONGS 6:1, 13

AUGUST 14

The change in the Shulammite woman's life had been so dramatic that even the lives of her friends had been transformed. Those who had known her the longest might even have been the most affected by the inner beauty now shining from her life. Although the Shulammite knew they were happy for her, she had been surprised when they began to ask her questions.

"What is so special about him?" they had asked. "We've never seen a love like the two of you share. Where does it come from?" Even more astonishing was the fact that they had begun to admire and even love him, too. Far from making her jealous, she realized that as much as the king loved her, he also had a kingdom filled with subjects who loved him, as well. As the months had gone on, the Shulammite's friends had even begun to look at her differently. Where once she had simply been their friend, now they were beginning to see her as a role model—someone worth emulating—in her own right.

One of the most amazing things about this intimate love story is the fact that the transformation in the Shulammite also brought about a change in her friends. Although Jesus yearns to fellowship with you as his beloved bride, he is also deeply concerned for the broken, hurting people around you. Sadly, many Christians become so self-absorbed in their own relationship with Christ that they lose sight of the fact that their healing has another purpose, one that goes far beyond their own needs. As much as God wants to heal you, he also desires to heal *through* you. As you allow the Lord to work in your life, your friends will begin to ask you questions about him, because nothing is more compelling than the testimony of a transformed life. As you answer their questions, some of them will even follow you into the arms of the very Savior who has changed you.

I am asking the Lord to open your eyes to the needs of the friends around you. This may require a change in your thinking. After years of being absorbed in your own personal search for healing, it may be hard for you to think about anyone but yourself. But God will not allow you to waste the pain of your past. In fact, the very process through which you were delivered will give you the wisdom and the compassion you need to help your friends find the same freedom you now enjoy. For you, the barriers you must cross to minister to others may also end up being the final steps in your own healing, as well. May the Lord help you to see those closest to you who need to experience His love and healing today.

HOW ABOUT YOU? IS YOUR RELATIONSHIP WITH GOD AFFECTING THE LIVES OF YOUR FRIENDS? IN THIS DEVOTIONAL, I SEE AGAIN HOW THE RELATIONSHIP WE HAVE WITH CHRIST IS NOT SIMPLY ABOUT US. YOUR RELATIONSHIP WITH GOD SHOULDN'T JUST AFFECT YOU; IT SHOULD ALSO RADICALLY AFFECT THOSE AROUND YOU.

Jeff Frankenstein

Lessons from the Life of the Shulammite:

OUT OF THE DESERT

Who is this coming up from the desert
leaning on her lover?

SONG OF SONGS 8:5

AUGUST 15

Although she had always loved gardens, the Shulammite's own soul had been a desert. In fact, much of the time, the stark, dry barrenness of her own heart had kept her from enjoying the natural beauty around her. Now, however, things were different. She had come out of the desert—not the geographical desert, but the desert of her own heart. Although her journey out of the desert had come at a great price, her beloved king had not let her face the journey alone. Every time she could feel herself beginning to falter, he was right there for her to lean on. Without the king's strength, her soul would have eventually withered and died, for she never could have gotten out of the desert on her own.

Like the Shulammite, you, too, are on a journey. God is slowly but surely leading you out of the desert. In fact, he is not merely taking you out of the desert—he is taking the desert out of you. Although this may sound strange, it is a critical point. Many people make the mistake of thinking they can escape their desert by moving to a different place or into a different phase of life. Single people with this mentality think that they will never be able to leave their desert behind until they are married. On the other hand, there are married couples who have deceived themselves into thinking that divorce is the oasis their soul desires. Tragically, if your heart is filled with bitterness, depression, anger, or rejection, no matter who you are with (or where you are), it will always seem like a desert.

It is also important for you to realize that once you are out of the desert, your relationships with the people around you will begin to change. Even those people you have always blamed for putting you in the desert in the first place will seem radically different to you. This is because the very attitudes in you that used to react to them are gone. For example, even if they still reject you, you no longer implode on the inside because your soul has been filled with the love and security of Christ. Do you see it yet? Once Christ has led you out of the desert, no one on earth has the power to ever place you there again.

You may be asking yourself, *How do I maintain this new place to which the Lord has brought me?* The answer is simple: Even as the Shulammite was leaning on her beloved, so you must lean on Jesus Christ through the promises of the Bible and the power of the Holy Spirit. When you are faced with the tests and challenges that will surely come, your answer does not lie in mustering up all the strength that your own humanity can find. No, in moments like these, you must cry out to God for the strength and power that only he can give. Never forget, however, that leaning on Christ is more than just effective crisis management. It is the posture he desires you to take for the rest of your life.

It is interesting to me that this story's heroine was leaning on her lover when she came out of the desert. Leaning to me is a picture of the fact that she had put her trust in the King. This is so important. No matter how strong I think I am, my only hope to make it through the deserts that all Christians face is to "lean" on the God that loves me so much.

Jeff Frankenstein

Lessons from the Life of Shulammite:
COME WITH ME

Come away, my lover,
and be like a gazelle
or like a young stag
on the spice-laden mountains.

SONG OF SONGS 8:14

AUGUST 16

Even the Shulammite herself could hardly believe the changes that had taken place in her life. Only months before, she had gotten so angry with the king that she had locked him out of her room and refused to leave. She had never forgotten the despair she had experienced as she lay in the shadows of her darkened room, behind the door she herself had locked. But now she had grown beyond merely responding to his overtures of love. In fact, she had become so secure in his love that even when he was busy with the matters of his kingdom, she would attempt to charm him away from his work. This might have become the king's favorite thing about their relationship. Although he had hundreds of people at his beck and call, she was the only person who had the security to seek him out even when he had not called.

It should be no different for you in your relationship with Christ. There is a place beyond merely responding to God where few people ever venture. Those who enter this place have become so intoxicated with his love that they seek him out even when all their needs have been met. Yes, whether he calls them or not, they continue to come. His love for them has so changed their hearts that there is no other place they would rather be, and no other presence whom they enjoy more. When God finds a person like this (and they are very rare), it brings tremendous delight to his heart.

Like Abraham, whom God called his friend, and Mary, the sister of Lazarus, whose petitions moved him to tears, the Lord will bring these people into a place of love and security beyond their imagination.

Furthermore, unlike the lions' dens and leopard haunts from which the king had earlier called the Shulammite, now he was appealing to her from special mountains filled with spice plants. Spices, which are known for both their fragrance and their taste, are a beautiful picture of some of the joys of serving Christ. Like a spice, the presence of Christ will bring a unique accent to every area of your life. Whether it is a new level of enjoyment in your most cherished relationships, or the fact that hurting people are drawn to you because of the fresh fragrance of Christ's love, the presence of God will definitely "spice up your life."

Although God commands your obedience, he also earnestly desires your intimate fellowship and friendship. As this revelation fills your heart, you will begin to walk in the security and the confidence that only a person who is both sought by God and seeking God will experience. You will also begin to enjoy a new measure of God's presence. Through this increased measure of his presence, like the Shulammite, you, too, will begin to experience new levels of abundant life and incredible joy.

This Devotional touches me because it is almost like the young woman had a role reversal. In the beginning, the king was seeking her; now she was seeking him. I think this is what God wants for all of us. He not only wants to do the seeking, He wants us to seek Him as well. This Devotional has encouraged me to seek him with more passion and desire.

Jeff Frankenstein

Lessons from the Life of Daniel:
IDENTITY THEFT

The king ordered Ashpenaz, chief of his court officials, to bring in some of the Israelites from the royal family and the nobility—young men without any physical defect, handsome, showing aptitude for every kind of learning, well informed, quick to understand, and qualified to serve in the king's palace. He was to teach them the language and literature of the Babylonians.... Among these were some from Judah: Daniel, Hananiah, Mishael and Azariah. The chief official gave them new names: to Daniel, the name Belteshazzar; to Hananiah, Shadrach; to Mishael, Meshach; and to Azariah, Abednego.

DANIEL 1:3–4, 6–7

AUGUST 17

Why didn't the king listen? Daniel wondered. Even though Jeremiah repeatedly warned King Jehoiakim not to rebel against Babylon, he refused to listen. Now the whole nation was paying for the king's folly: Judah's finest young men were being torn away from their families and taken to Babylon as hostages, and the king himself had been placed in chains, like a common criminal, for transport to Babylon.

As for Daniel, his heart was breaking because he had been torn away from his mother and father. Daniel knew life would never be the same for him or his family again. At only twelve years old, Daniel was on his way to Babylon. Tales of this wicked city had been used by Judean mothers to frighten their rebellious children for years; now, this city would be his new home.

Once in Babylon, Daniel would be forced to take a three-year program of courses including a thorough indoctrination into the culture, politics, and religion of that nation. After classes were over, the young men would enter the king's service.

Before they began their instruction, the Babylonians attempted to strip these boys of their Hebrew names. Although they gave Daniel a new name, deep in his heart he refused to accept it. Have you resisted the enemy's attempts to steal your name? The name I'm referring to has nothing to do with your parents, and everything to do with the names God has given you. In the Bible, people who trusted in Christ as their Savior are called God's servants, friends, and children. In fact, despite our struggles with sin, God even calls us saints. These names define both the *nature* of your relationship with God and the *person* he has made you to be.

The devil wants to steal the names God has given you, because once he has taken them, he has also robbed you of their inherent promises. For example, you cannot be called "ugly" and "unwanted" when God has named you "beautiful" and "treasured." Therefore, whether it is an attack of condemnation making you feel unworthy of your God-given name, or the peer pressure you face when you attempt to live up to that name, you must resist every attempt of the enemy to rename you. As you resist these attempts, you will grow in confidence and faith in God and man.

When I read this devotional about Daniel, I was reminded that the devil doesn't just want to steal our name, he also wants to redefine what our names really mean. Even the terms "evangelical" and "christian" have been portrayed in the media as being synonymous with harsh, rigid, uneducated, unloving, unthinking people. Although this, in most cases, couldn't be farther from the truth, it is important that we live up to the true meaning of the names we have been given in scripture.

Jeff Frankenstein

Lessons from the Life of Daniel:
UNDEFILED

[David said to the chief official], "Please test your servants for ten days: Give us nothing but vegetables to eat and water to drink. Then compare our appearance with that of the young men who eat the royal food, and treat your servants in accordance with what you see."

DANIEL 1:12–13

AUGUST 18

Nebuchadnezzar's chief official was stunned. No one, other than the king himself, had ever challenged him before. And his challenger was only twelve years old! Who did this young boy think he was, to tell him that he would not eat from the royal table? Yet, there was something different about the child; maybe he should agree to the child's demands. Daniel had begged the official to let him and three of his friends live off nothing but water and vegetables for ten days. At the end of that time period, if they were not healthier than all the boys who were eating from the king's table, Daniel had promised to eat the royal food.

Once the official had agreed to Daniel's proposal, it became the talk of the whole palace. "Who do these Judeans think they are to refuse Babylon's finest fare?" the servants whispered. But much to the court's amazement, at the end of ten days the appearance of Daniel and his friends could not be matched by any of the boys who were eating at the king's table. After this, they were never required to eat the royal food again.

If Daniel refused to eat from King Nebuchadnezzar's table (because he would have been in violation of the dietary laws given by Moses), surely you can take a similar stand for righteousness today. For you, however, there is more at stake than ceremonial food laws. You may be battling against sexual immorality, substance abuse, or an eating disorder. Whatever the case may be, God is well able to deliver you.

Like Daniel, however, there must be a new level of resolve in your heart. *Resolve?* you may be thinking, *I've never been able to muster up the willpower to defeat any of my thoughts before*. Fortunately, the resolve I am describing has nothing to do with human willpower. Philippians 2:13 promises that God can give you both the desire and the ability to do his will. Once you understand this, you will have the confidence you need to face the sin that is threatening to defile and dominate your life.

Daniel's commitment to live an undefiled life affected more than just his spiritual walk with God. Despite their austere diet, Daniel and his friends looked healthier and better nourished than all the other Hebrew young men who had defiled their consciences by eating the king's meat. It is no different for you today. Although following the ways of God may not give you an "extreme makeover," it will affect every area of your life.

If God could give a twelve-year-old boy the power to defy the king of Babylon, surely God can give you, as a Christian young person, the power to live for him. As fearful as this thought may seem to you, if you will simply trust God and follow him, like Daniel, he'll make you a burning light to your generation.
Jeff Frankenstein

Lessons from the Life of Daniel:
TEN TIMES BETTER

To these four young men God gave knowledge and under-standing of all kinds of literature and learning. And Daniel could understand visions and dreams of all kinds.

At the end of the time set by the king to bring them in, the chief official presented them to Nebuchadnezzar. The king talked with them, and he found none equal to Daniel, Hananiah, Mishael and Azariah; so they entered the king's service. In every matter of wisdom and understanding about which the king questioned them, he found them ten times better than all the magicians and enchanters in his whole kingdom.

DANIEL 1:17–20

AUGUST 19

The king announced that in every area of wisdom and understanding, Daniel and his friends were ten times better than all the magicians and enchanters in his whole kingdom. The king's other advisors had been humiliated by this assessment. How dare he compare them to these young adolescent boys from a barbaric nation?

As the boys' legends grew, everyone began to wonder about the source of their incredible wisdom. Nebuchadnezzar's chief official, how-ever, had ceased to wonder long ago. After watching these boys for three years, he knew the source of their wisdom was not natural at all, for the hand of their God was upon them in a powerful way. There was no doubt in his mind that all of them would rise to positions of great power in the Babylonian Empire.

How could these young men obtain such high levels of wisdom and knowledge in only three years? The Bible says that God gave them knowl-

edge and understanding in all types of literature and learning. He also gave Daniel the ability to interpret visions and dreams. If you have limited the anointing of God to things such as preaching, full-time Christian ministry, or the gifts of the Spirit, this verse probably amazes you. But no matter what profession God has called you into, he wants to anoint you with his power. Although you will still have to be disciplined in order to master your craft, God can supernaturally empower you to accomplish things within your profession that are humanly impossible.

God's desire to bring the Holy Spirit's power into every profession is vital for our culture today. If Daniel had limited God's power just to the interpretation of dreams and visions, he never would have been in the political position necessary to interpret Nebuchadnezzar's dream. God also wants to anoint you professionally in order to give you the platform you need to radically influence your culture. As you submit to power, he has the power to give you levels of ability and wisdom beyond your comprehension. I am convinced it is time for the Church to produce the greatest entertainers, entrepreneurs, scientists, athletes, authors, playwrights, and politicians the world has ever seen. As this happens, even the darkest centers of influence within our culture will be transformed.

All of the newsboys have experienced what this devotional describes. Because we have been willing to follow Him and consecrate ourselves to Him, He has given us the grace to touch people in a way that goes far beyond our talents and abilities. You, too, can experience this same blessing no matter what your career or profession may be. As you submit it to the Lord, He will do marvelous things through you.

Jeff Frankenstein

Lessons from the Life of Daniel:

THE POWER OF FRIENDSHIP

Daniel returned to his house and explained the matter to his friends Hananiah, Mishael and Azariah. He urged them to plead for mercy from the God of heaven concerning this mystery, so that he and his friends might not be executed with the rest of the wise men of Babylon. During the night the mystery was revealed to Daniel in a vision. Then Daniel praised the God of heaven.

DANIEL 2:17–19

AUGUST 20

News of the king's edict spread through kingdom, eventually reaching the wise men of Babylon. The magicians, sorcerers, and astrologers were in a panic because the king had ordered their execution. After years of being deceived, the king had had enough of these "pretenders." When they could not reveal to him the details of the dream he had—nor its interpretation—King Nebuchadnezzar ordered their deaths.

When the royal guards arrived at the home of Daniel and his friends to kill them, Daniel asked the commander for permission to speak to the king about his dream. When Daniel was presented to the king, he asked for time to pray before answering the king's request for an interpretation. Although King Nebuchadnezzar was still furious, he was also desperate to have his dream unveiled and interpreted. When Daniel returned home, he asked his three friends to support him with their prayers until God revealed the answers they needed. Although Daniel was confident he could *interpret* the king's dream, it was an entirely different matter to *reveal* the king's dream.

As Daniel prayed and waited on the Lord, both the dream's contents and its interpretation were revealed to him. When the king heard the revelation Daniel had received from God, he was so astonished that he fell prostrate at Daniel's feet. After acknowledging the power of Daniel's God, Nebuchadnezzar set Daniel and his three friends as rulers over the whole province of Babylon. Even more amazing than Daniel's revelation and interpretation, was the attitude he demonstrated throughout the whole process. He was deeply gifted in the interpretation of dreams, but he did not allow his gift to fill him with pride. On the contrary, with humility, he immediately went to his friends for help. Daniel realized that without their prayers he would never be able to solve the mystery that had been set before him.

No matter how gifted you may be, you will never lose your need for other Christians! In fact, this principle is so important, God himself will allow you to face circumstances designed to you remind you of your need for others. In my own life, I have found that God has used the prayers and counsel of my friends to repeatedly give me the wisdom I so desperately need.

It is also important to note that Daniel never forgot his friends. Unlike many Christians who quickly forget their friends when promotion or success comes, Daniel insured that his friends were blessed and promoted with him. He did not do this out of pity; Daniel realized that without their help and counsel, he would never be able to rule the province of Babylon. Some of the relationships God has given you will last a lifetime. No matter how successful you become, you will never outgrow your need for the wisdom and support their friendship provides.

Believe it or not, some of our greatest moments together as a band don't come in the concerts. They come behind the scenes as we experience the fellowship and mutual encouragement that walking together as friends can bring.

Jeff Frankenstein

Lessons from the Life of Daniel:

NEBUCHADNEZZAR'S JUDGMENT

[Nebuchadnezzar] said, "Is not this the great Babylon I have built as the royal residence, by my mighty power and for the glory of my majesty?"

The words were still on his lips when a voice came from heaven, "This is what is decreed for you, King Nebuchadnezzar: Your royal authority has been taken from you. You will be driven away from people and will live with the wild animals.... Seven times will pass by for you until you acknowledge that the Most High is sovereign over the kingdoms of men and gives them to anyone he wishes."

Immediately what had been said about Nebuchadnezzar was fulfilled.... His body was drenched with the dew of heaven until his hair grew like the feathers of an eagle and his nails like the claws of a bird. At the end of that time, I, Nebuchadnezzar, raised my eyes toward heaven, and my sanity was restored. Then I praised the Most High; I honored and glorified him who lives forever.

DANIEL 4:30–34

Despite the revelation God had given Daniel about his dream and the miraculous deliverance of the three Hebrew boys from the fiery furnace, Nebuchadnezzar still had not learned to fear the Lord. In fact, if anything, his pride and arrogance had only grown with the size of his kingdom.

AUGUST 21 **The fatal day finally came while he was walking on the** roof of the royal palace of Babylon. "I have built all of this by my power and for my glory," he exalted himself. God's response came like a lightning bolt from heaven: "You will live like an animal for seven years, then you will know that I am sovereign over all the kingdoms of men."

The Lord's words were immediately fulfilled. In everything but his appearance, he was transformed into a beast. After seven years had transpired, he had lost almost every shred of his humanity. But seeing the brokenness of Nebuchadnezzar's heart, in his mercy God reached down and healed his insanity. Even when he was restored to the splendor of his throne, the king continued to walk in humility.

What principles can we draw from this amazing story of redemption? First, like Nebuchadnezzar, when you continue to rebel, despite God's patience and kindness, sooner or later you will be judged. Never forget that no matter how long it takes, you will experience the consequences of your sin if you do not repent.

Second, although God directly judged Nebuchadnezzar with a horrible case of insanity, this was the direct result of his sin. In Psalm 73:22, David wrote that his bitterness and grief left him so senseless and ignorant that he began to live like a brute beast. However, at the end of seven years, God miraculously restored Nebuchadnezzar to both his right mind and to the fullness of his kingdom. This powerful demonstration of God's transforming power should fill you with hope. No matter how sin has destroyed you, God is able to heal you and to deliver you by his amazing power.

When I consider Nebuchadnezzar's stubborn pride and its consequences, two lessons are driven into my heart. First, no matter how long it takes, God is going to teach us (and sometimes it takes awhile!) Second, even when we have been shattered by the consequences of our sin, God in His mercy is still willing and able to deliver us.

Jeff Frankenstein

LESSOHS FROM THE LIFE OF DAHIEL:
FOURTH MAN IN THE FURNACE

Shadrach, Meshach and Abednego replied to the king, "O Nebuchadnezzar, we do not need to defend ourselves before you in this matter. If we are thrown into the blazing furnace, the God we serve is able to save us from it, and he will rescue us from your hand, O king. But even if he does not, we want you to know, O king, that we will not serve your gods or worship the image of gold you have set up."

DANIEL 3:16-18

AUGUST 22

Although Nebuchadnezzar acknowledged the power of God after his dream had been interpreted, the experience didn't really change him. In fact, shortly after his encounter with Daniel, the king built a model of the statue he had seen in his dream—a ninety-foot tall image made of gold. Nebuchadnezzar then issued a proclamation: Every person was to fall and worship the statue instantly when they heard the musicians play—or immediately be thrown into a blazing furnace.

As the exotic music began to play, everyone began to worship, but Shadrach, Meshach, and Abednego refused to bow to the image. The defiance of the three Hebrews was reported to the king. Furious, Nebuchadnezzar ordered that they bow down before the image or face the furnace. But their response to the king's threats stunned Nebuchadnezzar: "Our God is able to save us from the fiery furnace. We know he will rescue us from your hand. Yet, even if he doesn't choose to rescue us, we will never worship your gods or the golden image you have erected."

Nebuchadnezzar was outraged. After ordering the furnace to be heated seven times hotter than normal, he commanded his soldiers to bind the Hebrews and throw them into the fire. The blazing furnace was so hot, however, that some of the guards were killed while following the king's orders. But Shadrach, Meshach, and Abednego were totally unharmed because God himself had entered the furnace with them.

The king jumped up from his throne. "I thought you only threw three men into the furnace," he bellowed.

"That is correct, your majesty," one of his servants replied.

"Look for yourself," Nebuchadnezzar cried. "There are four men in the furnace, and they are not burned. One of them even looks like a son of the gods. Come out! Come out, O servants of the Most High God!" When the young Hebrew men came out of the furnace, the king and his advisors were even more amazed. They had not been singed or scorched, and there was no smell of smoke on them.

Although the three Hebrews were confident of God's deliverance, they had already determined to obey God—whether he delivered them or not. Unlike many believers who only obey God in order to escape a difficult situation, these courageous men were obeying God simply because it was the right thing to do. You will experience times when the only reward of your obedience is the pleasure it brings to the heart of God.

No matter what type of ordeal you are facing, God is able to meet you in such a way that you will be neither scarred nor marred. In fact, as you walk out of your furnace, your faith will be shining with new confidence, and your character will be purer than the finest gold.

This devotional forced me to be deeply honest with myself. Do I have the faith the three Hebrew young men had? Would I be willing to be thrown into a fiery furnace for the sake of my testimony? Although I realize that I will never know the answer until the time comes, I am asking God to help me grow in faith.

Jeff Frankenstein

Lessons from the Life of Daniel:

DANIEL AND THE LION'S DEN

So the king gave the order, and they brought Daniel and threw him into the lions' den. The king said to Daniel, "May your God, whom you serve continually, rescue you!"

… Then the king returned to his palace and spent the night without eating and without any entertainment being brought to him. And he could not sleep.

At the first light of dawn, the king got up and hurried to the lions' den. When he came near the den, he called to Daniel in an anguished voice, "Daniel, servant of the living God, has your God, whom you serve continually, been able to rescue you from the lions?"

Daniel answered, "O king, live forever! My God sent his angel, and he shut the mouths of the lions. They have not hurt me, because I was found innocent in his sight. Nor have I ever done any wrong before you, O king."

The king was overjoyed and gave orders to lift Daniel out of the den. And when Daniel was lifted from the den, no wound was found on him, because he had trusted in his God.

DANIEL 6:16, 18–23

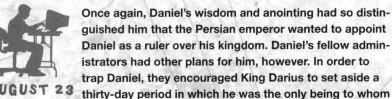

AUGUST 23

Once again, Daniel's wisdom and anointing had so distinguished him that the Persian emperor wanted to appoint Daniel as a ruler over his kingdom. Daniel's fellow administrators had other plans for him, however. In order to trap Daniel, they encouraged King Darius to set aside a thirty-day period in which he was the only being to whom people could pray. Despite the king's decree, Daniel was unmoved. With the windows of his palace opened wide, he faced Jerusalem and prayed. When the other administrators found Daniel praying, they reported him to the king. Although King Darius loved Daniel, he had no choice but to condemn him to death in the lions' den.

When the guards brought him to the mouth of the lions' den, Daniel could hear the roar of the beasts below. But Daniel was not alone. Where once there had been earsplitting roars, now there was silence, for every one of the lions' mouths had been sealed shut. With an angel of the Lord protecting him and the once savage lions curled up around him, he enjoyed a peaceful sleep.

No matter what pit the enemy has thrown you into, God is able to deliver you. No matter what type of spiritual lion is threatening to consume you, God can shut its mouth. You may be in financial peril, or you may feel like you are being eaten alive by the sin preying on your soul. Whatever the case, the same God who sent his angel to shut the lions' mouths is with you today.

However, your deliverance may not always be immediate. Even Daniel had to spend the night in the lions' den. Maybe that's where you are right now: although your problems have been silenced, you can still see their threatening forms all around you in the darkness. If this is where you are, take heart. God is testing your faith. He wants to see if your faith is as strong in the *presence* of your enemies as it is in their *absence*. As you pass this test, you will come out of your lions' den with a new testimony before God and man.

When I consider the story of Daniel in the lions' den, I am reminded afresh of God's power to deliver you and me. Paul tells us that no matter what we're facing, God will give us a way of escape. No matter what kind of lions' den you may be in, the same God that has always been there for me will be there for you, too.

Jeff Frankenstein

Lessons from the Life of Daniel:
DANIEL'S PRAYER

I, Daniel, understood from the Scriptures, according to the word of the LORD given to Jeremiah the prophet, that the desolation of Jerusalem would last seventy years. So I turned to the Lord God and pleaded with him in prayer and petition, in fasting, and in sackcloth and ashes.

While I was speaking and praying, confessing my sin and the sin of my people Israel … Gabriel, the man I had seen in the earlier vision, came to me in swift flight about the time of the evening sacrifice. He instructed me and said to me, "Daniel, I have now come to give you insight and understanding. As soon as you began to pray, an answer was given, which I have come to tell you, for you are highly esteemed."

DANIEL 9:2-3, 20-23

AUGUST 24

According to Jeremiah's word, the Babylonian captivity of God's people would last for only seventy years. That meant it was time for the people of God to go home, because the seventy years were over. Daniel realized that without fervent prayer, Jeremiah's prophecy would never be fulfilled. Daniel entered into a season of prayer and fasting. Even though he was probably the most righteous man on the face of the earth, Daniel identified with Israel's sins as if they were his own. "We have sinned," he cried out in anguish to the Lord. "We have not listened to your prophets."

Finally, Daniel's prayers reached a new level of fervency, as if he was pounding on the very gates of heaven. "O Lord, listen! O Lord, forgive!" Daniel pleaded. Then, he lifted up his face from the ground and saw an angel rapidly approaching him. It was Gabriel, the messenger angel of heaven.

"Daniel," Gabriel spoke, "you had your answer the moment you began to pray." Unlike many believers who simply wait on God to fulfill his promises, Daniel realized that without any action on his part, he would never experience the fullness of God's promises. It is the same for you today. Whether it is prayer and fasting, or repentance and faith, there is always a cost to fully possess the promises of God.

However, many Christians grow impatient. *What's taking God so long?* you may be wondering. If this is where you are, it is time to face the fact that you are not the one doing the waiting. In reality he has been waiting on you. He has been waiting on you to pray—and even fast. He is also waiting on you to acknowledge any sin in your life that could be hindering the fulfillment of his promises. Although fasting, brokenness, and repentance may be novel ideas to you, they are not new to God at all. It will take a faith-filled lifestyle of prayer and fasting to fully possess God's promises.

As I consider the depth and the discipline of Daniel's prayer life, I am reminded afresh of my own failures in this area. Although I love God with all my heart and am committed to daily time with God, like many Christians there are times that I miss it. This devotional impressed on me again the importance of seeking God and reading the Word on a daily basis.

Jeff Frankenstein

Lessons from the Life of Esther:
THE HAREM

 Mordecai had a cousin named Hadassah, whom he had brought up because she had neither father nor mother. This girl, who was also known as Esther, was lovely in form and features, and Mordecai had taken her as his own daughter when her father and mother died.

When the king's order and edict had been proclaimed,... Esther also was taken to the king's palace and entrusted to Hegai, who had charge of the harem. The girl pleased him and won his favor. Immediately he provided her with her beauty treatments and special food. He assigned to her seven maids selected from the king's palace and moved her and her maids into the best place in the harem.

ESTHER 2:7–11

AUGUST 25 As part of Babylon's despised Jewish minority, Esther's life had not been an easy one. Despite her great beauty, her life had already been scarred by personal tragedy. Her parents had died when she was very young, and she had no siblings. Now, because of her great beauty, she was being taken to the harem of King Xerxes. Only weeks before, Xerxes had divorced his beautiful queen after she refused to entertain his drunken friends. Esther's heart sank at the thought of trying to please this wicked man, known for his brutality. When she had been selected as a finalist in the nationwide search to find the next queen, she wanted to die. To this righteous Jewish girl, life in a harem was no better than life in hell itself. Esther had no idea that God would use her to save the people she loved so much.

Have you, like Esther, been shut up in a place you consider no better then hell? If you have, don't be discouraged. God may have placed you there for a purpose. If you are going to be effective in your placement, however, there are two things you need to understand.

First, Esther was terrified at the very thought of living in a harem. God, however, was not concerned. He knew that this undefiled young girl had both the consecration and the strength to remain pure. No matter how weak and wayward you may feel, God never makes a mistake. He would not have placed you where you are unless he intended to give you the power to walk successfully there. Whether you are a homeschooler facing the realities of a large public school, or a Christian student who is battling to walk with God on a college campus, God is well able to keep you and to help you stand strong for him.

Second, the harem was Esther's doorway to the throne. Without the training and preparation she received there, she never would have become queen. I have often found that the most difficult seasons in my life have proven to be doorways into times of incredible purpose. Remember, it doesn't matter how dark your own present circumstances may be or how dim your future may seem because God himself is preparing you to bring you into your divine destiny.

If God can sustain a young Jewish girl in the midst of a harem, there is no doubt in my mind that He can give you and me the strength to be successful for Him. Whether it's in our neighborhoods, schools or jobs, God can help us to stand.

Jeff Frankenstein

Lessons from the Life of Esther:
FAVOR

When the turn came for Esther ... to go to the king, she asked for nothing other than what Hegai, the king's eunuch who was in charge of the harem, suggested. And Esther won the favor of everyone who saw her.

ESTHER 2:15

AUGUST 26

When the doors of the harem closed behind Esther, she was heartbroken. How could she ever hope to maintain her purity and faith in a place of such darkness and intrigue? Yet, Esther soon became aware that she had reservoirs of inner strength. From the moment she arrived, every-one knew she was different. Even Hegai, the eunuch in charge of the harem, loved her. Her beauty was far deeper than her lovely face and beautiful figure. She was so filled with peace and tranquility that nothing seemed to bother her. Unlike the petty, jealous, insecure women who usually surrounded Hegai, Esther was humble, forgiving, and always ready to serve. Even the other women in the harem could not resist her other-worldly charms. Esther's joy was contagious; it lifted the spirits of everyone around her.

Yes, Hegai had said to himself, _this is the girl we need as our queen_. The old eunuch knew that Esther's humility and innocence was exactly what the kingdom needed. Therefore, he determined to do whatever it took to prepare her to win the king's favor. Esther was moved into the finest apartments and given special beauty treatments, and seven maids were commanded to serve her. Much to Esther's amazement, the same God who had been with her at home was also with her in the darkness of the harem.

How could this young girl gain such favor in the harem of King Xerxes? Although she was obviously a beautiful girl, it had nothing to do with her preference; the harem was probably filled with women who were equal to her in natural beauty. No, the secret to Esther's acceptance was the fact that she had an inner beauty that no one had ever seen before. Esther 2:9 says that Esther won Hegai's favor. In the Hebrew language, this means that she overwhelmed him with the grace in her life. When the old eunuch saw the righteousness, peace, joy, patience, and humility in Esther's life, he would have done anything to help her. No matter where God has placed you, he is well able to give you the same kind of favor Esther experienced.

Before you can fully walk in this favor, however, you must first understand it. Proverbs 3:3–4 teaches us that if a person walks in love and faithfulness, they will win favor in the sight of both God and man. The secret to God's favor is his *character*. As the character of Christ is formed in your life, it releases a magnetism that much of the world will find irresistible. Whether you are shining his light in your high school, on your college campus, or at your workplace, the same favor that opened miraculous doors for Esther will also open doors for you.

In this devotional, I was struck by the importance and power of God's favor in our lives. Even in the beauty-obsessed culture of the harem, Ester's character brought her tremendous favor. All of the newsboys realize that it is no different for us. When it comes to experiencing God's favor, our character is far more important than our talents.

Jeff Frankenstein

Lessons from the Life of Esther:
LIFELINE

Esther had not revealed her nationality and family background, because Mordecai had forbidden her to do so. Every day he walked back and forth near the courtyard of the harem to find out how Esther was and what was happening to her.

ESTHER 2:10–11

Despite Esther's amazing rise to prominence in the harem, there were still times when she felt starkly alone. Although she was surrounded by other girls and had even developed a few friendships with some of them, none of them shared her faith or values. "Thank God for Mordecai," she had

AUGUST 27 **whispered to herself repeatedly. Ever since her parents had died, he had been her father, big brother, and best friend. He still managed to get word to her every day, whether it was a softly whispered message through one of the harem's locked doors or words of encouragement he would send through the eunuchs. Mordecai had become her lifeline. The encouragement and wisdom she received from him on a daily basis were like brilliant rays of light in her darkness.**

No matter where God has placed you today, he wants to provide you with a lifeline—a person like Mordecai—to give you the encouragement, counsel, and accountability you need. In fact, the greater the darkness you are facing, the more important this type of lifeline becomes. Sadly, though important, this principle is virtually unknown in the church today. I have watched countless Christian young people go off to high school or college with no real commitment to maintaining the lifelines that God has been carefully developing in their lives. Whether these lifelines are their

parents, a Christian friend, or their youth pastor, they somehow lose these vital connections. For you, it might simply be a matter of geographical distance. Once you are far from home, the ones who have always "been there" for you gradually drift away from your heart, as well. Don't forget about your "old" friends when you begin to make new and exciting ones. And don't forget the teachings of your parents when you are out on your own. Keep your relationship with them strong, because they can continue to be God's lifeline for you. As Esther maintained her relationship with Mordecai through the walls of the harem, you should strive for your own vital relationships. Even if you've moved across the country to take another job or go to college, the counsel and support you need are only a phone call or email away.

This is not to say, however, that God will not continue to place new and different people in your life as you walk with him. When I look at the men God has placed in my life, I have known some of them for twenty-five years, and others for only ten. Although this pattern might be the same for you, it is also important that you maintain some form of relationship with your original "Mordecais." Don't forget: Even when Esther ascended to the throne, she never forgot the man who had walked her through the harem.

If Mordecai could remain in spiritual contact with Ester through the walls of the harem, there is no excuse for you and me to give up on the people we have been called to mentor or disciple. With all the technology at our fingertips, there is never any excuse for losing touch with the people God has brought into our lives.
Jeff Frankenstein

Lessons from the Life of Esther:
THE PREPARATION

Before a girl's turn came to go in to King Xerxes, she had to complete twelve months of beauty treatments prescribed for the women, six months with oil of myrrh and six with perfumes and cosmetics. And this is how she would go to the king: Anything she wanted was given her to take with her from the harem to the king's palace. In the evening she would go there and in the morning return to another part of the harem to the care of Shaashgaz, the king's eunuch who was in charge of the concubines. She would not return to the king unless he was pleased with her and summoned her by name.

ESTHER 2:12-14

AUGUST 28

Although Esther did not see it at first, later she would look back at the months she spent at the harem as some of the most important months of her life. While she had been frantic with worry about her purity, God had been far more concerned about her preparation for the throne. Nevertheless, despite her initial fears and misgivings, God was using the eunuchs, who now loved her like their own daughter, to prepare her for her divine purpose. The twelve months she spent under their kind tutelage laid the foundation for the rest of her life.

Maybe, like Esther, you're in the one place you never wanted to be. As far as you're concerned, if it wasn't the whim of chance, it must have been either the will of the devil or your own wanton desires that led you into this virtual "hell on earth." As hard as this may be for you to accept, I want to suggest another possible source. Could it be that the God of the universe has placed you in your little "corner of hell" because he wants to

prepare you for greater times of service ahead. Perhaps you are in a place of temptation today—but perhaps God has put you there for a purpose.

Temptation? you might be thinking. *I thought God would never tempt me!* Although God will never tempt you himself, he will allow you to be tempted because he wants you to see what he already sees in you—the reality of your own sin nature. Once you begin to deal with this sin, you will have officially entered the process of being prepared for your destiny.

Furthermore, even as Esther was probably surprised that God chose to use pagan eunuchs in her life, so you will be equally surprised by some of the people God chooses to mentor you. Whether it is your school's meanest teacher or the boss who can never seem to see your "true greatness," God knows exactly what you need. If you're smart, you'll learn as much as you can now from your parents and the kind people in your church. But no matter where you are today—or who God is using to prepare you—never forget that your loving God has given you an amazing purpose. If your preparation seems arduous, and at times even impossible to bear, it is only because your purpose is even greater than you have imagined.

Like Ester, I have experienced some very unique teachers and mentors in my life. In fact, one of my earliest piano teachers suggested to my mom that I quit and give myself to something other than music. Although his advice wasn't sound, God can even use comments like this for good in our lives.

Jeff Frankenstein

Lessons from the Life of Esther:
THE CORONATION

Now the king was attracted to Esther more than to any of the other women, and she won his favor and approval more than any of the other virgins. So he set a royal crown on her head and made her queen instead of Vashti. And the king gave a great banquet, Esther's banquet, for all his nobles and officials. He proclaimed a holiday throughout the provinces and distributed gifts with royal liberality.

ESTHER 2:17–18

AUGUST 29

The chief eunuchs were not surprised; they knew young Esther was destined to be queen from the first moment they had seen her. Although she was a beautiful girl, it was her kindness, love, joy, and meekness that had won the hearts of everyone in the harem. Because of Esther's profound humility, however, she had been totally shocked when the king had chosen her to become his queen. Who would have thought a little Jewish girl would rise out of the darkness of the harem to the power of Persia's throne? Mordecai, Esther's cousin, had always told her she had a destiny to fulfill. He had been convinced she was born for a special purpose. As she walked to receive her crown, she knew Mordecai had been right all along. With the adoring multitudes cheering and applauding, Esther knelt to receive her crown. Her coronation, however, was only the beginning, for God had exalted her for a purpose far beyond anything she could have imagined.

If God could take Esther—a young orphan from a persecuted minority—out of the darkness of the harem and raise her to the power of Persia's throne, what can he do for you? Even as God had a purpose for Esther's life, so he also has an amazing purpose for yours. Although you may never become a political king or queen on this earth, there is a divine purpose for your life. The apostle Paul wrote that all of us have been created with a specific task to accomplish (Ephesians 2:10). God is able to do things in our lives, through the power of the Holy Spirit, that are far beyond our own imagination (Ephesians 3:20). No matter where you are in your life, these Scriptures also apply to you. As you submit to the preparation required to complete his purpose in your life, you will be amazed to see the platform he gives you for the advancement of his kingdom.

You may be thinking to yourself, *What about my terrible past? Can God really use a person like me?* The answer to all these questions is, "Yes, absolutely!" In fact, God delights in using broken, wounded people to accomplish his purposes on the earth. Whether it was Esther, who lost both of her parents at a young age, or King David, who was despised by his own family, there is nothing in a person's past that will keep God from using them, as long as they submit their lives to him. If you will embrace God's purpose and submit to his preparation, he will bring you into a destiny beyond your comprehension.

When I consider God's amazing hand in the life of Ester, I cannot help but reflect on the circumstances of my own life. As an adopted child who recently discovered the identity of my biological parents, I am so thankful for God's hand and care in my life. By His grace, I was adopted by the very family I needed in order to come into my destiny. It is the same for you. No matter what your past looks like or what circumstances you are facing today, God is preparing you for your purpose.

Jeff Frankenstein

Lessons from the Life of Esther:
DIVINE PURPOSE

[Mordecai] also gave [Hathach] a copy of the text of the edict for their annihilation, which had been published in Susa, to show to Esther and explain it to her, and he told him to urge her to go into the king's presence to beg for mercy and plead with him for her people.

Hathach went back and reported to Esther what Mordecai had said. Then she instructed him to say to Mordecai, "All the king's officials and the people of the royal provinces know that for any man or woman who approaches the king in the inner court without being summoned the king has but one law: that he be put to death. The only exception to this is for the king to extend the gold scepter to him and spare his life. But thirty days have passed since I was called to go to the king."

ESTHER 4:8–11

AUGUST 30

Mordecai was beside himself with grief. After putting on ashes and sackcloth, he staggered, weeping and wailing, through the streets of the royal city. King Xerxes had issued an edict calling for the annihilation of the Jewish people. Now, as Jews throughout the Persian Empire fasted and prayed for their deliverance, Mordecai knew young Queen Esther was the only hope for their people.

When Esther heard about her cousin she immediately sent her servants to clothe and comfort him. Mordecai's response to her inquiry would change Esther's life forever—he sent her a copy of the king's wicked edict and pleaded with her to go into the king's presence and ask him to show mercy on her people.

After the eunuch relayed Mordecai's conversation to Esther, the young queen was more frightened than she had ever been. The king had not called her into his presence for thirty days. Under Persian law, anyone who approached the king without a royal summons would be executed—no exceptions. Despite her terror, she wondered—deep inside—if her people's peril was the very reason God had placed her on the throne.

Just as God placed Esther on the throne for a specific purpose, so he has given you, for reasons probably far beyond your comprehension, the position or title you hold today. Whether you are a class president, a team captain, a CEO, an editor, a professor, or a politician, God has given you the power you need to advance his kingdom on earth. Many of you, however, are afraid to use your God-given position for his purposes and his glory; you don't want to lose your position or its power. Remember, the same God who placed you in your current position also has the power to keep you there. If he doesn't, it is only because your next placement will be even more strategic than the one before.

Once you see God's sovereign hand in your work, you shouldn't be afraid to use the place of influence he has given you. This may involve bringing a new level of morality and ethics to your chosen profession. You may work within the legal or political system to change the laws destroying the very life of your nation. Whatever the case may be, never forget that God has sovereignly positioned you for the advancement of his kingdom and the fulfillment of his purposes for your life.

No matter how small your role may seem or what profession you're in, like Ester, your life has a purpose. Although you may not be able to see it now, as you allow God to work in you, you will not miss his purpose for your life. In my own experience, I have found that God can use the people who are setting up our equipment just as much as those of us who are performing on stage.

Jeff Frankenstein

Lessons from the Life of Esther:
OUR PERIL

When Esther's words were reported to Mordecai, he sent back this answer: "Do not think that because you are in the king's house you alone of all the Jews will escape. For if you remain silent at this time, relief and deliverance for the Jews will arise from another place, but you and your father's family will perish. And who knows but that you have come to royal position for such a time as this?"

ESTHER 4:12–14

AUGUST 31

Mordecai's reply did nothing to ease the young queen's fears. In fact, his challenge shook her to the very core of her being. He had told the eunuch to tell Esther that she would not escape death if the king's evil edict remained in effect. In fact, even if every other Jewish person in the kingdom was spared, she and her family could still die. Mordecai also challenged her with a probing question: "And who knows but that you have come to a royal position for such a time as this?"

With that divine question still resounding in her ears, Esther closed her eyes and put her face in her hands as she pondered the eunuch's report. Then she whispered to the eunuch: to tell Mordecai to gather together every Jew in Susa for a three-day period of prayer and fasting. At the end of this time she agreed to approach the king. With a heavy heart, the eunuch took the young queen's message back to Mordecai.

Many times, like Esther, we deceive ourselves into thinking our place in life will save us from the pain and destruction in our land. It may be our job security, net worth, family, influential friends, or the position of power we have achieved, but we mistakenly think these things can insulate us

from the horrible realities all around us. In my own experience, I have found this mindset cannot be farther from the truth.

For example, if you do not stand up and fight against abortion, sooner or later someone you love will be touched by its horror. Maybe, like the majority of Christians, when you look at the horrible problems plaguing the inner cities and poverty-stricken areas of our world, you simply raise your hand in thanksgiving that you do not live there. Sadly, this type of attitude almost guarantees that the problems of the inner cities will soon be coming to a neighborhood not far from you. No matter what you or your nation might be facing, God is calling you to use your *place* of influence to accomplish his purposes in your *sphere* of influence: your neighborhood, your city, state, country, and even your world.

It doesn't matter if you are performing in front of thousands of people or quietly setting up the chairs in your church, God has given you a place of influence. Whether your influence seems to reach multitudes or to just one person, never underestimate God's purpose for your life. I cannot count the times that I have watched the most unlikely person bring the very words that were needed.

Jeff Frankenstein

Lessons from the Life of Esther:
THE KING'S RECEPTION

On the third day Esther put on her royal robes and stood in the inner court of the palace, in front of the king's hall. The king was sitting on his royal throne in the hall, facing the entrance. When he saw Queen Esther standing in the court, he was pleased with her and held out to her the gold scepter that was in his hand. So Esther approached and touched the tip of the scepter.

Then the king asked, "What is it, Queen Esther? What is your request? Even up to half the kingdom, it will be given you."

"If it pleases the king," replied Esther, "let the king, together with Haman, come today to a banquet I have prepared for him."

ESTHER 5:1–4

SEPTEMBER 1

As Esther approached the king's throne room, her heart was pounding. With the lives of her people in danger, however, Esther knew that she had to approach the king. When Esther entered the king's inner chambers, his guards and officials were stunned to see her. When the king finally saw Esther, joy flooded his heart, and when the king held out the golden scepter, Esther approached the throne and touched the scepter's tip. As the whole court breathed a sigh of relief, the king opened the bounty of his kingdom to his young queen. As Esther wisely answered the king, she knew her people would be safe.

The same favor that had won Esther to the king's heart was also able to keep his heart. When the king saw the inner beauty that radiated from Esther, there was nothing in the world that he would not give her. As you continue to allow the character of Christ to be formed in your life, the favor that normally follows godly character will continue to grow in your life.

Because of her character, Esther risked her life in order to save her people. Even though she was his wife, Esther also knew that the king was a tyrant who had ordered the death of countless people. If Esther had the courage to approach him, surely you can have the boldness to approach the throne of the God who loves you so much. In fact, unlike Esther, who had to be summoned to the throne of her king, your king has given you twenty-four hour access to him! As a son or daughter of God you can approach your Father's throne at any time.

Tragically, some Christians seem to think that the God they serve is more like Xerxes than the loving God whom the Bible describes. If this is you, the Holy Spirit wants to give you a healthy image of your heavenly Father today. In John 14:8, Philip asked Jesus to show both him and the other disciples what the Father was like. The answer Jesus gave them is the same answer he has for you today: "Anyone who has seen me has seen the Father" (John 14:9). In other words, our loving heavenly Father is filled with compassion, mercy and grace. Even when he judges sin, he never ceases to love the people he has created. As this revelation fills your heart, allow it to give you the confidence you need to approach both God and man.

Our good works and deeds are not pre-conditions for God's love; they are just signs of repentance and salvation. God's love is unconditional. There is nothing you can do to add to it and nothing you can do to take away from it.

Peter Furler

Lessons from the Lives of Jeshua and Zerubbabel:

CYRUS'S TRANSFORMATION

In the first year of Cyrus king of Persia, in order to fulfill the word of the LORD spoken by Jeremiah, the LORD moved the heart of Cyrus king of Persia to make a proclamation throughout his realm and to put it in writing:

"This is what Cyrus king of Persia says:

"'The LORD, the God of heaven, has given me all the kingdoms of the earth and he has appointed me to build a temple for him at Jerusalem in Judah. Anyone of his people among you—may his God be with him, and let him go up to Jerusalem in Judah and build the temple of the LORD, the God of Israel, the God who is in Jerusalem.'"

EZRA 1:1–3

SEPTEMBER 2

Every official in the Persian Empire was astonished. King Cyrus had decided to let the people of God return to their homes in Jerusalem and Judea. While this news spread throughout the Jewish community, only one man was not surprised—Daniel. He had read Isaiah's prophecies about King Cyrus—that Cyrus would become a shepherd to the people of God and would allow them to return to Jerusalem and rebuild the temple (Isaiah 44:28). He had also read the prophecies of Jeremiah that predicted that Israel would only be held captive in Babylon for seventy years. When this time came to an end, Daniel began to pray. Now, as he read the edict of Cyrus, his heart was filled with thanksgiving for the mercy God had shown to his beloved people.

This story demonstrates one of the most remarkable answers to prayer in all of Scripture. If God can transform the pagan leader of a dark empire into the shepherd of his chosen people, imagine what he can do for the leaders of our world today! But until God raises up a group of men and women who will embrace the principles in which Daniel operated, we will never see the leaders of our society change.

Daniel based his prayer life on the promises of God's Word. The prophecies of Isaiah and Jeremiah inspired in Daniel the confidence he needed to persevere in prayer until his answer came. God's Word commands us to intercede for our leaders so that we can live peaceful and quiet lives in godliness and holiness (1 Timothy 2:1–2). When we look at our planet today, there are obviously many places where people do not have the freedom to live as a follower of Christ. Could it be that if we took Paul's command more seriously, the leaders of our planet would be changed?

Once Daniel had established his faith on the promises of God, he persevered until his answer came. Whether it was a simple prayer, deep intercession, fasting, or spiritual warfare, Daniel did what it took to see the will of God expressed on the earth. God wants to put that same heart in us today. He desires to breathe the fresh power of the Holy Spirit into our prayer lives. If you and I will take both the examples and the commands of Scripture seriously, God will use our prayers to change our leaders so the world they rule can also be changed.

DANiEL is one of my FAVORite people. He WAS in the WORLD But not of it. WhiLe the people of GOD were either whimpering OR. even worse, selling out to the cuLture. DANiEL WAS RunNinG the city whiLe the king WAS out chewing GRASS.

Peter Furler

Lessons from the Lives of Jeshua and Zerubbabel:

THE REMNANT

The whole company numbered 42,360, besides their 7,337 menservants and maidservants; and they also had 200 men and women singers. They had 736 horses, 245 mules, 435 camels, and 6,720 donkeys.

EZRA 2:64–67

SEPTEMBER 3

When Cyrus first proclaimed his edict, every Jew in the Persian Empire talked about going home. Whether they were wealthy or poor, all of them professed their willingness to rebuild the temple of the Lord. As the weeks passed, however, more and more Jews seemed to lose their desire to leave. Whatever their excuses were—and there were many—out of the thousands and thousands of Jews living in the Persian Empire, only 42,360 men and women decided to return home.

Among those going home were the leaders of the expedition, Jeshua, the high priest, and Zerubbabel. Although both of them had been highly successful in Persia, there was no doubt in their minds that God had called them to return to the land of Israel. Since his boyhood, Jeshua's heart had burned to see the great temple of God rebuilt. Older relatives had described the temple's grandeur and the pageantry and holiness of its ceremonies. Zerubbabel, on the other hand, wanted to do more than rebuild the temple: He longed to see the nation he loved reestablished. All his life, he had wanted to live in a country where the righteous laws of God, not the unjust statutes of man, were the rule of the day. Together,

Jeshua and Zerubbabel would lead this small remnant back to their ancient homeland.

Although you might be surprised that only 42,360 Jews went home, it would probably not be a greater number today. Typically, when God calls his people to embrace a divine mission or to accomplish a great task, there are very few who respond. If your commitment is based on what everyone else in your church or ministry does, you will probably never get anything done. Typically, only a small minority of God's people actually do the work of his kingdom. Even in the best of churches, it is the committed core that determines the effectiveness and the fruitfulness of their congregation.

The only question that really matters, however, is the question of what *you* will do. Will you share your faith? Will you pray and cry out for the advancement of God's kingdom on the earth? Will you make it your priority to build a strong devotional life and support the services and outreaches of your local church? If you will make the kind of commitment that I am describing, it will hardly matter what anyone else decides to do. If David, as a young teenager, was able to kill a giant, and fifteen-year-old Daniel changed an empire, what could God do with you? Do not forget that the accomplishment of God's purposes has never rested on large numbers. Gideon destroyed the hosts of Midian with three hundred men. And Jesus laid the foundations for changing all of human history with the help of only twelve men. So, when you look around and see that your prayer meetings are small or that few workers show up for your evangelistic outreaches, take heart. God is well able to use a remnant to accomplish his purposes on the earth today.

"LORD, help us not to grow tired or weary of doing your work. I ask today that you join me with your faithful people, so together we can know and serve your purpose."
Peter Furler

Lessons from the Lives of Jeshua and Zerubbabel:
THE ALTAR

When the seventh month came and the Israelites had settled in their towns, the people assembled as one man in Jerusalem. Then Jeshua son of Jozadak and his fellow priests and Zerubbabel son of Shealtiel and his associates began to build the altar of the God of Israel to sacrifice burnt offerings on it, in accordance with what is written in the Law of Moses the man of God. Despite their fear of the peoples around them, they built the altar on its foundation and sacrificed burnt offerings on it to the LORD, both the morning and evening sacrifices.

EZRA 3:1–3

SEPTEMBER 4

When the Jewish people had returned home, Jeshua and Zerubbabel had one priority. Even more important than building defensive fortifications, they knew that they must rebuild the altar of the Lord. To these men, this was far more than religious ritual. They realized that only the sacrifices of worship that God required would bring the manifestation of his presence that they so desperately needed. Without the protection that God's presence provided, they knew it was only a matter of time until their enemies attempted to destroy them.

How about you? Have you made building an altar a priority in your life? The altar I am talking about is not made of stone or dirt. It is the time you set aside to pray, worship God, and read your Bible. In fact, the sacrifices you make on the altar have nothing to do with animals and everything to do with you. God desires more than just your time, talents, and tithe. God desires to have all of you. In Romans 12:1, Paul urges us to present every part of our lives as a living sacrifice of worship to the God who loves us so deeply.

The altar God is calling you to build is probably far more important than you realize. The disciplines of the Christian life are not just a set of rituals that well-meaning preachers have made up to keep their congregations busy; it is through them that the devotional altar of your life is built. Without the disciplines of prayer, worship, and Bible study, you will never experience the joy, victory, and peace that only God's presence can bring. In the realm of the spirit, both God and the devil abhor a vacuum. Depending on what you choose, your life will either be filled with the joy and peace that only God's presence can bring, or you may well find your life filled with the depression, torment, and heaviness that only the enemy can bring.

Building your devotional altar should be one of the highest priorities of your life. My wife and I are so committed to this principle that we seek God both individually and as a couple every day. We have found that when we seek God together, we experience a level of spiritual oneness that we could not achieve in any other way. No matter what crisis you are in or what enemies you are facing, God has an answer for you at the altar. As you fill your heart with God's Word, and you lift up your needs in an attitude of worship and praise, he will meet your every need through the promises of his Word and through his Spirit.

"He who pursues righteousness and love finds life, prosperity and honor" (Proverbs 21:21). Like the Hebrews who placed their priority on building God's altar, so building your relationship with God must be the priority of your life.
Peter Furler

Lessons from the Lives of Jeshua and Zerubbabel:
THE ATTACK

When the enemies of Judah and Benjamin heard that the exiles were building a temple for the LORD, the God of Israel, they came to Zerubbabel and to the heads of the families, and said, "Let us help you build because, like you, we seek your God and have been sacrificing to him since the time of Esarhaddon king of Assyria, who brought us here."

But Zerubbabel, Jeshua and the rest of the heads of the families of Israel answered, "You have no part with us in building a temple to our God. We alone will build it for the LORD, the God of Israel, as King Cyrus, the king of Persia, commanded us."

Then the peoples around them set out to discourage the people of Judah and make them afraid to go on building.

EZRA 4:1–4

SEPTEMBER 5

Once they had erected the altar, the people of God began to rebuild the temple. Even more important to them than the city's gates and walls was the temple of God. After the temple's foundations had been laid, the people assembled for a time of celebration and worship. As the older people, who had seen the original temple, cried and wept, the young people shouted for joy. Yes, God in his mercy had restored his people to himself.

Not everyone in the land was celebrating, however. When their enemies heard that they had begun to rebuild the temple of the Lord, they were frightened. They knew that once God inhabited his temple again, they would lose their power. At first, their attempts to stop the rebuilding of the temple were cloaked in deception. They approached Zerubbabel and asked if they could help with the great project. "Let us help you," they pleaded. "We also want to seek the Lord." When this ploy failed, their attacks became more direct. After all their methods of intimidation had failed, they decided to pursue legal means. They hired counselors in hopes of convincing King Cyrus to rescind his edict and to order all work on the temple to cease.

It is vital that you see the connection between the warfare this Jewish remnant faced and the difficulties you face in your own life because the enemy of your soul is still making the same kind of attacks today. You can be sure that the moment you begin to build or rebuild the temple of the Lord in your life, the enemy will renew his attack. You can be sure that, whether you are purchasing property or constructing a building for the kingdom of God, the enemy will resist you with all his might. Therefore, if you are involved in any of these endeavors, you need to prepare yourself for war. Typically, the enemy will attack the relationships of the people involved in the project and the finances needed for its completion. He will also try to stir up opposition from political figures and the people who live around the property you are trying to buy. When these attacks come, it is critical that you maintain unity at any cost. Although the attacks of the enemy will come, the joy you receive from God's work in your life will far outweigh the pain of those attacks.

The enemy of your soul hates you reading God's word daily, praying, worshipping, walking with covenant relationship with church leaders, making disciples, training up the next generation of leaders, and therefore finding abundant life. I wonder what it is we're waiting for.

Peter Furler

THE ACCUSER

Then he showed me Joshua the high priest standing before the angel of the LORD, and Satan standing at his right side to accuse him. The LORD said to Satan, "The LORD rebuke you, Satan! The LORD, who has chosen Jerusalem, rebuke you! Is not this man a burning stick snatched from the fire?"

Now Joshua was dressed in filthy clothes as he stood before the angel. The angel said to those who were standing before him, "Take off his filthy clothes."

Then he said to Joshua, "See, I have taken away your sin, and I will put rich garments on you."

Then I said, "Put a clean turban on his head." So they put a clean turban on his head and clothed him, while the angel of the LORD stood by.

ZECHARIAH 3:1–5

SEPTEMBER 6

Jeshua and Zerubbabel were heartbroken. They felt they had failed God and the nation they loved. Yet, in the midst of their shame and failure, God had shown mercy on them and sent Haggai and Zechariah. Under the encouragement of Haggai, the Jewish exiles were filled with fresh faith.

Zechariah the prophet also brought discernment. Through his amazing ministry, both Jeshua and Zerubbabel had been able to see the spiritual forces arrayed against them. Although they had both felt a terrible

sense of oppression and shame, it was not until then that they realized the roots of this oppression were spiritual in nature.

In a vision, Zechariah had seen Jeshua (Joshua) standing before the throne of God with Satan at his right side to accuse him. Much to his amazement, God had rebuked the devil instead of rebuking Joshua. In fact, despite Satan's horrible accusations, Joshua was dressed in beautiful new garments and ushered into a new measure of God's presence and authority.

When Zechariah had finished describing this vision to Joshua, the high priest felt a sense of victory in his heart that he had not experienced for over a decade. After all the years of failure, God had not abandoned him. Maybe you find yourself in a place of utter failure and defeat today. The same God who sent his prophets to Joshua and Zerubbabel will rescue you!

Like Joshua, the source of your failure and shame may well be spiritual in its origins. In Joshua's case, he wasn't simply facing the might of the Persian Empire; he was under the attack of Satan himself. But despite the fact that Joshua was dressed in the filthy garments of unbelief and shame, the Lord still rebuked the devil for accusing him. No matter how you have sinned or failed, God will give you the strength to resist the enemy's accusations. Once this spirit of accusation has been exposed, you will be able to experience the cleansing and transformation that God desires for you.

"O LORD, OUR UNDERSTANDING FAILS BUT YOUR LOVE ENDURES. PLEASE RENEW OUR MINDS JUST LIKE YOU GAVE JOSHUA A NEW TURBAN."

Peter Furler

Lessons from the Lives of Jeshua and Zerubbabel:

MOUNTAIN MOVING

Then the angel who talked with me returned and wakened me, as a man is wakened from his sleep. He asked me, "What do you see?"

I answered, "I see a solid gold lampstand with a bowl at the top and seven lights on it, with seven channels to the lights. Also there are two olive trees by it, one on the right of the bowl and the other on its left."

I asked the angel who talked with me, "What are these, my lord?" He answered, "Do you not know what these are?"

"No, my lord," I replied.

So he said to me, "This is the word of the LORD to Zerubbabel: 'Not by might nor by power, but by my Spirit,' says the LORD Almighty.

"What are you, O mighty mountain? Before Zerubbabel you will become level ground. Then he will bring out the capstone to shouts of 'God bless it! God bless it!'"

ZECHARIAH 4:1–7

SEPTEMBER 7

The dream Zechariah received for Zerubbabel had been far more mysterious than the one he received for Joshua. In fact, even the great prophet himself had trouble interpreting it at first. He had seen a giant Jewish candlestick with an olive tree on either side; oil was pouring from the branches of the trees into this remarkable candlestick. As he pondered this vision, Zechariah received an amazing prophecy from the Lord. He told Zerubbabel the temple would not be rebuilt by Zerubbabel's might or power; it would only be completed by the anointing of the Holy Spirit. Although Zerubbabel was overwhelmed by the immensity of this task, God would give him the strength to complete it.

When Zechariah relayed this message to Zerubbabel, the shackles of unbelief and failure—which bound this great leader for fifteen years—were shattered. Zerubbabel rallied the people of God to finish the task they had started. The same God who anointed Zerubbabel to finish his divine task is also able to anoint you. It doesn't matter whether you have any strength or energy left at all. God will supply the power and strength you need to accomplish his will.

It is interesting to note that the candlestick (symbolizing the nation of Israel) was being fueled by two olive trees. These olive trees, which were gushing with oil, were a picture of Joshua and Zerubbabel. This analogy captures one of the secrets to moving in the power of God. When God finds a person who is willing to sink the roots of his or her life into his promises and power, that individual will have an unlimited supply of anointing and grace to achieve the purposes he or she has been given to accomplish. This is one of the reasons Paul commands us to be "rooted" in Christ (Colossians 2:7).

Yet once we have *received* the necessary anointing, we must learn how to *release* it. Although there are many ways to release the power of God, one of the most important is found in Zechariah 4:7. In this verse, God spoke to the challenges that Zerubbabel was facing. He then promised that Zerubbabel would accomplish this task. It is no different for you. If you will begin to speak the Word of God over the mountainous circumstances you are facing today, God will release his miraculous power on your behalf.

I Believe that this is A Word for us today and everyday. What a Revelation to Be Revealed "not By might, not By power, But By My Spirit, says the LORD."

Peter Furler

Lessons from the Lives of Jeshua and Zerubbabel:

A PRIEST ON THE THRONE

"Take the silver and gold and make a crown, and set it on the head of the high priest, Joshua son of Jehozadak. Tell him this is what the Lord Almighty says: 'Here is the man whose name is the Branch, and he will branch out from his place and build the temple of the Lord. It is he who will build the temple of the Lord, and he will be clothed with majesty and will sit and rule on his throne. And he will be a priest on his throne. And there will be harmony between the two.'"

ZECHARIAH 6:11–13

SEPTEMBER 8

These divine instructions were even beyond Zechariah's comprehension. God had told the prophet to make a crown and set it on the head of Joshua the high priest. This command was amazing, because nowhere in Scripture had a high priest ever been crowned as king. Although there had been a number of kings who loved to worship God, there had always been a clear separation between these two offices. As Zechariah contemplated this mystery, the Lord revealed to him that Joshua's crowning would symbolize the coming of a great Priest-King (the Messiah) who would rule God's people in the future. The Lord promised Zechariah that this great leader would rule Israel as a priest, with no tension between his priestly and kingly functions. Although Zechariah was greatly encouraged by this revelation, he realized its ultimate fulfillment was for another day.

Despite the fact that this prophecy speaks of Christ, it still contains some critical principles that can be applied to your life today. No matter who or what you have been called to lead, your natural leadership should be founded on your priestly ministry. In other words, the wisdom and strength you need to lead will flow out of the time you spend with God. Whether you are leading your family, a business, a team, a corporation, or an entire nation, the answers you need are found in the same place: the person and promises of our Almighty God.

Zechariah also stated there would not be any tension between the priestly and kingly aspects in Joshua's life. This is a critical promise, because many leaders have difficulty blending their devotional life into their business schedule. They wonder how they will ever find the time to pray and read their Bibles in an agenda filled with to-do lists. In reality, however, God does not call us to fit our devotional disciplines into our regular lives. He commands us, rather, to build our *whole* lives on these disciplines. When you begin to see everything flowing out of your time with God, you will never see prayer and Bible study in the same way again. Far from being a short "quiet time" you try to sneak in every day, your relationship with Christ and the disciplines associated with it will become the highest priority of your life. No matter how early you have to wake up or how creative you have to become, you will fight to protect this relationship. This revelation of your priestly ministry will change your life.

"Do not worry, saying "What shall we eat?" or "What shall we wear?" ... Seek first his kingdom ... And all these things will be given to you" (Matthew 6:31-32). This is probably one of the most important keys to an abundant life. If you will put God's kingdom first, he will help you take care of the rest.

Peter Furler

Lessons from the Life of Nehemiah:
THE PRAYER

The words of Nehemiah son of Hacaliah:

In the month of Kislev in the twentieth year, while I was in the citadel of Susa, Hanani, one of my brothers, came from Judah with some other men, and I questioned them about the Jewish remnant that survived the exile, and also about Jerusalem.

They said to me, "Those who survived the exile and are back in the province are in great trouble and disgrace. The wall of Jerusalem is broken down, and its gates have been burned with fire."

When I heard these things, I sat down and wept. For some days I mourned and fasted and prayed before the God of heaven....

"O Lord, let your ear be attentive to the prayer of this your servant and to the prayer of your servants who delight in revering your name. Give your servant success today by granting him favor in the presence of this man."

NEHEMIAH 1:1–4

SEPTEMBER 9

Nehemiah was heartbroken. Despite his position in the Persian Empire, he had never forgotten the ancient city of his people. When he heard that Jerusalem was still defenseless, he immediately began to fast and pray. With her walls broken down and her gates burned with fire, the city and its inhabitants had no respite from the fear and torment of their enemies. Finally, after Nehemiah had fasted and prayed for a number of days, a plan began to form in his heart. Although its timing would have to be perfect and would be extremely dangerous,

Nehemiah would risk anything for the people of God and the city he loved so much.

The same God who laid Jerusalem on Nehemiah's heart wants to give you a burden for your city today. You will never be able to receive a divine burden for your city, though, as long as you continue to insulate yourself from the pain around you. Nehemiah was not burdened for Jerusalem until he heard the reports of its condition—and it is no different for you. You must be willing to face the desperate plight of the city to which you have been called. Whether it is simply following the local news, or taking a drive through your city while you are praying, you will never feel what God feels until you have begun to hear what he hears and see what he sees.

Receiving God's burden for your city, however, is only the beginning of the process. Like Nehemiah, you must progress from being "burdened" for your city to being "broken" over your city. It is possible that this brokenness may only be achieved through concentrated periods of prayer and fasting. But the moment you ask God to break your heart over the pain of your city, you will find God's emotions welling up in you. Whichever your case your may be, this type of brokenness opens your heart afresh to receive the plan God has desired to give you all along. Once you have received his plan, as Nehemiah did, God will give you the exact timing and strategy you will need to see this plan gloriously fulfilled, and your city redeemed from its sin and path toward destruction.

"LORD let our hearts be broken by the things that break your heart." If you will faithfully pray this prayer, you will never be the same again.

Peter Furler

Lessons from the Life of Nehemiah:
THE CUPBEARER

I was cupbearer to the king.

In the month of Nisan in the twentieth year of King Artaxerxes, when wine was brought for him, I took the wine and gave it to the king. I had not been sad in his presence before; so the king asked me, "Why does your face look so sad when you are not ill? This can be nothing but sadness of heart."

I was very much afraid, but I said to the king, "May the king live forever! Why should my face not look sad when the city where my fathers are buried lies in ruins, and its gates have been destroyed by fire?"

The king said to me, "What is it you want?"

Then I prayed to the God of heaven, and I answered the king, "If it pleases the king and if your servant has found favor in his sight, let him send me to the city in Judah where my fathers are buried so that I can rebuild it."

Then the king, with the queen sitting beside him, asked me, "How long will your journey take, and when will you get back?" It pleased the king to send me; so I set a time.

NEHEMIAH 1:11 — 2:6

SEPTEMBER 10

As cupbearer to the king of Persia, Nehemiah had more access to the king than almost any other person in the empire. Whereas some of the king's officials would only see him periodically, Nehemiah saw him on a daily basis. Although the king loved and trusted him, Nehemiah had never asked the king for a favor. Now, however, it seemed that Nehemiah had no other choice, for King Artaxerxes was the only person who had the power to rebuild the defenses of Jerusalem.

After three months, Nehemiah knew the day had finally come. Until that time, he had managed to hide the grievous burden of his heart from the king. This time, however, it was different. No matter how hard he tried to smile, his emotions were overwhelming him.

"Nehemiah," the king inquired, "I have never seen you without a smile.

I know you are not sick, so you must be worried over some matter."

Although Nehemiah was frightened by the king's statement, he responded boldly. "My king, my face only reflects the pain of my heart. How can I be joyful any longer while the city of my fathers lies in ruins?"

"What do you want?" the king asked.

Nehemiah replied, "If it pleases the king, send me to rebuild the city of Jerusalem." When the king gave him permission to go, Nehemiah's boldness grew. "My king," he continued, "I also need royal protection and the materials required to rebuild the city's defenses." When the king granted this second request also, Nehemiah left for Jerusalem.

No matter what job or position God has given you, he has placed you there for his purposes. Although some believers are blinded by a desire for "affluence," God is far more concerned with their "influence." In fact, just as God used Nehemiah to influence the heart of the king, so he wants to use your influence to touch those around you. Christianity is filled with stories of how God has used humble, ordinary believers to change the "high and mighty" of our world. If you will simply make yourself available to God and his Spirit, you will be amazed to see how much he can use you.

TODAY, YOU might Be An AnsweR to A pRAyeR.
TODAY, YOU might Be An infLuence thAt
chAnges the futuRe.

Peter Furler

Lessons from the Life of Nehemiah:
OUR CHALLENGE

Then I said to them, "You see the trouble we are in: Jerusalem lies in ruins, and its gates have been burned with fire. Come, let us rebuild the wall of Jerusalem, and we will no longer be in disgrace." I also told them about the gracious hand of my God upon me and what the king had said to me.

They replied, "Let us start rebuilding." So they began this good work.

NEHEMIAH 2:17–18

SEPTEMBER 11

As Nehemiah examined Jerusalem's defenses with a small group of men, his burden for the city had only grown. No wonder the Jews who had returned from Babylon lived in such fear and torment. With no real fortifications, they had been easy prey for their enemies. As Nehemiah gathered a few men from the city together, he began to share the deep burden of his heart with them. "You see the trouble we are in," Nehemiah said to them. "Jerusalem is in ruins, and her defenses are shattered. We must rebuild her walls, or we will continue to be humiliated and disgraced by our enemies. God is with us, and the king himself has given his full support to our enterprise." When Nehemiah finished, he waited to see how these brave men would respond. As one man with one heart, they answered him, "Let us rebuild!" In the days to come, they would prove that their response had been more than mere words.

I am convinced that the words Nehemiah spoke to the men of Jerusalem are for you, as well. That's right—even as God called these men to restore their city, so he is calling you today to begin the transformation of your city. Like these men, you must see that your city's troubles are your own troubles. This is important because until you personally identify with the pain and trouble of your city, you will never be moved to action. It does not matter if there is violence in the school system or drugs being sold on your streets, sooner or later trouble will come to your neighborhood unless you are willing to fight for someone else's neighborhood.

It is also critical that you embrace the task of rebuilding your city's walls. When I speak of "walls" in this context, I am not describing the protection provided by policemen, sheriffs, and firefighters. I am talking of the spiritual protection which comes through a city's moral and spiritual life. No matter what type of programs you and I develop for our cities, they are doomed to failure without spiritual and moral protection. Whether it is praying for your city, strategic evangelism, church planting, or enacting godly legislation through the political process, you and I must rebuild the divine walls of protection around our cities.

Nehemiah also emphasized the fact that God's hand was upon them. If you will embrace God's purpose, you will also enjoy God's power and provision. When God finds a people who will accept the task of transforming their city, they will never lack the means necessary for its completion.

This is our time in history. We are on watch. We have a charge to keep.

Peter Furler

Lessons from the Life of Nehemiah:
RIDICULED

When Sanballat heard that we were rebuilding the wall, he became angry and was greatly incensed. He ridiculed the Jews, and in the presence of his associates and the army of Samaria, he said, "What are those feeble Jews doing? Will they restore their wall? Will they offer sacrifices? Will they finish in a day? Can they bring the stones back to life from those heaps of rubble—burned as they are?"

Tobiah the Ammonite, who was at his side, said, "What they are building—if even a fox climbed up on it, he would break down their wall of stones!"

NEHEMIAH 4:1–3

SEPTEMBER 12

When their enemies heard that the Jews were really rebuilding the walls of Jerusalem, they were incensed. Instead of attacking the inhabitants of Jerusalem directly, however, Sanballat and his men decided to break the spirit of God's people through mockery and ridicule. "What are these feeble, worthless Jews doing?" they laughed. "Will they really restore these walls? Will they ever finish this great work?" Then they sneered scornfully: "How will they even find the stones they need in these scorched heaps of rubble?" Under the leadership of Nehemiah, however, the work on the walls was not delayed. The more the Jews were ridiculed, the harder they worked.

Today, when you begin to threaten the enemy in your own life, he will respond with ridicule and mockery. Like Sanballat, he will question everything you are doing. He will do everything he can to make you quit. In my own circumstances, I have discovered that the more the enemy is threatened by something I am doing or considering, the more he will question it. For example, when the enemy begins to question the call of God on my life, it is a sure sign that my calling is scaring him to death! In fact, far from being beaten up by the enemy's questions, my faith is built up by his incessant queries.

The enemy also questioned the Jews' ability to bring the stones "back to life." In the New Testament, God refers to his people as "living stones" (1 Peter 2:5). I cannot count the times the enemy has questioned my ability to see an unbeliever converted or a struggling Christian transformed. Personally, I love it when he asks me this particular question, because conversion and transformation have nothing to do with my ability and everything to do with God's ability! In fact, I have found that reminding the devil of God's power incenses him more than almost anything else. Whether a person's life has been shattered by substance abuse, immorality, violent crime, or some terrible emotional wound, God is well able to make them live again.

It does not matter what you are facing today. Whether it is the spiritual darkness of your city or the pain of a broken marriage, the very fact that the enemy is questioning your faith is a sign God is on the move. Even if the people involved in the situation you are praying about seem beyond all hope, our God is well able to bring healing and full restoration to their damaged souls; all he needs is a vessel through whom he can do his work.

In no way should you let the devil define your life. He is the father of lies. God has "plans to prosper you and not to harm you, to give you hope and a future" (Jeremiah 29:11). Any voice contrary to this is a lie.

Peter Furler

Lessons from the Life of Nehemiah:
ON GUARD

 But when Sanballat, Tobiah, the Arabs, the Ammonites and the men of Ashdod heard that the repairs to Jerusalem's walls had gone ahead and that the gaps were being closed, they were very angry. They all plotted together to come and fight against Jerusalem and stir up trouble against it. But we prayed to our God and posted a guard day and night to meet this threat.

NEHEMIAH 4:7–9

SEPTEMBER 13

When Sanballat saw that ridicule and mockery had not stopped the rebuilding of the walls, he and the other leaders decided to gather their forces and attack the people of God. When Nehemiah received word of Sanballat's plans, however, he simply told the people to pray, post guards, and keep on working. Nehemiah realized unless they continued to rebuild the walls, they would never truly be protected. Therefore, he was determined to complete the walls of Jerusalem at any cost.   The tactics of the enemy have really never changed from Nehemiah's day until now. If Satan cannot stop you through ridicule and mockery, he will bring new levels of intimidation and conflict to your life. When this happens, two things are critical. First of all, never forget that the more you pray, the more the devil will pay. The enemy hates the prayers of God's people because he is powerless to withstand the divine power released by those prayers. Second, you must remember that there are times when prayer alone will not suffice. No matter how much you pray, if you leave the vulnerable areas of your life unguarded, the enemy will take advantage of these weaknesses. In Philippians 4:6–7, Paul tells us not to be anxious and worried about anything. He also promised that the peace of God would guard our hearts as we present our needs to God in prayer and thanksgiving. If you will simply give each of your worries to God, you will find that his peace will protect your soul from the stress and turmoil produced by anxiety and fear.

It is also important that you "guard" your life through holiness and purity—especially in the areas of movies, music, the Internet, or television. These forms of media are important battle lines, because the enemy seeks to plant seeds of destruction in your soul through what you see and what you hear. You may be thinking, *No one has the right to determine my entertainment choices.* Sadly, it doesn't matter what you think, because I'm not talking about just anyone's standards—I'm talking about God's. For example, God tells us that we should think only about those things which are true, noble, right, pure, and admirable (Philippians 4:8). Furthermore, even if you think the choices you have been making have not been affecting your spiritual life, you may be wrong. Once a person has defiled their conscience past a certain point, they are often not even convicted about the things that affect them the most. Allow God to work in this area of your life today.

Don't let tomorrow's worries rob God's purpose for you today. Don't worry about tomorrow—God is already there.

Peter Furler

Lessons from the Life of Nehemiah:
BUILDING AND FIGHTING

> Those who carried materials did their work with one hand and held a weapon in the other, and each of the builders wore his sword at his side as he worked. But the man who sounded the trumpet stayed with me.
>
> NEHEMIAH 4:17–18

SEPTEMBER 14

Nehemiah was concerned. Even though his strategic defenses had foiled the enemy's battle plans, work on the walls had ceased. He realized if he continued to respond to the threats of his enemies by keeping all of the workers deployed for battle, he would lose in the end, because the walls would never be rebuilt. After arming half of his workforce and posting them as guards around Jerusalem, he prepared the other workers to fight and build at the same time. Every builder was ordered to strap a sword on his side, and every handler of the materials was ordered to carry them under one arm while holding a weapon with the other hand. With the miraculous help of their God they would still finish the walls in record time. Like Nehemiah, there are times when we must build and fight at the same time. Whether it is your marriage, ministry, business, or church, when any of these things begin to threaten the enemy, he will do whatever it takes to stop their growth and development. When you find yourself in a season like the one I am describing above, it is important that you do the following things.

First, no matter how hard the enemy attacks you, you must continue to do the things that threaten him. I will never forget the first time I learned this lesson; I was developing a course on spiritual warfare. The doctor called my wife and informed her that she had cancer. When I heard this news, I was working at my computer. Everything in me wanted to stop and pray, yet when I tried to stop, I felt literally arrested by the Holy Spirit.

Don't stop and pray, He said. *Type and pray!*

At that moment, I realized that my wife's diagnosis of cancer and her treatment was trying to keep me from my mission. Once I saw this, I determined to complete this spiritual warfare course, no matter what it cost. Today, eight years later, thousands of people have taken this course, and my wife has no trace of cancer in her body.

Second, if you are going to continue to build when you are under attack, you must learn to fight and build at the same time. In the case of my wife's health, I would find myself praying and typing simultaneously; it was as if I was living out the very course I was developing.

Third, never forget that your enemy, the devil, is the ultimate bully. If you faithfully stand up to him through the power of God's Word, he will eventually look for an easier target to attack. No matter what you are building today, you must never forget that if you do your part, God will do his part. If you will fight for what God has told you to build, God himself will fight for you.

One of the many benefits of reading God's Word daily has been a new awareness toward him and his presence. This has led to a greater prayer life — praying in my car, in business meetings, or during a concert — like the men of Nehemiah who continued to build even when they were on guard duty, so I have learned to build my life by staying in a continual mind-set of openness and communication with God.

Peter Furler

Lessons from the Life of Nehemiah:

WHY SHOULD THE WORK STOP?

When word came to Sanballat, Tobiah, Geshem the Arab and the rest of our enemies that I had rebuilt the wall and not a gap was left in it—though up to that time I had not set the doors in the gates—Sanballat and Geshem sent me this message: "Come, let us meet together in one of the villages on the plain of Ono."

But they were scheming to harm me; so I sent messengers to them with this reply: "I am carrying on a great project and cannot go down. Why should the work stop while I leave it and go down to you?" Four times they sent me the same message, and each time I gave them the same answer.

NEHEMIAH 6:1–4

SEPTEMBER 15

By this time, Sanballat was desperate. With all of Jerusalem's walls totally rebuilt, only the gates were left to be hung for the project to be completed. Sanballat knew unless he could lure Nehemiah down off the walls, his plot was doomed to failure. If they could kill him or capture him, however, the gates would never be hung. But no matter how many messengers Sanballat sent to him, Nehemiah's reply was always exactly the same: "I am carrying on a great project and cannot come down. Why should the work stop while I leave it and go down to you?" Even when Nehemiah received a false document filled with accusations, he still refused to leave the task God had given him.

Like Nehemiah, you will find that as you draw closer to the completion of your God-given task, the enemy will become more desperate to stop you. The enemy's attempt to bring you down from what God has called you to build may well involve the job offer you have always desired—or the city where you've always wanted to move. Whatever the case may be, you know that if you accept the offer, you will never finish the assignment God has given to you.

Or, you may face a crisis of such magnitude that there is no time left for anything else. When things like this happen, you must not forget the words of Nehemiah: "I am carrying on a great project." No matter what you are facing, you must not forget the importance of what God has given you to do. Even if it seems small in your own eyes, never underestimate the value of your task in the overall plan of God for your church, campus, city, or nation.

Nehemiah also told Sanballat that he could not leave his task. It would have been one thing for him to say, "I *will not* leave my task," but he clearly said, "I *cannot* leave my task." Nehemiah said this because God himself had commanded him to rebuild the walls. It should be no different with us, because like Nehemiah, you and I have been assigned a task that we have been called to finish. Unlike many Christians who never conclude what they start, I want the words of Paul at the end of his life to describe my life, as well: "I have fought the good fight. I have finished the race. I have kept the faith" (2 Timothy 4:7). May these words become your own as you work on completing the task God has for you.

One of the saddest examples of this I see is someone called down off the wall of parenting to answer what they perceive is their call to ministry. Although this sounds noble, God never wants us to sacrifice our families for the sake of ministry.

Peter Furler

Lessons from the Life of Nehemiah:
FACING FEAR

 They were all trying to frighten us, thinking, "Their hands will get too weak for the work, and it will not be completed."

But I prayed, "Now strengthen my hands."

N E H E M I A H   6 : 9

SEPTEMBER 16

Nehemiah realized the greatest challenge he faced was not the forces of Sanballat and Tobiah. Instead, it was the fear and terror that their diabolical threats produced in his beloved people, the Jews. Nehemiah also realized that no matter how strong a man was, once fear had penetrated his heart, his strength and his faith would be broken. Therefore, Nehemiah declared war on fear—in all of its forms. Through the example of his steadfast faith, as well as the continual encouragement coming out of his mouth, Nehemiah was determined that panic and terror would not destroy his people.

It is no different for you today. Even as faith is your greatest friend, so fear is your greatest foe. In fact, fear is the enemy's version of faith; just as faith will bring you into the reality of God's promises, so fear will bring you into the reality of the enemy's tormenting threats. Although what you fear does not literally always come upon you, there is a magnetic quality to fear that can seem to draw you into the very things that terrify you. This is why, in many cases, the things people fear almost become self-fulfilling prophecies.

Fear also has a deadly corporate effect. That is why God commanded Gideon to release every soldier from his army who was afraid (Judges 7:3).

God realized that fear is highly contagious—the fear of one person can easily turn into an epidemic of panic.

If fear is so deadly, how can you and I combat it? First, we must fight fear with faith. I have learned that the confession of God's Word and the encouragement of my friends are the two primary ways to defeat fear. When I respond to the assaults of fear through the authority of God's Word, the power of my Master is magnified, and the threats of my fears are minimized. The help of my Christian friends is also critical in my battle against fear. In those times when my own faith is failing me, I can find a temporary place of refuge under the powerful shield activated by their faith-filled prayers for me.

Second, although we can *fight* fear with faith, we can only *defeat* fear through the love of God. John wrote, "There is no fear in love. But perfect love drives out fear" (1 John 4:18). When I am established in the revelation of God's love, I can trust him—no matter what I am facing. Even when my own faith seems shattered and broken, I remain confident because his faith for me is strong. In my own experience, I have discovered that God's love alone has the power to terminate fear and terror. People who have this revelation walk free from fear because they realize that no matter what they are facing, their God has promised to use it for the fulfillment of his purposes in their lives (Romans 8:28).

HERE AGAIN is ANotHeR seCRet 10 AN ABUhDANt LifE. GoD's Love mAKes me feARLess. ALive, I Am his messehGeR; DeAD I Am his Bounty. This ReveLAtioh hAS CHANGeD my Life. I ASK GoD to ReveAL it to you.

Peter Furler

LESSONS FROM the LIFE OF NEHEMIAH:
SHOULD I RUN?

One day I went to the house of Shemaiah son of Delaiah, the son of Mehetabel, who was shut in at his home. He said, "Let us meet in the house of God, inside the temple, and let us close the temple doors, because men are coming to kill you—by night they are coming to kill you."

But I said, "Should a man like me run away? Or should one like me go into the temple to save his life? I will not go!" I realized that God had not sent him, but that he had prophesied against me because Tobiah and Sanballat had hired him. He had been hired to intimidate me so that I would commit a sin by doing this, and then they would give me a bad name to discredit me.

NEHEMIAH 6:10–13

SEPTEMBER 17

Sanballat and his forces had become desperate. With only the city's gates left to be hung, Jerusalem's defense would soon be complete. In order to deceive Nehemiah, Sanballat hired a false prophet named Shemaiah. Shemaiah told Nehemiah that he needed to hide in the temple because men were coming to kill him. Nehemiah, however, saw through the false prophet's ploy and refused to be intimidated. "Should a man like me run away?" he asked Shemaiah. "Should I try to save my life by hiding in the temple?" With the last attempt of their enemies foiled, Nehemiah and his men quickly finished their work on the walls.

The questions asked by Nehemiah in his response to the false prophet are directly applicable to your life today. Maybe you find yourself in a situation in which you want to take flight and run away. Whether it is a troubled relationship that only seems to be getting worse, or a painful situation in your local church, even though you know God has placed you there, you still want to run away. In my own experience, I have found that once the enemy gets a person on the run, it is difficult for him to ever stop running again. Once the enemy learns how to manipulate you through fear, you will be running for the rest of your life—unless you turn around and face him through the power of God's Word.

Nehemiah's next question may be even more important than his first: Should you go into the church to save your life? Many Christians today simply see the Church as a place where their lives and the lives of those they love can be saved. Whether it is by hearing the message of Jesus as Savior and Lord or through learning the principles of childrearing, their local church has become a place of refuge from the wicked, cruel world around them. Although the Church is obviously meant to be an instrument of salvation, many Christians refuse to see it as anything beyond that. Tragically, this view of church has produced a generation of Christians who are more interested in escaping from the world than transforming the world. From Christian cruises to Christian television, believers have settled for the creation of their own culture instead of penetrating the dark culture that surrounds them. Unless you and I, like Nehemiah, are willing to stand and build what God has called us to build, the cities and nations we love so much will die.

> You may have been hurt by the church or by other believers, but never let that define you or cause you to run from the clear plan of God—his church.
>
> **Peter Furler**

THE GREATEST MAN IN THE EAST

In the land of Uz there lived a man whose name was Job. This man was blameless and upright; he feared God and shunned evil. He had seven sons and three daughters, and he owned seven thousand sheep, three thousand camels, five hundred yoke of oxen and five hundred donkeys, and had a large number of servants. He was the greatest man among all the people of the East. His sons used to take turns holding feasts in their homes, and they would invite their three sisters to eat and drink with them. When a period of feasting had run its course, Job would send and have them purified. Early in the morning he would sacrifice a burnt offering for each of them, thinking, "Perhaps my children have sinned and cursed God in their hearts." This was Job's regular custom.

J O B   1 : 1 – 5

What I feared has come upon me;
    what I dreaded has happened to me.

J O B   3 : 2 5

SEPTEMBER 18

Job was the greatest man of the East; his wealth was beyond human comprehension. Yet despite his wealth and prominence, he was still a humble, righteous man. The Scriptures say that he feared God and hated evil. Even still, in the midst of this remarkable man's life, there was a growing fear. The lifestyle of his children was breaking his heart. Unlike their father, they were spending an increasing amount of their time in revelry and idleness. Job had become so concerned over the state of their souls that he was rising early every morning to sacrifice burnt offerings in order to atone for the sins he feared they were committing. Unfortunately for Job, God was not the only one who had seen his growing fear. In another dimension, a malevolent creature was watching and waiting for the chance to destroy Job's life.

No matter how righteous or wealthy you have become, you also have an enemy who is always watching you. To the world, Job lived a charmed life. Humble, righteous, and wealthy, he was the man everyone wanted to be. Yet his incredible character and amazing riches were not able to insulate him from pain. Even though Jesus promised that Christians would face tribulations and trials in this life, many of God's people are still shocked and surprised by the unpleasant realities of their lives. Sooner or later, some painful challenge will threaten the tranquility you have come to expect. When this happens, you will either respond in fear or in faith.

Although Job was a man of faith, his sacrifices made for his children were made out of fear. We know this because after Job's children were killed, he said, "What I feared has come upon me; what I dreaded has happened to me" (Job 3:25). In your battles with the enemy, it is not enough for you to merely say or do the right thing. You can claim the name of Jesus and even tell the devil to get behind you, but if fear is in your heart, these expressions will have no power to defeat the enemy. No matter how wonderfully you have built your life, sooner or later, you will face a situation that forces you to choose between faith and fear. It is in these moments that the very foundations of our lives are revealed. If your life has built on the daily discipline of seeking God through the Word and prayer, your faith will not fail you.

In my life, I have found that fear is a trap. It will not stop trials or tribulation; it will only keep you exposed to them.

Peter Furler

Lessons from the Life of Job:
JOB'S ACCUSER

 One day the angels came to present themselves before the LORD, and Satan also came with them. The LORD said to Satan, "Where have you come from?"

Satan answered the LORD, "From roaming through the earth and going back and forth in it."

Then the LORD said to Satan, "Have you considered my servant Job? There is no one on earth like him; he is blameless and upright, a man who fears God and shuns evil."

"Does Job fear God for nothing?" Satan replied. "Have you not put a hedge around him and his household and everything he has? You have blessed the work of his hands, so that his flocks and herds are spread throughout the land. But stretch out your hand and strike everything he has, and he will surely curse you to your face."

The LORD said to Satan, "Very well, then, everything he has is in your hands, but on the man himself do not lay a finger."

Then Satan went out from the presence of the LORD.

JOB 1:6–12

SEPTEMBER 19

In a dimension far different than our own, the angels gathered around the throne of their beloved King. Yet something was tainting the purity of their celestial realm. Yes, it was him. Once a leader among the angelic hosts, Lucifer was now the enemy of both God and man.

"Have you seen my servant Job?" the Lord queried. "There is no one on the earth as righteous as he."

"Of course he is serving you," the devil replied. "With your blessing he has grown rich beyond comprehension."

God, however, had already determined that without testing, his beloved servant Job would not continue to grow.

"If you will allow everything he has to be destroyed, he will curse you," whispered Satan.

"Very well," the Lord said, "you may destroy everything Job has, but I forbid you to touch his person."

You may be wondering, *Why would the loving God of the universe allow his precious children to face the attacks of the enemy?* The answer to this age-old question is simple: There are times when no other being but Satan will do. That's right, when it comes to stubborn, hard-headed people like you and me, there are times when it takes the attack of the devil for God to teach us his most important lessons!

Humor aside, the fact of the matter is that we live in a fallen world with a very real foe. As a believer, you will face attacks from time to time. When this happens, you can be sure that God is more than able to use them as an instrument of change and transformation in your life.

I have found that there is nothing like the concentrated assault of the enemy to bring a new level of discipline and commitment to my spiritual life. Even the devil's temptations have positive benefits, because without them, you and I would never recognize the sin that is hidden in our souls. Never forget, however, that even when the Lord allows you to face the attack of Satan, his protection is still present. The same God who told the enemy that he could not touch Job's body, is also able to limit the enemy's attack on you as you walk in obedience to his will.

Even though the heart melts like wax, even though the soul faints, even though the eyes fail looking for the promise, remain faithful, remain faithful, and remain faithful.

Peter Furler

Lessons from the Life of Job:
JOB'S RESPONSE

At this, Job got up and tore his robe and shaved his head. Then he fell to the ground in worship and said:

"Naked I came from my mother's womb,
    and naked I will depart.
The LORD gave and the LORD has taken away;
    may the name of the LORD be praised."

In all this, Job did not sin by charging God with wrongdoing.

JOB 1:20-22

SEPTEMBER 20

When the enemy struck Job, he struck him with all his might. In less than a day, the wealth that Job had accumulated over a lifetime was gone. His oxen and camels had been carried off by raiding parties, and the servants guarding them had been brutally murdered. His sheep and the shepherds tending them had been slaughtered by burning fire that fell from heaven. If this was not enough, all of his children were killed when the house they were feasting in was destroyed by a violent desert wind.

Whereas most men would have begun to rant and rave against God, Job, after hearing the news of these disasters, simply tore his robe and fell to the ground in worship. As he continued to worship the Lord, those around him heard these words: "The Lord gave and the Lord has taken away; may the name of the Lord be praised."

These disasters, however, were only the beginning of Job's trials. When Satan saw that Job's faith remained strong even after he had suffered the loss of his children and all of his wealth, he asked God for permission to strike him with a terrible infirmity. Although God refused to allow Satan to kill him, he did grant the enemy his permission to afflict his precious servant. When Job woke up the next morning, he was covered in painful sores from the top of his head to the soles of his feet. And the trials and testings continued.

There are a few lessons we can learn from this story. Even though Job had many valuable holdings, they did not have a hold on him, and he was able to praise the Lord when everything he owned was taken away. No matter how many possessions you have, you must never allow these things to develop a hold on your soul.

Second, this story also gives us a critical insight into the nature of Satan. Far from giving up when Job successfully resisted his initial assaults, Satan continued his attacks until Job was broken and defeated. Many Christians have no idea how relentless Satan can be. Once they win a minor skirmish, they begin to live as if they have won the whole war.

No matter what you are facing, never forget that the same God who was at work in Job's life through his pain is also faithfully working in the midst of your suffering today.

YouR ResPoNse hAs sigNifICANce. This is one of my fAVoRite ResPoNses in the BiBle. JoB Loses everything. his FRIeNDs ARe woRse thAN eNemies. the oNly thing he hAs Left is his GReAtest Asset — A fAithfuL ResPoNse: "MAY the NAme of the LoRD Be pRAiseD!"

Peter Furler

Lessons from the Life of Job:
OUT OF THE STORM

 Then the LORD answered Job out of the storm.

JOB 38:1

SEPTEMBER 21

None of his friends had been able to help him. As the weeks went by, Job's bitterness only grew. Once he had been filled with praise and worship; now he cursed the day of his birth. The man who had walked with God as an intimate friend now saw the Lord as a monstrous, unfeeling, capricious tyrant. Even when young Elihu had brought the word of the Lord to him, Job's soul had been so filled with bitterness and anger that he refused to respond. Now, with all hope gone, he sat forlornly in the ruins of his once-vast holdings. With his soul in torment and his body racked by constant pain, death seemed to be his only way of escape. At that moment, he felt the presence of the Almighty. As he looked up, he saw a huge, billowing whirlwind coming toward him. Despite the force of its howling winds, he knew this was no ordinary storm. After weeks of terrifying silence, he heard the voice of God—for God was in his storm.

No matter what type of storm you are facing, it is critical that you learn to discern the voice of God that is present in the midst of it. Like Job, there will be times in your life when none of your friends will be able to explain the horrible storms that are battering you. In moments like these, it is important that you learn how to discern the voice of God. As we see in the story of Job, however, this is not always an easy matter. Although God had been in the middle of Job's storm from the very beginning, Job did not recognize his presence until the end.

There are several reasons for Job's failure to recognize God in his storm. First, Job had never experienced a storm of this magnitude before. His great wealth had insulated him from the problems of ordinary people. For many Christians, it is no different. When they experience a storm that is bigger than any they have experienced before, it is almost impossible for them to imagine that God could have anything to do with it. In the midst of the panic that is flooding their soul and the pain that is all around them, all they can see is the devil wherever they look.

Second, when you are in the middle of a major storm, it often takes the counsel of other people for you to discern God's hand. In Job's case, the friends who should have been able to help him were even more blind than he was. Far from being the horrible sinner they perceived him to be, Job was a choice servant of God who was simply undergoing a new level of divine transformation.

Third, as the storm continued, Job progressively grew more bitter and angry. In his darkened state he was unable to discern the presence of his loving God and best friend. If you fail to respond properly to the storms that come into your life, you will also lose your ability to fellowship with the God who is waiting for you in the eye of your storm.

Looking BACK over storms I've had in my life, I see how they tested my foundation and trust in Christ. Asking me where my hope lies, calling me to a deeper place. Stay strong and persevere — like Job, the best is yet to come.

Peter Furler

Lessons from the Life of Job:
SEEING HIM

"You asked, 'Who is this that obscures my counsel without knowledge?'
Surely I spoke of things I did not understand,
    things too wonderful for me to know.
"You said, 'Listen now, and I will speak;
I will question you,
    and you shall answer me.'
My ears had heard of you
    but now my eyes have seen you.
Therefore I despise myself
    and repent in dust and ashes."

JOB 42:3-6

SEPTEMBER 22

None of Job's questions had been answered, but it didn't matter anymore. In fact, for the last few hours, all God had done was question him. In the midst of the howling winds, the voice of God had cut through the darkness of his heart like a knife. The Lord had been right; he had lost sight of the God who had always loved him. Now, as he saw his mighty God afresh, he was pouring dust and ashes over his head. Although he had been covered in dust and ashes for days, this time was different. Before, he had been mourning over his situation, now he was grieving over his sin.

Have you seen the reflection of God in the horrors of your storm? Before you answer that too quickly, let me explain what I mean. It is one thing to hear *about* God, but it is an entirely different matter to *see* him.

For example, Saul, the persecutor who had heard about God all of his life, became the apostle Paul after he saw him on the road to Damascus. Moses was a fear-ridden fugitive until he met God in the burning bush. Sadly, despite all of our Christian books, CDs, messages, and television, we have produced a generation of Christians who know a lot *about* God without really *knowing* him. Perhaps you are asking, "How can I experience God like this?"

First, it is critical that you spend quality time with God on a regular basis. As you read the Word, worship him, and wait on him, the Holy Spirit will begin to make your heavenly Father real to you. In John 14:17, Jesus, speaking of his Father, said, "The world cannot accept him because it neither sees him nor knows him. But you know him ..." Although we will not be able to physically see God until we get to heaven, there is a place of knowing God that is almost like seeing him. As you are faithful in your spiritual disciplines, with the help of the Holy Spirit, you can be one of those who knows him in this way.

Second, through his friend's misrepresentation of God and the pain and bitterness in his own heart, Job was unable to see the reality of his loving God. In 1 Corinthians 13:12, Paul wrote, "We see but a poor reflection as in a mirror; then we shall see face to face." One of the mirrors through which we attempt to see God is our internal view of what God is like. If that internal lens had been distorted, you will find it almost impossible to see clearly the God who loves us so much. Never forget that the same God who revealed the light of his countenance in the darkness of Job's soul is more than able to reveal himself to you in a fresh way today.

There are so many distorted views of God out there — from TV shows to bestselling books and crazed cults. Guard your view of God. Anything contrary to his Word about him is a distortion.

Peter Furler

Lessons from the Life of Job:
THE POWER OF FORGIVENESS

After the LORD had said these things to Job, he said to Eliphaz the Temanite, "I am angry with you and your two friends, because you have not spoken of me what is right, as my servant Job has. So now take seven bulls and seven rams and go to my servant Job and sacrifice a burnt offering for yourselves. My servant Job will pray for you and I will accept his prayer and not deal with you according to your folly. You have not spoken of me what is right, as my servant Job has." So Eliphaz the Temanite, Bildad the Shuhite and Zophar the Naamathite did what the LORD told them; and the LORD accepted Job's prayer.

After Job had prayed for his friends, the LORD made him prosperous again and gave him twice as much as he had before. All his brothers and sisters and everyone who had known him before came and ate with him in his house. They comforted and consoled him over all the trouble the LORD had brought upon him, and each one gave him a piece of silver and a gold ring.

JOB 42:7–11

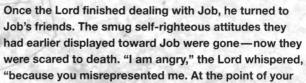

SEPTEMBER 23

Once the Lord finished dealing with Job, he turned to Job's friends. The smug self-righteous attitudes they had earlier displayed toward Job were gone—now they were scared to death. "I am angry," the Lord whispered, "because you misrepresented me. At the point of your friend's greatest need, you wrongly told him that some horrible sin in his life had brought my displeasure and judgment upon him.

You broke his heart and shattered his confidence in me. In your arrogance, you never realized that even in his darkened state, Job was far closer to me than you were.

"Bring seven bulls and seven rams to Job," the Lord thundered. "After you have sacrificed them for your sins, my servant will pray that I spare you the punishment that your folly deserves."

When Job's friends approached him with the animals that were to be sacrificed, he was a far different man. Even covered with dust and ashes, there was a radiance about him and a smile on his face. Far from being vindictive and bitter over their shameful treatment of him, Job embraced them in tears, and the offenses between them simply disappeared. Job prayed for his friends and they were forgiven. Job's prayers, however, did not merely affect his friends. When God saw the humility and purity of Job's heart, he determined to prosper him like never before.

Even though God had dramatically touched Job, his healing could not be completed until he was willing to forgive his friends. Some of you have been betrayed by your spouse. Even though God is at work to restore your marriage, your bitterness and unforgiveness has locked you out of the very miracle God is doing in your marriage. Others of you have been mis-judged and condemned by those who should have understood you that you now find it hard to be in their presence. Whatever the case may be, it is time for you to forgive.

Second, Job's ability to forgive ushered him in to the greatest pros-perity of his life. The same God who allowed you to face such loss is able to bring you into a season of blessing and prosperity that is beyond your comprehension. Never forget that no matter what you have lost, God can bring restoration to your soul as you open the doors of your heart through forgiveness and obedience.

When you can't forgive someone you become a slave to your hurt. Those who remember how much they are forgiven know how to forgive.
Peter Furler

Lessons from the Life of Job:
JOB'S END

The LORD blessed the latter part of Job's life more than the first. He had fourteen thousand sheep, six thousand camels, a thousand yoke of oxen and a thousand donkeys. And he also had seven sons and three daughters. The first daughter he named Jemimah, the second Keziah and the third Keren-Happuch. Nowhere in all the land were there found women as beautiful as Job's daughters, and their father granted them an inheritance along with their brothers.

After this, Job lived a hundred and forty years; he saw his children and their children to the fourth generation. And so he died, old and full of years.

JOB 42:12–17

As you know, we consider blessed those who have persevered. You have heard of Job's perseverance and have seen what the Lord finally brought about. The Lord is full of compassion and mercy.

JAMES 5:11

SEPTEMBER 24

Once again, Job was considered the greatest man in the East. Where once many had considered him a broken, embittered failure who had been judged by God, now everyone marveled again at his prosperity. As for Job, he was filled with kindness and humility, for a man who has lost everything is never the same when he gets it back. Even his children were different. The ten who had been born to him in the years since his trials were so responsible that Job even gave the girls their own inheritance. In many ways, Job's life had become a living

parable—where once people had talked about his trials, now they talked about the way God had blessed the end of his life.

No matter how you are suffering today, if you will continue to respond to God, he is well able to transform and bless your life, too. Far from the bitter end with which the enemy has threatened you, God has a better end to your story than you can even imagine! Although it may not include the wealth and prominence of Job, it will involve a measure of blessing that is beyond your current ability to comprehend.

Have you ever wondered why the end of Job's life was far better than the beginning? It obviously wasn't because God loved him any more than he had before the trials. I think it had to do with the fact that Job was no longer bound by fear. According to Job 3:25, God's precious servant had been tormented with the fear of losing his children and possessions. Now that he had faced the reality of every one of his fears, there was nothing left to fear, and this enabled him to enjoy a quality of life that he had never enjoyed before. It will be no different for you. As in the life of Job, once the fires of your current trial have burned away the ungodly attitudes that have been constricting your heart, you will be ushered into a new place of prosperity and joy.

This tells me that whether RICH OR POOR, the most FORTUNATE people on the EARTh ARe the feARLess.

Peter Furler

Lessons from the Lives of Zechariah and Elizabeth:
FAITHFULNESS

[Zechariah and Elizabeth] were upright in the sight of God, observing all the Lord's commandments and regulations blamelessly. But they had no children, because Elizabeth was barren; and they were both well along in years.

Once when Zechariah's division was on duty and he was serving as priest before God, he was chosen by lot ... to go into the temple of the Lord and burn incense....

Then an angel of the Lord appeared to him, standing at the right side of the altar of incense. When Zechariah saw him, he was startled and was gripped with fear. But the angel said to him: "Do not be afraid, Zechariah; your prayer has been heard. Your wife Elizabeth will bear you a son, and you are to give him the name John."

LUKE 1:6-9, 11-13

SEPTEMBER 25

Old Zechariah had finally been selected to go to Jerusalem and offer a sacrifice in the great temple. With tears in his eyes, he reported the joyous news to his wife. Although the Bible describes them as faithful, holy, obedient servants of the Lord, they were barren. After years of futility, they had aged past the point of hope. But God had other plans for his faithful servants. When Zechariah entered the courts of the temple to make the sacrifice, his heart was pounding—this was his crowning moment—he had been chosen to make an incense offering to the Lord.

Although Zechariah had been taught from childhood to believe in the God of his people, he had never experienced his presence or heard his voice. At that moment, the whole room began to change. It was as if the very glory of heaven was flooding into the inner court of the temple. As Zechariah wiped the tears from his eyes, he saw an angel standing near the altar of incense. Although he was terrified, the angel said, "Don't be afraid. Your prayers have been heard, and your wife, Elizabeth, will bear a son."

Even though Zechariah and Elizabeth had given up all hope of having a child, because of their faithfulness, their prayers were answered. God delights in people who will continue to do what he has called them to do, even when they have no sense of faith or anticipation left. Like Zechariah and Elizabeth, there may be a barrenness deep within your soul. If this is where you find yourself, take heart. Sooner or later, your faithfulness may bring you into the very presence of the God you have been serving.

After years of dutifully serving the God he never really knew, Zechariah finally stepped into the temple's inner courts and was overwhelmed by the presence and promise of God. Could it be that if you went a little deeper into God's presence that you might be equally surprised?

There have been countless times in my life that I have been mistakenly less than zealous about attending certain events like early morning men's prayer breakfasts, high school visits, or business meetings. Many times, however, I have found that the things I was reluctant to go to or do ended up being divine appointments. Just show up. To the faithful, he shows himself faithful.

Peter Furler

Lessons from the Lives of Zechariah and Elizabeth:

THE PAIN OF UNBELIEF

The angel answered, "I am Gabriel. I stand in the presence of God, and I have been sent to speak to you and to tell you this good news. And now you will be silent and not able to speak until the day this happens, because you did not believe my words, which will come true at their proper time."

LUKE 1:19–20

SEPTEMBER 26

Despite the glory of heaven and the angelic messenger who stood in front of him, Zechariah's heart was still paralyzed by the tentacles of unbelief that had been strangling him for years. "How can I be sure that what you're saying is true?" the old man whimpered. "I'm an old man, and my wife is well beyond the years of childbearing."

"I am Gabriel," the angel thundered.

When Zechariah heard these words, his heart filled with fear, for Gabriel was the chosen messenger of heaven.

"I stand in the presence of God," the angel said, "and He has sent me to you with a message you have rejected. Now, because of your unbelief, you will be silent until the day this great miracle takes place."

When Zechariah staggered out of the temple, his face was glowing with an unearthly radiance. Even though he was burning to describe his visitation to the waiting crowd, his unbelief had left him a voiceless mute. As the months progressed and the child grew in his wife's womb, the shame of his unbelief became even more painful than his inability to speak.

This strange story contains both an incredible message of hope and a stern warning. This story's message of hope is easy to see. Despite Zechariah's unbelief, his wife would still have a baby boy after years of barrenness. This should encourage all of us. If God only answered our prayers and fulfilled his promises when we were in a state of perfect faith, we would all be in trouble. Fortunately, when God has determined to bring forth his purposes in our lives, he is still willing to work, even when we are in a place of unbelief.

There is also, however, a warning in this story. Although Zechariah's wife still had the promised son, his unbelief destroyed his ability to enjoy the miraculous process he and his wife were experiencing. I cannot count the number of people I have seen in this very place. Even though God is at work in their marriage, business, or finances, their unbelief has struck them dumb. Far from being able to testify about what God is doing, their unbelief leaves them with nothing to say.

If this is where you are today, it's time to repent. Why settle for joyless change when God wants you to delight in this season of your life? If you will simply ask both God and the people he has placed in your life for help, they will give you the encouragement and strength you need to cut away the unbelief from your soul.

It seems like there are two types of Christians in the world: those who believe it when they see it and those who see it because they believed it. Now the first kind might catch the end of the blessing, but the last kind ride it from start to finish.

Peter Furler

Lessons from the Life of MARY:
MARY'S PROBLEMS

In the sixth month, God sent the angel Gabriel to Nazareth, a town in Galilee, to a virgin pledged to be married to a man named Joseph, a descendant of David. The virgin's name was Mary. The angel went to her and said, "Greetings, you who are highly favored! The Lord is with you."

LUKE 1:26–28

SEPTEMBER 27

She was young, beautiful, and in love. Although she hardly even knew the young carpenter, she had probably been betrothed to him for a long period of time. The last thing on her mind that day was the message she would soon be receiving from the angel of the Lord. After all, how could she ever imagine that she would be chosen as the Messiah's mother—the only woman in all of history to give birth as a virgin? As she continued down the dusty streets of an obscure town called Nazareth, God had other plans for this chosen young woman.

The story of the virgin birth is obviously one of the most miraculous events in all of Scripture. With all the mystery and theological implications which surround it, you and I can easily forget that Mary was a real person. The courage it took for her to perform her God-ordained role is normally taken for granted. It is easy to forget that on the day the angel appeared to her, she was a very scared little girl.

Although there are many lessons which can be drawn from her story, I want to concentrate on three of them. First of all, Mary lived in a small town in the region of Galilee. Her inconsequential little town was located in one of Israel's most backward regions. This is important because it illustrates the fact that God delights in bringing people out of obscurity into the limelight of his purpose for their lives. No matter where you are living, how educated you are, or what kind of job you have, none of these things should be a deterrent to the fullness of God's purposes in your life.

Second, Mary was a virgin. Her virginity, however, was not merely physical—it was spiritual, as well. Although it is hard to imagine what her personality was like, I believe there was a unique humility and hunger for God that characterized her life. With thousands of girls to choose from, God chose her. Surely Israel was filled with girls who were probably far more intelligent, beautiful, and even educated. Yet something in this young woman had captured the heart of God. No matter how you feel about your figure, form, or face, God is more concerned about what he sees in your heart.

Third, Mary was already betrothed to a man. Her encounter with God had the potential to destroy every primary relationship in her life. Why would Joseph ever believe that the Holy Spirit had made her pregnant? What about her parents? Even if Joseph didn't divorce her, and the village didn't stone her, she would be branded for the rest of her life. This may be the most frightening thing about being chosen by God. When God places his hand on your life, it has the potential to radically affect your most cherished relationships. Sooner or later, a relationship you value will be affected by your obedience to Christ. Yet in the end, the rewards of following him far surpass anything else you will ever experience.

> WhAt A FREEDOM to find out in life that we don't need to promote ourselves. LeAve that up to God and just Remain faithful, never forgetting that God promises to exAlt the humble.
>
> **Peter Furler**

Lessons from the Life of Mary:
MARY'S MESSAGE

The angel said to [Mary], "Do not be afraid, Mary, you have found favor with God. You will be with child and give birth to a son, and you are to give him the name Jesus."

"How will this be," Mary asked the angel, "since I am a virgin?" The angel answered, "The Holy Spirit will come upon you, and the power of the Most High will overshadow you. So the holy one to be born will be called the Son of God. Even Elizabeth your relative is going to have a child in her old age, and she who was said to be barren is in her sixth month. For nothing is impossible with God."

LUKE 1:30–31, 34–37

SEPTEMBER 28

Gabriel was amazed. Unlike almost every other human he had ever greeted, Mary was not afraid. Yes, the Almighty God had chosen well. Like the rest of the angels, Gabriel had been almost desperate to meet the young woman who had been chosen to bear the Messiah—God the Son, in human flesh.

"Mary," he whispered, "you have been chosen to bear the Messiah. You will give birth to a Son and name him Jesus."

With no hesitation, Mary asked him an amazing question, "Since I am a virgin, please explain to me how this is going to work."

"The Holy Spirit will come on you, and the presence and power of God will provide a covering over you. So the Holy Child who will be born to you will be called the Son of God."

If God can use a young teenage girl from a backwards town to change all of human history, what can he do through you? No matter how

impossible your calling is, or how unattainable your destiny may seem, nothing is impossible with God.

When the angel told Mary that the Holy Spirit would come upon her, he was revealing the very secret of her miraculous conception. Without the Holy Spirit's power, you, too, will never accomplish your divine purpose. As you submit to his work in your life, he will do miraculous things for you.

The angel also told that Mary that God's presence and power would overshadow, or cover, her. In the Bible, "covering" can be associated with authority. You will never experience the full reality of God's work in your life until you have submitted to his authority. The Bible calls this submission by another name: lordship. Sadly, many Christians have created a sad dichotomy between the role of Jesus as Savior and his role as Lord. Although they fully embrace him as Savior because they don't want to go to hell, they still have no real desire for his lordship in their lives. If you, like Mary, want to experience the reality of your destiny, you must accept Christ as Lord.

Choosing Jesus as Lord means choosing life. Jesus did not teach us that he came simply to save us from hell and then leave us to fend for ourselves until the Great Judgment Day. He taught us that he came to give us life, and life more abundantly. Choosing Jesus as Savior only can give you an assurance of heaven but it can also leave you with an empty, unfulfilled life. Making him Savior and Lord will lead you into an abundant life.

Peter Furler

Lessons From the Lives of Joseph And Mary:

MARY'S RESPONSE

 "I am the Lord's servant," Mary answered. "May it be to me as you have said." Then the angel left her.

LUKE 1:38

SEPTEMBER 29

Although Mary did not realize it, all of heaven was waiting on her reply that day. In fact, if the peoples of the earth had understood the decision she was making, they would have been waiting as well. Even Gabriel was wondering, for, unlike God, he was not omniscient. Yet as he contemplated the faith that was radiating out of her countenance, he knew in his heart that she would choose well. "I am the Lord's servant," Mary replied. After saying those words, she paused and took a deep breath. "May it be to me as you have said."

As Gabriel prepared to return to the celestial realm, he marveled at the faith he had found that day. For one so young, Mary was rapidly taking her place among the great heroes and heroines of his Master's kingdom.

Sooner or later, like Mary, you will face a choice that will determine your destiny. Although there probably will not be an angelic messenger standing before you, the implications of your choice will be serious nonetheless. Whether God's direction for your life comes through your Bible reading, a sermon, or a word from a trusted Christian friend, it does not matter. All that matters is how you choose. When this moment comes, the choice you make will determine whether you become a womb or a tomb for the word that God has spoken to you. If you respond properly, you will eventually give birth to the very purposes God has called you to fulfill. On the other hand, if you reject what God is saying, no matter how powerful the word may have been, it will die in you.

Where are you today? Has God called you to a seemingly impossible task? Has he given you something to do that is beyond the limits of your strength and wisdom? Whatever the case may be, the same God who has called you is well able to give you the strength to fulfill his purpose. Never forget that God promises to give you both the will and the ability to do his will (Philippians 2:13).

Your response has significance for more people than just you. Choose to be a womb for the purposes of God and both you and the world you live in will be blessed.

Peter Furler

Lessons from the Lives of Joseph and Mary:

MARY'S MENTOR

 "Even Elizabeth your relative is going to have a child in her old age, and she who was said to be barren is in her sixth month."

At that time Mary got ready and hurried to a town in the hill country of Judea, where she entered Zechariah's home and greeted Elizabeth. When Elizabeth heard Mary's greeting, the baby leaped in her womb, and Elizabeth was filled with the Holy Spirit.

In a loud voice she exclaimed: "Blessed are you among women, and blessed is the child you will bear! But why am I so favored, that the mother of my Lord should come to me?"

Mary stayed with Elizabeth for about three months and then returned home.

LUKE 1:36, 39–43, 56

SEPTEMBER 30

As Mary gazed at the angel's countenance, she was almost mesmerized. She knew she should be terrified, yet the kindness that radiated from Gabriel had filled her with peace and tranquility. Yet, in the middle of the mandate he had given her, he had informed her that one of her aging relatives, Elizabeth, was pregnant. Even though she had been in the midst of her own miracle, this amazed Mary, for Elizabeth was well beyond her childbearing years. After agonizing over whom she should tell first about her divine encounter, she realized that Elizabeth was the one person who might understand. Because she herself had been supernaturally touched by the Lord, she would be more inclined to accept Mary's miraculous tale.

When Mary finally got to the home of Elizabeth, she was filled with anxiety. If Elizabeth didn't believe her, who would? Deep inside, she knew that without human help, she would never be able to fulfill the mission God had given her. When she entered the house, Mary called out, "Elizabeth! It's Mary!" Before Elizabeth could speak, it was as if they both knew instantaneously that they shared a common destiny. "Blessed are you among women," Elizabeth cried. "Blessed is the child you will bear." Mary was stunned. With this divine confirmation, Mary began to worship and sing.

Have you found your Elizabeth yet—the person God desires to place in your life? Whether it is through your pastor, your parents, or a mature Christian of the same gender, God wants to give you the encouragement and mentoring you need. When Gabriel told Mary about Elizabeth, he knew she would need the strength and counsel of an older believer in order to face the tests and trials that her destiny would entail. If God can send Mary to Elizabeth, he can send you to the exact person you need today.

This is so true! In the last few years, one of the greatest blessings has been the men that God has placed in my life. The enemy will tell you that you don't need people in your life. Well, let me tell you that that is _his_ version. He is a liar. The enemy of your soul wants to keep you alone in your thoughts and battles. Surround yourself with the strong and you will stay strong. Surround yourself with leaders who know how to lead because they themselves have made themselves accountable to others.

Peter Furler

Lessons from the Lives of Zechariah and Elizabeth:
ELIZABETH'S CONFIRMATION

When Elizabeth heard Mary's greeting, the baby leaped in her womb, and Elizabeth was filled with the Holy Spirit. In a loud voice she exclaimed: "Blessed are you among women, and blessed is the child you will bear! But why am I so favored, that the mother of my Lord should come to me? As soon as the sound of your greeting reached my ears, the baby in my womb leaped for joy. Blessed is she who has believed that what the Lord has said to her will be accomplished!"

LUKE 1:41–45

OCTOBER I

Elizabeth had been overwhelmed by the Lord's mercy. Even though she had given up all hope of ever having a child, God had not forgotten her. There were times when she was still afraid—even though she knew that she was pregnant. But she *was* very old, and some days she had even wondered if the baby was still alive. She had experienced some faint sense of movement, but maybe it was just her imagination. Then she heard it. Not the voice of God, but the voice of young Mary. "Elizabeth!" At the sound of her name, the baby leaped inside her womb. It was an amazing moment. Two women, decades apart in age, had been brought together by God's common purpose for their lives—and their miraculous pregnancies.

This may be one of the most beautiful pictures in all of Scripture of the benefits of discipleship and mentoring. Although Mary obviously needed the strength, encouragement, and counsel that only her aging relative could provide, there were also benefits for Elizabeth. When Elizabeth heard Mary call her name, the child in her womb quickened, and she was filled with the power of the Holy Spirit. This power gave her the strength she needed to both encourage Mary and to successfully raise the young prophet she was carrying.

It is no different for you today. If you will embrace your responsibility to make disciples, like Elizabeth, you will be filled with new life and power. In my own experience, I have found that every time a younger Christian asks me for help, something comes alive in me. Their need for wisdom and counsel seems to draw a whole new level of God's anointing and the Word out of my soul. In fact, I have discovered that the best way for me to keep growing is by helping others to grow! After all, how can I not read my Bible and pray when other Christians have asked me to hold them accountable to do the same? The demands of mentoring a good disciple will require you to be a great disciple.

It is interesting to note that Elizabeth considered Mary's visit to be an honor. Unlike many self-absorbed Christians who have no desire to work with younger children or teenagers, Elizabeth realized that Mary and the generation she represented were the hope of her nation. Never forget that the need of our hour, and indeed every hour, is for Marys—young people who will birth the purposes of God for their generation—to meet with Elizabeths—older men and women who will mentor them in the faith.

God's design is for different generations to unite the Body of Christ. Satan's aim is to lie to each generation in order to convince them that any generation except theirs is irrelevant to God's purpose and plans. Don't believe the lies. Embrace God's design for every generation—it's always the best.

Phil Joel

Lessons from the Lives of Joseph and Mary:
JOSEPH'S DECISION

This is how the birth of Jesus Christ came about: His mother Mary was pledged to be married to Joseph, but before they came together, she was found to be with child through the Holy Spirit. Because Joseph her husband was a righteous man and did not want to expose her to public disgrace, he had in mind to divorce her quietly.

But after he had considered this, an angel of the Lord appeared to him in a dream and said, "Joseph son of David, do not be afraid to take Mary home as your wife, because what is conceived in her is from the Holy Spirit. She will give birth to a son, and you are to give him the name Jesus, because he will save his people from their sins."

When Joseph woke up, he did what the angel of the Lord had commanded him and took Mary home as his wife.

MATTHEW 1:18–21, 24

OCTOBER 2

Joseph was in agony. His beautiful young bride-to-be had just announced to him that she was pregnant. Not only that, an angel had told her that the child had been conceived through the Holy Spirit.

"Are you out of your mind?" Joseph stammered. He was so distraught over Mary's visit that he couldn't concentrate on his work. When he got home that night, he was still seething over the pain of her alleged betrayal. Despite his pain, however, he decided to privately divorce her. As he climbed into bed, his heart was in turmoil. Somehow, he couldn't believe that Mary was lying. When God saw the humility of Joseph's heart and his decision to keep Mary from dis-

grace, he was pleased. When Joseph fell asleep, Gabriel appeared to him in a dream and told him the truth.

When Joseph awoke the next morning, he sprinted to Mary's house. "Forgive me," Joseph whispered. "I should have never doubted you."

Joseph was a righteous man, but even he nearly missed the purpose for which he had been born. I have watched many people make the very same mistake that Joseph was contemplating. Although they continue to attend church and even read their Bibles, in their hearts they have quietly divorced themselves from the purposes of God for their lives.

Fortunately, instead of simply dismissing Mary as crazy, Joseph opened his heart to the possibility that her story might be true. When God saw that Joseph's heart was open , he immediately sent his angel to assure Joseph that Mary was telling the truth. If you, too, will open your heart to what you believe God is telling you, he will send you the confirmation you need. No matter where you are or what you are facing, God has the grace to enable you to respond to the message he has given you.

Joseph must have been a man of good character to begin with. But what God was after was to make him a man of GREAT character. God used this unusual and humiliating situation to build in Joseph the faith and character he would need to raise His own Son. Joseph's response in this testing time pleased God. Is your response to your current circumstances pleasing to God?

Phil Joel

Lessons from the Lives of Joseph and Mary:

NO ROOM IN THE INN

In those days Caesar Augustus issued a decree that a census should be taken of the entire Roman world. (This was the first census that took place while Quirinius was governor of Syria.) And everyone went to his own town to register.

So Joseph also went up from the town of Nazareth in Galilee to Judea, to Bethlehem the town of David, because he belonged to the house and line of David. He went there to register with Mary, who was pledged to be married to him and was expecting a child. While they were there, the time came for the baby to be born, and she gave birth to her firstborn, a son. She wrapped him in cloths and placed him in a manger, because there was no room for them in the inn.

LUKE 2:1–7

OCTOBER 3

By the time they had finished their journey to Bethlehem, Mary was exhausted. The baby was due at any moment. By this point, Mary was desperate for rest. "Joseph, isn't there any place we can stay?"

"There is one place," Joseph said.

"Let's take it!" Mary said anxiously.

"It's a stable, Mary."

"A stable?" she exclaimed. "Do you think God would want his Son to be born in a stable?"

"He may not have any choice," Joseph said.

No one on Bethlehem's crowded streets realized that this young woman was pregnant with their long-awaited Messiah. If the people had realized that Mary was pregnant with the Son of God, there would have been plenty of room in the inn. Whether it was the secret rooms they had reserved for their richest customers or their own beds at home, they would have found a place for the Messiah to be born.

Like the inhabitants of Bethlehem, many times we fail to recognize the hand of God on the people who pass through our churches and ministries. Perhaps because of their age, background, gender, or ethnicity, we miss the fact that the purposes of God are on their lives. When this happens, they do not receive the priority their calling requires, and we lose the blessing of participating in a divine moment.

Imagine for a moment how the people of Bethlehem felt when they discovered, years later, that the Messiah had been born in their city. Perhaps they agonized over the fact that they had closed their doors in the face of God's only Son. Sadly, they had missed their opportunity to participate in one of history's greatest miracles. How about you? Are you missing your opportunity to help someone else come into their destiny?

Don't let the enemy trick you into thinking that there is no room for you in God's kingdom or that you have nothing to share. No matter how old you are, the power of your testimony and the truth of the gospel in your life are always relevant.

Phil Joel

LESSONS FROM THE LIVES OF
JOSEPH AND MARY:
THE SHEPHERDS

And there were shepherds living out in the fields nearby, keeping watch over their flocks at night. An angel of the Lord appeared to them, and the glory of the Lord shone around them, and they were terrified. But the angel said to them, "Do not be afraid. I bring you good news of great joy that will be for all the people. Today in the town of David a Savior has been born to you; he is Christ the Lord. This will be a sign to you: You will find a baby wrapped in cloths and lying in a manger."

Suddenly a great company of the heavenly host appeared with the angel, praising God and saying,

"Glory to God in the highest,
and on earth peace to men on whom his favor rests."

When the angels had left them and gone into heaven, the shepherds said to one another, "Let's go to Bethlehem and see this thing that has happened, which the Lord has told us about."

So they hurried off and found Mary and Joseph, and the baby, who was lying in the manger.

LUKE 2:8–16

OCTOBER 4

It had been an ordinary night until the the heavens exploded in a celestial light show. As the startled shepherds attempted to cover their eyes from the burning radiance, an angel appeared and said, "Don't be afraid. I have come to bring you good news. The Messiah has been born in Bethlehem. You will know it is him when you find a babe wrapped in cloths, lying in a humble manger."

After hearing the good news, the shepherds knew they needed to visit the Holy Child. When they found him they came bursting into the stable and fell to their knees, worshiping the young babe with all their hearts. When the shepherds told Mary about the angel's message and the singing of the heavenly choir, Mary clutched the young babe. Yes, this was more than an ordinary child. He was the very Son of God.

Isn't it amazing that the first people to worship Christ on the earth were a band of simple shepherds? The shepherds saw the angelic host because they were in the fields. Spiritually speaking, fields can represent the place where God has called us to minister or serve. One of the keys to successfully walking with God is being faithful to the "field" to which he has called you.

God used the humble shepherds to encourage Mary and Joseph. Weary and alone, without friends or family, Mary and Joseph were probably in desperate need of encouragement. It is no different for you. Your experiences with the power and presence of God are never for you alone. Like the shepherds, God is encouraging you so you can become an encouragement to someone else. No matter how dark it may be in the field where you are serving, if you will simply keep watch, like the shepherds, you will be amazed at what God will do through you.

> As we watch and wait with hungry anticipation, we will find God's feast of provision and encouragement. It will always arrive at the perfect time.
>
> **Phil Joel**

Lessons from the Lives of Joseph and Mary:
SIMEON'S CONFIRMATION

Now there was a man in Jerusalem called Simeon, who was righteous and devout. He was waiting for the consolation of Israel, and the Holy Spirit was upon him. It had been revealed to him by the Holy Spirit that he would not die before he had seen the Lord's Christ. Moved by the Spirit, he went into the temple courts. When the parents brought in the child Jesus to do for him what the custom of the Law required, Simeon took him in his arms and praised God, saying:

"Sovereign Lord, as you have promised,
you now dismiss your servant in peace.
For my eyes have seen your salvation,
which you have prepared in the sight of all people,
a light for revelation to the Gentiles
and for glory to your people Israel."

The child's father and mother marveled at what was said about him. Then Simeon blessed them and said to Mary, his mother: "This child is destined to cause the falling and rising of many in Israel, and to be a sign that will be spoken against, so that the thoughts of many hearts will be revealed. And a sword will pierce your own soul too."

LUKE 2:25–35

OCTOBER 5

Like any other young couple, Mary and Joseph were excited. After all, it was the dedication of their firstborn son. Before the ceremony could even begin, however, a strange old man stepped out of the crowd and took the

child in his arms. It was Simeon, the prophet of the Lord. He turned to Mary and Joseph and began to bless them: "Mary, this child is uniquely destined. But his ministry will bring major changes in the nation you love. Many will speak against him. His pain will also be your pain, for you will feel as if a sword has pierced your very soul."

One important lesson we can take from Jesus' dedication in the temple is this: *It will cost you more than you can imagine to fully live out your divine purpose.* Joseph's purpose took him from his home to Bethlehem and then to life as a foreigner in Egypt until they were called to settle in Nazareth. Mary would watch as her firstborn son was rejected, brutally betrayed, and murdered on the cross. Yes, the pain she experienced would be as great as was the pleasure of his birth.

Your divine purpose will cost you. Whether it is an unexpected geographical move, a midlife career change, or the pain of being misunderstood by friends and family, who knows the price you will be asked to pay to follow God's will for your life? Only you can decide if you will pay the price to fully live out God's purpose. It is easy to become intoxicated with the vision of fulfilling your divine destiny. But in reality, your destiny has very little to do with your excitement and enthusiasm and everything to do with your discipline, dedication, and devotion. May the Lord begin today to open your eyes to the reality of his calling for your life.

As I've determined to see God's divine purposes carried out and fulfilled in my life. At times it has caused discomfort and misunderstanding — not just my own. But it has radically affected my friends and family as well. When we aim to please God, we might displease people. Yet, through it all, God remains faithful.

Phil Joel

Lessons from the Lives of Joseph and Mary:
WISE MEN

After Jesus was born in Bethlehem in Judea, during the time of King Herod, Magi from the east came to Jerusalem and asked, "Where is the one who has been born king of the Jews? We saw his star in the east and have come to worship him."

The star they had seen in the east went ahead of them until it stopped over the place where the child was. When they saw the star, they were overjoyed. On coming to the house, they saw the child with his mother Mary, and they bowed down and worshiped him. Then they opened their treasures and presented him with gifts of gold and of incense and of myrrh. And having been warned in a dream not to go back to Herod, they returned to their country by another route.

MATTHEW 2:1–2, 9–12

OCTOBER 6

They were stargazers—seekers of the truth—men who had spent their life in study and contemplation. When the unusual star had appeared months before, they knew a great king had been born. When they found him, though, it wasn't in a palace, but in a humble home. Although there was neither natural grandeur nor any appearance of wealth, the young mother who stood before them was the most regal-looking woman they had ever seen. She stood with a small toddler peeking from behind her robes as the wise men fell to their knees and began to worship the child. They could all feel the power and majesty that emanated from his small form. Other than Simeon, Anna, and the parents of Jesus, only the shepherds and the wise men recognized that a king

had been born when Jesus arrived. They recognized this divine moment because, unlike everyone else, they were watching the heavens. In Colossians 3:2, Paul wrote that you are to "set your minds on things above, not on earthly things." If you focus your attention on God's vision for your life and the advance of his kingdom, like the wise men, you, too, will experience the realities of his marvelous plan.

In addition, even though God's Son was born in obscurity, the Lord marked his birth with the appearance of an amazing star. When you are involved in ministry, you may feel that what you are doing is so insignificant that no one will ever take notice. If this is where you find yourself today, be encouraged. The same God who marked the birth of his Son with a burning star is able to divinely advertise what you are doing.

The Magi were able to give to the kingdom of God while it was still in its infancy. Though Jesus was only a toddler, they were discerning enough to realize that he was a divinely born King. No matter where you're going to church or what ministries you're involved in, God wants to give you discerning spiritual eyes like those of the ancient wise men—eyes that see beyond the natural into the essence of what God is doing on the earth today.

GOD is ALWAYS DOING new AND exciting things through those servants who truly desire to serve. It's never just "Business As usual." But it can Appear this way without Divine insight. The Kingdom of GOD AND its ADVANcement is ALWAYS exciting.

Phil Joel

LESSONS FROM THE LIVES OF JOSEPH AND MARY:
THE ESCAPE

An angel of the Lord appeared to Joseph in a dream. "Get up," he said, "take the child and his mother and escape to Egypt. Stay there until I tell you, for Herod is going to search for the child to kill him."

So he got up, took the child and his mother during the night and left for Egypt, where he stayed until the death of Herod. And so was fulfilled what the Lord had said through the prophet: "Out of Egypt I called my son."

After Herod died, an angel of the Lord appeared in a dream to Joseph in Egypt and said, "Get up, take the child and his mother and go to the land of Israel, for those who were trying to take the child's life are dead."

So he got up, took the child and his mother and went to the land of Israel.

MATTHEW 2:13–15, 19–21

OCTOBER 7

When the wise men left, Mary and Joseph fell to their knees in thanksgiving. They had never seen such rich gifts in all of their lives, and they had no idea what to do with the money.

That night as they were sleeping, an angel of the Lord appeared to Joseph in a dream. "Joseph, get up immediately. Take the child and his mother, and flee to Egypt. Herod will attempt to kill your son."

With no hesitation, Joseph immediately jumped out of bed. Once Mary had packed a few belongings, they fled into the night. The wise men's gifts would enable them to survive in the country to which God was sending them.

After a time in Egypt, Joseph had another dream. "Joseph, return to Israel, for those who were trying to kill God's Son are dead," the angel said.

This miraculous story of divine guidance and amazing escapes powerfully illustrates the realities that can be involved in following God. Mary and Joseph had no idea what it would cost to raise Jesus. Whether it was losing their carpentry business or moving to Egypt, all their well-laid plans and dreams about the future were altered forever.

You, too, can be sure that following God will dramatically affect the course of your life. This may entail living in places you never expected or even wanted to live. When I first got out of the army, I was bound and determined to return to the beautiful beaches of southern California. The Lord, however, had other plans. He kept me in the piney woods and humidity of North Carolina for twenty more years. When I finally got over my frustration and anger with God, I realized that he had known what he was doing all along. You may find yourself enrolled in a college you never wanted to attend or working at a job you would not have chosen. Whatever the case may be, never forget that God in his wisdom knows exactly where you need to be. Although following God can be filled with uncertainties, one thing is always sure: God has determined to bring you into the fullness of his plan and purpose for your life.

AS I READ this, I AM REMINDED of the lines of an old hymn: "TRUST AND OBEY, for there's no other way to Be happy in Jesus, than to TRUST AND OBEY."

Phil Joel

Lessons from the Lives of Joseph and Mary:
HAVE YOU LOST HIM?

Every year his parents went to Jerusalem for the Feast of the Passover. When he was twelve years old, they went up to the Feast, according to the custom. After the Feast was over, while his parents were returning home, the boy Jesus stayed behind in Jerusalem, but they were unaware of it. Thinking he was in their company, they traveled on for a day. Then they began looking for him among their relatives and friends. When they did not find him, they went back to Jerusalem to look for him. After three days they found him in the temple courts, sitting among the teachers, listening to them and asking them questions. Everyone who heard him was amazed at his understanding and his answers. When his parents saw him, they were astonished. His mother said to him, "Son, why have you treated us like this? Your father and I have been anxiously searching for you."

"Why were you searching for me?" he asked. "Didn't you know I had to be in my Father's house?" But they did not understand what he was saying to them.

LUKE 2:41–50

OCTOBER 8

Mary and Joseph hadn't even worried about Jesus during the first day of their trip home to Nazareth from the Passover. After all, he had never disobeyed them or even given them a moment of concern. Now, however, Mary was growing frantic. They had been journeying home from Jerusalem for a whole day, and they still hadn't found

him. "Joseph," she pled, "we've got to go back to Jerusalem." When they returned, they searched for him for two more days with no success.

Finally, they decided to search the temple. As they entered its courtyard, they realized that everyone was listening to a boy who was questioning the Sanhedrin. Even these esteemed teachers of the Law were stunned at the boy's questions. Although he was humble and deferential, he had a knowledge of the Word and a powerful authority that they had never seen before. Mary, however, was oblivious to anything but the fear she'd been experiencing. "Son! Why have you done this to us?" she cried.

"Mama," came his calm reply, "why were you looking for me? Didn't you know that I would be in my Father's house, doing his business?"

Have *you* lost sight of Jesus today? Could it be that, as in the lives of Mary and Joseph, Jesus has gotten down to business in your life, and you simply haven't recognized it yet? Some Christians seem to forget that God has more in mind for their lives than simply blessing them. They have forgotten that as much as he enjoys fellowshipping with them and meeting their personal needs, he also wants to use them to change the world. If you, like Mary and Joseph, have lost sight of his person and presence, you can easily find him again by embracing his purpose for your life.

ASSUMING THAT WE KNOW HOW AND WHERE JESUS IS WORKING CAN LEAD US INTO COMPLACENCY. IN THE PAST, THIS HAS CAUSED ME TO LOSE THAT UP-TO-THE-MINUTE LEADING OF THE HOLY SPIRIT. I DON'T WANT TO FEEL LIKE JESUS IS FOLLOWING ME AROUND BLESSING WHAT I'M DOING. I WANT TO BE FOLLOWING HIM AND BEING A PART OF WHAT HE IS BLESSING.

Phil Joel

Lessons from the Life of John the Baptist:

A VOICE IN THE WILDERNESS

In those days John the Baptist came, preaching in the Desert of Judea and saying, "Repent, for the kingdom of heaven is near." This is he who was spoken of through the prophet Isaiah:

> "A voice of one calling in the desert,
> 'Prepare the way for the Lord,
> make straight paths for him.'"

John's clothes were made of camel's hair, and he had a leather belt around his waist. His food was locusts and wild honey. People went out to him from Jerusalem and all Judea and the whole region of the Jordan. Confessing their sins, they were baptized by him in the Jordan River.

MATTHEW 3:1–6

OCTOBER 9

Even his parents realized he was a strange child. It wasn't just that he was a Nazarite; he simply loved to be alone. While other young men his age loved the revelry and life of Israel's towns and cities, John would spend hours in the solitude of the desert. By the time he was in his late teens, the prophetic calling on his life was growing clearer and clearer. Despite the fact that he had been raised to love the temple and the priesthood, he was growing increasingly angry over the hypocrisy and

spiritual contradictions that he saw in Israel's spiritual life. Finally, when he was thirty, it was as if the volcano of God's power in his soul erupted. His powerful message of repentance shattered the religious complacency of Israel. With thousands coming to be baptized, his ministry became the talk of the nation. "I am the voice of one calling in the desert," he thundered. "My job is to prepare the way for the coming of the Lord."

The story of John is important because, sooner or later, you, too, may be called to prepare people for the salvation they desperately need. In order to prepare Israel for the gospel that Jesus would preach, John was chosen to break up their hardened spiritual soil through both his austere lifestyle and his cutting message. John experienced amazing results, but this is not always the case. No matter how much you pray or how hard you preach, no one responds. You invite people to your Bible study or to church, and they don't show up. Everything in you wants to quit, but right now is no time to give up.

In 1 Corinthians 3:5–9, Paul wrote that every Christian has been assigned a divine task. In my own experience, I have found that some Christians are called to plow up the hard fields. Others may plant the seeds. A completely different group may reap the harvest. Only God knows which group you're currently a part of. If you're in a time of plowing right now, the seeds you are sowing in your school or workplace today may not grow into a harvest until later. It was no different for John the Baptist and Jesus. Although both of them preached to thousands, the fullness of their harvest never materialized until they were both no longer on the earth. No matter how hard your task may seem, God is at work to change the very place you are laboring, and if you are faithful to fulfill the task God has given you, sooner or later, the harvest will come.

I love this stuff! God is faithful. Always. As we remain faithful to him and to the tasks that he has set before us, our labors will not be in vain. Remain yoked to him and sooner or later the harvest will come.

Phil Joel

Lessons from the Life of John the Baptist:
JOHN'S IDENTITY

Now this was John's testimony when the Jews of Jerusalem sent priests and Levites to ask him who he was. He did not fail to confess, but confessed freely, "I am not the Christ."

They asked him, "Then who are you? Are you Elijah?"

He said, "I am not."

"Are you the Prophet?"

He answered, "No."

Finally they said, "Who are you? Give us an answer to take back to those who sent us. What do you say about yourself?"

John replied in the words of Isaiah the prophet, "I am the voice of one calling in the desert, 'Make straight the way for the Lord.'"

JOHN 1:19–23

OCTOBER 10

John's ministry had become the talk of the nation, and thousands were coming to hear his messages. Some people wondered if he was the prophet Elijah. Others speculated that he might be the Messiah. As for John, there was no doubt in his mind who he was.

Sooner or later, as you become successful in your chosen profession, people will begin to ask who you are. This may be one of the greatest tests a person can face, because there is nothing like success and the questions it brings to reveal a person's heart. John was asked three basic questions concerning his identity, which are still important for us today.

First, John was asked if he was the Messiah. When success comes,

it is easy for people to believe *they* are God's hope for their business, city, or church. But if this complex begins to take root in their soul, they will be destroyed by the pride and deception it brings.

Next, John was asked if he was Elijah. Elijah was the prophet who challenged four hundred prophets of Baal on his own. He was used to begin the salvation of Israel. Many Christians seem to have modeled their lives after the ministry of Elijah. In their own minds, they somehow see themselves as the lone prophet on the hill—the last one standing. If you allow this misconception to take hold, you will end up isolated from the people you desperately need in your life and vulnerable to the attacks of the enemy.

Third, John was asked if he was "the" prophet. Out of all three questions, this may be the one that most Christians will face. You may be tempted to think that you are "the" man or "the" woman—the one who has all the answers, anointing, and wisdom necessary for any situation. Tragically, if this type of pride permeates your soul, you will become an untouchable—a person that no one can correct or even speak to.

Questions like these, by their very nature, reveal what is in our hearts. John answered all of these questions by simply saying, "I am a voice crying in the wilderness." Despite all of his acclaim, he remained humble in his heart. In his own estimation, he was simply an empty vessel whom God had chosen to fill. I am asking God to give you that same attitude as you ponder this story today.

Identity—we are God's children, God's servants, God's soldiers. The nature of these roles requires constant submission. We must remain yielded to the Holy Spirit's authority, leading and counsel. We must also remain submitted to those whom the Lord has placed in our lives to speak truth to us and help us to remember who we are and who we are not.

Phil Joel

Lessons from the Life of John the Baptist:
JOHN'S TESTIMONY

Then Jesus came from Galilee to the Jordan to be baptized by John. But John tried to deter him, saying, "I need to be baptized by you, and do you come to me?"

Jesus replied, "Let it be so now; it is proper for us to do this to fulfill all righteousness." Then John consented.

As soon as Jesus was baptized, he went up out of the water. At that moment heaven was opened, and he saw the Spirit of God descending like a dove and lighting on him. And a voice from heaven said, "This is my Son, whom I love; with him I am well pleased."

MATTHEW 3:13–17

OCTOBER 11

For days John had felt it—the Messiah's coming was imminent. As he searched the crowd, he could feel the presence of the One he had been expecting. Then, the crowd parted, and a man stepped forward. It was Jesus of Nazareth, his own relative. He had grown up hearing from the lips of his mother the stories of this young man's miraculous birth. John had also been told by her that they shared a common destiny and a unique, divine purpose.

"Baptize me, John," Jesus said.

"I am not worthy to baptize you," John stuttered. For once, he even seemed to be speechless.

"I need you to baptize *me*," John said, looking at the ground.

"John," Jesus replied, "unless you baptize me, I will never be able to fulfill my divine mission." As John began to baptize him, Jesus came

up out of the water, the heavens were ripped open, and a beautiful dove fluttered down and gently lighted on Jesus' shoulder. The voice of God thundered, "This is my Son, whom I love; with him I am well pleased." This confirmed what John had expected; earlier, God had told him that the man on whom the Holy Spirit alighted and remained would be the long-awaited Messiah.

The baptism of Jesus was marked by three amazing signs: the heavens were torn open, the Holy Spirit descended on him, and the voice of God confirmed his true identity. When God finds a person who will truly serve him wholeheartedly, he delights in opening heaven on his or her behalf. I have seen the atmosphere of entire high school and university campuses change because God found a person who was willing to walk in such a way that heaven could be opened,.

God also wants to give you a new measure of the Holy Spirit. The amazing thing about Jesus is not the fact that the Holy Spirit descended on him but that he remained on him. Could it be that if you lived more like Christ, you would have a new measure of the Holy Spirit's power as well?

After Jesus had been baptized, God testified to the true identity of his beloved Son. Although he doesn't normally describe a person's virtues or reveal their secret identity in an audible voice, he does give them a unique measure of his confirming presence and convicting power. In fact, God doesn't have to say anything; everyone who comes into contact with them can feel God's supernatural approval and favor on their lives.

I know for myself, I must be aggressive when dealing with my sinful attitudes. I want the fullness of the Holy Spirit's power. There is no victory without hearts of purity.

Phil Joel

Lessons from the Life of John the Baptist:
JOHN'S SECURITY

The next day John was there again with two of his disciples. When he saw Jesus passing by, he said, "Look, the Lamb of God!"

When the two disciples heard him say this, they followed Jesus. Turning around, Jesus saw them following and asked, "What do you want?"

They said, "Rabbi" (which means Teacher), "where are you staying?"

"Come," he replied, "and you will see."

So they went and saw where he was staying, and spent that day with him. It was about the tenth hour.

JOHN 1:35-39

OCTOBER 12

Despite the national acclaim his ministry had drawn, John remained humble. In his mind, he had never been anything more than God's voice in a broken generation. When he baptized Jesus, his heart was filled with joy. Unlike other men, who might have been envious and insecure at the coming of Jesus, John was thankful that God had given him a part to play. Yet deep inside, he knew that as Jesus' ministry increased, his would naturally decrease. Now, as he stood with two of his closest disciples, he knew his time with them was almost over. As he placed his hands on their shoulders, he spoke out, "Look, the Lamb of God." As the disciples turned toward Jesus, John smiled at them and nodded his approval. Once they had his blessing, they turned away and began to follow the Messiah. In the days to come, these two young men would take their places among the closest disciples of Jesus.

Scripture clearly teaches that every Christian is called, like John, to make disciples (Matthew 28:19–20). John realized, however, that the ultimate purpose of discipleship is not to create a personal follower, but a follower of Christ. In the name of discipleship, many Christian leaders have created a following of people dependent on them. I am not saying that a time will come when these disciples no longer need godly people in their lives, but I am saying that God, not a human, should be the primary source of their counsel, encouragement, and guidance.

We also want to produce disciples who are able to hear from people other than their mentors. This is important because an individual who is only anchored to a church or ministry through one relationship can easily be dislodged. When a man or woman has learned to receive from more than one person in that church or ministry, he or she will have another Christian to turn to when the moment of testing comes.

No matter where you are in the discipling process today, I am asking God to make these truths real to your heart so that you will be able to advance the kingdom of God in your world.

The word "Rejoice" can be a frightening thing for some people. Maybe our trust has been betrayed or we have been let down by a moral failure of a mentor. We are all human and from time to time, we will let each other down. The purpose of discipleship is to secure a relationship with the one who will never let us down — Jesus. Don't let the past keep you from being mentored in Christ and in turn mentoring and discipling someone else.

Phil Joel

Lessons from the Life of Jesus:
LED INTO THE WILDERNESS

Then Jesus was led by the Spirit into the desert to be tempted by the devil. After fasting forty days and forty nights, he was hungry.

MATTHEW 4:1-2

OCTOBER 13

When Jesus came up out of the water, his whole being was energized by the power of the Holy Spirit. After a brief moment of fellowship with John, he could sense the deep drawing of the Holy Spirit. He was being led out into the depths of the wilderness. The deeper he went into the desert, the more he sensed his Father's presence. For forty days he prayed and fasted over the mission he had been given. At the end of his fast, already weakened from the desert's heat and lack of food, he sensed the approach of a malevolent, wicked presence. It was Satan, the archenemy of God and man. Although he had already been battling the enemy, this attack was different. In the hours to come, he would face an incessant onslaught of temptation from the enemy. His victory over Satan in the battle to come would create the spiritual breakthrough Jesus needed to proclaim the Gospel with power and clarity.

The first place the Holy Spirit led Jesus was into the wilderness to be tempted and tested by the devil. Mark even says that Jesus received this guidance the moment after he was baptized (Mark 1:12). Why would God lead his own precious Son into a violent confrontation with Satan in the depths of the wilderness at the very beginning of his ministry? This question is important because it is also critical for your life today.

First, Jesus was not simply being led into the wilderness. He was also being called into an intense forty-day period of fasting and prayer. During this time, Jesus received the instructions and strategy he would need to establish the kingdom of God on the earth. If the very Son of God needed to fast and pray at the beginning of his ministry, surely it will be no different for you and me.

Second, Jesus was led into spiritual warfare so that he could begin the process of breaking Satan's power over the human race by defeating him in open conflict. The same is true for you. No matter how much of God's anointing you may possess, you will never see the fruit you desire until you have broken the enemy's power through your prayers. In my own life, I have found that every season of victory and harvest is preceded by a season of intense spiritual warfare.

Third, the Scripture also says that Jesus was led into this time of prayer and battle immediately after his baptism. I have seen this same scenario played out in the lives of countless Christians. Whether they have just made a fresh commitment to Christ or received a new measure of his power, their receptiveness to God always brings the immediate retaliation of the enemy.

Sooner or later, the same God who led his Son into the wilderness for a time of testing and battle will lead you into a similar season. In fact, you may be in that very place today. If you are, take heart. No matter how weak you are or how intense the battle grows, the same God who led Jesus to victory in his conflict with the devil is also leading and guiding you.

In these times of testing and battles, fasting is an extremely valuable tool. We fast food to feast on the presence of God. When was the last time you fasted in order to draw nearer to God?

Phil Joel

Lessons from the Life of Jesus:
TEMPTATION

 The devil said to him, "If you are the Son of God, tell this stone to become bread."

Jesus answered, "It is written: 'Man does not live on bread alone.'" The devil led him up to a high place and showed him in an instant all the kingdoms of the world. And he said to him, "I will give you all their authority and splendor, for it has been given to me, and I can give it to anyone I want to. So if you worship me, it will all be yours."

Jesus answered, "It is written: 'Worship the Lord your God and serve him only.'"

The devil led him to Jerusalem and had him stand on the highest point of the temple. "If you are the Son of God," he said, "throw yourself down from here. For it is written:

"'He will command his angels concerning you
to guard you carefully;
they will lift you up in their hands,
so that you will not strike your foot against a stone.'"

Jesus answered, "It says: 'Do not put the Lord your God to the test.'"

LUKE 4:3–12

OCTOBER 14

After forty days of battling the enemy, Jesus hoped the conflict was over. But as he turned to leave the wilderness, he was struck with the full force of the enemy's temptation. He was tempted with bread, authority, and to test his own Father.

Like Jesus, you, too, will face three different types of

temptation as you follow God. John describes these temptations as the lust of the flesh, the lust of the eyes, and the pride of life (1 John 2:16, KJV). First, Jesus was tempted to turn a stone into bread when he was hungry. For us, the temptation may come in the area of food, sex, or substance abuse. This is probably the most basic of all temptations. Although it is the temptation most common to new Christians, I have also seen mature Christian leaders destroyed by their failure to overcome temptation in this area.

As we grow in God, our temptations become more sophisticated. Jesus was promised authority over all the kingdoms of the world if he would simply worship the devil. Sadly, I have watched many Christians succumb to the temptation—not to worship Satan, but to control their own lives. Once they become successful, they begin to refuse the very counsel and advice they craved when they were first born again. While they claim to be listening to God, in most cases, the only person they really listen to is themselves.

When his other temptations had failed, Satan challenged Jesus to jump off the temple. This was probably the most deadly temptation that Jesus faced. Even though Jesus was the Son of God, he knew that if he presumptuously jumped off the temple, his Father would not protect him. Unfortunately, many Christians are not this discerning. I am not saying that God cannot supernaturally protect us; I am saying, however, that we cannot always expect his protection and provision when we operate in presumption and pride.

No matter which of these temptations you are facing, it is critical that you follow the example of Jesus and use the Bible as you respond to them. As you respond to your temptations with Scripture, the power of God will be released both in you and through you.

We need to be able to quote Scripture and know its meaning in order to effectively combat the attacks of the enemy. I have found that memorization through meditation on a particular Scripture's meaning is best.

Phil Joel

Lessons from the Life of Jesus:
REPRIEVE

 When the devil had finished all this tempting, he left him until an opportune time.

LUKE 4:13

OCTOBER 15

When Satan finally left Jesus, he found himself teetering on the top of the temple. Despite the fact that he was fully God, he was also fully human. Consequently, he was at the point of absolute exhaustion. His battle with the enemy had been almost surreal. Much of it had taken place in the invisible world, and it left him partially dazed. Although his strength would recover, the lessons he learned would last him a lifetime. As for Satan, however, he did not give up. Far from being defeated, he was only waiting for another opportunity to strike Jesus with the full arsenal of his diabolical weaponry—the trials of the Savior were just beginning.

Sadly, it is the same for us today. No matter how many battles with temptation we have already faced, we will be constantly at war with our flesh and the devil until the day we die. Even during those times when we seem to be free from temptation, the enemy is simply looking for a better opportunity to attack us. Luke says that when the devil had finished tempting Jesus, he left him until an "opportune time" (or, a better opportunity).

In my own experience, I have found that there are three favorite times for the devil to attack the believer. When you are physically, spiritually, or emotionally weak, you can almost certainly expect the attack and temptation of the enemy. When you are in this weakened state, it is important that you do not try to face your time of temptation alone. Even as Jesus asked Peter, James, and John to stand with him when he faced the enemy's assaults in Gethsemane, so you must ask for help from other mature Christians.

Second, the enemy likes to attack Christians after they have experienced great victories. This is the case because many Christians grow complacent and sometimes even arrogant once they have experienced a tremendous success in their lives. In their euphoric state, they seem to forget that they are in a *lifetime* battle with the enemy. As their devotional disciplines begin to slip and their spiritual alertness is lost, the enemy assaults them with all of his might.

Third, no matter how mature you think you are, if you engage in a pattern of continual sin, your life will be opened up to the destructive blows of the enemy. Jesus understood this principle when he said, "The prince of this world is coming; he has no hold on me." Jesus had no fear of the enemy's attack because he realized there was no area of his life outside of the Father's control. You may be thinking to yourself by now, *Where does that leave me? There is definitely one area (or two) in which I am struggling.* If this is the case, like me, you can be thankful for the precious blood of Jesus. He promises to forgive us and cleanse us from the very sins we are struggling to overcome when we repent and confess them to him (1 John 1:9). No matter how many opportunities you have given the enemy up until now, the Lord is more than able to bring you into a whole new level of spiritual security.

Satan is tricky and his timing can be meticulous. At times, he has backed off and allowed me to fall prey to pride in my past victories. It's at these times that he's thrown darts at me and I've been hit in my complacent, smug state. We must remain vigilant, like soldiers on duty.

Phil Joel

Lessons from the Life of Jesus:

EMPOWERED

> Jesus returned to Galilee in the power of the Spirit, and news about him spread through the whole countryside.

LUKE 4:14

OCTOBER 16

Although Jesus was exhausted after his brutal battle with the enemy, he was still burning with his Father's purpose. When he returned to Galilee, everything seemed different. There was not just new power—there was also a new sense of authority. Even in Nazareth where he had grown up, they were amazed to see the dramatic changes in his life.

It should be no different in your life. Once you have received the Holy Spirit's fresh anointing and overcome the enemy's initial counterattacks, like Jesus, you, too, can experience a new measure of God's power. The full release of God's power will not come, however, without a cost. Even though Jesus had been endued with the Holy Spirit's power after his baptism, he did not attempt to fulfill his divine mission until his time in the wilderness was completed.

This is important, because we sometimes forget that Jesus was both fully God and fully human. As a human, Jesus gained a new sense of authority and confidence through successfully resisting the enemy's temptations. There was also something else that was being accomplished. Through his prayers, he was beginning the process of penetrating the very spiritual darkness that would blind the Jewish people to the truth that he was the Messiah.

As important as spiritual warfare was in the life of Jesus, it is even more important in your life today. As you successfully resist the power of temptation, it will give you the confidence you need to face the enemy in

the battles that lie ahead. There is also a measure of your experience that is directly transferable to the people to whom you are ministering. For example, most of the principles of spiritual warfare that I teach to other Christians are things that I have learned through my own struggle to resist Satan and his temptations.

Even more important is the fact that your victory over the devil will affect more lives than just your own. Like Jesus, the battles you are waging in your own wilderness are also affecting the spiritual receptivity of the people you have been called to reach. I have discovered that when the spiritual warfare becomes especially severe, it is a sure sign that I am not just fighting for myself alone. Even as I am struggling in prayer, God himself is breaking down walls of deception in countless lives through my prayers. No matter how severe your battle is today, never forget that the peril of the wilderness precedes the power of the Spirit.

My wilderness experiences have helped straighten out my priorities. This has allowed me to see and get rid of the junk that has inhibited me from experiencing the fullness of God's power.

Phil Joel

Lessoหs fROm the Life of Jesus:

THE MIRACULOUS CATCH

[Jesus] said to Simon, "Put out into deep water, and let down the nets for a catch."

Simon answered, "Master, we've worked hard all night and haven't caught anything. But because you say so, I will let down the nets."

When they had done so, they caught such a large number of fish that their nets began to break. So they signaled their partners in the other boat to come and help them, and they came and filled both boats so full that they began to sink.

When Simon Peter saw this, he fell at Jesus' knees and said, "Go away from me, Lord; I am a sinful man!" For he and all his companions were astonished at the catch of fish they had taken, and so were James and John, the sons of Zebedee, Simon's partners.

LUKE 5:4–10

OCTOBER 17

Jesus was speaking to Simon. "Take me out into the water so I can speak to the people." *Out in the water?* **Simon snorted to himself.** *This is a fishing boat, not a tour boat!* **Yet, he knew he had no choice but to comply.**

"Simon," Jesus said, "take the boat out into the deep waters. It's time to catch fish."

Catch fish? **Simon thought.** *What's this carpenter*—**then Simon remembered to whom he was talking. Despite his outward indifference, Simon's heart was touched by this man. "Master, I worked hard all night, and didn't catch anything. But because it's you commanding me, I will put the nets out again," he said.**

The moment the nets were in the water, they began to fill with fish. In fact, the nets were so full that they began to tear and break under the

strain of the catch. Frantically, Simon and Andrew began to signal for John and James to come and help them. Even with their help, the catch was so large that both boats began to sink under its weight. When Simon saw the immensity of the catch, he fell on his knees, sobbing, and said, "Lord, I'm such a fool that I didn't believe you!"

There are two main lessons that can be drawn from the story of Simon's miraculous catch. First, Jesus asked Simon to fish in the very place where he had caught nothing the night before. When Simon obeyed him, he pulled in the greatest catch of his life. Whether it is evangelism or business, when the Lord sends you back to a place where you've only known futility and even failure, you must be willing to go. If you are faithful to obey him, you may have the greatest catch of your life as well.

Second, even though Simon obeyed God, he didn't really believe there would be a catch. This type of unbelieving obedience may bring you the same heartbreak that it brought Simon. Simon lost part of his miraculous catch because his nets broke and his boats were sinking. If he would have had faith to prepare for the harvest that Jesus' command implied, he could have enjoyed the full harvest with which God had intended to bless him.

God wants to give you the harvest of your lifetime, as well! Faith plus obedience will begin to prepare you for the blessings God has intended for your life.

This challenges me to question myself in areas of preparation, education, ability, and availability. I want to be ready for whatever the Lord leads me into today. I also want to be preparing for the ways in which he may choose to use me tomorrow. This time next year, I hope to have a greater knowledge of the Word than I do today. I also hope for a greater level of personal purity and a greater prayer life.

Phil Joel

Lessons from the Life of Jesus:
WEDDING WINE

On the third day a wedding took place at Cana in Galilee. Jesus' mother was there, and Jesus and his disciples had also been invited to the wedding. When the wine was gone, Jesus' mother said to him, "They have no more wine."

"Dear woman, why do you involve me?" Jesus replied. "My time has not yet come."

His mother said to the servants, "Do whatever he tells you."

Nearby stood six stone water jars, the kind used by the Jews for ceremonial washing, each holding from twenty to thirty gallons.

Jesus said to the servants, "Fill the jars with water"; so they filled them to the brim.

Then he told them, "Now draw some out and take it to the master of the banquet."

They did so, and the master of the banquet tasted the water that had been turned into wine. He did not realize where it had come from, though the servants who had drawn the water knew. Then he called the bridegroom aside and said, "Everyone brings out the choice wine first and then the cheaper wine after the guests have had too much to drink; but you have saved the best till now."

JOHN 2:1–10

OCTOBER 18

He was enjoying being a simple guest. He had known both the bride and the groom, and was rejoicing in their happiness. But then his mother whispered, "Jesus, they have no more wine." This was more than just an embarrassment to the bride's parents. It would be a social nightmare that would reflect badly upon their reputations for years.

"Dear woman," he pled, "I don't want to be involved in this. It isn't time."

"Do whatever my son tells you," she said to the servants. At that moment, Jesus clearly felt his Father's presence and leading. His hour had come. Pointing at six stone jars, he commanded the servants to fill them with water. They complied and then took some jars to the head of the banquet. "This is the finest wine I've ever tasted," the banquet master bellowed. Through this miracle, Jesus revealed his glory and his disciples believed in him all the more.

Isn't it interesting that Jesus performed the first of his major miraculous signs at a wedding? I believe this reveals more than just his divinity—it also displays his love for the joy of marital love. In a world torn by the pain of divorce and the unfaithfulness of adultery, this story is good news. Maybe, like these newlyweds, the wine—the joy and life—in your marriage has run dry. If this is where you find yourself today, take heart. The same Jesus that turned this couple's water into wine is able to transform the very fabric of your own relationship.

It is important for you to remember, however, that Jesus and his disciples had been invited to the wedding. If you want the life and joy that Jesus can bring, you must invite him into the relationships you are in. His disciples had also received an invitation. The body of Christ has been given to you to help in the problems you are facing. You will never receive the fullness of the change you desire in the isolation of your home, but as you reach out for help, Jesus and his disciples are able to transform your marriage today.

I love the fact that Jesus loves marriage because so do I. I love being married. It's an ingenious design and works best when I'm following this design and nurturing my relationship with the LORD.

Phil Joel

Lessons from the Life of Jesus:
SAY THE WORD

When Jesus had entered Capernaum, a centurion came to him, asking for help. "Lord," he said, "my servant lies at home paralyzed and in terrible suffering."

Jesus said to him, "I will go and heal him."

The centurion replied, "Lord, I do not deserve to have you come under my roof. But just say the word, and my servant will be healed. For I myself am a man under authority, with soldiers under me. I tell this one, 'Go,' and he goes; and that one, 'Come,' and he comes. I say to my servant, 'Do this,' and he does it."

When Jesus heard this, he was astonished and said to those following him, "I tell you the truth, I have not found anyone in Israel with such great faith. I say to you that many will come from the east and the west, and will take their places at the feast with Abraham, Isaac and Jacob in the kingdom of heaven. But the subjects of the kingdom will be thrown outside, into the darkness, where there will be weeping and gnashing of teeth."

Then Jesus said to the centurion, "Go! It will be done just as you believed it would." And his servant was healed at that very hour.

MATTHEW 8:5–13

OCTOBER 19

Under Rome's harsh system of military justice, this centurion was used to being immediately obeyed. But this situation was beyond the realm of his experience. His beloved servant was suffering from a debilitating and painful paralysis. When he heard Jesus was visiting Capernaum, he asked the Jewish leaders to intercede on his

servant's behalf. "Jesus," they pleaded, "there is a Roman whose servant is in need of healing." This intrigued Jesus because he knew that he had been called to the Gentile world as well.

Before Jesus got to the house, he was met by the centurion. "Lord, please don't come to my house." the centurion pled, "I'm not worthy to be around you. Just speak the word and my servant will be healed." Jesus was stunned by the faith of this man and he cried out, "I've not seen anyone in Israel with this type of faith. Go, everything you've asked for will be done!" At that moment, the Spirit of God touched the centurion's servant, and he was healed.

God can intervene on your behalf—wherever you are! It doesn't matter if you are in the middle of a church service or serving on the mission field, the same God who healed the centurion's servant is able to care for your needs.

Fortunately, the centurion realized that the power of Jesus to heal was not based on his righteousness. In fact, even though he had built a synagogue, he still did not feel worthy for Jesus to enter his home. Many times before God does a miracle in our lives we hit what I call "the unworthiness barrier." Whether it is the condemnation of our own conscience or the accusation of the enemy, we feel unworthy to receive the miracle we are crying out for. But miracles are not earned! They are received through faith in the promises of a merciful God, who delights in meeting the needs of his precious children. Also, the centurion's servant was not healed through his own faith—he was healed through the faith of someone who loved him. Maybe this is the situation you find yourself in. The same God who healed the centurion's servant is able to act on your faith as well.

I'm asking myself, what things do I or those around me need healing for? What things have I given up on and no longer have faith to see healed? Am I still walking with a wound that God wants to heal because I've become used to my limp?

Phil Joel

Lessons from the Life of Jesus:
THE OTHER SIDE

[Jesus] saw Peter's mother-in-law lying in bed with a fever. He touched her hand and the fever left her, and she got up and began to wait on him.

When evening came, many who were demon-possessed were brought to him, and he drove out the spirits with a word and healed all the sick. This was to fulfill what was spoken through the prophet Isaiah:

"He took up our infirmities
and carried our diseases."

When Jesus saw the crowd around him, he gave orders to cross to the other side of the lake.

MATTHEW 8:14–18

OCTOBER 20

Peter's mother-in-law was in bed with a high fever. But no one expected what happened next. When Jesus walked into the room, without a second thought, he reached out and touched the sick woman's hand. Immediately, the fever left her and she got out of bed. She had been a believer in God all of her life, but she had never experienced his presence or felt his power in her body. As she began to serve Jesus in her home, the news of her healing spread throughout the town.

By evening, the whole town had gathered at the door of Peter's home. Scores of sick and demonized people were instantly healed. But despite the growing crowds around Peter's home, He told his disciples to get into a fishing boat and take him across the lake to the Gadarenes. When the disciples heard these instructions, they were astonished. The Gadarenes was one of the darkest areas of Israel. There were even communities of

Gentile pig farmers there—surely Jesus wouldn't bring his ministry to these wretched people!

Why would Jesus leave the incredible revival that had been initiated through the miraculous healing of Peter's mother-in-law? After all, the crowds were growing, and every sick person in the meeting had been totally healed. Wouldn't it have been more strategic for Jesus to stay and build a large church on the foundation of this amazing gathering?

Unlike many Christian leaders who live for the thrill of large crowds, Jesus was never impressed by the multitudes that flocked to him. He realized that without a dedicated core of trained disciples, there would be no one to lead and train his followers when he was gone.

Jesus knew that the darkened Gentile community on the other side of the lake was far needier than Peter's small town—they had no synagogue, no Bible, and they were unaware of the transformation The Messiah could bring. Therefore, as much as Jesus desired to minister to his own people, he was compelled by his Father to bring the Gospel to these others who were hurting and broken.

Right now, God may be calling you to go to the "other side." Jesus will bring you into the lives of needy, wounded people. No matter how different they are from you, or how much you abhor their lifestyle, they are part of the reason you were created. Be a shining light in the dark places of this world.

> There have been times when the Lord has led me into something great and I've been guilty of subconsciously saying to him, "Thanks. But I've got it from here." That's always the moment he leaves and the move of God turns into a move of man. "Lord, keep me yielded and sensitive to your leading."
>
> **Phil Joel**

LESSONS FROM THE LIFE OF JESUS:
THE SOLITARY PLACE

At daybreak Jesus went out to a solitary place. The people were looking for him and when they came to where he was, they tried to keep him from leaving them. But he said, "I must preach the good news of the kingdom of God to the other towns also, because that is why I was sent." And he kept on preaching in the synagogues of Judea.

LUKE 4:42–44

OCTOBER 21

While everyone else was sleeping, Jesus was praying. Despite the fact that Jesus was God, every fiber of his being had been drained by the release of miracle power in the evening meeting. The needs of the people had been almost overwhelming. The cries of the demon-possessed and the groans of the sick were still ringing in his ears. Yet, he knew that for him, prayer was more important than sleep. It was almost impossible for him to pray during the daylight hours. The disciples were filled with questions, and the crowds were always looking for him. So now, as he continued to pray, he sensed a growing burden for the Gadarenes. All of his life, he had heard about the horrible spiritual condition of this darkened Gentile community. After a number of hours had passed, his tranquility was broken by the voices of his disciples.

"Everyone is looking for you!" they shouted. "What are you doing here? Why aren't you resting?"

"Quiet," Jesus said. "It's time for us to go."

"Go? The meetings are just getting started!" they objected.

"There are other places that need us more," Jesus replied.

In the middle of rising acclaim and unbelievable pressure, Jesus had already learned a lesson most Christians never learn. No matter how busy he was, spending time with his Father remained the highest priority of his life. Jesus realized that without the refreshing of his Father's presence and the providence of his Father's words, he would quickly lose his effectiveness.

Have you learned this lesson yet—the lesson that time with God is the very foundation of success in your life? If you haven't, the lack of spiritual discipline is already affecting you more than you even realize. If this is where you find yourself today, remember it is never too late to start seeking the God who has been waiting for you to pursue him.

It is also crucial for you to realize that devotional consistency will not come without a fight. Luke tells us when the people found Jesus in prayer, they tried to keep him from leaving them (Luke 4:22). Like Jesus, you will find that the needs of the people you love the most will pull you away from your time with God—if you do not guard that time arduously. For you, the ringing of the telephone and the busyness of your schedule may become your greatest enemies. Or you may have to battle to detach your emotions from the stressful pace of life you are forced to endure. Remember, your time with God is priceless. No matter how early you have to get up in the morning, or how radically you have to adjust your schedule, every precious moment you spend with God translates into hours of strength and faith for your life.

Amen! Amen! Amen! For me, the start of my day — the first fruits — belong to God. It's vital for me to spend the first part of my day meeting with him and hearing from him. The busier I get the more important this time becomes.

Phil Joel

Lessons from the Life of Jesus:
THE UNEXPECTED STORM

Then he got into the boat and his disciples followed him. Without warning, a furious storm came up on the lake, so that the waves swept over the boat. But Jesus was sleeping. The disciples went and woke him, saying, "Lord, save us! We're going to drown!"

He replied, "You of little faith, why are you so afraid?" Then he got up and rebuked the winds and the waves, and it was completely calm.

The men were amazed and asked, "What kind of man is this? Even the winds and the waves obey him!"

MATTHEW 8:23–27

OCTOBER 22

Even though many of the disciples had fished these waters all of their lives, they were scared to death. The raging storm had come out of nowhere. The howling winds had driven the waves to such a height that the boat was already in danger of sinking. Peter and the other experienced sailors among them realized that without a miracle, they would die. To make matters worse, Jesus was sound asleep. *Didn't he care about them?* "Jesus!" they screamed. "Save us, Lord!" they implored him. "We're all going to drown!"

"Why are you afraid?" he asked. When he stood to his feet, they were even more amazed. Without a hint of fear in his eyes, or a trace of panic in his voice, he sternly rebuked the screaming winds and the crashing waves. Immediately, the winds ceased, and the churning sea gradually subsided. *What kind of man is this, that even storms obey him?* the disciples wondered.

The disciples experienced the worst storm of their lives on the very lake where many of them made their living. You may find that your place of

employment becomes a battlefield when you attempt to bring the Gospel to your co-workers. Or you may face unexpected storms in places where you've always known tranquility and peace. This is simply a normal part of the Christian life.

But despite the horrible storm they were facing, they were never in any real danger, because Jesus was on the boat. Once they had awakened him, he easily quelled the storm that was threatening them. There will be times when you feel you have to "awaken" Jesus. Although you realize he is present in your life, it may seem as though he has become blind to your peril and deaf to your cries. In moments like these, it is important that you do not give in to discouragement and despair. If you will simply cry out to him in persevering prayer, he will rise up to answer your need.

No matter where you have followed Jesus, no matter what type of situation you are in, he is well able to quell the storms buffeting your soul. Whether these storms are in your family, church, or business, he is nonetheless the absolute Lord over each one of them, and out of the storms, only he can bring lasting peace.

It is a fact that, even in the midst of God's perfect will, we may still find ourselves in terrible storms. This gives us the faith we need to face our storms with confidence.

Phil Joel

THE PURPOSE OF THE STORM

Leaving the crowd behind, they took him along, just as he was, in the boat. There were also other boats with him. A furious squall came up, and the waves broke over the boat, so that it was nearly swamped. Jesus was in the stern, sleeping on a cushion. The disciples woke him and said to him, "Teacher, don't you care if we drown?"

He got up, rebuked the wind and said to the waves, "Quiet! Be still!" Then the wind died down and it was completely calm.

He said to his disciples, "Why are you so afraid? Do you still have no faith?"

They were terrified and asked each other, "Who is this? Even the wind and the waves obey him!"

MARK 4:36–41

OCTOBER 23

"Lord!" they screamed. "Help us! Master! Wake up! Teacher! Don't you see our peril?" No matter how loudly they shouted, or how many of his titles they used, the howling winds drowned out their voices. The longer the storm lasted, the more their panic grew.

"Doesn't he even care about us?" they yelled to one another. "Why did we even follow him in the first place? We're all going to die!"

After Jesus had calmed the storm, however, and the disciples' panic had subsided, they were left to face the heart attitudes that the storm had exposed. The disciples had called on him by every powerful name they could think of: Teacher, Master, and Lord. Still, he did not respond to them immediately because he was after something far deeper—the fact that they didn't really believe his love for them. Like the disciples, your own heart attitudes will be tested. God will allow you to stay in the storm until your ungodly attitudes and false perceptions of him are fully exposed.

"Don't you care?" they cried. Has your own storm revealed a similar misconception of God in your heart? If it has, it's time for you to repent. God, in his love, allows you to face storms—it is the only way he can get you to face those attitudes raging beneath the surface.

The disciples also told Jesus they were drowning. This fatalistic statement captured the unbelief remaining in their hearts. Even though Jesus was in the boat with them, they still struggled to believe that he had the power to save them. It was beyond their comprehension that anyone could calm the storm in time to rescue them. This was why they were so amazed when the storm subsided after Jesus simply rebuked the wind and the waves.

Where do you find yourself today? Has your storm become so horrible that you have given up all hope of rescue? Fortunately, your unbelief is no deterrent to God's ability. The same God who calmed the storm that threatened his unbelieving, fearful disciples can calm your storm today. In fact, calming the storm of circumstances *around* you is easier for God than calming the storm of unbelief raging *inside* you. If you will be faithful to *deal* with what your storms *reveal*, even the winds of unbelief howling through the depths of your soul can be made to submit to Jesus' words.

Sometimes I look back at situations where I've panicked and become fearful and anxious. Then I've seen the Lord provide for my need in a miraculous way and, quite honestly, I've had to repent for my lack of faith. As I've repented, I've almost felt God laughing as if to say, "See, I told you!"

Phil Joel

THE DEMONIAC AT YOUR DOOR

When Jesus stepped ashore, he was met by a demon-possessed man from [Gerasenes]. For a long time this man had not worn clothes or lived in a house, but had lived in the tombs. When he saw Jesus, he cried out and fell at his feet, shouting at the top of his voice, "What do you want with me, Jesus, Son of the Most High God? I beg you, don't torture me!" For Jesus had commanded the evil spirit to come out of the man.

When the demons came out of the man, they went into the pigs, and the herd rushed down the steep bank into the lake and was drowned.

When those tending the pigs saw what had happened, they ran off and reported this in the town and countryside, and the people went out to see what had happened. When they came to Jesus, they found the man from whom the demons had gone out, sitting at Jesus' feet, dressed and in his right mind; and they were afraid.

LUKE 8:27–29, 33–35

OCTOBER 24

As they approached the shore of the Garasenes, Jesus could feel a dark, demonic presence. Unlike his disciples, Jesus had not been fooled by the true nature of the storm they had experienced. When he had sensed its supernatural origins, he had rebuked it as he would a demon.

The moment Jesus and his disciples stepped ashore, they were confronted by a powerful, insane demoniac. Totally unclothed, with remnants of chains still hanging from his hands and feet, he screamed wildly and thrashed about. When Jesus commanded the demons to come out of him, the man cried out, "What do you want with me, Jesus, Son of the Most High God? I beg you, don't torture me!"

"What is your name?" Jesus asked.

The demons snarled in reply, "They call us Legion, for there are many of us. Don't send us back to the abyss. Let us make our new home in that herd of pigs."

"Go," Jesus answered them.

As soon as the demons had entered the pigs, they stampeded into the lake and drowned. The demoniac, however, had been transformed. The people of the town were all frightened, for the change which had taken place was remarkable. Typically, when the enemy cannot drive you away through a demonic "storm" of circumstances, he will confront you through a person who seems beyond all help. But Jesus recognized that he was not confronting a mere human being. Instead of attempting to reason with the man, he confronted the demonic forces that were tormenting him. Many Christians make the mistake of trying to reason with a person who is deeply bound by the enemy. You must engage the enemy through prayer *before* you attempt to set the captive free.

Despite the man's horrible bondage, he was dramatically set free after only one encounter with Jesus. Remember, no situation is too difficult for God. No matter how long someone has been under attack, our Mighty God has the power to transform his or her life.

Sometimes circumstances seem insurmountable and it is then that I'm forced to remember that it's not about me and my ability. Instead, it's about God's ability and my availability to pray and be led by the Holy Spirit.

Phil Joel

Lessons from the Life of Jesus:
THE AMAZING REACTION

Those who had seen it told the people how the demon-possessed man had been cured. Then all the people of the region of the Gerasenes asked Jesus to leave them, because they were overcome with fear. So he got into the boat and left.

LUKE 8:36-37

OCTOBER 25

The disciples were astonished. *How could these people ask Jesus to leave?* **they wondered in frustration. After all, the man who had haunted their dreams for years had been totally transformed through their Master's words. Yet no matter what they had tried to say, the people clearly wanted them gone. As the disciples got in the boat to leave, they doubted they would ever set foot on these shores again. Their loving God, however, had not given up on the broken people of this darkened region.**

How could these people want Jesus to leave after he had demonstrated the powers necessary to completely change the human soul? The Bible says they were frightened, but what could be so frightening about a man set free? First of all, I believe they were alarmed by the mass suicide of their pigs. They knew that Jews considered pigs to be unholy, defiled creatures that no righteous person would eat. They probably wondered, *If Jesus is destroying our pigs now, what will be next?* **This is typically how unsaved people think. Instead of being excited when their unbelieving friends are dramatically set free from immorality or substance abuse, they're threatened by the changes they see—because they themselves have no desire to change.**

They were also alarmed by the amazing authority Jesus possessed. If Jesus could bring the most feared demoniac in the region under his full control, what would he do to a normal human? *After all*, they may have surmised, *who wants a God who can control us, when we could have a nice, tame idol under our own complete control?* It is no different in the cultures of our world today. Everyone wants a cosmic buddy or a divine helper. Almost no one, however, is looking for a sovereign Lord. If you've been saved for any length of time at all, you've probably already experienced the strange reactions I am describing. In fact, if you're more recently saved, you may be in the same situation that Jesus and his disciples encountered—the changes in your life are threatening the very people you're trying to reach. They may even be trying to get you demoted or kicked off the team. No matter what you may be facing, you have no cause for despair. The same God who had a plan for the Gerasenes has a plan to move through you.

Like the disciples, I have found myself being led by the Lord into situations that begin great and then turn sour. Sometimes these adverse reactions need to be lovingly confronted. Other times, like in this story, we are called to leave or back off. "Lord, give me discernment and wisdom to hear you and obey you even when circumstances get strange or the reactions of people surprise me."

Phil Joel

Lessons from the Life of Jesus:
THE UNFULFILLED REQUEST

The man from whom the demons had gone out begged to go with him, but Jesus sent him away, saying, "Return home and tell how much God has done for you." So the man went away and told all over town how much Jesus had done for him.

LUKE 8:38–39

When they had crossed over, they landed at Gennesaret. And when the men of that place recognized Jesus, they sent word to all the surrounding country. People brought all their sick to him and begged him to let the sick just touch the edge of his cloak, and all who touched him were healed.

MATTHEW 14:34–36

OCTOBER 26

The pain was gone! Where once he had been filled with darkness and torment, now his whole being was pulsing with joy and vitality. The demoniac was finally in his right mind again—if he had ever really been in his right mind at all before that day. After years of hearing voices, now even they were gone. The whole world seemed different because Jesus had set him free. As far as he was concerned, he would follow this man to the ends of the earth. There was no one he even wanted to be with besides the man who had delivered him. Yet Jesus had other plans for him. "You can't go with me," Jesus told him.

"Can't go with you?" the man desperately replied. "What if the demons try to come back? What will I do? Everyone here is afraid of me, and they even hate you. Don't you see? You'll be leaving me alone with no friends," the man pleaded.

"Return to your home," Jesus commanded him, "and tell everyone there what I have done for you."

Jesus' treatment of this man opposes everything we are teaching in the Church today. Surely he would need hundreds of counseling hours, and, on a weekly basis, at least two or three different therapy groups. After all, the Bible says that a person needs to be discipled. Although this man was obviously an exception to the usual way Jesus trained and discipled people, his story illustrates one dramatic truth: There is almost nothing on this planet more powerful than a real testimony. Once the people of the Gerasenes had overcome their initial feelings, Jesus knew that many of them would be radically influenced by this man's compelling story. The consistent fruit they would see in this man's life would eventually cause them to ask the right questions and lead them to a relationship with God.

Jesus was right. In Matthew 14:34–36, we find that Jesus received a completely different reception when he visited the Gerasenes for the second time. When they recognized him, people came from everywhere, begging to be healed. The manifestation of God's presence was so powerful that people were healed by simply touching Jesus' cloak. This demonstrates, like no other story in Scripture, the power of one person's testimony. If you, like this story's demoniac, will be faithful to proclaim what Jesus has done for you, who knows what he will also do through you?

Sometimes I forget or undervalue the power of my own testimony of what God has done and is still doing in my life. "LORD, I pray for more opportunities to share the story of you and me with others."

Phil Joel

Lessons from the Life of Jesus:
NIGHT VISITOR

Now there was a man of the Pharisees named Nicodemus, a member of the Jewish ruling council. He came to Jesus at night and said, "Rabbi, we know you are a teacher who has come from God. For no one could perform the miraculous signs you are doing if God were not with him."

In reply Jesus declared, "I tell you the truth, no one can see the kingdom of God unless he is born again."

JOHN 3:1–3

OCTOBER 27

It was the talk of Jerusalem. The young prophet from Galilee had physically driven the money lenders out of the temple's courts. He had even boasted that he could rebuild the whole temple in three days if it were ever destroyed again. Jerusalem's religious leaders, in particular, were in an uproar. "How dare this young zealot impose his authority on our traditions?" they complained. "The next time he visits Jerusalem, we'll be ready."

One member of the Sanhedrin, however, had a very different reaction. Although he had initially been angered by the young man's zeal, Nicodemus could not deny the miracle power Jesus possessed. He also realized that only someone sent from God could demonstrate this type of power and authority.

Therefore, Nicodemus decided to visit Jesus and question him. That night, he crept out of his home and went to where Jesus was staying. When the disciples saw him standing at their door, they were stunned. What could this old man want with their Master? Surely he was there to harm him or deceive him. But Jesus instructed them to let him in.

"Rabbi," Nicodemus said, "many of us know you are a teacher sent from God. Otherwise, you would not have the miraculous powers we see in your life."

"You'll never understand unless you are born again, Nicodemus," Jesus replied.

"Born again? How can an old man like me enter his mother's womb for a second time?" Nicodemus asked. He did not realize Jesus was talking about a different kind of birth.

I am convinced that you, like Jesus, will have night visitors who have seen clear evidence of God's work in your life. Even if you've never done a miracle, your testimony will be so compelling that they begin to question the meaning of their own lives. When they do come, however, it is important that you handle them with both gentleness and integrity. It is important for you to remember these visitors must be "born again" before they can even begin to understand many of the truths of Jesus. Many Christians today seem to think good logic and solid reasoning can replace the power of repentance. They go into elaborate discourses on the existence of God and his love for a fallen humanity, while they gingerly avoid the demand of God that people repent. Although wisdom and timing are essential, people must repent and believe if they are ever to see God and his amazing kingdom.

Are you ready? Have you prepared yourself to help the people whom God is sending into your life? Whether any of them have come to you yet or not doesn't matter. Even if you cannot see them, they are on the way!

"LORD, I ASK you to pREpARE me AND equip me to BE of use AS you seND LOST people my wAy."

Phil Joel

Lessons from the Life of Jesus:
A PATCH JOB

Then John's disciples came and asked him, "How is it that we and the Pharisees fast, but your disciples do not fast?"

Jesus answered, "How can the guests of the bridegroom mourn while he is with them? The time will come when the bridegroom will be taken from them; then they will fast.

"No one sews a patch of unshrunk cloth on an old garment, for the patch will pull away from the garment, making the tear worse. Neither do men pour new wine into old wineskins. If they do, the skins will burst, the wine will run out and the wineskins will be ruined. No, they pour new wine into new wineskins, and both are preserved."

MATTHEW 9:14–17

OCTOBER 28

Jesus had expected the Pharisees to resist him. Unless they were willing to give up their self-righteousness and hardened religiosity, there was no other way they could respond to his message. However, when John's disciples, along with the Pharisees, challenged the fact that Jesus' disciples weren't fasting yet, Jesus had been astonished. How could the disciples of John, the very man who had been sent by the Father to prepare the way for Jesus' coming, question the validity of his ministry? Then Jesus realized that, like the Pharisees, John's disciples also had traditions that were threatened by the Gospel.

As much as their challenges saddened him, Jesus knew he had to give John's disciples an answer. "You can't take a piece of unshrunk cloth and use it to patch a tear in an old garment. If you do, the patch will come loose from the garment you have attempted to repair, and the tear will only end up worse." When Jesus gave the disciples of John this strange analogy, he was telling them that a "patch job" would not work. In other words, he was warning them not to selectively accept only the parts of his message that they liked. Unless they embraced everything he was saying, their lives would never change, and in some cases, they might even become worse.

It is no different in our world today. Many people are coming to Jesus for a "patch job." While they desire his help for their marriage, children, or finances, they reject the fullness of his message and resist his authority in their lives. Tragically, this approach to Christianity is doomed to failure. For example, if a couple tries to build their marriage on Christian principles without the power of Christ coming through conversion, those efforts will be doomed to failure. Without the power to forgive and the unconditional love for each other that only Christ can supply, all the wonderful principles in the world will never give couples the marriage they desire.

Jesus is not interested in giving you a "patch job." He wants to do far more, through the application of his principles, than just to mend the "tears" in your life; he wants to make you a brand new person. This reality, however, can only be actualized through the acceptance of his entire message. If you avoid the realities of repentance and faith, your patched-up life will tear apart under the stresses and pressures that all of us face.

"LORD Jesus, ARE thERE Any REALities of fAith AND REpentAnce thAt I hAve Kept At ARM's LENGth? IF so, pLEASE REVEAL them to me (GENtLY)!"

Phil Joel

Lessons from the Life of John the Baptist:
I MUST BECOME LESS

They came to John and said to him, "Rabbi, that man who was with you on the other side of the Jordan — the one you testified about — well, he is baptizing, and everyone is going to him."

To this John replied, "A man can receive only what is given him from heaven. You yourselves can testify that I said, 'I am not the Christ but am sent ahead of him.' The bride belongs to the bridegroom. The friend who attends the bridegroom waits and listens for him, and is full of joy when he hears the bridegroom's voice. That joy is mine, and it is now complete. He must become greater; I must become less."

JOHN 3:26–30

OCTOBER 29

John the Baptist was coming to the end of his earthly ministry. Slowly but surely, the crowds were thinning out. Deep inside, he knew that once the crowds were gone, Herod or the Jews would try to kill him.

His disciples approached. "Rabbi, do you remember that man named Jesus you baptized? Everyone is leaving your ministry and going to him. It isn't right; he's even baptizing more people than you are!"

As he looked into the eyes of his earnest disciples, John took a deep breath before answering. "I've told you before, I am not the Messiah. Never forget, he is the Bridegroom, and the bride belongs to him. Don't you see? My joy, as his friend, is to help him find his bride."

"But Rabbi, what will happen to you?" his disciples objected.

"He must become greater. I must become less." With these words, John demonstrated the humility that was at the foundation of his phenomenal success. Sooner or later, no matter what profession you are in, someone else will begin to eclipse you. You may be a pastor whose church is being outgrown by a newer church in town, or a business person who has lost your prominence to a younger competitor. Whatever your vocation, God wants to give you the heart of John today.

John told them the bride belongs to the Bridegroom. This meant that the goal of John's life was not for people to find out about him but to find out who Jesus was. His greatest joy in the world was not in his personal success, but in the ultimate success of God's kingdom.

Although all of us realize we are to do whatever it takes to "make Jesus greater," there are times when this principle applies to other people as well. Sooner or later you will have to *decrease* for others to *increase*. If you don't follow this principle, the ministry or business you claim to love may languish after you are gone.

Do you understand it yet? Life is not about you and your ministry (or career). In the end, it's about advancing the kingdom of God and pointing people toward Christ. Accepting this brings far greater joy than you could ever experience if you simply live for yourself.

The music business is so competitive—even the Christian music business. But we must not compare ourselves and our success against the success of others. The questions John's disciples were asking him were essentially: "Who are you in light of Jesus?" And "Now that Jesus has come, what are you going to do?" No matter what business you are in, these are pretty good questions for all of us, don't you think?

Phil Joel

Lessons from the Life of Jesus:
THE WOMAN AT THE WELL

Jesus answered, "Everyone who drinks this water will be thirsty again, but whoever drinks the water I give him will never thirst. Indeed, the water I give him will become in him a spring of water welling up to eternal life."

The woman said to him, "Sir, give me this water so that I won't get thirsty and have to keep coming here to draw water."

He told her, "Go, call your husband and come back."

"I have no husband," she replied.

Jesus said to her, "You are right when you say you have no husband. The fact is, you have had five husbands, and the man you now have is not your husband. What you have just said is quite true."

"Sir," the woman said, "I can see that you are a prophet."

The woman said, "I know that Messiah" (called Christ) "is coming. When he comes, he will explain everything to us."

Then Jesus declared, "I who speak to you am he."

JOHN 4:13–19, 25–26

OCTOBER 30

Jesus' disciples left him by a well to rest during their long trip through Samaria. He saw a woman approaching the well and knew that she was trying to avoid the other women in the town. As she looked around furtively before approaching the well, Jesus could feel the deep torment and rejection of her soul.

"Woman," he said, "will you give Me a drink?"

"You're a Jew," she said, "and I am a Samaritan woman. Why would you ask me for a drink, since your kind hates us?"

"If you knew the gift of God, and who I was, you would ask me for a drink," Jesus replied.

Everything in her wanted to respond to him. He was unlike any man she had ever met before. There was no lust or cruelty in his eyes. In fact, she desperately wanted to weep and open her heart to him.

"If you only drink from this well, you'll thirst again. If you drink from my waters, you'll never thirst again, because they will create a spring of living water in your heart."

"Sir, I beg you. Give me this water."

Are you thirsty today? Whether you're an unbeliever or a thirsty Christian, God is able to quench the deep thirst of your soul. Like the woman at the well, you will first have to traverse the barriers, in your own soul, that stand between you and Christ. For her, this meant confronting her prejudice toward Jews, her distrust of men, and her religious traditions. Your barriers may be far different, but whatever they are, they must be confronted. You must also be willing to deal with the sin that is choking your soul and see them in the light of God's Word so that you can repent from them and be free at last.

EVERY DAY we need to DRINK pHYSICALLY. AND SpiRI- tuALLY iT's no DiffeReNT. I wAKE up thirsTy AND must go to the weLL. ONLy time ALone with GOD in his WORD AND tHROUgH pRAYeR wiLL quench the thirst I'm feeLING.

Phil Joel

Lessons from the Life of Jesus:
NEW FOOD

Just then his disciples returned and were surprised to find him talking with a woman. But no one asked, "What do you want?" or "Why are you talking with her?"

Meanwhile his disciples urged him, "Rabbi, eat something."

But he said to them, "I have food to eat that you know nothing about."

Then his disciples said to each other, "Could someone have brought him food?"

"My food," said Jesus, "is to do the will of him who sent me and to finish his work."

JOHN 4:27, 31-34

OCTOBER 31

When the disciples of Jesus returned with his lunch, they never even bothered to ask him why he had been talking to the Samaritan woman. "Eat, Rabbi," they urged him. "Aren't you hungry? You should be starving by now."

"I have food to eat that you know nothing about," Jesus replied.

"Know nothing about?" they said to each other. "Maybe someone else brought him lunch."

Jesus simply looked at them and sighed, "My food is to do the will of him who sent me, and to finish his work."

This may be one of the most profound statements in all of Scripture. The disciples could not figure out why Jesus wasn't hungry. They didn't realize he had already eaten! The food that had satisfied him, however, wasn't natural—it was spiritual. Ministering to the Samaritan woman had satisfied the deepest hunger of his soul.

Sadly, most Christians never learn this. They seem to think that satisfying their spiritual hunger is all about hearing God's Word. Whether it is a great sermon, a deep teaching, or a wonderful tape series, they truly think these are the things that will satisfy the hunger of their hearts. When the ministry of one church doesn't satisfy them, they simply look for another church. If that doesn't satisfy them, they watch some other dynamic preacher on Christian television or buy a few more books to read. Although it is wonderful to listen to God's Word, these Christians fail to realize that hearing alone will never satisfy them. Jesus told the disciples that his secret food was not *hearing* about God's will, but *doing* God's will. This concept is vital for your life, because all the teaching in the world will not satisfy this intrinsic need.

Even worse is the fact that hearing God's Word without applying it will cause you to lose your spiritual appetite. Just as physical activity increases your natural hunger, so spiritual activity will increase your spiritual hunger. If this is where you find yourself today, maybe you should try changing your lifestyle before you try changing churches. Could it be that making your first disciple will satisfy you far more than all the teachings you've heard about discipleship or all the books you've read on the subject? I believe it will—in fact, you will discover one of the secret joys most Christians never experience: the satisfaction of doing God's will and finishing his work.

THIS IS GOOD STUFF! I'M SO CHALLENGED BY THIS!
Phil Joel

Lessons From the Life of Jesus:
THE HARVEST

"Do you not say, 'Four months more and then the harvest'? I tell you, open your eyes and look at the fields! They are ripe for harvest. Even now the reaper draws his wages, even now he harvests the crop for eternal life, so that the sower and the reaper may be glad together. Thus the saying 'One sows and another reaps' is true. I sent you to reap what you have not worked for. Others have done the hard work, and you have reaped the benefits of their labor."

JOHN 4:35–38

Jesus was amazed—the harvest was all around them. Yet, because of their self-absorption and their ethnocentricity, the disciples were totally blind to this fact. Finally, when he couldn't bear their oblivion any longer, he spoke to them.

NOVEMBER 1

"Stop saying in your hearts, 'The harvest hasn't come.' Open your eyes and look around! Even now, I am reaping a harvest. Thus far, you've experienced a harvest for which you haven't toiled. Others have done all the hard work, while you simply enjoyed the benefits." The words of Jesus to his disciples are as needed now as they were then. Most of us are also blind to the burgeoning harvest all around us.

Blind? **you may be thinking.** *How am I blind? I am in the middle of dry, hardened soil. All I can do is plow!* **If this is how you really think, you need to deeply reflect on the words of Christ.**

First, Jesus told his disciples to stop thinking that the harvest would take place only in the future. To the majority of Christians I know, the harvest is something that is always coming—but never actually arrives. "The

harvest is coming! Get ready!" they cry. Sadly, as long as the harvest is put off to the future, we will continue to miss the harvest all around us today.

Second, Jesus told the disciples to open their eyes. He realized that they were so absorbed in their personal needs that they had totally missed the spiritual hunger in the woman at the well. He also knew that the only harvest in which they were interested was a Jewish harvest. That is why he told them to look at the fields. Even though the Jewish field might not have been ready for harvest, other ethnic fields were ripe. It is no different for you and me today. Many times, when the people who are like us are not open to the Gospel, we don't bother to look for other opportunities. Just because our suburban neighbors are not receptive to the Gospel doesn't mean the inner city isn't wide open for evangelism.

Third, when Jesus said, "Even now, the reaper draws his wages; even now, he harvests," he was speaking of himself. While his disciples had been totally absorbed in their lunches, Jesus had been busy opening up a whole new region for the kingdom of God.

The disciples were reaping where they had not sown. They had merely been subsisting off the hard work of others. Everyone wants to reap, but few want to do the hard work of plowing and sowing. Until God finds a generation of Christians who are willing to do "the hard work," the Church will not experience the continual cycle of harvest that God desires.

It is time for you to stop living for your own needs. You must rise above your own ethnic or national identity and see that you are also a citizen of a larger kingdom—the kingdom of God. Once you understand this, you will begin to see a harvest you have never seen before.

This is why RACISM is so WICKED At its CORE. To SAY that one RACE is ABove the otheR. is totALLY uNBiBLicAL. GOD is no RespecteR of peRsons. He mADe us ALL AND Loves us ALL equALLY. If it's GOOD enough FOR him, it's GOOD enough FOR me.

Duncan Phillips

Lessons from the Life of Jesus:

THE WOMAN AT THE WELL

Many of the Samaritans from that town believed in him because of the woman's testimony, "He told me everything I ever did." So when the Samaritans came to him, they urged him to stay with them, and he stayed two days. And because of his words many more became believers.

They said to the woman, "We no longer believe just because of what you said; now we have heard for ourselves, and we know that this man really is the Savior of the world."

JOHN 4:39–42

NOVEMBER 2

Before Jesus could even finish correcting his disciples, the crowds began to gather. The woman Jesus had met at the well had now become a well of life herself, and her testimony created a deep thirst throughout the people in Sychar. The disciples were incredulous as the Samaritans begged Jesus to stay in their city and preach to them. All their lives, the disciples had been taught that Samaritans were dark, bestial creatures who would never be able to fully understand the truth. Jesus, however, knew better. He stayed in Sychar for two days, teaching the people and answering their questions. When he finally left, the small town had been transformed. She who had been treated like an outcast was now toasted as a heroine. "We no longer believe in him because of what you said," the people told her. "Now that we have heard him for ourselves, we believe this man is the Savior of the world."

God wants to do more than give you a drink from his well of life. He wants to make you into a well of living water, so that others will also be able to drink from your life. Sadly, most of the Church has emphasized getting a *drink* far more than becoming a *well*. This is part of the reason that many Christians have no real interest in the kingdom of God beyond the satisfaction of their own needs. Even worse is the fact that many of these same Christians quietly drop out of the church once their depression is gone or their marriage is better. After all, why should they continue to go to church when their whole purpose for going there in the first place has already been fulfilled?

If this is your attitude, God wants to deal with your heart today—because the people around you are desperate for a well. You must not continue to think that some anointed evangelist or incredible pastor is going to be used by God to touch all of your friends. In most cases, your friends will want to take their first spiritual drink from a trusted source, and whether you like it or not, the water they desire the most is probably the life they see flowing out of you.

This reminds me of James 4:14. We are all eternal beings. This life on earth is but a fleeting "puff of smoke" compared to eternity. "Lord, may we all diligently seek your face and your kingdom while we still have breath." Matthew 6:33.

Duncan Phillips

Lessons from the Life of Jesus:
THE POOL OF BETHESDA

📖 There is in Jerusalem ... a pool... called Bethesda.... Here a great number of disabled people used to lie — the blind, the lame, the paralyzed. One who was there had been an invalid for thirty-eight years. When Jesus saw him lying there and learned that he had been in this condition for a long time, he asked him, "Do you want to get well?"

"Sir," the invalid replied, "I have no one to help me into the pool when the water is stirred. While I am trying to get in, someone else goes down ahead of me."

Then Jesus said to him, "Get up! Pick up your mat and walk."

JOHN 5:2-8

NOVEMBER 3

Bethesda was the most amazing pool in the whole world. Periodically, an angel from heaven would miraculously stir the pool's waters. When this happened, the first person to get into the pool would be instantly healed. People came from near and far for the chance to be healed.

One of the men around the pool had been waiting for thirty-eight years. By now, he had no money left to hire people to help him into the pool, and his friends had all given up. Yet he still lay there, in hopes that his day of healing would come. Sadly, he had become so fixated on the pool's promise that he did not realize that One far greater than an angel was walking through the crowd. He was Jesus Christ, the Messiah.

Jesus was deeply moved when he arrived on the scene. Everywhere he turned, he could feel the despair gripping the people around the pool.

When he saw the man who had been waiting for thirty-eight years, he could sense the stirring of his Father's presence, and he asked the man, "Do you want to be healed?"

"I want to be healed," he replied, "but I have no one to help me into the pool. I've been trying to get in for years, but every time, someone else goes in just ahead of me."

Looking deeply into his eyes, Jesus said, "Get up. Pick up your mat and walk." At these words, the man's whole body was divinely energized. Without even thinking about it, he picked up his mat and walked.

Much of the Church today has what I call the "Bethesda complex." They seem to believe they can only be healed in some dramatic church service or extraordinary Christian meeting. Like the man at Bethesda, they have become so focused on the place or way in which they expect to be healed that they have lost sight of the Person who can heal them at any place he chooses.

Jesus Christ is asking you the same question that he asked the paralyzed man: "Do you want to be healed?" If you do, stand up and follow him. He promises to give you the strength to obey him. As you stand in response to his command. he will begin to heal you through and through.

It's been my experience that the Father will never ask us to do anything unless he gives us the strength to do it. That is the heart of a Father. Read Isaiah 40:28-31.

Duncan Phillips

WHERE ARE THE LEADERS?

Jesus went through all the towns and villages, teaching in their synagogues, preaching the good news of the kingdom and healing every disease and sickness. When he saw the crowds, he had compassion on them, because they were harassed and help-less, like sheep without a shepherd. Then he said to his disciples, "The harvest is plentiful but the workers are few. Ask the Lord of the harvest, therefore, to send out workers into his harvest field."

MATTHEW 9:35-38

One of those days Jesus went out to a mountainside to pray, and spent the night praying to God. When morning came, he called his disciples to him and chose twelve of them, whom he also designated apostles.

LUKE 6:12-13

NOVEMBER 4

No matter how tired he was, Jesus never ceased to be compassionate. Where others would have seen the crowds as just a collection of dirty, sweating, selfish people clamoring for their needs to be met, he saw help-less sheep who desperately needed someone to shepherd their troubled souls. As the crowds continued to grow, his burden became even heavier. Finally, after a long night in prayer, his Father spoke to him.

"Select twelve from among your disciples, and give them the author-ity to do what you have been doing." As Jesus stood up from his time of

prayer, a burden was lifted from his shoulders. It was time to send these young leaders out to reap the harvest.

Many leaders around the world are praying the same prayer that Jesus prayed. They, too, are burdened by a huge workload and weighed down by the endless needs of the people in their congregations. Sadly, unlike Jesus, many of them have no disciples from whom they can select the leaders they need. They have never paid the price to truly "make disciples." This may be one of the greatest needs of the modern-day Church. We need strong leaders, but first we need people to be trained as disciples so they can become those leaders.

In the Bible, great leaders were first great disciples. It should be no different today. Until a person has learned the skills it takes to successfully follow Christ, how can they really lead others? Furthermore, if no one has ever spent the time it takes to train these disciples, where will they get these skills in the first place? No one is born into the kingdom of God with all the skills they need to follow Christ. Like babies in the natural world, we all need "grown-up" Christians to nurture and train us. We follow Jesus' instructions when we make disciples. Making disciples is at the very heart of God's plan to change our hurting world.

There are many religions around the world that have stolen this truth of discipleship and used it very successfully to do great harm. How much more powerful is discipleship when the truth of God's word is behind it? This is an art that must be reclaimed. If half the christians in the world would each make one disciple, the church would grow by fifty percent. If we continued this, we could win the whole world for Jesus in a few short years. Then we could all go home to be with Jesus! Hallelujah!

Duncan Phillips

Lessons from the Life of Jesus:
WHY BOTHER JESUS?

Seeing Jesus, [Jarius] fell at his feet and pleaded earnestly with him. "My little daughter is dying. Please come and put your hands on her so that she will be healed and live."

Some men came from the house of Jairus, the synagogue ruler. "Your daughter is dead," they said. "Why bother the teacher any more?"

Ignoring what they said, Jesus told the synagogue ruler, "Don't be afraid; just believe."

When they came to the home of the synagogue ruler, Jesus saw a commotion, with people crying and wailing loudly.

After he put them all out, he took the child's father and mother and the disciples who were with him, and went in where the child was. He took her by the hand and said to her,..."Little girl, I say to you, get up!" Immediately the girl stood up and walked around.

MARK 5:22–23, 35–36, 38, 40–42

NOVEMBER 5

Jairus, one of the rulers of the synagogue, was frantic with fear because his precious little daughter was dying. When he saw the people gathering around Jesus, he pushed through the crowd and fell at the Lord's feet. "Please, my little girl is dying. Come and put your hands on her so that she will be healed," he implored Jesus.

Jesus turned and went with Jairus. But soon men from Jairus' house met them and they were bearing bad news. His little girl was gone. "Don't bother the teacher anymore," they told him.

Although everything in Jairus wanted to crumble, he saw a confidence in the eyes of Jesus that filled his soul with faith. When they arrived at the house, everyone was screaming and wailing and crying. Taking the small girl's parents and three of his disciples with him, Jesus entered the child's room and simply said, "Little girl, I say to you, get up." Immediately, the girl stood up and began to walk around.

Sooner or later, like Jairus, you will face a crisis beyond anything you have ever experienced. There are three critical things for you to remember at this time.

First, everything in you (and most of the people around you) will be telling you not to bother God anymore. You will have to choose to ignore these voices and choose to listen to what God is saying. Ignore the unbelief around you and listen to his Word and you will have taken the first step on the pathway to your miracle.

Second, *words* of faith were not enough to see the little girl resurrected; it was going to take an *act* of faith. You must choose to believe *and* take a step of faith.

Third, when Jesus entered the home of Jairus, the atmosphere was permeated with despair, grief, and unbelief. So he turned out every person who was harboring unbelief. While those without faith waited on the outside, the few who truly believed witnessed the miracle.

No matter what you're asking God for today, you're not bothering him. However impossible it may seem, there is nothing he cannot do for those who choose to believe.

WHAT A GREAT STORY OF FAITH AND HEALING. Sometimes I think it's HARDER to see these MIRACLES living in the WEST. WE ARE SO BLINDED BY intellectuALISM AND MATERIALISM. THERE IS nothing WRONG with MATERIAL things in themselves, BUT they CAN BLIND US spiritUALLY. WhEN YOU HAVE nothing LEFT BUT simple childLiKe FAITH, the FATHER is FREE to DO MIRACLES.

Duncan Phillips

Lessons from the Life of Jesus:
FALLING AWAY

 After Jesus had finished instructing his twelve disciples, he went on from there to teach and preach in the towns of Galilee.

When John heard in prison what Christ was doing, he sent his disciples to ask him, "Are you the one who was to come, or should we expect someone else?"

Jesus replied, "Go back and report to John what you hear and see: The blind receive sight, the lame walk, those who have leprosy are cured, the deaf hear, the dead are raised, and the good news is preached to the poor. Blessed is the man who does not fall away on account of me."

MATTHEW 11:1-6

NOVEMBER 6 After John the Baptist had challenged the legitimacy of King Herod's marriage to his brother's wife, the king imprisoned him. Now, as he sat alone in the dampness of his lonely, dark cell, John began to question the ministry of the very man he had come to proclaim. Perhaps Jesus had forgotten him. After all, if he was truly the Son of God, he had the power to rescue him. John began to wonder if Jesus was living in a state of compromise and preaching a weak message.

John's followers had been telling him all the stories. While John had lived an austere life in the depths of the desert, Jesus had been seen eating dinner with sinners and going to parties in the homes of Pharisees. Finally, out of the darkness of his soul, John sent some of his followers to ask Jesus if he was truly the Messiah. Although this question hurt Jesus, he knew that his precious co-laborer and relative had grown depressed in the bowels of Herod's dungeons.

"Go back to John. Be honest with him. Tell him what you have seen and heard," Jesus said. "There are miraculous healings everywhere I go, and the dead are even raised. Tell him I am also preaching my Father's good news to all people. Also, most importantly, tell him this: Blessed is the man who does not become offended and fall away from me."

How could John the Baptist be in danger of falling away? What had offended him so deeply that he would question the very man whose ministry he had been sent into the world to confirm? These questions are important because sooner or later, you, too, like John, may be tempted to become offended at God.

When sincere Christians become offended with God, one of three things is normally involved. First, like John, they have been placed in difficult circumstances. They feel imprisoned emotionally, physically, financially, or spiritually, and darkenss gradually distorts their sense of reality. Second, many Christians have been personally disappointed. It's likely that John did not expect Jesus to leave him in prison. When these expectations were not met, his soul plummeted into despalr and offense. Finally, some Christians have the wrong concept of God's kingdom. It might have been hard for John to understand how Jesus could befriend sinners or spend time in the home of a Pharisee.

Wherever you are today, I beg you not to become offended with God. If you wait on him, he will bring to light his purposes for your life in the midst of your darkness.

We DoN't hAve the "LuxuRY" of tAking offense. We have ALL DeAlt with AND felt it. It's something thAt we ALMost feel is Due us if we've Been offeNDeD. "I hAve the Right to Be offeNDeD BecAuse they hurt me." UNfortuNAtely, offense hAs A myriAD of BeDfellows — ie. BitterNess, ANgeR. AND ReveNge — ALL of which cAN cARRY us DowN A veRY DARK RoAD. Let it Go toDAY.

Duncan Phillips

Lessons from the Life of Jesus:

WHO WILL FEED THE FIVE THOUSAND?

When Jesus looked up and saw a great crowd coming toward him, he said to Philip, "Where shall we buy bread for these people to eat?" He asked this only to test him, for he already had in mind what he was going to do.

Philip answered him, "Eight months' wages would not buy enough bread for each one to have a bite!"

Another of his disciples, Andrew, Simon Peter's brother, spoke up, "Here is a boy with five small barley loaves and two small fish, but how far will they go among so many?"

Jesus said, "Have the people sit down." There was plenty of grass in that place, and the men sat down, about five thousand of them. Jesus then took the loaves, gave thanks, and distributed to those who were seated as much as they wanted. He did the same with the fish.

When they had all had enough to eat, he said to his disciples, "Gather the pieces that are left over. Let nothing be wasted."

JOHN 6:5–12

NOVEMBER 7

Jesus and his disciples were exhausted. It wasn't just because of the continual needs of the multitudes who were following them. This time, they were also facing the news of John the Baptist's death. Suddenly they saw a huge crowd coming up the mountainside.

"Philip," Jesus said. "Where will we get the money to feed all these people?"

Why is he asking me that? Philip wondered. *He's the Messiah.* "Lord," Philip replied, "eight months' wages couldn't buy enough bread for each of these people to even have a small bite."

Then Andrew spoke up: "Lord, there is a boy here with five small barley loaves and two little fish. But what good will that do?" This is exactly what Jesus had been waiting for, because when he had asked Philip about money, he had been testing him.

"Have the people sit down," Jesus said. Jesus took the small lunch and prayed over it. When he and his disciples then distributed it to the five thousand men and their families who were present, there were still twelve baskets of food left. When the crowds saw this amazing miracle, they began to say, "Surely this is the Messiah!" Some of them even wanted to forcibly make Jesus the king of Israel.

Whether you like it or not, the day may come when Jesus will test you, too, just as he tested Philip. Even though Jesus already knows exactly what he is going to do, he may allow you to face a financial need that is totally beyond your resources. You may face it as an individual or as part of a church or ministry, but whatever the case, this story holds a number of important lessons for you.

First, no matter what type of financial need you may be facing, Jesus already has a plan to provide for it. Second, when you are faced with a need that is far beyond your own resources, it is because God himself has planned to meet that need miraculously. Jesus knew that neither he nor his disciples had enough money to feed the thousands of people who were crowding around them. He simply wanted to see if they would give the little bit they had in hopes that he would multiply it.

Third, it may take giving to release God's miraculous provision. Even though the disciples probably had a little bit of food or money, they never offered it. But one boy gave his lunch, and Jesus did the rest. Never forget that giving is the secret to releasing God's miraculous provision in your life and in the lives of those you love. As you give, you will leave behind the limitations of human planning and enter the realm of God's provision.

He even asked us to test him on this. Read MALACHI 3:8-12.
Duncan Phillips

Lessons from the Life of Jesus:
WALKING ON THE WATER

Jesus made the disciples get into the boat and go on ahead of him to the other side, while he dismissed the crowd. After he had dismissed them, he went up on a mountainside by himself to pray. When evening came, he was there alone, but the boat was already a considerable distance from land, buffeted by the waves because the wind was against it.

During the fourth watch of the night Jesus went out to them, walking on the lake. When the disciples saw him walking on the lake, they were terrified. "It's a ghost," they said, and cried out in fear.

But Jesus immediately said to them: "Take courage! It is I. Don't be afraid."

"Lord, if it's you," Peter replied, "tell me to come to you on the water."

"Come," he said.

Then Peter got down out of the boat, walked on the water and came toward Jesus.

MATTHEW 14:22–29

NOVEMBER 8

When the crowds finally left, the disciples were exhausted, so Jesus told them to head back across the Sea of Galilee. The disciples were ecstatic to be going home. Hours later, however, all their joy was gone. The wind was making all progress toward the shore impossible. No matter how hard they rowed they were still stuck in the middle of the lake.

Jesus prayed for many hours, and then, seeing his disciples still struggling in the water, he stepped onto the lake and broke into a brisk walk. When the disciples first saw him, they screamed in terror: "It's a ghost!"

Jesus said, "Don't be afraid. It's me!"

"Lord!" Peter hollered. "If it's really you, tell me to walk out to you."

"Come!" Jesus said. While the rest of the disciples watched in astonishment, Peter jumped to his feet and began to run toward Jesus on the water.

Like the disciples, the day will come when you will face a storm beyond your strength. No matter how hard you try, you will find your progress impeded. That is why this story's lessons are so critical for your life.

First, even though the disciples were exhausted, they still should have prayed for help. Sometimes the times we want to pray the least are the times we need to pray the most. Second, they had already been struggling for a number of hours before Jesus rescued them. The Lord, in his wisdom, may allow you to come to the end of your own strength so you can experience the fullness of his divine might. Third, when Jesus walked past on the water, he was demonstrating to them the power of God's Spirit. At the very moment their strength was breaking, he showed them the importance of walking in the power of God. Fourth, instead of simply waiting in the boat, Peter joined Jesus on the water. When you find yourself stuck, Jesus may call you to join him by stepping out in faith.

Remember, no matter how the storms of life are beating against you, Jesus can give you the power to overcome. No matter how high the waves or how forceful the winds, he who has called you out of the boat is both your Lord and the Lord of the storm.

"The effectual, fervent prayer of a righteous man avails much." Read James 5:13-19.
Duncan Phillips

Lessons from the Life of Jesus:
CRUMBS FROM THE MASTER'S TABLE

Leaving that place, Jesus withdrew to the region of Tyre and Sidon. A Canaanite woman from that vicinity came to him, crying out, "Lord, Son of David, have mercy on me! My daughter is suffering terribly from demon-possession."

Jesus did not answer a word. So his disciples came to him and urged him, "Send her away, for she keeps crying out after us."

He answered, "I was sent only to the lost sheep of Israel."

The woman came and knelt before him. "Lord, help me!" she said.

He replied, "It is not right to take the children's bread and toss it to their dogs."

"Yes, Lord," she said, "but even the dogs eat the crumbs that fall from their masters' table."

Then Jesus answered, "Woman, you have great faith! Your request is granted." And her daughter was healed from that very hour.

MATTHEW 15:21–28

NOVEMBER 9

She was scared to death. Canaanites like her never approached Jewish men. The hatred between their races was ancient, but her daughter's plight had made her desperate. A demon was tormenting her precious child. After hearing reports of Jesus' miracles, she believed he was her last hope.

"Lord," she pleaded, "Son of David, have mercy on me." Uncharacteristically, Jesus didn't bother to answer her. "Get rid of her, Lord," the disciples urged Jesus.

Finally, Jesus answered, "I only help Jews." Most people would have walked away angrily, but she fell on her knees and continued to plead with him. "Why should I give the bread of God's children to the dogs?" Jesus replied. "Yes, Lord, you're right," she said, "but even dogs eat the crumbs that fall from their master's table."

Jesus was astonished. "Woman, you have great faith! Your request is granted," he said. Her daughter was healed at that very moment.

As harsh as the replies of Jesus may seem, he was not being unkind. In fact, he was testing this woman's faith and demonstrating the barriers we must overcome so we can receive God's best for our lives.

First, because of the historic enmity between the Canaanite people and the Jews, this woman had no right to expect the Jewish Messiah's help. Desperation, however, forced her to cross the barriers of ethnic hatred in order to find healing.

Second, even though the woman pled with him, initially Jesus remained silent. Many times, when you are in a moment of crisis, God will remain silent. He wants you to persevere and come into a deeper faith as you pursue him.

Third, this desperate woman faced the rejection of Christ's closest followers. Sooner or later, in your pursuit of God, one of his people will offend you. But if you allow your pain or rejection to keep you away from God, you may never experience the reality of his promises to you.

Where are you in your journey? You may be in the place where God is silent. Or you may feel rejected by his servants. Wherever you find yourself, God has more than crumbs for you. He stands ready to bring you to his overflowing table of blessing.

This woman was amazing. She pushed past culture, gender, religion, slander from Christ's followers, and even the silence of the Lord himself for the love of her daughter. "Lord, let me emulate this woman's abandon for your glory."

Duncan Phillips

Lessons from the Life of Jesus:
IN WHAT ARE YOU REJOICING?

 The seventy-two returned with joy and said, "Lord, even the demons submit to us in your name."

He replied, "I saw Satan fall like lightning from heaven. I have given you authority to trample on snakes and scorpions and to overcome all the power of the enemy; nothing will harm you. However, do not rejoice that the spirits submit to you, but rejoice that your names are written in heaven."

LUKE 10:17-20

NOVEMBER 10

As the seventy-two disciples returned from their first mission, many of them were ecstatic. "Jesus! You're not going to believe it! Even demons listened to us when we used your name!" they cried. "Lord, it was just amazing! The power was flowing out of our lives like a river."

Jesus smiled as he looked at them. "I saw Satan himself thrown out of heaven, and I've given you authority to smash his kingdom," he said. "But it is not wise for you to place your joy in these things, because the foundation of your joy must be your citizenship in my kingdom."

Even though the cities of Korazin and Bethseda had not repented after he had just ministered there, Jesus' own joy had not been dampened. "Thank you, Father," he said. "You have hidden the secrets of your Kingdom from the wise, and revealed them to people with hearts like little children."

In this simple conversation, Jesus revealed to his disciples one of the secrets of a joy-filled life. He warned them not to derive their joy from the successes of their ministry, but from their citizenship in heaven. He did this because he realized their successes would not always be constant. Just as Jesus felt rejection in the cities where he had preached, he knew that sooner or later his disciples, too, would encounter failure. Whether it was a demon that didn't respond to them or a person who wasn't healed, it was inevitable that they would not always achieve the success they desired. When they met with failure—and their joy was not based on eternal realities—they would end up joyless and despairing.

This principle is the same for you today: Whatever profession you are in, it is dangerous to make your success the basis of your joy. If you do, you will find your joy will be fleeting at best, because it is based on what is temporal. Although my successes and the successes of those I love have brought me tremendous happiness, I have never made the mistake of making them the source of my joy. Instead, I have found that God's love for me—and the fact that I am a part of his family—are the continual source of my joy. I say *continual* because, like God himself, they never change. As you ask God for the revelation I am describing, he will fill your life with a level of joy beyond anything you can imagine. This type of joy, unlike your happiness, will remain constant, no matter what your life may bring.

"The joy of the LORD is our strength." That passage confused me for years. How can you get strength from having a laugh? Once your joy is rooted in knowing your eternal home, not only joy but peace, love, and all the fruits of the Spirit will be increasingly apparent. Our joy is in the assurance of our salvation.
Duncan Phillips

Lessons from the Life of Jesus:
DISTRACTED

As Jesus and his disciples were on their way, he came to a village where a woman named Martha opened her home to him. She had a sister called Mary, who sat at the Lord's feet listening to what he said. But Martha was distracted by all the preparations that had to be made. She came to him and asked, "Lord, don't you care that my sister has left me to do the work by myself? Tell her to help me!"

"Martha, Martha," the Lord answered, "you are worried and upset about many things, but only one thing is needed. Mary has chosen what is better, and it will not be taken away from her."

LUKE 10:38–42

NOVEMBER 11

Although many houses were open to Jesus, by the end of his life there were very few places where he was truly at home. One of them was the home of Martha. Along with her siblings, Mary and Lazarus, she was one of Jesus' best friends. Martha was a never-ceasing bundle of energy. A natural perfectionist, she needed all of her strength to refrain from screaming a rebuke at her sister, Mary, on the day that Jesus came to visit. Although everyone considered Mary the truly spiritual one, Martha wondered about her motives. Maybe her "spirituality" was just an excuse to be lazy.

This time, though, Mary had gone too far. As usual, she was sitting around, being spiritual, while Martha was working like a slave. Martha was fuming. Finally, in exasperation, she turned to Jesus for help.

"Lord, don't you care that my sister isn't helping me? Here she is, wasting time while I'm getting everything ready. Tell her to help me!"

"Martha," Jesus replied, "why are you so worried about the condition

of your house? Only one thing should be your heart's priority, and Mary has chosen it. Your house won't last, but Mary will experience the fruit of her choice for eternity."

This story has been repeated in various ways to women around the world. People cry, "Don't be a Martha!" or, "Be a Mary, who simply spent time with Jesus." In reality, this story, like most in the Bible, has very little to do with gender. Furthermore, Jesus was not rebuking Martha for being administrative, organized, or busy. His rebuke had nothing to do with the perfection of her house, and everything to do with the priorities of her life. Martha had been so busy in preparation for Jesus' visit that she had forgotten how to enjoy her Visitor. Like Mary, she, too, should have found the time to sit at his feet.

Martha's mistake is almost universal among Christians. Many believers have lost sight of his person in their zeal to advance his purpose. If your *work* for God has taken priority over your *waiting* on God, you are one of the very people I am describing. Sadly, lack of time in God's presence will eventually result in a lack of the very power we need to serve him. If this is where you are today, it's time for you to make a shift in your priorities. Instead of criticizing those in your church who seem to spend all their time in prayer and worship, take a serious look at your own life. Never forget that the prayerless life is the powerless life, and the life without his presence will always lead to a life without his passion. God is looking for people who will burn with the purpose of Martha, yet pray with the passion of Mary.

GReAt Lesson! We're ALL Guilty of living hur-
Ried lives. I've had times where I've ActuALLY
felt guilty for taking an afternoon nap
OR taking A day off. Learning to Rest is A
very positive And BiBLicAL concept. Even God
ALmighty took A day off to Rest After cReAting the cosmos.

Duncan Phillips

Lessons from the Life of Jesus:
DANGER ZONE

After this, Jesus went around in Galilee, purposely staying away from Judea because the Jews there were waiting to take his life. But when the Jewish Feast of Tabernacles was near, Jesus' brothers said to him, "You ought to leave here and go to Judea, so that your disciples may see the miracles you do. No one who wants to become a public figure acts in secret."

Therefore Jesus told them, "The right time for me has not yet come; for you any time is right. The world cannot hate you, but it hates me because I testify that what it does is evil."

JOHN 7:1–4, 6–7

NOVEMBER 12

Jesus was in danger. Although there were places where he could still minister safely, Jerusalem was not among them. His brothers, however, did not understand this. They did their best to talk him into going to Jerusalem so he could continue to build the popularity he had been experiencing. Jesus, however, knew better. "It doesn't matter when you go to Jerusalem," he told them, "For me, my Father's timing is vital."

Jesus knew what some Christians never learn. The more dangerous you become to the devil, the more danger you experience. Jesus threatened the very foundations of the satanic kingdom. Therefore, the enemy was looking for every opportunity to destroy him. When you begin to threaten the enemy, he will begin to threaten you. In my own experience, I have discovered that there are three different levels of spiritual warfare.

First is what I call a target of opportunity. In the military world, certain planes fly a prescribed route, looking for any target to present itself—like a tank out of its bunker. As you grow in God's strength and power, though,

you will be seen as a prime target for enemy attacks because you are attacking him.

The second level of warfare is the one described in the story we have been discussing. There were certain places, like Jerusalem, that were more dangerous for Jesus than others. Sometimes when we go to another country to minister or attempt to reach certain people, we will encounter unusual levels of opposition. Rejoice when you see this happen, because it means that you are doing powerful work for the Lord.

Third, by the end of his ministry, Jesus couldn't minister publicly among the Jews without risking his life. Some of you may even experience this level of warfare. There are some people whose lives or ministries threaten the kingdom of hell to the point that they live under the incessant attack of the enemy. Even though they walk in the joy and protection of their Father, they know that the enemy is stalking them, and they live accordingly.

No matter what type of warfare you are experiencing today, God will give you the strength you need to stand against evil attacks. As you grow through his Word and hide in his protection, you will be able to withstand anything the enemy brings your way.

The WORD says that the enemy ROAMS the eARTh seeking whom he MAY DeVOUR. The Devil hATes US so much that he WOULD KiLL US if he hAD the chAnce. We ARe mADe in the imAGe of christ, so we ARe A constAnt Reminder of the One thAt expeLLeD him fRom heAven. We must Live with this DAnGer in mind, But ALso in the joy of Knowing thAt we ARe hiDDen in the BLOOD of Jesus!

Duncan Phillips

Lessons from the Life of Jesus:
THE POOL OF SILOAM

As he went along, he saw a man blind from birth. His disciples asked him, "Rabbi, who sinned, this man or his parents, that he was born blind?"

"Neither this man nor his parents sinned," said Jesus, "but this happened so that the work of God might be displayed in his life. As long as it is day, we must do the work of him who sent me. Night is coming, when no one can work. While I am in the world, I am the light of the world."

Having said this, he spit on the ground, made some mud with the saliva, and put it on the man's eyes. "Go," he told him, "wash in the Pool of Siloam" (this word means Sent). So, the man went and washed, and came home seeing.

JOHN 9:1-7

NOVEMBER 13

The crowd was astonished. Jesus hadn't just touched the blind man—he'd placed a mud pack over his eyes. "Go," he told the blind man, "wash in the Pool of Siloam." When the man obeyed Jesus, he was instantly healed.

Maybe you've wondered why this man wasn't healed the first time Jesus touched him. Although it's true that healing can be progressive, there is a far deeper lesson in this story, and the key is that Jesus told the man to wash in the Pool of Siloam. The word *Siloam* means "sent," and it is similar to the word from which we derive the term *apostle* ("sent one"). When the blind man chose to obey, he was both healed and given the assurance that he had been chosen by Jesus for a purpose.

I have met a number of Christians like the blind man in this story. Although Jesus has done extensive work in their lives, they are still blind to the purpose for which Christ sent them into the world. Many well-meaning Christians either have no idea what their destiny is or have no concept of God's purpose for their lives. And until they are exposed to the realities of "apostolic Christianity," they will remain unseeing. When I use the term *apostolic*, I am not describing a denomination or a specific church. I am talking about the reality of being sent by God into the world to advance his kingdom. As much as I delight in hearing a tremendous teaching or a great evangelistic message, I would not be the Christian I am today without the impassioned apostolic men with whom God has called me to walk. Their burning desire to plant churches and advance the kingdom of God to the uttermost regions of our planet keeps me from being blind to the realities of the larger world that I have been called to reach. Whatever it takes, I encourage you to expose yourself to the type of dynamic ministry I am describing. Once you have washed in these waters, your life will never be the same again.

When talking with fans on the road, their biggest source of confusion is their calling. Most people don't know what they are called to do. I think maybe this might help. A part of every Christian's calling is to make disciples. The last thing that Christ said before he left was, "Go to all the nations and make disciples." I'm convinced that if we start here, our personal calling will follow. Read Matthew 28:18-20.

Duncan Phillips

Lessons from the Life of Jesus:
IT'S GOOD FOR US TO BE HERE

After six days Jesus took with him Peter, James and John the brother of James, and led them up a high mountain by themselves. There he was transfigured before them. His face shone like the sun, and his clothes became as white as the light. Just then there appeared before them Moses and Elijah, talking with Jesus.

Peter said to Jesus, "Lord, it is good for us to be here. If you wish, I will put up three shelters—one for you, one for Moses and one for Elijah."

While he was still speaking, a bright cloud enveloped them, and a voice from the cloud said, "This is my Son, whom I love; with him I am well pleased. Listen to him!"

When the disciples heard this, they fell facedown to the ground, terrified. But Jesus came and touched them. "Get up," he said. "Don't be afraid." When they looked up, they saw no one except Jesus.

As they were coming down the mountain, Jesus instructed them, "Don't tell anyone what you have seen, until the Son of Man has been raised from the dead."

MATTHEW 17:1–9

NOVEMBER 14

When Jesus had asked Peter, James, and John to climb up a mountain with him, they were not surprised. They knew how much he liked to pray in solitary places. This time, though, it was different. Heaven itself seemed to come into the earth. With the glory of God streaming down upon him, the face of Jesus shone like the sun, and his clothes were dazzling and brilliant. As if this were not enough, Moses and Elijah appeared and began to talk to Jesus about his upcoming ordeal.

"Jesus!" Peter finally shouted. "If you'd like, I will build three tabernacles—one for you, one for Moses, and one for Elijah." Feeling very pleased with himself, Peter hardly noticed that he was being enveloped in a dense, bright cloud.

"This is my Son, whom I love. With him I am well pleased. Listen to him!" the Father said.

Have you ever wondered why God did not want Peter to build three tabernacles on the mountain? First, unlike Moses and Elijah, who were mere men, Jesus, as the Son of God, was divine. Therefore, if God had any desire for Peter to build a tabernacle, it would only have been for his Son. God wants us to keep focused on Jesus and not get distracted by even his most godly servants.

Second, I am convinced that God did not want Peter to build any tabernacles because he did not want the Mount of Transfiguration to become a permanent place of worship. In fact, the only thing the Father wanted built on that mountaintop was the faith of his Son's disciples. Their newfound faith would be desperately needed to deal with what lay ahead.

We would all prefer to stay on the mountaintop with Christ if we could. Whether these spiritual mountaintops are glorious church services, dynamic conferences, or poignant personal encounters, we'd like to live in these moments forever. But mountaintop experiences were never meant to become permanent places of refuge. They are meant to give us the fresh faith and power we need to meet the needs of our hurting world.

It is so wonderful to be given a little taste of heaven. Incredibly refreshing! Yet we must never forget the purpose of this glimpse is to strengthen us for the battles in the valley below.

Duncan Phillips

Lessons from the Life of Jesus:
HE STAYED AWAY

Now a man named Lazarus was sick. He was from Bethany, the village of Mary and her sister Martha. This Mary, whose brother Lazarus now lay sick, was the same one who poured perfume on the Lord and wiped his feet with her hair. So the sisters sent word to Jesus, "Lord, the one you love is sick."

When he heard this, Jesus said, "This sickness will not end in death. No, it is for God's glory so that God's Son may be glorified through it." Jesus loved Martha and her sister and Lazarus. Yet when he heard that Lazarus was sick, he stayed where he was two more days.

JOHN 11:1–6

NOVEMBER 15

Lazarus was deathly ill, but his sisters, Mary and Martha, weren't terribly worried. There was no doubt in their minds that Jesus would rush to their home the moment he heard about the illness. After all, they were among his best friends. Much to everyone's amazement, however, Jesus did not respond immediately to the urgent need of his friend. In fact, the Bible says that even though Jesus loved Lazarus and his sisters, he stayed where he was two more days. By the time he arrived, Lazarus was dead, and his sisters were heartbroken.

Why did Jesus stay away when his best friend was dying? He obviously had the power to heal him—yet he left him to die. This question is important because sooner or later, all of us will face a similar situation. At some point of great need in our lives, God will stay away. Although there are a number of reasons why he does this, there are two that are the most pertinent for the situations most of us will face.

First, unlike us, God does not become hopeless as the severity of our crisis grows. To Jesus, it didn't really matter if Lazarus was merely dying, or already dead. He knew that he had the power to easily handle either one of these scenarios. The problem was that some of Lazarus's family members and friends did not share that confidence. The sicker Lazarus became, the more their discouragement grew. Have you ever felt this way? Your limited view of God's power and the unbelief of your heart might have left you vulnerable to the fear and discouragement that came as your situation grew worse.

The second reason that Jesus stayed away at the time of his friend's dire illness was that he had far more in mind than simply healing Lazarus. He wanted to give Mary, Martha, and Lazarus the faith they would need to face his own imminent death. Therefore, healing Lazarus would not be enough. Giving them the necessary faith would take his friend being raised from the dead. It is no different for you today. There are times when Jesus is far more interested in building your faith than he is in immediately alleviating the painful crisis of your soul. When these times come, he may allow your situation to worsen, simply because it takes a great crisis to build a great man or woman of faith. But he will remain faithful to not place on you more than you can bear, and ultimately he will build the strength, courage, and faith in your heart through these difficult times—if you continue to trust in him as the One who knows what's best for you and who holds you in the palm of his hand.

Imagine the audacity and even betrayal Martha and Mary must have felt when Jesus didn't respond the way they had expected. His ways are not our ways. Our character is so much more important to him than our comfort. No pain, no gain!

Duncan Phillips

Lessons from the Life of Jesus:
ANSWER OR ACTION

"Lord," Martha said to Jesus, "if you had been here, my brother would not have died. But I know that even now God will give you whatever you ask."

Jesus said to her, "Your brother will rise again."

JOHN 11:21–23

NOVEMBER 16

When Jesus arrived in Bethany, Lazarus had already been in the tomb for four days. Mary and Martha's home was filled with their friends who had come to comfort them. When Martha heard that Jesus was on the way to her home, she went outside her village and waited for him. *Why has he taken so long?* she wondered. *Maybe he doesn't love us as much as I'd thought.*

"Jesus," she said in an agonized voice when she saw him, "if you had been here, my brother would not have died. Yet I know that your Father will grant you anything you ask."

"Your brother will rise again, Martha," Jesus responded.

"I know he will at the resurrection," Martha said tearfully.

"I am the resurrection," Jesus whispered.

Martha was so numb with grief that she was unable to hear what Jesus was really promising.

When Mary heard from Martha that Jesus had arrived, she ran to him. Unlike Martha, who simply spoke to him, she fell, weeping, at his feet. "Lord, my brother wouldn't have died if you had been here," she said.

Jesus was so deeply moved by her entreaties that he began to weep himself, and said, "Where did you bury him?" It was time for Jesus to raise Lazarus from the dead.

In the middle of this miraculous story, we find an amazing contrast. Although both sisters told Jesus that if he would have been there, their brother wouldn't have died, they got completely different responses. Martha got an answer, while Mary got action. This was nothing to do with how much Jesus loved them. It was a matter of proximity and intimacy. Mary simply had more ability to move his heart because of the time they had spent together. Although Martha served Jesus with all her heart, she had never taken the time to develop the level of intimacy with him.

Where are you today? Are you like Martha, settling for simple answers when you could be seeing God in action? If so, it's not too late for you to develop the type of divine intimacy I am describing. All it will take is the daily discipline of quiet time spent with God. As you embrace this discipline, in time, it will become a delight—the delight of a person spending time with their best friend. In this place, your relationship with God isn't simply about principles. Rather, when you're together with your Master, you can feel his heart and sense his desires. There was no doubt in Mary's mind that Jesus would raise her brother from the dead. She knew him well enough to know that was his intention. Her tears were simply an outward manifestation of what Jesus was already feeling in his heart. When you, like Mary, have paid the price to come into this place, you will be amazed to see that God is not simply a God of answers. He is a God of action.

LocAtion, LocAtion, LocAtion. A RcAL estAte term, But it WoRKS foR this stuDy. MARy hAD A speciAL "LocAtion" in the LoRD's heARt BecAuse of the time she spent in pRAyeR AnD fellow-ship. In ReAL estAte, LocAtion empoweRs the owneR to BRing moRe "GolD." MARy's GolD WAS to move Jesus' heARt to Action. ReAD this soBeRing pAssAge of MAtthew 7:21-23.

Duncan Phillips

Lessons from the Life of Jesus:
LOOK UP

Jesus, once more deeply moved, came to the tomb. It was a cave with a stone laid across the entrance. "Take away the stone," he said.

"But, Lord," said Martha, the sister of the dead man, "by this time there is a bad odor, for he has been there four days."

Then Jesus said, "Did I not tell you that if you believed, you would see the glory of God?"

So they took away the stone. Then Jesus looked up and said, "Father, I thank you that you have heard me. I knew that you always hear me, but I said this for the benefit of the people standing here, that they may believe that you sent me."

When he had said this, Jesus called in a loud voice, "Lazarus, come out!" The dead man came out, his hands and feet wrapped with strips of linen, and a cloth around his face.

Jesus said to them, "Take off the grave clothes and let him go."

JOHN 11:38–44

NOVEMBER 17

When Jesus came to the tomb of Lazarus he asked for the huge stone to be rolled away from the tomb's mouth. Martha was resistant. "Lord, are you sure you want to do this?" she asked. "He's been dead four days, and the odor of his decaying body will be horrible."

"Martha," Jesus replied, "didn't I tell you that if you believed, you would see God's glory?"

Then Jesus simply looked up toward heaven. "Father, I thank you that you have heard me." And then Jesus spoke in a loud voice: "Lazarus, come out." When he had spoken these words, a hush fell over the crowd. Much to their amazement, a rustling sound came from the tomb and Lazarus came shuffling out, still wrapped in his grave clothes.

All of us are confronted by the death and decay of something of great value to us, at some point in our lives. It may be a dead marriage or a business. Or you may face the death of the church or ministry you love so much. When this happens, you will either look up or look in. When Jesus was faced with Lazarus's death, he did not spend his time gazing into the tomb and wondering how he would ever resurrect this deteriorating corpse. Instead, he looked up to the One who has power over death: his beloved Father. With this heavenly perspective Jesus brought Lazarus back from the dead.

No matter what you're facing today, your only hope is to look up. Pull your eyes away from the darkness and hopelessness of your situation. Lift your hands in praise, even in the midst of your despair, and you cannot help but look up. If you fix your eyes on God's promises, you'll find the power you need to resist the downward spiral of despair and defeat that loss produces. Once these principles have been burned into your heart, you can face death the way Jesus did; in the words of Paul, death will have "lost its sting" (1 Corinthians 15:56).

As we are confident in our salvation, the "sting" of death is just that - only a sling. A sting is not a hugely painful experience in eternal terms. We may experience pain, but in the light of eternity, it will soon be a faded memory. To Jesus, the death of Lazarus was only a sting that he could easily rectify.

Duncan Phillips

Lessons from the Life of Jesus:
WAS IT WASTED?

Six days before the Passover, Jesus arrived at Bethany, where Lazarus lived, whom Jesus had raised from the dead. Here a dinner was given in Jesus' honor.... Mary took about a pint of pure nard, an expensive perfume; she poured it on Jesus' feet and wiped his feet with her hair. And the house was filled with the fragrance of the perfume.

JOHN 12:1-3

"Leave her alone," said Jesus. "Why are you bothering her? She has done a beautiful thing to me.... She poured perfume on my body beforehand to prepare for my burial. I tell you the truth, wherever the gospel is preached throughout the world, what she has done will also be told, in memory of her."

MARK 14:6, 8-9

NOVEMBER 18

Lazarus's friends had come to rejoice with him in his new life and to honor Jesus. But while everyone else was celebrating life, deep inside, Jesus knew he was about to face death. Someone else in the room was beginning to sense the same thing: Mary, Martha's sister. Always sensitive to the needs of Jesus, she took a pint of very expensive perfume and began to pour it over his feet. Then, when she had finished with the perfume, she slowly wiped his feet with her hair. As the fragrance of her sacrificial worship filled the room, the other guests began to grumble. "Why is she wasting that perfume?" they muttered under their breath. "She could have sold it and given the money to the poor." Even one of the apostles, Judas Iscariot, objected to her sacrifice and rebuked her.

"Leave her alone," Jesus said. After pausing, Jesus said tenderly, "Wherever this Gospel is preached, the story of her sacrifice will also be told."

In this story of extravagant worship, there are a number of important principles worth noting. First, it is one thing to see Jesus as your Friend but it is an entirely different matter to know him as your Lord. Jesus was surrounded by people who loved him, yet only Mary recognized his impending sacrifice and anointed him in preparation. Her costly gift was an act of worship.

Second, Mary's valuable gift filled the whole room with its fragrance. The more it costs you to worship, the more powerful your worship becomes. Never forget that just one sincere worshiper, like Mary, has the ability to affect the entire atmosphere of a place.

Third, some of the people at the feast accused Mary of wasting the costly perfume; in the same way, there will always be people in your life who will consider your worship and praise a waste of time and energy. These people will affect your spiritual purity and passion if you listen to them.

Remember—it is never a waste to worship God with all your heart. Like Mary's perfume, your worship will be like a fragrance that flows to all those around you. As you touch the heart of your Lord and Friend, he will bring you into a fresh place of fellowship and intimacy with him.

WORShiping the FAther is incREDIBLy powerful. It REALLy gets his Attention. The First Line of the LORD's PRAyer, which I Believe is A guide to how we shoulD pRAy, begins with worship: "HALLoweD Be yOUR hAme" (MAtthew 6:9 – 13).

Duncan Phillips

Lessons from the Life of Jesus:
VIRTUAL REVIVAL

[The disciples] brought the donkey and the colt, placed their cloaks on them, and Jesus sat on them. A very large crowd spread their cloaks on the road, while others cut branches from the trees and spread them on the road. The crowds that went ahead of him and those that followed shouted, . . .

"Hosanna in the highest!"

When Jesus entered Jerusalem, the whole city was stirred and asked, "Who is this?"

MATTHEW 21:6–10

As he approached Jerusalem and saw the city, he wept over it and said, "If you, even you, had only known on this day what would bring you peace—but now it is hidden from your eyes. The days will come upon you when your enemies will build an embankment against you and encircle you and hem you in on every side. They will dash you to the ground, you and the children within your walls. They will not leave one stone on another, because you did not recognize the time of God's coming to you."

LUKE 19:41–44

NOVEMBER 19 As far as his disciples were concerned, Jesus had won. With thousands of people praising him as they entered Jerusalem, what else could their Master want? Even the Pharisees had commented that the whole world was following him. The adoring crowds had become so frenzied in their worship that they were creating a pathway for his donkey to walk on by laying their cloaks on the ground. Yet despite what seemed like his greatest moment of triumph, Jesus was weeping. When he had seen Jerusalem in the distance, his heart broke. "Jerusalem," he had wept, "if only you had realized what was happening to you today. Now, you will end up being totally destroyed because you did not recognize God coming to you."

Like Jesus' disciples, many Christians today might have considered this moment the high point of Jesus' ministry. After all, there was incredible praise and a gigantic crowd. Tragically, the only revival on the streets of Jerusalem that day was a virtual revival. Many of the very people who were shouting his praises would be screaming for Jesus' death only days later. Jesus realized that Jerusalem's fickle crowds were not welcoming him as the Messiah who would be Lord over their lives; they were simply celebrating the fact that he had the power to meet their needs. This distinction is important for you to understand because Jesus is never satisfied with merely having a follow*ing*. He wants follow*ers*.

As in the streets of Jerusalem, much of what is passing for revival in our time is no more than virtual revival—there is no lasting fruit. People shout and praise. Some are even converted. Yet, for the most part, cities are not transformed, the majority of people who make professions of faith fall away, and immorality does not decline. May God help us to distinguish between real revival and virtual revival as we seek his face today.

I don't want to someday be a burnt-out musician talking about the "good old days" of a virtual revival that doesn't last. I want to be part of one of the greatest outpourings of God's glory till the return of our Savior.

Duncan Phillips

Lessons from the Life of Jesus:
SEED FAITH

Jesus replied, "The hour has come for the Son of Man to be glorified. I tell you the truth, unless a kernel of wheat falls to the ground and dies, it remains only a single seed. But if it dies, it produces many seeds. The man who loves his life will lose it, while the man who hates his life in this world will keep it for eternal life."

JOHN 12:23–25

NOVEMBER 20

As Jesus entered Jerusalem, he learned that some of the Gentile converts to Judaism wanted to meet him. The disciples were ecstatic. Could it be that the whole world would embrace their Master's message? Jesus' reply to the Gentiles, however, stunned them. Rather than being euphoric over the crowd's thunderous praises, he seemed sober, even sad. "The hour has come for the Son of Man to be glorified," Jesus replied.

To be glorified? the disciples wondered. *Why doesn't he look around? This is the ultimate glory.*

Jesus sighed and spoke again. "I tell you the truth, unless a grain of wheat falls to the ground and dies, it will remain a single seed. But if it dies, it produces many seeds."

You and I live in an era of the Church in which there has been much talk about seed faith. To some people, seed faith is a financial concept. They believe that if you sow a small seed into God's kingdom, you will be blessed with an abundant financial harvest. Others believe that seed faith is the key to mountain moving. In other words, even if your faith seems small, you can still move the mountainous obstacles that are in your path by simply exercising your faith. Although there is truth in both of these concepts, neither expresses the kind of seed faith that Jesus describes in John 12:24. This is the purest form of seed faith because it does not involve your money or your mountain. It involves your life.

Do you have that type of God-given faith? People with this kind of faith have no trouble humbling themselves because they know that God is able to exalt them again if he chooses. They are not afraid to die to their position, purpose, or prosperity. Like Jesus, they realize that until they die to everything but the Father's will, they will never accomplish the purposes they have been living for in the first place. Christians with a true understanding of seed faith do not fear being buried like a seed in the soil of God's will for their lives. Whether their burial involves giving up the prominent position they have held in their company or business, or stepping into a less visible ministry in the church they love, they know the time they spend buried will bring a divine germination to their faith that will produce an incredible season of fruitfulness in their lives.

Jesus said that when a person dies, he does not remain alone. The death Jesus describes is not just the death of our aspirations, dreams, and plans. It is the tearing down of our willfulness and self-absorption. People who fail to deal with these sinful attitudes will find themselves void of intimacy with God and with fellow Christians. Are you ready to experience the ultimate form of seed faith today? If you are, it will affect more than your money and your mountains. It will shake the world around you, as the character of Christ is freshly manifested in your life.

This story speaks to me of multiplication. Jesus had to leave this earth for his disciples to really come into their full destinies. Also, as we die to self and disciple people, the multiplication effect can be enormous. Today's millions of christians came from Jesus, then twelve, then to what we have today. We're a lot closer than we think.

Duncan Phillips

Lessons from the Life of Jesus:
THE REAL ISSUE

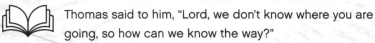

Thomas said to him, "Lord, we don't know where you are going, so how can we know the way?"

Jesus answered, "I am the way and the truth and the life. No one comes to the Father except through me. If you really knew me, you would know my Father as well. From now on, you do know him and have seen him."

Philip said, "Lord, show us the Father and that will be enough for us."

Jesus answered: "Don't you know me, Philip, even after I have been among you such a long time? Anyone who has seen me has seen the Father. How can you say, 'Show us the Father'?"

JOHN 14:5–9

NOVEMBER 21

The disciples were frightened. Although Jesus had told them that he would come back, he had left no doubt in their minds that he was going to leave them. He told them to trust in God, but they didn't know how to cope with the anxiety in their hearts. Finally, Thomas spoke up. "Lord, if we don't know where you're going, how can we know the way there?" he asked.

"I am the way," Jesus said. "Trust me. In fact, if you really knew me, you'd know exactly what my Father is like."

At that point Philip couldn't hold back the deepest concerns of his heart any longer. "Show us what your Father is like, and we won't be afraid to trust you anymore."

Turning to them with a smile, Jesus said, "My Father is just like me."

Many times, like the disciples of Jesus, Christians today don't have a problem with direction, but they have a problem with discernment—discerning what God the Father is really like. Some people have been so torn apart by the destructive forces of sin and the shame it brings that they can only see God through the lens of their own pain. They can't imagine how God could ever love them. Others have been involved in a religious tradition that has misrepresented God's nature as distant, angry, and unforgiving. When our souls believe these lies, unbelief and an inability to trust God result.

If you, like the disciples, find yourself in a place where having faith is hard, it could be that you need to rework your basic image of God. Fortunately, the answer Jesus gave to his fearful followers is the same answer that he offers us today: "If you have seen me, you have seen my Father." In other words, God the Father is just like God the Son. Far from being distant and harsh, he is loving, kind, patient, and filled with mercy.

In Romans 8:15–16, Paul says that we can call God "Daddy" because the Holy Spirit gives us the revelation that we are God's children. Ask God to fulfill this Scripture in your life today, and you will be amazed at the change it will bring.

Having children was a revelation to me. The moment my daughter was born I was overwhelmed with love for her. I would have given anything for her, even though we had just met. Becoming a father gave me a greater insight into God's love for us. There is nothing we can do to make the Father love us more and nothing we can do to make him love us less. His love is unconditional.

Duncan Phillips

SATAN ENTERED HIM

But one of his disciples, Judas Iscariot, who was later to betray him, objected, "Why wasn't this perfume sold and the money given to the poor? It was worth a year's wages." He did not say this because he cared about the poor but because he was a thief; as keeper of the money bag, he used to help himself to what was put into it.

JOHN 12:4–6

Jesus answered, "It is the one to whom I will give this piece of bread when I have dipped it in the dish." Then, dipping the piece of bread, he gave it to Judas Iscariot, son of Simon. As soon as Judas took the bread, Satan entered into him.

"What you are about to do, do quickly," Jesus told him, but no one at the meal understood why Jesus said this to him. Since Judas had charge of the money, some thought Jesus was telling him to buy what was needed for the Feast, or to give something to the poor.

JOHN 13:26–29

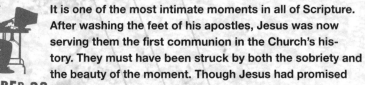

NOVEMBER 22

It is one of the most intimate moments in all of Scripture. After washing the feet of his apostles, Jesus was now serving them the first communion in the Church's history. They must have been struck by both the sobriety and the beauty of the moment. Though Jesus had promised to return, none of them knew if they would ever have a moment like this with him again. Little did they know, however, that a dark, malignant entity was at work. He had been stalking one of their number for months. Slowly but surely, the enemy had been able to exploit an area of weakness in this disciple's heart, and now was time to spring his trap.

When Jesus looked up at his disciples, he wore a deeply pained expression on his face. "One of you will betray me," he whispered.

"Ask him who," Peter said in John's ear. "Who is it, Master?" John asked.

"The one I give the bread to will betray me," Jesus replied. At that moment, just as Judas touched the bread in his Master's hand, the dark forces he had been entertaining made him their slave. Without another word, he rushed into the night to betray his Master into the hands of his enemies.

Think about it. How could one of the original twelve apostles, a man personally discipled by Jesus in the world's greatest accountability group, become filled with a demon during a communion service?

Unfortunately, all the discipleship and spiritual covering in the world will not protect you if you are living in secret sin. It is clear from Scripture that Judas was a thief, stealing money from the ministry funds of Jesus, and his financial dishonesty opened the door to a more serious level of temptation. When he had the opportunity to betray Jesus for forty pieces of silver, he did not hesitate.

If you're living in habitual secret sin, sooner or later, the enemy will try to exploit it, and there is no telling how many people will be affected. If you want deliverance today, and I believe you do, you can no longer keep your sin a secret. Go to one of the Christian leaders that God has placed in your life and ask for their help. But also never forget that no matter how far you've already fallen, the Scripture says, "Though a righteous man falls seven times, he rises again" (Proverbs 24:16).

READ ROMANS 2:1 - 16. I WOULD RATHER HAVE the EMBARRASSMENT THAT TRANSPARENCY CAN BRING WITH A TRUSTED FRIEND, THAN TO EXPERIENCE THE HORRIBLE CONSEQUENCES OF SIN.
Duncan Phillips

Lessons from the Life of Jesus:
PETER'S PRIDE

"Simon, Simon, Satan has asked to sift you as wheat. But I have prayed for you, Simon, that your faith may not fail. And when you have turned back, strengthen your brothers."

But he replied, "Lord, I am ready to go with you to prison and to death."

Jesus answered, "I tell you, Peter, before the rooster crows today, you will deny three times that you know me."

LUKE 22:31–34

NOVEMBER 23

Judas was not the only apostle about whom Jesus was concerned on the night of his Last Supper. "Simon, Simon," he said to Peter, "Satan has asked my permission to grind your life like kernels of wheat being made into flour. I have prayed for you, though, Simon, that your faith won't fail you. When you've returned from your testing, strengthen the faith of your brothers."

"What are you talking about, Lord?" Peter boasted. "I am more than ready to be imprisoned and even to die for you."

Jesus answered him sadly. "Peter, before the rooster crows, you will deny me three times."

"No way, Lord!" Peter burst out. "Don't you remember? You called me the rock! I don't care if I have to die. I will never disown you."

Peter's foolish dismissal of Christ's warnings cost him dearly. In the hours that followed, he ran for his life in the Garden of Gethsemane and denied Jesus three times. How could Peter ignore the repeated warnings of God's only Son? Sadly, in the very same way, we often refuse to listen to people who have been called to mentor us. When God is going to warn us, he often uses other people. We then have to choose whether or not we will listen—or remain in a state of pride.

Pride? I don't have any pride! you may be thinking. But pride has a way of hiding—even from us. Typically, prideful people think they are among God's most humble children. If this describes the attitude of your heart, it may be time to get the opinion of another person. Your spouse, boss, coworker, pastor, or best friend will probably be able to tell you the truth.

Pride is one of the most destructive sins because it blinds people to the counsel and help they need in their walk with God. Even worse is the fact that pride produces a deceptive confidence that keeps us from seeking the help of people and the help of God.

If this is where you are today, swallow your pride and ask for forgiveness. God opposes the proud, but gives grace to the humble (1 Peter 5:5). Ask him for his grace today.

PRIDE is WILY. MTV AND HOLLYWOOD PROMOTE it TO RELIGIOUS STATUS. The BIG houses, LUXURY CARS, AND money in most music videos MAKE pRIDE into A viRtue. It DISGUISES itself As conFIDENCE OR even self-esteem. It CAN BLIND you to GOOD ADVICE AND feel SO pAinful when pRODDED. FOR A REMEDY FOR this DECEptive sin. READ PROVERBS 16:18 AND 1 John 2:15 - 17.

Duncan Phillips

Lessons from the Life of Jesus:
THE OIL PRESS

Jesus went with his disciples to a place called Gethsemane, and he said to them, "Sit here while I go over there and pray." He took Peter and the two sons of Zebedee along with him, and he began to be sorrowful and troubled. Then he said to them, "My soul is overwhelmed with sorrow to the point of death. Stay here and keep watch with me."

MATTHEW 26:36–38

NOVEMBER 24

As he walked toward the Garden of Gethsemane, Jesus could already feel the pressure of his coming confrontation. Although he'd been battling the enemy for the last three years, he knew this would be different. Like his battles with Satan in the wilderness, this would be one of the defining moments of his earthly life. This time, however, he was taking Peter, James, and John with him into the conflict.

Over the next few hours, while Jesus prayed, the oppression was so great that he was literally sweating blood. All the while, his closest friends slept. Finally, the Father sent an angel to strengthen him for his coming ordeal.

What lessons can we learn from Jesus' battle with Satan in the Garden of Gethsemane? First of all, though his disciples failed him, the principle of inviting people into your conflicts with the enemy is still vital. No matter how hard the enemy attacks, it is hard for him to defeat me when I have both God's power and my brothers and sisters on my side. This powerful combination has brought me safely through many battles.

Second, Jesus faced down the enemy with the power of his Father through prayer. If you depend on your own strength in the battle against the enemy, you will not be able to withstand his onslaught. Only through God's power can you stand strong.

Third, when his disciples failed him, Jesus' heavenly Father sent an angel to strengthen and encourage him. In the same way, if you cry out to God, he will give you all that you need to face down your adversary, the devil.

The word *Gethsemane* means "oil press." This garden was the place where olives were made into valuable and useful olive oil through intense pressing. God allows you to experience tremendous pressure so that you can be used for his purposes. So when you face the "press," pray hard and reach out to your spiritual family to stand with you. Instead of simply being pressed, you will press through to the victory God has for you.

I cannot imagine the pressure and stress that Jesus must have felt — a pressure that caused him to sweat drops of blood. Though obviously not to the same extent as Jesus, my own Gethsemane experiences have been traumatic as well. But the LORD has always provided comfort, and the final result was always good. Like a spiritual workout; these experiences hurt at the time but result in a stronger spirit.

Duncan Phillips

Lessons from the Life of Jesus:
THE ROOSTER'S CROW

 Now Peter was sitting out in the courtyard, and a servant girl came to him. "You also were with Jesus of Galilee," she said.

But he denied it before them all. "I don't know what you're talking about," he said.

Then he went out to the gateway, where another girl saw him and said to the people there, "This fellow was with Jesus of Nazareth."

He denied it again, with an oath: "I don't know the man!"

After a little while, those standing there went up to Peter and said, "Surely you are one of them, for your accent gives you away."

Then he began to call down curses on himself and he swore to them, "I don't know the man!"

Immediately a rooster crowed. Then Peter remembered the word Jesus had spoken: "Before the rooster crows, you will disown me three times." And he went outside and wept bitterly.

MATTHEW 26:69–75

NOVEMBER 25 By the time Peter ran out of the Garden, fear had a tight grip on his soul. At first, he had tried to play the hero, cutting off the ear of one of Jesus' attackers. His bravado, however, had quickly waned when Jesus rebuked him and healed the man. Now with the shame of his failure weighing on his conscience, he was easy prey for the enemy's temptations and torments. When he finally made his way to the courtyard of the building where Jesus was being questioned, he was immediately confronted—not by a burly temple guard, but a simple servant girl.

"You were with that Jesus! I saw you!" she said.

"I was never with him. You're a crazy woman," Peter quickly replied as he hurried past her.

When he attempted to slip out, another girl saw him. "This fellow was with Jesus," she shouted.

"It's not true! I swear it!" Peter said, lying to protect himself.

Later, when he was trying to warm himself by the fire, a man said, "I can tell by your accent you're a Galilean. You must be one of that Jesus fellow's disciples!" This time, Peter was so afraid that he began to call down curses on himself, and swore, "I don't even know the man."

Just as he was finishing his passionate denials, the rooster crowed. When he had made his way out of the building, he wept and sobbed bitterly. This time, however, there would be no running away—he couldn't run from himself.

Maybe, like Peter, you've been weeping bitterly over the pain your sin has brought to the life of someone you love. If so, take heart. Even though the crowing rooster reminded Peter of his folly, it was also a cause for faith, because roosters only crow at the first light of a new day. Though Peter couldn't see it then, the brokenness and humility he would experience through his denials of Christ would usher in a new day of power and anointing.

Far from signifying your bitter end, the crowing rooster also symbolizes your fresh new beginning. If you will respond to the conviction that follows your sin, you, too, can walk into a future that is bright and new.

The FATHER DESIRES to expose OUR SiN, not to humiliate us But to BRING it to the Light. The enemy Loves secret sins Because they give him power over us. But once our sin is exposed in the Light of GOD'S Love, its power evaporates Like ice in the midday sun.

Duncan Phillips

Lessons from the Life of Jesus:
THE ROAD TO EMMAUS

Now that same day two of them were going to a village called Emmaus, about seven miles from Jerusalem. They were talking with each other about everything that had happened. As they talked and discussed these things with each other, Jesus himself came up and walked along with them; but they were kept from recognizing him.

When he was at the table with them, he took bread, gave thanks, broke it and began to give it to them. Then their eyes were opened and they recognized him, and he disappeared from their sight. They asked each other, "Were not our hearts burning within us while he talked with us on the road and opened the Scriptures to us?"

LUKE 24:13–16, 30–32

NOVEMBER 26

Cleopas and his friend were tired, frustrated, and discouraged. Although they'd always considered themselves faithful disciples of Jesus, this was too much. He'd been dead for three days. Despite all his hints about coming back, Jesus was nowhere to be found. Despite the fact that the tomb was empty and his body was gone, they still wondered where he was.

As they looked up from the discussion they were having, they noticed that someone was walking along the road with them. "What are you talking about?" the stranger asked.

They couldn't believe it. "Are you just a visitor around here? Don't you know the things that have happened?" they asked in surprise.

"What things?" the man asked. They explained how Jesus of Nazareth was a great prophet who had been killed three days ago. His tomb was empty, and his body couldn't be found, so no one really knew where he was.

When they had finished their tale, the man began to explain the Scriptures that talked about the Christ. *Who is this man who is talking with us?* they began to wonder. *It's almost like we've met him before. Whoever he is, he can sure teach the Scriptures.* When they finally stopped for the night, they convinced the man to stay with them. As they sat at the dinner table, the stranger took the bread, prayed over it, and broke it. At that moment, their eyes were opened, and they knew it was Jesus. But before they could even say a thing, he disappeared. *How could we be so blind?* they wondered. Forgetting their dinner, they immediately returned to Jerusalem to tell the disciples that Jesus was alive.

This may be one of the most humorous stories in all of Scripture. Two of Jesus' faithless disciples were griping and murmuring about the fact that they couldn't find him—when he was right in front of them! As much as we may want to laugh at this story, however, in reality, unbelief is no laughing matter. It has the ability to blind you to the reality of God in your life. No matter how close he is to you, or what he has done for you, unbelief has the power to make it seem as if he has never been there at all.

All of us have had conversations with God similar to that of Cleopas and his friend. "God! Where are you?" we cry. What makes these conversations so ironic, even absurd, is the fact that if we really believed God had left us, we wouldn't be talking to him at all!

Even when you feel you are completely alone, you are actually closer to God than you realize. Ask the Holy Spirit to burn away the fog of unbelief that has kept you from recognizing the reality of God's person and work in your life.

UhBeLief AhD DisoBeDiehCe seem to GO hAhD in hAhD. PART oF the REASoh we sih is Due to unBeLief thAt the FAtheR is ABLe to Do whAt he hAs pROmiseD AhD DowhRight ReBeLLioh AGAihst whAt we khow to Be tRue.

Duncan Phillips

Lessons from the Life of Jesus:
LOCKED UP

On the evening of that first day of the week, when the disciples were together, with the doors locked for fear of the Jews, Jesus came and stood among them and said, "Peace be with you!" After he said this, he showed them his hands and side. The disciples were overjoyed when they saw the Lord.

Again Jesus said, "Peace be with you! As the Father has sent me, I am sending you." And with that he breathed on them and said, "Receive the Holy Spirit. If you forgive anyone his sins, they are forgiven; if you do not forgive them, they are not forgiven."

JOHN 20:19–23

NOVEMBER 27

Even though Jesus was alive, his apostles were still acting as if he were dead. They were hiding behind locked doors in the very place where he had shared his Last Supper with them. They were furtive and fearful, wondering when the Jews would come and kill them. Peter and John had both seen the empty tomb. John had believed, but Peter still wondered. Mary Magdalene even claimed to have had a conversation with him. Where she was concerned, they weren't sure what to believe. After all, she had been possessed by seven demons.

Jesus had a different plan for his fearful followers, and he came to visit them. Locked doors were nothing to the resurrected Son of God. Without a second thought, he simply stepped through the wall and appeared in their midst. The disciples were stunned. "Peace," Jesus said. When the disciples saw the nail prints in his hands and the wound in his side, they were filled with an unearthly joy, for they knew their Master had been raised from the dead. Jesus, however, quickly silenced their celebration. "Peace," he said to them again. "As the Father has sent me, I am sending you." Then he breathed on them and said, "Receive the Holy Spirit." This was like no other breath they had ever felt before—they felt refreshed and somehow ignited with fire at the same time. Where once they had been shackled by fear, now they were mastered by peace.

Initially, this story is one of the saddest in all of Scripture. Even though Jesus had been gloriously raised from the dead, his closest followers were fearful, worried, and exhausted. More tragic still is the fact that many Christians are still living this way two thousand years later. Maybe that's where you are. Perhaps you are living as if his resurrection never took place.

Thankfully, the same Jesus who walked through the wall of the Upper Room is also able to penetrate the walls of unbelief in your life. He's not rebuking you. Instead, he is saying, "Peace! See my hands? See my side? You don't have to be afraid."

Jesus also wants to send you to minister to others. Even as the Father sent him, he is going propel you into the harvest field. He will dramatically transform you by the power of the Holy Spirit. Even as he breathed on his disciples, he's coming to breathe into your life in a fresh way today. Never forget that receiving the Holy Spirit's power is a lifestyle. The apostle Peter was breathed on by Jesus, empowered by the Holy Spirit in Acts 2, and filled by the Holy Spirit again in Acts 4. It can be the same for you. No matter what your prior experience with the Holy Spirit has been, he wants to fill you with fresh power for the fight that you are called to win.

HOLY SPIRIT, BREATHE ON ME. UNFORTUNATELY, SOME PEOPLE HAVE MARGINALIZED THE HOLY SPIRIT SAYING IT'S NOT FOR TODAY. BUT I BELIEVE THAT'S WHERE OUR AUTHORITY LIES.

Duncan Phillips

Lessons from the Life of Jesus:
THE NET DIDN'T BREAK

Simon Peter, Thomas,... Nathanael,... the sons of Zebedee, and two other disciples ... went out and got into the boat, but that night they caught nothing.

Early in the morning, Jesus stood on the shore, but the disciples did not realize that it was Jesus.

He called out to them,... "Throw your net on the right side of the boat and you will find some." When they did, they were unable to haul the net in because of the large number of fish.

Then the disciple whom Jesus loved said to Peter, "It is the Lord!" As soon as Simon Peter heard him say, "It is the Lord," he wrapped his outer garment around him ... and jumped into the water. The other disciples followed in the boat, towing the net full of fish, for they were not far from shore, about a hundred yards.

Simon Peter climbed aboard and dragged the net ashore. It was full of large fish, 153, but even with so many the net was not torn.

JOHN 21:2-8, 11

NOVEMBER 28

When Simon Peter told the other apostles that he was going fishing, he had more than a simple desire to catch fish. Deep inside, he was wondering if he would ever be used to catch men again. Even though Jesus had been raised from the dead, Peter felt that he had lost his calling when he denied Jesus three times.

After fishing all night, they hadn't caught even one fish. Then they heard a voice that was vaguely familiar. "Cast your net on the right side of the boat, and you will find some fish," the man promised. The minute they

obeyed, the net began to be filled with fish. The harvest was so abundant that they could not even bring it into the boat. "It's the Lord!" John cried. Without hesitation, Peter plunged into the water. The other disciples followed behind in the boat, pulling the huge net of fish. Even though there were 153 fish, the net did not break.

What lessons can we learn from this miraculous catch of fish? First, despite Peter's failure, the Lord never gave up on him. Even though Peter had denied him, Jesus still had an amazing calling for his life.

Second, when Jesus first called Peter and Andrew into ministry, he told them to take their boat out into the lake and let their nets down—only then did a miraculous catch result. This time, they only had to move their net to the right side of the boat for the miracle to occur. The longer you follow God, the smaller his adjustments in your life will need to be.

Third, during that first miraculous catch the nets broke (Luke 5). Now, even though the nets were filled, they did not break. God was getting them ready for the catch of their life. God uses his people and the relationships they form as a strong net for his harvest.

God has not given up on you, either. Even if everything in you wants to give up, this is no time to quit. God is telling you to put your net on the other side of your boat and receive the catch of your life!

I see the net as us, the church, tethered and tied together. As a spirit-empowered, word-based church tightly knitted together, we can "catch" the harvest that's all around us.

Duncan Phillips

Lessons from the Life of Jesus:
NEW MAN

Jesus said, "Feed my sheep. I tell you the truth, when you were younger you dressed yourself and went where you wanted; but when you are old you will stretch out your hands, and someone else will dress you and lead you where you do not want to go." Jesus said this to indicate the kind of death by which Peter would glorify God. Then he said to him, "Follow me!"

JOHN 21:17–19

NOVEMBER 29

There on the beach, after a breakfast of fish, Jesus spoke with Peter. "When you were younger, you dressed your-self any way you wanted, and went wherever you wanted to go. When you're older and truly mature, you will willingly stretch out your hands and allow other people to dress you any way they want, and you will be led to places you don't even want to go." After these sobering words, Jesus spoke two more: "Follow me!"

Peter had come to the defining moment of his life—he was now faced with the price he would have to pay to follow Christ. Although Jesus' analogy spoke of the death Peter would one day die, it also signified Peter's need for a new attitude that would bring him into his divine destiny.

First, the Lord told him that when he was mature, he would stretch out his hands. This speaks of being teachable and submissive. The old, obstinate, arrogant, stubborn Simon would not be tolerated anymore. God was requiring Peter to be broken so he could truly follow the Lord.

Second, when Jesus told Peter that he would not be able to dress himself anymore, he was telling him that he would need to be defined by his relationship with Christ alone and not by external things.

Third, the Lord told him that someone else would lead him. Even though he would be the leader of the twelve, he still had to be willing to receive the leadership and direction of other men. Peter's ability to submit to the leadership of others would be critical to the fulfillment of his destiny.

Fourth, he would not only be led; he would be led to places he did not want to go. This new attitude would be significant to his ministry. Later, when the Holy Spirit told him to go and preach at the house of a Roman soldier, Peter obeyed, even though he hated the very thought of preaching to Gentiles. Through his obedience, the house of Cornelius became a place of revival.

Today, if you will become pliable in the hands of God and in the circle of your spiritual family, there is nothing God cannot do through your life. Are you ready to grow up spiritually? If you will simply place your life completely in God's hands, he will use you to lead his people into their destinies.

The LORD has called us to full maturity. As fruit ripens on the tree it has a sweet taste and is good to eat. Imagine if the grape never ripened on the vine. It would be cut down as useless. May the LORD never think of me as useless because of immaturity.

Duncan Phillips

Lessons from the Life of Jesus:
WHAT ABOUT HIM?

Peter turned and saw that the disciple whom Jesus loved was following them. (This was the one who had leaned back against Jesus at the supper and had said, "Lord, who is going to betray you?") When Peter saw him, he asked, "Lord, what about him?"

Jesus answered, "If I want him to remain alive until I return, what is that to you? You must follow me."

JOHN 21:20-22

NOVEMBER 30

Wouldn't you know it? Peter thought. *Right when the Master gives me the good news about the horrible death I'm going to die, who should be skulking behind us, but his special little buddy, John.* After choking down his feelings, Peter said submissively, "What about him?"

What about him? Jesus might have thought. Yes, it was definitely time to deal with Peter's insecurity and jealousy of John. Jesus answered, "If I want him to remain alive until I return, what business is that of yours? Follow me, Peter."

Although Peter remained outwardly quiet, on the inside, he was distressed. *Remain until he comes?* Peter might have wondered. *That just isn't fair! I'm going to be martyred, and he's going to live forever?*

In my own experience, almost every Christian I've ever met has a person like John in their life—someone to whom they tend to compare their life. Typically, these comparisons include murmuring, griping, and wondering why that person is being treated better than they deserve. After all, if that person has fooled everyone, they have probably fooled God. Sadly, beneath all the accusations and comparisons, there is typically an inordinate desire to have what that other person has. Whether it is their significant other, their looks, their position, their blessing, or their brains, it doesn't really matter. Sooner or later, you will have to face the fact that the only person you can ever be is the person who God has made you to be. That is why these types of comparisons are so futile and frustrating. Why should you spend your time growing resentful and even bitter over something you'll never have, or someone you'll never be?

Even more tragic is the fact that the very people who spend all their time comparing themselves to others have very little time left to compare themselves to Jesus, the one Person they should be trying to emulate. It's time to turn your eyes back toward Jesus. He has been waiting for your gaze, because the Scripture says that we are transformed into his likeness as we contemplate him (2 Corinthians 5:18). May you be changed into his image more every day as you apply the promise of this passage to your life.

What is it within us that thinks the grass is always greener on the other side of the fence? We do it without thinking. His car is nicer; she is prettier; their house is bigger. Most often, it's the temporal things we covet. But it's all going to burn anyway. Seek first his kingdom and all these things will be added (Matthew 6:33).

Duncan Phillips

Lessons from the Lives of the Apostles:
WHY ARE YOU LOOKING UP?

 So when they met together, they asked him, "Lord, are you at this time going to restore the kingdom to Israel?"

He said to them: "It is not for you to know the times or dates the Father has set by his own authority. But you will receive power when the Holy Spirit comes on you; and you will be my witnesses in Jerusalem, and in all Judea and Samaria, and to the ends of the earth."

After he said this, he was taken up before their very eyes, and a cloud hid him from their sight.

They were looking intently up into the sky as he was going, when suddenly two men dressed in white stood beside them. "Men of Galilee," they said, "why do you stand here looking into the sky? This same Jesus, who has been taken from you into heaven, will come back in the same way you have seen him go into heaven."

ACTS 1:6–11

DECEMBER 1

Although they had been filled with the Holy Spirit and freshly commissioned by Jesus, some things among the disciples had not changed at all. "Lord," the apostles asked, "are you going to restore the kingdom to Israel now?" Once again, it was hard for them to see beyond their own needs and the immediate needs of their people.

Jesus answered them by saying, "It's not for you to know all the times and dates of what's going to happen. Instead, you will receive power when the Holy Spirit comes upon you, and you will be my witnesses in Jerusalem, Judea, Samaria, and to the ends of the earth."

When Jesus had finished speaking, he was taken up in a cloud before their very eyes. The disciples were awestruck as they contemplated this incredible mode of transport. Long after he was hidden from their eyes, however, they were still peering into the sky, wondering when he would return, what it would be like, and what place humble servants like themselves would have in his kingdom. Finally, as they continued to stare off into the heavens, two angels appeared to them and said, "Why are you standing here, looking into the sky? Jesus will come back the same way you have seen him go."

The same question asked by the angels is applicable to us: "Why do you stand here, looking into the sky?" If it is truly possible to become so "heavenly minded" that you're no "earthly good," that is probably the very state of many modern-day Christians. The heavenly mindedness I am talking about, however, has nothing to do with holiness, commitment, and true spirituality, and everything to do with dates, times, and idle speculations about when Jesus is coming to rescue them from the evils of the culture in which they live. In reality, it is not *what* you believe about the end times, but *how* you believe it.

If you are so busy looking up into the heavens that you have forgotten your mission on the earth, it's time for you to change. God wants to send you into your city with a new passion and fervor. Far from being concerned with escaping the final judgment, your concern should be how to take as many people with you as possible, no matter how or when he comes back!

As wonderful as it is to be excited about heaven, we'll have plenty of time to enjoy it when we get there. Right now, God wants us to concentrate on reaching the earth. As tempting as it is to spend time thinking about the return of Christ, our real job is to get as many people as possible ready for that great day — whenever it comes.

Jeff Frankenstein

LESSONS FROM THE LIVES OF THE APOSTLES:

PENTECOST: MOMENT OR MODEL?

"I am going to send you what my Father has promised; but stay in the city until you have been clothed with power from on high."

LUKE 24:49

They all joined together constantly in prayer.

ACTS 1:14

When the day of Pentecost came, they were all together in one place. Suddenly a sound like the blowing of a violent wind came from heaven and filled the whole house where they were sitting. They saw what seemed to be tongues of fire that separated and came to rest on each of them. All of them were filled with the Holy Spirit and began to speak in other tongues as the Spirit enabled them.

Those who accepted his message were baptized, and about three thousand were added to their number that day.

ACTS 2:1-4, 41

DECEMBER 2

God's Spirit was shaking Jerusalem. The city had never before experienced such an intense manifestation of God's power. With flames of fire resting on their heads, and languages they'd never spoken coming from their mouths, they were empowered with the very Spirit of God. Crowds gathered around them. Thousands were radically saved. The city continued to be shaken for years.

Fortunately, we don't have to just imagine what it must have been like to see a whole city shaken by the power of the Holy Spirit. Although the day of Pentecost was a unique, divine moment, it is also a model for what God can do in our cities and nations today. The same God who shook Jerusalem can also radically shake *your* city when you follow God's plan for revival.

A trained, dedicated cell of disciples was at the core of the Pentecost revival. Their commitment and dedication brought them a divine bond that they would need to withstand the extraordinary pressure that would come.

These disciples were obedient to God's call to return to Jerusalem and wait. As we focus on what God is asking of us, he will give us the power we need to see not only our churches, but also our cities changed for his glory.

The disciples joined together in constant prayer until the power came. God is still calling us today to commit ourselves to the prayer that precedes revival.

Scripture says the disciples were all together, in one place, both literally and in their hearts. Their unique unity was the foundation God would use to build his Church.

It is critical that we understand the importance of God's timing. We can't predict when revivals are coming, but we can follow the principles involved in birthing them, knowing that God will be faithful in his good time. I am convinced that when God finds a core of believers who are willing to pray in unity for their city, he will answer their prayers!

When I think of the Apostles God used to change the world, it fills me with hope and encouragement. They were filled with insecurities, unbelief and pride. But because of their faithfulness they were slowly changed. Despite the problems I've faced, God has been faithful to change me so that I might be used to change the world.

Jeff Frankenstein

Lessons from the Life of Peter:
PETER'S POWER

Then Peter, filled with the Holy Spirit, said to them: "Rulers and elders of the people! If we are being called to account today for an act of kindness shown to a cripple and are asked how he was healed, then know this, you and all the people of Israel: It is by the name of Jesus Christ of Nazareth, whom you crucified but whom God raised from the dead, that this man stands before you healed."

ACTS 4:8–10

Peter and the other apostles replied: "We must obey God rather than men!"

ACTS 5:29

DECEMBER 3

At every critical moment, God was using Peter to define what he was doing and bring salvation to thousands of people. When some in the crowd on the day of Pentecost accused the apostles of being drunk, Peter stood up and quieted them with an exposition on one of Joel's ancient prophecies. After he and John had been arrested for their proclamation of the Gospel, Peter boldly preached the Good News to the whole Sanhedrin. Far from being fearful, he was confident in the face of their withering questions. When the Sanhedrin confronted the apostles another time, Peter led them all in proclaiming that they would obey God rather than men. He who had fled from the Garden in terror and denied Jesus three times out of fear, was now the leader of them all.

How could this hard-headed sailor be transformed into one of God's greatest leaders? First, Peter had been broken. As a person submits to Christ in the midst of their trials and difficulties, those places of hardness

and obstinacy in their souls are shattered. Peter was pretty full of himself when he began his walk with Jesus, but his failures left him a broken man. The broken pieces of Peter's life were reconstructed so that he became the "rock" that the early Church would so desperately need.

Second, Peter's brokenness prepared him to be emptied of himself. In Philippians 4:7 it says that Jesus made himself nothing, or emptied himself. Unlike Jesus, who was sinless, it took a great deal of brokenness for Peter to truly begin the process of emptying himself. Once it began, however, Peter's soul found freedom from the pride, self-will, and stubbornness that had bound him.

Once he was emptied, the process of being filled with the power and might of the Holy Spirit could begin. Through Jesus' work in his life, Peter gained a humble heart. This humility gave him the foundation he needed to contain the incredible outpouring of the Spirit that he would receive. The Peter who took a stand after the day of Pentecost was a man filled and completely transformed by the Holy Spirit.

In spite of your failures, God can bring you through the brokenness you are experiencing. As you respond to him, you will find yourself being emptied of yourself and filled with his power. Never forget, the same God who transformed Peter is able to transform you!

AS MUCH AS ALL OF US WANT TO BE WHOLE PEOPLE, MANY TIMES THE PATHWAY TO WHOLENESS BEGINS WITH BROKENNESS AND PAIN. IN MY OWN LIFE I HAVE FOUND THAT GOD WILL WORK THROUGH MY CIRCUMSTANCES TO BREAK THE PRIDE THAT IS KEEPING ME BACK. HUMILITY PRECEDES EXALTATION.

Jeff Frankenstein

Lessons from the Life of Peter:
THE BEGGAR AT THE GATE

Then Peter said, "Silver or gold I do not have, but what I have I give you. In the name of Jesus Christ of Nazareth, walk." Taking him by the right hand, he helped him up, and instantly the man's feet and ankles became strong.

While the beggar held on to Peter and John, all the people were astonished and came running to them in the place called Solomon's Colonnade. When Peter saw this, he said to them: "Men of Israel, why does this surprise you? Why do you stare at us as if by our own power or godliness we had made this man walk? By faith in the name of Jesus, this man whom you see and know was made strong. It is Jesus' name and the faith that comes through him that has given this complete healing to him, as you can all see."

ACTS 3:6–7, 11–12, 16

DECEMBER 4

Peter and John were simply on their way to pray. As they approached the temple gate, Peter spotted the beggar. He'd seen him countless times, but this time he saw the man through the eyes of God. Peter's heart burst with compassion. "I don't have any money," Peter said, "but the one thing I do have, I give to you. In the name of Jesus Christ of Nazareth, walk." For the first time in his life, the man was walking, leaping, and shouting. The people in the temple were astonished.

There are several important lessons here about how the miraculous power of God operates. First, when Peter called out to the crippled man, he said, "Look at *us*," speaking of himself and John. He realized that

John's faith was just as important as his own for this man's healing to be accomplished. We must never forget that God delights in using a team.

Second, when the beggar had been dramatically healed, Peter asked the crowd a question that revealed the humility of his heart: "Why do you stare at us?" After his previous failures, Peter wanted no glory or attention for himself. When God finds a man or a woman like this, he is delighted to use them as a mighty vessel for his power.

Third, Peter and John told the crowd that the man had not been healed through their power. They realized that the crippled man's healing had nothing to do with their own ability—they were simply the vessels through which God's power could be displayed.

The same God—who brought Peter out of the darkness of his failures and into the fullness of God's purpose—desires to bring you into your destiny, too. If you will allow God to work in your heart, you can become a vessel of his power in our hurting, broken world.

Like you, as much as I want to be holy, it has always been important for me to remember that the foundation of everything I have from God is the gift of righteousness I received when I got saved. No matter how much the devil tries to accuse me and condemn me, I can stand before God in confidence because of the precious blood of his Son. I have learned that this is one of the most important secrets of walking in the power of God.

Jeff Frankenstein

Lessons from the Life of Peter:
PETER'S PICNIC

Peter went up on the roof to pray. He became hungry and wanted something to eat, and while the meal was being prepared, he fell into a trance. He saw heaven opened and something like a large sheet being let down to earth by its four corners. It contained all kinds of four-footed animals, as well as reptiles of the earth and birds of the air. Then a voice told him, "Get up, Peter. Kill and eat."

"Surely not, Lord!" Peter replied. "I have never eaten anything impure or unclean."

The voice spoke to him a second time, "Do not call anything impure that God has made clean."

This happened three times, and immediately the sheet was taken back to heaven.

While Peter was wondering about the meaning of the vision, the men sent by Cornelius found out where Simon's house was and stopped at the gate.

While Peter was still thinking about the vision, the Spirit said to him, "Simon, three men are looking for you. So get up and go downstairs. Do not hesitate to go with them, for I have sent them."

ACTS 10:9–17, 19–20

Although he had heard Jesus' mandate for them to take the Gospel outside of the Jewish world, Peter was struggling to overcome the traditions of his upbringing that told him to steer clear of Gentiles. God was patient with Peter, though. He was sending him some clear signs to help him

DECEMBER 5 **get past these obstacles.**

One day, when he was supposed to be praying, he was so hungry that he kept thinking about lunch. As his mind drifted, he fell into a trance. He saw heaven open, and a gigantic sheet being lowered down to the earth by its four corners. The sheet contained all kinds of animals that Jewish law called unclean. As he looked on, God's voice spoke to him: "Get up, Peter. Kill, and eat."

Peter resisted this command, but the vision repeated itself three more times.

Then a group of men appeared at his door, sent by a God-fearing Roman centurion named Cornelius. The Holy Spirit told Peter he was to go with them. Peter obeyed, and Cornelius's whole family was radically transformed when Peter explained the Gospel to them. And with this one Roman family the evangelization of the Gentile world began.

Many of us, like Peter, are in danger of missing out on being used by God because we consider the people he is sending us to be so "unclean" that we shouldn't even bother reaching out to them. Despite Peter's powerful anointing, he still had trouble seeing beyond the traditions of his own culture.

But there was no mistaking God's word. "Get up, Peter. Kill and eat," the Lord had commanded. "Stop calling anything impure that I have made clean." With these words echoing in his ears, Peter chose to obey. And if you will be faithful to reach out to the people God asks you to, he will be faithful to cause wonderful changes in their lives through your obedience.

Even as Peter had ethnic and cultural barriers that kept him from reaching out to the Gentiles, all of us have barriers in our own lives. Whether it is national pride, religious perspectives, or the values we are raised with, all of us will need God's adjustment so we can see all people through his eyes.

Jeff Frankenstein

Lessons from the Life of Peter:
PETER'S PERIL

The night before Herod was to bring [Peter] to trial, Peter was sleeping between two soldiers, bound with two chains, and sentries stood guard at the entrance. Suddenly an angel of the Lord appeared and a light shone in the cell. He struck Peter on the side and woke him up. "Quick, get up!" he said, and the chains fell off Peter's wrists.

Then the angel said to him, "Put on your clothes and sandals." And Peter did so. "Wrap your cloak around you and follow me," the angel told him. Peter followed him out of the prison, but he had no idea that what the angel was doing was really happening; he thought he was seeing a vision. They passed the first and second guards and came to the iron gate leading to the city. It opened … and they went through it. When they had walked the length of one street, suddenly the angel left him.

Then Peter … said, "Now I know without a doubt that the Lord sent his angel and rescued me from Herod's clutches and from everything the Jewish people were anticipating."

ACTS 12:6-11

DECEMBER 6

James, the brother of John, had become the first of the apostles to be martyred. When Herod saw that James's murder had pleased many of the Jews, he decided to have Peter killed, as well. With Peter, however, he decided to take special care. He ordered four squads of soldiers to guard Peter. He was chained between two soldiers, bound with two chains, and sentries were posted at the door of his cell.

All the while, the Church was praying for Peter's deliverance. The night before his trial, an angel woke the soundly sleeping Peter. "Quick, get up," the angel said. As Peter rubbed his eyes sleepily, the chains miraculously fell off his wrists. He thought he was having a vision. When they passed the guards and the locked gate swung open, Peter realized he was free. God's angel had rescued him from Herod's evil grasp.

What lessons can we learn from this remarkable story of deliverance? First, the prayers of the Church were a decisive factor in Peter's release. We should never underestimate the power held in prayer.

Second, when the angel came to Peter, he was sleeping soundly—the peaceful sleep of faith. Peter was confident in the God who had rescued him before. In my own life, the divine deliverances and miracles I have experienced in the past give me the faith I need to calmly face the future.

Third, despite all of Herod's extra guards and chains, the Lord rescued Peter easily. No matter how tightly the enemy has bound you, your God is more than able to deliver you.

Fourth, Peter didn't realize that he was really free until his deliverance was complete. Sometimes when God is delivering us, it may not seem real. When your deliverance is complete, however, it won't just seem like a dream. It will be a dream come true.

When I think about Peter's miraculous deliverance, I am reminded again of the power of the God I serve. This story gives me the confidence I need to face the devil's attacks because I know that God can always deliver me.

Jeff Frankenstein

Lessons from the Life of Philip:
SAMARIA'S REVIVAL

Those who had been scattered preached the word wherever they went. Philip went down to a city in Samaria and proclaimed the Christ there. When the crowds heard Philip and saw the miraculous signs he did, they all paid close attention to what he said.

Now for some time a man named Simon had practiced sorcery in the city and amazed all the people of Samaria.... But when they believed Philip as he preached the good news of the kingdom of God and the name of Jesus Christ, they were baptized, both men and women. Simon himself believed and was baptized.

When the apostles in Jerusalem heard that Samaria had accepted the word of God, they sent Peter and John to them.... Peter and John placed their hands on them, and they received the Holy Spirit.

ACTS 8:4–6, 9, 12–14, 17

DECEMBER 7

After his dear friend, Stephen, had been brutally murdered, Philip had been forced, along with thousands of other Christians, to flee Jerusalem. Yet, even in the midst of his turmoil and pain, he knew that the Church was not merely being scattered; it was being sown—they were being pushed out of Jerusalem and Judea so they could reach Samaria, and, ultimately, the uttermost parts of the world.

When Philip entered Samaria and began to preach, the Lord confirmed his words with miraculous healings. So many people were healed that the whole city was filled with joy. Even Simon, a powerful sorcerer, began to follow Philip. With all of Samaria blazing with revival, the apostles sent Peter and John to help Philip. Although multitudes of Samaritans had been converted and baptized in water, none had yet received the power of the Holy Spirit. Through the ministry of Peter and John, the Spirit came upon them as well.

Despite the horror of the Church's persecution, Philip had a deep faith that assured him that God himself was sending his people out of Jerusalem. Acts 8:4 says, "Those who had been scattered preached the word wherever they went." The word *scattered* is, at its root, an agricultural term. It means to plant many seeds by throwing them onto fertile ground. Like Philip, there may be times when God works through some painful time in your life to spread the seeds of the Gospel.

Philip's faith also helped him minister to Samaritans—the social outcasts of his day. Jesus' mission took priority over his own cultural sensitivities. And when he began to preach the Word, the Lord confirmed his message with multiple miraculous healings. If you will simply follow God, like Philip, there is no telling how he may use you.

Philip did awesome work for God, but he was also part of a larger team. When the apostles heard that revival had broken out in Samaria, they sent Peter and John to help him—and Philip welcomed their help. Never forget that no matter who you are, you will always be more effective when you work with a team.

Like Philip, allow the humble tasks of service you perform in your local church to develop your faith. Long before I was preaching, I was teaching four- and five-year-olds, setting up chairs, and cutting the grass. As you are faithful to give yourself to ordinary things, God may call you to do extraordinary things.

Why GOD WAS ABLE to use Philip so mightily? Although he had MANY GOOD tRAits, I believe it WAS his humility that BROUGht him into the fullness of WhAt GOD hAD for him.

Jeff Frankenstein

Lessons from the Life of Philip:

DIVINE APPOINTMENT

Now an angel of the Lord said to Philip, "Go south to the road—the desert road—that goes down from Jerusalem to Gaza." So he started out, and on his way he met an Ethiopian eunuch ... on his way home ... in his chariot reading the book of Isaiah the prophet. The Spirit told Philip, "Go to that chariot and stay near it."

Then Philip ran up to the chariot and heard the man reading Isaiah the prophet. "Do you understand what you are reading?" Philip asked.

"How can I," he said, "unless someone explains it to me?" So he invited Philip to come up and sit with him.

As they traveled along the road, they came to some water and the eunuch said, "Look, here is water. Why shouldn't I be baptized?" ... Philip and the eunuch went down into the water and Philip baptized him. When they came up out of the water, the Spirit of the Lord suddenly took Philip away, and the eunuch did not see him again, but went on his way rejoicing.

ACTS 8:26–31, 36–39

DECEMBER 8

Philip was astonished by the angel's message. *Go south to the road, the desert road?* Although the angel's instructions made absolutely no sense, Philip obeyed. As he walked down the road, an important official from Ethiopia passed in his chariot.

The Holy Spirit immediately spoke to Philip: "Go to that chariot, and stay near it."

Philip sprinted after the rapidly departing chariot. When he finally caught up with it, he called, "Do you understand what you are reading?"

The man was reading from the book of Isaiah and he asked Philip up into his chariot to explain the passage to him. The official joyfully accepted the Gospel and Philip baptized him in a nearby body of water. The Ethiopian returned home to lay the spiritual foundations for what would become an incredible revival in his nation.

Maybe you, like Philip, find yourself walking on a road into the desert. If this is the case, don't despair. Even if you have no idea where you are going, God is still at work in your life. Perhaps, just around the bend, there is a divine appointment waiting for you! Some of the paths we are called to have nothing to do with *where* we're going, and everything to do with *who* we're going to meet along the way. If you will maintain a good attitude and follow the Holy Spirit's leading, you, like Philip, may end up being uniquely used by God.

Some Christians, however, refuse to embrace this new path. They don't want to leave the place they're currently enjoying, or they fear stepping into an uncertain future. But when you refuse to obey God, you will end up regretting it. When you stay in a place after your purpose there has already been accomplished, you will grow stagnant and miserable.

Other people will finally obey God and go. Sadly, because of their hesitation, they may have already lost their moment of divine opportunity. Although God can still use them in the future, that opportunity will have already come and gone.

No matter how confused you may be today, do not be slow to obey! Who knows who is waiting for you around the next bend?

WHAT AN AMAZING STORY. PHILLIP WAS WILLING TO LEAVE A PLACE OF HIGH VISIBILITY AND LARGE CROWDS TO MINISTER TO ONE PERSON ON A DESERT ROAD. AFTER PONDERING THIS DEVOTIONAL, I WAS LEFT WITH A NEW DESIRE TO WALK IN THE SIMPLE OBEDIENCE THAT CHARACTERIZED PHILIP'S LIFE.

Jeff Frankenstein

LESSONS FROM THE LIFE OF BARNABAS:

BUILDING BLOCK OF THE NEW TESTAMENT CHURCH

When [Barnabas] arrived [in Antioch] and saw the evidence of the grace of God, he was glad and encouraged them all to remain true to the Lord with all their hearts. He was a good man, full of the Holy Spirit and faith, and a great number of people were brought to the Lord. Then Barnabas went to Tarsus to look for Saul, and when he found him, he brought him to Antioch. So for a whole year Barnabas and Saul met with the church and taught great numbers of people. The disciples were called Christians first at Antioch.

ACTS 11:23–26

DECEMBER 9

His name was Joseph, and he had been raised in a Levite family on the island of Cyprus. As revival swept through Jerusalem, he sold a field and gave the money to the disciples. As they came to know him, the disciples realized he had a tremendous gift of prophecy, and they renamed him Barnabas, which meant "son of encouragement," or "son of prophecy." This committed man was at the very heart of what God was doing in Jerusalem. When no one else in the church trusted Saul (who later became the apostle Paul), Barnabas sponsored him.

When revival broke out in Antioch, the apostles sent Barnabas there, and he went without hesitation. Through his leadership, multitudes of people were added to the Antioch church. When he needed a new staff member, he journeyed to Tarsus and searched for Paul to add him to his team. Later, after he and Paul were sent out together from Antioch, the

Holy Spirit made it clear that Paul, not Barnabas, should be the leader. Instead of resisting this direction, Barnabas readily submitted to the Holy Spirit's leading. Anointed, humble, and always encouraging, Barnabas was the ultimate team player.

There are several lessons we can learn from the life of this humble servant of God. First, unlike many Christians who are convinced they know exactly what God has called them to do, Barnabas allowed himself to be defined by the other apostles: they named him Barnabas because he had the gift of prophecy. In my own life, I have discovered that no matter what I think God has called me to do, he will always use other people to confirm it. In other words, if I'm the only one who thinks I am called to be an apostle, I am probably not one.

Second, Barnabas had the willingness to reach out to people who were much less than perfect. Whether it was Saul, the church's worst persecutor, or young John Mark, who abandoned his ministry duties, Barnabas never gave up on people. Through Barnabas's encouragement, Saul became Paul, and John Mark was given a second chance.

Barnabas had the unique ability to change the spiritual atmosphere around him, because he had the gift of encouragement. Whenever people were around Barnabas, their spirits were lifted up, and their faith was strengthened.

God wants to give you the same spirit Barnabas had. Whether it is allowing other Christians to help you find your calling, or being willing to be sent out into the harvest field, the qualities Barnabas demonstrated are essential for your life, as well.

In Christian music, I have met countless people who seem to think that only God can lead them. Unlike Barnabas, who sought to be mentored, these people rarely feel any need for the counsel and direction of other Christians. Tragically, in many cases, the cost they pay is more than they ever bargained for.

Jeff Frankenstein

Lessons from the Life of Barnabas:
BARNABAS AND JOHN MARK

Paul said to Barnabas, "Let us go back and visit the brothers in all the towns where we preached the word of the Lord and see how they are doing." Barnabas wanted to take John, also called Mark, with them, but Paul did not think it wise to take him, because he had deserted them in Pamphylia and had not continued with them in the work. They had such a sharp disagreement that they parted company. Barnabas took Mark and sailed for Cyprus, but Paul chose Silas and left, commended by the brothers to the grace of the Lord.

ACTS 15:36–40

Only Luke is with me. Get Mark and bring him with you, because he is helpful to me in my ministry.

2 TIMOTHY 4:11

DECEMBER 10

Despite Paul's tendency to be critical and insensitive, Barnabas had always been able to get along with him. This time, however, it was different. Paul was refusing to let Barnabas's nephew, John, accompany them on their next ministry trip. Although the young man had abandoned them on the island of Cyprus, Barnabas still felt that he deserved another chance. Finally, when the argument could not be resolved, Paul and Barnabas decided to go their separate ways. Paul found another prophet named Silas and continued his missionary journeys. Barnabas took young John back to Cyprus. He realized that unless the young man confronted his failures, he would never be changed. Despite the prominence of John's mother in the Jerusalem church, Barnabas realized that John had never really been discipled. In the years

to come, under the gentle hand of Barnabas, young John would become Mark, and he would write the book of the New Testament that bears his name. Peter would call him his son, and even Paul would ask for his help again.

The story of young John becoming Mark may be one of the most beautiful examples of discipleship in all of Scripture. Many scholars believe that when Mark was a young boy, he had been with Jesus and his disciples in the Garden of Gethsemane. He might have been the young man referred to in Mark 14:51, who, when one of the guards snatched the clothes from his fleeing form, ran out of the Garden naked. Sadly, these patterns of fear stayed with John Mark.

You can be raised in a wonderful church and have Christian parents who teach you well, but you still need discipleship. Despite John Mark's great destiny, and the fact that he was a participant in some of the greatest events of the early Church, he was never fully transformed until someone mentored him. The greatest need of our generation is not more churches, ministries, or services; it is discipleship. The mandate of Jesus has not changed. We have been called to go into every ethnic group, make converts, and train them to follow Christ. Without this training, they may still go to heaven, but they will never have the skills or the will to bring heaven to this earth.

When I think about the fact that Paul and Barnabas argued so sharply that their friendship was hurt, it makes me want to guard the relationships God has given me all the more.
Jeff Frankenstein

Lessons from the Life of Paul:
SAUL'S CONVERSION

Saul was still breathing out murderous threats against the Lord's disciples. He went to the high priest and asked him for letters to the synagogues in Damascus, so that if he found any there who belonged to the Way, whether men or women, he might take them as prisoners to Jerusalem. As he neared Damascus on his journey, suddenly a light from heaven flashed around him. He fell to the ground and heard a voice say to him, "Saul, Saul, why do you persecute me?"

"Who are you, Lord?" Saul asked.

"I am Jesus, whom you are persecuting," he replied. "Now get up and go into the city, and you will be told what you must do."

The men traveling with Saul stood there speechless; they heard the sound but did not see anyone. Saul got up from the ground, but when he opened his eyes he could see nothing. So they led him by the hand into Damascus. For three days he was blind, and did not eat or drink anything.

ACTS 9:1–9

DECEMBER 11

Saul was on his way to persecute the church in Damascus, filled with a burning hatred toward Christians. But there was a small crack in the hardened religious armor guarding Saul's soul. As much as he had hated Stephen's faith, he could not help but respect the way the young martyr had died. He still couldn't forget the expression on Stephen's face when he had looked up to heaven, nor would he ever forget Stephen's final words: "Lord, do not hold this sin against them." In fact, whenever he recalled these words, Saul shuddered on the inside.

Yet, Saul thought, this was not the time to be thinking about Stephen. As he shook off his feelings of remorse, a blinding light out of heaven flashed around him. Jesus himself appeared and everything changed in that instant. When Saul got up from the ground he was totally blind, and totally different. After his men led him into Damascus, Saul sat for three days in the darkness until a man named Ananias came and restored his sight—he had been blind both physically and spiritually, but now he could truly see.

Believe it or not, you probably have a "Saul" or two in your life today. They may show no outward signs of being interested in the Gospel. In fact, they may even be antagonistic to the very mention of Christ. But in each one there is a growing crack in his or her spiritual armor—a soft spot that is ready to be touched by Jesus' love.

We need to be sensitive to the Holy Spirit's leading so we don't miss the "Sauls" that God has placed in our lives. Ask God today to open your eyes and allow you to see the people around you the way he sees them. Perhaps when he has answered your prayer, you will be amazed to see a "Saul" who needs your touch in order to be released from his or her spiritual blindness. In your obedience, you will play a part in God's design for a "Paul" to be birthed into his kingdom.

I have learned from experience that it is hard to recognize the "Sauls" that God has placed in my life. Whether it's their demeanor, reputation or attitude, many times it's easy to miss the fact that the Holy Spirit is working in a person's life. The story of Saul's conversion brings home the fact that I, too, could be dismissing the very people that God wants to touch.

Jeff Frankenstein

Lessons from the Life of Paul:
ANANIAS'S DECISION

In Damascus there was a disciple named Ananias. The Lord called to him in a vision, "Ananias!"

"Yes, Lord," he answered.

The Lord told him, "Go to the house of Judas on Straight Street and ask for a man from Tarsus named Saul, for he is praying. In a vision he has seen a man named Ananias come and place his hands on him to restore his sight."

"Lord," Ananias answered, "I have heard many reports about this man and all the harm he has done to your saints in Jerusalem. And he has come here with authority from the chief priests to arrest all who call on your name."

But the Lord said to Ananias, "Go! This man is my chosen instrument to carry my name before the Gentiles and their kings and before the people of Israel. I will show him how much he must suffer for my name."

Then Ananias went to the house and entered it. Placing his hands on Saul, he said, "Brother Saul, the Lord — Jesus, who appeared to you on the road as you were coming here — has sent me so that you may see again and be filled with the Holy Spirit."

ACTS 9:10-17

DECEMBER 12

Ananias was wrestling with the Lord. God had told him to go to the house of Judas and to ask for a man from Tarsus named Saul. That is where the problem began. Everyone knew Saul was a murderous persecutor of the Church. "Lord," Ananias prayed anxiously, "I've heard many reports about Saul. He's coming to arrest us and persecute us."

"Go," the Lord said. "He is my chosen instrument to the Gentile world, as well as the people of Israel." And so, Ananias obeyed and left for the house of Judas. Through his obedience, Saul became Paul, and all of history was changed.

Even as Paul had to wait three days in the darkness of his blindness while God dealt with Ananias, so there are also people waiting on you. God's Spirit is drawing people to Jesus, but these people need someone who can help them understand this call from God in their hearts. That's where you and I come in. We have to look beyond their reputations and history so that they don't have to sit in darkness any longer. What will it take for you to become the one who can be used to transform the life of another?

Like Ananias, you must be a disciple. You need to be following Jesus and seeking to be more like him. If you are not a disciple yourself, you will never be able to make one.

Ananias was also able to hear the voice of God. Unless you are sensitive to the Holy Spirit and his voice, you may well miss the opportunities he has for you. As you listen to the Lord, you will receive the instructions you need to change your world.

Finally, you must choose faith over fear. Evangelism can be a very scary thing. But if you allow your faith to grow and God's love to flow within your heart, you will be able to overcome your fears and help to make the toughest "Sauls" into the greatest leaders in the world today.

Like Ananias, many times our life comes down to a choice between fear and faith. Because of his faith, he was able to approach the very man that the rest of the church was hiding from. His simple faith and obedience resulted in the transformation of the Apostle Paul — one of the church's greatest leaders.

Jeff Frankenstein

Lessons from the Life of Paul:
SAUL'S DISCIPLESHIP

Placing his hands on Saul, [Ananias] said, "Brother Saul, the Lord—Jesus, who appeared to you on the road as you were coming here—has sent me so that you may see again and be filled with the Holy Spirit." Immediately, something like scales fell from Saul's eyes, and he could see again.

[Saul] began to preach in the synagogues that Jesus is the Son of God. All those who heard him were astonished and asked, "Isn't he the man who raised havoc in Jerusalem among those who call on this name?" ... Yet Saul grew more and more powerful and baffled the Jews living in Damascus by proving that Jesus is the Christ.

After many days had gone by, the Jews conspired to kill him, but Saul learned of their plan. Day and night they kept close watch on the city gates in order to kill him. But his followers took him by night and lowered him in a basket through an opening in the wall.

ACTS 9:17-18, 20-25

DECEMBER 13

When Ananias placed his hands on Saul, Saul's sight was fully restored. Fortunately, he had lost more than the scales that had been on his eyes; he'd lost the scales that had been on his heart. In the days to come, under the mentorship of Ananias, Saul began to preach the Gospel in Damascus. His preaching was so powerful that the Jews could not refute his arguments. In anger, they conspired to kill him. When the church in Damascus heard of this plan, they lowered Saul over the city's wall in a basket, and he escaped.

How could this new convert, only days old in the Lord, preach the Gospel with such power and precision? Saul's source of power was found in the dramatic nature of his conversion and the discipleship he had received through Ananias. To make disciples who can be used of God from the very moment they are saved, it is important for us to understand what Ananias did.

First, after hearing what the Lord had to say about Saul's future, Ananias revealed this destiny to him. When a young believer is given even a small glimpse into his or her destiny, they will be more motivated to embrace the disciplines of the faith.

Second, Ananias introduced Saul to the power of the Holy Spirit. The role of the Spirit in the believer's life is critical to the process of discipleship. New Christians need to be taught how to respond to his conviction and walk in his power, so that they can reach the fulfillment of their destinies.

Third, Saul received individual attention from Ananias. Although small groups can play a role in the discipleship process, every Christian needs individual attention and mentoring. One-on-one interaction provides the atmosphere they need to truly become transparent, and to ask the questions they might be embarrassed to ask in a group setting.

When we encourage young believers with their divine destiny, and introduce them to the realities of God's Word and the power of his Spirit, they will in turn help change their schools, neighborhoods, and cities, just like Saul.

It was interesting to me that God told Ananias to tell Paul about his calling. I think God did this because he realized that Paul would not have had the motivation to endure the trials and hardships that were to come unless he had seen what God had called him to do. Once you can see your destiny, your sufferings and trials will have new meaning.

Jeff Frankenstein

Lessons from the Life of Paul:

WE ARE ONLY MEN

In Lystra there sat a man crippled in his feet, who was lame from birth and had never walked. He listened to Paul as he was speaking. Paul looked directly at him, saw that he had faith to be healed and called out, "Stand up on your feet!" At that, the man jumped up and began to walk.

When the crowd saw what Paul had done, they shouted … "The gods have come down to us in human form!" The priest of Zeus, whose temple was just outside the city, brought bulls and wreaths to the city gates because he and the crowd wanted to offer sacrifices to them.

But when the apostles Barnabas and Paul heard of this, they tore their clothes and rushed out into the crowd, shouting: "Men, why are you doing this? We too are only men, human like you. We are bringing you good news, telling you to turn from these worthless things to the living God, who made heaven and earth and sea and everything in them." Even with these words, they had difficulty keeping the crowd from sacrificing to them.

ACTS 14:8–11, 13–15, 18

As Paul scanned the crowd in Lystra, he saw a man with faith in his heart, and he knew that, although the man had been lame from birth, it was time for him to be healed. "Stand up on your feet," Paul cried out. Without hesitation, the man jumped up and began to walk.

When the crowd saw this miracle, they responded by heading to the temple to get the priest so they could make sacrifices

DECEMBER 14

to them. Paul and Barnabas, however, would have nothing to do with the crowd's attempts to worship them. They tore their clothes and rushed into the crowd, shouting, "Why are you doing this? We are only men!"

Sooner or later, like Paul and Barnabas, someone is going to try to give you the level of honor due only to God himself. How you handle this test may well determine your future success in the kingdom of God. Paul and Barnabas were not flattered by the crowd's acclaim. Instead, they tore their clothes as a sign of grief, and rushed into the crowd, telling the people they were only human. How will you respond when people attempt to give you glory that belongs only to God? If you handle these moments correctly, God will continue to bless you with the anointing you need to walk out your purpose in his Kingdom.

God has called you to preserve his honor in a culture that celebrates human achievement. May God give you the grace to serve him among your generation!

It shouldn't be any surprise that the people of Lystra found it far easier to worship humans as if they were gods instead of worshiping God himself. Sadly, I have seen this tendency in the lives of people over and over again. No matter what they try to say, it is clear that many of them are more enamored with God's servants than they are with God himself.

Jeff Frankenstein

Lessons from the Life of Paul:
THE DISPUTE

Some time later Paul said to Barnabas, "Let us go back and visit the brothers in all the towns where we preached the word of the Lord and see how they are doing." Barnabas wanted to take John, also called Mark, with them, but Paul did not think it wise to take him, because he had deserted them in Pamphylia and had not continued with them in the work. They had such a sharp disagreement that they parted company. Barnabas took Mark and sailed for Cyprus.

ACTS 15:36–39

DECEMBER 15

They'd been friends for years. In fact, Paul was more indebted spiritually to Barnabas than to any other man. Although Ananias had initially discipled the apostle, Barnabas had been his chief mentor and constant friend. When no one in the Jerusalem church would trust Paul, Barnabas had been willing to sponsor him, at the risk of his own reputation. Later, after Paul was in Tarsus for a number of years, Barnabas had traveled there in order to bring him back to Antioch. Even when the leadership shifted from Barnabas to Paul, Barnabas still loved him and supported him. This was not always an easy matter, for, unlike Barnabas, who was known for kindness and encouragement, Paul was quick to speak and, at times, hot-tempered.

No matter how Barnabas had pled with Paul to allow his nephew John to be allowed to rejoin their ministry team, Paul had refused. Finally, Barnabas had had enough. By the time the argument had ended, their friendship was severed, and their days of ministry together were over.

How could these two incredible men of God allow their friendship and ministry partnership to be destroyed like this? First, Paul and Barn-

abas were not simply friends. Their partnership was at the heart of the most effective ministry team in all of Christianity. In my own experience, I have discovered that the more strategic your friendship becomes to the advancement of God's kingdom, the more danger it is in. No matter how long you have been friends, or how many good times you have had, if you do not vigilantly guard your relationship, the enemy will find a way to destroy.

Second, there may have already been tension between Paul and Barnabas. Perhaps Barnabas was secretly frustrated with the fact that he was no longer the team leader. Even if he was handling it well, Paul's style and manner of dealing with people was radically different from his own. If you do not deal with the tensions that will arise in any relationship, sooner or later, they will blow it apart.

Third, a family member was involved in their relational conflict. This is one of the enemy's favorite ways to destroy a strategic friendship—to use family tensions to ruin a relationship.

Although there is no evidence that Paul and Barnabas ever worked on the same ministry team again, there are a number of comments in Paul's prison epistles that would lead us to believe that there was at least some measure of healing in their relationship. This can also be the case in your life. No matter how far you have grown apart from the friend you once loved, God is able to bring healing if you open your heart to both him and your friend.

Although I enjoy all my friendships, those that also involve kingdom partnerships are especially enjoyable. They must, however, also be more carefully guarded. When one of your relationships becomes vital to the advancement of God's kingdom, you can be sure that it will be tested.

Jeff Frankenstein

Lessons from the Life of Paul:

TIMOTHY'S CIRCUMCISION

He came to Derbe and then to Lystra, where a disciple named Timothy lived, whose mother was a Jewess and a believer, but whose father was a Greek. The brothers at Lystra and Iconium spoke well of him. Paul wanted to take him along on the journey, so he circumcised him because of the Jews who lived in that area, for they all knew that his father was a Greek.

ACTS 16:1–3

DECEMBER 16

Although Timothy's father was not a believer, both his mother and his grandmother were strong Christians. In fact, their family was considered one of the pillars of the Christian community in Derbe. When Paul met Timothy, he knew immediately that the young man had an incredible destiny, and so he asked Timothy to join him and Silas on their missionary journeys. Timothy was ecstatic at the thought of traveling with the legendary apostle Paul and the mighty prophet Silas. After all, what young Christian man wouldn't want to be a part of this great ministry team? His enthusiasm, however, was soon to be sorely tested. As they made preparations to leave, Paul informed Timothy that he could not accompany them unless he was willing to be circumcised. Timothy almost turned pale at the thought. It was one thing for a Jewish baby to be circumcised, but he was a grown man. Yet if that was the painful price he had to pay for his destiny, it would be worth it.

Sooner or later, all Christian young people, like Timothy, will have to pay a price for their destinies. Although it may not be circumcision, it could be something equally painful. Whether it is through the loss of a cherished significant other, or the alteration of their well-laid plans for their future, there is usually a period of intense dealings right before they proceed into their destiny.

Many times, these dealings include what the Bible calls "spiritual circumcision," the cutting away of the old nature and attitudes from the human soul. You can be sure that no matter what God has called you to do, there will be a time of intense "cutting" before you are prepared. He will cut into every attitude that resists his will for your life. No matter how committed and submitted to his will you may be, whole new levels of dealing await you as you journey on into your destiny.

At times, these dealings will take place in some of the most private and sensitive areas of your life. You may experience this intense dealing in the midst of your most cherished relationships. Or you may find God dealing with the strongholds of immorality and fantasies deep within your heart. Whatever the case, if you run from the sharp two-edged sword of God's dealing, you will also be running from his will for your life. May God give you the grace to pay the price as you stand on the threshold of your destiny.

As much as we all love being used by God, the preparation is not always easy. Although God won't take a knife to us, he will cut us with sword of his Spirit. In my own life, God has cut away more things than I care to enumerate.

Jeff Frankenstein

Lessons from the Life of Paul:
PAUL'S CONFUSION

Paul and his companions traveled throughout the region of Phrygia and Galatia, having been kept by the Holy Spirit from preaching the word in the province of Asia. When they came to the border of Mysia, they tried to enter Bithynia, but the Spirit of Jesus would not allow them to. So they passed by Mysia and went down to Troas. During the night Paul had a vision of a man of Macedonia standing and begging him, "Come over to Macedonia and help us." After Paul had seen the vision, we got ready at once to leave for Macedonia, concluding that God had called us to preach the gospel to them.

ACTS 16:6-10

DECEMBER 17

By the time Paul reached Troas, he was thoroughly confused. No matter where he tried to go, the Holy Spirit stopped him. When he went to bed that night, sleep was almost impossible. Finally, he drifted off, and in the middle of the night, God revealed his plan to Paul through an extraordinary vision. In the vision, a man from Macedonia began to plead with Paul: "Come over to Macedonia and help us!" After seeing the vision, Paul knew he and his team had been called to preach the Gospel in Macedonia.

If you have ever been confused about God's will for you, this account can bring great comfort. After all, if the anointed apostle Paul could become confused about God's direction in his life, you and I shouldn't feel so bad! Fortunately, there is more than just encouragement in this story—there is guidance.

First, the province of Asia would eventually become the most fruitful field in Paul's whole ministry, but the Holy Spirit would not allow Paul to evangelize there yet. It was a matter of God's timing. Perhaps Paul was not yet ready for the battles he would face in Asia, so the Holy Spirit made Paul wait until the time was right.

God knows the right time for you to take the next step in your destiny. It can be hard to wait, but if you attempt to jump into an area of service prematurely, you will have neither the grace nor the strength for the battles you will face.

Second, Paul was forbidden to go into Bithynia. Unlike the province of Asia, Paul was not called to go to Bithynia at all. Even worse than trying to walk into a phase of your destiny prematurely is trying to walk into a destiny that is not yours. You will never find true satisfaction outside of being the person God has called you to be.

Third, when Paul's anxiety had calmed and he fell asleep, God spoke to him. Sometimes you just need to rest and wait for God to show you the next step. In his dreams, God called Paul to Macedonia, not only because the Macedonians were ripe for evangelism, but also because they would later provide Paul with the resources he would need to penetrate Asia. Every phase in your destiny is preparing you for the next phase.

No matter how confused you may be in your own journey, God is at work to bring you into his will. As you come to a place of rest, God will not fail to speak to you.

AS MUCH AS PAUL WANTED TO GO INTO ASIA, IT WASN'T TIME. LIKE PAUL, I KNOW EXACTLY HOW IT FEELS TO HAVE A TIMING PROBLEM. OVER AND OVER AGAIN, GOD HAS TAUGHT ME THAT NO MATTER HOW BADLY I WANT SOMETHING, HIS TIMING IS ALWAYS PERFECT.

Jeff Frankenstein

LYDIA'S CONVERSION

From Troas we put out to sea and sailed straight for Samo-thrace, and the next day on to Neapolis. From there we traveled to Philippi, a Roman colony and the leading city of that district of Macedonia. And we stayed there several days.

On the Sabbath we went outside the city gate to the river, where we expected to find a place of prayer. We sat down and began to speak to the women who had gathered there. One of those listening was a woman named Lydia, a dealer in purple cloth from the city of Thyatira, who was a worshiper of God. The Lord opened her heart to respond to Paul's message. When she and the members of her household were baptized, she invited us to her home. "If you consider me a believer in the Lord," she said, "come and stay at my house." And she persuaded us.

ACTS 16:11–15

DECEMBER 18

Lydia was one of the most prominent business people in Philippi—and she was hungry for the Lord. Although she had sought God through the Jewish faith, she still hadn't satisfied the deepest longings of her heart. One day when she was praying with a group of women by the river, she was approached by a stranger. An excellent judge of character, Lydia knew immediately that this was no ordinary man.

Paul, too, realized there was something different about this woman. She was completely open to God's will in her life. In the days to come, this woman would be instrumental in the founding of the church at Philippi.

Although Lydia's encounter with God was not as dramatic as some in the Bible, the results of her changed heart also changed a whole city. The Bible says "the Lord opened her heart to respond to Paul's message." When the Gospel deeply penetrates a person's heart, there will be lasting fruit. Never forget that it is our job to proclaim the Gospel, but it is God's job to transform the heart.

After her own conversion, Lydia's whole household was saved. This probably included her blood relatives, servants, and employees. Lydia's story is an important model to follow. Once a person is saved, it is important that they be encouraged to reach out to the people closest to them immediately.

The Bible also says she "persuaded" Paul's team to stay in her home. Usually it is church leaders who do all of the persuading! They spend all of their time trying to persuade reluctant Christians to do the things they have been called to do. But Lydia had been so transformed by God's Spirit that she was the one doing the persuading. As a leader, there is nothing I enjoy more than a Christian who asks me to give them the mentoring and the training they need.

God wants to open the hearts of the people around you, just like he opened the heart of Lydia. As he does this work in their hearts, you will be amazed by the radical change people will experience in their lives.

What an amazing story of the power of one person to make a difference. Through the life of Lydia, her whole household was saved and her city was radically touched. This story makes me aware of the fact that we should never underestimate the impact of just one person coming to Christ. As tempted as I am to become enamored with large numbers, every conversion is powerful.

Jeff Frankenstein

Lessons from the Life of Paul:
PRISON REVIVAL

About midnight Paul and Silas were praying and singing hymns to God, and the other prisoners were listening to them. Suddenly there was such a violent earthquake that the foundations of the prison were shaken. At once all the prison doors flew open, and everybody's chains came loose.

ACTS 16:25-26

DECEMBER 19

The revival had started with Lydia, and now there was a burgeoning church in her home. But this victory would mean retaliation from the enemy. Paul and Silas were confronted by a slave girl who predicted the future. She made great profits for her masters. Paul couldn't bear her pain and he cast the demonic spirits out of her. When her owners realized their livelihood was gone, they took Paul and Silas to be tried by the authorities.

Paul and Silas were imprisoned, with their feet fastened in stocks. And yet, within hours, the whole prison was resounding with Paul and Silas's praise and worship. And then, at midnight, God struck the prison with a violent earthquake. Every door flew open, and every prisoner's chains fell loose.

Even though God had called Paul and his team into Macedonia, hardships and battles still awaited them. Many Christians seem to believe that God will never call them into times of trouble and difficulty, but this is not true. The bigger the mission God calls us to, the bigger the attacks from the enemy will be when we seek to accomplish that mission.

When Paul and Silas were brutally beaten and thrown into a dungeon, other prisoners heard their praises. No matter how difficult your circumstances may be, you always have an audience. God may allow you to face adversity and crisis for the people who will be listening to you and who need to hear God's love through your words.

Also, their deliverance came at midnight. Although a new day had begun, it was still shrouded in darkness. Perhaps a new day has dawned in your life, but you are still unable to see it. If that is where you are, worship while you wait for the light!

When the earthquake struck, *every* cell door swung open, and *every* chain fell off. In the same way, your deliverance will also affect those around you. God may allow you to be brought low so he can use you to bring others up out of their darkness. As you praise in your midnight hour, you will ignite the explosive power of the Holy Spirit you so desperately need, and your deliverance will also give birth to the deliverance of those around you.

Just as Paul and Silas turned their prison into a mission field, I have watched members of my own family do the same thing. In one case, one of my family members who suffered and overcame cancer is now ministering to people who are dealing with the same condition.

Jeff Frankenstein

Lessons from the Life of Paul:
MODEL CHURCH

When they had passed through Amphipolis and Apollonia, they came to Thessalonica, where there was a Jewish synagogue. As his custom was, Paul went into the synagogue, and on three Sabbath days he reasoned with them from the Scriptures, explaining and proving that the Christ had to suffer and rise from the dead. "This Jesus I am proclaiming to you is the Christ," he said. Some of the Jews were persuaded and joined Paul and Silas, as did a large number of God-fearing Greeks and not a few prominent women.

But the Jews were jealous; so they rounded up some bad characters from the marketplace, formed a mob and started a riot in the city.

A C T S   1 7 : 1 – 5

For we know, brothers loved by God, that he has chosen you, because our gospel came to you not simply with words, but also with power, with the Holy Spirit and with deep conviction. You know how we lived among you for your sake. You became imitators of us and of the Lord; in spite of severe suffering, you welcomed the message with the joy given by the Holy Spirit. And so you became a model to all the believers in Macedonia and Achaia.

1   T H E S S A L O N I A N S   1 : 4 – 7

The enemy had struck the new church at Thessalonica. After a number of the city's inhabitants had been saved, a group of Jewish leaders incited a mob against the church. The leaders of the new church sent Paul and Silas out of

DECEMBER 20 **the city to save their lives. They had only been preaching**

there for two or three weeks and according to 1 Thessalonians 3:5, Paul was deeply concerned for the young church's ultimate survival.

In spite of the forces arrayed against it, this church did survive. Even though the time Paul spent with them was short, the power of the Holy Spirit enabled him to accomplish a great deal in a short period of time. God had done a deep and lasting work in the hearts of these new believers that was true and lasting.

Another key to their success was that the Thessalonians imitated their leaders—they were deeply committed to discipleship and followed closely after those that God had sent to guide them. The Thessalonians not only *listened to* the messages preached by Paul and Silas, but they also *did* what they saw Paul and Silas doing. Their willingness to follow the godly example of their leaders allowed them to grow at an amazing rate.

In addition, even though this new church experienced tremendous hardship, they received Paul's message with the joy that comes only from the Holy Spirit. The Thessalonians' ability to maintain joy in the middle of terrible circumstances helped them to persevere in their battles.

Unlike many leaders, who make their messages so palatable that their people are never prepared for a life of anything but blessing, Paul and Silas prepared their congregation for hard times. If the church today would simply follow their example, more Christians would run *to* the fight instead of *away* from it. As you ponder these principles today, may God give you the grace to help *your* church become a model church.

PAUL'S TRAINING OF THE THESSALONICAN CHURCH IS A MODEL FOR US ALL. INSTEAD OF PROMISING THEM AN EASY LIFE OF BLESSING, HE PREPARED THEM FOR THE TRIALS AND TROUBLES THAT ALL OF THEM WOULD FACE.

Jeff Frankenstein

Lessons from the Life of Paul:
THE ATHENS ASSIGNMENT

When I came to you, brothers, I did not come with eloquence or superior wisdom as I proclaimed to you the testimony about God. For I resolved to know nothing while I was with you except Jesus Christ and him crucified. I came to you in weakness and fear, and with much trembling. My message and my preaching were not with wise and persuasive words, but with a demonstration of the Spirit's power, so that your faith might not rest on men's wisdom, but on God's power.

1 CORINTHIANS 2:1-5

DECEMBER 21

We live in a day when many people place a tremendous emphasis on apologetics and the intellectual defense of the Gospel. Although these disciplines have their place, they will never be enough to pierce the veil of darkness that blinds the minds of our postmodern generation. Like Athens of Paul's day, the great educational centers of our world will never be transformed merely by logic and brilliant theological presentations. Unless we, like Paul, learn to rely on the simple message of the Gospel and the power of the Holy Spirit, we will never be able to win the world we have been called to reach.

Many times, when we are attempting to reach brilliant or highly educated people, we are tempted to deal with them on their own level. Although some of this can be very helpful, and it is important to understand the arguments for the Christian faith, only the Holy Spirit can transform the heart. Remember, it doesn't matter how intelligent you think you are or even how educated you may be, if you are a Christian, you have been armed with the most powerful weapon known to man: the Gospel of Jesus Christ. According to Paul, this Gospel has the power to demolish every argument against it (2 Corinthians 10:4). As we rely on the Holy Spirit and faithfully proclaim this Gospel, we will see our cultures deeply penetrated by the power of God's Word.

I WAS REMINDED AFRESH WHILE READING THIS DEVOTIONAL OF JUST HOW IMPORTANT THE WORK OF THE HOLY SPIRIT IS. MANY TIMES, WE ARE TEMPTED TO RELY ON OUR OWN WISDOM AND TRAINING WHEN WE ARE SHARING THE GOSPEL. ALTHOUGH TRAINING AND KNOWLEDGE ARE IMPORTANT, I CONTINUALLY REMIND MYSELF THAT ONLY THE HOLY SPIRIT CAN CHANGE THE HUMAN HEART.

Jeff Frankenstein

LESSONS FROM THE LIFE OF PAUL:
REVIVAL CORE

While Apollos was at Corinth, Paul took the road through the interior and arrived at Ephesus. There he found some disciples and asked them, "Did you receive the Holy Spirit when you believed?"

They answered, "No, we have not even heard that there is a Holy Spirit."

So Paul asked, "Then what baptism did you receive?"

"John's baptism," they replied.

Paul said, "John's baptism was a baptism of repentance. He told the people to believe in the one coming after him, that is, in Jesus." On hearing this, they were baptized into the name of the Lord Jesus. When Paul placed his hands on them, the Holy Spirit came on them, and they spoke in tongues and prophesied.

ACTS 19:1–6

DECEMBER 22

Paul had been to Ephesus before, but this time it was different. He was not here to simply visit the city—he was here to see the city changed. When he arrived at the synagogue, he found a small group of twelve disciples. Although Scripture isn't clear, they'd probably all been converted under the ministry of Apollos. As Paul looked into their eyes, he saw a deep hunger for the truth and a steadfast commitment to God's kingdom.

"Did you receive the Holy Spirit when you believed?" he asked them.

"We've never even heard of the Holy Spirit," they replied. After questioning them, Paul realized they'd never even heard the full message of the

Gospel. All they really knew was the baptism of John the Baptist. Once he had preached the full Gospel of Christ to them, he laid hands on them, and they were struck by the power of the Holy Spirit. As they began to pray in tongues, and even prophesy, Paul knew he had found the core group of men it would take to transform the great city of Ephesus.

When this group of Ephesian disciples opened their lives to the ministry of Paul, they had no idea how things would change for them. Not only would they discover things about the Christian faith they had never experienced, but they would leave the safety of the synagogue to confront the pagan culture around them. From twelve disciples they would grow into a citywide church of thousands. Extraordinary miracles would become ordinary, and even witches and warlocks would leave their evil practices and turn to the Lord. By the time the revival had subsided, every Jew and Greek who lived in the province of Asia would have heard the Word.

If the Lord walked into your business, high school, or college campus today, would he find a committed group of disciples? Would he find even one person who was willing to be freshly filled with the power of the Holy Spirit in order to bring life and transformation to their sphere of influence? Would anyone be willing to venture out of the safety and security of their Christian group for the sake of the Gospel?

It doesn't take much for God to change a business, a university, or even a city. All he needs to begin the process is a small group of disciples. Once he has found a group of men and women who will pay the cost, there is nothing he cannot do with them and through them. Although you may not experience what the church at Ephesus experienced, you will be brought into a place of service and effectiveness beyond your wildest dreams.

> MANY times we ALL get CAUGHT up too much in OUR GRAND plAns AND GiGAntic events. Although these things CAN Be GREAT, none OF us ShOULD eveR FORget the ABiLity OF GOD to chANGe history though just A hANDFul OF commiTTeD peOpLe.
>
> **Jeff Frankenstein**

Lessons from the Life of Paul:
THE SCHOOL OF TYRANNUS

Paul entered the synagogue and spoke boldly there for three months, arguing persuasively about the kingdom of God. But some of them became obstinate; they refused to believe and publicly maligned the Way. So Paul left them. He took the disciples with him and had discussions daily in the lecture hall of Tyrannus. This went on for two years, so that all the Jews and Greeks who lived in the province of Asia heard the word of the Lord.

ACTS 19:8–10

DECEMBER 23

After three months of preaching in the synagogue at Ephesus, Paul knew it was time for a strategic change. After praying for God's direction, he decided to plant a church in the lecture hall of Tyrannus. Following two years of preaching daily in the lecture hall, the whole city was aflame in revival, and the whole province of Asia had heard the Gospel.

What was so strategic about Paul leaving the synagogue and moving his evangelistic efforts to the lecture hall of Tyrannus? First, Paul wasn't just leaving the synagogue. He was leaving the hardened, resistant soil of the Jewish community in Ephesus. Unlike many Christians, Paul was not interested in simply winning his own friends or ethnic group to Christ, but instead he always searched for the most receptive spiritual "soil" of a region. He found this receptivity in the Gentile citizens of Ephesus.

Second, when Paul went to the school of Tyrannus, he was penetrating one of the city's major centers of influence. Unlike the insulated, cloistered religious world of the synagogue, the lecture hall of Tyrannus was a place where ideas were exchanged and philosophy was discussed. It was also a place where the city's brightest young people were being molded and shaped for the future. Paul realized he would never be able to transform the *culture* of Ephesus if he did not first transform the *campuses* of Ephesus.

It is no different for us today. If we are not committed to reaching the university campuses of our society, we will never be able to change the world. Here millions of young people are trained and educated, while their professors shape the values of every facet of our society through their writing and research.

Evangelizing these campuses, however, will be no simple matter. The name of the man who owned the lecture hall where Paul was ministering was *Tyrannus*, which means "tyrant." Whether his mother and father named him that, or that was the name given to him by his students, we do not know. Whatever the case, the word *tyrant*, or *tyranny*, describes one of the major barriers we will face in our attempts to penetrate the world's campuses. Although universities are reputed to be places where the free exchange of ideas is welcomed, this is usually not the case. If your ideas have anything to do with the validity of the Christian faith, the divinity of Christ, or moral absolutes, they are frequently unwelcome and may even be brutally suppressed. Yet, despite the battles that must be waged to liberate the campuses from their intellectual and moral tyranny, these strategic centers of influence are worth all the effort it will take to win them, because winning them is the key to winning our whole world.

When I think back on my own years in college, it's not hard for me to realize the importance of this story. As much as college campuses claim to be the intellectual lights of our world, they are some of the darkest places in the world. Many of the kids on these campuses are groping for answers that these institutions are not equipped to give.

Jeff Frankenstein

Lessons from the Life of Paul:
EXTRAORDINARY MIRACLES

God did extraordinary miracles through Paul, so that even handkerchiefs and aprons that had touched him were taken to the sick, and their illnesses were cured and the evil spirits left them.

ACTS 19:11-12

DECEMBER 24

No one could even comprehend it. Simple healings were one thing, but these miracles were a whole different matter. Everyone knew that Paul, the leader of the Ephesian church, was also a tentmaker. In order to financially support himself and his team, he was preaching all day and working with leather all night. People were so desperate to be healed from their diseases and delivered from their demonic bonds that they had begun to visit Paul in his shop. Much to their amazement, Paul didn't even have to touch them. Anything he had touched would heal them. Whether it was one of the sweaty leather aprons on which he had been working, or one of the leather cloths he was using to wipe his brow or clean his hands, the same anointing flowing out of Paul was sometimes present in these ordinary articles. People couldn't believe it; everyone wanted one of these items. Although handkerchiefs were more plentiful, aprons were even in higher demand because they could be cut up and used to heal multiple diseases. Fueled by these manifestations of God's power, the revival continued to grow in strength and numbers.

The Bible says God did extraordinary miracles through Paul during the Ephesus Revival. What was most extraordinary about the miracles, though, had nothing to do with the people who were healed, and everything to do with the means through which they were healed. The revival had grown to such a magnitude that people were being healed through the means of simple articles such as sweat rags and aprons. What lessons can we learn from this story's amazing events?

First, Paul wasn't just anointed as a preacher; he was also anointed as a businessman. Unlike the majority of modern-day Christians, Paul saw no validity in a view of the world divided between the sacred and the secular. As far as Paul was concerned, whether he was preaching or stitching together a tent, it was all God's work. Therefore, he fully expected the presence and power of God to be working through whatever he was doing.

It should be no different with you today. Does God only change people at the services of your local church, or can he transform them just as easily where you live, work, or go to school? Never forget, the same God who moved powerfully in Paul's tentmaking shop wants to move in you and your profession today.

Second, if God could heal a person through one of Paul's sweat rags, what might he be able to do through you? The same God who released healing power through simple, ordinary objects desires to release his power through ordinary people as well. If you will simply submit to him and ask for the faith to move in his power, you will be amazed to see the people he uses you to touch. Remember, even as people came running to Paul's shop for a touch from God, so he wants to bring them on the run to you.

It is amazing to me that Paul's anointing did not end when the church meeting was over. Whether he was serving as an apostle or a leather worker, God's power was working through him. This should encourage all of us to believe for God to work through us no matter what our profession is.

Jeff Frankenstein

THE SEVEN SONS OF SCEVA

Some Jews who went around driving out evil spirits tried to invoke the name of the Lord Jesus over those who were demon-possessed. They would say, "In the name of Jesus, whom Paul preaches, I command you to come out." Seven sons of Sceva, a Jewish chief priest, were doing this. [One day] the evil spirit answered them, "Jesus I know, and I know about Paul, but who are you?" Then the man who had the evil spirit jumped on them and overpowered them all. He gave them such a beating that they ran out of the house naked and bleeding.

ACTS 19:13–16

DECEMBER 25

The seven sons of Sceva had learned the secret to casting out demons. After following Paul around town, they determined that it was this Jesus fellow's name that seemed to work, and they decided to try it out.

When the young men surrounded the demoniac, they immediately began to chant: "In the name of Jesus, whom Paul preaches, I command you to come out." Before they knew it, the evil spirit in the man was answering them back: "I know Jesus. In fact, I've heard about Paul, too. But who do you think you are?" The next thing they knew, the demoniac had jumped on them and was beating them to a pulp. Before they could stop him, he'd even ripped off their clothes. By the time he was finished, they were running for their lives, bleeding and naked.

This story presents us with one of the most important lessons in the whole Bible about the use of spiritual power. The seven sons of Sceva thought the power was in the method. As long as they had the right name, the correct intonation, and the exact posture, they thought the demon had to flee. Unfortunately for them, the demon knew the difference between a religious formula and true authority. Many Christians have learned the same lesson which the sons of Sceva learned and felt the same sense of futility and powerlessness when they tried to use the name of Jesus or some other Christian expression to be released from the enemy's assault.

Maybe that's where you are today. When you tell the devil to get behind you, he simply attacks you from another angle. When you rebuke the devil, you can almost hear him laughing. Whether you like it or not, the problem is not in the words. It's in your heart. Like God, the devil knows true spirituality when he finds it. If what is coming out of your mouth is not in your heart, it will have no power. The only type of Christians whose authority the enemy respects are those who are clearly under the authority of Christ themselves. This is the true secret of all spiritual authority.

If Christ is not the Lord of your life, and if you are not walking under his authority, all the Christian slogans and trite sayings in the world are not going to save you. Wherever you are today, and no matter what type of spiritual attack you are facing, it's not too late for you to discover the type of authority I am describing. If you will freshly place yourself under the Lordship of Christ and deal with the sinful inroads which Satan has made into your heart, you, too, can experience true biblical authority.

Whether we like it or not, true spiritual authority does not consist of having the right verbiage. It comes instead from having the right relationship with God. The demons fled from Paul not because of what he said but because of who he was in Christ.

Jeff Frankenstein

Lessons from the Life of Paul:

RAISING EUTYCHUS FROM THE DEAD

On the first day of the week we came together to break bread. Paul spoke to the people and, because he intended to leave the next day, kept on talking until midnight. There were many lamps in the upstairs room where we were meeting. Seated in a window was a young man named Eutychus, who was sinking into a deep sleep as Paul talked on and on. When he was sound asleep, he fell to the ground from the third story and was picked up dead. Paul went down, threw himself on the young man and put his arms around him. "Don't be alarmed," he said. "He's alive!" Then he went upstairs again and broke bread and ate. After talking until daylight, he left. The people took the young man home alive and were greatly comforted.

ACTS 20:7–12

DECEMBER 26

The last time he had been in Troas, Paul had not squandered his opportunity to spread the Gospel. Instead of being absorbed in his own problems, he had begun the process of planting a church there. Now, as he was finishing his mission in the province of Macedonia, he stopped in Troas to spend seven days with the new church. When he came to the last day of his visit, he decided to extend the meeting. As might be expected, not everyone was happy with this decision.

About midnight, a young man named Eutychus just couldn't take it anymore. He was sitting on the ledge of an open window, but the fresh air could no longer keep him awake. Finally, when he could resist no longer, he fell into a deep sleep. Tragically, while he was sleeping, he slipped off the ledge and fell three stories to his death. When Paul heard what had happened, he immediately stopped the meeting and ran downstairs. After throwing his arms around the young man's broken, bleeding corpse, Paul cried, "Don't be alarmed. He's alive!" Eutychus had been raised from the dead.

Although this story has some humorous elements, it contains a number of serious lessons for our time. Like Eutychus, it is so easy to become apathetic about the things of God and the church—but that is a place of danger. From what I've seen, the average Christian teenager loses their exuberance and their passion for Christ long before they lose their purity. What is your relationship with God like today? Have you lost your passion? Have you fallen asleep in your walk with God, even though you are in the church?

Take care if you have fallen asleep, because that is when Eutychus fell to his death. Although Scripture doesn't say, I would imagine that no one ever realized that Eutychus was gone until they heard the commotion in the streets below. He simply quietly slipped off the ledge and died. But when Paul heard that Eutychus had died, he stopped the meeting and went down to where the young man had died. Once he had thrown his arms around the young man, he raised him from the dead. This is an important point for you. It is possible to be raised back from the dead even if you have fallen asleep! God is pursuing you and wants you to bring you back into that dynamic place of fellowship with him. Are you like Eutychus—falling asleep in the light? It's time to wake up!

EUTYCHUS WAS ONLY RAISED FROM THE DEAD BECAUSE THE PEOPLE OF HIS CHURCH WERE WILLING TO LEAVE THE MEETING AND COME TO HIS RESCUE. WHETHER WE LIKE IT OR NOT, MOST OF THE REAL WORK OF GOD'S KINGDOM IS DONE OUTSIDE THE CHURCH. UNTIL WE REALIZE THIS, WE WILL NEVER SAVE THE EUTYCHUSES OF THIS WORLD.

Jeff Frankenstein

Lessons from the Life of Paul:
DO NOT BE AFRAID

After the men had gone a long time without food, Paul stood up before them and said: "Men, you should have taken my advice not to sail from Crete; then you would have spared yourselves this damage and loss. But now I urge you to keep up your courage, because not one of you will be lost; only the ship will be destroyed."

ACTS 27:21–22

DECEMBER 27

Paul tried to warn them that their voyage would bring the loss of their ship and their cargo. Sadly, they chose to watch the winds instead of listening to the word of God's servant. Although the voyage started out smoothly enough, Paul, his fellow prisoners, and the whole crew were in terrible danger. The winds and the waves battered the ship so violently that the crew was forced to throw the cargo overboard. Finally, after battling the storm's fury for a number of days, everyone on the ship had given up hope—everyone, that is, but Paul. An angel appeared to Paul in the midst of the storm and told him not to be afraid because he would reach Rome. God also told Paul that he would spare the lives of everyone who was sailing with him. When Paul spoke to the ship's company and told them this news, they were filled with fresh confidence and faith. Although the ship would be destroyed on a sandbar, not one person aboard the ship would lose his life.

Could it be that, like Paul, you have been placed in the midst of a horrible crisis for the purpose of saving those around you? If so, this is no time for you to give in to despair. The same God who promised Paul his life and the lives of those around him is also able to deliver you and those you love today.

Even though Paul had been brought on the trip as a prisoner and had warned them that horrible storms were coming, he refused to become resentful and bitter. Bitterness will eat away the very confidence you need to survive. But when you let go of your anger, God will be able to bless you in the midst of the storm.

Even though the storm literally tore the ship to pieces, Paul did not allow fear to rule his heart. Even if you are feeling the powerful forces of a storm in your life, you can choose to be confidently led by the promises of God's Word and instead of being defeated by the howling winds of fear.

No matter what type of storm you are facing today, it's not time to jump ship. If the winds are howling, put your trust in God alone and stand firm. Never forget that your storm is not just about your life. It is also about the lives of those you love. Therefore, as you hold fast, they, too, will experience the protection and the power of God's promises.

This is another example of why we should have faith in the midst of the storm. No matter what storm you're going through, this passage should encourage you. Even though Paul's ship was being destroyed and his life was threatened, he never lost his peace or his joy because he knew that God could deliver him.

Jeff Frankenstein

Lessons from the Life of Paul:
SHAKE IT OFF

Once safely on shore, we found out that the island was called Malta. The islanders showed us unusual kindness. They built a fire and welcomed us all because it was raining and cold. Paul gathered a pile of brushwood and, as he put it on the fire, a viper, driven out by the heat, fastened itself on his hand. When the islanders saw the snake hanging from his hand, they said to each other, "This man must be a murderer; for though he escaped from the sea, Justice has not allowed him to live." But Paul shook the snake off into the fire and suffered no ill effects. The people expected him to swell up or suddenly fall dead, but after waiting a long time and seeing nothing unusual happen to him, they changed their minds and said he was a god.

ACTS 28:1–6

DECEMBER 28

Just as Paul had predicted, the ship ran aground on a sandbar. Although the Roman soldiers had wanted to kill all of the prisoners to keep them from escaping, their centurion, in order to spare Paul's life, forbade them to carry out their plan. Now, as they were floating and swimming toward the distant island, they were simply thankful to be alive. When the haggard survivors finally came ashore on the island of Malta, only Paul realized that their shipwreck was more than a tragic accident. Despite the fact that Paul was cold and exhausted, he sensed that God had a work to do in this strange place.

Paul had been so lost in his thoughts that he never saw the serpent that lunged out of the wood he was carrying and sank its fangs into his hand. Everyone was stunned. While the crew wondered how this could happen to such a righteous man, the inhabitants of the island speculated

that Paul must be a horrible criminal because this snake never failed to kill its victims. Paul, however, simply raised his arm and violently shook it back and forth until the snake was thrown into the fire. With no evidence of swelling in his body or any other sign that he had even been bitten, Paul calmly continued to collect the wood that was needed for the fire.

What has bitten your life today? Some of you may have been bitten by financial disaster or unemployment. Others of you have been deeply bitten by rejection or the betrayal of someone you love. Even now, the venom of those cutting words is coursing through your veins. Maybe, like the inhabitants of Malta with Paul, some people are even suggesting that it's all your fault—that you're simply getting what you deserved. No matter how badly it hurts, it's time for you to shake it off. *Shake it off?* you may be thinking. *It's paralyzed me. I can barely move.* In my own life, I have found that beginning to move is the most difficult part. As faith stirs up in your spirit and holy anger toward the devil rises in your breast, you will have the confidence you need to violently shake off the devil's bite. As you begin to raise your hands in praise and cry out to God in prayer, the very fist you make to pound on heaven's doors will staunch the bleeding of your soul. There is nothing you cannot shake off of your life into the burning fires of God's passion. No matter what type of diabolical serpent it may be, it is no match for the authority given us by Jesus. Whatever has shaken your life, it's time for you to shake back!

What amazes me the most about this story is Paul's response to being bitten by a highly poisonous serpent. Instead of panicking and screaming for help like I probably would have done, he simply shook it off into the fire and went about his business. No matter what has bitten you. You can shake it off.

Jeff Frankenstein

Lessons from the Life of Paul:
MALTA REVIVAL

There was an estate nearby that belonged to Publius, the chief official of the island. He welcomed us to his home and for three days entertained us hospitably. His father was sick in bed, suffering from fever and dysentery. Paul went in to see him and, after prayer, placed his hands on him and healed him. When this had happened, the rest of the sick on the island came and were cured. They honored us in many ways and when we were ready to sail, they furnished us with the supplies we needed.

ACTS 28:7-10

DECEMBER 29

It didn't take long for the reports of Paul's miraculous healing to spread throughout the small island. When Publius, the chief official of the island, heard the story, he took Paul and some of his companions into his home. After Paul arrived, he discovered that Publius's father was sick in bed with a burning fever and dysentery. After Paul healed him, revival was ignited on the island. Before Paul left Malta, every sick person on the island had come to the meetings and had been healed.

What an amazing God we serve! Even when we feel that our lives have been totally blown off course by the storms raging around us, God is in full control. For you, the storms of your life may simply subside. Or you may find yourself shipwrecked in a place you never thought you would be. If the latter scenario best describes your life, be encouraged! God is not only going to give you a better boat—he's going to give you a better life. Like Paul, you will be embarking on another divine phase of your destiny.

Only you, however, can determine the outcome of this new phase. If you sulk or pout about the things you have lost, the best you can expect is to be rescued from the wreckage of your storm. Conversely, if you can acknowledge God's hand in the midst of your storm, you may ignite a revival in the very place where you thought you were washed up. Have you been shipwrecked on the shores of a new city, a new job, a new school, or a new church? It doesn't matter. As you trust God's sovereign hand in your circumstances and display his character in your life, who knows what he will begin to do through you?

This is a tremendous example of God's provision. Paul and his shipmates were shown considerable kindness and hospitality by people that had never even met them before. In fact, they gave them all the supplies they needed before they set sail again. This story is an awesome testimony of the power of God to meet our needs through the people he places in our path.

Jeff Frankenstein

Lessons from the Life of Paul:
HOUSE ARREST

> Now I want you to know, brothers, that what has happened to me has really served to advance the gospel. As a result, it has become clear throughout the whole palace guard and to everyone else that I am in chains for Christ.

PHILIPPIANS 1:12–13

DECEMBER 30

Paul's movement throughout the city was restricted. At times, he had even been chained between two Roman soldiers. Yet his spirit had never been more free. Paul realized that even his chains were for the sake of the Gospel. Not only did he write a number of letters to the churches he had visited, but he also led many of the emperor's personal guards to Christ. Through these divine contacts, Scripture tells us that even members of the emperor's own household became Christians. Instead of spending his time in bitterness and despair, Paul realized that his house arrest had been ordered by God.

Maybe you, too, feel like you are under house arrest. You may be facing physical illness that keeps you at home or in the hospital. You may be in a dead-end job or enrolled in a school you dislike. Regardless of what you are facing, determine to maintain a godly attitude, and allow your spirit to rise above the circumstances that are shackling you. If you will make a commitment to do this, you will be amazed at what God can do through you. For those of you who are facing sickness or physical weakness, could it be that God has sent you to care for the very people who are caring for you? Maybe your lengthy recovery has been ordered by God to give you the time you need to draw closer to him. If your job or school seems like a prison to you, maybe God has chosen to keep you there because you still have work for him to do there.

Like Paul, you may feel that you've been chained to people that you would rather not be. Whether you are working with them or taking a class with them, no matter how hard you try, you can't seem to avoid them. Even as Paul was able to look beyond the swords of his captors and into their hearts, so God wants to show you the hearts of the people around you today. He has a purpose for bringing these people into your life.

No matter how trapped you feel or how truly imprisoned you may be, God himself has "arrested" you for a purpose. He has brought *your plans* to a halt in order to allow you to participate in *his plan* for your life. As you praise him in spite of your prison, he will not fail to accomplish his purposes in your life.

Could it be that the very place you're sick of being is the place where you're needed most? Maybe, like Paul, you feel chained to people you don't even want to be around. If that's the case, you're not alone. I've felt the same way myself at times. If you'll simply trust God, you'll be amazed to see what he will do through you in the very places you despise. In my own life, some of the things that I felt horribly stuck in have been just what I needed to prepare me for my next phase in life.

Jeff Frankenstein

Lessons from the Life of John:
PATMOS

I, John, your brother and companion in the suffering and kingdom and patient endurance that are ours in Jesus, was on the island of Patmos because of the word of God and the testimony of Jesus. On the Lord's Day I was in the Spirit, and I heard behind me a loud voice like a trumpet, which said: "Write on a scroll what you see and send it to the seven churches: to Ephesus, Smyrna, Pergamum, Thyatira, Sardis, Philadelphia and Laodicea."

REVELATION 1:9–11

DECEMBER 31

John was very likely the last of the twelve apostles still living. He was an old man, but his passion for God and his prophetic insight were still very much intact. When John was younger, Jesus had called him and his brother James the "Sons of Thunder" because they once had wanted to call down fire on some of Jesus' enemies. Now, however, he was the apostle of love—kind, charitable, and patient. His greatest joy was not found in ministering to people, but in ministering to the Lord. Even in his old age, the Roman government considered him a threat, so they had exiled him to the island of Patmos. To John, his exile was not a punishment. After all, he simply got to spend more time with the One he loved beyond all other beings: Jesus Christ, the Son of God. One day, while worshipping and waiting on the Lord, John saw his Friend. This time, however, Jesus did not come as the Broken Healer. He came in the full glory of his resurrection as God's Triumphant Son.

Even though John had undergone untold suffering, including the martyrdom of many of his best friends, his spirit was neither embittered nor broken. The man who had leaned his head on Jesus' breast at the Last

Supper continued to maintain his friendship with his beloved Master. The same should be true with you. If you will simply draw close to the Lord and receive from his strength, you, too, will be transformed, instead of deformed, by your pain.

Even though John had been exiled to an island, away from every person he held dear, the Bible says that he was in the Spirit on the Lord's Day. In other words, he was not discouraged, angry, despairing, or disconsolate. Instead, he was filled with thanksgiving for God's provision in his life and open to whatever his Master had to say.

No matter where you find yourself or how terrible your circumstance may be, it is critical that you stay in the Spirit. You may be in a place far away from everything and everyone you love. You and your family may have been transferred to another city, or you may be serving on a distant military base; everything in you longs for what you have lost. If this is where you are, get back in the Spirit! As you draw near to him, the same God who stepped into John's life on the lonely island of Patmos will step into your life, as well. Through the promises of God's Word and the praises of your lips, you can be lifted to a place where God can speak to you. Not only will God freshly reveal his purposes to you, but he will also give you the power to pursue them.

MANY OF US PROBABLY WOULD HAVE BEEN BITTER IN JOHN'S CIRCUMSTANCES. AFTER ALL, MOST OF HIS BEST FRIENDS WERE DEAD AND HE HAD BEEN IMPRISONED ON A LONELY ISLAND. WHEN I THINK BACK OVER MY CHRISTIAN LIFE, I HAVE SEEN MORE PEOPLE THAN I CAN EVEN COUNT WHO HAVE BEEN HURT BY THE BITTERNESS OF THEIR OWN HEART. JOHN, HOWEVER, KNEW THAT NO MATTER HOW HARD HIS CIRCUMSTANCES WERE, HE DID NOT HAVE THE RIGHT TO BE BITTER. THIS IS AN IMPORTANT LESSON FOR ALL OF US TO LEARN.

Jeff Frankenstein

At Inspirio, we love to hear from you—your
stories, your feedback,
and your product ideas.
Please send your comments to us
by way of email at
icares@zondervan.com
or to the address below:

inspirio

Attn: Inspirio Cares
5300 Patterson Avenue SE
Grand Rapids, MI 49530

If you would like further information
about Inspirio and the products we
create, please visit us at:
www.inspiriogifts.com

Thank you and God bless!